G. Sims (German Sims) Woodhead

Practical pathology: a manual for students and practitioners

G. Sims (German Sims) Woodhead

Practical pathology: a manual for students and practitioners

ISBN/EAN: 9783742832870

Manufactured in Europe, USA, Canada, Australia, Japa

Cover: Foto ©Thomas Meinert / pixelio.de

Manufactured and distributed by brebook publishing software
(www.brebook.com)

G. Sims (German Sims) Woodhead

Practical pathology: a manual for students and practitioners

PRACTICAL

PATHOLOGY.

A MANUAL FOR STUDENTS AND PRACTITIONERS.

BY

G. SIMS WOODHEAD, M.D., F.R.C.P.Ed.,

FELLOW OF THE ROYAL SOCIETY, EDINBURGH; DIRECTOR OF THE LABORATORIES
OF THE CONJOINT BOARD OF THE ROYAL COLLEGES OF PHYSICIANS (LOND.)
AND SURGEONS (ENG.), FORMERLY DEMONSTRATOR OF PATHOLOGY
IN THE UNIVERSITY OF EDINBURGH; AND PATHOLOGIST
TO THE ROYAL INFIRMARY, EDINBURGH.

WITH ONE HUNDRED AND NINETY-FIVE COLOURED ILLUSTRATIONS

THIRD EDITION.

EDINBURGH AND LONDON:
YOUNG J. PENTLAND.
PHILADELPHIA: J. B. LIPPINCOTT COMPANY.
1892.

PRINTED FOR YOUNG J. PENTLAND.

EDINBURGH: 11 TEVIOT PLACE.   LONDON: 38 WEST SMITHFIELD, E.C.

PREFACE TO THE THIRD EDITION.

In placing a third edition of this work before his readers, the Author feels that he incurs a greater responsibility than any he has before assumed in connection with it.

During the last decade great advances have been made in the methods of studying Pathology; students are more thoroughly grounded and trained in Practical work, and the general standard of Pathological knowledge is now, certainly, much higher than it was, even ten years ago. It is therefore the more necessary that any one essaying to offer instruction in Practical Pathology should take the greatest care to bring his descriptions into line with the results obtained by Modern Methods. A sense of this responsibility and further experience in teaching, and of the needs of both student and teacher, have impelled the Author to enlarge the scope of the work and to alter it, very materially, in several respects.

The chapter on Methods has been brought well up to date; a chapter on Inflammation and Healing of Wounds has been added, and other matter, especially as regards the naked eye appearances of Diseased Organs has been introduced. Special attention has been paid to arrangement, much repetition has been avoided, and the references to methods of Hardening, Preparing, and Staining, have been so arranged as to interfere as little as possible with the continuity of the text. In short, the work has been almost entirely re-written, and so re-cast as to make it available not only as a

Practical Handbook for the Class-room and Laboratory, but also as a book useful for Home Study in connection with Practical work. The number of illustrations has been increased from 162 to 195, and many of the original figures have been redrawn or replaced by drawings of more typical specimens.

To those friends who have so freely placed their time and specimens at his disposal, the Author returns his most hearty thanks: to Mr. G. C. Cathcart, M.B., C.M., who has carefully revised the proof sheets and made most valuable suggestions for the improvement of many of the descriptions; to Drs. Alexander Bruce (*vide* Figs. 139-40), G. F. Crooke (*vide* Figs. 5, 6, 16, 38-9), H. Alexis Thomson (*vide* Figs. 126-7-8, 132-3), and John Thomson (*vide* Figs. 40-1), for the use of microscopic specimens from which some of the new drawings have been made; to Prof. Michael Foster, Dr. C. S. Sherrington, and Messrs. Macmillan & Co., for permission to use the figures in Foster's Physiology from which Fig. 138 was prepared; and to Messrs. G. A. Fothergill, R. Muir, J. T. Murray, and W. A. Scott for their faithful delineations of the specimens entrusted to their care.

G. S. W.

LONDON, *June* 1892.

PREFACE TO THE SECOND EDITION.

Owing to the continued demand for this work, the preparation of a second edition has become necessary. The favourable criticism which the first edition evoked from the Medical Press, and the Profession generally, has greatly encouraged the Author in this undertaking. Some valuable suggestions contained in the criticisms have been adopted, while others have been passed over only after careful consideration had made it evident that their adoption would materially alter the plan of the work.

Every page has been carefully revised, parts have been re-written, and much new matter has been introduced.

The number of illustrations has been increased, many of the plates have been re-drawn, and several, which in the first edition were copied from other sources, have been replaced by original drawings.

The Author hopes that he has thus been able to make this edition an improvement on the first, and trusts that it may be regarded as worthy of at least equal favour by those for whom it is intended.

He renews his thanks to those friends mentioned in the Preface to the First Edition, all of whom have again assisted him. He would also thank most cordially Mr. G. Lovell Gulland and Mr. Arthur Clarkson for Drawings, and Mr. J. Milne Chapman, M.B., M.R.C.S., for the great care and labour he has expended upon the chapter which he has contributed.

G. S. W.

Edinburgh, *December* 1884.

PREFACE TO THE FIRST EDITION.

WHILST there are, in abundance, systematic treatises upon Pathology, and the results of researches of those most eminent in the Pathological world are within the reach of all, there is yet a want of a guide to the practical work involved in the study, preparation, and examination of Morbid Tissues. This want, so great as to have become almost a reproach to Pathologists, the author of this hand-book has endeavoured to supply. Though vast strides have recently been made in this branch of medical study, one of the most important bases of Clinical Medicine, the Student and the Practitioner have had very scant opportunity of thoroughly acquainting themselves with the appearance of Diseased Organs and Tissues. Acquaintance with naked eye and microscopic appearances of diseased structures is necessary for the comprehension and appreciation of recent pathological researches, and can be acquired only by a diligent use of the scalpel and microscope.

The necessity for such practical work was recognised abroad earlier than in our own country. At the present time practical teaching in Morbid Anatomy and Pathological Histology is more general than was formerly the case in our Medical Schools. The Author hopes that his work will greatly aid both Students and Practitioners in familiarising themselves with the methods and results of pathological inquiry, and that it will prove to be an adequate introduction to Systematic Pathology. It is not designed to displace so much as to aid and supplement oral instruction in Practical Pathology, and to prepare the Student for the Lecture-room, and for the study of more systematic text-books.

The plan adopted is to follow the tissue from the body to the microscope, to describe the method of making the *post mortem* and naked eye examinations, and of preparing the various structures for microscopic investigation. The more important changes of each organ are indicated, though all the changes which occur could not possibly be considered in the space at command. In all cases the aim has been to describe at least the more important typical lesions. In as many instances as possible, illustrations, which are not mere diagrams, are added. Most of the original Drawings have been made from Sections prepared in the course of the work of the Edinburgh University Practical Pathology Class. They may therefore be accepted as representing as faithfully as possible the appearances which may be recognised by any normally intelligent and dexterous student. The copied Drawings, taken from the best sources, are, as far as possible, acknowledged in the descriptions.

The Author is greatly indebted to numerous writers for many of the facts adduced, but has preferred to acknowledge generally his indebtedness rather than to cumber his work with individual references. He is constrained to mention with gratitude the late Professor Sanders's Course of Pathology, and Professor Hamilton's and Professor Greenfield's Courses of Practical Pathology, on the outlines of which two practical courses the work is based. To Professor Greenfield (who kindly allowed the Author to make what use he thought fit of notes taken of his course of Systematic Lectures), he is indebted for much valuable assistance. The Author has found that Professor Ziegler enunciates views similar to those of Professor Greenfield upon the Pathological Histology of

Granular Contracted Kidney and Acute Phthisis. He therefore
feels it incumbent upon him to record that Professor Greenfield's
investigations were completed and published in Papers and Lectures
before Professor Ziegler's excellent Manual of Pathology appeared,
and that the two sections (Kidney and Lung) of the present work
were already printed when the corresponding sections in Ziegler's
Pathology appeared.

Such descriptions as occur of the Normal Histology of various
organs are based mainly on Klein and Noble Smith's admirable
work.   Only such points are referred to as may prove to be of very
great assistance in following pathological changes.   Every student
is advised to make himself thoroughly acquainted with Normal
Histology before commencing the study of Morbid Tissues.

In the section dealing with Parasites, the general plan has been
departed from in some measure.   A few comparatively full descriptions are offered, and in addition merely a list of the more important
forms.

As the work was written at intervals between the discharge of
more pressing duties, the Author is prepared for many imperfections
in it.   He thanks most warmly Mr. Robert Robertson, M.B., C.M.;
and Mr. Mason, for the very full Index which they have compiled ,
Mr. J. Tatham Thompson, F.R.M.S., for many of the Drawings ; Dr.
Bendall, and Messrs. W. E. Hoyle, M.A., R. J. Harvey Gibson,
M.A., Chas. Kennedy, M.B., C.M., W. B. Mackay, M.B., C.M., and
R. Muir for Drawings ; Messrs. C. W. Cathcart, F.R.C.S. (*vide* Fig.
67), and W. O. Williams, M.R.C.V.S. (*vide* Figs. 161 and 162), for
the loan of preparations from which Drawings have been made.

G. S. W.

EDINBURGH, *October* 1, 1883.

CONTENTS.

CHAPTER XIV.

TUMOURS.

CHAPTER XV.

ANIMAL PARASITES.

CHAPTER XVI.

VEGETABLE PARASITES.

LIST OF ILLUSTRATIONS.

———◆———

PRACTICAL PATHOLOGY.

CHAPTER I.

POST MORTEM EXAMINATION.

1. Instruments required.—

(*a.*) Two or three "section" knives, strong enough to be used as cartilage knives. The handle must be strong and thick, so that it may be grasped firmly in the palm of the hand ; the blade stout, with the belly curved and sharpened up to the point, which should be well rounded off. With the knives (Fig. 1) made for me by Mr. Gardner of Edinburgh, there is little or no danger of punctured *post mortem* wounds.

(*b.*) A couple of scalpels, such as are supplied in the ordinary dissecting cases.

*(*c.*) For dividing the costal cartilages, Coats recommends a knife with "a triangular blade, the edge being straight, and forming an angle of about 35° with the back, which should be very strong and thick ; the handle should be strong, and the blade prolonged through it from end to end" (Lindsay Steven).

(*d.*) Two curved bistouries; one probe-pointed, the other sharpened up to the point.

*(*e.*) A hollow ground razor (Heifor's army razor), or better, a Valentine's knife, for cutting thin sections of fresh tissues.

(*f.*) A long thin-bladed knife, about one inch broad and ten or twelve inches long, for making complete sections through the various viscera. This is especially useful for cutting into the brain,

---

* Those marked with asterisk are not absolutely necessary for use in private houses, but they should be in every *post mortem* theatre.

but one rather shorter, though of similar make, is frequently used for cutting into the other organs. For the first incision into the brain a thin narrow knife, about one-third to one-half inch in breadth, and ten or twelve inches long, is also exceedingly useful, but by no means necessary.

(*g.*) A couple of pairs of dissecting forceps.

*(*h.*) Two pairs of double hooks well blunted, with chain, and a couple of copper spatulæ.

(*i.*) Two pairs of scissors; "one pair large, having one blade with the point rounded off, the other sharp ; the other pair small, one blade probe-pointed, the other sharp-pointed."

(*j.*) A pair of intestine scissors, with a long curved and blunt-pointed blade with a hook turned backward, and a shorter square-ended blade which closes behind the curve, so that the curved blade is never cut out of the bowel.

(*k.*) A blowpipe, preferably with a stop-cock.

(*l.*) Several blunt probes, of different sizes.

(*m.*) A small bone-saw, with a strong moveable back and fine teeth, well set, and one with long curved handle for sawing through the laminæ of the vertebræ.

(*n.*) A metal catheter, No. 8, and several flexible catheters.

(*o.*) A mallet—or steel hammer with a hook at the end of the handle, which is very useful in laying hold of and lifting the calvaria—and steel chisel, in the shape of a capital T; the blade and cross piece of the chisel should each be about 6 inches in length, and the blade, one inch broad, may be made with a guard at a distance of about one-third of an inch from the point. This guard is of use when the skull-cap is being removed, but it interferes with the use of the chisel for other purposes, such as taking out the spinal cord, so that when the guard is adopted a second straight steel chisel should be added to the list of instruments.

(*p.*) One pair of strong bone-forceps, the two ends of the handles of which should be at least two inches apart when they are forcibly gripped in the hand.

(*q.*) Three or four large straight flat "packing" needles, half a dozen curved needles, of different sizes, and some strong thin twine.

(*r.*) A pair of caliber-compasses, with graduated cross-bar, or a narrow wooden foot-rule graduated in inches and centimetres. A yard or metre tape or steel band measure finely graduated in inches and centimetres. A series of graduated cones, from one-tenth inch to two and a half inches diameter, for measuring the various orifices. A large well graduated glass measure of about twenty ounce capacity, or even larger; this may be used for holding specimens, especially if it is fitted with a ground-in stopper. A smaller graduated beaker - shaped one ounce glass measure, which is often useful for taking out fluid from small sacs and pouches in the peritoneal cavity.

(s.) A large trocar and cannula, or a flexible tube with rigid walls, to which a stomach pump may be attached, may be very useful for drawing off large accumulations of fluid, especially in cases of dropsical effusion.

(t.) A pair of scales, with weights from one-quarter ounce to fourteen pounds.

(*u.*) Blue litmus papers and turmeric papers. A weak solution of iodine, made by adding one drachm of tincture of iodine to eight or ten drachms of water. A solution of sulphide of ammonium to test for free iron derived from blood pigment, as in cases of pernicious anæmia.

(v.) A good magnifying glass and a compound microscope with accessories, such as slides, cover glasses, a couple of needles in handles, a small phial of neutral solution (three-fourths per cent. solution of common salt in distilled water). (§ 37).

FIG. 1.

Of these instruments, those for cutting must all be perfectly clean and sharp, as nothing is more likely to interfere with the accuracy of the results of an examination than a set of blunt instruments—except want of method. It is needless to say, however, that *post mortem* examinations have to be made without many of the above instruments (and the lack of some of them should never be put forward

as a reason for not making an examination), but these, or substitutes for them, should be obtained when possible.

2. In the *post mortem* theatre of an infirmary all instruments, a good table, a plentiful supply of hot and cold water, and all the requisites for sponging the body and washing out the cavities should be provided. The best form of table is a slate slab six feet long and two feet broad with the corners rounded off, a bead round the edge, and so hollowed out that all fluids run to the lower or foot end, at which is a grating with a waste-pipe running to the centre, where the table is supported by a hollow iron pillar, on which it can easily revolve. A waste pipe passes down the central pillar; the height of the table should be about 2 feet 9 inches.[1] Above the table a good "star" gas light is essential for work in dark weather, and along with the gas pipe a pipe for the supply of water should be brought to a point above the middle of the table, to which an india-rubber hose may be attached; the hose should be kept out of the way by means of a hook, or some similar contrivance, when not in use. The gas and the water should both be controlled from a point within reach of the operator; this is usually done by having taps similar to those used in billiard rooms placed in the wall near the head of the table. For supporting the head and neck, a block about 15 inches long, 3 inches thick, and 9 inches broad, with half a circle with a radius of 6 inches cut out from one side, should be used; a number of blocks of a similar size, but without the excavation, and a few wedge-shaped blocks are also useful. For the examination of organs, a slate table, from 18 to 20 inches broad, with a couple of flat bottomed slate sinks, each 3 feet long and 4 inches deep, one fitted in at about 2 feet from each end, and with 2 feet between them, is a very convenient arrangement. The sink at the left should be used for washing out the intestines, and a nozzle should be fitted running parallel to, and about an inch from, the bottom of the sink, at the left hand corner. In the right hand sink it is well to have an ordinary tap to the right, and a pillar tap with a rose attached by a short indiarubber connection, about 4 or 5

---

[1] By a fulcrum and lever arrangement underneath the table, the body may be weighed as it lies in position.

inches long, so that it hangs vertically, when not in use, from an arm projecting from the back of the sink, this arm being so jointed that it can be turned out of the way of the operator. Hand-basins, with an abundant supply of hot and cold water, should also be within easy reach.

Where the examination has to be conducted in a private house, the following matters should be attended to beforehand :—

A good firm kitchen table is to be placed in the room where the cadaver is lying. (If this cannot be obtained, the coffin lid, or a door removed from its hinges and supported by a couple of chairs, is a good substitute.) The room should be well lighted, and as large and airy as possible ; where it is small the windows should be thrown wide-open. A piece of stout Mackintosh should be spread over the table. A couple of wash-hand basins must be procured, two empty pails, a plentiful supply of water, hot and cold, a bottle of 1–20 carbolic acid (watery solution), some turpentine, and some carbolic linseed oil, 1–5. Dr. Lindsay Steven recommends a mixture of thymol—half a drachm, and vaseline—one ounce ; and Dr. Harris of Manchester always uses a mixture of beeswax and vaseline, worked up in a mortar in such proportions that they form a kind of paste.

Clean rags, a number of newspapers, three or four sponges, a piece of soap, and several towels, are essential.

The hands of the operator are first thoroughly washed with warm water and turpentine ; a stream of cold water is then allowed to run over them ; after which they should be thoroughly anointed with the carbolic oil ; or if this is not at hand, with olive oil or lard, or with one of the above mixtures. The palms of the hands should then be carefully wiped with a clean dry cloth, in order to allow of a firm grip of knives, or other instruments, being taken. From time to time during the section the stream of cold water should again be run over the hands, or they should be dipped and rubbed in a bowl of cold water placed between the legs of the subject. When the section is completed, the hands are thoroughly washed, first with cold and then with warm water, soap, and turpentine, and when the hands are clean, some of the carbolic lotion is poured over them, and allowed to soak in, before they are finally wiped.

If the skin is cut, scratched, or pricked, the hands should be at once cleansed, the wound sucked, and pure nitric acid or strong acetic acid applied to it; it should then be covered with a layer of flexile collodion, with good waterproof plaster (Seabury and Johnson's), or with an indiarubber finger-cap. If the hands are already cut indiarubber *post mortem* gloves, *with long sleeves*, should always be used.

In all private cases the *post mortem* examination should, if possible, be made before the body is "dressed," but if this has already been done the operator should always see that it is again dressed before he leaves.

3. As much information as possible should be obtained from the medical attendant, the friends of the patient, and from the police, in order that search may be made for special features due to accident or disease, and, before the section is commenced, a careful note should be made of the time at which the patient died, the interval (in hours) that has elapsed between the death and the examination of the body, and the external temperature and the temperature of the body. This is of considerable importance, as upon these factors depend the condition or state of preservation of the organs, and the degree of *post mortem* change, and it enables the observer in many cases to decide whether certain changes are *ante mortem*, or whether they have come about subsequent to the death of the patient.

4. The body, having been placed in the supine position, with a block under the shoulders and the head hanging well down, a careful and systematic examination of the external appearances of the body must be made, and the results noted down in as clear and accurate a manner as possible. This may be done in the following order :—

Name, age, and sex (for reference), occupation, name of physician (and number of ward if in hospital), date of death and date of examination ; height (from vertex of the head to sole of the foot, in a line with the external malleolus); circumference around the shoulders ; circumference of skull around frontal and occipital protuberances (in the case of a child the shape of the cranium, the various diameters, and the condition of the sutures and of the fontanelles should also be noted); the amount of adipose tissue, and the apparent state of nutrition of the body, whether it is emaciated or well-nourished; the muscular development; and the shape and appearance generally of the head, thorax, and abdomen.

Next note the colour of the various parts of the body. Such parts as are reddened or otherwise discoloured should be firmly pressed upon with the fingers, and then examined to see whether the colour still remains *or not.* These discoloured patches should also be incised, and the colour of the tissues and the condition of the small vessels noticed. *Post mortem* lividity is always most marked in the dependent parts, except where pressure is exerted from the contact of the body with the table. Unlike the colour that arises from ecchymoses it disappears on pressure. When ecchymoses are cut into, the blood is found in the subcutaneous tissue, and can not be pressed out. A dark Fuller's earth blue or livid red colour, arranged in branching lines, is often seen on the surface, especially about the sides of the neck and on the chest and arms. This is due to decomposition of the blood in the surface veins, and the diffusion of the colouring matter of the blood into the subcutaneous tissues. A careful search must be made for abrasions or eruptions, extravasations of blood, bed sores, ulcers, or any other evidences of a diseased condition, such as pigmentation of the skin or mucous membranes, or around old cicatrices, and these must be carefully described and recorded; scars, wounds, &c., on any part of the body, and their appearance, size, and position are also noted.

Determine what degree of *post mortem* rigidity has appeared or still remains in the various muscles of the body. Note whether there is any green coloration of the abdomen over the intercostal muscles, or in any part of the body. Such coloration, when present, points to the presence of pus or inflammatory products beneath, and is usually met with in cases of peritonitis and pleurisy, especially when the fluids have become purulent, and over abscesses. Observe the eyelids, the tension of the eyeballs, the appearance of the cornea, and the relative size of the pupils. Examine the various orifices of the body—the nose and the ears for discharges of any kind, and for foreign bodies which may have become impacted; the mouth, about which should be noted the colour of the lips, the appearance and position of the teeth and of the lower jaw, and the relation of the tongue to these. Here also look for foreign bodies, and in the fauces and larynx. Note the condition of the breasts, the state of distention of the abdomen, and see whether there are "linea albicantia" or not. The organs of generation are now to be examined for any abnormality or growth, and a careful search is to be made for any evidence of Inguinal or Femoral Hernia. (In the child it should be noted whether the testicles have descended.) The anus is to be examined in a similar manner for growths, scars, or fissures. In addition to the above it should be noted, in the case of a child, whether the anus is perforated or not, the condition of the umbilicus and the umbilical cord, the presence or absence of *vernix caseosa,* and the condition of the various epiphyses, especially of that at the lower end of the femur, which should be gradually cut away in very thin slices.

5. In making all *post mortem* examinations it is necessary to have certain well defined rules of procedure ; and although, in a small minority of cases, these rules cannot be adhered to in their entirety, they nevertheless form a basis on which to work regularly and methodically. It will be found that the various sets of rules adopted by eminent pathologists are mostly based upon Virchow's method—a method which, with more or less modification, has found almost universal favour. In the following short *resumé* of the various steps to be taken in conducting a *post mortem* examination there is nothing original ; it is an outline of a system that has been found to be exceedingly convenient, and very thorough. It is based upon that given by Virchow.[1]

6. It may be laid down as a cardinal rule that, where possible, *all* the cavities of the body are to be examined, and also that they

---

[1] Those who require a full and accurate description of the manner of conducting medico-legal sections should consult Virchow's "Method of performing *Post Mortem* Examinations, with Special Reference to Medico-Legal Practice," translated from the German by Dr. T. P. Smith ; also "*Post Mortem* Handbook for Clinical and Medico-Legal Purposes," by Thomas Harris, M.D., Lond., M.R.C.P.; and "A Text Book of Pathology" (Introductory Chapters), by Prof. Hamilton of Aberdeen.

are to be examined in a regular order (head, thorax, abdomen), which order should be rigidly adhered to, unless there be very good reason for departing from it. In certain cases the abdomen or the thorax may be opened and examined first; as for instance, when there is good reason to suspect some grave lesion or lesions in the viscera contained within one or other of these cavities, and where the removal of some of the organs might disarrange the relative positions of the diseased parts; otherwise, it is desirable to keep to the order and plan as closely as possible.

Before opening the head, however, it is well to open the other cavities, and make a preliminary examination of certain of their contained viscera. This may be done as follows :—

7. Stand on the *right* side of the body, and with a strong sharp knife, held in the palm of the hand, make a single incision through the skin and subcutaneous tissue of the neck, commencing at the symphysis of the chin, continuing it down the middle line of the sternum cutting down to the bone, then through the muscular wall of the abdomen, passing round the umbilicus, and extending to the pubes ; this part of the incision not being carried deeper than the subperitoneal tissue. When the neck is not to be examined the lower margin of the thyroid cartilage, instead of the symphysis menti, may be taken as the upper extremity of the incision. At one point, a little below the ensiform cartilage, carefully dissect through the peritoneum ; pass the fingers of the left hand through the opening so made ; raise the abdominal wall and complete the incision by cutting from within outwards, so as to avoid injuring any of the organs which are situated near the surface in the middle line. Examine the cut surface of the muscle, and note any peculiarity, such as pallor, hyaline patches (met with in Enteric Fever), or minute opaque white points,—encapsuled trichinæ, which are found specially in the recti muscles ; then make a careful search for any adhesion ; should such be present, note its position before disturbing any of the organs. At the same time notice the relative position of the liver, the stomach, intestine, and other viscera to the costal and ensiform cartilages. As soon as the body is opened, and before oxidation of the colouring matter of the blood can be brought

about by the presence of air, observe the colour of the liver.
Look carefully for perforations, fæcal matter in the peritoneal
cavity, constrictions of the intestine; examine the state of distention of the stomach; look for points of adhesion, perforation,
or any evidence of inflammation. It is to be remembered that
in all cases an external or a cut surface of an organ must be
examined at once, and the colour noted, though these surfaces are
also to be examined later, when the blood has become oxygenated,
and has assumed the bright red colour commonly associated with
arterial blood. The position of the diaphragm is to be carefully
noted (the normal height on the right side is at the level of the
fourth rib or the fourth intercostal space, on the left side, at the
level of the fifth rib); and lastly, any fluid contained within the
cavity is to be removed, measured, and examined, and any sign
of inflammation, lymph, foreign body, or tumour is to be examined
and accurately localised. The examination of the abdomen must,
for the present, be carried no further; a partial examination of the
thorax must now be made.

8. The soft tissues are most easily reflected from the chest by
grasping firmly with the left hand the abdominal muscles attached
to the lower ribs and drawing on them, whilst the knife is carried
with long sweeps along the margins of the costal cartilages for some
distance on to the ribs, and then, always cutting in the same
direction, the whole of the costal cartilages, and three or four inches
of the outer ends of the ribs and clavicle, are exposed. In order
to obtain more room for examination of the abdominal cavity, it
is often convenient to cut the attachments of the recti tendons just
above and on each side of the symphysis pubis. Then remove
the sternum. With a strong cartilage knife cut through the sterno-
costal cartilages as near to the end of the ribs as possible, and cut
downwards, outwards, and backwards, following the line of the
attachment of the ribs to their cartilages, commencing with the
second rib and passing down to the ninth, the line of incision
gradually curving outwards, this curvature becoming greater as
the floating ribs are reached and cut through. If care be taken
to carry the knife in an oblique or slanting direction, the cartilages

are cut through with comparative ease, but unless this direction be taken, it is often a matter of very great difficulty to divide these tough cartilaginous structures. When the cartilages have become ossified it is found impossible to divide them with a knife. Then, as the object is to gain free access to the chest cavity, the best plan is to divide the ribs with the saw or bone-forceps at some distance from the cartilages, great care being taken not to injure the visceral pleural sacs. Having separated the ends of the ribs, raise the sternum with the left hand, and carefully cut away the bone from the soft tissue beneath, making one cut downwards (towards the feet) to separate the diaphragm from its attachments to the lower end of the sternum, two lateral cuts above the curve already described, and then, after passing up the hand to feel for any mediastinal tumour or aneurism, pass the knife upwards to the manubrium, taking care not to injure the pericardium. Cut through the cartilage of the first rib (which is very frequently ossified), and disarticulate the clavicle. To divide the first costal cartilage the knife must pass a little further outwards than for the second rib, and, on account of the frequent ossification, it is often necessary to use the bone-forceps, even when the other cartilages have been readily divided with the knife. According to Virchow, "The best way to proceed is to insert the knife" (which should always be sharp and narrow) "with its edge looking upwards and forwards, under the cartilage of the first rib, below its inferior border, and then cut upwards and forwards." Divide the sterno-clavicular ligament, and turn the sternum backwards.[1] The next step is to open the pleural sacs, notice the position, state of distention, colour, and general appearance of the lungs, and look for any fluid, noting carefully whether it is blood-stained or not, then pass the hand between the two pleural surfaces, and make sure of the presence or absence of any adhesions or foreign body or tumour. Carefully remove and measure any fluid which may be present, just as in the case of the abdomen. Do not for the present attempt to remove the lungs, but note the condition of the mediastinum, the size and appearance

---

[1] I prefer to disarticulate the manubrium sterni, as on several occasions I have seen nasty scratches inflicted by the sharp edges of the divided bone, when the sternum has been sawn from the under side and broken across.

of the thymus gland, and the appearance of the vessels outside the pericardium; then open the pericardial sac by two incisions at right angles to each other, both extending from the lower and right side of the heart, one directly upwards, and the other outwards to the left side. Look for points of adhesion, especially near the great vessels; notice the appearance of the surfaces of the heart and pericardium, and remove any serous fluid which may be in normal quantity, or in greater or less excess, also look for any blood, and again feel for any tumour or aneurism that might be present; and lastly, note the state of distention or contraction of the various chambers and vessels of the heart. Not until this point is reached can we commence to remove any of the viscera, as such removal is necessarily accompanied by a considerable loss of blood, which drains away from the heart, and so may alter very considerably the state of distention of the cavities of that organ, and its relations to the other viscera, and to the external landmarks.

9. The dissection now goes on regularly, commencing with the head and neck, and then passing downwards, taking the thorax and abdomen in order.

Head.—After a careful external examination of the head for wounds, ecchymoses, or disease, has been made, an incision is carried transversely over the vertex of the skull from behind the right ear to a similar point on the opposite side, cutting *outwards* after transfixing the skin, so as to cut away no more hair than is absolutely necessary, and also to keep the edge of the knife in good order. If this is not done, the hair should be carefully parted along the line of incision. Reflect the skin and pericranium over the occiput and over the forehead, exposing the occipital protuberance and the eminences over the frontal sinuses. Then carefully examine the soft tissues and the outer surface of the bones for any abnormal appearances, or for fractures or depressions; carry the knife round the skull at the level above indicated, and divide any adherent soft tissues and the temporal muscles (or turn down the temporal muscles with their aponeuroses), and saw through the dense outer layer and part of the inner porcellanous layer of bone in this circular direction, taking care not to allow the saw to pass through the whole thickness of the skull. During this sawing, an assistant with his hands protected with a strong towel holds the head. The left hand of the operator should also be protected by a cloth. To complete the separation of the skull-cap use the mallet and steel chisel, breaking through the remainder of the inner table, unless a fracture of the bones of the skull is suspected, in which case it is better to use the saw more freely, even at the risk of injuring the membranes or the brain. In sawing through the calvaria, take care, in all cases, to go as deep as you intend at any one place before you leave it. Then, using the cross-bar as a lever, detach the skull-cap from the subjacent membranes. In most cases this is readily enough managed, but in persons who have suffered from chronic alcoholism, or who have been subjected to hard knocks or rough usage, it is not such an easy matter, owing to the presence of adhesions. In children, too, where the bones are still growing rapidly, there is, almost invariably, adhesion of the skull-cap to the dura mater beneath. In such cases, it is better to combine the removal of the bony cap with the next stage and take out the brain with skull-cap attached. Where the skull-cap can be detached, the appearances of the inner surface of the skull-cap, any thin points, or extreme thickening, and the outer surface of the dura mater and the meningeal vessels are to be noted, and the superior longitudinal sinus is to be laid open and examined.

Next make a small opening into the dura mater on each side, just above the bony margin, and pass in at each of these openings in turn a curved probe-pointed bistoury, carrying it to the mesial line on each side, backwards and forwards, so as to thoroughly divide the membrane; then with a pair of scissors cut through the attachment to the crista galli, and draw back the membrane,[1] falx cerebri and all, from the surface of the brain, leaving it attached at the position of the meeting of the sinuses. Examine its inner surface, the exposed arachnoid and pia mater, and then proceed to remove the brain. Whilst these operations are being carried on, the following amongst other points should be carefully noted :—

---

[1] Hamilton recommends that the falx should not be removed from the longitudinal fissure, because, if the brain has to be injected with a hardening fluid, this is apt to disturb the vessels.

The quantity of blood in the membranes and in the cerebral cortex; the quantity and nature of the fluid in the subarachnoid space; the breadth and depth of the sulci, and the breadth of the convolutions; any flattening or depressions, discoloration, or other marked alteration, such as lymph on the surface; hæmorrhage of any kind; tubercle granulations on the pia mater, especially along the fissure of Sylvius, and at the vertex. Learn to distinguish these from the Pacchionian granulations for which they are sometimes mistaken.

With the fingers of the left hand draw back the frontal lobes, and carefully detach the olfactory bulbs from the cribriform plate with the handle of a scalpel; then, passing the fingers gradually further and further back, so as to support the brain, divide the optic nerves and the internal carotid vessels with a sharp scalpel as near their bony channels as possible. Passing backwards, divide the third nerves, the fourth pair as they lie in the margin of the tentorium cerebelli, and the sixth nerves, which are divided along with the tentorium. In the same manner the fifth and seventh are cut with the sharp bistoury, which is further carried along the margin of the tentorium, freely dividing that membrane at its point of attachment to the petrous portion of the temporal bone. Cut through the eighth and ninth nerves, then, with a long sharp-pointed bistoury, divide the cord as low down in the canal as it is possible to reach, and carefully tilt the brain backwards from the cranial cavity with the right hand, supporting it beneath with the left. Lay it aside until the examination of the inner surface of the dura mater at the base of the skull is completed.[1] Here look for any altered conditions or new growths. Slit open the various sinuses, and note their contents (as the state of distention of the right auricle has been already observed, it is not a matter of very great importance that the escape of blood should be prevented), examine the various vessels at their points of entrance to the skull, after which the dura mater may be detached with a chisel, and the bones at the base of the skull examined, especially the petrous portion of the temporal bone.

---

[1] To support the brain on the table, twist a cloth into a roll, make a circle with it, in the hollow of which the organ may rest.

10. Weigh the *brain*,—average weight of encephalon, male, 49-51 oz.; female, 44-45 oz.—and note its relative weight to that of the body. Then dissect it. In making this dissection it is necessary (as in the dissection of all the viscera) to have two ends in view :—*1st.* To make as complete a naked eye examination as possible ; *2nd.* To have the organ so cut up that it will be possible to replace each separate part in its proper position, to enable the operator to examine the organ as a whole, or to take any small portion from a precise given area. These ends may be attained in one of several ways, but it will be well here to give two methods, by either of which this examination may be made thoroughly and well. In either of these methods, Virchow's cardinal rules for the attainment of the object in view should be constantly borne in mind. They may be summed up as follows :—(1.) Make bold, free incisions by traction through the thickest, broadest, and longest part of the organ ; (2.) Leave the fibrous covering of the organ, some of the vessels, or some of the parenchyma of the organ, to keep the sections attached, at one edge.

(*a*.) Virchow's method slightly modified.—With a long, thin, narrow-bladed knife cut horizontally from within outwards into the hemisphere, just above the level of the corpus callosum, leaving the upper part of the brain attached to the lower, by the pia mater only, at its outer margin ; make a similar incision into the opposite hemisphere. Then examine the lateral ventricles before any excess of fluid has time to escape, by cutting vertically down into the corpus callosum at a distance of one-sixteenth of an inch from the mesial plane, until at a depth of one-eighth of an inch the knife comes directly into the lateral ventricle. This incision is to be extended both backwards and forwards for some distance, in order to expose the "body" of the ventricular cavity (here also note the quantity of fluid that escapes). Then divide and sub-divide several times the upper portion of the cerebral hemispheres already turned outwards, always cutting from within outwards, and leaving some of the pia mater intact to hold together the wedge-shaped lamellæ. To open into the anterior horn of the ventricle cut horizontally into the frontal lobe a little below the level of the body of the cavity, removing the brain substance above the incision.

The posterior horn is opened up in a similar fashion, the horizontal incision here, however, being made in a plane about three-quarters of an inch lower.

Now separate the pons, medulla, and cerebellum from the brain proper by cutting towards the mesial line in a plane the anterior border of which is just in front of the pons, the other border lying immediately behind the posterior pair of the corpora quadrigemina. A similar incision is made from the opposite side, when the cerebellum, medulla, and the upper part of the cord may be removed, and examined later.

" Having determined the contents of the lateral ventricles, the state of their walls and venous plexus, and the condition of the septum," says Virchow, "the latter is taken hold of with the left hand, close behind the foramen of Monro, the knife is pushed in front of the fingers through this aperture, and the corpus callosum cut through obliquely, upwards and forwards, and then all these parts (corpus callosum, septum lucidum, and fornix) are carefully detached from the velum interpositum and its choroid plexus.   After these two latter have been exposed, we have to examine the state of their vessels and tissue.   Then the handle of the scalpel is passed from the front under the velum, which is thus detached from the pineal body and corpora quadrigemina, the state of these parts is determined, and the third ventricle now exposed."

Then open into the aqueduct of Sylvius by making a vertical incision through the corpora quadrigemina.   The corpora striata and optic thalami are further examined by means of numerous incisions, " whose common starting-point is the peduncle of the cerebrum. However great the number of these incisions may be—and it is necessary here to make numerous cuts—the relationship of the parts may always be closely preserved in consequence of the connection between each separate portion and the peduncle of the cerebrum."

Cut through the peduncles of the cerebellum, after which make free incisions into this organ in the positions already mentioned (*i.e.*, to get sections having as large a surface as possible).

Treat the pons, medulla, and upper part of the cord in a similar manner, the transverse incisions to be at intervals of about from one-eighth to one-quarter of an inch, the pia mater and dura mater being left uncut on the anterior surface to bind the sections together, and keep them in position.

In some few cases, as, for example, in the brains of hydrocephalic children, where there is great distention of the ventricles, it is sometimes found convenient to do the first part of the dissection into the ventricles whilst the brain is still *in situ*, or immediately after the skull-cap has been removed, and the membranes examined. In this way all risk of laceration of brain tissue and escape of fluid is done away with.

(*b.*) The other method—one especially adapted for the exact localisation of lesions on the cortex and the secondary changes in the lower parts of the brain after it has been carefully hardened—is that adopted by D. J. Hamilton from the French school. After removing the brain, injuring the carotid and vertebral vessels as little as possible, it is carefully injected with Müller's fluid for a week or two (see *Text Book of Pathology*, vol. I., p. 57), and then further hardened in Müller's fluid for several months. The cerebellum, medulla, and pons are then removed as in the first method, and a series of slices is made at right angles to the vertex, the brain being mounted on a board and all the sections being made parallel to one another, and at right angles to the superior longitudinal fissure, each slice being from one-sixth to one-half of an inch in thickness; the first section includes the tips of the frontal lobes, and the last the tips of the occipital lobes. Each slice is carefully examined, and then, by means of a small parchment or metal label, numbered and put aside for further more minute examination.

A modification of this method will also be found useful in certain cases. It consists in making vertical, more or less longitudinal, sections of the brain; the cerebellum, medulla, and upper part of the cord being left *in situ*. Where it is suspected that cortical lesions are followed by secondary degeneration descending to the cord this method is especially useful, as by making the sections in somewhat different planes the lesion may be pretty accurately followed.

11. The directions for taking out the *cord* may be now given, but it is better not to proceed with this until the thoracic and abdominal viscera have been taken out, when, of course, the body is so much lighter.

The directions given by the German medico-legal authorities [1] are those which are almost universally followed.

The vertebral column is opened from behind. Place the body in the prone position with a large block supporting the thorax, and divide the skin and subcutaneous fat exactly over the spinous processes; and remove cleanly the nucleus "from the sides of these latter, and from the arches of the vertebræ. . . .

"Then, by means of a chisel, or a vertebral saw, if at hand, the spinous processes, together with the adjoining portions of the vertebral arches, are to be detached and removed." A pair of strong bone forceps, especially if bent at an angle on the flat as recommended by Dr. Savage, will prove extremely useful in removing the arch after the laminæ have been partially cut with the saw or chisel. The removal is commenced as low as possible—at the 2nd or 3rd lumbar vertebræ. "The dura mater is now exposed, and after its external surface has been examined, it is to be carefully slit open longitudinally, and the presence of any serum or extravasated blood, or other abnormal matters, is to be determined.

"The colour, appearance, and general condition of the posterior portion of the pia mater are next to be noticed, and the consistence of the spinal cord is to be ascertained by gently passing the finger over it.

"The roots of the nerves are next to be divided on both sides by a longitudinal incision; the lower end of the cord is to be carefully taken out, its anterior connections are to be gradually separated, and, finally, the upper end is to be removed from the occipital foramen.

"In carrying out these directions great care must be taken that the spinal cord be neither pressed nor bent. When removed, the condition of the pia mater on the anterior aspect is first to be examined; then the size and colour (external) of the spinal cord are to be noted; and lastly, numerous transverse incisions are to be made with a very sharp and thin knife, to determine the internal

---

[1] *See* Dr. T. P. Smith's translation, *loc. cit.*

condition of the spinal cord, both of its white strands and of the grey substance." (These incisions should not be carried through the dura mater, which should be left attached to the posterior surface of the cord in order to keep the segments in serial position.) "The dura mater is then to be removed from the bodies of the vertebræ, and the dissector is to examine for extravasation of blood, injuries, or alterations in the bones or intervertebral cartilages." The cavity should then be carefully examined for thickening or fracture of the bone, for caries, and for evidence of pressure of any kind, such as hæmorrhage, tumours, or tubercular masses.

12. To return to the examination of the contents of the thoracic cavity. The various cavities of the *heart* must be opened separately whilst that organ still maintains its relative position to the surrounding structures. It is rotated from right to left, so that the right border of the heart may come to the front, and an incision is made into the right ventricle, commencing at the base, the knife being gradually withdrawn as it nears the apex. In the same plane make an incision into the right auricle from about midway between the two venæ cavæ to very near the base of the heart, then remove, measure, and examine the blood from the right auricle, and examine the tricuspid opening with the fingers, from the auricle, taking care not to interfere in any way with the segments of the valve. In the same way, measure and examine the blood taken from the right ventricle.

To open the left auricle, make an incision, still in the same plane, between the left superior pulmonary vein and a point just on the same side of the coronary vessels (in order that these latter may be left intact).

The left ventricle is also opened by a single cut from "just behind the base" to "just short of the apex," at a distance of about half an inch from the septum. The blood is removed from these two cavities and examined as before, and the size of the mitral orifice determined (see below).

Remove the heart by dividing the aorta and pulmonary artery at some little distance from it ; note the size of these vessels, the thickness of their walls, or any abnormal condition, and then carefully clear out all coagula, not only from these vessels, but also from the various orifices, and test the competence or incompetence of the aortic and pulmonary valves by means of a stream of water. To do this with the aortic opening, place the tips of two fingers—one in the right auricle and another in the left, and with the tips of one or two fingers of the other hand draw on the pulmonary artery. In this way an equal traction is made at three points, around and in the same plane as the closed valve. Allow water to run in from above, and see whether it runs away or not. If it does, and the water sinks rapidly, cut away the aorta down to within about one inch from the level of the valve, and note at what point the water escapes.

The pulmonary artery is to be tested in the same manner, by fixing the margins of the vessel with the tips of the fingers of both hands, and allowing the water to run in. Take the cone diameters of the various orifices where possible. To make the examination more complete, the cavities of the heart are still further opened up ; the right ventricle, by passing a pair of bowel scissors into the opening already made, and cutting towards the pulmonary artery, care being taken to avoid injuring the "anterior papillary muscle of the tricuspid valve with its chordæ tendinæ." To open the left ventricle, cut with the scissors from the apex close to the septum into the aorta, passing "midway between the pulmonary orifice and the left auricle." The auricles are further opened by incisions, one running from the opening of the superior vena cava to that of the inferior vena cava, and that for the left running between the openings of the pulmonary veins. When the cavities are fully opened up, the appearances of the tricuspid and mitral valves are to be carefully observed, any thickening, contraction, roughening, or new growth, being fully noted and described. Then examine the endocardium, its colour, and the appearance of the muscle beneath, look for clots, especially in the right auricular appendix. Observe the consistence of the muscular tissue by compressing between the fingers, and then slit open the coronary vessels with a pair of probe-pointed scissors or a probe-pointed bistoury, look for contractions, atheromatous patches, and so on. Measure the length of the various cavities, the thickness of their walls, and weigh the heart. Average weight given by different authors—male, $9\frac{3}{4}$ to 13 oz., also given at 312 grammes ; female, 9 to 10 oz. and 225 grammes—the highest weight in each case being the most accurate. After which examine the aorta for dilatations or abnormal conditions of the inner coat especially; also examine carefully the pulmonary veins.

TABLE OF MEASUREMENTS OF THE NORMAL HEART.—*Hamilton.*

DIAMETERS OF ORIFICES.		CAVITIES AND WALLS.	
Aortic,	·9 to 1 in.	Left Ventricle,	3 to $3\frac{1}{4}$ in.
Mitral,	1·2 to 1·4 in.	Wall, $\frac{1}{4}$ in. (at thinnest) to $\frac{1}{2}$ in. (at thickest).	
Pulmonary Artery,	1·1 to 1·2 in.	Right Ventricle,	$3\frac{1}{16}$ to $3\frac{3}{4}$ in.
Tricuspid,	1·5 to 1·8 in.	Wall,	$\frac{1}{4}$ in. (over all).

13. *Lungs.*—After careful examination of the serous surfaces, which are usually somewhat altered in appearance if there is any fluid present, a careful search is made for any abnormal appearances. If there is any considerable quantity of blood in either of the pleural cavities, the aorta should be examined for aneurismal dilatations. This should also be done where there has been any evidence of pressure on either the lungs or the bronchi. To remove the lungs, seize the upper lobe with the left hand, and cutting from above downwards and backwards through the vessels and bronchi, as far from the point where they enter the lung as possible, and then through the broad pulmonary ligament. The left lung should be first removed and then the right, each being placed on its own side of the body on the table. Average weight—male, right lung, 24 oz., left lung, 21 oz.; female, right lung, 17 oz., left lung, 15 oz. If there are adhesions, localised or general, which cannot be broken down with the fingers, the costal pleura must be dissected away along with the lungs. Whilst breaking down these adhesions, or when working in the thoracic cavity, it is well to get an assistant to hold the reflected mass of skin and muscle over the ends of the ribs, especially when the cartilages are ossified, or where the saw has been used. Examine the outer surface of the lung for fibrinous exudation, colour, minute hæmorrhages, fibrous adhesions, nodules, excessive pigmentation along the lines of the interlobular septa, miliary tubercles in the same position, emphysematous bullæ, gangrenous sloughs, consolidated patches, cicatrices, or any other abnormal appearances, and note the colour of these patches, whether gray (catarrhal), yellow or caseous (tubercular), or red (infarction). Note whether these latter are wedge-shaped (at the free border) or rounded (in the substance of the lung). This can only be made out after the lung has been incised. Then make a long free cut from apex to base, commencing at the outer rounded surface, and passing to the root, so as to bisect the bronchial glands, leaving the two portions attached by the vessels and bronchi forming the root of the lung. Then examine the cut surface, note the amount of blood on the surface, and how much may be squeezed out on pressure; note also how much air and serum may be squeezed out (œdema), and the colour of the serum (dirty brown in brown induration, bloody in acute congestion). Examine scrapings and consolidated patches, &c., as seen on surface ; further examine the consolidated patches, and see if there are any cavities in them. Note the number and extent of these if present, especially when they are near the apex. Look at the walls and at the pleura above them ; note their relations to the bronchi. Try the specific gravity of any consolidated or suspicious patches by placing them in water and noting whether they float or sink.

Observe the condition of the fibrous septa and of the pleural covering of the lung, the *bronchial glands* (enlargement, caseation, pigmentation), and then with a pair of scissors slit open the branches of the bronchus and pulmonary artery ; note the appearances of these lining membranes, and also look for foreign bodies, clots, new growths, or any obstructive mass.

14. It is seldom necessary to examine the parts about the side of the *face* and *ear ;* but when this is necessary, the various structures may all be exposed by continuing the vertical incision over the skull, down behind the ears to the neck, throwing the skin forward, so that it may be replaced at the conclusion of the dissection. (§ 29).

15. In the *neck* open the carotid sheath at once, after reflecting the skin, muscles, and fascia of the side of the neck and the floor of the mouth, and examine the vessels, the vagus, and the sympathetic ganglia ; then dissect out the larynx, œsophagus, and pharynx *en masse,* and remove them along with tongue and soft palate by cutting through the muscles passing from the hyoid bone to the lower jaw, close behind the symphysis menti, and cutting along the rami back to the base of the skull. Free the upper part of the pharynx behind draw forward the tongue below the jaw, and then cut through the soft parts immediately behind its hard attachment, and remove the pillars of the fauces, the floor of the mouth being thus entirely detached. With the bowel scissors open up the œsophagus from behind; the larynx and trachea are also to be cut up from behind, care being taken to avoid injuring the œsophagus. The epiglottis and vocal cords can then be examined. Open the Eustachian tubes and examine for new growths, the condition of the mucous membrane, and then examine in turn the thyroid and salivary glands, the tonsils, and the cervical lymphatic glands.

Complete the examination of the abdominal cavity.

16. Take out the *omentum*, noticing any abnormal growths or appearances, redness, lymph, colloid mass, tubercle, thickening, contraction, or constriction of the intestine.

17. After noting the position and taking measurements whilst the organ is still *in situ*, remove the spleen by cutting through its vessels and peritoneal attachments. Weigh the organ (normal weight— male, $5\frac{1}{2}$ oz.; female, $4\frac{3}{4}$ oz.) and examine the capsule for thickenings or alterations in colour. Make a free incision through the thickest and longest part; note the colour, consistence, amount of blood exuded, the appearances of the trabeculæ, and of the Malpighian bodies. Pour a watery solution of iodine over the surface, and examine again, especially the Malpighian bodies. If there are any cicatrices, swelling, or other evidences of infarction, make other incisions in various directions.

18. Remove and examine each *kidney* separately, first the left, and then the right, placing each on its own side of the body; take out at the same time the corresponding suprarenal capsules and the semi-lunar ganglia. To remove the kidney make "a vertical incision through the peritoneum, external to and behind the ascending or descending colon; the intestine is to be pushed aside, and the kidney detached from its connections," by a single cut of the knife near the hilus. Remove the fat and other tissue from the capsule and weigh the organ ($4\frac{1}{2}$ oz. in the male, a little less in the female; left a little heavier, than the right), and examine the outer surface for evidence of surrounding inflammation, then make an incision from the convex outer border of the organ down to the pelvis ; note the relative thicknesses of the medulla and cortex, normally about 7:3 (Hamilton gives it 3:1). If there is any marked deviation from these proportions, examine the organ most carefully, and notice the amount of blood exuding from the cut surface, the colour of the cortex and of the medulla, especially at the bases of the pyramids. Then strip off the capsule, see whether it is thickened, adherent, or laminated. Examine the surface for "granulations," cysts, tubercles, cicatrices, depressions or elevations, or persistent marking out of the lobes ; note the state of distention of the venæ stellatæ, the colour of the surface, and so on, after which try the consistence of the organ.

Note the size, patency, and thickness of the walls of the arteries in the boundary area, the regularity and the size of the Malpighian bodies, the appearances of the interlobular vessels in the cortex and the straight vessels and tubules in the pyramids, noting changes or accumulations in the tubules, especially near the apices of the papillæ ; look for cysts, and then examine the condition of the mucous membrane of the calyces, pelvis, and of the ureter, the latter of which should be slit up with a probe-pointed bistoury, unless it is deemed desirable to remove the kidney, bladder, and ureters together for more careful examination outside the body.

Stain a section with a watery solution of iodine (§ 1), and examine especially the Malpighian bodies and straight vessels.

In examining the kidney always commence at the capsule and work systematically towards the pelvis.

19. The *suprarenal capsules* are to be described as to size, colour, consistence, and appearances on section (induration, caseation, waxy appearance, for which apply the watery solution of iodine); examine along with them the *semilunar ganglia* of the corresponding sides, and any firmness of these ganglia is to be noted, or any signs of inflammatory thickening or pigmentation, where such are present. Preserve both of these structures for microscopic examination.

20. The *bladder* is next opened *in situ*, and any peculiarity of the mucous membrane—pouches, thickening of the walls, papillomatous growths, deposits of ammoniacal phosphates—observed. Remove the contents of the pelvis, and examine the *prostate, vesiculæ seminales,* and *urethra* for signs of inflammation, enlargement, or stricture; the *testicle* and *spermatic cord* are also examined for caseation, enlargement, or other changes.

21. In the female look for evidence of injury to the wall or peritoneal covering of the uterus; remove and note the condition of the *vagina,* search for ulceration, or new growths on the *os uteri.* Examine the *uterus,* noting its size, the thickness and consistence of its muscular wall, the condition of the mucous membrane, the corrugations (*arbor vitæ*) at the neck, the appearances of the vessels, and also any new growths, and their positions; note the condition of the broad ligaments and the fallopian tubes; and look for corpora lutea, cicatrices, cysts, or new growths in the ovary.

22. Next cut out the *rectum* after placing on it a couple of ligatures; slit it up, and examine its mucous membrane; look for fissures, stricture due to new growths or other causes, for varicose conditions of the veins, &c.

23. At this stage Virchow insists that the *duodenum* and *stomach* should be examined for adhesions, perforations, or any other abnormal appearances, and should then be opened *in situ* by an incision (made with a pair of scissors) running longitudinally along the anterior surface of the duodenum and the greater curvature of the stomach. In all cases where it is suspected that traces of poison may be found in the stomach, the organ should be removed before it is opened, and at as early a stage of the examination as possible. A couple of *double* ligatures are passed, one round the upper end of the œsophagus, the second round the lower part of the duodenum. The interval between the parts of each double ligature should be at least an inch, in order that there may be no danger of the string slipping. Remove the stomach, with its contents, and then empty these contents into a clean bottle, after cutting the ligature at the duodenal end, after which the stomach may be examined. It is sometimes recommended that this method should be adopted in every case, and it certainly has the great advantage of cleanliness. Hamilton's plan of first making a short opening along the lesser curvature and then taking the cone diameters of the two orifices is an admirable one. It may be carried out either when the stomach is opened *in situ* or after it has been removed. Determine the contents of the duodenum, "above and below the papilla biliaria; then this papilla should be examined, and its contents gently pressed out; then, by pressing on the gall bladder, we should determine the presence or absence of obstacles to the flow of bile; and, lastly, the *ductus communis choledochus* should be slit up. Then the *vena cava* should be examined, especially where death from suffocation is suspected, and, all this having been done, the liver should be removed. It is quite useless to pass a probe along the gall duct, for our being able to introduce a probe into the orifice is no evidence whatever that the portio intestinalis was pervious during life."

The *stomach* should be examined at the same time as the duodenum, and any thickening of the pylorus, congestion, or ulceration of the mucous membrane noted.

24. Many pathologists remove the *liver* first, but it is better, in many cases, to leave it until this stage, in order that the relations of the organ itself, and of the gall duct and bladder to the stomach, duodenum, and head of the pancreas may be determined. To free it carry the knife through the arch of the diaphragm along the left border of the liver, then pulling the organ forward, sweep through the falciform ligament, and cut through the remaining attachments to the diaphragm, posteriorly. Slit open the gall bladder and look for watery or inspissated bile, gall stones, or any other abnormal condition; weigh (average weight—in the male 48-50 oz., in the female 41-42 oz.) and measure, note the shape, consistence, and resistance, and examine the external surface for thickenings or any abnormal appearance. Make sections through its substance transversely (from right to left), leaving the sections united by one edge at the under surface of the organ; note the toughness of the tissue as the knife passes through it, and test its consistence and friability with the fingers, observe the amount of blood contained, the size of the vessels, the appearance of the capsule on section, the amount of connective tissue, the colour and appearance of each zone of the lobules (before and after the addition of iodine solution),

and the size of the lobules; look for new growths, such as cancer, sarcoma, or tubercle.

After the removal of the liver, the stomach and duodenum, if not already removed, may be drawn upwards and excised by cutting parallel to the vertebræ through the head of the pancreas, and then pulling forward and cutting through the various posterior attachments.

25. Then examine the *pancreas*, especially at its attachment in the curve of the duodenum, for tumours or cysts, which are usually found in the head,—the part that lies in the curve,—and take out the semilunar ganglia, if this has not been done when the kidneys were removed; it is to be remembered that in some cases this is much easier to do at this stage, when the pancreas has been got out of the way, than earlier.

26. The *mesentery* and *intestines* are examined *in situ*, and any adhesions, new growths, enlarged glands, the condition of the *vessels* and *lymphatics* should be observed; then, taking hold of a loop, with a sharp knife cut through the attachment of the mesentery close to the intestine. The two extremities of the intestine have already been tied, and nothing remains to be done but to put on a double ligature at about one foot above the large intestine, drawing the intestine from the abdominal cavity as this is done; send a stream of water through it to wash out its contents, unless there are special reasons for examining these in the different parts of the intestine; and then slit up the bowel with the bowel scissors, taking care to cut through the walls at the point of attachment to the mesentery. Examine the mucous membrane for thickenings or changes in the various structures, congestion, ulceration, sloughing, perforation, and so on; at the same time examine the mesenteric attachment for tubercle nodules along the lines of the lymphatics; typhoid swellings and ulcers are to be specially looked for, just above and below the ileo-cæcal valve, whilst the valve itself should always be most carefully examined for tubercular ulceration, and, "in every case of peritoneal inflammation examine carefully the vermiform appendage." Apply iodine to the mucous surface.

27. Lastly, examine the *retro-peritoneal glands, thoracic duct, recep-*

taculum chyli, aorta vena cava, and the large trunks going into the pelvis; and also, if necessary, examine the sympathetic nervous trunks.

In certain cases other structures have to be examined, or more particular attention has to be paid to certain parts; but the necessity for doing this will be indicated by the clinical history of the case. In such cases special dissections must be made.

28. Where it is necessary to remove the whole eye two saw cuts should be made, one vertically downwards through the frontal bone and the roof of the orbit, in a line corresponding to the inner side of the orbit as one extreme, and the inner side of the optical foramen as the other, the other line being drawn from the outer side of the orbit to the outer side of the optic foramen. As soon as the bone is cut through a sharp tap forward behind the frontal bone will cause the horizontal plate to tilt up; this allows of a complete dissection of the eye being made. The ring around the orbit foramen may be left *in situ* by chiselling through the thin plate of bone that lies in front of it. If the whole eye is removed, however, the face is somewhat disfigured, and as in most cases it is quite sufficient to remove the posterior half of the globe, all that is necessary is to smash in and remove the thin orbital plate of the roof with a pair of strong bone-forceps. The muscles and nerves can then be dissected out, and the posterior half of the eye may be removed with a pair of sharp-pointed scissors, the parts being held in position by a pair of forceps. A scrap of dark-coloured cloth held in position behind the pupil, with cotton wadding, prevents any disfigurement.

29. The temporal bone with its petrous portion containing the internal ear may be taken out and examined after removal of the brain by stripping off the dura mater from the base, dissecting off the skin and muscle, and detaching the external ear from the bone and disarticulating the jaw; then taking the margins of the temporal bone as the base of a pyramid, the apex of which is a little beyond the inner extremity of the petrous portion, two saw cuts are carried almost vertically downwards so as to bound the pyramid, and then with a bone chisel and mallet the whole temporal bone may be removed, after which it may be softened in a decalcifying fluid, or the internal ear may be dissected out with a small saw, a pair of sharp well-fitting bone forceps, and a sharp gouge and chisel. The internal ear or tympanic cavity and mastoid cells may also be opened up with the aid of the above instruments.

30. The following method of examining the nose is one that I have sometimes used since I read Dr. Harris' little hand-book, from which the description is taken :—

"After the brain has been removed, and the base of the skull has been examined, the body of the sphenoid bone, a little in front of its line of union with the basilar portion of the occipital bone, is divided transversely with the aid of a chisel, and then by means of a small saw the base of the skull is divided along a line running on either side from the extremities of the incision in the body of the sphenoid, through the middle fossa on the outer side of the cavernous sinus, and thence forward through the lesser wing of the sphenoid to the anterior fossa, where the inner part of the orbital plate of the frontal bone on both sides is divided as far as its anterior extremity, and then the extremities of these incisions are united by a transverse one across the front part of the perforated plate of the ethmoid bone. We are then enabled, by means of a chisel and a pair of bone forceps, to remove the portion of the base of the skull included between the lines of incision, and to examine the interior of the nasal cavities."

AVERAGE WEIGHTS OF ORGANS.

Table used in the Post Mortem Room of the Royal Infirmary, Edinburgh.

	MALE.		FEMALE.	
	lbs.	oz.	lbs.	oz.
Human Brain,	3	1½	2	1½
„ Heart,	—	11	—	9
„ Lungs,	2	13	2	—
„ Liver,	3	5	2	12
„ Pancreas,	—	3	—	2¾
„ Spleen,	—	6	—	5½
	Right.	Left.	Right.	Left.
	oz.	oz.	oz.	oz.
„ Kidneys,	5¼	5¼	4¾	5

CHAPTER II.

PATHOLOGICAL HISTOLOGY.

31. *Instruments required.*—To the student entering upon this department of pathological investigation, who has not already made himself, to some extent, master of histological methods, a few words are necessary as to the selection of the apparatus most commonly used in carrying on microscopic work.

First, as to the microscope itself; this should, if possible, never be bought without the assistance or advice of some one well qualified to decide on the merits of the instrument.

It may help the student in his selection, however, if a short description of a good compound microscope, such as is suitable for pathological work, be given.

The pedestal must be firm and steady, either a tripod with a good broad base, or a horse-shoe. Fixed into this is a column of sufficient thickness to ensure strength, and jointed just below the stage, to allow of the whole instrument being inclined, or even bent to a right angle, if necessary, the tripod should be so based that the stand remains perfectly steady in this positon. The stage should be immovably fixed into the pillar at a convenient distance from the base, *i.e.*, not so high that the arms may not rest on the table when the fingers of the left hand are moving the slide over its surface. The transverse diameter of the stage should not be greater than the length of the ordinary glass slide—three inches. The antero-posterior diameter must not be less than two inches and a half. On each side of the pillar there should be a brass clip fixed into holes in the stage. These are of use in fixing an object in any desired position for examination, and also for controlling the movement of the slide when a high power is used.

Mechanical stages should be avoided, except for use with very high powers, for two good reasons,—they add enormously to the expense of the instrument, and, for continued work, the manipulation of the screws tires the hand much more than does the movement of the slide by means of the fingers over the simple stage. In the centre of the stage is an aperture about five-eighths of an inch in diameter. Attached to the under surface of the stage is a thin circular plate of metal, in which are cut some five or six holes, varying in size from 1-24th of an inch to three-quarters of an inch in diameter, and so placed that, when the metal disc revolves, the centre of each of these holes is in succession brought under the centre of the aperture in the stage, which should always be smaller than the largest hole, and should be tapered off from below upwards, especially where the thickness of the stage exceeds a quarter of an inch. This arrangement is of considerable importance when low powers are used.

In order to bring the metal disc and the apertures of the diaphragm nearer to the objective, the under surface of the stage may be bored or recessed. For ordinary work this is not necessary, but when higher powers are used with the smaller apertures of the diaphragm, or where it is wished to transmit oblique light through the specimen under examination, it is essential. At or near the circumference of the disc should be small depressions or indentations, into which a spring catch drops as the centre of each opening comes to the centre of the opening in the stage. The edge of the disc is milled, and its surfaces are blackened. At one side of the stage a slight recess is usually cut out, or the milled edge projects slightly, so that the disc may be readily turned by the tips of the fingers. For convenience of working, Brown's "Iris" diaphragm is much to be preferred to the disc form, but it adds about twenty shillings to the cost of the microscope. The removable "stop" diaphragms, though very perfect, are now seldom used.

Under the stage, and fixed to the pillar above the joint, is a moveable mirror, which can be focussed on the object. For ordinary work a slightly concave reflecting surface is used, but for work with very low powers, or with an achromatic condenser, a flat surface is necessary. These mirrors are used for the illumination of objects by transmitted light, or light sent through the object to the eye of the observer; it is therefore especially useful in the examination of transparent objects, which form by far the greater proportion of those which fall to be

studied by the pathologist. In most cases the light is passed
through at right angles to the plane of the section ; but where the
tissues are very delicate or very transparent, it may be thrown from
beneath obliquely, by which means a shadow picture is produced,
and even delicate structures are brought out distinctly.

The part of the microscope above the stage is, however, the more
important. Of this it will be well to describe two forms, and point
out the special advantages of each.

The first form has an arm fixed at right angles to the pillar ; into
this arm is screwed a hollow split tube, about two inches and three-
quarters in length ; working in this is a telescopic tube, composed of
two segments, measuring, when closed, about five inches, and when
drawn out to the full extent, seven inches in length.[1] In this case the
coarse adjustment is effected by giving a spiral motion to the telescopic tube in the split tube. When the parts are kept *perfectly clean*,
this adjustment answers admirably, even with moderately high powers;
but when the tubes are allowed to get at all dirty, the force exerted at
the end of the lever is apt to render the joints of the microscope
somewhat shaky. Otherwise, this is the simplest and cheapest form
of coarse adjustment, and, where no nose-piece is used, it is also the
best and the most convenient, as the tube can be quickly withdrawn
when the lenses are to be changed.

Perfect cleanliness is all that is needed to keep this part of the
microscope in good condition ; and it is to be remembered that on
no account is oil to be used, its effect being merely to clog the tubes
by accumulating in the slits in the side of the tube. The sliding parts
should be polished from time to time with a *little* powdered French
chalk.

The fine adjustment is made by means of a milled head placed at
the upper end of the pillar. If this is good, the screw should work
perfectly steadily, and not "lose time"—*i.e.*, the slightest turn of the
screw should alter the focus, and the alteration should be smooth and
steady, and not in jerks. Neither the coarse nor the fine adjustment
when moved should give rise to the slightest lateral movement of the
image in the field.

---

[1] The "English" tube is usually ten inches long, and requires lenses specially
corrected for that length.

The feature wherein the second form differs from the first is in the method of making the coarse adjustment, which is effected by means of a rack and pinion movement. This, like the fine adjustment, should be attached to the pedestal, and not to the end of the arm which supports the body of the microscope. The pinion is worked by means of "milled heads;" it should work smoothly and without any "loss of time." The rack with oblique teeth is perhaps the best that is made.

To the body of the microscope is attached a Bull's-Eye Condenser, consisting of a plano-convex lens, at the end of an arm which is fixed by a universal joint into a moveable split ring fitting around the split tube, or it may be fixed to a pedestal or standard. By means of this arrangement the condenser may be made to focus light directly on to the object under examination, such as a section of waxy liver stained with iodine, or an opaque object, from which it is reflected to the eye. (Care must be taken to have the condenser at right angles to the rays of light.) In some microscopes the condenser is fixed to the stage, where, however, it is usually in the way.

The optical parts of the microscope are naturally the most important—the eye-piece and the objectives. In selecting these, take care to obtain such as will give a magnification of about 50 for the low power, and 300 with the higher combination. In the case of the Hartnack, these are approximately given with a No. 3 eye-piece, and objectives Nos. 3 and 7; in the microscopes of English make, ocular No. 3, with five-seventh inch to one inch and one-sixth or one-seventh inch ($80°$—$100°$ angle of aperture—Hamilton) objectives; and in Zeiss's microscopes, ocular No. 3, with objectives A and D. Lower and higher powers may be afterwards obtained for special investigation, but the above lenses will be quite sufficient for ordinary work. In selecting the lenses, note the following points, testing by means (1) of a thin film of blood, and (2) salivary corpuscles. The lens must be perfectly achromatic; the low power should have good definition and a *flat field*. In regard to the low power this last point is of special importance, as with it the general outlines of the structure are first examined, and it is as necessary to have as much of the tissue under observation, in focus, at one time as possible.

Focus the blood corpuscles in the centre of the field, and then

c

observe whether the corpuscles at the margin of the field are equally distinctly seen.

The higher power should have *good definition ;* the field should also be flat ; but this is not a matter of such great moment as the clear definition of delicate structures, such as those seen in a salivary corpuscle.[1]

32. The following most useful accessory apparatus may with advantage be procured :—

A double or triple nose-piece properly centred. This will prove a great saving of both time and trouble, especially where the rack and pinion coarse adjustment is used. Zeiss's new sliding apparatus is equally convenient where the rack and pinion movement is used, and much more so where the adjustment is made by means of the sliding tube.

An achromatic condenser made by one of the English makers, a

---

[1] The demand for good and cheap microscopes has now become so great that a considerable number have lately been offered to the student. From actual experience the author can recommend almost any of the following instruments as being very good and reliable ; but he has no doubt there are others in the market almost, if not quite, as good and cheap. For cheap instruments, those made by Beck (The Star), £3 : 3s., Reichert, £3 ; 10s., Leitz, £3 : 10s. and £5 : 5s., and H. Crouch, £5 : 5s. and upwards. A little more expensive is Hartnack's No. III. A., with ocular No. 3 and objectives Nos. 3 and 7, which cost about £7 : 10s. (The fine adjustment and the higher power objective are exceedingly good, but the lower power lens is not always good, and great care should be taken in selecting this objective.) It has a steady horse-shoe stand. Similar microscopes of very great excellence are made by Nachet and Verick, both of Paris. Carl Zeiss of Jena furnishes a stand, V b, with ocular No. 3 and objectives A. and D., for about £9. The lenses made by this maker are uniformly good.

Of the English microscopes, the following may be relied upon as of thoroughly good workmanship, and possessing good optical appliances :—Pillischer's " International," with five-eighths of an inch and one-seventh of an inch objectives, and two eye-pieces, price £7 : 10s. ; a capital microscope for students. The " New International," somewhat higher in price, is also a good microscope.

R. & J. Beck's " Economic " microscope, with two eye-pieces, objectives one inch and one-eighth of an inch, £8 : 8s., also a good instrument, very firm and steady ; and the " Pathological " is really a first-class microscope.

Swift & Son's " Improved Wales's American " microscope, with one inch and one-fifth of an inch objectives, and No. 3 eye-piece, £8, and H. Crouch's " Histologist " microscope, £5 : 5s. and £6 : 6s., or the same maker's " Biologist " microscope, £9 : 9s., are all admirable students' microscopes.

Powell & Leland's oil condenser, or an Abbe's illuminator, is essential when micro-organisms are to be studied.

A paraffin lamp, with a blue glass chimney, or, what answers equally well, an argand gas burner fitted with a blue glass chimney. (This combination may be obtained for about 7s. 6d.)[1]

A micrometer eye-piece and a stage micrometer.[2]

A camera lucida, Abbé's, made by Zeiss, or one made by Nachet's of Paris.

A warm stage or a constant temperature hot-box to enclose the microscope (Zeiss).

DIRECTIONS FOR WORKING WITH THE MICROSCOPE.

33. Clean the front of the objective and both lenses of the eye-piece with a piece of soft chamois leather, a silk handkerchief, or a camel hair pencil, using, if the glasses are greasy, a little weak ammonia or benzine. Take out the draw-tube, screw on the No. 3

Of the more expensive microscopes one of the best is Zeiss's, made in various qualities, of which Nos. IV. to I., ranging in price from £7 : 10s. to £15, may be selected. This is the price of the stand only ; the other appliances, optical and mechanical, may be had up to any sum that the purchaser may feel inclined to expend. For high powers the best objectives are Zeiss's one-eighth inch, or the one-twelfth inch oil immersion by the same maker. Very good and cheap immersion lenses are made by Seibert, successor to Gundlach of Berlin, whose one-sixteenth inch water immersion lenses give exceedingly good definition with even a moderate light. Price, with correction, £3 : 18 : 6 ; without correction for thickness of cover glass, £3 : 3 : 6. Agent in London for both Zeiss and Seibert is C. Baker ; Kanthack is Zeiss's London representative. Very good higher priced microscopes also are made by Reichert and Leitz. The apochromatic lenses made by Powell & Leland and Zeiss are splendid objectives, and will stand almost any eye-piecing that can be obtained with the compensating oculars ; whilst Ross's stands have made a world-wide reputation, though they are scarcely available for students. The high power lenses made by most of the English makers are excellent in quality, but where expense is no object, those made by Powell & Leland should certainly be procured.

[1] A small electric lamp, fitted under the stage, giving a good white light, is now made, which answers admirably for microscopic work. The Kochs-Wolz lamp, price 15s., is also most convenient. It consists of a bent glass rod along which the light is transmitted from a lamp to the under surface of the microscope stage.

[2] Directions for determining the magnifying power of a lens or a combination of lenses, and for measuring the actual size of cells and bacteria are given in all the technical works on the microscope.

or low power objective, put in the No. 3 eye-piece, close the telescope tube and replace the draw tube; then bring the lens nearly down to the level of the stage, and illuminate the field by reflecting the light upwards, from the sub-stage mirror, through the largest aperture of the diaphragm. The best light that can be obtained for the purpose is a north light, not too bright, reflected from a bank of white cloud; for night-work, a lamp as already described may be used. A screen of white tissue paper or of ground glass placed before the lamp will modify both the heat and the glare of the light; whilst, if the flame be too yellow, a globe containing a solution of ammoniated sulphate of copper may be used. Look through the eye-piece with one eye, but keep both eyes open. If any specks are visible in the bright field, turn the eye-piece, and if the specks move, they are on the eye-piece and not on the objective. If there is simply blurring or cloudiness in parts of the field, the objective is still dirty, and should be more carefully cleaned. Place a slide on the stage, gradually draw the tube *upwards*, or work it upwards with the coarse adjustment, moving the slide over the stage with the left hand, and look down the tube, until the specimen comes into view in the bright field. Then with the fine adjustment bring the object accurately into focus.

By commencing with low powers near the stage (about a quarter of an inch away) there is less danger of bringing a very low power, say a two or four-inch objective, down on the slide.

In all cases, the general features of the object should be first carefully studied under the low power, from which study much is to be learned.

Place in the centre of the field any part of the object which is to be further examined, and screw on the high power lens, or turn round the arm of the nose-piece to which the high power lens is attached. Centre a small aperture of the diaphragm. The objective is then brought to a distance of a quarter of an inch from the stage, and is gradually brought *down* by means of the coarse adjustment to the point at which the outline of the specimen may be clearly seen (the directions given above as to looking through the microscope whilst the object is being focussed still being borne in mind); then focus more carefully with the fine adjustment, and use the aperture of the diaphragm, which, whilst allowing the passage of sufficient light, enables you to obtain the sharpest definition. It must be remembered that it is always necessary to use a smaller aperture when a specimen is unstained than when it is stained. In using the high power, the beginner will from time to time bring the lens down into the Canada balsam or other mounting fluid, unless very great care be taken to attend to the directions given. When this occurs, it is well to remember that the Canada balsam may be dissolved off by means of a drop of clove oil, which should, however, be removed at once, or it will loosen the lenses, which are usually "set" in Canada balsam.

In reading the above directions, it will be noticed that nothing has been said about changing the eye-piece. This is intentional, and the student will find that it is better to accustom himself to a single eye-piece, and to alter the magnifying power by means of the objectives, rather than by the eye-piece. With a *perfect* lens, any eye-piece may be used, but where there are the very slightest defects in the lens, these are, of course, magnified by the higher eye-pieces, which magnify only the image given by the objective. The same remark holds good as regards the lengthening of the tube. When possible, work with the shorter tube, for, although greater magnifying power is obtained when the tube is drawn out, the definition is not so good, except with first-class lenses, and in a very strong light.[1]

The student should accustom himself to work with the microscope in a vertical position, as the fingers can move the slide much more steadily over a level stage,—fluids should always be examined on a horizontal stage. With the high power, the clips gently pressed down on to the slide will prove of very great service in controlling its movements. A list of the apparatus and reagents required is given on page 112, *et seq.*

Before setting to work, see that both slides and cover glasses are perfectly clean. The slides, as a rule, are pretty free from grease or hard film when they are supplied, and can be readily cleansed by

[1] With the apochromatic lenses as now constructed this does not hold good, but as the student is not likely to use these except when he has become accustomed to the use of the microscope, it is not necessary to go into that question.

thoroughly washing them in clean water, and drying them carefully with an old cloth ; but new cover glasses are sometimes coated with grease, or with a hard film, which cannot be got rid of by water alone. To cleanse them, put them into a shallow glass or porcelain dish, and cover them with some strong acid (nitric, sulphuric, or acetic), leave them for a couple of hours, pour off the acid, and wash well with clean water, then with methylated spirit, after which they should be dried with an old handkerchief. Once clean, they should always be held by the edges ; they should never be laid down flat, but should be tilted up against some convenient object, such as the microscope or the reagent stand, until required. Cover glasses may be cleaned in large quantities, left in water or in clean spirit in a covered vessel, and dried as they are required for use.

Examination of Fresh Tissues.

34. For the pathologist, even more than for the student of histology, it is necessary to examine tissues in a fresh condition. In making such examinations, the tissues must be bathed in a medium which will not change either the appearances or the vital properties of their various elements more than is absolutely necessary, and where possible, tissue elements should be examined in the fluid in which they are normally bathed. Pus, blood, fluid secretions, and sediments, usually contain sufficient fluid to allow of the corpuscles being easily mounted ; and when mounted, the corpuscles remain comparatively unchanged, until the quality of the fluid is altered by evaporation, or until the altered temperature begins to tell upon them. Where larger sections or fragments are to be examined or where the fluid is too thick, it is necessary to extemporise a neutral medium in which to bathe the tissue. In the case of gland tissue, nerve fibrils, splenic pulp, and other like delicate and unstable tissues, such a fluid is essential. Any of the following may be used :—

1. Aqueous humour taken from the anterior chamber of the eye of a newly killed ox, after puncturing the cornea with a triangular knife. This, of course, is available only in small quantities.

2. Serous fluids, such as that taken from the pericardial sac (which

is always procurable in the *post mortem* room), hydrocele fluid, amniotic fluid, or even blood serum, which are not so readily obtained.

3. An artificial serum may be made by adding to 1 part of egg albumen, 9 parts of neutral salt solution (see No. 5).

4. To any of these serous fluids, iodine may be added to form *iodised serum.* It is prepared by adding

> 1 part tincture of iodine to
> 100 parts of the serous fluid.

To each ounce of the fluid add a couple of drops of carbolic acid, and filter. This may be kept for some time, but should be prepared fresh whenever opportunity occurs. Its disadvantages are that it alters the tissues slightly, and stains them yellow.

5. *Salt solution.*—Three-quarters per cent. solution of sodium chloride is practically a neutral solution; it alters the tissues but slightly, never causes any swelling, and is easily prepared by heating sodium chloride to redness, cooling it over sulphuric acid, and dissolving $7\frac{1}{2}$ parts by weight in 1000 parts by measure of distilled water.

35. Tissues teased out and mounted in any of the above fluids, retain an almost normal appearance and structure for a sufficient length of time to allow of a careful examination. Snip off a small fragment with a pair of curved scissors, put it on a clean glass slide with a *small* quantity of the neutral fluid (a single drop is usually quite sufficient). There should always be enough to allow of the tissue being bathed in the fluid, without air-bubbles being allowed to creep in, but never sufficient to float the cover glass. With one of the needles fix the piece of tissue at one margin, and with the other tear off small fragments; these smaller fragments are fixed with one needle, and torn with the other in the same manner, until they are small enough to be examined. Put on a cover glass, and then place on the stage of the microscope. In this operation a simple or dissecting microscope will prove of great assistance. This may be easily extemporised from the bull's eye condenser by fitting a ring of blackened cardboard into the brass frame on the plane surface of the condenser. It is used as a simple lens, leaving it

attached to the body of the microscope, or fastening it to any
upright bar, say of a retort stand. (The perforated cardboard, the
student will understand, acts as a diaphragm.)

36. *Method of applying a cover glass.*—Take a cover glass by the
edges between the forefinger and thumb of the left hand. Allow
the edge to the left to come in contact with the left edge of the
drop of mounting fluid. Then with a needle held *under* the right
hand allow the right edge to descend slowly, taking care that the
cover drives the fluid evenly before it and encloses no air bubbles.
If the cover is perfectly clean, the operation is readily enough per-
formed; but if it is at all dirty, a considerable crop of air bubbles
is sure to result, in spite of the greatest care. Any air bubbles in
the mounting or examination medium should be carefully removed
with the point of a needle before the cover glass is applied.

37. The salt solution is also used in the process known as "pencilling." A thin section of the tissue cut fresh and placed on a glass
slide is covered with the fluid, and then beaten with a camel hair
pencil. By this method the cells of a section of a lymphatic gland
are set free from the network of delicate tissue in which they lie, and
the different elements may be readily examined.

A similar result may be more effectually obtained by shaking the
section in a test tube containing a quantity of the salt solution.

38. Scrapings of fresh organs should also be examined. To
obtain these, first squeeze and wash out as much blood as possible
from the surface, then carrying the knife at right angles to this surface, scrape off some of the juice, dilute it with neutral salt solution,
and examine at once. All fluids rich in cells may be treated in this
fashion. Where the cells are not plentiful the fluid may be allowed
to stand in a conical glass, and the sediment is then removed with a
pipette, and examined in the same manner.

39. Lastly, thin sections of fresh tissues should always be examined both unstained and stained.

To make a section of most fresh tissues with an ordinary razor is a
matter of very great difficulty, and in its place a Valentine's knife

may be used. This instrument is set to cut sections of a certain thickness between its two parallel blades; it is first *drawn by a single movement* through the organ of which a section is to be made, then suddenly turned, and a sharp cut is made at a considerable angle to the first, so as to separate the section. The blades are then unscrewed under water (it is best to use the saline solution in which to manipulate the sections so made), and the section is transferred to a slide.

A more satisfactory plan of making fresh sections in the *post mortem* room is by means of Cathcart's microtome (§ 85). A drop of gum placed on the plate is nearly frozen, and a thin slice of the tissue to be cut is placed on this, a little more gum is painted round the edges (the tissues are frozen just firm enough to allow of their being cut easily); make sections and mount. Sections so made are thin enough to be mounted and stained for a more complete examination at a later period, though of course they do not remain unaltered for an indefinite length of time.

40. To mount these sections, float them in a large quantity of water or salt solution, then taking the slide in the left hand, plunge it into the water in such a position that its under surface forms an angle of about 60° with the table; by moving the slide gently to and fro the section is brought from the bottom of the basin (if it has sunk); then, with a needle in the right hand, gently draw one edge of the section on to the slide, fix it there, and withdraw the slide from the water when the part of the section last in the water is floated out on to the slide. The slide is now turned round, and the margin which was first fixed may be floated out in the same way; and underlying or overlapping edges all round are similarly treated until the section is spread out, perfectly flat, on the glass slip.

Remember, in doing this (1) to draw the margin a little beyond the centre of the slide when fixing the first edge, in order that the section may be near the centre; and (2) after fixing the edge with the needle, not to touch the section with the needle again, but to trust entirely to the movement in the water to spread out the crumpled edges. Put on a cover glass (§ 36) and examine. A second section should be stained.

The best stains for these fresh specimens are picro-carmine (§ 98); methylaniline violet (§ 106); fuchsin (§ 114); methylene blue (§ 116); aniline blue black for nerve cells (Bevan Lewis) (§ 112); and osmic acid (§ 110). Mount in glycerine (§ 151); Farrant's solution (§ 152); or Canada balsam (§ 155).

Fluids used for the purpose of macerating and isolating tissue elements without hardening them.

41. In some cases it is almost impossible to tease out fresh sections so as to obtain anything like satisfactory results. By macerating them in one of the following fluids, however, it is found that the tissue elements or cement substances may be so altered that the constituent parts are readily separated. In doing this it must be remembered that the object is not to harden the tissues, but to isolate cells or fibres, and only a small quantity of the macerating fluid should be used for each fragment of tissue. The following are amongst the most useful :—

1. *Weak alcohol.* 1 part 96 per cent. spirit to 2 parts water (Ranvier). Macerate for twenty-four hours.

2. *Iodised serum* (§ 34) dissolves the intercellular cement substance in about thirty-six hours. It is also useful for macerating white nerve fibres.

3. *Common salt, ten per cent. solution,* may be used to soften the cement substance of white fibrous tissue. It is useful in the study of fibromata, osteo-sarcomata, and similar growths.

4. *Caustic potash, forty per cent. solution,* may be used for isolating the cells of non-striped muscle—myoma uteri. This seldom takes longer than from twenty minutes to an hour. Tease out, stain with picro-carmine (§ 98), and mount in Farrant's solution (§ 152). If time is available, and it is wished to obtain a permanent preparation of the muscle cells from such growths, use—

5. *Nitric acid, twenty per cent. solution.*—Place small fragments of the muscular tissue in this fluid, and leave for twenty-four hours; wash well in water, tease, stain, and mount in glycerine. By this method the connective tissue is softened, and the muscle cells are hardened. A similar fluid for isolating nerve structures may be used :—

Glycerine	.	1 part.
Water . .	. . .	3 parts.
Strong nitric acid	. . . .	1 part.

Mix thoroughly. Place small fragments of the tissue in this fluid, leave for three or four days, and then wash well with distilled water.

6. *Ordinary Müller's fluid* (§ 59) may be used as a macerating fluid for nerve tissues, small pieces of which are left in a few drops of the medium for two or three days, and then teased out. They may then be examined in glycerine, water, or saline solution.

7. *Dilute chromic acid* ·1 per cent. May be used for the same tissue.

8. *Perosmic acid* 1 per cent. Especially useful for defining the outlines of cells and for fatty tissues, which should be allowed to macerate for from twelve to twenty-four hours before any attempt is made to tease them out.

9. *Acetic acid*, one per cent. for five or ten minutes, and then chromic acid ·1 per cent. for twenty-four or forty-eight hours. Stain in picro-carmine and examine in glycerine or Farrant's solution (Arnold).

These methods assume special importance in the study of the elements of which morbid growths are composed. For the various methods of artificial digestion, which are sometimes useful to the pathologist, the student is referred to special handbooks on Histology.

42. It is often necessary to inject the vessels of an organ or of a tissue before it is cut up or hardened. In making injections for this purpose it is to be remembered that, in most cases, the patient has been dead for twenty-four hours, and that not only have the tissues undergone considerable structural changes, but they have become considerably lowered in temperature. For these reasons, a gelatine injection fluid cannot be forced into the smaller ramifications of the blood-vessels, unless certain precautions are taken to prevent the too rapid solidification of the gelatine. The tissues must be carefully heated throughout to 100° F., or 38½° C. In some cases such elevation of temperature might give rise to considerable alterations in the tissues, especially where there is much epithelium, the cement substance of which has already become somewhat changed during the period that has elapsed since death; here it is

necessary to use what may be spoken of as a *cold injection*, or one which is fluid at the ordinary temperature.

43. *Cold Injection Fluid, No.* 1.—*Richardson's Blue.*

Dissolve ten grains of ferric sulphate in 1 ounce of distilled water. Then dissolve 32 grains of ferrocyanide of potassium in 1 ounce of distilled water; and add the ferric sulphate solution gradually, keeping the mixture well shaken in a bottle as it assumes a beautiful greenish-blue fluid, then add 2 ounces of water and 1 ounce each of glycerine and alcohol, shaking the mixture vigorously. Hamilton recommends that the two salts should be dissolved in a mixture of the glycerine and water (taking half of the total quantity for each), and then mixed as above, 10 grains of oxalic acid should then be rubbed up with the fluid in a mortar, after which the alcohol is added. The oxalic acid prevents any fading of the blue. This fluid is always ready for use, but, before injecting, it is well to give the bottle a good shaking. This precipitate is so fine that the injection may be used for filling the smallest capillary blood-vessels. For instance, in a leg amputated for a circular ulcer, this injection, forced into the tibial vessels, passes readily into the vascular loops near the surface of the ulcer, giving rise to a blue colour, where before the injection there was the characteristic raw red appearance of ordinary granulation tissue.

44. *Cold Injection, No.* 2.

Soluble Prussian blue, which may be bought ready prepared, is also a very convenient material with which to make a cold injecting fluid. Dissolve 2 parts of soluble Prussian blue in 100 parts of distilled water; add a few drops of hydrochloric or acetic acid before using.

After being injected the organ should be plunged into weak methylated spirit (equal parts of spirit and water), to which a few drops of hydrochloric acid have been added; it is left in this for twenty-four hours, after which it may be cut up and the hardening process continued; or it may be hardened from the first in Müller's fluid (§ 59), or picric acid (§ 71). Sections should again be washed in weak acid and mounted in camphor mounting fluid (§ 153), or in Canada balsam (§ 155).

Kollmann's cold carmine injection may also be used. It is prepared by dissolving 1 gramme of carmine in 15 drops of liq. ammonia to which 20 cc. of glycerine is added. This is added to a mixture of 1 gramme of common salt dissolved in 30 cc. glycerine, and the whole is diluted with 50 cc. of distilled water.

45. For capillary injections Cohnheim used a mixture of one part of aniline blue in 600 parts of 5 per cent. salt solution; and Hamilton recommends a ¼ per cent. watery solution of aniline blue-black, either alone or combined with 5 per cent. gelatine. These are both true solutions, and there are no particles, however fine, to become impacted in the minute blood vessels.

Rutherford mentions two injection masses used by Ludwig.

The first of these—asphalte, dissolved in chloroform and filtered, —is used for injecting the bile ducts. The special advantage of this fluid is "that chloroform, being an extremely mobile fluid, flows readily along the vessels, and that it readily evaporates and leaves them filled by a solid black mass."

The second, "a solution of alcannin, in turpentine or in chloroform, is used by Ludwig for injecting lymphatics. The solution is of a bright red colour. Both the turpentine and the chloroform flow readily. When the latter is employed the chloroform evaporates, and leaves the alcannin in the vessels."

46. Nitrate of silver cannot, as a rule, be employed by the pathologist as an injection, as the tissues are dead before he can deal with them, and nitrate of silver does not act at all readily upon dead tissues. In the case of tumours, however, which may be obtained at once, thin slices of the tissue may be injected by absorption. Thin sections are placed in a half per cent. solution of nitrate of silver (§ **118**), where they are left for twelve hours. They are then transferred to a solution of equal parts of methylated spirit and glycerine. The sections should be mounted in glycerine.

47. The following injection masses are solid at ordinary temperatures, and can only be used in the case of animals newly killed or where the parts to be injected can be warmed to blood-heat.

Carmine Gelatine Injection Mass.

a. In a mortar pour 8 parts by measure of liq. ammonia on 4 parts by weight of carmine, when an almost black paste will be formed if the carmine is pure; to this add 50 parts by measure of distilled water, and set the solution aside to filter.

b. In a tall glass jar, cover 10 parts by weight of pure gelatine (Cox & Coignet's) with distilled water; allow to stand until all the water is absorbed, and the gelatine is thoroughly softened.

Warm solution (*a.*) in an earthenware jar or basin, placed in a pan of water (kept nearly boiling on a gas jet or near the fire), and add the gelatine; stir thoroughly, and add a ten per cent. solution of acetic acid, drop by drop, until the alkalinity of the ammonia is neutralised and the fluid even slightly acid.

The point at which this takes place will be recognised by the fact that the pungent odour of the ammonia is gradually lost, and that of acetic acid substituted, and also that a precipitation of the carmine takes place, indicated by the fluid losing its bright carmine transparent colour and turning to a dull brownish red. In order to preserve this solution a small quantity of salicylic acid may be added. After injection keep the organ or tissue for twenty-four hours in equal parts of spirit and water, to which has been added acetic or hydrochloric acid (1 part to 100). Continue hardening as directed (§ **57**) with spirit.

48. *Soluble Prussian Blue and Gelatine Injection Mass.*

Dissolve 5 parts by weight of soluble Prussian blue in 60 parts by measure of distilled water; add gelatine mass (*b.* of § **47**), warm, and add the salicylic acid. Harden the tissues as above directed.

In these injection masses the pigment is soluble in alkaline solutions, but is precipitated by acids; hence it cannot diffuse through the tissues, whilst the gelatine still keeps it in a state of exceedingly fine division. This form of injection has the very great advantage over the fluid injections, that it keeps the vessels distended, as the gelatine is rapidly hardened by the action of the alcohol, and is not driven out when the injection tube is withdrawn on the following day.

49. A solution of gelatine prepared as above, but without the colouring material, is also an extremely good distending mass. It is perfectly clear, but takes on stains, especially carmine, very readily.

50. *Hoyer's Transparent Yellow Injection* :—

(*a.*) To two volumes of a cold saturated solution of bichromate of potash add 1 volume of gelatine solution containing 1 part of gelatine to four of water.

(*b.*) To 2 volumes of cold saturated solution of sugar of lead add 1 volume of a similar gelatine solution; keep these separate. When required for use heat (*b.*) nearly to boiling point and gradually pour in (*a.*), stirring continuously. This injection is so fine that it will run into the lymphatics.

Injecting Apparatus.

51. I. Cannulæ of different sizes, which are generally made of brass. The cannula should have a projecting rim near the nozzle, so that when tied it cannot slip out of the vessel; there should also be a cross bar, to which the threads may be fixed after tying round the rim. This acts as a further preventive to the slipping out of the cannula.

For very small cannulæ, glass tubing drawn out and cut beyond the thinnest part, so as to form a bulb, may be substituted for the brass. Notch the glass with a fine triangular file, and then round off the edges in a blow-pipe flame.

FIG. 2.

II. (*a.*) A brass syringe of at least 4 or 6 ounce capacity; for silver injections a glass or vulcanite syringe should be used.

(*b.*) A constant pressure apparatus.

III. A piece of brass tubing with a stop-cock.

All the cannulæ are made to fit one end of the brass tube (an

adapter of indiarubber tubing may be used for the glass cannulæ).
The other end of the brass tube receives either the nozzle of the
syringe or the tube from the constant pressure apparatus.

52. Select the nozzle which appears to be about the size of the
vessel to be injected.   Make an oblique incision into the vessel, and
push in the cannula ; pass a piece of thin but strong twine around the
vessel and the cannula, and tie firmly, drawing the tube back until
the rim comes against the knot ; make a second knot, and pass the
two ends of the twine around the transverse bars on the tube, and
make them fast.   Into the open tube drop the injection, drop by
drop, until it is full ; put in the stop-cock tube with the tap open ;
fill it in the same way, and turn the tap off.   Fill the syringe with
the injection fluid, and then turn the nozzle upwards, drive the
piston up gently, until all air bubbles are expelled and only the fluid
comes.   Open the stop-cock and allow the fluid to drop in as before ;
when the tube is filled, put in the nozzle of the syringe and slowly
rotate the handle of the piston, and force home, gradually driving the
injection into the vessels.   *This cannot be done too slowly and steadily.*
The syringe may have to be filled several times, and each time the
same routine must be gone through, in order, as far as possible, to
keep out air from the vessels.

53. In place of the syringe, the constant pressure apparatus may be
used with advantage, as by it the pressure may be graduated with
extreme nicety, and the injection may be made to run very slowly.
Ludwig's mercury pressure apparatus, or some modification of it, is
usually employed ; but Stirling's water pressure apparatus is perhaps
at once the cheapest, the most readily made, and quite as convenient
as any.   It is constructed as follows :—Fit a large wide-mouthed
bottle and a smaller one with corks.   In the larger cork bore four
holes, and in the smaller one, two.   Into two of the four holes in
the larger cork fit two straight tubes, one passing nearly to the
bottom of the bottle, the other passing for a distance of half an inch
only through the cork.   On this latter tube should be a stop-cock,
and fitted above it a mercurial manometer by which the pressure is
to be measured.   This consists simply of a flattened ꝏ-shaped tube

one bend of which is filled with mercury, fixed to an index board marked off in inches or centimetres.   Into the other holes fit a

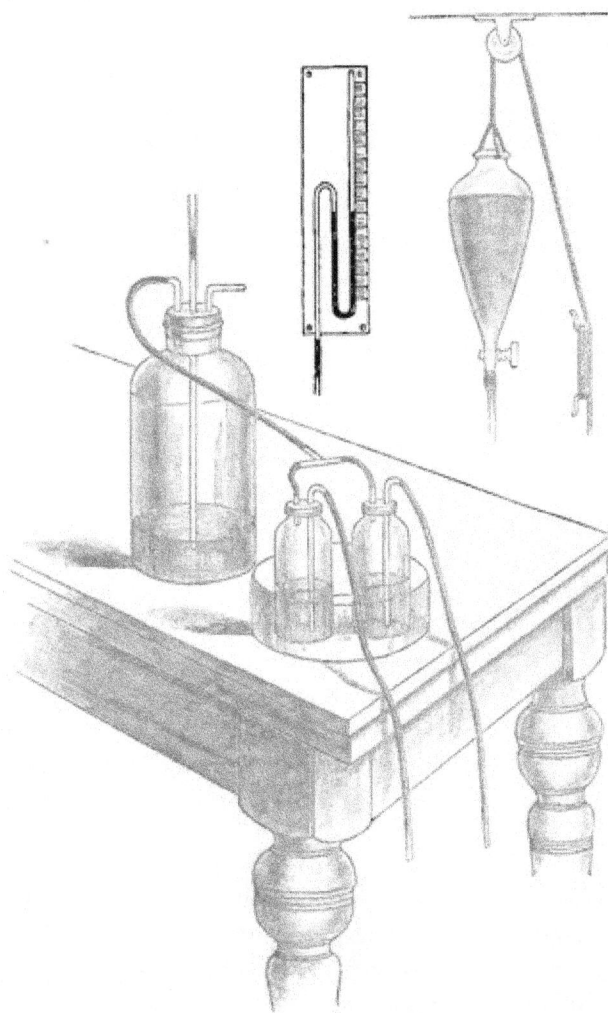

FIG. 3.—Constant pressure apparatus as described.   The fourth tube, with stop-cock for allowing ingress and egress of air, not represented in the diagram.

couple of tubes bent at right angles, each passing through the cork and projecting into the bottle for about half an inch, one of them having a stop-cock on the horizontal part of the tube. Into the two holes in the smaller cork are fitted bent tubes, one of which passes to the bottom of the bottle, the other passing in for only half an inch. A tin or glass cylinder holding a couple of pints or more of water, or a Winchester quart bottle, fitted with the neck down into a large funnel, is suspended from a pulley fixed to the ceiling of the room by a cord, by means of which it can be raised or lowered at pleasure. An indiarubber tube is carried from the bottom of the cylinder, or of the funnel, to the straight tube which passes to the bottom of the larger vessel. Instead of the above, pressure from a water main may be used. From the open bent tube of the larger bottle a piece of flexible tubing is carried to the shorter bent tube in the smaller bottle, and attached to the longer bent tube in the smaller bottle is a flexible tube with a nozzle which will receive the stop-cock tube fitted into the cannula. The smaller bottle is filled with in-jection fluid, and both corks are fitted. The stop-cock on the short tube bent at right angles (in the larger bottle) is closed, and the tin vessel or bottle is gradually raised; the water runs into the large bottle by the tube passing to the bottom; the air in this large bottle is gradually compressed, and is driven into the smaller bottle, and as the pressure on the surface of the fluid increases, it is driven out of the bottle and into the vessels which are to be filled. The pressure in the vessels is indicated on the manometer. This pressure is very readily regulated by merely raising or lowering the tin from which the water gets its "head," or by regulating the amount of water flow-ing from the main. The pressure should commence at half an inch of mercury, and be very gradually raised to three or four inches, according to the nature of the organ or tissue which is to be injected. In cases where it is necessary to make double injections, two, three, or even four small bottles containing different coloured injections may be used, but with care equally good results may be obtained with the above simple apparatus.

When the gelatine injection mass is used, the organ and the bottle containing the mass, or the syringe, must both be placed in a vessel of water, which should be maintained at a constant temperature of about (never above) 104° F. (40° C.) for an hour before the injection, and during the time that the injection is running.

N.B.—Always fill the tubes with the injection fluid before attaching to the cannula (the cannula having been already filled), in order that no air may get into the vessels.

METHODS OF HARDENING TISSUES.

54. As already mentioned, it is an extremely difficult matter to obtain good sections of fresh tissues, and even when sections have been obtained, the structural elements absorb water so freely that they do not remain sufficiently well defined, and the examination invariably proves more or less unsatisfactory. To get over these difficulties—*i.e.* to obtain thin sections, to obviate this absorption of water, and see the tissues in the natural state—it is found necessary to harden them, or to " fix the tissue elements as nearly as possible in their normal form and volume."—(Rutherford.)

In this fixing process, the protoplasm of the cells is toughened and rendered less liable to take up fluids. When working with normal tissues which have been removed from the body immediately after death, it is necessary to take the greatest care in carrying on the hardening process, and this care is even more necessary with pathological specimens that have been in the cadaver for at least twenty-four hours, and have therefore undergone considerable change, even in cold weather. For successful pathological investigation so much depends on this preliminary work, that the student is advised to pay attention to the most minute details in connection with it.

GENERAL DIRECTIONS.

55. *a.* Cut up the organ with a *sharp knife* or razor (taking care to make clean cuts, and not to drag or tear the tissue) into blocks about one inch square and half an inch thick, or into cubes, each side of which should measure not more than about three-quarters of an inch. Where tissues are to be hardened rapidly, as in absolute alcohol, such small cubes should always be prepared. These cubes should, in most cases, be taken from different parts of the organ or tissue to be examined, but one piece from the surface of an organ, with the capsule still attached, should always be included. In the case of the kidney, a triangular piece, including a portion of the cortex as the base of the wedge, and a medullary papilla as the apex should be taken. Small portions from the different parts of a tumour—growing margin, centre, and intermediate area—should always be taken. Hollow organs, such as stomach, bladder, or intestine, should first be slit open and then tacked down, with the mucous surface upwards, to pieces of board. Delicate membranes, such as omentum, pia mater, &c., are best prepared by pinning them down to pieces of cork which are first floated in dilute hardening fluids. Large sections of whole organs should be laid in a flat-bottomed dish, or tied to wood or glass plates, with a layer of cotton wadding between the plate and the section, as may be found most convenient.

b. Put the tissues away *at once* in the hardening fluid.

c. Put a piece of rag or some cotton wadding, saturated with the hardening fluid, in the bottom of a wide-mouthed jar, on this, place four or five of the blocks of tissue, then a second layer of rag or wadding, a second layer of tissue, and so on, the proportion of tissue to fluid never being greater than 1 to 20. Fill the jar with fluid, label distinctly with the name, age, and sex of the patient, the organ, the supposed morbid condition, and the date and time of the commencement of the hardening process, and its nature. Put it away in a cool dark place, an underground cellar being as good a place as can be used; but immediately before putting away, take the opportunity of changing the position in the bottle of the pieces of tissue. This is especially necessary when spirit is used.

d. At the end of twenty-four hours pour out the fixing or hardening fluid, carefully wash out the jar, and rinse the tissue thoroughly with water to get rid of any blood or other deposit which may have settled, and which would, if left, seriously interfere with the hardening process; add fresh fluid. As a general rule fluids should again be changed at the end of the third day, and then weekly for two or three weeks.

e. Each time the fluid is changed the tissue should be carefully examined, and its consistency ascertained. When hardened properly, tissues should be tough and firm, never brittle, as they are apt to become if the hardening process is carried too far or has been done imperfectly.

f. After being hardened slowly, the tissues are removed from the fluid, generally about the end of the second to the eighth week, according to the fluid used, and if not hardened in spirit they are washed for several hours in water until no further yellow colour is given; after which they are transferred to a mixture of equal parts of methylated spirit and water for a couple of days, and then to methylated spirit, in which they are left until required. The spirit may become cloudy, in which case it must be changed, and again as often as the cloudiness makes its appearance.

g. It is an extremely difficult matter to give definite instructions as to the fluid to be used in individual cases, but the following general rules will materially assist in determining what hardening fluid should be used.

(1) Corrosive sublimate solution—saturated solution—7·5 per cent. may in all cases be used as a preliminary fixing reagent. It stops putrefactive processes and fixes the protoplasm at once. It or Flemming's solution is most valuable for perfectly fresh material.

(2) Where a tissue is hard and firm, and not likely to shrivel on the abstraction of water, and where, too, it is not thought necessary to keep the blood in the organ, methylated spirit may be used. Tissues hardened in spirit are very readily stained with logwood or with the aniline dyes.

(3) For very delicate tissues, or where there is much blood in the tissue to be hardened, or when it is very soft or œdematous, use Müller's fluid.

(4) Osmic acid is an extremely useful fixing and hardening reagent for small objects of very delicate structure. It may also be used for hardening the salivary glands, small particles of tissue in which there is fatty degeneration, &c.

(5) If the presence of bacilli or bacteria is suspected, use absolute alcohol. In some cases, however, a previous treatment with Müller's fluid will be found to be attended with considerable advantage.

(6) Hamilton recommends chromic acid for the lungs, especially
for such as are affected with anthracosis or emphysema.

(7) For the retina and for very delicate nerve tissues, a mixture
of three parts Müller's fluid and one part of methylated
spirit, well cooled before it is used, is a very useul
hardening reagent.

HARDENING FLUIDS.

56. *Absolute alcohol* hardens tissues very rapidly. When preparing
the intestines, stomach, and pancreas, dip the pieces into methylated
spirit, and then place in a bottle in sufficient absolute alcohol to cover
them ; at the end of twenty-four hours again wash in methylated
spirit, after which pour over them about twenty times their volume
of alcohol. For tubercle, anthrax specimens, etc., plunge small
pieces at once into a large quantity of absolute alcohol, and allow
them to remain until thoroughly hardened, the process usually being
complete in from three to ten days.

57. *Methylated spirit* is used principally to complete the hardening
process, but it may also be used as above for very firm tissues, especially where there is a large proportion of fresh epithelium, as in cancers,
skin, etc. If used alone, as for waxy liver, it is changed at the end
of twenty-four hours, and again at the end of a week. Tissues
hardened in this way are ready for examination at the end of a fortnight. With most tissues hardened in spirit, it is well to put them
away in equal parts of spirit and water, and only to put them into
strong spirit at the end of twenty-four hours ; or at this stage to add
weak spirit again, and then at the end of forty-eight hours change into
strong spirit. When changing the spirit it is specially necessary to
wash away the precipitated blood, which will be found to have
accumulated in considerable quantities on the specimens, and at the
bottom of the bottle. This deposit, if left, interferes very much with
the proper hardening of the specimens. Change the spirit at the
end of the first week, and cut the tissue at the end of a fortnight. In
combination with other fluids, methylated spirit is of very great value.

58. *Corrosive sublimate (bichloride of mercury).*—Where tissues are moderately fresh, and often even where slight putrefactive changes have commenced, it is an exceedingly good plan to stop the putrefaction and to fix the elements of the tissue as far as possible by the use of bichloride of mercury before hardening them in spirit. Dissolve 7·5 grammes of bichloride of mercury in 100 parts of normal saline solution (·7 per cent. common salt in water). In this, place portions of tissue about the size of a small bean, and allow them to remain for from 6 to 24 hours, then wash thoroughly in water, after which place them in a 30 per cent. solution of spirit to which a few drops of tincture of iodine have been added, the iodine serving to combine with and precipitate all the mercury that is left in the tissues, re-dissolve in weak iodide of potassium solution and wash thoroughly ; then place the pieces in 50, 75, and 90 per cent. spirit and absolute alcohol, each for 24 hours, after which the specimens may be embedded and cut.

Chromic acid, alone or in the form of some salt, is very frequently used as a hardening reagent. Of the combinations into which it enters—

59. *Müller's fluid* is the most useful, especially in the preparation of delicate tissues, in which it fixes the protoplasm of the cells rather than hardens them, and thus causes but little shrinking of the tissues, so that for congested organs or mucoid tissues it is invaluable. To prepare it, take of

Potassium bichromate, .	.	2¼ parts.
Sodium sulphate, . .	.	1 part.
Water, . . .	. . 100	parts.

Care is to be taken to put in only one volume of tissue to twenty of fluid, as with all other methods. Change the fluid at the end of the first, third, and seventh days, and then at the end of each week till the end of the fifth ; transfer to water for several hours after the tissue has been in the fluid for six or eight weeks, and then again to dilute methylated spirit ; leave in this for from twenty-four to forty-eight hours, and then preserve in strong methylated spirit. The great advantages of Müller's fluid are, that there is no great danger of over-hardening, and although the process takes a considerable time, the results are almost invariably satisfactory ; that the red blood corpuscles remain unchanged in shape and take on a greenish tinge ; and that many tissues hardened in it afterwards take on various stains more readily than when hardened in alcohol.   It appears that the sulphate of sodium can penetrate almost any tissues, and where it once gets in the bichromate salt can follow.   Consequently, it is not so essential that the pieces should be small, and this fluid may be used where it would be inconvenient to cut up the tissue into small cubes.   Commence the hardening process as soon as the structures are taken from the body, and carry on, for the first few days at any rate, in a cool dark place.

60. *Müller's fluid and spirit* is recommended by Hamilton for hardening nerve tissues, brain, spinal cord, retina, intestinal muscle and glands.   It is composed of

Müller's fluid, ...	3 parts.
Methylated spirit, ...	1 part.

Cool thoroughly before using, and follow the directions given for hardening with Müller's fluid.

61. *Bichromate of potash* (saturated solution) may also be used for hardening pieces of tissue of considerable size, especially of the brain. It must be used in large quantities, to which carbolic acid is added (one or two grains to the ounce), and the fluid is not changed, but is kept saturated by the addition, from time to time, of crystals of the bichromate salt.   It hardens slowly—in six or eight weeks.   Keep in a cool dark place.

62. For hardening brain tissue to be stained by Weigert's method, Erlicki's fluid may be used :—

Potassium bichromate, .	2˙5 parts.
Cupric sulphate, . .	˙5 parts.
Water, ...	100 parts.

At the ordinary temperature this fluid hardens tissues in eight or ten days.   At 40° C. tissues are hardened in four to five days.   This method, however, gives rise to more shrinking of the tissues than the Müller fluid method.

63. *Bichromate of ammonia*, as a two per cent. solution, may be used either to harden or complete the hardening of the nerve centres but it may be employed for almost any tissue.   Use at least twenty volumes of fluid to one of tissue, change at the end of the first, third, and seventh days, and at the end of the second, third, and fifth weeks.

64. Where it is desired to harden tissues more rapidly, a solution of *chromic acid* may be used. The solution should not be stronger than one-sixth per cent., or the outside only of the cube is hardened, and the tissue is rendered brittle. Where this or any of the following chromic acid compounds are employed, it is to be remembered that the pieces of tissue must be very small indeed (except in the case of the lung); they should never be more than one-sixth of an inch in thickness and half an inch in diameter. Use twenty volumes of the fluid to one of the tissue. Change at the end of twenty-four hours, again on the second and third days, and then every third day until the tissue is hard and tough. A careful examination should be made about the eighth day to see that the hardening is progressing properly; for if the tissues are left in the chromic acid mixture too long they become exceedingly brittle. Wash well, allowing a stream of water to run over the material for several hours; then place it in equal parts of methylated spirit and water, leave for twenty-four hours, and transfer to pure methylated spirit.

65. In place of pure chromic acid a mixture of *chromic acid and spirit* (Klein) may be used :—

Chromic acid, one-sixth to one-third per cent. solution, 2 parts.
Methylated spirit, ... 1 part.

Change the fluid three times—once a day for three days; after this gradually increase the proportion of spirit in the fluid, until at last only methylated spirit is used. Such a method answers admirably for hardening the lung; the process is completed in about a fortnight if the fluid is changed once every three days after the alteration in the proportion of the fluids has commenced.

66. Flemming's solution for fixing nuclear figures in fresh tissues, tumours, scars, &c. :—

Chromic acid, 1 per cent.,	.	15 parts.
Osmic acid, 2 per cent.,	.	4 parts.
Glacial acetic acid,	.	1 part.

Use 10 to 20 parts of fluid to 1 of tissue. Allow to remain in this for one to three days; but tissues may remain for weeks, even exposed to sunlight, with no bad results. Wash thoroughly in water before cutting. After being fixed in this fluid, tissues may be hardened by passing through 30, 50, 70, and 90 per cent. spirit (one day each) and then into absolute alcohol. Embed in paraffin (§ 93) or celloidin (§ 90).

67. In the same way may be used Fol's fixing fluid :—

Chromic acid, 1 per cent.,	25 parts.
Osmic acid, 1 per cent.,	2 parts.
Acetic acid, 2 per cent.,	5 parts.
Water,	68 parts.

68. *Ammonium chromate.*—Five per cent. solution, filtered, and kept in a stoppered bottle, hardens small pieces of tissue, or pieces of the mesentery or omentum in twenty-four to forty-eight hours, and is especially useful in studying cell structure. In employing this mixture, cut the tissues into very small pieces, not more than about one-sixth to one-quarter inch in diameter; place in about ten to fifteen volumes of the fluid; leave until hardened (never for longer than forty-eight hours); wash thoroughly in water, and cut at once, or transfer to weak and then to strong spirit, which will preserve the tissue until required.

69. *Nitric acid.*—Brook recommends for fresh tissues a preliminary fixation with 5-10 per cent. of nitric acid. (Altmann uses 3 per cent.). The method of procedure is as follows :—Place small pieces of tissue in the nitric acid solution for from one to two hours; wash thoroughly in 50 per cent. methylated spirit; change this two or three times to get rid of the acid, and then keep in 75 per cent. methylated spirit until the tissues are required to be cut. Before cutting place the pieces for a day in 90 per cent. spirit, and then for an equal time in absolute alcohol.

None of the above hardening media give a permanent colour to the tissues; but the two following not only harden, but also stain them.

70. *Osmic acid.*—As a hardening reagent osmic acid is extremely useful for small pieces of delicate tissue, such as nerve fibres, retinal cells, and the like. It is used as one-sixth to one-half or even one per cent. solution. The tissue is allowed to remain in this, carefully protected from the light for about six, eight, or twenty-four hours, according to its size and nature. From osmic acid transfer the tissue to 75 per cent. spirit, in which it may be kept until required ; or after washing well in distilled water it may be placed at once in the gum and syrup solution, frozen, cut, and mounted in Farrant's solution, or better still in acetate of potash ; glycerine being continually browned by the acid, unless the sections, before mounting, are thoroughly washed in water, or in water and glycerine. Osmic acid appears to tan the tissue, "fixing the tissue elements without producing a granular precipitate, or causing shrivelling."—(Rutherford.)

71. *Picric acid saturated solution.*—Fill a bottle with distilled water, add excess of crystals of picric acid, and simply fill up with water as the fluid is used, keeping crystals in the bottle to maintain saturation. Tissues, always in small pieces, should never be allowed to remain in this for more than from twenty-four to forty-eight hours ; wash out the picric acid with 30 per cent. spirit, gradually raising the strength of the spirit to 75 per cent. In this way much of the swelling of the connective tissue element is prevented. The great advantages of this method are that it hardens rapidly, and that tissues so hardened stain most beautifully with picro-carmine. It is especially useful for tumours and epithelial or epidermic structures, for mesentery, and for small pieces of gland.

72. *Kleinenberg's picric acid*, for hardening soft sarcomata, myxomatous tissues, and embryonic tissues, is usually made as follows :—

Saturated watery solution of picric acid,	100 parts.
Strong sulphuric acid, . . .	2 parts.

Filter to remove a yellow precipitate which is formed,
and add

Distilled water, ...	300 parts.

This will harden the above tissues in from three to twelve hours.

73. *Fixing by heat.*—For his work on the spleen Professor Sanders

used a method that is still employed in Germany for such organs or
tissues as contain fluid albumen which it may be wished to coagulate *in
situ*, as in cases of œdema of the lung, nephritis, &c. Small half-inch
cubes of such material are plunged into boiling water for from one to
three minutes, and then hardened in spirit as above.

74. Most tissues, when hardened in the above solutions, may be
transferred to the gum and sugar solution, in which they will keep
perfectly well for an indefinite length of time, if sufficient carbolic
acid is added to the mixture (§ 81).

DECALCIFYING SOLUTIONS,

are used for removing lime salts from bone and teeth, and at the
same time hardening the organic matter.

75. *Picric acid saturated solution*, made as above.

It takes some time (two or three weeks) to decalcify bone, unless
the pieces are small, when eight or ten days may be sufficient; it is
especially useful for softening young bones. Use a large quantity of
the fluid, and add crystals from time to time; it is not necessary to
change at all until the bone is ready for cutting; when ready, wash
out the picric acid by soaking in water for two or three days, and
transfer first to weak and then to strong spirit to harden and preserve
the specimen.

76. *Chromic and nitric acid fluid* is made as follows :—Take of

Chromic acid, .	1 part.
Distilled water, .	200 parts.

Dissolve, and add

Strong nitric acid,	2 parts.

Put small pieces of bone into twenty times their volume of the fluid ;
change every third day until the end of the second week ; wash well
in water for twenty-four hours, and transfer first to weak and then
to strong spirit (§ 68).

The best results are obtained by this method ; the organic parts of
the bone are hardened, whilst the nitric acid removes very thoroughly
all the calcareous materials.

77. *Perenyi's softening fluid :—*

Chromic acid, ·5 per cent., .	3 parts.
Nitric acid, 10 per cent., . .	4 parts.
Absolute alcohol, ...	3 parts.

Use large quantities of this fluid, change regularly until the bone is softened, then place in 70 per cent. alcohol for one day, and then in absolute alcohol for four or five days. Unless this process is conducted very carefully the after staining is a very difficult matter.

78. *Nitric acid.*—Five per cent. nitric acid may be used for decalcifying bone and fixing the softer tissues as above, but a further hardening with spirit (§ **68**) is always necessary.

SIMPLE DECALCIFYING SOLUTIONS.

79. *Hydrochloric acid,* 10 per cent. solution. This removes the calcareous matter very thoroughly, but it must be remembered that it causes fibrous tissues to swell up. It is useful, however, for softening injected bone. When it is wished to prevent the swelling of the softened fibrous tissue Von Ebner's solution may be used.

80. *Von Ebner's solution.*—To prepare this take of

Common salt, ...	10 parts.
Water, . .	100 parts.
Hydrochloric acid, ...	1 part.

Another formula for Von Ebner's solution (v. Kahlden).

Common salt, ...	2·5 parts.
Hydrochloric acid, .	2·5 parts.
Alcohol, .	500 parts.
Water, ...	500 parts.

Use two or three hundred volumes of either of these to each volume of bone, and add sufficient acid, day by day, to thoroughly decalcify the bone. When this is attained, the bone may be bent like a piece of indiarubber. It should then be thoroughly washed in water for a few hours, and transferred to a ten per cent. salt solution until all acid reaction disappears (change the salt solution daily). Mount the sections in the ten per cent. salt solution.

81. *Waldeyer's Chloride of Palladium Solution* (v. Kahlden)—

    Chloride of Palladium, . .   ·01 part.

    Hydrochloric acid, 1 per cent.,   . 1000 parts.

Used as Von Ebner's solution. The tissues are afterwards hardened, first in weak and then in stronger spirit (§ **68**).

Methods of Cutting Sections.

82. Freezing and other microtomes are now to be obtained so cheaply, that it is unnecessary for the busy student to waste time in learning to cut sections by hand. Various modifications of the freezing method have been suggested from time to time. Of these D. J. Hamilton's method is the most perfect, especially as it involves no danger of overfreezing. To prepare the tissues proceed as follows :—

Remove the hardening fluid from the tissue, especially if spirit has been used, by a prolonged immersion (say for twenty-four hours) in water, which should be constantly changed by allowing a very small stream from the tap to fall into the vessel in which the tissue is being washed. Then transfer to a mixture of gum, B. P. strength,[1] two parts, syrup[2] one part; for retina, brain, or cord, gum five parts, syrup four parts. Allow the tissue to remain in this mixture for from twenty-four to forty-eight hours, or even longer. To each of these fluids add three drops per ounce of a strong solution of carbolic acid prepared by adding one part of Calvert's No. 4 carbolic acid to two parts of water, or saturate (boiling) with boracic acid, to prevent the formation of fungi. If this be attended to, the tissue may be left soaking in the solution for an indefinite length of time, and at the end will "cut" perfectly, if it has been properly hardened in the first instance. The microtome is cooled down to such a point that a drop of gum (B. P. solution) placed on the die or disc (to be afterwards described) is frozen. The tissue which has been soaking in the gum and syrup is taken out with a pair of forceps, carefully

[1] Gum acacia, one lb. is dissolved in eighty ounces of cold water.
[2] The syrup is made by boiling one part of crystallised sugar in one part of distilled water until the whole of the sugar is dissolved.

dried in the folds of a soft cloth, put to soak for a few minutes in gum, and then adjusted as required on the surface of the cooled disc; gum is painted around it to keep it in position, and to form with it a solid firm mass, which may be cut in a single section. The mass is frozen just so hard that it will cut like a piece of cheese; when softer than this, it is not sufficiently frozen, when harder, it is very difficult to cut, especially if the sections are of considerable size.

83. A capital embedding material, recommended by Professor Hamilton, especially for unsoftened bone and other brittle substances, is a mixture of equal parts of a saturated solution of gelatine (gelatine simply washed, covered with water, allowed to soak for twenty-four hours, and then heated in a water bath) and gum and sugar solutions. A piece of bone, say, is transferred from the gum and syrup solution to the above warm mixture, where it may remain for several hours or even days, after which it is allowed to cool; it is then cut out in a square block of the mixture, the whole being frozen on the metal disc. The sections are transferred at once to a slide, and the gelatine may be removed by carefully washing with warm water; or the section may be stained and mounted with the gelatine, still keeping the tissues *in situ*. This method may be used for other tissues, especially when immersion in ether or chloroform would act injuriously upon them.

84. Hamilton, to whom we owe nearly all the good embedding processes used in the freezing method, has succeeded in combining the celloidin with the gum and sugar process. After the tissue is hardened it is placed (if it has not already been hardened in spirit) in methylated spirit for three or four days, the fluid being changed daily. It is afterwards immersed in a mixture of equal parts of alcohol and ether, in which it is left for two days, then from one to four days, according to the size of the piece of tissue, in a syrup of celloidin, dissolved in equal parts of ether and absolute alcohol. Then pour a somewhat stronger celloidin solution into a paper box or a pill box and embed in the centre of this the piece of tissue. Allow the fluid to be exposed to the air for some time; until it partially hardens (the longer it is exposed the harder it ultimately becomes), then plunge the whole into strong methylated spirit, and leave it until the celloidin is quite hard. This mass is now soaked in water for twenty-four hours, and then in a mixture of gum and syrup in the proportion of one to two. During this latter part of the process the fluid may be kept at a temperature of about 40° C. with advantage, as it then passes much more readily into the tissues. The procedure is afterwards just the same as in the case of the ordinary freezing method.

The Freezing Microtome.

85. Of this there are several very convenient forms, but it will be necessary here to describe four only—one for ether freezing, two for freezing with ice, and a compound microtome. For an instrument which is ready for use at a moment's notice, Cathcart's ether microtome appears to be undoubtedly the best, and from the student's point of view it has several very great advantages. It is portable, very clean to work with, its initial cost is moderate, and it can be very inexpensively worked. It is based on a hardwood frame, which is firmly fixed to the table by means of a clamp; screwed to this is a hollow cylinder, on the top of which is a roughened zinc plate. On each side of the zinc plate is a strip of glass cemented to the wooden frame. By means of a screw with a fine thread, the hollow cylinder, and with it the zinc plate, is raised or lowered at will, through a distance of a quarter of an inch. A double tube is introduced into the hollow cylinder, through one part of which air is driven by a small indiarubber ball. This stream of air rushing over the mouth of the second tube (which is connected with a bottle of ether) creates a vacuum, and ether is drawn through a small hole; the stream of air completely vaporises the ether in the chamber under the zinc plate, the temperature of the plate is very rapidly reduced, and the piece of tissue, fixed in position with gum (§ 82), is frozen.

The best instrument to use for making the sections is the blade of a carpenter's smoothing plane, used either with or without a wooden handle (recommended by Dr. Delépine). It works on two glass runners, so that the centre of the blade comes in contact with nothing but the material to be cut, and consequently it remains sharp much longer than where there is simply a hole in the glass plate, as in some of the other microtomes. The elevating screw is worked with the left hand, and the knife with the right. In very hot weather it may be found necessary to stop cutting now and again, to use the spray and keep the tissue frozen, or the freezing apparatus may be handed over to an assistant. The screw which raises the disc should be lubricated with glycerine, not with oil, which freezes too readily.[1]

This instrument is valuable for the *post mortem* room; for cutting hardened specimens it is also extremely useful and economical, as pieces of tissue up to a quarter of an inch thick may be cut with the expenditure of little more than a halfpenny worth of ether.

Ice-Freezing Microtomes.

86. Of these, Rutherford's and Williams's are undoubtedly the best. Rutherford's consists of a freezing-box, covered with a gutta-percha non-conductor, having an outflow pipe at one corner. This box surrounds a well, in which is placed a hollow cylinder with a thread on the inner wall, and covered in at the top with a grooved disc. Into the hollow cylinder, and into a fixed nut a screw is so fitted that when it is turned the cylinder rises or falls. Above the well, and partly covering it in, is a metal plate covered with glass, on which the knife works. Before commencing to work with this instrument, have ready some finely powdered ice or snow, some coarse salt, a little glycerine, some thick gum, a piece of clean cork (a fresh cut surface of a pickle bottle cork answers very well), and a clean cloth. Screw the cylinder up to the surface, take it out, and smear a very small quantity of glycerine over the screw in the well, on the inner and outer surface of the cylinder, and on the inner surface of the well; then screw down the cylinder until there is

---

[1] This instrument, with all necessary apparatus (except the knife, for which an extra charge is made), may be obtained from A. Frazer, Teviot Place, Edinburgh, price 17s. 6d. The planing-iron may be obtained for about a shilling from any tool warehouse.

E

sufficient depth to take in the tissue. Fill the freezing box with
alternate layers of the powdered ice and salt, taking care to keep
the drain freely open, and keep thoroughly mixed until a "hoar frost"
makes its appearance on the outer surface of the gutta-percha.
Pour on to the notched die at the bottom of the well a drop of gum
solution, made by adding one part of gum to two parts of water.
Remove the section from the gum and syrup solution, and place it
on the drop of gum as soon as the first sign of freezing of the gum
is seen at the margin. Hold it in the required position until it is
firmly fixed. Then pour into the well sufficient gum to cover the
specimen completely; place the cork over the well, and keep in
position with a weight until the freezing process is completed. The
best knife to use with this microtome is undoubtedly the planing-
iron, already recommended for the Cathcart microtome. Remove
the sections from the knife with a camel's hair pencil, and treat as
below (§ 89).

Professor Rutherford has recently devised an additional piece of
apparatus, by means of which the ice microtome may be rapidly
converted into an ether-freezing microtome.

87. Williams's ice-freezing microtome (made by Swift) is also an
excellent instrument. By the aid of this, sections may be cut very
rapidly with but little practice. The freezing box consists of a round
wooden tub with an outlet pipe. The inner surface of the box is
pitched or tarred to render it water-tight. In the centre of this is a
stout brass pillar, screwed firmly down. On the upper surface of the
pillar, dies of various sizes may be screwed for the reception of larger
or smaller specimens. Covering the box is a lid, on which, embedded
in pitch cement, is a plate of glass. In the centre of this lid is a
round opening, through which the die is adjusted to the level of the
upper surface of the glass. The cutting part of the apparatus consists of a razor, fitted into a triangular frame supported on three
legs; each leg is a screw, one in front and two behind, and by
raising or depressing these screws the distance of the triangle from
the plate may be altered at will, and with the triangle, the razor.
The edge of the razor is thus let down when the triangle is depressed
in front, by simply turning the front screw out of the frame. (Thus,

instead of bringing the tissue up to the razor, the edge of the razor is brought down to the tissue.) Fill the ice-box with salt and ice, layer upon layer, until the box is full; in summer this must be carefully attended to, but in winter the tissue will be frozen sufficiently hard if the box be but half filled. Fasten down the lid, screw in one of the dies, and fix on to it the tissue to be cut, as above described (§ 86). By means of the three screws bring the razor down to the level of the tissue, taking care to have all three legs equal in length. Grasp the tripod in the two hands, and with the forefinger give the large head of the screw at the apex of the triangle a turn through a very small angle, and push the frame, and with it the knife, obliquely forwards, keeping the three ivory tipped legs resting firmly on the glass plate. A thin section will thus be made, the thickness of which is graduated by the angle through which the front screw is turned. The thawing gum is quite sufficient to keep the knife moistened. Remove the sections with a camel's hair pencil.

Frazer's Combination Microtome.

88. Frazer has succeeded in combining in a cheap and simple form the Williams and the Cathcart microtomes. His apparatus has the additional advantage that it may also be used for making sections of tissues embedded in paraffin.

89. If the tissue is very delicate, the sections must be transferred separately to a glass slide by means of a camel's hair pencil, where they are floated out and washed in a mixture of methylated spirit one part, to two parts of water. With ordinary tissues, however, the sections are transferred at once to a basin of water, where they may be left from two to six hours (according to the temperature), after which the water should be changed and the sections left for a quarter of an hour, in order that the syrup and gum may be thoroughly washed out. If it is then found that air bubbles are entangled in the sections, they should be well washed in methylated spirit and afterwards in water. They may be stained and examined at once; or if this should not be convenient, they may be kept in

a mixture of equal parts of methylated spirit and glycerine, or in a
fluid, made as follows :—Take of

Glycerine,	15 parts.
Water, . . .	15 parts.
Carbolic acid 1-2c, ...	1 part.

In place of this methylated spirit may be used, especially if the
sections are unstained.

For the method of cutting sections of whole organs, see Hamilton's
Pathology, and the author's paper in the *British Medical Journal*,
vol. i., 1888, p. 737.

CELLOIDIN EMBEDDING.

90. Tissues after being hardened are transferred to various grades
of spirit, then to absolute alcohol, and are placed for twenty-four hours
or longer, according to the size of the blocks, in a mixture of equal
parts of alcohol and ether. From this they are transferred to a very
thin celloidin syrup, made by dissolving shavings of celloidin in equal
parts of ether and alcohol, then to a stronger, and, lastly, into a good
stiff syrup of the same material. Then take a piece of wood (not
cork, which gives slightly in the jaws of the clamp) cut across
the grain, and pour over this cross-grained surface a quantity of
ether until no more bubbles make their appearance. Over this prepared surface pour some of the thick celloidin, and on this embed
the soaked tissues. Bank up well with the thick celloidin syrup,
allowing it to dry for some time until there is a good firm film, add
more celloidin, again dry, and then immerse in a large quantity of
methylated spirit until the whole is thoroughly hardened. This
method may be used for embedding the spinal cord or brain tissue,
and may also be utilised in making large sections of bone.

91. Celloidin embedded specimens are best cut under spirit, and
for this purpose I have devised a modification of the Schanze
microtome, of which the following is a description :—To the
knife-block that runs in the groove I have affixed a second bevelled
plate, so adjusted that it throws down the point of the knife about
two inches. This bevelled block is sufficiently long to carry both
the knife and the steadying clamp that runs to the end of the

blade. It will be evident that the knife will not run parallel to the ground, but somewhat obliquely. To the body of the microtome there is fixed by moveable clamps a nickelled copper tray, only about a quarter of an inch deep where it is attached, but two and a quarter inches deep at its outer part. In the bottom of the tray is a rounded opening, five and a half inches in diameter, through which the specimen clamp passes. The space between the margin of the opening and the rod supporting the clamp is filled in by an india-rubber bag (Nachet's plan), fixed by a wire to a flange around the opening, and by a nut with a washer around the clamp-supporting rod. The tray is filled with spirit, which cannot escape except by special taps, but the specimen can be raised by means of the screw, the indiarubber bag allowing considerable movement but preventing the escape of the spirit. At one corner of the tray is a grating with a tap beneath by which the spirit may be drawn off, whilst in the indiarubber bag there is also a tube with a Mohr's clip, through which the remainder of the spirit may be removed. At each end of the body of the microtome is a ring with a binding screw, in which a rod may be fixed to prevent the knife point or heel coming in contact with the ends of the tray. For sections three or four inches square this arrangement is absolutely necessary. The apparatus was made for me by Hume, Edinburgh; it may also be obtained from A. H. Baird, Edinburgh.

SERIAL SECTIONS (CELLOIDIN).

92. For mounting serial sections of specimens cut in celloidin I now use Al. Obregia's modification of Weigert's method. (1) Make a solution of sugar candy in water, about as thick as ordinary syrup. To 30 cc. of this add 20 cc. of 95 per cent. alcohol and 10 cc. of a solution of pure dextrine of the consistence of syrup. Spread a thin layer of this over a slide and allow it to dry in a warm place, protecting it from dust ; keep for several days.

(2) Dissolve photoxylin, 6 grms., in a mixture of absolute alcohol 100 cc., ether (pure) 100 cc. ; allow it to stand, and pour off the clear part. Both this and No. 1 may be readily preserved in stoppered bottles. Celloidin may be used instead of No. 2. Cut pieces of satin cooking paper (which is thin and leaves no particles

on the sections) the size of the slides, place in a flat dish with
the smooth surface upwards, and moisten with 95 per cent. alcohol.
Remove the sections with similar paper, and arrange on the slips in
the dish, spreading them well out with a pencil moistened in alcohol.
Then remove the paper with its sections and lay it, with the
sections upwards, on folded blotting paper until all fluid is absorbed,
then place the paper, face downwards, on a prepared slide, so that
sections come in contact with the dextrine; place blotting paper
over it, press lightly with the finger, and remove the paper,
leaving the sections on the prepared layer. Then pour over the
slide solution No. 2 and wave in the air until all cloudiness disappears. Number, etc. Put the slide into pure water, which dissolves
off the sugar, when the whole film comes easily away from the glass,
leaving one side quite uncovered, so that all processes of staining,
washing, and dehydrating may go on more quickly than when both
surfaces are covered with a collodion film. For brain sections this is
an exceedingly good method, as the medium is not stained by either
carmine or hæmatoxylin, although it is stained by aniline colours,
which, however, may be removed by means of strong acids.

SERIAL SECTIONS (PARAFFIN).

93. More recently the paraffin methods of embedding have been so
perfected that much time may often be saved by using paraffin when
it is essential to obtain serial or specially thin sections. Small pieces
of tissue that have been well hardened and then soaked for twenty-
four hours in absolute alcohol are immersed in *clean*, pure turpentine,
placed in a covered porcelain crucible. This is put into a warm
chamber, where it is gradually heated up to the melting point of the
paraffin that is used, and left for from three to twenty-four hours. It is
then transferred directly to melted hard paraffin at 53° C. (very delicate
objects should be passed through several softer paraffins); the tissue
is allowed to soak in the melted paraffin for several hours, and is then
transferred to a paper boat or metal mould full of melted paraffin.
It is kept in position with warm needles and is cooled rapidly by
floating the boat in water. There should be no turpentine left in the
tissue or in the paraffin. When the specimens are to be stained in
bulk they should be taken from 75 per cent. spirit, stained, and then

passed through 90 per cent. spirit and absolute alcohol, after which they are treated as above; or they may be taken from the turpentine and first transferred to a mixture of turpentine and paraffin for twenty-four hours, after which they are passed into pure paraffin.

In place of turpentine, benzol or chloroform may be used in paraffin embedding. When the tissues have been in absolute alcohol, either before or after staining, immerse in a small porcelain crucible or test-tube, in equal parts of chloroform and alcohol. The specimen—which at first floats—after a time sinks, when the mixture should be replaced by pure chloroform. As soon as the specimen again sinks, pour off most of the liquid and add to what remains scraps of solid paraffin; place in a chamber heated to 53° or 54° C., and gradually add more paraffin. Keep the specimen at the above temperature until no smell of chloroform is given off, then embed in a paper boat or metal mould as above described, and cool at once in water. These paraffin blocks are best fitted to moveable dies. Fix the die in a large cork, warm in a bunsen flame, then carefully heat the under surface of the paraffin block and press it firmly down on to the die, which should be forthwith plunged into cold water, this at once causing setting of the paraffin between the die and the block. Pare the block down to a rectangular form, leaving a small border of paraffin around the margins of the tissue.

Where bones are to be embedded softer paraffin should be used, and where Webster's method of cutting large sections in paraffin (*Laboratory Reports*, R.C.P.Ed., vol. iii.) is used, it is always of very great advantage to embed in the softer mass.

94. Any of the microtomes already mentioned may be used for cutting these paraffin sections. The one that I now use is the Rocking microtome of the Cambridge Scientific Instrument Company, which —with dies instead of a hollow tube, and some other improvements suggested by G. Brook and myself, and carried out by Frazer of Edinburgh — is a capital instrument. The German and French makers also turn out very good instruments, but they seem to me to have no special advantages over the above, of which it is not necessary to give a description, as full directions are sent out with every instrument.

95. *Fixing serial sections on the slide where paraffin is used* as the
embedding medium. When sections are very friable, or when serial
sections are to be made, it is well to fix the sections on the slide by
one of the following methods.

Meyer's method :—Take of filtered white of egg and glycerine, equal
parts ; mix thoroughly, and add a crystal of thymol, or salicylic acid,
or some scraps of camphor. On the slide, in the position in which
the sections are to be fixed, spread as thin and equable a layer as
possible of this mixture, using the edge of a clean glass slide as
a kind of " scraper." Float out the sections on warm water (10° less
than the melting point of the paraffin used), lay them in the desired
position on this film of albumen, and heat the slide over a bunsen
flame until the albumen is fixed or coagulated and the paraffin
melted. Wash off the melted paraffin with *warm* turpentine or with
Persian naphtha, pouring on several relays of the fluid until the
whole of the paraffin is removed. Then immerse the slide with its
adherent sections first in methylated spirit, then in turpentine or
clove oil, to get rid of the granularity of the albumen, and mount
in Canada balsam. If the sections have not already been stained
" in bulk " they may be easily stained after the paraffin has been
dissolved out by the naphtha and they have been washed in spirit.
Hæmatoxylin and eosine, borax carmine or any of the ordinary
staining reagents may be used for this purpose. The sections are
afterwards dehydrated thoroughly with absolute alcohol, cleared up
in clove oil, and mounted in balsam, or picro-carmine ; stained
specimens may be mounted in Farrant's solution. Instead of using
albumen and glycerine, the sections may be arranged by means of
a camel hair pencil moistened with alcohol on a slide moistened
with alcohol. The slide is then warmed and the sections adhere
moderately firmly, and on raising the temperature still higher the
paraffin may be melted, after which it may be dissolved off by means
of naphtha, xylol, or turpentine. The sections are then rinsed with
alcohol if they are to be stained on the slide, after which the method
of procedure is as above.

96. Schällebaum's collodion fixing method may be used where the
sections have been stained in bulk. A mixture of one part

collodion, three parts clove, or lavender, oil is spread in a very thin layer with a glass rod, or the edge of a glass slide, on the slide, the sections are placed in position on this and then warmed over a water bath or naked flame until the clove oil has been evaporated; the sections are then washed with turpentine to get rid of the paraffin, and are mounted in benzol balsam. If the naked flame be used the paraffin and clove oil may be blown out of the mass by means of the breath or of a hand blower similar to that employed by Kühne in his staining and mounting manipulations; wash with turpentine and mount in balsam.

Using Al. Obregia's method for sections cut in paraffin, they are arranged on the surface of the dried syrup with a camel hair pencil, flattened out and heated in a warm chamber kept at 57-60° C. for ten minutes, when the sections have a tendency to become more perfectly spread out. The paraffin is first removed with good blotting paper, then with xylol or turpentine, after which the slide is placed in absolute alcohol for a few minutes, and quickly into photoxylin solution; dry for ten minutes, then wash in water and stain. To dehydrate afterwards use 95 per cent. spirit, and to clear use pure carbolic acid crystals, 1 part, to xylol (pure), 3 parts.

METHODS OF STAINING SECTIONS.

97. In all cases sections should be examined first unstained; but the examination, if confined to this, would be very incomplete, as much may always be learned from a study of the tissues after they have been acted upon by various special reagents. Whatever may be the nature of the reagents employed, each is used for the purpose of bringing into greater prominence special structures, or to differentiate one tissue from the others in which it lies. Thus it has been found that certain vital parts of cells are more deeply stained by most staining reagents (carmine, etc.) than are the surrounding parts; that a few reagents, such as picric acid, have a special affinity for the formed material of the cell; that the cement substance between cells may be specially picked out, as by nitrate of silver; or, that certain parts may become "cleared up," so that other structures may be seen more distinctly.

In the following directions given for staining tissues special prominence will be accorded to such methods as are found to be most useful to the pathological histologist, which methods, none of them very complicated, usually give most satisfactory results.

98. *Picro-Carmine.*—By far the most useful staining reagent at present in the hands of the histologist is Ranvier's picro-carmine staining fluid or picro-carminate of ammonia. When the fluid is properly prepared and the staining process is well carried out, the most brilliant double-staining effects are obtained.

It is prepared as follows :—Take of

Pure carmine, .	1 part.
Strong ammonia,	3 parts.
Distilled water,	3 parts.

Dissolve the carmine in a test tube with the ammonia and water. To this add two hundred parts of a cold, saturated, and filtered solution of picric acid, and mix thoroughly. Place the fluid in a basin and cover with a clock glass (with the concave surface upwards to keep out dust, and to allow of the moisture falling back into the basin, so that the exposure to the sunlight may be prolonged), and allow it to evaporate in *strong sunlight*, testing it every few days by staining a section of skin, until the nuclei and fibrous tissue are stained distinctly pink, and the epithelial cells, especially those of the horny layer, are stained yellow. The best double-staining is usually given before the fluid has evaporated down to half its bulk, and at this stage it is sometimes found that crystals of picric acid are deposited in the tissues. To obviate this, it is necessary to add ten or twenty parts of distilled water to the fluid that remains. To prevent the growth of fungi add from two to six drops of 1-20 carbolic acid solution to each ounce of the fluid ; filter, and keep in a glass - stoppered bottle. Some workers use the fluid without any evaporation at all, and appear to obtain fairly satisfactory results.

To stain a section, lay it out flat on the glass slip (§ **40**), drain off the superfluous water, and run several drops of the staining fluid (not diluted) over it; allow it to stand for from three to five minutes exposed to sunlight, covered with a watch-glass to keep off the dust. (In winter it is well to warm the slide on which the section is being stained gently over a spirit lamp, as slight heat causes the tissues to stain both more rapidly and more brilliantly.)

Do not wash the section, but simply run off the superfluous fluid by tilting the slide, and then wipe round the section with the thumb, or with a very soft clean cloth; but be careful not to remove the whole of the staining fluid, as any slight excess is gradually taken up by the tissues after the section has been mounted either in Farrant's solution (§ **152**) or in glycerine (§ **151**), to which from one to five per cent. of formic acid has been added. The full effects of the stain are not seen at first, but after the section has been mounted for two or three days, especially if a small quantity of the staining fluid has been left on the section, and if the slide has been kept in a warm place, a beautiful selective double-stain is found. Tissues of high vitality and fibrous tissue are stained brilliant crimson or pink, whilst the formed material of epithelial cells, elastic tissue, and dead material are stained yellow. Thus, in a section of the skin, the horny layer, the stratum Malpighii, hairs and muscles, are stained various shades of yellow, whilst the nuclei of the cells in the deeper layers of the epidermis are stained crimson, as also is the tissue of the cutis vera. In a section of a scirrhous cancer the stroma assumes a delicate pink stain, the indifferent tissue, which is made up of rapidly proliferating connective tissue corpuscles and leucocytes, takes on a rich crimson colour, whilst the cancer cells are stained yellow, the nuclei appearing of the same tint as the cells of the indifferent tissue.

In a tubercle "follicle" the double-staining also comes out well. The centre of the giant cell takes on a canary yellow colour; surrounding this is usually a zone of nuclei stained brilliant orange-red, and outside this again is the reticulum with the endothelioid cells stained crimson; the condensed fibrous-looking capsule at the periphery being stained pink, and the small round cells much as in the indifferent tissue of the scirrhous cancer. When caseation has commenced in the centre, the yellow mass assumes a somewhat granular appearance and loses its brightness. When it is wished to mount the section in Canada balsam, special precautions have to be taken to retain the picric acid stain. Stain the section for a longer time, as much as an hour being sometimes necessary ; then wash in glycerine to which 1 per cent. of hydrochloric acid has been added, and that has been tinged with picric acid ; dehydrate with alcohol, also coloured with picric acid, clear in clove oil, and mount in balsam. For some purposes this gives very good results, but it is not so generally useful as the Farrant's method.

99. *Picro-lithia Carmine.*—In place of ammonia, carbonate of lithia may be used to hold the carmine in solution. It is prepared as follows :—

> Pure carmine, ... 2·5 parts.
> Saturated watery solution of carbonate of lithia, 100 parts.
> Saturated watery solution of picric acid, . 200 parts.

The fluid is ready for use at once, but should always be filtered before it is used.

100. *Carmine staining fluid* is especially useful for sections of the central nervous system, and for structures in which are considerable quantities of fibrous tissue. As a staining reagent for most tissues, it has been superseded by logwood and picro-carmine. To prepare it, take of

> Pure carmine, . 1 part.
> Strong ammonia, . 1 part.
> Water, ... 50 parts.

Triturate the carmine in a mortar, add sufficient water to form a paste, and then add the ammonia, when the paste will at once turn from a bright red to almost black if the carmine is pure. Add the rest of the water, and keep the solution in a glass-stoppered bottle in which is suspended a piece of camphor.

After carefully washing out picric acid or any of the chromates, a section may be stained rapidly by spreading it out on the glass slide, (§ **40**), and running a drop or two of the solution over it ; allow it to stand for from three to five minutes, and then wash in water for a couple of seconds, and rapidly transfer to acidulated water (eight drops of acetic acid to a pint basinful of water). This last part of the operation must never be neglected, as the carmine is held in solution by an alkaline fluid, and is only precipitated in the tissues when the fluid is rendered acid. Where the stain is properly selective, the nuclei and fully formed fibrous tissue are stained carmine and a delicate pink respectively; other formed material remains unstained, or is only slightly tinted. The axis cylinders of medullated nerve fibres are stained brilliant carmine, as are also the nerve cells of the cord, etc., the latter not so deeply. A more selective stain is obtained by staining the sections slowly in a watery solution. The sections are afterwards treated in the same way. The sections so stained may be mounted in glycerine or Farrant's solution (§ 152), or when it is wished to clear up the section still further it may be mounted in Canada balsam (§ 155).

101. *Alum carmine* sometimes gives very good results, but it is as a rule a somewhat disappointing stain. Method of preparation :—

Dissolve carmine (pure), ...	2 parts.
And alum, . . .	6 parts.
In water, ...	100 parts.

Boil for an hour, allow to cool, and filter. Add a crystal or two of thymol.

Sections may be left in this ten minutes or twenty-four hours as they never over stain; wash thoroughly in water and mount in balsam.

102. *Borax carmine.* For a good differential stain, borax carmine is one of the best that can be used, especially as it may also be used for staining in bulk specimens that have been fixed in nitric acid and hardened in methylated spirit or absolute alcohol.

Borax, ...	2 parts.
Distilled water, ...	50 parts.

Boil, and add while boiling, carmine 1¼ parts; continue the boiling for 10 minutes. Allow to cool and add equal bulk of 70 per cent. alcohol in distilled water. Allow to stand for three or four days, and filter before using. Small pieces, or sections, are left in this until they are sufficiently deeply stained, and then decolorised for from two to three minutes for sections, or sixteen to eighteen minutes for blocks in the following :—

Alcohol, . . .	. 70 cc.
Distilled water, . .	. 30 cc.
Hydrochloric acid, .	. 4 drops.

Then place in methylated spirit for an hour, and in absolute alcohol for twenty-four hours. Leave in clove oil over night (until it sinks, when it is sufficiently cleared up). Then put into pure turpentine or embed, as above, in paraffin (§ 93). Sections stained in borax carmine may be afterwards stained with Ehrlich's hæmatoxylin with very good results.

103. *Logwood Staining Fluid.*—This is especially useful for bringing out the nuclear structures in the tissues, and it has the special advantage that it also stains the protoplasm of cells slightly, and the fibrillar elements in the tissues. It may be made in any of the following ways :—Take of

(*a*) Extract of hæmatoxylin, .   3 parts.

    Alum, .   .   1 part.

    Glycerine,   200 parts.

    Water, ... 400 parts.

Mix the extract, alum, and water, and allow to stand for four days, shaking well three or four times a day. Add the glycerine, and boil down to five-sixths of its original bulk, throwing in two or three grains of alum, whereupon the colour becomes much more brilliant. Add a crystal of thymol dissolved in alcohol, in order to preserve the fluid.

(*b*) Cook's method of making logwood solution, which is also an exceedingly good one. Take of

    Extract of hæmatoxylin, .   .   6 parts.

    Alum, ...   6 parts.

    Cupric sulphate, .   .   1 part.

    Distilled water, ... 40 parts.

(Great care must be taken that none of the ingredients contain any trace of iron.) Grind the alum and cupric sulphate in a mortar, and add the extract of hæmatoxylin, mix thoroughly, and add sufficient water to form a thin paste. Leave this for one or two days, add the remainder of the water, and filter.

(*c*) Barrett prepares a very good logwood stain as follows :—

    Common extract of hæmatoxylin, .   6 parts.

    Benzoate of soda,   4 parts.

    Distilled water,   200 parts.

Mix and allow to stand for one day, then add 10 grammes of potash alum; filter as required, using equal parts of stain and of distilled water; stain for five minutes. The great advantage of this fluid is that it is ready for use twenty-four hours after the ingredients are mixed. Add a crystal of thymol, dissolved in alcohol, to prevent the formation of fungi.[1]

To stain sections, filter about half a drachm of (*a*) or ten drops of (*b*) [to (*b*) add half a drachm of distilled water] into a watch-glass; allow the sections to remain for about three or four minutes in (*a*), or half a minute in (*b*); wash well in water, and mount in Canada balsam (§ **155**).

> *Note.*—Never put more than two or three sections at a time into the watch-glass, or they cling together, and are un-equally stained. Should the staining be too intense, place the sections in a watch-glass, pour a few drops of strong acetic acid over them, then wash thoroughly and mount. V. Kahlden recommends that, for the purpose of getting rid of "over stain," sections should be washed thoroughly in a 1 per cent. solution of acetic acid, and then for twelve to twenty-four hours in distilled water.

(*d*) For many kinds of work Ehrlich's acid hæmatoxylin is greatly to be recommended, especially as a ground work for double and triple staining. Dissolve hæmatoxylin, 2 parts, in 60 parts absolute alcohol. To this add 6 parts of glycerine and 60 parts of water, both of which are previously saturated with alum, and 3 parts of glacial acetic acid. The great advantage of this solution is that it does not cause over staining nearly so readily as some of the other hæmatoxylin preparations. It should be kept exposed to the light for three or four weeks, and then carefully filtered before being used.

104. *Eosine* used as a one-tenth per cent. solution gives a beautifully transparent stain, and one which will remain unaltered for a considerable length of time. It may be used in watery solution, especially for muscular tissue of the heart, etc., or as an alcoholic solution for staining the coloured blood corpuscles. It stains nucle

---

[1] A very good logwood staining fluid is made by Martindale, London.

pink, but these are better brought out by exposure of the sections to the action of the logwood staining fluid (§ 103) for a few seconds after they have been stained with the eosine solution.

To stain with eosine, filter a few drops of the solution into a watch-glass containing distilled water; place the sections in this, and allow them to remain for a minute or two. Wash in water slightly acidulated with acetic acid. Mount in Farrant's solution (§ 152), acidulated glycerine (§ 151), or balsam (§ 155).

105. *Eosinated Hæmatoxylic Glycerine.*—This reagent, as recommended by J. Renaut, appears to be specially useful for staining specimens hardened in chromic acid compounds, or in osmic acid, which are not well stained by carmine and picro-carmine. It is a differential stain which in many respects is equal to picro-carmine.

The protoplasm of muscular tissue takes on the eosine, and is coloured bright rose, the nuclei a deep violet; red blood corpuscles are stained brick red; axis cylinders of nerves, violet.

Prepare the solution as follows :—Take 300 grammes of neutral viscid glycerine and saturate it with potash alum, warming the solution gently and then allowing it to cool. To this add, drop by drop, a concentrated watery solution of eosine, until a slight opacity appears.

If a deeper eosine stain is required, it may be obtained by mixing ordinary glycerine, saturated in the same manner, with the alum saturated solution, until the required tint is obtained. Filter by means of an exhaust filter through fine paper, supported by a platinum cone or well pierced parchment paper. This fluid should have a rose colour by transmitted light, and a peculiar fluorescent yellow green by reflected light.

To this solution add, drop by drop, a concentrated solution of hæmatoxylin in alcohol, gently warmed and shaken to ensure saturation.

The alcoholic solution of hæmatoxylin should be added to the eosinated glycerine until the mixture becomes a "beautiful violet purple," but still retains the green fluorescence. Should the fluorescence disappear, more eosinated glycerine must be added, until the green colour is again distinctly seen. Filter, and keep in flasks covered with perforated paper. "At the end of three or four weeks, when all smell of alcohol has disappeared, filter again as above, and preserve the fluid in stoppered bottles."

Sections hardened in the chromates may be stained in from five to ten minutes, but those hardened in osmic acid require a longer time —one to six hours. The fluid may be used as a mounting fluid, the cover glasses being held in position by Canada balsam, or some other cement.

Sections may also be mounted in Canada balsam if they are first washed in a weak, watery (distilled) solution of eosine, and then cleared up in eosinated alcohol and oil of cloves, in which one per 1000 of eosine has been dissolved ; or camphor mounting fluid saturated with eosine may be used. For specimens to be mounted in Canada balsam, however, this method has no special advantages.

Specimens which have been hardened in osmic acid become blackened after a time, but the violet and rose colours may be restored by passing under the cover glass a drop of a mixture of 1 part formic acid to 200 parts of glycerine, the formic glycerine being replaced by hæmatoxylic glycerine, either pure or, if the rose colour is not deep enough, mixed with eosinated glycerine.

Hæmatoxylic glycerine is prepared by adding a saturated solution of "hæmatoxylin" to glycerine saturated with potash alum, as above described. When the required strength is attained, the liquid should still be quite clear, and on being mixed with water there should be no precipitation of violet granules. If these appear, add a little more glycerine. Filter, and keep in flasks protected from dust, but to which air is allowed to gain access. This fluid serves as a very good and clean logwood stain.

106. *Methylaniline violet* is one of the most useful of the aniline dyes, especially to the pathological histologist. With certain normal tissues it gives a double stain, and in tissues in which there is waxy degeneration the affected parts are most accurately differentiated from the normal tissues. It may be used as a strong watery solution, but by far the best and most reliable preparation is the "Telegraphen Tinte," prepared by A. Leonhardi of Dresden. The sections are placed in a

watch-glass, with about half a drachm of the staining fluid of the watery solution of either the ordinary methylaniline violet or of the ink, of such a strength that when held up before the window in a three-quarter inch test tube, light is allowed to pass readily. Leave the sections in this for two or three minutes ; then wash well in water for half an hour, and mount in glycerine, either pure, or, as recommended by Cornil, slightly acidulated with acetic acid. Farrant's solution may also be used as a mounting medium. With any of the above media the staining is retained for a considerable time. Do not use dammar or Canada balsam, as both the clove oil and alcohol dissolve out the colour, and even the chloroform which is sometimes used as a solvent for the dammar or balsam dissolves out the methylaniline freely, so that the colour, especially where the section has been imperfectly washed, is gradually discharged from the tissue, is diffused, and the section becomes blurred and muddy looking. Methyl violet gives two reactions, a red violet and a blue violet ; these are very well seen in hyaline cartilage, where the matrix takes on the red violet stain, and the cells the blue violet ; or again, in "waxy degeneration," where the "waxy" material takes on the red violet stain, whilst the healthy tissues take on a blue colour, in some instances almost a slaty blue. If it is not convenient to mount these stained sections at once, they may be kept in preservative fluid (§ 89), but not in alcohol, which discharges most of the colour from the tissues ; even that which remains being too diffuse. For fresh tissues, epithelial structures, salivary corpuscles, or cells from the vagina or urethra, it is extremely useful. Used as a dilute watery solution (one or two per cent.), it brings out nuclei and connective tissue corpuscles. Fresh tissues stained with methyl violet should be mounted in "a saturated watery solution of potassic acetate." Methyl violet is also useful as a staining reagent for micrococci and bacteria, which take up the stain and retain it firmly, even when washed in alcohol ; so that sections containing such organisms may be mounted in glycerine or Farrant's solution, after they have been well washed in very dilute acetic acid, or they may be washed in alcohol, clarified with clove oil and turpentine, and then mounted in dammar mounting fluid or Canada balsam (§ 155). Thierfelder recommends that specimens in which waxy degeneration is present should first be stained with the methyl violet, and then washed in a saturated solution of oxalic acid, which discharges most of the colour from the normal tissues, leaving them a dull slaty grey, but intensifies or brightens the red violet stain of the waxy tissues.

107. *Iodine staining solution* is made by adding water to tincture of iodine until it is about the colour of a very dark sherry or brown vinegar. It should never be very strong for microscopic work. Waxy tissues stained with this reagent appear rich mahogany brown when the section is examined by reflected light, the normal tissues yellow; when examined by transmitted light, however, the waxy material assumes a lighter yellow than the surrounding healthy tissues, than which it is much more translucent. It must be remembered that the granules of glycogen in liver cells assume the same mahogany brown colour when stained with iodine solution, as do also some of the cells in growing bone. To stain a section, place it in a watch-glass, and pour over it a small quantity of the solution; allow it to stand for ten minutes; wash rapidly in water, and mount in iodine mounting fluid (see below)—never in Farrant's solution or glycerine, or the staining fades, the iodine diffusing rapidly into the mounting medium. Another method may be used: the section is floated out on a slide, and a small quantity of the fluid is dropped on with the glass rod; this is allowed to stand for a few minutes, then a drop of the mounting fluid is added, and the cover glass is lowered on to the specimen. Where iodine is used the solution in which the section is mounted must be kept saturated with iodine, and as this is very volatile, the cover glass must be at once cemented with French glue, Canada balsam, or some such cementing substance.

To make the iodine mounting fluid, take of

Liquor iodi. (B.P.),	3½ parts.
Glycerine,	6 parts.
Water,	6 parts.
Mix, and add, carefully picked gum arabic, about,	6 parts.

Keep in a stoppered bottle, stirring or shaking regularly, until the whole of the gum is dissolved. Allow the fluid to stand until all air bubbles have risen to the surface, and then decant into a small stoppered bottle to which a glass rod is fused (§ **162**). This fluid is used as a preserving medium for sections stained with iodine.

108. To obtain the blue reaction with *iodine and sulphuric acid* in waxy organs, treat the sections in a test glass with a sherry coloured watery solution of iodine for about half an hour; then immerse them in a 4 per cent. solution of sulphuric acid until the blue colour makes its appearance. Mount in glycerine (§ **151**), or Farrant's solution (§ **152**). This is an extremely delicate test for waxy material, but unfortunately it succeeds only in some cases, though in the hands of some observers extremely satisfactory results have been obtained.

109. *Methyl green.*—As a one per cent. watery solution this gives a beautiful rose pink reaction with waxy material, staining the normal tissue a bluish green. Bolles Lee points out that this reagent has several additional advantages. It does not overstain; it is very penetrating, kills cells instantly without causing swelling or other change of form, and preserves them for several hours. It may also with advantage be combined with weak solutions ('1 to 1 per cent.) of osmic acid, by which mixture tissues are both fixed and double stained. Mount in xylol balsam (§ **155**), but remember that alcohol dissolves out this stain very rapidly, hence the section should not remain very long in this fluid, nor should it remain long in the clove oil, which also quickly discharges the colour.

110. *Osmic acid*, perhaps the most delicate of all staining reagents, is invaluable for staining fat and nerve fibres. It may be kept as a one per cent. watery solution, made by breaking the glass tube in which it is supplied in a mortar, and triturating with one hundred parts of distilled water. It should be kept cool in a glass-stoppered bottle, well protected from the light by a covering of brown paper closely gummed to the bottle. It may afterwards be diluted as required.

When required as a staining reagent it is used as a one-twelfth to one-sixth per cent. solution. The sections to be stained are placed in a small quantity of the fluid carefully protected from the light, and left for from one to twelve hours, after which they are washed in distilled water, and mounted in Farrant's solution (§ 152), or glycerine (§ 151) ; never in Canada balsam or dammar. This staining reagent blackens fat, the myeline of white nerve fibres, the outlines of fibres and cells, at the same time giving the substance of these structures a greenish grey or olive green tinge.

111. *Aniline blue black* is especially useful for staining sections of the nerve centres, bringing into special prominence the nerve cells, which are stained a slaty blue colour.—(Bevan Lewis.)

It is made as follows :—Take of

Aniline blue black, .	1 part.
Water, ...	40 parts.
Dissolve and add rectified spirit, . .	100 parts.

Keep in a stoppered bottle, filter a few drops into a watch-glass, and add eight or ten volumes of alcohol. Stain the section from a half to three minutes, and mount in Canada balsam (§ 155). For ordinary tissues use a one per cent. watery solution, allow the sections to remain in this for a few minutes, and mount in balsam. If the staining is too deep, Stirling recommends soaking of the sections for a time in a two per cent. solution of chloral hydrate.

112. Bevan Lewis' special method of staining fresh nerve tissues :— Freeze a piece of fresh brain or cord in gum on an ether microtome. Cut sections and remove them one by one into cold water, from which spread out at once on a glass slide. With a pipette pour on each a few drops of two per cent. osmic acid solution, leave the sections in this from one to two minutes, then wash thoroughly in water, and stain on the slide with the one per cent. watery solution of aniline blue black for one or two hours. Examine at once or mount in acetate of potash or glycerine. Sections which are to be mounted in balsam should first be well washed in water then allowed to dry thoroughly (well protected from the dust), covered with balsam and mounted.

113. *Gentian violet,* as recommended by Weigert for staining tubercle bacilli, is prepared by adding twelve parts of a two per cent. watery solution of gentian violet to one hundred parts of a saturated solution of aniline oil water.

To prepare this saturated aniline oil water, take of

Aniline oil, . .	1 part.
Distilled water, .	3 parts.

Shake well every half hour for three or four hours, and decant the water as the oil settles to the bottom. The commercial aniline is about a twelfth of the price, but it is said not to answer the purpose so well. For ordinary staining with gentian violet, a two per cent. watery solution, to which is added a crystal or two of thymol dissolved in alcohol, may be used. When mounting in xylol or benzol balsam, do not leave the section too long in either the alcohol or the oil of cloves, both of which reagents dissolve out the staining fluid very rapidly.

114. *Fuchsin.*—A concentrated watery solution of acid fuchsin should also be prepared by those who intend to investigate the pathology of the nerve centres. The method of staining these tissues with fuchsin will be referred to under the heading of special staining methods, and the various methods of staining bacilli will also be more fully described.

Basic fuchsin is now used instead of magenta for staining tubercle bacilli, cells, fibrous tissue, blood corpuscles, &c.

115. *Bismarck brown,* prepared as follows, is an exceedingly useful contrast stain, and is also invaluable for staining sections of bone and young granulation tissue. Take of

Bismarck (aniline) brown,	1 part.
Alcohol anhyd., .	10 parts.
Distilled water, . .	100 parts.

The sections must be stained slowly, and the water in which the staining fluid is suspended should contain about ten per cent. of methylated spirit. Make a straw-coloured solution, and allow the sections to remain in this for several days. Mount in Canada balsam (§ 155). Where used as a contrast stain, pour a few drops of the strong solution into a watch-glass, and allow the section to remain in this for about ten minutes.   This gives a very transparent brown colour to the nuclei and the margins of the cells, leaving the protoplasm almost unstained.

This reagent may be used as a glycerine (two to four per cent.) solution. Heat the Bismarck brown with glycerine in a test tube, then allow to cool, stain the section for a couple of hours or more, wash well in distilled water and mount in Canada balsam.   It will be found of great advantage to allow the section or cover-glass on which is the dried film to remain for a few minutes in a weak solution of carbolic acid before transferring it to the staining fluid.

When time is an element of importance, a stronger solution may be obtained by making the solution in boiling water or in 40 per cent. alcohol, either of which will take up 2-3 per cent. of the Bismarck brown.   Such a solution will stain sections in about five minutes, and will also allow of their being washed with absolute alcohol.

116. *Methylene blue* is used as a contrast stain ; it is also a very good stain for muscle fibre.

To prepare a saturated solution of methylene blue, take of

Methylene blue,	.	1 part.
Alcohol anhyd.,	.	15 parts.
Distilled water, .	.	35 parts.

When the fluid is to be used, dilute with about five times its volume of water.   Mount muscle stained by this method in glycerine (§ 151), or Farrant's solution (§ 152).

It may also be used as a simple watery solution ; 1-2 per cent.

117. *Gold chloride* is of comparatively little use to the pathologist, except in the case of tissues which can be transferred at once to the staining fluid.   In the examination of the morbid conditions of the cornea it is, however, an extremely valuable reagent, as also in the cases of tumours and of nerve terminations in muscles which have been removed from the body during life.   It should be remembered that it can be used to best effect only within a quarter of an hour of the removal of the part from the living body. It may be used in any of the following ways :—

(*a.*) Soak the tissue as soon as removed from the body in a half per cent. solution of chloride of gold, until it assumes a lemon colour; then expose in one per cent. acetic acid solution to strong light, until it assumes a purplish tinge. Sections thus prepared show connective tissue corpuscles (corneal corpuscles, cartilage cells), nerve fibrils, especially those of small size, and ganglion cells, stained reddish purple. Mount in glycerine (§ 151).

(*b.*) Ranvier's method gives extremely good results; its only disadvantage is that, during the process, epithelial cells are removed. It is especially useful for staining nerves, &c., in dense tissue.

Filter the juice of a lemon through clean starchless muslin. Soak small pieces of perfectly fresh tissue in this for about five minutes; wash out the lemon juice with distilled water, and then transfer to a one per cent. solution of gold chloride, in which allow it to remain for half an hour. Again wash in distilled water, after which keep the tissue in a stoppered bottle, carefully protecting it from the light for twenty-four hours, during which time it should be exposed to the action of a 20 per cent. solution of formic acid. At the expiration of this period a purple colour should have made its appearance. Again wash in distilled water, and preserve in glycerine (§ 151).

(*c.*) An exceedingly good modification of the gold method, especially for nerve tissues, is Beckwith's modification of Freud's.

Pieces of nerve centres, or nerves, are hardened (*not* over hardened) in Erlicki's fluid, and then, though not necessarily, in alcohol. Sections are rinsed with water and placed for three or four hours in a one per cent. solution of gold chloride, after which they are washed with water, treated with a 20 per cent. solution of caustic soda for three minutes, then with a 10 per cent. solution of carbonate of potash for thirty minutes, the superfluous fluid is drained off, and the sections are placed from five to fifteen minutes in a 10 per cent. solution of iodide of potassium. They are washed in water, dehydrated, and mounted in balsam.

This method gives most beautiful results, picking out the delicate nerve fibrils and axis cylinders in a most remarkable manner. One of the great secrets of success is that the specimens should be taken directly into the gold solution, the knife being wetted with water instead of with alcohol.

(*d.*) Sandmann's gold process also gives good results.

Thin pieces of fresh muscle are immersed in ordinary sulphurous acid in a test tube for from one to eight days. The acid is then replaced by a considerable quantity of distilled water, this is boiled quickly, then poured off; another lot of distilled water is added and boiled, the process being repeated three or four times, cold distilled water is then added, and the test tube is shaken vigorously until the muscle is broken up into fragments. The fibrils are then placed in a weak solution of chloride of gold, two or three drops of a one per cent. solution of the gold chloride being added to 10 cc. of distilled water; leave in this for from three to ten minutes until the fibres are yellow, and then wash in a very dilute solution of acetic acid, two or three drops to 10 cc. of distilled water. Boil in this fluid until the fibres assume a bluish colour, wash out with water, and examine in glycerine, though the tissues may be mounted in any other mounting medium.

118. *Nitrate of silver* is used specially to bring out the intercellular substance on any epithelial or endothelial surface, in which it is reduced by light to the black oxide of silver. It is also used as a stain for the intercellular substance of cartilage, and for the laminated intercellular tissue of the cornea, though, if the tissues be exposed for a considerable time in the silver solution, the nuclei, and even the protoplasm of connective tissue, epithelial or fat cells may become more or less blackened. To the pathologist it is specially useful in the study of the eye and of tumours of epithelial type, as most other tissues have been dead for some time before they come into his hands. For demonstrating the structure and relations of the alveoli of cancerous growths, this reagent is perhaps the most valuable at command. Take a very thin section of the tissue to be stained as soon as it is removed from the body, and wash well in distilled water to remove all chlorides, which would at once throw down the silver as a white precipitate. Expose it to the action of a large quantity of half per cent. solution of nitrate of silver for from five to ten minutes (until it becomes somewhat whitened); wash in water (not distilled), and expose to diffuse daylight until a delicate brown colour makes its appearance. Care must be taken to protect the specimen from the direct action of the sun's rays, or the tissues soon become quite opaque and very deeply stained. Preserve these specimens (if not mounted at once) in a mixture of glycerine two parts, and water one part, to which has been added five to ten drops of acetic acid to each ounce of the mixture. These stained sections may also be preserved in a mixture of equal parts of spirit and glycerine. Mount in glycerine (§ **151**).

119. *Perchloride of iron.*—Mrs. Dr. Hoggan recommends that sections of epithelioma, papilloma, &c., should first be treated with water and a dilute solution of nitrate of silver and methylated spirit, then with a two per cent. solution of perchloride of iron, and lastly, with a two per cent. solution of pyrogallic acid. By this method the nuclei of epithelial cells are stained very distinctly, and the processes of the prickle cells of papillomas are well brought out. A weak solution of tannic acid or of gallic acid in alcohol may be used instead of the pyrogallic acid for the purpose of reducing the iron salt. The weaker the solution the longer the time required for the reduction, and the better are the results obtained.

SPECIAL STAINING METHODS.

120. For some time I was very much prejudiced against the use of safranin, but after the results I saw obtained by Gulland, and after reading Bolles Lee's warning about the variety of the kinds of safranin, I made another attempt to use it, this time with the most successful results, especially in those cases where I wished to obtain accurate nuclear staining. Lee says, "Before thinking of working with this important reagent, you should go to Grübler or to Münder and order the safranin you want, specifying whether you want it for staining nuclei or for staining elastic fibres, or for what other purpose you may require it." Certain forms are more soluble in water than others, points that must be borne in mind in connection with the special methods found in the following sections.

121. *Pfitzner's Safranin Solution.*—This is specially useful for making out nuclear figures in fresh tissues or in tissues that have been hardened in Fol's solution (§ **67**) bichloride of mercury (§ **58**), &c. :—

Dissolve safranin, .	1 part,
In alcohol, . .	100 parts.

Allow this mixture to stand for several days, then add 200 parts of water. Stain the sections in the solution for 24 hours, wash thoroughly in water, and remove any excess of stain from the tissues with absolute alcohol, examining the sections on the slide under the microscope from time to time as the process of decolorisation is proceeding.

If the specimen is stained in bulk the excess of stain should be removed by soaking the piece of stained tissue in a ·5 per cent. solution of hydrochloric acid in absolute alcohol. By this method the active nuclei are stained bright red, the resting nuclei much less brightly ; safranin is also a very good stain for fibrous tissue.

122. *Adamkiewicz's Safranin Method for Nerve Tissues.*—First place the sections in water weakly acidulated with nitric acid, then in a tube of concentrated watery solution of safranin until they are well stained, wash in methylated spirit, then in absolute alcohol acidulated with nitric acid, and lastly with water similarly acidulated ; after which the sections are stained in methyl blue, cleared up with alcohol and clove oil, and mounted in balsam.

123. *Weigert's Method for Central Nerve Tissues.*—Stain a section hardened in Müller's fluid (§ **59**), bichromate of potash (§ **61**), or Erlicki's fluid (§ **62**), for twenty-four hours in a concentrated watery solution of acid fuchsin (soda salt of rose aniline sulphate). Wash in water and transfer to an alkaline solution of alcohol ("viz., 100 cc. of absolute alcohol with 10 cc. of a solution made by dissolving 1 gramme of fused caustic potash in 100 cc. of absolute alcohol, and filtering), for a few seconds, until the first sign of the grey nerve tissue of the section becomes visible ;" wash in water, "which must not be acid," and dehydrate with absolute alcohol saturated with sodium chloride, to preserve the colour of the section. Clear with oil of cloves, and mount in Canada balsam (§ 155). In sections prepared in this manner, the medullated nerve fibres stand out as brilliant red lines or points, even those in the anterior horns of the spinal cord. The sheath, or part of the sheath, is stained by this method. "The ganglion cells and connective tissue (especially in sclerosis), with the pia mater, vary in tint from a pale to an exquisite blue, which latter is increased by rinsing the sections in a solution of 1 part of hydrochloric acid to 5 of water, and then washing thoroughly in water before dehydrating them with alcohol. These tissues can also be stained blue by hæmatoxylin," "before or after colouring with the acid fuchsin." For the central nervous system, according to Weigert, this is invaluable, but for peripheral nerves it is of no use. To Weigert, also, we are indebted for the following method of staining the myelin sheath of the nerves of the nerve centres ; the sheath taking on a blue stain, the neuroglia light yellow, and the ganglion cells a brown tint. After the tissues have been thoroughly hardened, a piece embedded in celloidin (§ 90) is transferred to a saturated solution of neutral acetate of copper, diluted with an equal volume of water, the whole being kept at a temperature of from 35° to 45° C. The tissues become green, and the celloidin bluish green. Take of

A. Water, ... 90 parts.
     Saturated solution of lithium carbonate, 1 part.

B. Hæmatoxylin, . . 1 part.
     Absolute alcohol, . . . 10 parts.

When required, mix equal parts of *A* and *B*, and dilute somewhat. Leave the sections in this solution for any length of time between one and twenty-four hours, taking care to keep the temperature at from 35° to 45° C. Wash well in water, and transfer to a solution of

     Borax, . . . 2 parts.
     Ferrocyanide of potassium, 2½ parts.
     Water, . . . 200 parts.

Allow the sections to remain from half an hour to two or three hours, according to the thickness of the section and the intensity of the logwood stain. Again wash well in water, treat the section with alcohol, then with xylol, and mount in Canada balsam or dammar mounting fluid.

124. *Pal's Modification of Weigert's Method.*—Pal uses the same hæmatoxylin staining fluid, but afterwards transfers his sections (previously washed in a dilute lithium carbonate solution) for about half a minute into a ¼ per cent. solution of permanganate of potash freshly prepared, and then to the following

Oxalic acid (pure),	.	1 part.
Sulphite of potash,		1 part.
Distilled water,	.	200 parts.

for a few seconds, until the "grey" matter loses all colour, the "white" matter remaining moderately deeply stained blue. Wash thoroughly, clear, and mount, or give a contrast stain with eosin or picro-carmine. Pal gives a special formula for the hæmatoxylin solution, but it appears to have no special advantage over Weigert's solution.

125. *The Pal-Exner Method.*—This method is specially valuable for obtaining stained sections rapidly. The method of procedure is as follows :—Fresh brain or cord is hardened for two days in 10 times its bulk of ½ per cent. osmic acid ; fresh solution being added on the second day. It is then washed carefully in water, placed for a short time in absolute alcohol, and embedded in celloidin or paraffin. The sections are then cut into glycerine, washed in water, stained and differentiated by Pal's method, and mounted in the usual manner.

126. *Special Triple Stain for Bones and other Sections which are to be Photographed.*—Ehrlich's triple stain specially valuable for photographic work :—

  A. Ehrlich's acid hæmatoxylin.
  B. Make a saturated watery solution of Rubin S. (One of
    fuchsin series.)
  C. Make a similar solution of methyl orange. (A good
    "ground" stain.)

Stain the sections in equal portions of the logwood (filtered when used) and distilled water for from five to fifteen minutes, wash well in distilled water and, if necessary, with very dilute acetic acid, to discharge the stain from everything but the nuclei and then leave in tap water until the desired shade of blue is obtained, or wash with a very dilute solution of ammonia, in which case, however, there is some risk of precipitation taking place. Then place in a watch glass containing equal proportions of *B* and *C* for from ten to thirty minutes; wash freely in ordinary water, dehydrate and mount in Canada balsam.

This method is exceedingly useful for decalcified bones, and for other tissues where good contrasts are desired.

Preparation for Microscopic Examination of Tissues and Fluids containing Bacteria.

127. In connection with the manipulation of sections and fluids in which the presence of bacteria is suspected, it must be remembered that the greatest cleanliness is requisite—not only apparent but absolute; and to obtain this absolute cleanliness the apparent must first be attended to. No spot or blemish of any kind should be seen on any of the instruments used; the point of the knife or the platinum needle which conveys the fluid must be carefully polished; the cover glasses and slides thoroughly washed with acid and then with alcohol and distilled water, the watch glasses and other utensils should be treated in a similar manner, and the whole carefully heated to a temperature above that at which organisms can exist —150° C. This is most easily done by passing them carefully through the flame of a spirit lamp, though it is very convenient to have a hot air chamber in which the various utensils may be kept when not in use.

128. *Examination of Bacteria.*—Bacteria unstained, in fluids may be simply examined in a drop of the fluid without any preparation at all, or they may be prepared according to Baumgarten's method (*Lancet*, 15th July 1882). Take a small quantity of sputum, blood, or other fluid, with a needle and smear it on a cover glass, press another against it, and wipe away any superfluous fluid that may appear at the edges with a bit of blotting-paper.   Separate the cover glasses, when each will be found to be covered on one side with a very thin film.   Allow this to dry, and then, if the material contains any albumen, holding one of the cover glasses in a pair of forceps, pass it several times through the flame of a spirit lamp, by which process the albumen is coagulated.   The preparation is then immersed in a solution of a couple of drops of 33 per cent. solution of caustic potash added to a watch-glass of distilled water·   Press the cover glass down on a slide, and examine under a high power (× 600), when the bacilli may be distinguished as small rounded or rod-like bodies, micrococci, bacilli, &c.

" In order to preclude the possibility of confounding the bacilli of tubercle and leprosy with those of other species, the cover glass may be raised and placed aside until the layer of fluid on its under surface is dry, when it should be passed two or three times through a gas flame ; it is then covered with a drop of ordinary watery solution of aniline violet, or any other nucleus tinting aniline colour.   All the putrefactive bacteria are then seen under the microscope as deeply stained blue or brown bodies (according to the staining reagent used and its strength), while the tubercle bacilli remain absolutely colour-less, and can be seen with the same distinctness as in the ordinary potash preparation.   The whole process does not occupy more than ten minutes."

129. Where, however, bacteria are to be examined *in situ* in sections, the following method may be employed :—A fresh speci-men, or one hardened in absolute alcohol (§ 56), should be cut into a number of thin sections (§ 82 *et seq.*), from these the gum is dissolved with warm distilled water, to which has been added a small quantity of pure carbolic acid ; they are then transferred to a watch-glass con-taining absolute alcohol, where they are left for a few minutes ; then to ether ; afterwards to a strong solution of acetic acid.   Wash well in water, and transfer to a two per cent. solution of warm caustic potash or soda.   By this treatment all fat granules, which may be mistaken for micrococci, all small crystals, which are sometimes mistaken for bacilli, granular looking fibrin, and even differentiation of structure, are removed, and only the resistant groups or strings of micrococci or bacilli can be distinguished. Where there are masses of considerable size, within vessels or connective tissue spaces, this method is invaluable, especially for the removal of all elements which could be mistaken for micrococci or bacteria; and where there is any doubt at all in the mind of the observer, this method should certainly be adopted. Where, however, there are no large masses, and where, although the presence of single micro-organisms is suspected, they cannot be distinguished, Weigert's and Koch's method should be adopted. This consists essentially in staining either the parasites alone, or the parasites and the nuclei, with a watery solution of some of the aniline colouring reagents.

130. Sections or cover glass preparations are immersed in a saturated watery solution of gentian violet, methylaniline violet (ten minutes), methyl blue (thirty minutes), or Bismarck brown (twenty-four hours), in which they must be allowed to remain until they are deeply stained; the time required for staining varies with the temperature and the reagent used. When the colour is deep enough the sections are washed for a few seconds in distilled water, then in weak acetic acid, and again in distilled water. If the nuclei are to be left tinted, the section is at once mounted in Canada balsam (§ 155,) great care being taken that the sections are not allowed to remain for too long a time in either the alcohol or the clove oil. In place of the watery solutions, a saturated alcoholic solution of almost any of the germ-tinting aniline colours may be made up in considerable quantity, and diluted as required with about ten times its bulk of distilled water. All the staining reagents should be carefully kept from both dust and light, *and should always be filtered* before they are used. This method is exceedingly useful for the demonstration of the presence of micrococci. If the nuclei are to remain unstained, and the tissues are to be cleared up as much as possible, the section is first stained as above, washed in distilled water, and then transferred to a 5 per cent. solution of carbonate of potash, by which the colouring matter is discharged from all the tissues of the host, but is left in the bacilli or micrococci. The section is then mounted in either Canada balsam (§ 155), Farrant's solution (§ 152), or glycerine (§ 151). This method is

especially valuable for the demonstration and enumeration of bacilli contained within vessels or in thick sections, as in intestinal mycosis, where the anthrax bacilli are to be observed *in situ* in the capillary vessels of the intestinal villi. For pus, blood, and other fluids the so-called dry method is, perhaps, the most convenient. The fluid to be stained is smeared on a cover glass in a very thin layer, which is best obtained by pressing two cover glasses together. The thin film on the glass is first slowly dried, either at the ordinary temperature or by holding it at some distance away from the spirit lamp or gas flame; the glass is then held with a pair of forceps, and passed rapidly through the flame—the smeared surface away from the flame —until the whole of the albumen in the stratum is coagulated. In doing this the glass should first be held at some distance from the flame, and then passed thrice rapidly through it, great care being taken not to *scorch* the film. It may be stained at once, or, if carefully protected from moisture and dust, it may be left for future treatment. Stain with one of the above fluids, floating the cover glass, smeared side down on the surface of the fluid; wash in distilled water, again dry carefully, and mount at once in Canada balsam (§ **155**). It may be mentioned that although Canada balsam is most frequently used for preserving these bacilli, Farrants' solution (§ **152**) and glycerine (§ **151**) are both excellently adapted for this purpose, especially in the case of sections of tissues and of tubercle bacilli.

131. One of the best general stains for bacteriological work is *Kühne's methylene blue* solution. 1·5 grammes of methylene blue is dissolved in 10 c.c. of absolute alcohol and 100 c.c. of a 1 to 20 watery solution of carbolic acid. Specimens are stained in this fluid from five minutes to two hours, although sections may be left in it for a whole day without becoming over-stained. They are then carefully washed in distilled water, then with acidulated water, made by adding a couple of drops of hydrochloric acid to 100 c.c. of water. As soon as the sections become a pale blue colour they are transferred to a solution of lithium water made of the strength of about 1 part of lithium carbonate to 20 of water; they are then thoroughly washed in pure water, dehydrated by means of absolute alcohol in which a little methylene blue may have been dissolved, placed in aniline oil, which may or may not contain a small portion of methylene blue in solution, and rinsed in pure aniline oil. After this treatment they are transferred to terebene, in which they are left for about a couple of minutes. They are then washed in two lots of pure xylol and mounted in Canada balsam (§ 155). Almost any organisms may be stained by this method, even the glanders bacillus coming out fairly distinctly.

132. *Gram's method.*—The sections to be stained by this method should be kept in absolute alcohol from which they are transferred to the ordinary gentian violet and aniline water solution (Weigert's or Ehrlich's), (§ 95), and left for from one to three minutes (tubercle bacilli should be left from twelve to twenty-four hours) ; wash for two or three minutes in alcohol, and then in a solution of 10 parts iodine, 20 parts of iodide of potassium in 3000 parts of water, until the dark blue violet is replaced by a dark purple red. Wash once or twice in alcohol, until most of the colour has disappeared ; then clear up in oil of cloves, until the whole of the colour is washed out from the sections. Mount in balsam (§ 155 *b*). The nuclei and tissues are stained yellow, and the micro-organisms, if present, are deep blue or almost black. After the bleaching process, the nuclei may be stained with eosin, vesuvin, or Bismarck brown ; the sections are then washed in alcohol, and mounted in balsam (§ 155 *b*), glycerine (§ 151), or glycerine jelly (§ 154). Cover glasses, with thin films of sputum, &c., are treated in exactly the same manner.

133. It should be noted that although most micro-organisms may be stained by this method, those found in typhoid fever form an exception. For the *staining of the typhoid or glanders bacillus*, an alkaline solution of methylene blue is recommended by Loeffler. This may be prepared by making a $\frac{1}{10}$th per thousand watery solution of caustic potash, and adding one-third the bulk of a saturated alcoholic solution of methylene blue. The stained section or cover-glass is rinsed for about a second in a one per cent. solution of acetic acid, which has been tinged to the colour of Rhine wine by the addition of a watery solution of tropæolin, washed quickly with distilled water, then with absolute alcohol, cleared up with cedar oil, and mounted in benzole or xylol balsam (§ 155 *b*).

134. *Kühne's Modification of Gram's Method* is perhaps superior to the original. He stains with a two per cent. dilute alcoholic solution of gentian violet (§ 113), to which has been added one-sixth of its bulk of a one per cent. watery solution of ammonium carbonate, or with a similar solution of Victoria blue, without the ammonium carbonate, for about five or ten minutes. The preparations are then rinsed in water, and are placed in Gram's iodine solution (§ 132) for two or three minutes; they are then washed in water, dehydrated with fluoresceine alcohol, which is prepared by dissolving one gramme of yellow fluoresceine in 50 c.c. of absolute alcohol, the part undissolved being allowed to settle at the bottom, the supernatant part only being used. Keep the bottle filled with alcohol until the whole of the fluoresceine is dissolved. The section is washed in pure alcohol, then with aniline oil, and mounted in xylol balsam (§ 155 *b*).

135. *To Demonstrate Flagella on Bacilli* (*Loeffler, Trenkmann*). —Make a potato broth composed of two parts cooked potato, mashed and boiled in ten parts of distilled water; carefully sterilise,[1] and on this make a cultivation of the required organism. A drop of the culture is then diluted from five to ten times by means of distilled water. If the organisms will not grow on this potato broth they may be cultivated in meat bouillon, which must be diluted forty or fifty times before it is used for microscopic examination, or on gelatine plates, the cultivations in this case being diluted about one hundred times. A drop of the diluted fluid is spread on a cover-glass; on this a drop of 10 per cent. alcohol is allowed to fall, the whole is dried in the open air or in a warm room at a temperature of 40°C.; the bacilli are then mordanted in a solution made up as follows : —10 per cent. tannin solution 20 parts, water 80 parts, cold saturated solution of sulphate of iron 5 parts, fuchsin or methyl violet 1 part ; to this mixture add a drop of hydrochloric, acetic, or sulphuric acid in some cases, or of an alkaline solution in others. Put a few drops of this on a cover glass, heat until steam rises, wash in distilled water,

[1] See any text-book on Bacteriological Methods.

and then in absolute alcohol until all colour is removed. Repeat this process, and stain in a neutral aniline or carbolic acid water solution of fuchsin. This will bring out flagella most beautifully. Cholera bacillus, vibrio Metchnikovi, spirillum rubrum, spirillum concentricum, and proteus vulgaris, all stain on the addition of larger or smaller portions of acid. With alkali, the bacillus crystallosus, micrococcus agilis, and the typhoid bacillus, all show flagella. The glanders bacillus, although said to be motile, has, apparently, no flagella.

136. Specimens of tissue to be examined for *tubercle bacilli* should be hardened in alcohol. Sputum or other fluids should be examined as cover-glass preparations—a description of the preparation of which has already been given (§§ 128 and 136). In making a sputum preparation a small caseous portion, if such be present, should always be selected, and, as it is somewhat difficult in certain cases to spread out the sputum on the cover-glass, it is well to use Kühne's method of employing a concentrated solution of borax with which to dilute it. The borax and sputum are taken in equal parts and thoroughly shaken in a suitable glass vessel, or worked up in a mortar, after which it is an easy matter to spread the mixture in a thin layer on the cover-glass, in the ordinary manner. Nummular sputa from cavities may also be broken down by the addition of a watery solution of carbonate of ammonia; this substance is partially volatilised as soon as the cover-glass is heated, and what remains is broken up by the acid in the after treatment of the specimen.

137. *To stain tubercle bacilli in sections.*—Wash the section thoroughly in distilled water, transfer to Weigert's solution of gentian violet (§ 113), and warm gently in a test tube until steam rises; the section will be sufficiently stained in half-an-hour. If the fluid is not warmed the section must be left for twenty-four hours. When sufficiently stained, again wash the section thoroughly in distilled water and transfer to a twenty-five per cent. solution of nitric acid, where it must be left until all colour has disappeared (about half a minute). Again wash in distilled water, after which stain for ten minutes in Bismarck brown (§ 115) rinse with absolute alcohol, place for a second or two in oil of cloves, and immediately transfer to turpentine (the preliminary immersion in clove oil prevents the curling up and stick_ ing of the specimen) after which the section may be mounted in Canada balsam (§ 155 *a*). In place of gentian violet and Bismarck brown other aniline colours may be used.

138. *Ehrlich's method for staining tubercle bacilli.*—Take of—

Pure aniline, . .	5 parts.
Distilled water, . . .	100 parts.

Shake well and pass through a moistened filter; to the filtrate add a saturated solution of fuchsin, methyl violet, or gentian violet, till precipitation commences. Here also the rapidity of staining varies with the temperature.

The best contrast is obtained with methylene blue (watery solution, § 116).

139. The bacilli in *cover-glass preparations of sputum* may be stained in the same way. They are allowed to float face downwards in the staining fluid, for from five minutes to half an hour, according to the strength and temperature of the fluid. They are then removed, washed in distilled water, transferred to a solution (1-4) of nitric acid, as the ordinary solution (1-2) usually proves too strong (though it is here not so important that the solution should be weak, as it is in the case of delicate sections, which are difficult to manipulate after being treated with the stronger fluid). Leave in this for about half a minute, and transfer to distilled water, wash thoroughly, and use a contrast stain (§ 116), wash in absolute alcohol, clear up in turpentine, and mount in Canada balsam (§ 155 *a*).

140. *The Ziehl-Neelsen Method of Staining Tubercle Bacilli.*— This is a modification of the Weigert-Ehrlich method. The sections or cover-glasses are stained in Neelsen's solution, made as follows :— Fuchsin, 1 part, dissolved in 10 parts of alcohol, to which solution 100 parts of a 5 per cent. watery solution of carbolic acid is added ; this is heated until steam rises pretty freely. The cover-glass preparations are stained in three or four minutes, or even less ; sections are usually sufficiently deeply stained in seven or eight minutes. In the cold, they may be left for twelve or even twenty-four hours. The superfluous fluid is drained off, and the preparations are placed for a second or two in alcohol (90 per cent.), then in a 25 per cent.

solution of sulphuric acid, when the pink tinge should immediately be replaced by a yellowish brown. The preparations are then washed in alcohol, and if they are sufficiently decolorised they are transferred to a solution of lithium carbonate (§ 131). They may afterwards be stained with a watery solution of methylene blue, cleared up with clove or aniline oil, turpentine, and xylol, and mounted in Canada balsam (§ 155). Exceedingly good results are obtained by this method, which is preferable in many respects to the aniline oil method. In place of sulphuric acid, nitric or hydrochloric acid may be used, and for clinical work, in order to shorten the process, the methylene blue may, with advantage, be mixed with the acid, the decolorising and contrast staining being carried on in one process (*Gabbet, B. Fränkel*, § 143).

141. *Kuhne's Triple Staining Method for Tubercle Bacilli in Tissues.*—Sections taken directly from alcohol are stained for a couple of minutes in Grübler's nuclear black, diluted with three or four volumes of water. They are then washed in lithium carbonate solution (§ 131) until the sections assume a light grey tone. Rinse in water, and dehydrate in alcohol for five minutes. Stain in Ziehl's fuchsin for ten minutes (§ 140) ; again wash in water, decolorise in fluoresceine alcohol. Wash in alcohol and then place in methyl green aniline oil for five or ten minutes.

This is prepared as follows :—

> Take methyl green sufficient to cover a shilling.
> Aniline oil,   .   10 c.c.

Rub up in a mortar and transfer to a bottle. Allow the undissolved part to settle, and add two drops of the clear supernatant fluid to a watch glass of pure aniline oil, transfer to some ethereal oil, such as terebene, etc., and xylol (see § 131).

By this method a very delicate differentiation of the tissues is obtained. The bacilli are stained red, and are not hidden by the nuclei or other structures which stand out in various shades of transparent blue green. Other colours, such as gentian violet or methylene blue may be dissolved in the aniline oil, and variations of the nuclear stain may be obtained.

142. For cover-glass preparations, Kühne, after staining with the carbolic acid and fuchsin solution (§ 140) and removing the colour, obtains a contrast stain by adding two or three drops of a concentrated solution of picric acid in aniline oil to a watch glass containing pure aniline oil. A drop of this placed on the slide before the cover-glass is lowered into position, gives a sufficiently yellow contrast stain to cause the red tubercle bacilli to stand out very prominently. To keep as a permanent preparation the aniline oil is driven off by means of a hand blower, and the specimen is mounted in Canada balsam (§ 155 *b*).

143. Another rapid method of staining tubercle bacilli on cover-glass preparations is one I have frequently used, and which has been strongly recommended by Fränkel, Gabbet, and Liebman. After staining in carbolic acid fuchsin (§ 140) and washing thoroughly with distilled water, keep the covers for one minute in the following solution :—

Methylene blue,	1·5 grammes.
Absolute alcohol,	30 c.c.
Sulphuric acid, .	20 c.c.
Distilled water, ...	50 c.c.

Wash in water or in weak alcohol, and examine fresh, or mount in balsam (§ 155 *b*).

144. Czaplewaski, to avoid the use of acids, after staining with carbolic acid fuchsin (§ 140), holds the cover-glass in a pair of forceps with the film upwards, and runs over it sufficient staining fluid to cover its surface, holds it over a small flame until the fluid is thoroughly heated, but not long enough to cause drying at any point. The superfluous fluid is poured off and the cover-glass is passed from six to ten times through a concentrated solution of yellow fluoresceine, to which an excess of methylene blue has been added, the whole being filtered. This fluid removes the colour from everything but the tubercle bacilli. To obtain a good contrast stain, the cover-glass, still held in the forceps, is passed from ten to twelve times through the concentrated alcoholic solution of methylene blue, washed quickly in clean water, and mounted in balsam. The whole process takes only some two or three minutes; but where the specimens are to be mounted permanently it is better to wash in 70 per cent. alcohol, and not in water.

145. To demonstrate tubercle bacilli in tuberculous milk, the best plan is to pass the milk through a centrifugal apparatus and to take the sediment for examination, as almost the whole of the bacilli that were originally in the milk will be found along with the mucus and solid particles in this sediment. Where it is not possible to obtain the use of such apparatus, the milk should be allowed to stand for from twelve to twenty-four hours in a glass "separator," such as is used by chemists, or in a conical or funnel-shaped vessel surrounded by ice. The sediment with the contained bacilli is drawn off from the separator by the tap placed at its lower part, or the cream and the upper layers of the milk may be carefully removed by means of a syphon, then with a pipette a few drops of the milk from the bottom of the funnel are taken, dried on a cover-glass, and examined in the ordinary way. In place of the separator or other funnel-shaped vessel, I have used, at Mr. Coghill's suggestion, a long wide burette (which can always be obtained), in which to allow the milk to stand. In drawing off the sediment from the separator or burette the first few drops are rejected, the fluid from immediately above the stop-cock, which contains most of the bacilli, being taken.

Other Reagents used in the Preparation and Mounting of Sections.

146. *Acetic acid.*—One part glacial acetic acid to four parts water is extremely useful for dissolving albuminoid substances, and for bringing the nuclei of certain cells, such as pus cells or white blood corpuscles, into special prominence. It is also used for making more transparent sections of tissues, such as lymphatic glands or the spleen. It seems to act by dissolving or causing swelling of the albuminoids, thus rendering them homogeneous, and throwing up certain structures into greater prominence. A stronger solution is used to neutralise logwood when the stain is too deep (§ 103), and a weaker solution (one drop to the ounce) to fix carmine in the tissues by precipitation (where strong carmine is used as a rapid staining reagent) before the sections are washed and mounted.

Beale's mixture of glycerine, one ounce, and glacial acetic acid, five drops, may also be used for clearing up tissues in the manner above recommended.

147. *Caustic potash or soda,* forty per cent. solution, is extremely useful for clearing up sections of fresh tissues, or any tissues which are to be mounted in glycerine or Farrants' solution, both of which fluids again, having a higher refractive index than water, increase somewhat the transparency of tissues. Reference has already been made to its use in separating muscular fibres (§ **41**).

148. *Ether and Chloroform.*—These fluids are especially used for dissolving out fat from tissues. When such tissues are fresh it is necessary to drive out the water by which fat is protected from the action of the ether or chloroform by means of absolute alcohol.

Place the section in a watch-glass containing absolute alcohol until all the water is removed (which will be the case as soon as the milkiness disappears), when the section should be transferred to a vessel containing ether or chloroform. Allow it to remain in one of these fluids for a few minutes, and transfer first to alcohol, then to a weak solution of acetic acid ; stain and mount.

149. *Bicarbonate of soda,* five per cent. solution, is used, principally, for neutralising the acid hardening fluids (picric acid or chromic acid) before staining with such reagents as logwood. This is done after the sections are cut. This solution also removes much of the yellow picric acid stain. Staining may then be proceeded with in the ordinary manner.

FLUIDS USED IN MOUNTING SECTIONS.

150. *Clove oil* is usually employed to render stained tissues more transparent before they are mounted in Canada balsam or in dammar varnish. Clove oil is one of the most powerful of the volatile oils, and is very frequently used, as it is so agreeable to work with ; but it is a powerful solvent of aniline colours, so that where the tissues are stained with these dyes, turpentine, aniline, oil, and xylol, carbolic acid, creosote, bergamot oil, cedar wood oil, origanum oil, lavender oil, &c., may be used instead of the clove oil, as in the mounting of tubercle bacilli (§ 137). Before the oil of cloves or any other of these clearing reagents can be applied to the section, all water must be abstracted by means of absolute alcohol. The method of procedure is as follows :—After staining the section, wash well in water to remove all the staining fluid not actually taken up by the tissues ; pour about a drachm of absolute alcohol into a watch-glass, and into a second, a similar quantity of the clearing reagent ; remove the section from the water with a needle and absorb from it as much of the moisture as possible by means of a piece of blotting-paper or a soft cloth, allowing the free end of the section just to touch one of these absorbent materials ; place the section in absolute alcohol, allowing it to remain for two or three minutes without attempting to spread it out ; then transfer with a dry needle to the ethereal oil (clove, bergamot, &c.), when the alcohol, rapidly diffusing, carries the edges of the section with it, and the section is spread out on the surface of the fluid. It must not be left for an instant after it is clarified (this should never take longer than half a minute if the section has been properly dehydrated) as some of these oils render the tissue extremely brittle and friable. To transfer the section to the slide, pass the blade of the copper lifter, after carefully smearing it with the clarifying medium, under the section as it is spread out on the surface of the oil, fix one margin of the section with the point of a needle and lift it from the watch-glass ; have the blade as nearly horizontal as possible, so that the section still floats in oil on the blade ; bring the blade down parallel on to the slide, *which must be perfectly dry*, and, fixing the edge of the section with the point of the needle, gently *withdraw* the copper lifter, leaving the section on the slide. Tilt the slide to allow any superfluous oil to drain away, dry carefully with a soft cloth, put on a drop of Canada balsam or dammar varnish, lower a cover-glass on the section and press it down with the handle of the needle—any air bubbles which may have become entangled in the tissues being by this means driven out. In a day or two the cover-glass becomes perfectly firm, and the preparation will bear any amount of knocking about. For the method of clearing up with aniline oil and xylol, see § 131; and for the carbolic acid and xylol method, see § 92.

151. *Glycerine*, or some fluid in the composition of which it is an important constituent, is the most useful fluid for the preservation of thin sections which are to be transferred at once from water to the slide. Where pure glycerine alone is used, as for extremely delicate tissues (thin sections of lung or peritoneum), the section is placed on the slide (§ 40), superfluous moisture is drained away or removed with a soft cloth, and a small drop of the fluid is dropped on to the section with a glass rod; the size of this drop can only be determined experimentally, but it is always better to err on the side of too large a drop, as air bubbles are not then such frequent intruders under the cover-glass. Lower the cover-glass on to the section (§ 36) and press down gently with the handle of the needle to expel air bubbles, which, with glycerine, only too frequently get in, and are then with very great difficulty driven out. All superfluous fluid at the margin of the cover-glass must be removed with the aid of a small glass pipette, and a brush slightly moistened with water; the slide should be carefully dried with a soft cloth, and cemented in the course of an hour or two. The advantages of glycerine as a mounting fluid are its simplicity and its clarifying property, in the case of sections unstained, or stained with the metallic staining reagents, and more particularly in the case of those tissues which are to be examined with high powers. Its disadvantages are, that it is extremely hygroscopic, does not dry at all, and so does not fix the cover-glass; that it sometimes clears up sections too much, and that it causes fresh white fibrous tissue to swell up and look almost gelatinous. In place of glycerine, Farrants' gum and glycerine fluid is now usually employed.

152. *Farrants' Mounting Fluid.*—Take of
Water,
Glycerine,
Arsenious acid, saturated solution (satu-
rated by boiling),   .   .   equal parts.
Mix well in a covered jar, and add about half the bulk of picked gum

arabic ; allow these to stand for three weeks, stirring daily, or until
the whole of the gum is dissolved.   Then filter through coarse filter
paper, or allow the filtrate to stand for a further period of a couple of
weeks, when the air bubbles will have come to the surface, and any
dirt will have settled to the bottom.   Decant into a one-ounce stoppered phial, to the stopper of which a glass rod is fused.   Use in
the same way as glycerine.   If too much gum be used, the tissues
are apt to become slightly granular, whilst, if there is too much
glycerine, the tissues become transparent, and the solution does
not dry properly at the edge of the cover-glass, which remains
unfixed.

This is one of the most useful of all the media for preserving
all but "completely" clarified sections for microscopic examination.
It combines most of the advantages of glycerine with few of its disadvantages.   It does not cause such marked swelling of fresh tissues,
nor does it render sections quite so transparent as does the glycerine,
though it clears them up very appreciably, especially after they have
been mounted for a few days.   It also acts as a preservative medium,
on account of the presence of the arsenious acid : and the glycerine,
by its affinity for water, keeps the section moist, until the fluid at
the edge of the cover - glass dries.   By this drying the cover-
glass is fixed slightly by the gum, and after the specimen has been
mounted for two or three days, the slide may be cleaned, and the
cover-glass cemented with Hollis's glue, indiarubber solution, or
gelatine solution (§ **159**).   The only real disadvantage of this fluid
is that sections kept in it for a number of years often become
somewhat cloudy and slightly granular.

153. *Camphor Mounting fluid,* recommended by Hamilton, is
sometimes used in place of Farrants' solution, in which to mount
sections stained or injected with fluid that might be affected by
arsenious acid.   For instance, sections taken from an organ
injected with Prussian blue must be mounted in a fluid which contains no arsenious acid, that substance causing decolorisation of the
iron blue.

This fluid consists simply of Farrants' medium, in which the
arsenious acid solution is replaced by camphor water.   Take of

Camphor water,   .   2   parts.

Glycerine, ...   1   part.

Pure picked gum arabic,   .   .   .   1½ parts.

Prepare as for Farrants' solution, and keep a piece of camphor floating in the fluid. Employ as glycerine or Farrants' solution.

154. *Glycerine Jelly*—

Pure gelatine,   .   .   30 parts.

Distilled water,   .   .   70 parts.

Glycerine, ...   100 parts.

Alcoholic solution of camphor,   .   .   5 parts.

Allow the gelatine to stand in the distilled water for twelve or twenty-four hours until perfectly softened, boil and strain through a warm filter or a felt jelly bag, add the glycerine and the camphor, mix thoroughly, and warm as required. Be very careful to avoid air bubbles, and keep the slide warm until the cover-glass is in position. Keep the medium in small bottles and immerse in water warm enough to keep it fluid when it is in use.

CANADA BALSAM AND DAMMAR VARNISH.

155. These mounting fluids may both be used for deeply stained sections, especially where it is necessary to bring into strong relief the stained parts of the tissue. They can be used only where the tissues have been previously dehydrated with alcohol (§ 150), and cleared up with some substance (clove oil or turpentine) with which they will amalgamate. Each fluid has its special advantages and each its special disadvantages, the latter being that Canada balsam is said to have a somewhat yellow tint, and hence is not fitted as a mounting medium for sections that are to be photographed, but sections mounted in it keep perfectly well for years. If properly prepared, and not too thick, this is merely a theoretical drawback, as I have seen most beautiful photographs of sections mounted in Canada balsam. Sections mounted in dammar varnish, as a rule, become somewhat cloudy and granular after they have been kept for a year or two; but when fresh they are beautifully transparent, and the medium itself is perfectly free from colour, so that it is admirably adapted for photographic work. To prepare Canada balsam mounting fluid, heat the ordinary Canada balsam gently for about twenty-four hours in a covered vessel ; allow it to cool to a yellow vitreous looking mass ; take of this   100 parts.

Chloroform,	. .	47 parts.
Turpentine,	. . . . .	47 parts.

Dissolve the Canada balsam in the chloroform and turpentine, and filter through fine cotton wool. The fluid must be kept in a stoppered bottle which has previously been carefully dried, and rinsed out first with absolute alcohol, and then with turpentine and benzole. It must be kept in a dry place.

(*a.*) If the Canada balsam is to be used for mounting stained bacteria, especially tubercle bacilli, the chloroform must be replaced by benzole, or better still, xylol, neither of which is nearly so powerful a solvent of the aniline colours as is the chloroform.

(*b.*) Xylol balsam may be prepared by simply dissolving the dried and hardened balsam in sufficient xylol to give a mounting medium of the required consistence, 90 of xylol to 100 of balsam.

156. Dammar varnish is prepared as follows :—Take of

Gum dammar, .	. 2 parts
Gum mastic,	1 part.
Turpentine,	4 parts.
Chloroform,	. . . . 2 parts.

(These proportions may vary somewhat as a thinner or a thicker fluid is preferred, but the above proportions give very good results.)

Mix in an earthenware jar, or wide-mouthed bottle, stirring and agitating until the gums are dissolved, then filter through coarse filter paper into small stoppered phials, to the stoppers of which glass rods have been fused.

CEMENTING OF COVER GLASSES.

157. For this purpose various solutions have been suggested, but the same great difficulty almost invariably presents itself, that whatever substance is used the glycerine sooner or later leaks out. With Farrants' solution there is not the same difficulty, it being quite sufficient, after carefully cleaning the slide, and allowing the gum in the Farrants' solution to partially fix the cover glass, to run a ring of

gold size, French glue, Hollis's marine glue, or indiarubber solution around the margin of the cover glass. It may then be left for twenty-four hours, after which a ring of zinc white cement may be laid over the ring already painted on, and this may be repeated in the course of a day or two, when the first layer has become properly set.

158. Zinc white cement is composed of—

Benzole, . .	8 parts.
Gum dammar, .	8 parts.
Oxide of zinc, ...	1 part.

Mix the gum dammar and the benzole, filter through cotton wadding, after which add the oxide of zinc, mix in a mortar, and again filter through the wadding.

This cement forms a very workable material, and when set is as hard and firm as enamel. After a time, however, it usually becomes brittle and cracks, so that it is far the best plan to use it in combination with one or other of the cements already mentioned.

Slides treated in this manner will, if properly cemented in the first instance, keep perfectly free from leakage for years.

159. For sections mounted in glycerine Dr. Marsh suggests gelatine solution as a cement for first fixing the slide, the gelatine readily mixing with the glycerine in its immediate neighbourhood, and preventing its further escape.

He places a small quantity of gelatine in a narrow glass beaker, covering it with water, and allowing it to take up as much of the water as it will. Any superfluous water is poured off, the mixture is heated, and three or four drops of creosote are added to each ounce of the fluid; keep in a small bottle, and each time that the mixture is needed, it is "rendered fluid by immersing the bottle containing it in a cup of warm water." The slide must be perfectly freed from glycerine by the aid of a camel hair pencil and a damp cloth. A ring of the gelatine fluid is painted round the edge of the cover-glass. As soon as this is set, paint it over "with a solution of bichromate of potash, made by dissolving ten grains of that salt in one ounce of distilled water." He recommends that "this application of bichromate of potash should be made in the daytime, as the action of daylight upon it, in conjunction with the gelatine, is to render the

latter insoluble in water;" wash well in methylated spirit to remove
all the glycerine, and then run on a ring of zinc white ; this may be
repeated until a good firm ring is obtained.

160. In applying these various rings, it is well to use a "turn-table."
This is a heavy brass disc about three and a half inches in diameter,
which should work smoothly on a conical pointed pivot fixed to a
solid piece of wood.   On the disc are usually marked or engraved a
series of concentric rings, each of which should correspond in size to
one of the ordinary cover-glass sizes.   A couple of brass clips are
affixed, which serve to keep the slide in position when the cover-glass
is "centred."   Self centring turn-tables are now also much used.
With a goat-hair or short stiff camel-hair brush lay on first a ring of
the size or other cement, and when this is dry, paint on a ring of the
zinc white.   In working with the cements, always keep the brushes
clean.   This is most conveniently and thoroughly done by means
of warm water for the size, glue, or gelatine, and turpentine or
benzole for the zinc white.   When the zinc white becomes too
thick to run readily, it may be diluted with benzole.

161. Label the slide with the name of the tissue, the disease, date
of *post mortem* examination, method of staining and mounting
employed, and the date of mounting.   It is now ready for future
examination.   Slides so prepared should be kept in the flat trays
mentioned below, carefully protected from both light and dust.

162. In addition to apparatus mentioned (§ 32), the following will
be required :—

  a. A razor and a couple of scalpels, similar to those already pro-
      cured.   (§ 1.)
  b. Three or four strong needles firmly set in hardwood handles.
      These should be quite smooth, free from rust, the point perfect,
      and not hooked or twisted.   They should be cleaned from
      time to time with emery paper, and then with chamois leather.
      Glass rods, drawn out to points, and blunted, curved, or
      straight, may sometimes be used instead of these needles.
  c. A couple of pairs of scissors ; one pair straight and probe-
      pointed, the other pair sharp-pointed and curved on the flat.

Those used by ophthalmic surgeons answer the purpose admirably.

d. A copper lifter, with a stem about 3¾ inches long, and two blades—one about 1 inch × ¾ inch, and the other ⅝ inch × ⅜ inch. The stem should be flat and the blades, continuous with it, very thin, so that they may be bent to form any angle. The edges must be perfectly rounded and smooth. Nickel and platinum lifters, now made of very good quality, may be used instead of the copper lifters.

e. Six or a dozen deep watch glasses, or "Syracuse" glasses with flat glass covers.

f. Two or three test glasses and half a dozen test tubes.

g. Half a dozen white earthenware pint basins, and about a dozen rounded shallow glass trays or capsules. These may be replaced by what are known in the glass trade as clock glasses.

h. Two or three small glass tube pipettes, for removing fluids of various kinds from the edges of the cover glasses after sections have been mounted.

i. Several goat hair pencils for cementing slides, and a similar number of camel hair pencils for the manipulation of sections, in the process known as pencilling.

j. Six dozen glass slides with ground edges, 3 inches × 1 inch.
Four do.   do.   do.   3 inches × 1½ inches.
Eight dozen extra thin circular cover glasses, ⅞ inch in diameter.
Five or six dozen   do.   do.   1¼ inch diameter.
One ounce square cover glasses for use when Canada balsam is the mounting medium.

These, of course, may be replaced from time to time as they are used, but it is well to have at least these numbers, if the student intends to examine the various morbid tissues which come under his notice.

k. Labels for slides.

l. A small box for carrying six or a dozen slides, and a cabinet to hold about ten dozen slides, should be obtained, in order that the specimens may be kept clean and well arranged.

N.B.—The slides on which sections are mounted should always be kept *flat* in trays, or in upright boxes.

H

m. A soft linen cloth. An *old* pocket handkerchief is, perhaps, the best cloth one can use.

n. Drawing materials. A couple of black lead pencils—HB and HHHH.

Half a dozen lithographic pens.

A small box of moist water colours (which may be used as inks for the lithographic pens), with brushes.

Some ordinary mounts to be cut into drawing cards.

o. Two or three packets of white filter papers.

p. A freezing microtome (§§ **85-88**).

q. A spirit lamp or Bunsen burner.

For cutting in paraffin or celloidin, the following additional apparatus will be required :—

r. A small copper water oven, with thermometer and gas regulator, so that a temperature of from 54° to 60° C., as required, may be maintained.

s. A packet of silk "kitchen" paper.

t. Two or three photographic "developing" dishes.

u. A few blocks of wood, 1 inch or more square, cut across the grain.

v. Special microtomes (§§ **91-94**).

LISTS OF REAGENTS.

163. The following reagents, which should be in one-ounce glass-stoppered bottles, will also be required. Those marked *R* should have a glass rod nearly as long as the bottle fused into the glass stopper. The end of this rod must be well rounded, *not* pointed. Those marked *W* should be in wide-mouthed glass-stoppered bottles.

REAGENTS IN GENERAL USE.

R. Ranvier's picro-carmine staining fluid (§ **98**, p. **74**), or
Picro-lithia carmine (§ **99**, p. **76**).
Logwood staining fluid (§ **103**, p. **78**).

R. Carmine staining fluid (§ **100**, p. **76**).
Alum carmine (§ **101**, p. **77**).
Borax carmine (§ **102**, p. **77**).
Methylaniline violet (§ **106**, p. **81**).

R. Iodine staining fluid (§ **107**, p. **83**).
Eosine, $\frac{1}{10}$ % solution (§ **104**, p. **79**).

W. Osmic acid, 1 % solution (in bottle covered with brown paper (§ **41**, p. **43**, and § **110**, p. **84**).
Acetic acid, 1 to 4 (§ **146**, p. **104**).

R. Glacial acetic acid (§ 146, p. 104).
R. Caustic potash, 40 % (§ 41, p. 42, and § 147, p. 105).
 Ether (§ 148, p. 105).
 Chloroform (§ 148, p. 105).
 Neutral saline solution, ⅔ % solution of common salt (§ 34, p. 39).
 Bicarbonate of soda, 5 % solution (§ 149, p. 105).
 Absolute alcohol (§ 150, p. 105).
 * Aniline oil (§ 140, p. 101).
R. Oil of cloves, xylol, creosote, and turpentine (§ 150, p. 106).
R. White of egg and glycerine (§ 95, p. 72), or
R. Collodion and clove oil (§ 96, p. 73).
 Solid paraffin—hard and soft (§ 93, p. 70).
W. Celloidin (§ 90, p. 68 ; see also § 92, p. 69).
 Large bottles containing—
 Methylated spirit.
 Distilled water.

MOUNTING FLUIDS.

R. Farrant's solution (§ 152, p. 107).
R. Glycerine (§ 151, p. 107).
R. Iodine mounting fluid (§ 107, p. 83).
R. Canada balsam (§ 155, p. 109), or Dammar mounting fluid (§ 156, p. 110).
W. Glycerine jelly (§ 154, p. 109).
R. Camphor mounting fluid (§ 153, p. 108).

CEMENTS AND SOLVENTS.

W. French glue, gold size, or a solution of indiarubber (§ 157, p. 110), or
 gelatine (§ 159, p. 111).
W. Zinc white cement (§ 158, p. 111).
W. Benzole (§ 158, p. 111).

SPECIAL REAGENTS.

 Strong ammonia (for fungi, &c.).
 Lithium carbonate solution (§ 131, p. 97).
R. Carbonate of ammonia solution (§ 136, p. 100).
R. Borax solution (§ 136, p. 100).
 Saturated solution of oxalic acid (§ 106, p. 82).
R. Aniline blue black (§ 111, p. 85).
R. Gentian violet (§ 113, p. 85).
R. Fuchsin (§ 114, p. 86, and § 140, p. 101).
 Bismarck brown (§ 115, p. 86).
R. Methylene blue (§ 116, p. 87).
 Methyl green (§ 109, p. 84).
 Safranin (§§ 120-2, pp. 90, 91).
 Weigert's stains and reagents (§ 123, p. 91 *et seq.*).
 Pal's fluid (§ 124, p. 93).
 Ehrlich's stains (§ 126, p. 93).
 Gram's iodine decolorising fluid (§ 132, p. 98).
 Loeffler's stain for flagella (§ 135, p. 99).
 Kühne's stains (§ 141, p. 102).
 Renaut's eosinated hæmatoxylic glycerine (§ 105, p. 80).

* Gold chloride, ½ % solution in distilled water (§ 117, p. 87).
* Silver nitrate, ½ % solution in distilled water (§ 118, p. 89), for tumours, &c.
* Perchloride of iron solution (§ 119, p. 90).
  * The bottles in which these three reagents are kept should be carefully
    covered with brown paper, as should also the aniline oil bottle.

Nitric acid, 20 % solution in distilled water (§ 41, p. 42, and § 137, p. 100).
Sulphuric acid, 10 to 25 % solution in distilled water (§ 140, p. 101).
Hydrochloric acid (§ 79, p. 61).
Picric acid, saturated solution (§ 75, p. 60).

WORKS FOR REFERENCE.

1. A Manual of General Pathology. J. Payne, 1888.
2. A Text-Book of Pathology. D. J. Hamilton, 1889.
3. A Text-Book of Practical Histology. W. Stirling, 1881.
4. Bacteria and their Products. Woodhead, 1891.
5. Botanical Micro-Chemistry. V. A. Poulsen, Trans. by Trelease, 1884.
6. Course of Elementary Practical Physiology. Foster and Langley, 1884.
7. Course of Practical Histology. Schäfer, 1877.
8. Das Mikroskop und die Mikroskopische Technik. Heinrich Frey, 1886.
9. Die Methoden der Bakterien Forschung. Ferd. Hueppe, 1890.
10. Die Pathologisch-histologischen Untersuchungs methoden. George Schmohl
    in Lehrbuch der Pathologischen Anatomie, Bd. I., 1889, Birch-Hirschfeld.
11. How to work with the Microscope. L. S. Beale, 1879.
12. Manuel d'Histologie Pathologique. Cornil et Ranvier, 1881.
13. Manual for the Physiological Laboratory. Harris and Power, 1891.
14. Manual of Pathology. J. Coats, 1890.
15. Methods of Research in Microscopical Anatomy and Embryology. C. D.
    Whitman, 1885.
16. Microskopische Technik. C. Friedländer, 1889.
17. Mittheilungen aus dem K. Gesundheitsamte, Vol. I., 1881, and Vol. II., 1884.
18. Outlines of Practical Histology: A General Account of Histological
    Methods. W. Rutherford, 1876.
19. Pathological Mycology. Section I. Methods. G. S. Woodhead and A. W.
    Hare, 1885.
20. Practical Histology and Pathology. Heneage Gibbes, 1885.
21. Practical Pathology. J. Lindsay Steven, 1887.
22. Practical Microscopy. G. E. Davis, 1889.
23. Practicum der Pathologischen Histologie. Oskar Israel, 1889.
24. Praktische Anleitung zum Mikroskopischen Nachweis der Bakterien im
    tierischen Gewebe. II. Kühne, 1888.
25. Section Cutting and Staining. W. Colman, 1888.
26. Technik der Histologischen Untersuchung Pathologisch - Anatomischer
    Präparate. C. v. Kahlden in Ziegler's Lehrbuch der allgemeinen und
    speciellen Pathologischen Anatomie, 1890.
27. The Microscope and its Revelations. W. B. Carpenter, 1881.
28. The Microscope in Medicine. L. S. Beale, 1878.
29. Traité Technique d'Histologie. L. Ranvier, 1875-78.
30. Traumatic Infective Diseases. Robert Koch, Trans. New Syd. Soc., 1880
    (German, 1878).

And other Works already mentioned.

CHAPTER III.

INFLAMMATION, ORGANISATION, AND REPAIR.

INFLAMMATION OF THE OMENTUM.

164. The most convenient structure in which to examine the earlier processes of inflammation is the omentum, which is a typical example of a serous membrane—a transparent membrane composed of (1) delicate connective tissue fibrils and (2) connective tissue cells. It contains also (3) a few elastic fibres, and is traversed by a network of (4) vascular and lymphatic channels and spaces. The membrane is completed by an investing layer of (5) flattened endothelial cells similar to those met with on other serous surfaces. Between these cells there appear small orifices or stomata, by which a free communication is kept up between the large serous peritoneal cavity (which may thus be looked upon as an exceedingly large lymphatic space), and the smaller lymph spaces and channels in the omentum itself.

In this clear vascular membrane we may readily follow the changes that take place both in and around the vessels and in the fixed tissues, although in the process of inflammation the membrane becomes somewhat more opaque, swollen, and succulent than it is under normal conditions. In a case of acute peritonitis (as soon after death as possible, as the endothelial cells, by a kind of *post-mortem* maceration, are very quickly separated from their trabeculæ), cut out with a pair of fine sharp-pointed scissors a thin piece from the mesentery, or better still from the omentum, spread it out on a slide, stain (§ 98), and mount in a drop of glycerine (§ 151); cement (§ 159). If the specimen cannot be mounted at once, transfer to Müller's fluid, diluted to one-half the ordinary strength (§ 59), gradually increase the proportion of Müller's fluid for a few days, and then keep in preserving fluid (§ 89), mount and treat as above, or as in §§ **103-155** or **106-152**.

To the naked eye the appearances are very much like those presented in inflammation of any serous surface (see § **166**). In the very early stages there is simply a rosy flush of the membrane, which is accompanied by a loss of the characteristic glistening appearance of a healthy serous surface. This is due to exceedingly minute projections, some of which are caused by the distension of the blood vessels, others by minute accumulations of proliferating cells or small patches of coagulated extravasated lymph. Later, the amount of lymph thrown out may become enormously increased, when a layer of soft fibrinous lymph is formed on the surface, especially where any two layers are brought in contact.

If now we examine a piece of such a membrane during the early stage of inflammation, stained and mounted as above, the following appearances may be observed.

(× 50.)—There is (1) considerable distension of the small vessels, especially of the venules. Although the distending mass consists mainly of red blood corpuscles, there is a larger proportion than usual of stained (white) blood corpuscles.

(2) Around the distended venules is an accumulation of leucocytes, evidently the result of diapedesis or migration; this may be easily made out at those points where the capillary or small venules after the capillaries open into the larger venules, as the leucocytes collect in the angles at their junction. (3) There is also a marked increase in the number of the flattened endothelial cells, some of which are still adhering to the connective tissue or fibrous trabeculæ, while others are lying free in the trabecular spaces. In consequence of the rapid proliferation that is going on, most of these cells are smaller than normal, but in the very early stages, when some of the cells appear to be separated directly by the rapid effusion of fluids beneath them (the fluid elements that pass out from the distended vessels may be much increased in amount), they are still of considerable size, and retain much of their normal contour and appearance. (4) The connective tissue or fixed cells that lie on the delicate fibrillar stroma are also undergoing rapid proliferation.

(× 300). — The distended vessels are now readily enough demonstrated, the venules being surrounded by a large number of leucocytes, which can only have escaped from the engorged

vessels. There is also evidence of increased activity of the
endothelial cells, which are undergoing rapid proliferation. Little
groups of very regularly shaped cells, or single cells, are seen
lying in the spaces of the network ; some of these cells are elongated, others are pear-shaped, whilst others again are irregularly
rounded, most of them staining deeply and undergoing rapid
proliferative changes. The origin of some of these cells can

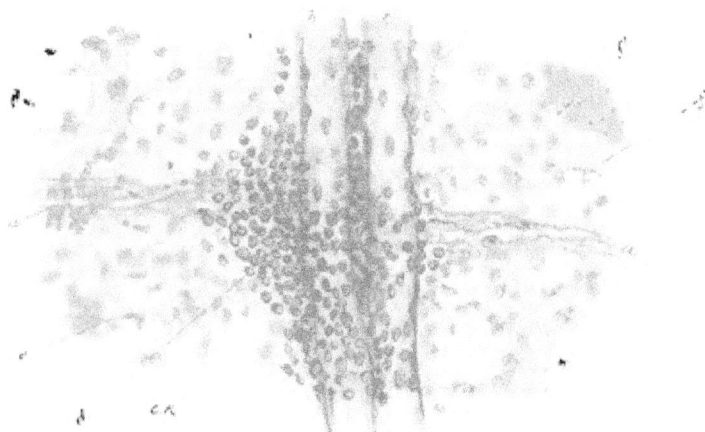

FIG. 4.—Early inflammation of peritoneum, taken almost immediately after death. Stained with logwood. (× 300.)
  a. Capillaries, arterial and venous.
  b. Larger venule.
  c. Larger arteriole.
  d. Accumulation of leucocytes at the angle formed at the junction
      of *a.* and *b.*
  e. Fibrous trabeculæ of the peritoneum.
  ff. Endothelial cells, proliferated, some detached from trabeculæ.

be traced to the fixed connective tissue elements, others to the
endothelial cells that cover the network and give it its characteristic shiny appearance ; some of the larger endothelial cells bulging
from the trabeculæ are multinucleated, whilst others appear to
be undergoing degenerative (especially fatty) changes. It should
be observed that a very large number of the proliferated cells are
contained within the lymph spaces, into which they appear to have
made their way by the channels by which the fluids ordinarily pass

from the vessels into the lymphatics; this, of course, does not apply
to the fixed connective tissue and lining endothelial cells, though here
again we may assume, from what may be observed in our specimen,
that the proliferative changes are merely an exaggeration of the
normal processes of multiplication and regeneration of the cells. In
the later stages of inflammation, where there is great exudation of
lymph, or where organisation has taken place, the microscopic
appearances are very similar to those met with on any other inflamed
serous membrane (such as the pleura or pericardium) (§ 166).

ACUTE METASTATIC MILIARY ABSCESS OF THE HEART IN ULCERATIVE ENDOCARDITIS.

165. In certain cases of ulcerative endocarditis small yellow points,
sometimes almost microscopical in size, but more frequently the size
of a millet seed, are seen in the muscular wall of the heart. These
are specially numerous, or to be more accurate, are specially well
seen near the endocardial surface. They are also met with in other
organs and in the subcutaneous connective tissue, and appear to be
due to the presence of septic emboli which, derived from the breaking
down vegetations in ulcerative endocarditis and composed of a network of degenerating fibrin in which are entangled cells and micrococci, become fixed in the small terminal or capillary vessels of the
various organs. These abscesses are usually multiple, and they
follow most closely the distribution of the blood-vessels. If they
can be examined at a sufficiently early stage, the appearances
represented are extremely characteristic. Each has a small yellow
or yellowish grey centre; then comes a grey, sometimes translucent, zone which, before shading off into the normal tissue, is
frequently surrounded by a delicate red or reddish purple zone. In
some cases, on account of the rapidity with which the breaking down
of the tissues is going on, this hyperæmic zone is so ill defined that
it can scarcely be distinguished; in the immediate neighbourhood of
the minute abscesses, or even in their substance, small hæmorrhages are often found. Harden (§ 58) a small piece of the muscle
from the wall of the left ventricle, care being taken to note that it
contains one of the small abscesses; stain the sections by Gram's
method (§ 132), using a contrast stain.

($\times$ 50).—The abscess can at once be recognised. In its centre is an oblique section of a vessel, plugged, at this point, with a mass of micrococci, which stands out very prominently. The wall of the

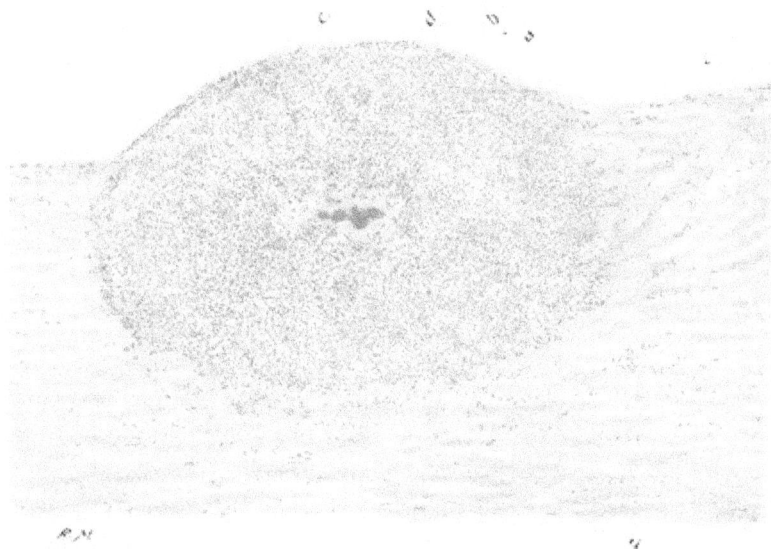

FIG. 5.—Acute metastatic miliary abscess immediately under the endocardium, from a case of ulcerative endocarditis; stained by Gram's method, but only partially decolorised; contrast stain—eosin. ($\times$ 50.)

   a. Mass of micrococci (which may be partly of *post-mortem* growth, impacted in a small blood-vessel).
   b. Altered, partly " digested," wall of the blood-vessel, with a similar change in some of the surrounding tissue. This tissue is imperfectly stained, and is almost homogeneous.
   c. Mass of leucocytes and proliferated fixed connective tissue cells, forming a kind of barrier between the dead normal tissues; between them fragments of unstained muscle may be seen.
   d. Proliferating cellular layer of the endocardium. A mass of flattened cells.
   e. Margin of abscess, near which the larger connective tissue cells are always most numerous. The line of demarcation is very distinct. .
   f. Small vessel in which are a large number of leucocytes.
   g. Small vessel seen in transverse section. A small collection of leucocytes is seen in the perivascular lymphatic space.

vessel and the small amount of remaining surrounding tissue are both somewhat homogeneous in appearance; immediately outside this we come on an enormous number of leucocytes, with here and there a few larger cells, which are to be looked upon as proliferating fixed connective tissue cells. Under this power little but these cells can be made out in the abscess area.

At the margins of the abscess the transition from abscess to muscular tissue is very abrupt, the leucocytes along with the digestive enzymes of the micrococci, apparently causing rapid disintegration of the muscular fibre. At one or two points a slight increase in the number of nuclei between the muscle fibres may be observed. Near the inner part of the wall of the heart, the proliferation of the endocardial cells is well marked, this proliferation gradually tailing off on each side of the "pointing" abscess, so that over the endocardial surface of the abscess is a thickened cellular layer. This resembles very closely the condition met with in endarteritis. The ends of the muscle fibres abutting on the abscess are somewhat irregular, and are evidently in process of being absorbed. In the immediate neighbourhood of the abscess, and in what is evidently part of the plugged vessel, there is an increase in the number of leucocytes within the lumen of the vessel. These leucocytes appear to have collected at this point in large numbers, partly in consequence of the obstruction to the blood-flow immediately beyond.

(× 300).—The structure of the abscess is now more evident ; the mass filling the lumen of the vessel is seen to be made up of small cocci ; immediately around this mass the wall of the vessel and fragments of muscle are quite homogeneous and are very imperfectly stained. In the unstained area, seen under the low power, are numerous nuclei, apparently those of dead or degenerated leucocytes which do not take on the stain nearly so deeply as do those in the surrounding tissues. Between these nuclei are granular fragments of muscle fibre which have lost much of their ordinary or typical structure and appearance. Outside this area comes a zone of leucocytes deeply stained, evidently very active, with here and there a larger cell with one or two deeply stained nuclei, derived, apparently, from the fixed connective tissue cells. At the extreme margin of the abscess these fixed connective tissue cells are more numerous; the muscle fibres look like " ghosts " of fibres, fragments of the sheath remaining, with, here and there only, fragments of much degenerated or vacuolated granular muscular fibre. Between these fragments, and even between the healthier muscle fibres, leucocytes are making their way in considerable numbers. The thickening of the endocardial layer with the proliferation of the cells forming it is well marked, especially at the margin of the abscess (not shown in Fig. 6). These cells are arranged in flattened, comparatively regular layers, lying immediately beneath the endocardial surface; they may be traced over the round celled mass, of which the main part of the abscess is composed. The distended vessel in the immediate neighbourhood of the abscess

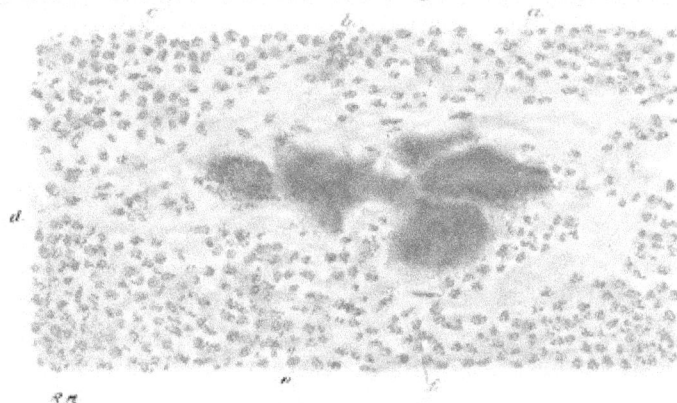

FIG. 6.—Acute miliary abscess immediately under the epicardium, from a case of ulcerative endocarditis, stained by Gram's method, but only partially decolorised; contrast stain—eosin. (× 420.)

a. Plugs of micrococci. These have made their way into or even through the wall of the vessel.
b. Altered (digested?) vessel wall.
c. Leucocytes thrown out in large numbers immediately around the vessel.
d. Altered (digested?) muscle fibre around vessel.
e. Digested leucocytes, very imperfectly stained, in the immediate neighbourhood of the micro-organisms, some of them are seen to contain large numbers of these micrococci.
f. Larger and more elongated connective tissue cells.

contains a considerable number of leucocytes, and a number of cells with proliferating nuclei, and a large mass of formed material around. The endothelial cells lining the vessel are also proliferating, and it appears probable that some at least of the larger cells seen are derived from this endothelial lining.

In this specimen we have an exceedingly good illustration of the process of abscess formation. A micrococcus, probably the staphylococcus pyogenes aureus or albus, or the streptococcus pyogenes

(§ 173), has made its way with an embolic mass to the minute vessels in the walls of the heart; this embolus becomes impacted in tissues that are already altered by malnutrition ; in a medium now at rest, in which the products of these or similar organisms are contained, the micrococcus is enabled to proliferate and so give rise to a large mass of organisms (this may have been continued after death). As in all cases of inflammation the blood vessels in the surrounding area, especially the minute venules and capillaries have become dilated ; there has been slowing of the blood current and emigration of leucocytes. The products of the micro-organisms acting on the tissues in their immediate neighbourhood have set up a kind of digestion of the muscle fibres and other tissues, so that nuclei now degenerating take on stains very imperfectly or not at all. Following or accompanying this, there has been a further migration of leucocytes from the distended vessels into the degenerating area, these leucocytes gradually making their way from the margin to the centre of the abscess, and removing the degenerative products. In this process a number of the "phagocytes" are destroyed and disintegrated by the peptonising products of micro-organisms, and at the stage at which this abscess is examined there appears to be an area immediately around the proliferating organisms, outside which the leucocytes are kept at bay by the micro-organisms or their products, or in which their presence is no longer required. As the abscess increases in size, more and more of the central leucocytes become digested, but in the immediate neighbourhood a reinforcement of leucocytes forms a barrier to the advance of the bacteria, either merely temporarary or more permanent in character, according to the vitality of the tissues on the one hand, and the activity of the micro-organisms on the other. As a rule, these micro-organisms cannot obtain a foot-hold in the circulation of healthy individuals, but wherever there is malnutrition, or lowered vitality of the tissues through injury or previous inflammation, the organisms are able to obtain a coign of vantage from which they are enabled to attack surrounding tissues, though, as is well known even in the case of acute abscesses, localisation sooner or later usually occurs.

It is stated that bacteria usually gain access to the tissues by means of the blood vessels, and in very acute cases this is undoubtedly the case, but it is now proved that in many cases these micro-organisms spread, though of course not so rapidly, by the perivascular and other lymphatic channels.

PLEURISY AND PERICARDITIS.

166. The series of changes in cases of inflammation of the different serous membranes bear a very striking resemblance to one another, and much of what has been written in describing peritonitis may be taken as holding good for inflammations of the pleura and pericardium. There are, of course, minor differences of structure, not so much of the membrane itself, as of the tissues beneath it, which may, to some extent, modify the appearances of the inflamed surface, just as there may be apparent or superficial differences in wounds healing by first or second intention or by granulation, although the processes are practically identical.

These inflammations of the pleural or pericardial surfaces may be considered in three stages. In *the first stage*, that of congestion, the vessels of the superficial layers of the serous membrane are simply distended with blood so that a rosy flush, extending over the surface, appears, the larger vessels being seen tolerably distinctly through the layer of endothelial cells, which even at this early stage are slightly clouded, so that the glistening appearance is lost. As this is identical with what is seen in early peritonitis (§ 164), it is unnecessary to give any further description of the microscopical changes, except to state that the lymph spaces appear to be increased in size, and to contain a larger amount of fluid and cellular elements than do those in normal tissues. In *the second stage*, during which there is an effusion of serous fluid and coagulable lymph from the congested vessels on to the pleural surface, the changes are more marked; whilst in the third stage, where organisation is taking place in this lymph, there is absorption of the fluid, softening and partial absorption (or even suppuration) of the exuded products, and the formation of new connective tissue, which gradually takes the place of the fibrin. This process of inflammation and repair is usually described as passing through four stages, but for descriptive purposes the above arrangement is quite accurate enough.

On naked·eye examination there appears to be little regular sequence, the appearances varying very considerably in the three stages ; but on microscopical examination it will be found that the sequence of events is quite definite, the various processes following one another in regular course, and, as in the case of a healing wound, varying only according to the amount of fluid or coagulable lymph that is thrown out and the power of the tissues to bring about absorption.

Leaving the first stage as sufficiently described under peritonitis, let us examine the second stage, in which the pleura is cloudy and granular, and the surface dry. On careful examination a thin layer of soft plastic lymph, which can be scraped off as a delicate slightly elastic film with the finger nail, may be observed covering the deeply congested surface. On section, the pleura is found to be somewhat thickened and œdematous, whilst the lung tissue immediately beneath may be slightly consolidated ; it is always congested. Harden (§§ 59 or 64), stain and mount (§§ 98-152).

(× 50).—If the pleurisy be simple, the changes are observed principally in the superficial or dense layer of the pleura. There is distension of the blood vessels, swelling of the fibrous tissue, and even at this stage exuded leucocytes are seen as bright pink dots around the turgid blood vessels. On the surface of the pleura is a delicate, almost transparent, layer of fibrin, very unequal in thickness, in which, scattered through its substance, are a few small pink nuclei (leucocytes).

(× 300).—The dots around the vessels are stained leucocytes or wandering cells, though a few of them, even at this early stage, are probably proliferating connective tissue corpuscles. The transparent layer on the surface resembles very closely the material that is found in the pulmonary alveoli in acute pneumonia in the stage of red hepatization, the delicate filaments of fibrin running in all directions and forming a network, in the meshes of which are entangled coloured and colourless blood corpuscles, sometimes in considerable numbers. This film of lymph is usually thrown out on the endothelial surface, so that beneath the delicate coagulum the swollen endothelial cells may sometimes be seen in profile as spindle-shaped cells with pink-stained nuclei. Sometimes, however, these cells are detached by the exudation, and are found entangled in the fibrinous lymph, some distance from their original position.

This is all that is to be seen in the case of a simple pleurisy, but pleurisy, it must be remembered, is an almost constant accompaniment of pneumonia. In such a case it is found that the vessels of the deep layer are congested, and that numerous leucocytes are collected around them; there is also some slight swelling of the bands of fibrous and elastic tissue, so that, in addition to the layer of exuded fibrinous lymph described below, there is always some thickening or swelling of the pleura proper.

When effusion of serous fluid takes place into the pleural cavity, there is usually formed a thick soft elastic layer on the pleural surface, which presents a peculiar honeycombed appearance, especially if the quantity of fluid be small. Sanders likened this to the appearance obtained when two slices of bread and butter were pressed together and then separated; if fluid is present in considerable quantities, the surface is smooth. The layer of lymph may be stripped off as a soft, easily broken membrane, leaving the pleural surface perfectly smooth. A section from such a case is found to present much the same appearance as the specimen above described, except that the fibrinous layer is considerably thicker and more granular looking. It contains a greater number of leucocytes, and stains somewhat more deeply, often of a peculiar brick red tinge, although it still retains some of its transparency. Around the vessels are numerous exuded leucocytes and proliferated cells; the lymphatics appear to be choked up by granular fibrinous lymph, with which, in a well stained section, they may be seen to be filled.

In what may be described as *the third stage*, organisation is taking place in the lymph which forms a kind of scaffolding on or in which new connective tissue is formed, though there is no organisation of the lymph itself. The fluid part of the exudation has been absorbed, the two inflamed surfaces have come together; a temporary adhesion has been brought about by the sticking together of the two surfaces of soft lymph, and the lung has become adherent to the wall of the chest.   This adhesion may be readily broken down, but it is impossible to detach the whole of the lymph from the pleural surface ; and at the points from which it can be detached the surfaces are left rough and irregular, and evidently something more than the pleura remains.   Harden a portion of such a lung (§§ 59-64) ; stain and mount (§§ 98-152).

(× 50).—The section under consideration was taken from a case in which the pleurisy was of some standing, and where organisation had commenced in the deeper layer of the lymph ; the pleura was extremely thickened, whilst on the surface was a layer of soft lymph, as described above.

Here there is evidence of considerable congestion of the inter-alveolar capillaries.   The vessels in the wall of the bronchus, and in the interlobular septa, are all filled with blood.

Around these vessels considerable numbers of stained nuclei are readily distinguishable.   Passing outwards, the pleura is seen to be considerably thickened, and the distinction into two separate layers is in great part lost ; the deeper layer appears to be made up of swollen fibres, between which the blood-vessels are numerous and are filled with coloured blood corpuscles.   The superficial layer is composed of a more delicate nucleated reticular tissue, in which may be seen large sinuses, lining the walls of which are a few coloured blood corpuscles ; there are also numerous smaller vessels which appear as loops or branching lines, all of them with their long axes more or less perpendicular to the surface.   At certain points these vessels appear to have ruptured, several masses of green (red) corpuscles lying free in the young tissue being seen near these cavernous spaces.   Above this a layer of pink cellular tissue, into which vascular loops, recognised as green lines bounded by elongated and flattened connective tissue cells, may be seen running perpendicularly or slightly obliquely to the surface.   Scattered here and there are a few small brick-red masses, which may be recognised as remnants of fibrin.   Near the free surface the new tissue is composed almost entirely of granular-looking fibrin.   It takes on the picro-carmine staining as a deep brick-red colour, whilst very little light is allowed to make its way through.   Young vessels, in the form of Y-shaped lines, or of more or less perfect loops, may be

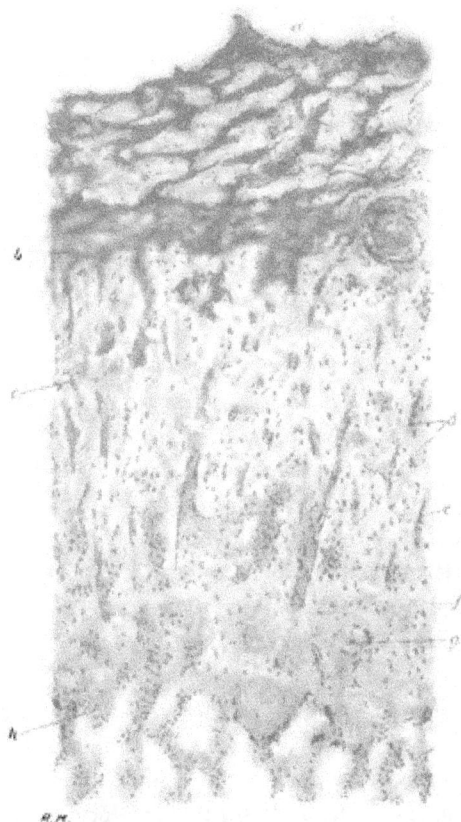

FIG. 7.—Section of thickened inflamed serous membrane (pleurisy). Stained with picro-carmine. (× 50.)

a. Network of fibrinous lymph on the surface, with deeply-stained leucocytes in its meshes.
b. Fibrinous lymph in which organisation is commencing.
c. Remains of fibrin in organising tissue.
d. Newly-formed vessels (vascular loops).
e. Larger fibro-plastic cells and plasma cells.
f. Elastic lamina marking division between the superficial and deep layers of the pleura.
g. Larger well-formed vessels in the deeper layer of the pleura. Pigment in the perivascular and other lymph spaces.
h. Lung tissue, somewhat congested. Numerous deeply-stained nuclei (of leucocytes, epithelial cells, and connective tissue cells).

   Note the passage of the new vascular loops from the engorged vessels of the thickened deep layer to the organising tissue of the superficial layer.

I

seen pushing their way from the more fully organised layer into this fibrinous mass; around them in this position are small masses of red blood corpuscles. Between the young vessels, and running along with them, are numerous young connective tissue cells, some rounded, others elongated or spindle-shaped, and forming definite lines. The nuclei of these cells are deeply stained, but it is somewhat difficult to distinguish any protoplasm around the nuclei under this power. In the brick-red granular lymph, which is found near the surface, or which remains between the two "granulating" layers, groups of leucocytes, and young connective tissue cells, are present sometimes in considerable numbers. In rare cases there is present a delicate translucent layer of newly-effused fibrinous lymph, like that already described in the second stage, and entangling both coloured and colourless corpuscles in its meshes.

($\times$ 300).—The congestion of the vessels around the air vesicles in the interlobular septa, in the peribronchial tissue, and in the layers of the pleura, is readily made out. These vessels are distended and packed with small greenish corpuscles. Around them the stained exuded leucocytes and young connective tissue cells with their nuclei are seen in large numbers; and if these latter are more carefully examined, in one of the interlobular septa, some of them are seen to be rounded, others are oval, others again are more or less spindle-shaped. Some are nothing but deeply stained nuclei, others have, in addition to the nucleus, a surrounding mass of protoplasm, and in certain cases this protoplasm is distinctly vacuolated, the nucleus being pushed to one side. Where the cell is spindle-shaped, the protoplasm is frequently slightly fibrillated.

Examine the part of the pleura in which, under the low power, the large open sinuses are seen. Here there is evidently a considerable quantity of new connective tissue, and the original deep pleural layer can only be distinguished by the presence of the pigment in the lymphatics. Above this is a delicate, clear, yellow (elastic) wavy line, dividing the deep from the superficial layer of the pleura, the latter of which is gradually lost in the new or organised tissue, which is made up of numerous rounded, branching, or spindle-shaped cells, each with a distinct nucleus. Between these cells is a variable quantity of delicate fibrillated stroma. Towards the deeper part

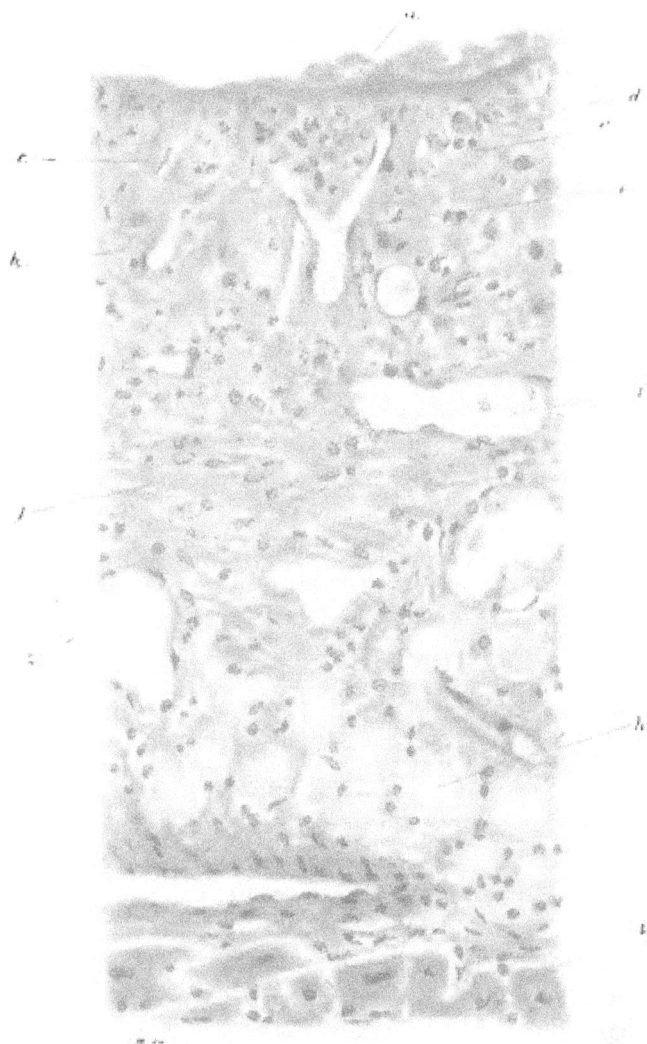

Fig. 8.—Section from case of organising pericarditis stained with logwood and eosin. (× 300.)

a. Thin layer of fibrinous lymph but little altered, on surface of new membrane. *b.* Altered degenerating fibrinous lymph in which organisation has commenced. *c.* Leucocytes, emigrated from new vascular loops. *d.* Connective tissue cells carried into fibrin along with vascular loops. *e.* Oblique and transverse section of vascular loops, probably derived from the large sinuses (*f* and *g*) immediately below. These are merely the distended, pre-existing blood-vessels of the epicardium. *e'.* Small blood-vessel, apparently formed from endothelial cells of connective tissue. *h.* Fatty tissue of deep layer of the epicardium. *i.* Muscle fibres of wall of heart. *j.* Layer of well-formed connective tissue cells immediately below the young organising tissue, the passage of connective tissue cells from this into the superjacent fibrinous mass along with the loops of blood-vessels is well seen.

are vessels with relatively thick, well organised walls, in some of which can be discerned a distinct muscular coat, and an endothelial lining. These appear to be the pre-existing vessels of the pleura, which in some instances are considerably dilated, and are almost invariably filled with coloured blood corpuscles (stained green). Nearer the surface are numerous large rounded or oblong openings, the walls of which are formed of one or several layers of compressed or flattened connective tissue cells, or nucleated spindle-shaped cells. Some of these spaces are quite empty, but others, as already seen under the low power, contain coloured blood corpuscles.

Observe the small capillary channels in the connective tissue. These small vessels are of the very simplest structure. The lumen is bounded on each side by a single or double row of elongated spindle-shaped cells, which may be seen running in various directions; but the majority of them run at right angles to the surface, though from the number of transverse branches near the surface it is evident that these capillaries are really in the form of loops, with the convexity of the loop outwards. Between the double row of cells a single row of coloured blood corpuscles may be seen. These capillary loops (Fig. 9) are in structure very much like the vessels found in ordinary granulation tissue, or in the substance of a sarcoma, and, as in those positions, so here, the blood has in some cases made its way from the capillary into the surrounding tissue, the delicate vascular wall yielding to any very slight sudden increase of blood pressure. In this specimen small extravasations have occurred near the transverse or superficial parts of the loops.

Under this power, too, examine the lines of spindle-shaped connective tissue cells, arranged in two groups, one set passing at right angles, the others parallel, to the surface. These rows of the first set are frequently separated by lines of green discs or coloured blood corpuscles, so that they may be looked upon as the cells of which the walls of the young blood-vessels running at right angles to the surface are built up. The cells of the second set are placed with their long axes more or less parallel to the surface; they also are spindle-shaped, and have lying between them a clear pink homogeneous material, coagulated fibrin or fibrinous lymph, which, as a rule, presents but little trace of fibrillation. Passing towards the free surface, the fibrinous lymph becomes more noticeable, and is seen as large brick-red granular masses, in which are a few vessels surrounded by a number of more or less rounded cells. In this part of the lymph the organisation is at its very earliest stage. The walls of the vessels are of purely embryonic type, and are formed of cells—some of them a little

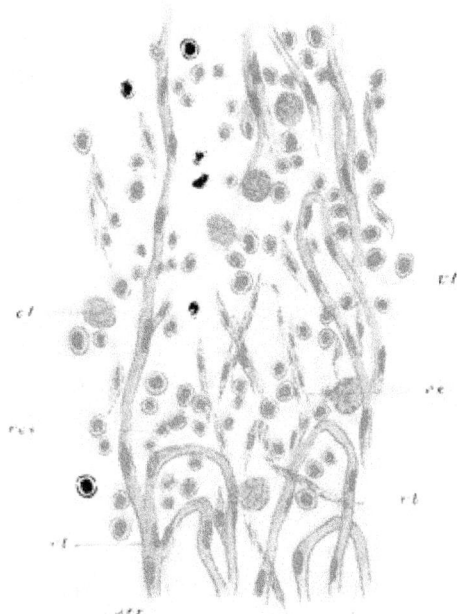

Fig. 9.—Loops of blood-vessels in organising tissue on a serous surface. Section stained with picro-carmine. (× 300.)

    v.l.   Loops of vessels fully formed, the structure of which is very readily observed.

    c.s.   Double rows of spindle-shaped connective tissue cells, from which the embryonic vessels are formed. Most of these cells are arranged with their long axes at right angles to the surface.

    c.l.   Large cells met with in all granulation tissue derived from connective tissue cells.

    r.c.s.   Small round cells or leucocytes.

flattened—laid end to end, between which are the rows of red blood corpuscles. In some parts of the section it is difficult to distinguish any vessel wall; the blood corpuscles appear to be simply pushing their way into the fibrin, but some of the sections of vessels are of considerable size, and are surrounded by both leucocytes and young connective tissue corpuscles in considerable numbers. Near the surface the connective tissue cells are not merely embryonic, they are comparatively scarce. On the surface of the brick-red granular mass there is frequently a layer of lymph of very recent formation, which consists of a network of fibrin similar to that described as present in the air vesicles in acute pneumonia during the stage of red hepatization. Entangled in this network are a few white blood corpuscles, not nearly so many as are found in the air vesicles ; there are also numerous red blood corpuscles. This layer has already been described as occurring in a recent pleurisy, so that it has probably been exuded some considerable time after the layer in which organisation is now so far advanced.

HEALING OF WOUNDS.

167. In describing healing of wounds it is necessary to bear in mind that although the process is essentially the same in all cases, the appearances and results are modified very much according to the loss of tissue, and according to the amount of extraneous or temporary supporting material that is thrown out into or left in the wound, which for the time may serve as a scaffold, but which afterwards has to be absorbed by new tissue ; and, further, according to the amount of stimulation or external irritation, so that we have all intermediate stages between healing by first intention and healing of an ulcerated surface, where, owing to the large gap that has to be filled up by newly formed tissue, much of which plays a merely temporary part, the processes of disintegration and death go on very rapidly, the formative process always being slightly in the ascendant.

If a clean incision with a sharp knife be made into the soft tissues, the hæmorrhage be allowed to cease, and all blood be carefully sponged away before the two cut surfaces are again brought together, and if these surfaces are kept in close apposition by gentle pressure, it will be found that in the course of a few hours the wound is so far healed that it requires some little effort to again open it up, and in three or four days healing may be almost complete.

Should one be fortunate enough to obtain a wound that is healing directly in this fashion during any of the stages, it will be found that the amount of exudation of albuminoid material or lymph is exceedingly small, only just enough being thrown out to form a glazing over the cut surfaces; this may be seen during about the first twelve hours. There is little distension of the blood-vessels, so that the surfaces are only slightly redder than normal. If a section (stained, § 98, or §§ 103, 104) taken from between the two surfaces be examined, the granular coagulated fibrinous lymph may be readily distinguished as a thin fibrinous layer in which, even at this stage, especially in the neighbourhood of the distended vessels, a slight increase in the number of leucocytes may be readily enough made out (both × 50 and × 300). Should the specimen be obtained the day after the wound has been made, the number of leucocytes is usually very considerably increased (so much so that to the naked eye the surface has now a regular greyish opaque covering instead of a transparent glaze); there is also evidence of proliferation of the fixed connective tissue cells in the immediate neighbourhood of the incision. The amount of fibrin is somewhat diminished, and what remains is invaded by leucocytes and larger round cells, the former of which have escaped from the distended vessels, the latter being derived from proliferation of the connective tissue cells as already described. Shortly after this all that remains along the line of the incision is slight increase in the number of the various cellular elements; the whole of the fibrin, which first becomes granular, is gradually absorbed, and if the edges of the epithelium have been brought close together, the wound may appear to be perfectly healed. This line of cellular tissue can, however, be distinguished for at least four or five days after the union is apparently complete. It is best seen under the low power, and should be always carefully searched for.

As has very frequently been observed, if the film of coagulated fibrin is merely sufficient to keep the lips of the wound in temporary apposition, the process of organisation can go on under the very best possible conditions; the less tissue there is to remove by the leucocytes, and the less bridging across the connective tissue cells and the embryonic blood-vessels have to do, the shorter will be the time required for the process of organisation and healing.

In the following specimen most of the characteristic processes met with in a more slowly healing wound may be followed.

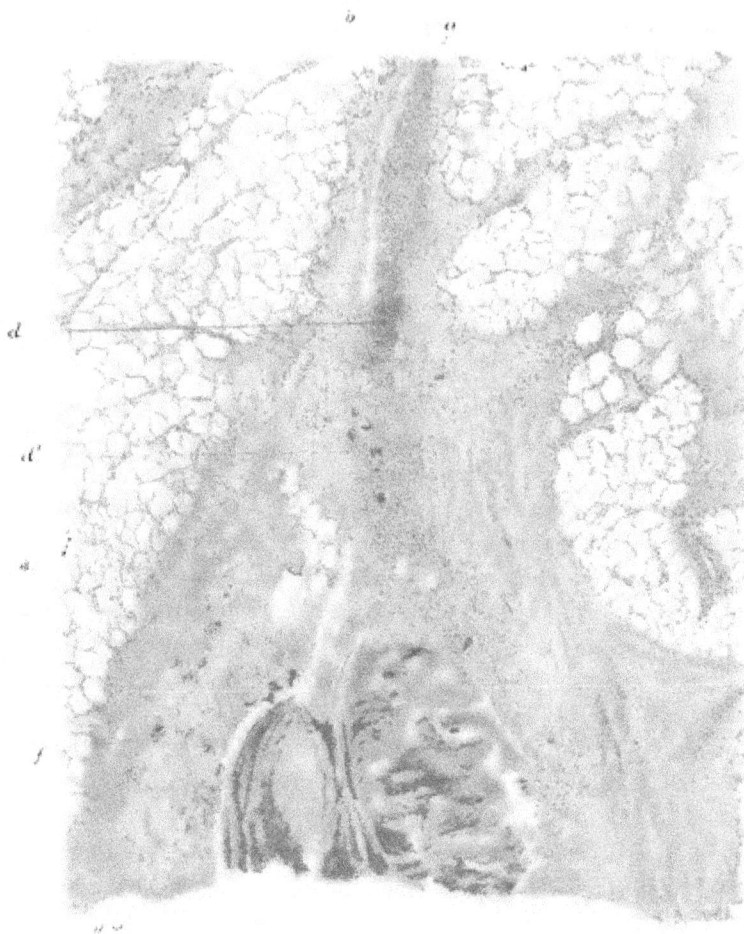

FIG. 10.—Deeper part of healing wound taken from a stump forty-eight hours after operation. Stained with logwood and eosin. (× 50.)

a. Leucocytes and proliferated connective tissue cells along the line where the two surfaces are not brought into accurate apposition. More marked on the right side than on the left. b. Part of remaining fissure. c. Adipose tissue. d. Mass of cellular tissue in which is altered blood pigment. Red cells absorbed and broken down by the leucocytes and connective tissue cells. d'. Smaller mass of pigment contained within cells. e. Pigmented fat cells. f. Other masses of pigment, some free, some within the larger cells. g. Altered blood clot surrounded by mass of cellular tissue. This must be absorbed before complete healing can take place; absorption carried on by leucocytes and invading connective tissue cells carried in by loops of new blood-vessels. Most vascularity and granulation tissue are seen where apposition is least perfect.

168. In a section taken from the end of a healing stump at about forty-eight hours after amputation, and in which the epithelial covering had at points become continuous as a thin blue line, the following appearances may be observed. Harden (§ 58), stain and mount (§§ 98 and 152).

(× 50).—At the point where the incision was made the corium has been partially replaced by a small mass of adipose tissue which has thus been brought into contact with the corium of the opposite flap. At the point of apposition there is considerable infiltration of leucocytes, both at the margin of the corium and at the edge of the fatty tissue. In addition to this, however, there is evidently a proliferation of the fat cells, with a corresponding, perhaps a preliminary, absorption of fat globules. Deeper down in the line of incision is a space in which a small clot of blood has evidently intervened between the two apposed margins; around this clot is marked proliferation of the connective tissue cells, and a number of black and golden brown pigment particles are seen lying in their immediate neighbourhood. Passing still further down it may be noted that where the adipose tissue surfaces have come together the fat globules have been absorbed, and that accompanying this is proliferation of the connective tissue cells; still further down is a mass of blood from which the absorption of the pigment has not yet gone very far, although there is great proliferation of the connective tissue cells around, many of which appear to contain particles of pigment. It may be observed that at the surface the epithelium has grown over a thin film of connective tissue which has brought about adhesion of the margins; the proliferation of the nuclei at the margin of the wound, *i.e.*, between the adipose tissue and the outer corium, is very well marked along the whole line of incision, but at one or two points there is an enormous increase in the number of stained nuclei. Wherever these nuclei are in excess there appears to have been an extravasation of blood, whilst the fat globules appear to be undergoing absorption.

In many places where, apparently, such extravasation has occurred, small round cell tissue, the granulation tissue of the surgeon, has taken the place of the fat, and in the cells is found a considerable quantity of altered blood pigment; there is also pigment at the margins of some of the fat cells, both where the fat has been invaded by the newly formed tissue and where it is comparatively free ; in the deeper part, where the extravasation of blood is considerable, the small round cell tissue around the clot may be very readily distinguished.

(× 300).—The continuous layer of epithelium may now be traced more distinctly as a very thin film across the surface of the wound ; below this is a delicate layer of connective tissue, in which, however, it is impossible to distinguish any blood-vessels, though there are distended capillaries running up to its very margin. Beneath this is a sinus of considerable size, apparently part of the incision that has remained unhealed ; along each side of the sinus is a mass of adipose tissue, whilst on one side is an accumulation of leucocytes actually between the individual fat globules, whilst here and there are larger cells, apparently delicate connective tissue cells, with dividing or divided nuclei.

In the corium, at the margins of the incision, we find a similar state of matters, but although the leucocytes are not so numerous, the larger cells, derived from the connective tissue cells by pro- liferation, are present in greater numbers, and stand out more prominently. At the bottom of this sinus the adipose tissue and the fibrous tissue of the corium have met in a line in which the two sets of cells are so blended that it is impossible at first sight to distinguish one from the other. A few small vascular loops are seen running towards this cellular junction, but only one or two small channels can be made out in the cell mass itself. Following the line of incision small fissures are met with at one or two points, from which, it may be gathered, that adhesion is not perfect along the whole line. This is especially well marked in those areas where the fibrous tissue on one side is very dense, and where the increase in the number of the cells appears to be confined entirely to the flap in which is contained the adipose tissue. A little further down where the junction is taking place between two small bands of adipose tissue, the adhesion is very perfect; the cells from the two sides are perfectly indistinguishable, but no blood-vessels can be made out in the cellular mass, although no doubt they are present, as they are to be seen in considerable numbers between the elements of the fatty tissue in the immediate neighbourhood of the wound. The large spaces in which blood has collected have a very characteristic appearance; they are surrounded by delicate cellular tissue, and in some cases where the blood has been absorbed a mass of granulation tissue has actually taken the place of the blood. In the cells of this and in the surrounding lymph spaces, numerous pigment granules are found. These are usually much darker in colour than the pigment stained fat globules found in the immediate neighbourhood of the clot or enclosed within the granulation tissue. In some places the remains of the blood clot may still be seen surrounded by the granulation tissue cells, many of which contain a large quantity of pigment, so much, in fact, that it is possible to make out simply a mass of granules with the outline of a cell, none of the protoplasm being stained as to indicate that we have actually to deal with a cell. Some of these pigmented cells are of large size, and are then much more like the large endothelioid cells, sometimes spoken of as giant cells. Wherever the line of junction is incomplete there appears to be little cell proliferation, at least on one side. Adhesion and organisation take place most rapidly where we have delicate connective or adipose tissue, usually at some little distance away from the surface, except where large masses of coagulated lymph or blood have been poured out; it appears that where this has occurred, the coagulum has all to be absorbed through the agency of leucocytes or fixed connective tissue cells before the regular organising process can take place. In some parts of the section where effusion is reduced to a minimum, all that remains to indicate the position of the healing process, is a thin line of deeply stained nuclei (the nuclei of leucocytes, the more direct the union the fewer of these there are, and of fixed connective tissue cells); it is not always possible, as we have seen, to follow the blood-vessels into or through this delicate cell mass, and it appears that organisation may take place without the formation of new vessels if the tissues on the two sides of the wound can be approximated sufficiently closely. At whatever stage these healing wounds are examined we find that, until the granulation tissue becomes well organised, there is usually evidence of vascularisation and of traces of the scaffolding of fibrinous lymph in which the new tissue is formed, so that even in the comparatively late stages of organisation little patches of granular or amorphous matter are seen, brick red or orange in the specimens stained with picro-carmine, or dirty brown, or reddish purple, in specimens stained with logwood and some

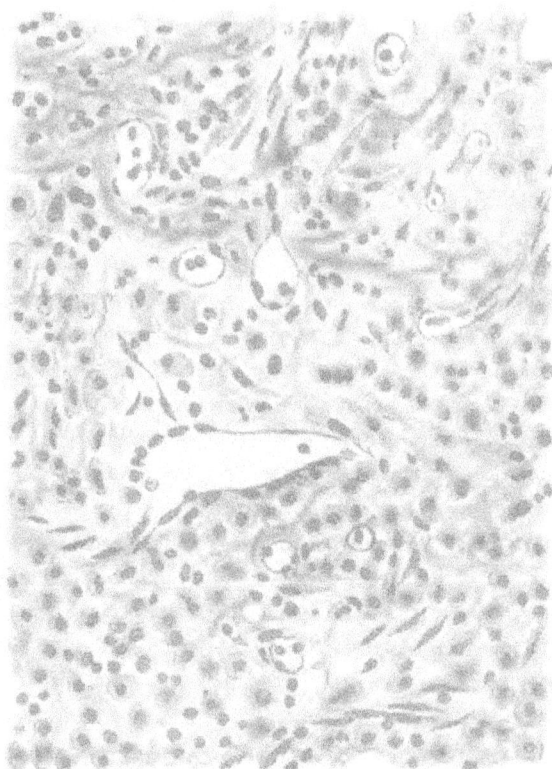

FIG. 11.—Healing wound near surface (three or four days after incision?)   Section stained with logwood and eosin.   (× 400.)

a, a', a''.   Fibrinous lymph in process of absorption.

b.   Small embryonic blood-vessel, containing a leucocyte and surrounded by primitive perivascular lymphatic space.

b'.   Larger vascular space from which smaller vessels (*b''*) open out.

c, c', c''.   Rows of cells indicating the course of new blood-vessels. Sometimes these appear to be buds from pre-existing vessels, at others parallel rows of connective tissue cells (*c'''*) which eventually form definite channels, into which the blood passes from point to point.

d.   Large connective tissue cells (formative or fibro-plastic) from which new tissue is formed.

e.   Large connective tissue cell, nucleus of which is undergoing indirect division, and shows mitotic figures.

f, f', f''.   Leucocytes in a blood-vessel, and in the connective tissue spaces.

contrast stain. As the healing process goes on and hæmorrhages are absorbed, the patches of effused blood become more yellow, the pigment being separated from the red blood corpuscles in the degenerating clot by the active phagocytes of the new tissue. It is sometimes held that it is necessary to have a perfectly clean granulation surface in order that the epithelial covering may grow over any healing surface from the margin, but in carefully prepared sections of healing wounds I have very frequently been able to make out the epithelial layer gradually creeping along the granulation tissue, and making its way between this tissue and the layer of fibrinous lymph covering it, dissecting the lymph from the outer granulation tissue. It is also said that the epithelium does not advance until the vascular loops in the granulation tissue have become obliterated, but although this is partially true (for these vessels gradually lose their embryonic character, become fewer in number, and also become better supported), these vessels persist for some time after the wound is closed in by the epithelial covering. It is only later that most of them become obliterated.

The method of formation of these vessels, and the way in which they are obliterated, must be considered after we have examined a healing ulcer, and the organisation of lymph on other surfaces.

HEALING ULCER.

169. Ulceration usually takes place in tissues of low vitality, especially where there is a tendency to venous engorgement and œdema ; it may also occur as the result of injury or over tumours. In these cases there is simply a destructive process, the dead tissue appearing as moist grayish fragments on the irregular ulcerated surface, on which scattered hæmorrhages occur. The characteristic features of such an ulcerated surface are loss of tissue and the dirty gray sloughing patches, some of which are seen to be separating. There is frequently very great œdema in the tissues around, so that the loss of substance usually appears to be greater than it actually is, the fluid escaping from the ulcerated surface, but being pent up in the comparatively healthy tissues around. In the history of almost all ulcers there comes a period at which healing takes place, the sloughs gradually separating and leaving a clean red surface covered with a very fine transparent film; sometimes this film becomes slightly opaque and grayish, and from it there is found constantly separating a fluid (pus) often very readily removed, leaving the surface perfectly clean. Examining such an ulcer carefully where the healing process has begun, it will be found that the loss of tissue has in some way been compensated for, the fleshy granulating surface now coming up to the level of the margins of the wound; if this granulating surface be roughly handled or pricked, it is found to be exceedingly vascular, especially towards the centre; nearer the margins it is usually slightly paler. At the extreme margin a delicate pellicle may be seen, at first red, then slightly bluer than the granulating tissue, further out purple, then blue, and gradually shading off from this into the white of the surrounding normal cutaneous tissue; this is known as the healing margin, and the opaque appearance is due to the growth inwards of the epithelial cells which gradually cover the granulation tissue. Remove the margin of such an ulcer. Harden (§ 58). Cut (§ 82, *et seq.*). Stain and mount (§ 98, or §§ 103, 104).

(× 50).—Near the central portion of the ulcer there will be found on the surface a thin layer of disintegrating cells, some of which are swollen and hyaline, others granular, but all of them imperfectly stained; they take on a brown coloration with picro-carmine, or red with logwood and eosin. Between these cells we find coagulated fibrinous lymph, usually in very small quantities. Beneath this layer which corresponds to the grayish layer of pus, there may be seen, though not where healing is going on rapidly, small scattered spaces filled with blood; these are partly lined by flattened endothelial cells, and appear to be dilated embryonic capillary vessels, which, unprotected by tissues near the surface, become over distended, and small hæmorrhages result, either at or near the surface. Immediately below this fibrinous and cellular layer comes a course of transverse vessels, evidently the convex arches of loops of capillaries, as from them the bundles of spindle-shaped cells may be traced downwards, first in an oblique direction, and then at right angles to the surface. Both in front of and behind these loops are numerous spindle and round cells; the smaller round cells, which are found in little groups, are evidently leucocytes which have escaped from the dilated vessels, in the immediate neighbourhood

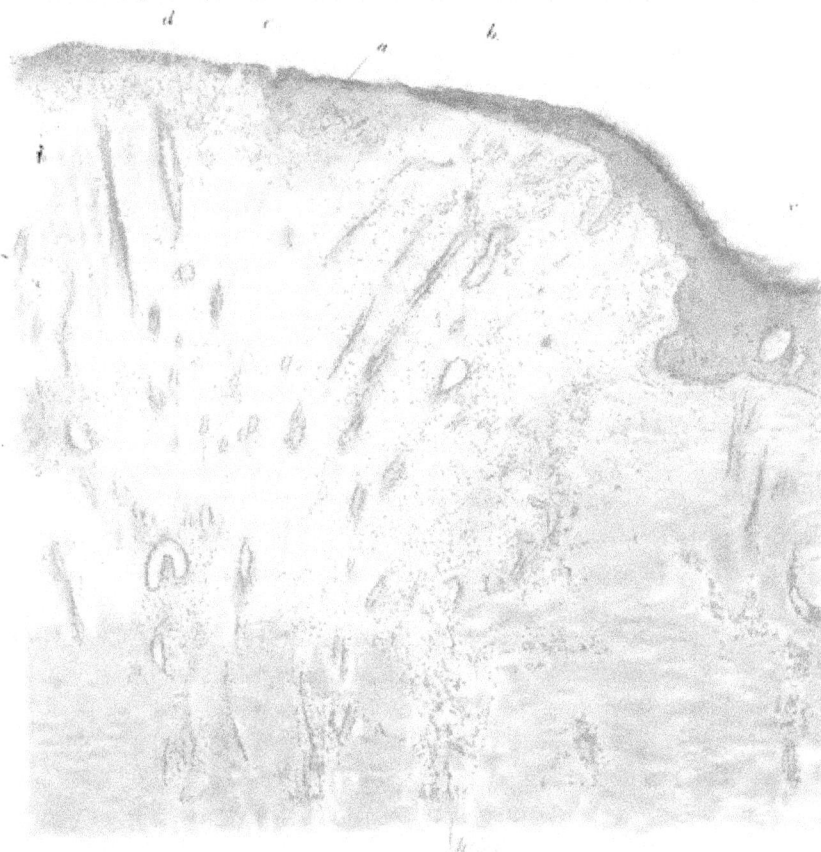

FIG. 12.—Section from a healing ulcer of the leg. Stained with logwood and eosin. (× 20.)

  a. Layer of fibrinous lymph and pus cells lying on the granulating surface.
  b. Invading margin of epithelium.
  c. Epithelial layer with well-formed papillæ, due to dipping down of processes into spaces between loops of vessels.
  d. Connective tissue cells and active leucocytes near the surface and around the sections of transverse portions of vascular loops (*e*).
  f. Longitudinal or limb parts of vascular loops passing to the surface.
  g. Groups of leucocytes around the young blood-vessels.
  h. Older, more perfectly formed, vessels shooting from the deeper tissues.
  i. Corium proper, composed of hard fibrous tissue.
  j. More cellular new tissue in which vessels still remain, although the new tissue is now covered in by a well-formed epithelial layer.

of which they are always found. The spindle cells and larger round cells with distinct nuclei and a well-marked protoplasmic body are found between the vascular loops. Near the surface the spindles run parallel to the axis of the blood-vessels, both in the curved and in the straight parts of the loops, but in the deeper layers of granulation tissue many of the spindle cells run at right angles to the axis of the vessels, giving rise to a peculiar basket-work appearance, the bundles of cells appearing to interlace backwards and forwards, behind and in front of the new vessels. At one or two points are seen large plasmodial cells, some of them with several nuclei, almost like bone osteoclasts, but not quite so large nor with so many nuclei; these appear to be simply Ziegler's fibroplastic cells; large single nucleated cells are also present in enormous numbers wherever the organisation is at all advanced, in fact, wherever the blood-vessels have made their way. Here, also, the larger plasma cells, with their small deeply-stained points, are very numerous. These may be seen distinctly under the low power.

On tracing the course of the new blood-vessels it will be found that they all come from the deeper layer of healthy tissue, and wherever buds are leaving these tissues there is usually an accumulation of leucocytes around sinuses of considerable size from which the new blood-vessels are given off, though, in many cases, they appear to be given off directly from the older vessels without any previous formation of sinuses.

Passing now to the margin of the ulcer where the epithelium is creeping in, it will be seen that the blood-vessels, although not nearly so prominent, nor so regularly arranged, can still be seen passing up to the under surface of the epithelium. The connective tissue cells are more regularly arranged; a large number of the leucocytes disappear, and only spindle and branching cells remain; these usually form a delicate, almost myxomatous-looking cellular tissue. Sometimes, however, in the deeper layers, we have still a large number of leucocytes surrounding the vessels that remain, and it is only as we pass outwards and away from the ulcer that the number of nuclei becomes diminished, the blood-vessels become better developed, and the tissue becomes more truly connective in type. Quite away from the wound we get the usual pink fibrous tissue basis with a small number of elongated nuclei lying between or on the bundles of pink fibres.

Coming now to the epithelium, we find that it creeps inwards by lateral extension from the margins of the ulcer, evidently growing from pre-existing epithelium; at first it undergoes very rapid

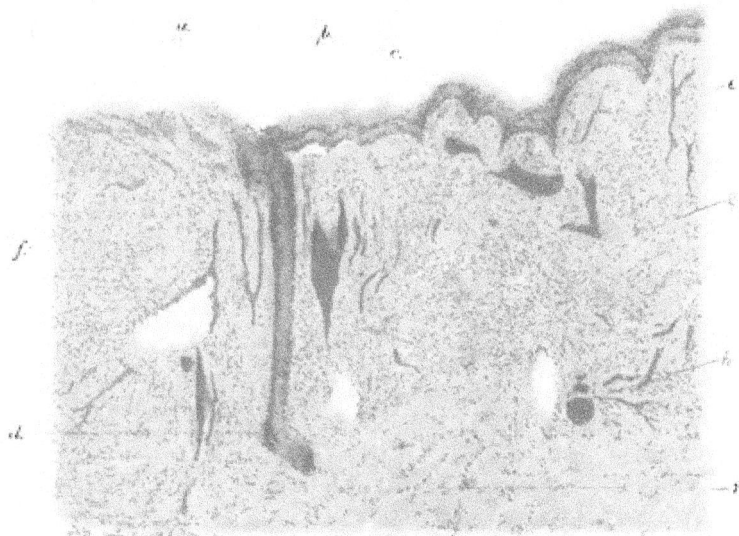

FIG. 13.—Section of injected healing ulcer stained with logwood and eosin.   Injected with carmine gelatine.   (× 70.)

   a. Transverse branches of vascular loops near the surface filled with the injection mass.
   b. Vertical limbs of these same loops.
   c. Thin layer of covering epithelium.
   d. Process of epithelium growing down into a deep depression, just at what should be the healing margin.
      The epithelium is only just commencing to get beyond this now that the pit is filled.
   e. Young vessels which ultimately form vessels of new papillæ.
   f. Cellular granulation tissue in part of wound not yet covered in.
   g. Cellular granulation tissue in part of wound covered in.
   h. Large vascular sinuses filled with injection mass.
   i. Well-developed fibrous tissue of the true corium.   Some cellular infiltration and proliferation are seen between the fibrous bundles.

degenerative change, and there is seen, on an irregular layer of squamous epithelium, a distinct yellow horny or degenerated layer. This ingrowth at the margin follows the irregularities of the granulating surface, and should there be any marked pit or depression, the epithelium grows down into it, sometimes for a considerable distance,

K

giving rise to the formation of a kind of epithelial barrier which, in some instances, interferes very materially with the healing of the wound. (Hamilton gives this as one of the chief causes of the slow

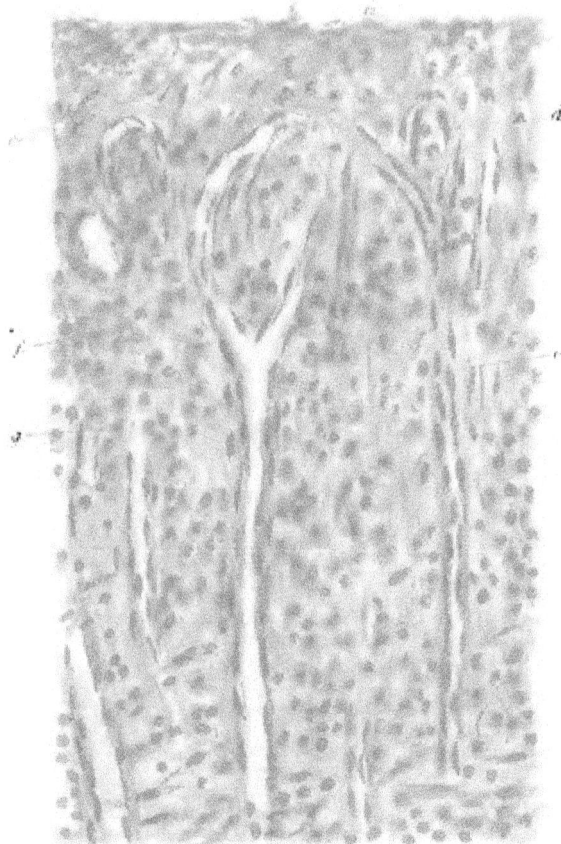

FIG. 14.—Granulating ulcer stained with picro-carmine. (× 300.)

a. Fibrinous coagulated lymph at the surface of the wound.
b. Small round cell, probably a leucocyte.
c. Spindle-shaped connective tissue cell.
d. Vascular loop, transverse part.
e. Vertical limb of same. Evidently formed by double rows of elongated cells.
f. Leucocytes and rounded connective tissue cells.
g. Spindle-shaped connective tissue cells.
h. Transverse spindle-shaped cells (with basket work arrangement) which ultimately form firm fibrous tissue and cause constriction of many of the new vessels.

healing of ulcers.) In consequence of these irregularities the thickness of the layer of epithelium, even at the healing margin, varies considerably at different points, but it may be observed that

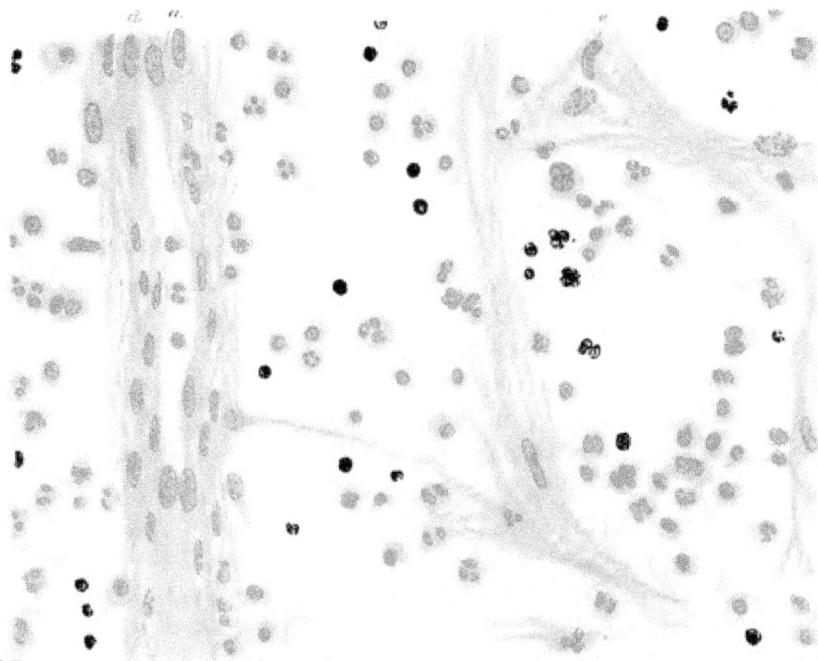

FIG. 15.—Section from healing ulcer of leg. Stained with logwood and eosin. (× about 600).

    a. Wall of fairly well-developed blood-vessel, in which are both red and white blood corpuscles.

    b. Connective tissue cell with nucleus, outside the vessel (in adventitia).

    c. Free, rapidly dividing connective tissue cells.

    d. Nuclei of lining endothelial cells of a vessel.

    e. Nucleus and protoplasm of fixed connective tissue cell lying on a bundle of fibrous tissue.

    f. Large cell in which the nucleus is undergoing mitotic or karyokinetic division.

    g. Spaces filled with œdematous fluid separating fibrils, and allowing the cells to be seen more distinctly.

    It is probable that the imperfectly stained and irregular bodies in some of the cells are really partially digested leucocytes or other material taken up by the " macrophages."

it does not vary more than, in fact not so much as, on ordinary cutaneous surfaces; it is owing to these irregularities that new papillæ are formed when the healing process is completed.

(× 300.)—All the above points may be made out more readily. Special attention should be paid to the following points:—The degenerating surface where hyaline cells and fragments of fibrin may be easily distinguished; the structure and arrangement of the blood-vessels with the surrounding connective tissue cells; the connective tissue cells each with its distinctly stained nucleus and the protoplasmic area around,—these are rounded, spindle-shaped, or irregularly branched; and the leucocytes, with their deeply stained nuclei and comparatively small quantity of protoplasmic cell body.

The giant cells, or fibro-plastic cells, plasma cells (or mast cells?), should also be observed; also the blood corpuscles lying between the parallel lines of flattened endothelial or connective tissue cells which constitute the blood-vessels of the granulation tissue.

In the connective tissue cells indirect division of the nucleus can very frequently be made out, whilst here and there large well-formed fibro-plastic cells lying on bundles of fibrous tissue may be seen just at the margin of the ulcer, especially where the tissues are œdematous, i.e., where there is an accumulation of fluid in the spaces between the cells and between the fibres, the elements of fibrous tissue and the nucleated cells may be seen very distinctly (see Fig. 15, which is taken from the margin of a somewhat œdematous very slowly healing ulcer). The healing process in an ulcer is very similar to that met with in other positions to which reference has already been made. The development of the cicatricial tissue may be readily followed, as the connective tissue cells gradually give place to fibrous tissue, the protoplasm of the cell becoming converted into a fibrillated matrix, whether by secretion or by direct differentiation of the protoplasm it is difficult to say.

"VEGETATIONS."

170. In acute endocarditis or aortitis the structure of fibrinous vegetations may be easily determined. It will be at once observed that the process of formation is very similar to that which takes place where there is exudation of fibrinous lymph and organisation in the coagulated exudate on a pleural or pericardial surface. Such vegetations, which usually occur where the valves are brought into apposition, or as the result of irritation by friction in the wall of the

aorta, may appear as small or larger semi-transparent, or opaque greyish or greyish-yellow wart-like bodies, projecting for some little distance into the blood-stream ; they may be easily detached with the finger, crumble down readily, and on section are somewhat laminated, and at points blood stained. When separated from their base they leave a rough slightly projecting surface. Harden a valve or piece of the aorta with attached vegetation (§ 59). Stain (§§ 98, 103, 104).

(× 50).—The fibrinous lymph, as it is laid down, is directly in contact with the blood stream ; consequently an enormous number of leucocytes, many of them more or less broken down are deposited not only on the surface, but also in the spaces between the layers of coagulated fibrin which have from time to time been deposited from the blood. Deeper down where the fibrin is not in contact with the blood-stream and where corpuscles have not been carried from the tissues below, the leucocytes have disappeared and the granular coagulated lymph is in all respects like that met with on other serous surfaces from which the leucocytes have disappeared during the process of fibrin formation. We have simply a net work of strands of coagulated fibrin. There is lamination even in a small clot such as this, *i.e.*, we have a layer of fibrin in which there are no corpuscles (probably made up in great part of *blood* "*plaques*"), then a layer in which the fibrin has in its meshes a large number of leucocytes and red blood corpuscles, and so on in alternate layers. This, of course, depends on the size of the clot, and is of much the same nature as the lamination met with in an aneurism, in which the clot is usually formed in very regular layers. Below the clot comes a layer of granulation tissue to which it is firmly adherent, and small blood-vessels appear to be making their way from the granulation tissue into the fibrinous mass. Embedded in this granulation tissue are small masses of fibrin which are evidently being absorbed by the advancing granulations. Below this, strands of muscle fibre and a large amount of connective tissue, in which some of the blood-vessels are enormously dilated, are seen ; there are also a number of blood-vessels around which connective tissue cells are developed in considerable numbers; the vessels in this layer are tortuous. Between the elastic laminæ the amount of new tissue is very considerable; it is made up, principally, of large fixed connective tissue cells, with granular protoplasm and well marked nuclei, a few leucocytes being distinguished here and there, especially in the

FIG. 16.—Vegetation on the wall of the aorta immediately above the valves, from a case of acute aortitis. Stained with logwood and eosin. (× 20.)

    a. Vegetation, smooth on its surface, composed of a reticulum of fibrin, in the meshes of which are numerous leucocytes.
    b. Indications of lamination near the surface.
    c. Central part of vegetation in which the fibrin contains very few leucocytes. See also *d*, near blood-stream.
    e. Vertical limbs of vascular loops in the granulation tissue.
    f. Position of transverse loops, not well shown in the drawing.
    g. Mass of superficial cells of granulation tissue, embedded in which we find small points of degenerating fibrin.

immediate neighbourhood of the blood-vessels. These leucocytes are usually in small groups, and are especially well marked at those points where the granulation tissue appears to be growing at the expense of the muscular and elastic fibres.

Examine the specimen systematically and note the appearance of the surface of the fibrin; owing to the pressure and friction of the blood-stream that flows over it, it has acquired a smooth slightly compressed surface; note the reticulum of fibrin (red with eosine) with the enormous number of leucocytes (small deep blue points) embedded in it; in the centre of the mass the fibrinous reticulum contains no leucocytes. Below this comes another layer in which the leucocytes are numerous, and finally a layer in which there are few. This fibrinous vegetation rests on a zone of granulation tissue, which, like other granulations, is made up of small loops of embryonic blood-vessels, some of which appear to be projected directly from the dilated vessels immediately below, others to be of entirely new formation. The vessels from which the loops are projected are distended, and are frequently surrounded by small masses of leucocytes into which the loops appear to project. Near the surface of the granulation tissue, and between the loops of the vessels with their accompanying cells, may be seen small irregular masses of homogeneous or slightly granular fibrin in process of absorption; deeper down it has already disappeared. The cells in this deeper layer have at this stage developed a quantity of protoplasm around their nuclei, so that here the intervals between the nuclei appear to be greater than near the surface.

Here then are all the conditions present on an inflamed serous surface on which organisation is taking place, the only marked difference being that a great part of the fibrinous clot is deposited, not from the small distended vessels coming to the inflamed surface, but from the blood passing over it, consequently the organisation of this clot is not nearly so far advanced as it is on a pleural surface where the changes in the deeper tissues are much more marked than they are in this specimen. It must be remembered that organisation invariably takes place from subjacent tissues, and that channeling or tunneling of a clot is not true organisation. The fact that the leucocytes in the lumen of the vessel cannot give rise to organising connective tissue cells near the surface of the clot, where there can be no question of want of nutrition, is a very strong argument against the formation of any connective tissue from ordinary leucocytes. On the other hand, where we have the young

connective tissue cells in large numbers in the deeper layers, into
which they can be carried or make their way very readily along with
advancing blood vascular loops, the formation of new connective
tissue invariably goes on rapidly.

(× 300.)—All the above features are now more distinctly seen.
In the wall of the aorta the laminæ are broken up, there is considerable dilatation of the vessels of supply, numerous branches—
many of them little more than embryonic capillaries—to be seen
running in the altered coat, are given off from the larger vessels.
At the junction of these small vessels with the larger branches,
from which they spring, leucocytes and young connective tissue cells
accumulate in large numbers ; but it will be noted that as the surface
on which the fibrin is thrown out is approached, more leucocytes
are present, but connective tissue cells, though still numerous, are
not nearly so well developed as in the deeper layers.   The vessels
that are pushing their way into the fibrin have a very rudimentary
structure, they consist simply of flattened cells arranged in double
rows, with blood-corpuscles lying between them.   Around each of
these vessels, rudimentary as they are, is a space sometimes bounded
only by compressed fibrin, with a cell nucleus here and there, but very
frequently by a layer of flattened cells, so that even at this early stage
a kind of peri-vascular lymph space (see fig. 18) is formed, in which
leucocytes are sometimes present in considerable numbers.   At certain points the vessels are passing singly into the fibrinous scaffolding,
but at others, whole groups of vascular loops project into it, carrying
with them a quantity of comparatively well formed connective tissue.
From these little bundles of loops small budding vessels, which are
quite distinct in structure and appearance from the larger projected
vessels, may be formed.   Where these are shooting upwards the
number of leucocytes in the fibrin is exceedingly small, this latter
forming a net-work of delicate threads.   Still nearer the free surface
the leucocytes, derived from the blood stream, and deposited in
layers on the surface of the vegetation, are very irregular in shape,
and are usually much broken down, though they still may take on a
distinct logwood stain.   Amongst the larger cells, many of which
appear to be undergoing irregular division, are numerous very minute
corpuscles, often deeply stained, which may be the result of the

disintegration of the leucocytes, though some of them are possibly blood plates ; here and there altered red blood corpuscles or little specks of pigment may be seen in large numbers. At no point near the clot is there any trace of lining endothelium left, but at the margin there is marked increase of the intima with extreme vascularisation, even at the point where it is not actually covered by the coagulum ; the proliferating connective tissue cells and distended blood-vessels in the inflamed and thickened intima being distinctly visible.

Relation of Inflammation to Repair.

171. It will be gathered from the description given of healing and of abscess formation, that in those cases, and even in injury to the tissues, inflammation plays a very prominent part, that it is, in fact, in most cases an essential factor in localising necrosis and in bringing up new tissue to repair any loss. At the same time it must be borne in mind that all inflammation is dependent upon irritation, and that any one of its features can be looked upon only as part of a complex process, and that in those cases where there is an actual breach of continuity the amount of inflammation may be very slight if the loss of tissue is small, or if the bruising is slight and the parts be again brought into very close apposition. Healing by direct union is then associated with but little evidence of inflammation either in the form of pain, swelling, heat, or redness. Where, however, tissues are bruised, or where the gap to be filled up is of considerable size, then inflammation ensues, the severity and extent of which are entirely determined by—(1) the amount of direct damage done to the tissues and of the irritation to which they are in the first instance subjected ; (2) the subsequent irritation by organisms, chemical irritants, pressure, chafing, &c. ; and (3) the amount of dead material or temporary scaffolding that has eventually to be removed.

Looked upon in this light, inflammation, though theoretically necessary only in a minor degree, is practically associated with most of those conditions that come under the observation of the pathologist. This fact is brought into still stronger relief when it is remembered that inflammation must be looked upon as comprising all those reactionary phenomena that are manifested by the various tissues when they are subjected to long-continued or very powerful abnormal stimulation.

Inflammation is not associated merely with the changes that take place in the walls of the blood-vessels, nor with those that occur in the lymphatic and connective tissue systems that surround the vessels, nor with those only that may be observed in cells lining large endothelial sacs, the cells that cover the omentum, the parenchymatous cells of the various organs, the cells lining the alveoli or the bronchial tubes of the lung, or, in fact, with any single set of tissues; although it is a manifestation of the reactions of the tissues as a whole to increased noxious stimulus, it is not dependent upon any one of these sets of tissues for its perfect development. Inflammatory changes may occur in a tissue entirely devoid of ordinary blood-vessels just as certainly as it may occur in tissues in which we can find no epithelial cells, but if these structures are present in any tissue subjected to irritation, they will, as a matter of course, take part in the general inflammatory process.

For the inflammatory changes in different organs we refer to the sections in which special diseases are described; but it may be well here to recapitulate generally certain facts connected with inflammation, abscess formation, and repair.

In the first place, cells that, under ordinary conditions, proliferate, do so much more rapidly under stimulation; such proliferated cells, embryonic in character, are endowed with the general characters of primitive protoplasm, they are more motile, more plastic, and appear to exhibit a greater power of ingesting foreign bodies; under continued abnormal stimulation these characters are retained and even accentuated, but when the stimulation is gradually diminished the embryonic cells revert to their original adult form, and give rise to the formation of tissue similar to that which, under normal conditions, they were engaged in building up. The more highly cells are specialised the less readily do they lose their form and functions under stimulation without being entirely destroyed, and the less readily do they revert to their original form when the stimulation is removed. It is found, as a matter of fact, that if the irritation be long continued, these higher cells are apt to be superseded by those of the lower connective tissue types. If this be borne in mind it will be an easy matter to understand how it is that various fibroid changes are met with in organs in which normally most of the cells have a specialised function, and the amount of connective tissue is comparatively small. Then, again, degenerated specialised cells always appear to act as foreign bodies, and until they or their *debris* are removed there can be no return' to health ; even those which retain a certain amount of vitality being unable to return to the normal or to carry on their function in any satisfactory manner.

SUPPURATION.

172. Under irritation a certain number of cells are usually so stimulated that their protoplasm is never again able to return to its normal condition, the cells die (poisoned or overstimulated) and must be removed to make way for others. How this takes place can best be seen in the abscess already described (§ 165). When a plug containing pyogenic micro-organisms becomes impacted in a small vessel, or when micro-organisms find their way from without into tissues that have their vitality impaired, the organisms acting on the proteids of the tissues, or in process of their own development, give rise to the formation of a poisonous chemical substance which, acting as an irritant, or by its direct digestive action on the protoplasm, brings about a process of degeneration which has been compared to that induced by the enzymes when acting on albumenoid materials ; in the immediate neighbourhood of these organisms both highly organised cells and connective tissues are in fact digested. This digested material at once commences to act as a foreign body, and it will be found that around and gradually invading it are numerous small round nucleated cells, the majority of which appear to have come from the blood-vessels. Most of these, as Cohnheim pointed out, are probably leucocytes, especially when the process goes on rapidly, but there are also seen a number of larger cells, which, apparently, can only be derived from the fixed connective tissue cells, —the endothelial cells lining the lymph spaces around the vessel. These cells, the result or manifestation in this position of the presence of inflammatory processes — emigration and proliferation — play a most important part, both in localising the area of activity of the products of micro-organisms and in removing dead or effete matter.

They are thrown out as soon as the irritation commences, but where the number of micro-organisms is large, and where they are able to form a considerable quantity of their special ferment or irritant matter, the cells first thrown out, although attacking both the organisms and their products, usually succumb and go to swell the quantity of dead material; this may go on time after time until a large mass of dead cells has accumulated in the neighbourhood of the septic embolus. Sometimes the process of breaking down of the tissues and cells is so perfect, and the quantity of fluid escaping with these cells is so large, that a considerable area of tissue may become resolved into "pus," which is made up of many dead leucocytes, of a few living ones, of a quantity of fluid derived from the distended blood and lymph vessels, of digested "fixed" tissues, and of micro-organisms, usually in various stages of degeneration.

Whether the quantity of digested tissue (in which the presence of peptones may actually be demonstrated) be large or small, there is usually a zone outside the mass of pus in which the leucocytes take on the usual staining reactions, and are therefore nearer a condition of health. If these marginal cells be examined, it will be found that they frequently contain very minute vacuoles, and that embedded in their substance are more or less perfectly stained micro-organisms, *i.e.,* micro-organisms in various stages of degeneration. Metschnikoff observing this, has concluded that these cells act as "phagocytes" or cells that devour dead tissues and noxious organisms. There can be little doubt that these cells do take up micro-organisms, but whether before or after the micro-organism is dead is an exceedingly difficult point to settle, for it must be remembered that micro-organisms may be very distinctly stained, even after they are dead, if degeneration has not commenced; it must also be borne in mind that what organisms can do cells can also effect, and that these leucocytes throwing out a digestive fluid, or at any rate some material detrimental to the existence of micro-organisms, may prepare the organisms, killing and even partially digesting them, taking them into their protoplasm as inert matter, and there continuing the process of digestion.

It will be remembered, however, that in addition to the small cells above described, larger connective tissue cells are found, such cells usually being numerous where the process is already, to a certain extent, localised by the leucocytes, so that in the outer part of the wall of an abscess they may usually be very distinctly made out. At this stage they appear to have very much the same function as the smaller cells, and one can often see within the protoplasm of these large nucleated cells, small spaces enclosing granular imperfectly stained leucocytes, red blood corpuscles, or, it may be, particles of pigment derived from red corpuscles, in fact, any dead or partially degenerated material with which they may come in contact. These, as above noted, are always more numerous where the process of localisation is complete, and it would appear that they take up and carry on slowly the work of digestion of foreign tissues which the leucocytes commenced ; and, comparing the process to a battle between organisms and the cells, a simile that is often used, the leucocytes may be described as the light cavalry which can be rapidly brought up and massed at any one point ; whilst the larger cells, derived from the fixed connective tissue, may be looked upon as the heavy infantry which completes the work and afterwards repairs the damage that has been done by the invading army. The leucocytes are spoken of by Metschnikoff as "microphages," the larger cells as "macrophages." All the changes met with in inflammation are associated with the necessity of bringing up these cells to the point at which injury occurs ; all the processes of healing are connected with the necessity of making good in as perfect a manner as possible the damage that has been done ; the two processes, therefore, cannot usually be dissociated. The processes of inflammation clearing the ground of dead or effete material, and laying the foundation, or rather forming the scaffolding, on which the processes of repair are afterwards carried on.

On incising a swelling which we know from experience would ultimately become converted into an abscess, it is found that although in some cases there is great accumulation of fluid in the lymph spaces, the tissues are firm and hard ; from these hard tissues there slowly exudes a quantity of comparatively clear fluid. In the swelling there is usually a small central point, yellow and opaque, but not yet distinctly softened ; whilst throughout the section, on examination with a hand lens, smaller opaque points may be seen, with here and there a number of glistening areas. A considerable amount of blood escapes from the cut surface, this indicating engorgement of the dilated vessels. If the swelling be examined at a sufficiently early stage, it may be determined by microscopic examination that the lymph spaces are enormously distended with coagulated fibrin, with leucocytes, and with proliferating connective tissue cells (these latter are not very numerous), whilst embedded in the fibrin are many micrococci, usually arranged in definite chains, or in little heaps. It is an exceedingly difficult matter to obtain sections of abscesses in this stage, but this condition is here described in order that the process of suppuration may be followed and understood in its later stages, especially in those cases in which the irritant organisms have made their way to the part by means of the lymphatics.

Pus.

173. If the pus from an acute abscess be examined (× 450) immediately after it is evacuated (§ **130**) the pus corpuscles (some of them still distinctly stained, others undergoing fatty and granular degeneration) may be readily distinguished. Most of these corpuscles are leucocytes, though here and there a larger cell may be found. Between the cells, and in some few instances actually within them, various forms of bacteria, usually streptococci, may be found. Sometimes, however, the cocci are arranged in pairs or in tetrads, or they may be arranged in small irregular heaps. In the early stages of pus formation bacteria are almost invariably demonstrable, but in the later stages, when the abscess is opened, it is often difficult to find a single micro-organism, even where the suppuration is very extensive.

Some of these pus corpuscles, during the very early stages (or when taken from an inflamed mucous surface), when examined on a Stricker's warm stage, still exhibit amœboid movement; they send out little processes, retract them, undergo change of shape, and generally behave much as do leucocytes under similar conditions. In the later stages of suppuration most of the cells have lost their amœboid movement, they are fatty and granular, the granularity becoming more and more distinct as the cells undergo further degeneration. If a drop of acetic acid be

run under the cover-glass it will be found that the protoplasm of the
pus cell is gradually cleared up, and as evidence of increased
activity of the cell at some earlier period, it is now found that the
nucleus has become divided into small fragments, usually three or
four in number. Large cells are rarely met with in pus, except as
large granular masses, which are evidently degenerated connective

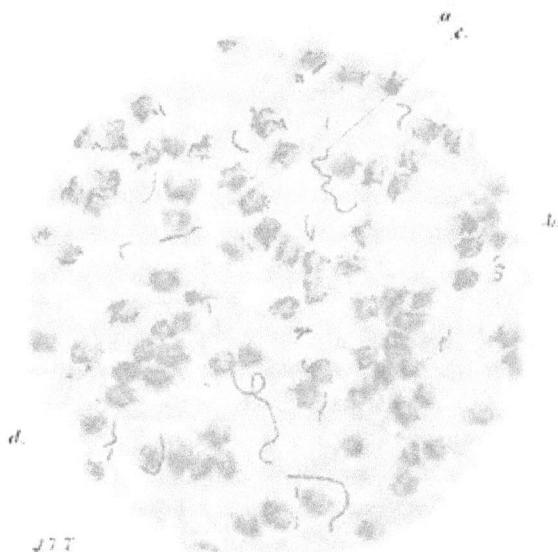

Fig. 17.—Pus from an acute abscess at time of evacuation. Dried
and treated with methyl violet. (× 700.)
  a. Pus corpuscles, between which may be seen the thin film of
      coagulated albuminoid material.
  b. Pair of micrococci. Diplococcus.
  c. Chains of micrococci. Streptococci.
  d. Sets of four. Tetrads.

tissue cells. In most pus, unless it be very liquid, small fragments of fibrous tissue may be distinguished, but these fragments
are very irregular, and evidently form only a small part of the
connective tissue of the area in which suppuration has taken place ;
there is also a quantity of finely granular material which does not
readily take on stains, and probably consists merely of *debris*,
broken down cells, and dead blood plates. Chemically, pus is an

albuminoid fluid holding in solution or suspended in it the original constituent materials of the tissues (more or less degenerated), the various salts and organic substances that these tissues contained, plus a large number of degenerating leucocytes, a number of micro-organisms, peptones, leucine, and other proteid derivatives which can only be looked upon as the result of the digestive action exerted on the tissues (a) by certain definite micro-organisms, and (b) probably by leucocytes.[1]   It is somewhat difficult to determine how the microbes act, but it is now very generally accepted that certain micro-organisms have the power of attacking bruised or partially devitalised tissues; on these they are supposed to exert a kind of digestive action; they use them as food, and in growing and multiplying excrete or separate from these albuminoid materials, poisonous products which act either directly on the tissues, or are absorbed into the blood and lymph vascular system, whence they may act either on the nerve centres or on the organs by which they are excreted, especially on the kidney and intestine; they there set up irritation which may give rise to grave inflammatory changes.   These organisms have been described in various forms of suppuration, but the most important are diplococcus citreus conglomeratus, staphylococcus cereus flavus, staphylococcus cereus albus, staphylococcus pyogenes aureus (micrococcus osteomyelitis), staphylococcus pyogenes citreus, staphylococcus pyogenes albus, streptococcus pyogenes, micrococcus pyogenes tenuis, bacillus pyocyaneous, bacillus saprogenes (several forms), bacillus pyogenes fœtidus.   Although many other organisms which appear to have a secondary pyogenic action have been found in certain specific diseases, such as glanders, tubercle, leprosy, &c., it is scarcely necessary to more than mention them.

The dead leucocytes in pus must be looked upon as the cells that have been brought up rapidly to interfere with the spread or diffusion of the products of the micro-organisms; a large number of these cells coming into contact with the poison in a concentrated form may succumb to its action, but before doing so they are able to deal with a certain quantity of the poisonous material, breaking it

---

[1] For the exact composition of pus refer to any of the systematic text-books.

down and rendering it inert. Other cells are constantly being brought up to assist these, until at length the bacteria are completely hemmed in; they live for a short time on the dead tissues, but being localised by the barrier of leucocytes, they ultimately die either from inanition, or because they are poisoned by their own products. It is found very frequently on opening an abscess that no organisms can be seen, those that were originally present appearing to have undergone degenerative changes, and to have been taken up and digested by the "phagocytes" or devouring cells.

SUMMARY OF PROCESSES OF REPAIR.

174. If a collection of pus be not of very large size it may ultimately be absorbed; the leucocytes at the margin do part of the work, but the bulk of it is carried on by the larger connective tissue cells, which, after some time, where foreign bodies are present, proliferate. The wall of an abscess, in the later stages, may be looked upon as a granulating surface, similar in many respects to that of an ulcer, throwing off dead cells; the vascular loops, the exudation of leucocytes, the proliferation of connective tissue cells, are much the same in both cases, and it is on the presence of these that healing depends after the pus has been evacuated or absorbed. The changes that occur in the connective tissue cells have already been referred to, and it appears that to them must be assigned the power of forming new tissue. The leucocytes may play a very important temporary part, but it is that of scavenging; the connective tissue cells, on the other hand, whilst continuing the scavenging process, and helping to remove the leucocytes that have already done their work, ingesting them and utilising them as food, have a further work to do; they form not only the new connective tissue, but also the embryonic blood-vessels, the new blood-vessels being apparently nothing more than tubes formed of large connective tissue cells of endothelial type. The mere mechanical protrusion of vessels, on unsupported surfaces, may be an important factor in vascularisation, but there are certainly other and even more important processes which can usually be followed near the surface of a healing

wound.   Growing from the cells which actually form the walls of the
minute vessels, or from cells immediately surrounding them there may
frequently be observed single rows or small columns of cells, which
appear to shoot outwards into the fibrinous lymph.   Into these small
columns the blood gradually makes its way as a channel or lumen is
formed, between which and the original vessel communication is then

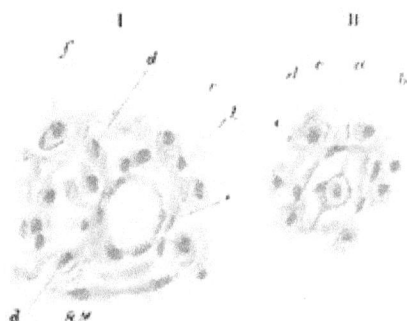

FIG. 18.—Young vessels from the granulation tissue of a healing
wound.   Stained with eosin and logwood.   (× 450.)

  I. *a.* Lumen of young vessel.
    b. Embryonic wall.
    c. Perivascular lymphatic space.
    d.d. Cells or buds shooting out from thickened mass of proto-
        plasm and cells at one side of the vessel.   It is from such
        buds that the new vessels are formed.
    e. Layer of cells forming outer boundary of newly formed peri-
        vascular space.
    f. Large connective tissue cell.
  II. Transverse section of a very young vessel.
    a. Lumen in which is a leucocyte.
    b. Wall of vessel (simply a couple of flattened endothelial, con-
        nective tissue cells).
    c. Rudimentary perivascular lymph space.
    d. Imperfect cellular lining of this space.
    e. Large connective tissue, fibro-plastic cell.

maintained.   In some cases this new vessel appears to grow outwards,
and the proliferation of the cells to take place always a little in front
of the advancing column of blood ; but in others it appears as though
there is first a single row of cells, which, proliferating, gradually gives
rise to a more complicated column, and then, rapidly opening up,
receives the blood.   It is only when the surface is neared that this

column of cells appears to give off branches, and it is after the branching commences that the loops are formed by the junction of the lateral processes; the pushing out of loops in the manner in which it is usually described is not of frequent occurrence so far as can be made out from the examination of a considerable number of specimens, the transverse portion of the loop being formed at a comparatively late stage of vascularisation. Once formed the vessels may give off other branches, but their walls gradually become more fully developed and the branches thrown out become fewer in number. In all these cases it is found that around the vessel there is usually a space, due, probably, to the alteration, from time to time, in the size of the vessel, and for the necessity that exists for some space in which may accumulate the fluid and cell elements that escape from the vessel. This space is ultimately bounded by a layer of connective tissue cells, a peri-vascular lymph space being thus formed. In the vessels in an old healing wound the walls are usually much thicker than in those of a recent one; this is due, apparently, partly to proliferation of the cells which form the intima, giving rise to what might be spoken of as an endarteritis, and partly to the formation of a kind of external coat from the connective tissue around—periarteritis. Along with this thickening of the vessel wall, as in the case of the healing ulcer (§ 169), we see in the deeper layers of the granulation tissue numerous spindle shaped cells which, running parallel to the surface, form a kind of interlacing net-work with the blood-vessels; as these become older and developed into connective tissue they gradually contract, help to constrict the blood-vessels, and so cut off a supply of blood which is no longer necessary for the nutrition of the more fully developed fibrous and connective tissues.

It will thus be seen that all these inflammations and healing processes are very intimately bound up one with another. On serous surfaces, as already described, it is found that every step is merely preparatory to a succeeding one, and that in many, or even in most cases, temporary makeshifts are resorted to in order to prepare the way for the formation of more permanent structures. First, there is the dilatation of the blood-vessels accompanied by softening of the cement substance between the endothelial cells and emigration of leucocytes (probably through this softened cement substance), and effusion of serum ; all this resulting from some injury or irritation to which the tissues are subjected, the various processes at this stage being set up in order to check or counteract the action of the irritant.

When these exudations have done their work and have localised the area of action of the irritant or injury, and have formed a sharp line of demarcation between the healthy and the abnormal tissues, they have no longer any function, they are foreign bodies, and as such must be removed.   Acting as foreign bodies, and along with the other irritants, they induce proliferation of the fixed connective tissue cells ; this is accompanied by the formation of blood-vessels, which remain in existence as long as they are required ; the process of healing is complete, and the tissues return as far as possible to their normal condition, though it usually takes a long time for the extra fibrous tissue to become absorbed ; in fact, it is doubtful whether this ever does take place completely.

If these facts are borne in mind most of the processes of inflammation and healing in other organs may be readily enough understood, and it is because of their great importance in this respect that the general plan of a practical work has been departed from in order that attention may be drawn to them as early as possible.

CHAPTER IV.

THE LIVER.

175. The weight of the normal liver when taken from the body is about 3 lbs. The surface is smooth, and the capsule has a glistening appearance, is of a bluish pink colour, and is fully though not tensely distended. The glistening appearance is due to the reflection of the

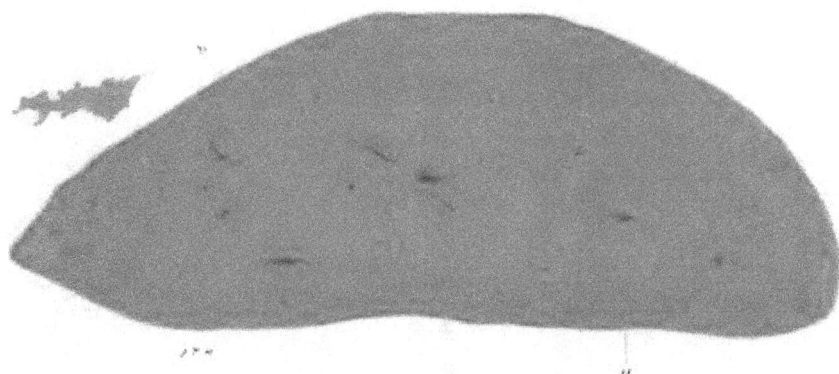

Fig. 19.—An almost normal liver in which there was only slight fatty infiltration, *a* (where the outlines of the lobules are more distinctly marked). The size of the lobules is here indicated.

    a. Branches of the portal and hepatic veins, seen in transverse and longitudinal section.
    b. Sections of lobules. Approximate size.
    c. Capsule of liver.

peritoneum over the surface of the organ, and is not observed at the posterior border, where the peritoneum is absent.

Beneath the capsule, and through the delicate subcapsular tissue, the lobules or small subdivisions of the liver substance can usually be seen, they vary in size from about 1-20th to 1-16th of an inch in diameter. The substance of the liver "cuts" readily, but is firm and close; the surface of a section of a healthy liver is of a dull chocolate colour, and the outlines of the lobules are usually very indistinctly marked. The capsule is thin and delicate, and only here and there very fine bands of connective tissue may be seen passing into the deeper part of the liver substance. In the cut section a number of large openings, mostly branches of the hepatic vein, are seen. The gall bladder is usually semi-distended, with a brownish-yellow bile, which may be readily pressed through the common duct into the duodenum.

176. For the preparation of such a liver for microscopic examination, see §§ 55, 59, 82, and 98.

Examine carefully, in order—(1) the capsule and the inter- and intralobular tissue; (2) the portal vein; (3) the hepatic artery;

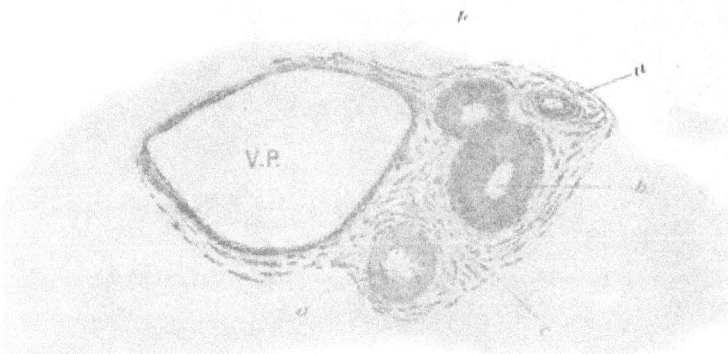

FIG. 20.—Contents of portal canal of dog. (Klein and Noble Smith). See also Fig. 39, p. 197.
V.P. Section of the portal vein, with large lumen and comparatively thin wall.
    a. The small branches of the hepatic artery, with thickened walls.
    b. Sections of bile ducts, each with a regular layer of nucleated columnar epithelium and a small orifice.
    c. Connective tissue, continuous with Glisson's capsule, supporting the various structures in the canal.

(4) the hepatic vein; (5) the bile ducts; and (6) the liver cells, or parenchyma of the organ. Always keep to this order in examining sections of either the diseased or the healthy liver.

On the outer surface of the capsule of a liver, put to harden immediately after death, is found a layer of endothelial cells, the serous layer proper; beneath this is a layer of irregular connective tissue, in which are yellow elastic fibres, and, deeper still, a layer of lamellated connective tissue, merely a continuation of Glisson's capsule, which plays a most important part in perihepatitis and polylobular cirrhosis. Continuous with the subcapsular tissue are processes of similar lamellæ—with flattened branching connective tissue cells between— running at intervals into the substance of the liver, where they are found in what are known as the portal canals. In the human liver

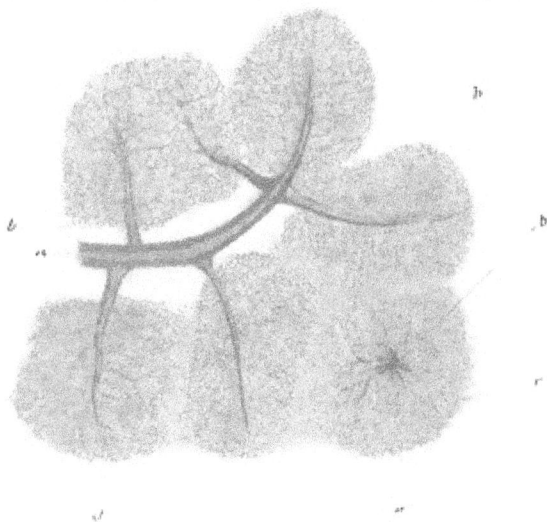

Fig. 21.—Diagrammatic representation of the structure of a small portion of the liver, altered from Quain's *Anatomy.*

    a. Sublobular vein, into which the central veins, or hepatic venules (*b*) open.
    c. Interlobular fissure, in which run the portal vein, &c. ; running from the portal vein to the central vein are the portal capillaries, *d.*
    e. The parenchymatous tissue, or gland substance proper, composed of masses of polyhedral cells.

there is little or no connective tissue between the individual lobules, but running along with the larger branches of the portal vein is a considerable quantity. It will be well to state at once that a study of a single lobule of the liver, and a single portal canal, will give the key to the structure of the whole organ as usually described.

The portal canals are the large spaces in a section of the liver, in which are seen the openings of the branches of the portal vein. In each of these canals are found (see Fig. 20)—(1.) A large opening (*v*), the portal or interlobular vein, which brings the blood from the alimentary tract to the liver. The walls of this vessel are comparatively thin. (2.) One or two small branches of the hepatic artery (*a*) with thick walls. These have the same structure as small arterioles in other tissues and organs. (3.) Small bile ducts (*d*) in any one of which the wall is of considerable thickness as compared with the lumen. Forming the inner part of this thick wall is a distinct layer of nucleated columnar epithelium.[1] These various structures are embedded in the connective tissue (*c*), which has

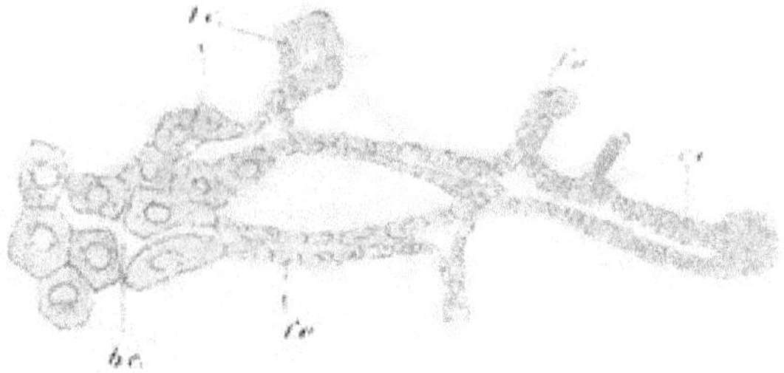

FIG. 22.—Commencement of biliary channels, and structure of smaller bile ducts (after Klein and Noble Smith).
b.c. Biliary canaliculi in the angles between adjacent liver cells.
l.c. Liver cells, slightly modified, just before the commencement of the bile duct proper, with its lining of flattened epithelium, *f.e.* (intermediary portion of the duct).
c.e. Cubical epithelium of the somewhat larger bile duct.

entered the liver at the hilus, along with the vessels, and now leaves the portal canals to run in the smaller portal spaces, and sometimes even between the lobules, forming a supporting framework for the liver substance proper. Examine a section through a lobule near the portal canal. It may be described as a mass of polyhedral cells arranged around a central (hepatic) vein. Piercing this mass of

[1] Remember the distribution of these vessels when the search for a lobule is entered upon. To find a lobule, look first for several portal spaces, which may be recognised by the fact that they contain *several* openings. Draw imaginary lines from these spaces to a common centre. Near this centre will be found a *single* opening—the hepatic vein, the centre of a lobule. The periphery of this lobule is marked by lines joining the several portal spaces running at right angles to those drawn towards the centre.

cells, and running from the portal vein, at the periphery, towards the centre, are numerous capillary vessels, bringing the blood into very close contact with the liver cells. Around these vessels are numerous lymphatics. Between individual cells, or rather at the angles between several cells, are the bile capillaries, which in their most minute ramifications are simply channels between adjacent liver cells, or actually within their substance (*see* § 184). These intra- and inter-

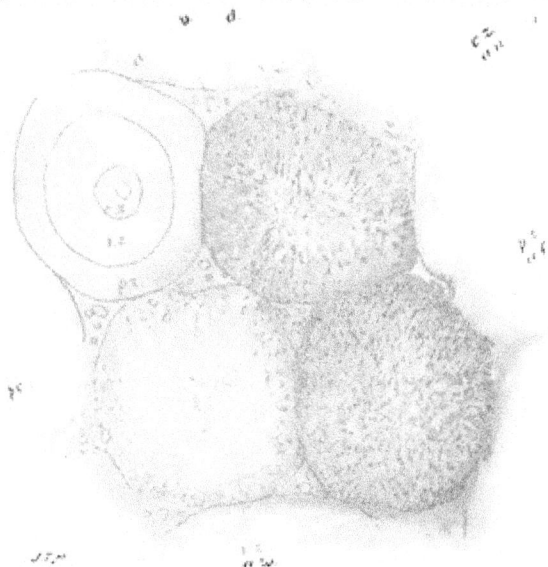

FIG. 23.—Diagrammatic representation of lobules of the liver, divided into zones.

b.c. Portal canal, in which are contained the following structures :—*d.* Bile duct. *v.* Portal vein. *a.* Hepatic artery. *a.n.* Area in which chronic venous congestion is first manifested. *a.w.* Area in which waxy change is met with. *a.f.* Area of fatty infiltration. These three areas correspond to the central (*c.z.*), intermediate (*i.z.*), and peripheral (*p.z.*) zones.

cellular channels are continued into the bile ducts, the epithelial cells of which appear to be derived from the same source as the liver cells.

The central veins of a group of lobules open into a larger branch of the hepatic vein—the sublobular vein (Fig. 21). On transverse section through one of these groups of lobules the arrangement is diagrammatically represented in Fig. 23, in which the following

structures are seen :—(1) Those situated at the angles between the
lobules ; and (2) the mass of liver cells perforated by the various
structures already mentioned, including the hepatic or intralobular
vein. For convenience of description this section of the lobule is
mapped out into three distinct zones. These are—(1.) The peripheral or portal zone, which, as its name indicates, is situated at the
periphery of the lobule, and occupies one-third of the diameter of
the section (area of fatty infiltration). (2.) Within this is the
intermediate zone, or, as it is sometimes named, the zone of the
hepatic artery, which, roughly speaking, also occupies one-third
of the diameter. It is named the zone of the hepatic artery from
the fact that the venous capillaries of the hepatic artery are supposed
here to empty their contents into the portal *venous* capillaries
which run between the inter- and intralobular veins (area in which
waxy degeneration is first met with). (3.) And lastly, there is the
central zone, or that of the hepatic vein, situated in the centre of the
lobule (area in which chronic venous congestion is first manifested).
At the periphery of the lobule are the small branches of the portal
vein, which empty their blood into the intercolumnar or portal
capillaries. Klein holds that there are, in consequence of
the mass of liver cells being *pierced* by the portal capillaries, short
transverse masses of the liver cells running at right angles to the
radiating columns of the network of cells. The liver cells making up
these columns are polygonal in shape, and have an extremely
granular appearance ; as a rule a single oval nucleus is to be observed,
which stains deeply with carmine, &c. ; a cell wall may also be
demonstrated—(Haycraft). Throughout the cell, granules of glycogen
and brown pigment are seen, whilst in a liver removed from an
animal killed shortly after food has been taken, globules of fat are
noticed in the cells of the peripheral zone. The granular appearance
of the protoplasm is due to the existence of an intranuclear and an
intracellular plexus, to be made out only with the aid of a very high
magnifying power. The imaginary spaces at the margins of the
lobules, joining the interlobular spaces, are spoken of as the interlobular fissures.

Sabourin, working from a pathological point of view, came to the
conclusion that the above description of the liver was not altogether

satisfactory ; he resuscitated the old theory, in support of which he was able to adduce considerable evidence, that the structure of the liver is essentially the same as that met with in other acinous glands. Delépine, on the basis of independent anatomical and physiological observations, holds that the columns of liver cells are really tubes with a fine lumen, and that instead of being arranged around the terminal hepatic veins as above described, they form small pyramidal masses which correspond to the lobules of other glands, so that the centre of the lobule, as described by him, is the portal canal with its bile ducts, portal veins, and hepatic arteries ; the columns of cells converging towards the bile ducts, and gradually becoming continuous with them. Near the portal space the diverging columns of liver cells are smaller, and have the character of intermediate tubes ; further away from the portal space, *i.e.*, in the intermediate zone as hitherto described, the cells are larger, whilst in the central zone they are again considerably smaller. Taking the centre of the lobule as at the portal space, and the interlobular fissures as occupying the position of lines drawn between the various hepatic veins, the above description might be repeated, simply changing the centre to the periphery,—the connective tissue forming the supporting frame work in the centre of each lobule,—and we have an acinous arrangement of tubes all converging to a central collecting bile duct, the structure of the liver thus being made to conform to that usually given for other acinous glands. A study of this arrangement enables us to understand many of the problems connected with secretion by the liver which, otherwise, are unintelligible. It may perhaps be said that it is difficult to recognise the arrangement of the tubes of a healthy liver, and this undoubtedly is the case, except when one set of them happens to be entirely in the plane of the section. We have to do with an organ in which there is so little interstitial tissue and in which there are so many confusing anastomoses that a section in such a plane can seldom be obtained. A careful study of the grouping of the liver tubes will, however, show that in many places their arrangement suggests quite as close a connection with the portal vessels as with the hepatic veins.

Cloudy Swelling of the Liver.

177. This condition is usually found in organs taken from patients who have died during the course of certain acute febrile conditions, especially those of septicæmic origin, or yellow fever, scarlatina, small-pox, and similar diseases. It is also met with in the early stages of phosphorus, arsenic, antimony, alcohol, or sulphuric ether poisoning. It is really an inflammatory condition, and is described by Virchow as a parenchymatous inflammation. It is also spoken of as molecular degeneration.—(See Fatty Degeneration, § **179**).

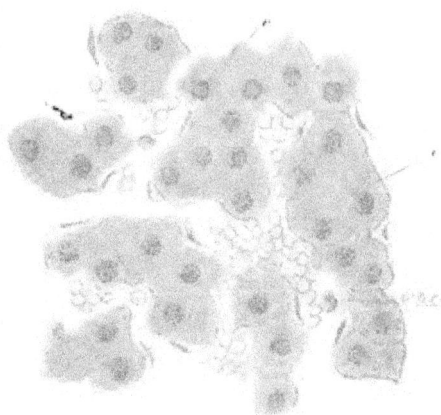

Fig. 24.—Cloudy swelling of the liver cells. Section stained in picro-carmine. (× 450.)

   l.c. Liver cells, swollen and granular ; small globules are seen here and there, and the nucleus is slightly obscured.

   c. Capillary vessels between the columns of liver cells ; containing red blood corpuscles (green), and, *w.b.c.*, white blood corpuscles (carmine).

   e. Endothelial cells forming the walls of the intercolumnar capillary vessels.

On naked eye examination the capsule is tense, the liver is swollen, although paler than normal (due to the diminished amount of blood in the *capillaries*), and, instead of having a clear glistening appearance and firm substance, is somewhat opalescent and flabby. Harden (§ **55**), and stain (§ **98**).

(× 50).—The lobules are rather more distinctly outlined than usual, owing to a slight increase in the number of connective tissue nuclei (due both to proliferation and to exudation) in the interlobular fissures ; the capillaries are seen to be compressed by the columns of swollen liver cells (and by exuded leucocytes).

(× 300).—The cells in the portal zone, where the change is always most readily seen, are distinctly swollen ; they have lost their polygonal form, and are much more rounded than healthy liver cells ; the protoplasm of each cell appears to be exceedingly granular and cloudy (probably due to an alteration in the thickness of the rods which make up the intracellular plexus), and the nucleus is somewhat obscured. In some cases the cells are undergoing a process of division or breaking down ; where this is far advanced the cell may consist almost entirely of a mass of granules, the nucleus having disappeared. On the addition of a drop of acetic acid to such a specimen, the granules disappear, and the protoplasm and nucleus of the cell resume their normal appearance.

It is probable that here, very frequently, as in the heart, cloudy swelling is nothing but an early stage of fatty degeneration.

FATTY INFILTRATION OF THE LIVER.

178. Fatty infiltration, Lipomatosis, or Adiposis of the liver cells, is found during the physiological process of digestion, and is only a pathological condition where there is an exaggeration and continuance of the normal periodic process. It may be due to an excessive supply of alcohol, or of such substances as fatty matter, maltose, or sugar, or to defective oxidation and assimilation of these substances ; but the essential factor in this condition appears to be that the fat is derived principally from without, and does not necessarily involve the breaking down of any protoplasm, though it is usually accompanied by impaired function of the cell, and may, ultimately, end in true fatty degeneration. It is found in patients who have died from phthisis, scrofula, cancer, and wasting diseases generally, and, as a rule, is unaccompanied by marked jaundice or ascites.

On naked eye examination, the organ is enlarged, smooth, paler or yellower in colour than normal. The capsule is tense and glistening, and the anterior margin of the liver is considerably

thickened and rounded. The tissue pits on pressure,—the indentation remaining for some time after the pressure is removed,—and is
friable. The lobules are usually distinctly marked out, each having a
pale yellow ring at its periphery, and a brownish red or purple
centre : this may be seen even through the capsule. On section, the

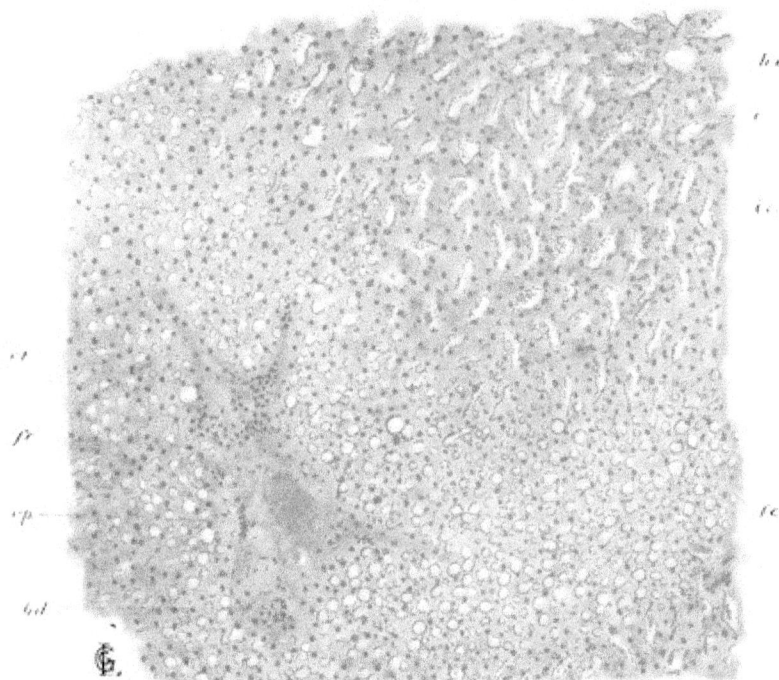

FIG. 25.—Drawing of portion of a lobule of a large fatty liver.
Section stained with picro-carmine. (× 100.)

h.v.	Central or hepatic vein.
c.	Capillaries distended with blood.
l.c.	Columns of healthy liver cells.
f.c., f.c.	Liver cells in the peripheral zone in an advanced stage of fatty infiltration.
b.d.	Small bile duct lined with cubical epithelium.
v.p.	Portal vein distended with blood.
c.t.	Connective tissue and bile duct in longitudinal section of an interlobular space.

general pallor is distinctly marked, and, in addition, the tissue
has a peculiar yellow mottled appearance. Though the actual
weight of the organ may be considerably increased, the specific
gravity may be so much diminished that a piece will float in water.

When the surface is scraped droplets of oil—readily recognised if the scraping is floated on water—collect on the knife. Harden (§ 59), and stain (§§ 98-110).

(× 50).—Examine a single lobule. In the early stages the infiltration is confined to the peripheral or portal zone, that part of the lobule where the blood is emptied from the portal vein into the portal capillaries. Under this power the droplets of fat are usually large, though they vary in size, and in the more advanced stages they tend to run together, and to form large, clear, strongly refractile droplets, which appear to distend the liver cell, and push the nucleus to one side. In very advanced cases the cells of the

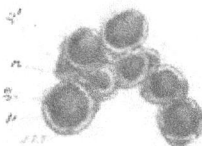

FIG. 26.—Cells from fatty liver (infiltration). Stained with osmic acid. (× 300.)

> *n.* Thin film of protoplasm, forming, along with the nucleus, *n.*, all that is left of the proper substance of the liver cell.
> *g.* A *single large* droplet blackened by osmic acid, and therefore of a fatty nature, contained within the wall of protoplasm. It will be observed that the nucleus is distinctly seen, and is pushed to one angle of the cell, giving rise to the so-called "signet-ring" appearance.
> In one cell only are there two droplets of fat, g^1.

intermediate zone, or even those of the whole lobule may be infiltrated; it is then difficult to distinguish the mass from ordinary adipose tissue.

(× 300).—The liver cells most affected, especially those in the peripheral zone, have lost their polygonal form and are swollen and rounded. Each cell is made up of a thin film or wall of protoplasm, enclosing one or perhaps two or three droplets of fat (stained black by osmic acid). In the picro-carmine stained section observe that one angle of the cell remains, and that in this angle the nucleus, deeply stained, and standing out very prominently, is situated. The liver cell, with its nucleus pushed to one angle, and the thin film of protoplasm surrounding the globule of fat is in this stage said to be like a signet ring. In consequence of the swelling of the cells, and of their being pressed together, their outlines or boundaries are somewhat indistinct and obscured.

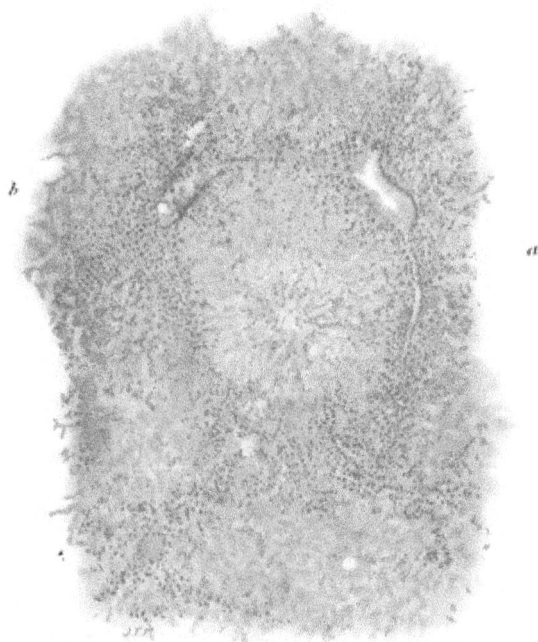

FIG. 27.—Drawing of fatty infiltration of the liver (with fatty degeneration at the periphery of the lobule only). Stained with osmic acid. (× 50.)

    a. Transverse section of central or hepatic vein.
    b. Portal canal with various openings. (See Fig. 20.)
    c. Peripheral zone of a lobule, in which are the infiltrated and degenerated cells,—the fat globules are stained black with osmic acid.

FATTY DEGENERATION OF THE LIVER.

179. Fatty degeneration is to be looked for in the livers of patients who die during the course of wasting or exhausting diseases. It is also constantly met with as a sequel to cloudy swelling, following

continued fevers, and the exhibition of those poisons already mentioned (§ 177), which act by interfering with the proper oxidation of the tissues. It is also seen in Addison's disease, in anæmia, and in phthisis, where, in addition to imperfect oxidation, there is decreased vitality of the tissues as a part of a general malnutrition or debility. It is frequently met with in patients who have succumbed to malignant growths, especially in those who have been attacked by cancer. Although it is impossible to draw a sharp line of demarcation between this and fatty infiltration, the conditions differ considerably in both naked eye and microscopic characters, and as they are met with in slightly different diseases it is found more convenient to treat of them under separate headings.

From the physical characteristics of the tissues, both naked eye and microscopic, the liver when affected with fatty degeneration is known as the atrophic or wasted form of fatty liver. The organ, in the advanced stage of the process, and where a large number of the cells have become affected, is markedly wasted, the weight and specific gravity are both diminished, and the capsule is somewhat wrinkled. On section the colour is brown or brownish-yellow, the peripheral zone usually being paler than the remainder of the lobule ; the tissue appears to be more or less opaque, but pale and friable, breaking down readily under the finger.

Harden (§ 59), cut (§ 82 *et seq.*), and stain (§§ 110 and 98).

(× 50).—The lobules are distinctly outlined, the liver cells are atrophied, and in these atrophied and somewhat angular cells are seen a number of small fat globules, each with a dark outline and a clear centre. These droplets of fat are usually said to be small, but there are several in each cell which may run together to form larger globules ; they give the characteristic black reaction with osmic acid, and are always in greatest number near the periphery of the lobule ; though, in advanced cases, the process extends throughout the lobule. The capillaries are usually dilated, and stand out prominently. In a picro-carmine stained specimen a number of exuded leucocytes may be seen as bright crimson points along the lines of the interlobular fissures, and in the interlobular spaces.

(× 300).—The cells are much shrunken, and have an angular outline. Scattered throughout the protoplasm of the cell are numer-

M

ous oil globules, never of any great size; for, although some of them may run together, they do not as a rule form a single large droplet unless the cell is much degenerated. Such of the protoplasm as remains is extremely granular, and the nucleus, when it can be made out, occupies the centre of the cell, though, in the majority of cases, it, like the protoplasm, is undergoing division and is breaking down. In consequence of the atrophy, the outlines of individual cells are easily made out.

180. Where fatty degeneration has been brought on more rapidly, as in the case of phosphorus poisoning, the decrease in size of the

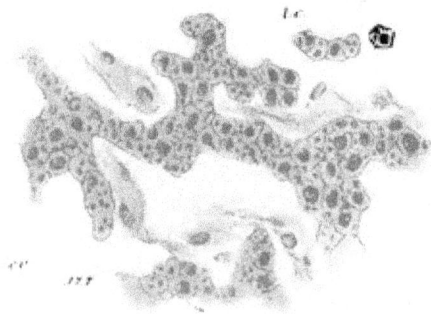

FIG. 28.—Drawing of liver cells undergoing fatty degeneration, taken from near the centre of a lobule. Stained with osmic acid. (× 300.)

l.c. Liver cells arranged in columns. The outlines of these cells are very distinctly marked. The nucleus is not visible in most of the cells, which are small, and have in their protoplasm several droplets of fat,—these droplets varying very much in size, but usually they are comparatively small.

c.v. Capillary vessels and delicate connective tissue,—the nuclei of both of which are seen slightly stained by the osmic acid.

liver is not so marked nor is the weight diminished; there are certain other characteristic features to which special attention must be drawn.

The liver is pale, but at certain points—or it may be almost throughout the whole of the organ—patches of bile-stained tissue and small punctiform hæmorrhages, especially under the capsule, are frequently to be seen. These are due to the rupture of the small bile ducts and arteries, the walls of which are found to have undergone fatty degeneration. In consequence of the bile-staining, the whole organ is frequently of a canary yellow, or even a darker yellow, colour. It is not much decreased in size. On examination under the microscope, the protoplasm of the liver cells appears to be almost replaced by fat globules, which in this case are of considerable size—much larger than in ordinary fatty degeneration, as here there is no time for absorption of the fat to take place.

From the descriptions given above it will be seen that it may sometimes be a difficult matter to determine whether we are dealing with a case of fatty infiltration or fatty degeneration.

It has been said that infiltration is due to the deposition within the cells of fat that has been derived from without, and that degeneration is due to the protoplasm of the cell itself supplying the material from which the fat is formed. In both cases there is incomplete oxidation, but the physiological occurrence of fat in the cells of the liver, after a meal, which may be taken as the type of the process of infiltration, and which results from the splitting up of proteids as the result of *external metabolism,* has a very different significance from true fatty degeneration which results from the breaking down of the protoplasm itself—*internal metabolism.*

As a matter of fact, we find that in fatty infiltration the greater part of the protoplasm of the liver cell is not destroyed ; it, along with the nucleus which also remains active, is simply pushed aside to form a comparatively active film around the large fat globule, whilst in fatty degeneration there are evidently grave nutritive changes in the protoplasm—such of it as remains unconverted into fat, is extremely granular—and the nucleus, retaining its normal position, is evidently undergoing marked degenerative changes, as it does not readily take up any staining reagent. In the one case, if the fat is removed both protoplasm and nucleus assume their normal appearance, whilst in the other, if the fat is removed, nothing but a small mass of granular protoplasm, with an imperfectly stained nucleus, is left.

WAXY LIVER.

181. Synonyms, "Bacony" Liver, "Lardaceous" (*Lard,* Fr.), (*Speck Leber,* Ger.), "Waxlike," "Amyloid," "Albuminoid" Liver.

Waxy liver is met with in patients who have suffered from

certain diseases in which suppuration has been profuse or long continued.   It is very frequently found in cases of chronic phthisis, especially where the discharge from the cavities, so characteristic of this disease, has been going on for some time, in empyæma, in bone disease accompanied by suppuration, and in syphilis, congenital or acquired, notably during the tertiary stages.   It is also said to occur in certain other diseases, such as chronic dysentery and leuco-cythemia, and after acute rheumatism.

It is difficult to determine whether this is a true degeneration or simply an infiltration, as it appears to depend upon two sets of conditions—(1) changes in the connective tissue elements, especially connective tissue fibrils and basement membranes; (2) an infiltration of these with certain unknown proteid materials, separated apparently directly from the blood in patients in whom *caseation* and *chronic suppurative processes* are going on.

Waxy liver derives most of its synonyms from some supposed physical resemblance to smoked ham, boiled bacon fat, and so forth.   The organ is, in uncomplicated waxy disease, enlarged in all directions, is more square than normal, and the anterior margin is somewhat thickened and rounded, though not so markedly so as in the fatty liver.   The capsule is smooth, glistening, thin and transparent, and so tense that the organ does not lie flat when placed on its anterior surface, the middle only coming in contact with the platter on which it rests, the edges being well raised.   To the touch the substance is firm and hard, like a piece of india-rubber; it is indented with difficulty by pressure of the finger, and the indentation disappears almost as soon as the pressure is removed.

In advanced cases the fresh section has a firm sharp edge, and a peculiar pink colour, somewhat like that of smoked ham or salmon; the tissue is anæmic.   A thin section is translucent, and its surface has the appearance of being covered with a very thin layer of gelatine.

On examining a lobule closely, in an organ in which the disease is not very advanced, it will be possible to divide it, roughly, into three zones: the peripheral or outer zone, of a pale opaque yellow colour, forms a kind of ring; within this comes the intermediate zone, which is broader than the peripheral zone, and of the peculiar translucent appearance mentioned above; whilst within this again is a zone which varies somewhat in colour, but is usually a little paler than the normal liver substance. This latter constitutes the healthiest part of the lobule.

Pour a watery solution of iodine (§ 107), over the fresh surface, and a selective staining is at once obtained. The translucent ring is stained a deep mahogany, red or brown, the other zones assuming a canary yellow colour. This translucent or mahogany brown area

FIG. 29.—Section of "waxy" liver. Unstained. (× 50.)
 a. Capillaries of intermediate zone, which have undergone waxy
        change—glassy, translucent.
 b. Small branch of hepatic artery.
 c. Central or hepatic vein.
 d. Liver cells of the peripheral zone, brownish-grey and opaque.
 e. Angular, somewhat atrophied, opaque degenerating liver cells
        around the central veins. None of the liver cells are waxy.

is the portion of the lobule in which the lardaceous material is deposited. Harden (§ 57), and cut (§ 82 *et. seq.*).

(× 50).—Examine an unstained section without a cover glass. It will at once be observed that in the intermediate zone of the lobule there is a series of columns of somewhat compressed liver cells, whilst between these are irregular, translucent, glassy-looking, or homogeneous streaks. These streaks, as will be found later, are the capillary vessels, the walls of which have undergone waxy change. This hyaline or vitreous appearance is exceedingly characteristic of waxy liver, and once recognised can never again be mistaken for anything else. The cells in the central zone

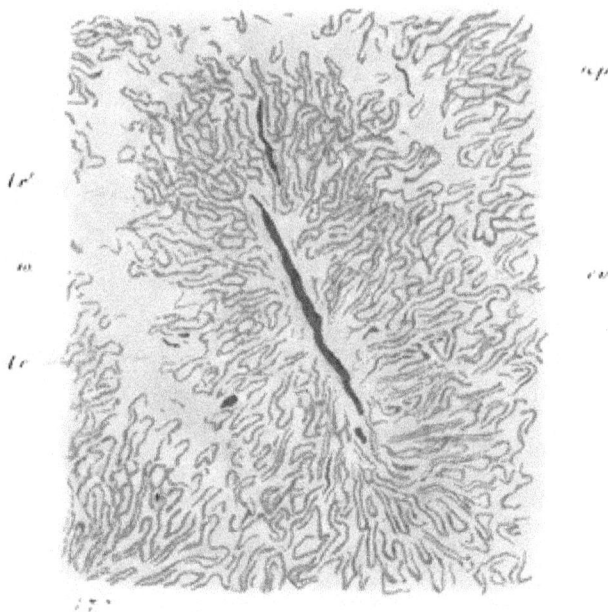

Fig. 30.—Drawing of waxy liver, stained with iodine, and examined by reflected light. Lobule cut through vertically. (× 70.)
w. Capillaries in intermediate zone—waxy. Stained dark brown.
c.v. Central or hepatic vein.
v.p. Small branch of portal vein.
l.c. Liver cells and unaffected capillaries in the peripheral zone. Stained yellow.
l.c.   Do.   do.   in the central zone.

appear to be comparatively healthy, whilst those in the peripheral zone are either healthy or are undergoing fatty infiltration; in both positions they can be readily recognised by their browner, more opaque, appearance. Allow a drop or two of the watery solution of iodine to run over the specimen from one margin, and then examine it by transmitted light, when the liver cells in the central zone appear to be stained a dark-yellow or brownish-yellow colour, the fatty globules and liver cells in the peripheral zone are canary yellow, and the homogeneous streaks assume a deeper yellow tinge. Whilst looking at the specimen, alter the angle of the mirror so as to turn off the light from below the stage; the homogeneous streaks now appear to be of the dark-brown colour similar to that observed

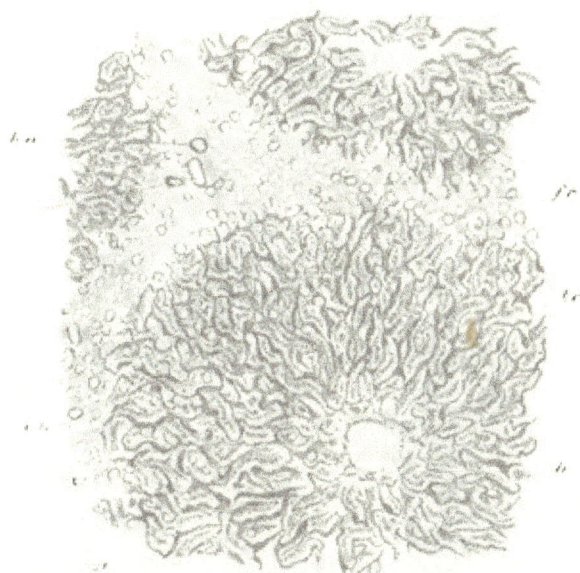

FIG. 31.—Drawing of waxy liver, stained with methylaniline violet. (× 100.)

h.a. Small branch of hepatic artery in portal space, middle coat waxy. Stained red violet.
p.v. Portal vein.
f.c. Liver cells in peripheral zone (fatty infiltration).
c.w. Capillaries in intermediate zone—waxy.
l.c. Atrophied liver cells between waxy capillaries.
h.v. Central or hepatic vein.

with the naked eye, and the liver cells previously dark now appear yellow. Mount this specimen in the iodine mounting fluid (§ 107).

(× 300).—It will be noticed that in the liver cells are a few granules (glycogen) which take on the same staining as does the waxy material, for which, however, they must not be mistaken, as it is found that although glycogen gives the same reaction with iodine, when stained with methylaniline violet, which gives a blue reaction, it may be distinguished from the waxy material.

(× 50).—In a specimen so stained (§ 106), the homogeneous material has taken on a beautiful rose pink or red violet colour; the other tissues are slaty blue. This characteristic reaction defines

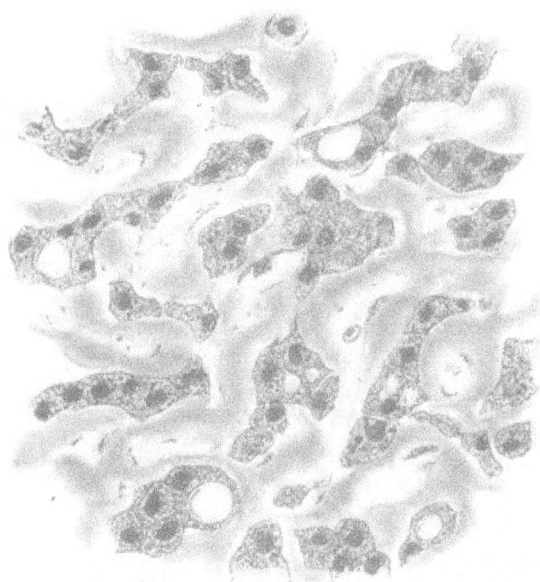

FIG. 32.—Drawing of waxy degeneration of liver. Methylaniline violet. (× 450.)

c.w. Walls of waxy capillaries, thickened, hyaline, red violet.
e.c. Endothelium of capillaries, *not* waxy.
l. White blood corpuscle.
a.c. Atrophied liver cells.
f.c. Fatty infiltration of liver cells ; f.c.³, smaller globules of fat in atrophied cells.

most accurately and minutely the waxy tissues. In the portal spaces, the small arterioles of the hepatic artery are stained rose pink—this coloration is confined more especially to the middle coat of the vessel. In the intermediate zone of the lobule, where the change is most advanced, the cells are more angular than usual, are attenuated looking, and even with this power may be observed to be granular and atrophied; they seldom or never give a pink reaction, as they usually remain perfectly free from any waxy change, though they frequently undergo fatty infiltration and degeneration. In certain cases, especially where the waxy change has involved the capillaries of the peripheral zone, the wall of the portal vein may be similarly affected, in which case, of course, it gives the rose pink reaction.

(x 300).—The arteriole in the portal canal is affected as follows:— The middle coat is picked out, and if a longitudinal section be examined, certain areas or bands only of this (not the muscle fibres) are seen to be affected. Later, the fibrous part of the inner coat becomes more or less involved, especially in its deeper layers, but the endothelial cells lining the vessel, although frequently granular and fatty looking, still give the blue reaction. If the branches of the portal vein are involved, the affection is similarly localised to the connective tissue fibrils.

The capillaries in the intermediate zone are found to be the special seat of the waxy change. The walls are enormously thickened, and in many cases the lumen appears to be obliterated, so that little is to be seen but thick bands of translucent homogeneous material, stained a beautiful rose pink colour, between which lie bands or rows of liver cells. These cells, atrophied and angular, are in many cases undergoing fatty degeneration; the nucleus is in its normal position, but is somewhat obscured, and the outline of the cell is distinctly marked; there is seldom any pink reaction to be seen in any part of the cell.

The capillary vessels in this position, simple though their structure is, are to be considered as being really made up of three coats; (1) a single layer of endothelial cells (the capillary wall proper) in immediate contact with the blood current; outside this is (2) a thin membranous or reticular structure, or basement membrane, composed of connective tissue fibrils, or possibly, elastic tissue; and (3) external to this again are connective tissue cells, the processes of which are connected with the basement membrane; these are spoken of collectively as peri- thelium. The waxy change takes place in the basement membrane or in the connective tissue filaments, between the two layers of cells. In some cases, however, it is extremely difficult to make out these perithelial cells, the swollen basement membrane apparently coming into direct contact with the parenchymatous liver cells (as seen in Fig. 32). The delicate filaments become enormously swollen, and ultimately become so prominent that they overshadow the other structures. The endothelial cells are granular and fatty. This enormous thickening of the walls of the capillary vessels brings about two results,— one from the extension inwards — gradual narrowing, and ultimately, complete obliteration of the lumen of the vessel ; another from the extension outwards—the compression of the columns of liver cells, leading to atrophy and molecular disintegration of the proper substance of the liver.

A third method of staining is to dip the section into a watery solution of iodine, and then convey it to a 7 or 8 per cent. solution of sulphuric or other mineral acid. Virchow originally used a very strong acid. He also uses a saturated solution of chloride of zinc for the same purpose. He describes the reaction as blue with the lardaceous material, and yellow with healthy tissues. The other methods, however, are more certain and more convenient, though it will be well to try this method where a very delicate reaction is required.

When the causes of waxy disease are compared with those which induce fatty and other changes of the liver it will be readily understood why it is so frequently found complicated with fatty infiltration, fatty degeneration, tubercle of the liver, cirrhosis and syphilitic scars. All these conditions, when present, modify the typical form of the waxy liver to a greater or less extent, a fact that must always be borne in mind when an examination of such a liver is made.

CHRONIC VENOUS CONGESTION OF THE LIVER.

182. Synonyms, "Nutmeg" or "Cardiac" Liver, "Cyanotic Atrophy." Nutmeg liver is seen in cases where there has been cardiac disease, or extensive lung disease, such as emphysema, chronic phthisis (fibroid). It is met with in any condition where there is pressure on the inferior vena cava, or where there is any obstruction to the return of the venous blood to the thoracic cavity. Where the primary lesion is in the heart, say at the mitral valve, a corresponding condition is found in the lungs, in the kidney, spleen, intestines, and in the portal system generally, so that amongst other symptoms during life are diarrhœa, hæmorrhoids, chronic intestinal catarrh, varices, and ascites. The causes are, to a very great extent, mechanical :—there is increased pressure in the hepatic vein, this pressure manifesting itself by its effects first in the central or intralobular veins, and later in the sublobular

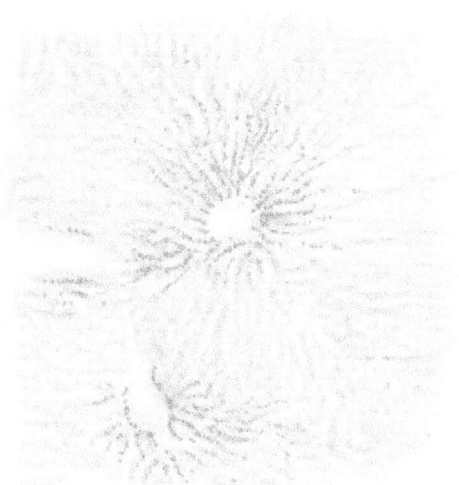

FIG. 33.—Early "Nutmeg" liver, unstained.   (× 70.)
  h.v. Central vein dilated, walls thickened.
  c.c. Dilated capillaries in central zone.
  l.c. Pigmented and compressed liver cells in central zone.
  p.c. Unaltered cells in peripheral zone.

veins and intermediate and peripheral parts of the portal capillary veins, all this leading to enlargement of the liver. *On naked eye examination* the capsule is tense, thin, and translucent ; in the later stages the liver appears to be atrophied and tough, but still contains a considerable quantity of blood, which gives to the section a very dark red colour ; the capsule is thickened in patches, and may have on its surface (especially where ascites has been present) small villous growths—papillomatous growths, as they are sometimes incorrectly called. The openings of the hepatic veins are enlarged, and therefore appear to be more numerous.

Examining a *lobule* in the earlier stages, it will be observed that it can be divided into three zones, each of which may be distinctly

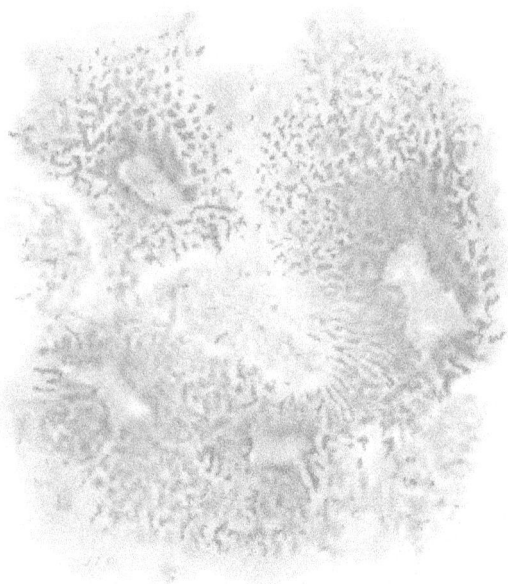

FIG. 34.—Section of "Nutmeg" liver—advanced. (× 50.)
  a. Dilated central vein, the wall of which is thickened and fibrous-looking, with here and there some golden yellow pigment scattered in its substance.
  b. Capillaries in the central zone, greatly dilated and filled with blood, with thickened walls similar in appearance to the thickened walls of the central vein.
  c. Liver cells of the peripheral zone.
  d. Capillaries in the peripheral zone, not greatly distended.
  e. Branches of the portal vein distended.
  f. Bile ducts, lined with more or less cubical nucleated epithelium.

seen. The central zone is deep red in colour, and is engorged with blood; external to this is the brownish-yellow intermediate zone, the yellow tinge here being due to bile-staining, whilst the peripheral zone is pale and fatty looking. To this peculiar colour arrangement the name "nutmeg" is given, and as the name refers simply to the appearance of the tissue, it is perhaps as good a one as can be used.

Virchow's name of "red atrophy" is applied either to localised patches of congested tissue or, in the later stages of the disease, where the whole liver has become shrunken, and where the congestion extending throughout the lobule has done away with the nutmeg appearance. Harden (§ 59). Mount (§ 152), one section unstained and one stained (§ 98).

(× 50).—The central or hepatic vein is considerably dilated, so that the lobules are distinguished much more readily than in the normal liver.

The capillaries leading to this central opening are also dilated, and are frequently filled with blood. Between the dilated capillaries the liver cells are atrophied, angular, compressed, and granular looking, and in the immediate neighbourhood of the central vein they contain granular masses of brown or orange red pigment.

(× 300).—The walls of the dilated vein and its surrounding capillaries are considerably thickened; in some cases they form distinct fibrous bands and circles. The pigment in the cells situated in the inner part of the lobule is seen much more distinctly in the periplast of the cells, and does not obscure the nucleus, unless the cell is entirely filled with the colouring matter. The shrinking and atrophy of the liver cells are very marked, and in some cases small fat globules are seen lying scattered throughout the angular mass of protoplasm which represents the cell.

The atrophy of the liver cells is due to the pressure of the blood distending the capillaries; as these vessels become swollen, varicose, and tortuous, the columns of liver cells between them are compressed. In the later stages, the liver cells may have disappeared from the immediate neighbourhood of the central vein, and there is left simply a cavernous structure, made up of the fused walls of capillary vessels, forming bands of fibrous-looking tissue, between which are spaces filled with blood.

In certain cases bands of fibroid or hyaline tissue, continuations of the fibroid vascular walls in the central zone, run to the periphery, and so cut up the lobules into distinct segments. Along with this hyaline thickening there is sometimes an apparent increase in the amount of connective tissue in the interlobular spaces and fissures. This gives rise to a form of cirrhosis, peculiar to the nutmeg liver, which is often seen in the later stages of the disease.

In the peripheral zone, well-marked fatty infiltration is often met with, the presence of which is probably accounted for by the slower passage of the blood through the portal system, in consequence of the obstruction to the outlet of blood from the hepatic vein, which brings about the following results :—

In consequence of the obstruction to the outlet of the blood from the vena cava, the hepatic vein cannot empty its contents so readily, and in turn the obstruction is felt in the sublobular, the central or intralobular veins, the intercellular capillaries, and lastly, in the portal vessels ; there is a partial stasis of the blood. In addition to this the liver cells are somewhat compressed and hampered by the increased pressure from the dilated and thickened capillary vessels, and their nutritive activity is impaired.

Common Cirrhosis of the Liver.

183. Synonyms, "Gin-drinker's" Liver, "Hobnail" Liver, "Polylobular Cirrhosis," "Coarse Cirrhosis," "Alcoholic Cirrhosis," "Granular" Liver.

In this condition the liver is, especially in the later stages, considerably diminished in size. It is firm to the touch, and its consistence may be compared to that of a piece of soaked leather. On the surface are a number of small projections about the size of the head of a hobnail or "tacket," and between these are depressions or fossæ. On section, the deeper layer of the capsule—Glisson's capsule proper—is more or less thickened and opaque, the whole organ is usually yellow, and is paler than normal, the pallor being always most marked in the fossæ or depressions between the projecting hobnail-like nodules. The tissue is firm and tough, and greyish-red gelatinous-looking bands of fibrous tissue are seen running in various directions throughout the substance of the organ, cutting it up into a series of areas of parenchymatous cells. These areas are of various sizes, usually from one-sixth to a quarter of an inch in diameter (a lobule being from one-sixteenth to one-twentieth of an inch in diameter); they are of a tawny yellow colour, as a result of bile-staining. As a rule the cells of several lobules are grouped together in the mass of liver tissue, each being bounded by one of these fibrous capsules.

The fibrous bands near the surface are continuous with the deeper thickened layer of the capsule, into which they run at the

FIG. 35.—Drawing of a section of common cirrhosis of the liver. Stained with picro-carmine. (× 20.)

f.t. Bands of newly formed fibrous tissue running into the substance of the liver, and cutting it up into masses of cells of various sizes.

l.c. Indicates the margin of a mass consisting of a number of lobules.

l.c¹. Indicates a portion of a lobule surrounded by newly formed fibrous tissue.

c.v. Central vein of a lobule.

v. One of the newly formed vessels, supplying the fibrous tissue with blood from the hepatic artery.

point of depression around the hobnail elevation, and it is owing to the contraction of these bands that the elevations and depressions are formed, the former consisting apparently of a yellowish brown mass of cells, which is pushed by the contracting fibrous bands in the direction of least resistance, *i.e.*, to the surface.

Harden (§§ 59 and 57), and stain (§§ 98, 103, and 104).

(× 20).—At the margin of the section the thickening of the capsule is seen as a mass of pink fibrous tissue, from which bands of different sizes may be observed running down into the liver substance from the lowest parts of the sulci.   Between these fibrous bands are masses of liver cells, made up of six, eight, or ten lobules, corresponding in position to the elevations above mentioned.

The fibrous bands run along with the *medium sized* branches of the *portal vein*, some of which are apparently slightly diminished in size by the pressure of the newly formed tissue around them.   It is often difficult to distinguish the individual lobules, as there is, especially in the earlier stages of the disease, no increase in the tissue in the smaller interlobular spaces and fissures, whilst, owing to the pressure exerted by the contracting fibrous bands in the larger portal spaces, the lobules are pressed together, and the central vein may be partially obliterated.

(× 300).—In the newly formed bands of fibrous tissue are enormous numbers of rounded extravasated cells, each with a nucleus, and surrounded by a small envelope of protoplasm. Amongst these are other cells of larger size, which are apparently derived from the proliferating connective tissue cells.   In the later stages it may be observed that the number of round nuclei is apparently much diminished, whilst in place of them appear (according to the method of staining) pink or delicate blue bands of fibrillated tissue ; scattered at intervals through this are numerous elongated nuclei,—the nuclei of flattened connective tissue cells, around which a fibrillated periplast has been formed.   The more advanced the disease, and the more contracted the organ, the more fibrous does this fibro-cellular tissue become, until in some parts it may be represented merely by a band of contracting cicatricial tissue.   This fibrous tissue in some cases, however, is exceedingly vascular, and by injection it may be proved that this vascularity is due to the formation of new capillaries and small vessels, which derive their blood supply from the pre-existing small branches of the hepatic artery.   These new vessels, embryonic in character, often consist of mere channels lined by a single layer of endothelial or flattened connective tissue cells, and are frequently filled with blood, especially if the tissue has been preserved in Muller's fluid. Hence, if a fresh "cirrhotic" liver is injected with a fine injection mass—carmine, say—the bands of fibrous tissue become deeply coloured.

The bile ducts are probably unaltered in number or size, though *relatively* their number appears to be greater.   In the logwood stained

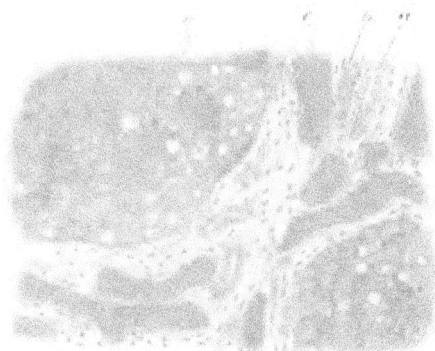

FIG. 36.—Section of common cirrhotic liver (after Thierfelder), (× 300 slightly reduced), in which are two masses of liver cells, between which is a band of fibrous tissue running in the portal space.

a.a. Small bile ducts lined by epithelial layer.
b.   Nuclei of connective tissue corpuscles.
c.   Newly formed blood-vessels, supplied by the smaller branches
        of the hepatic artery.
d.   Sections of intercolumnar or portal capillaries filled with blood.
e.   Globules of fat in the compressed and degenerating liver
        cells.

specimen they are seen, in longitudinal section, as double rows of nuclei; but in the picro-carmine stained specimen both nuclei and protoplasm of the epithelial cells lining the smaller ducts may be readily made out, especially when seen in transverse section.

The masses of cells, composed of groups of lobules, are at all points somewhat closely pressed together, the cells sometimes containing globules of fat.

At the periphery of the masses of lobules, thin bands of fibrous or

N

fibro-cellular tissue may be seen shaving off layer after layer of liver cells, the size of the masses being gradually cut down. The cells so cut off and compressed between the layers of fibrous tissue soon lose their nuclei, and become flattened and angular, the protoplasm of the cell becomes granular, and sometimes contains droplets of fat or pigment granules. Eventually these cells disappear. This cutting off of layers of cells is very characteristic of the polylobular form of cirrhosis.

To sum up: the change consists essentially in an increased growth of fibrous tissue in Glisson's capsule, and in the prolongations from

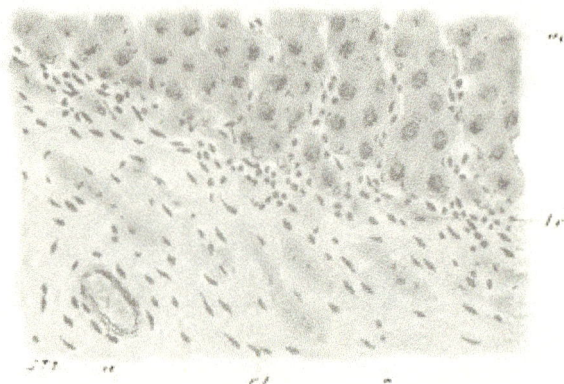

FIG. 37.—Section of common cirrhosis of the liver, stained with picro-carmine. (× 300.)

c.c. Columns of liver cells at the margin of a group of lobules. Between these columns young connective tissue is seen.

f.c. Liver cell infiltrated with fat.

l.c. Atrophied and flattened liver cells shaved off from the main body by the encroaching connective tissue, c.t.

a. Small branch of the hepatic artery.

it, which run along with the larger or medium sized branches of the portal vein. These branches of the portal vein become constricted by the surrounding growth of connective tissue, so that the larger branches of the portal system become dilated, as a result of which there may be great dropsical effusion. This continues, unless, or until, an anastomatic venous circulation is set up (1) through the veins in the suspensory ligament and around the obliterated umbilical vein,[1] or (2) through new or distended veins in the thickened capsule.

---

[1] Traité d'anatomie descriptive, par Ph. C. Sappey, p. 341.

The biliary passages are little affected, and jaundice very seldom makes its appearance during the course of this disease. The lobules are pressed together, and their outlines are lost. The liver cells undergo degenerative changes.

There is a less common form of alcoholic cirrhosis, in which the organ is greatly enlarged; the naked eye appearances are much like those met with in the following, or biliary, form; but we find that the distribution of the connective tissue is not so regular, the liver parenchyma is cut up into masses of very various sizes, and in the cells marked fatty degeneration and infiltration are met with. The splitting off of cells from the periphery of the masses points to the fact that here the disease advances rapidly and is similar to, but more advanced than, the common form. The biliary form of cirrhosis may sometimes be simulated, the connective tissue then running into the substance of the lobules, and new bile ducts being formed.

ACUTE INTERSTITIAL HEPATITIS.

If we examine a section of a cirrhotic liver, in the later stages only, it is difficult to understand the exact nature of the process, but if, at the same time, we can examine a section of a liver taken from a case of some such disease as small-pox, measles, scarlet fever, typhoid or other specific fever, in which a marked cellular infiltration occurs in the portal canals, and sometimes even along the course of the intercolumnar capillaries, we may often derive material assistance in the determination of the sequence of events. There is evidently advanced cloudy swelling of the parenchyma of the organ; in addition, it may be noted that in the portal spaces, in which there is undoubtedly an increase of blood, there are usually peculiar grey or red gelatinous-looking points which can only be understood on microscopical examination. Harden (§ 59) a piece of a liver from a case of one of the above diseases in which these appearances are presented; stain (§§ 103, 104).

(× 50).—Note the evidences of cloudy swelling (§ 177). In the medium-sized and smaller portal canals, and sometimes along the portal fissures may be seen a large number of deeply stained nuclei, evidently the result of emigration of leucocytes from the vessels, or of proliferation of the fixed connective tissue cells, or of both of these processes. These masses of cells (the grey gelatinous points above-mentioned) appear to be more intimately associated with the branches of the portal vein than with the other structures in the portal canals, and their distribution coincides almost exactly with

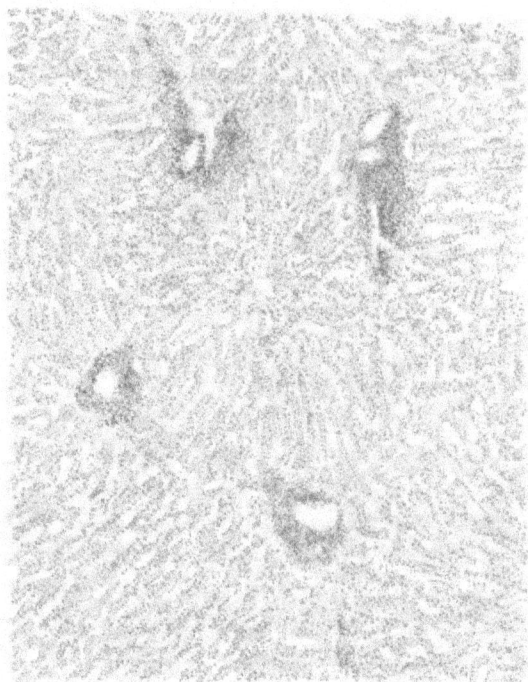

FIG. 38.—Early acute interstitial change in the liver of a patient who died from scarlet fever, stained with eosin and logwood. (× 50.)
    a. Small portal spaces in which the interstitial changes are well-marked—cell emigration and proliferation.
    b. Interlobular fissures in which similar new cellular tissue is seen.
    c. Hepatic vein.
    d. Liver cells, swollen and somewhat cloudy.

the distribution of the connective tissue seen in the commoner forms of cirrhosis.

(× 300).—Note the cloudy swelling of the liver cells, the distinct walls of the capillary vessels in the portal zone, and the increase in the number of leucocytes around the vessels in this area. In the portal spaces the emigrated and proliferated cells are well seen; the columnar epithelium of the bile ducts is slightly more granular than usual, but otherwise these marked inflammatory changes have affected

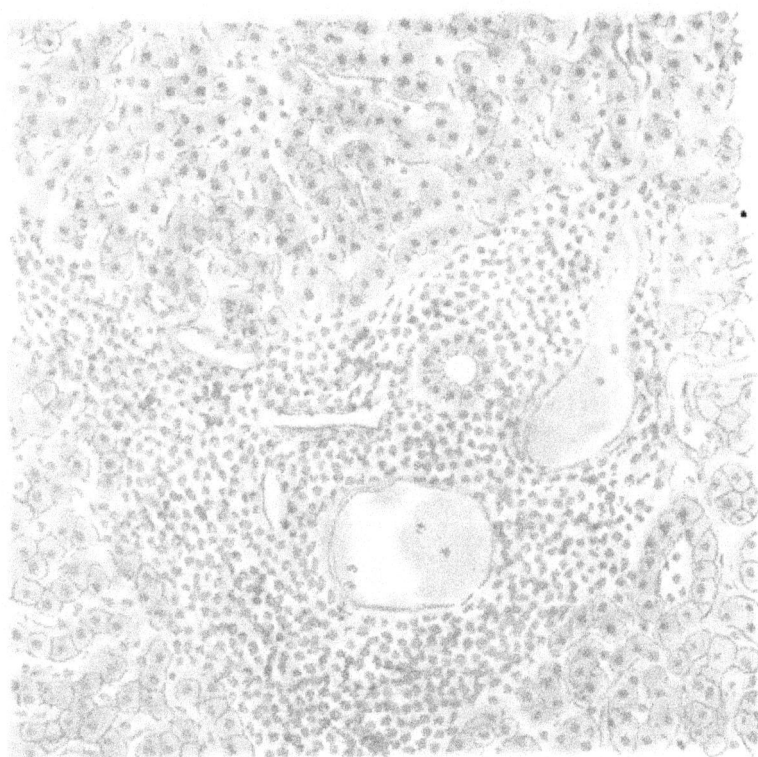

FIG. 39.—Early acute scarlatinal interstitial hepatitis. Stained with methyl green and fuchsin. (× 300.)

    a. Liver cells in a condition of cloudy swelling.
    b. Intercolumnar capillaries with distinct walls, and containing numerous leucocytes.
    c. New tissue in portal space, traces of fibrillated tissue to be seen.
    d. Small bile duct with well formed columnar epithelium.
    e. Branch of portal vein.
    f. Small branch of hepatic artery.

the bile duct in a relatively slight degree. The portal veins with their thin walls are evidently somewhat compressed by the large amount of new tissue surrounding them. From the commencing fibrillation of the protoplasm of the cells (the nuclei of which come out so prominently), it is evident that even here the process of connective tissue formation has already begun, and it must be assumed that many of the nuclei seen are those of proliferating connective tissue cells. If now we consider that this formation of fibrillated tissue had been allowed to advance still further, as it undoubtedly does in more chronic cases, we should be able to see that this acute inflammatory interstitial hepatitis, with its accompanying acute parenchymatous changes, may gradually pass into the cirrhotic form, in which the contraction of the fibrous bands, interfering with the vascular supply of the liver tissue, and also with its nutrition by actual pressure, may gradually give rise to the features that are so characteristic of common chronic cirrhosis. It should be noted, however, that there may be very similar appearances in the early stages of acute abscess formation in which the new cellular tissue, in place of going on to fibrous tissue formation, becomes degenerated, probably owing to the presence of pus forming microorganisms. The abscesses formed under these conditions differ very little, if at all, either in position or in structure, from the typhoid lesions to be afterwards described (§ 191). Bear in mind the above condition when considering the following.

"Biliary" Cirrhosis.

184. Synonyms, "Hypertrophic (?) Cirrhosis," "Monolobular Cirrhosis," "Hyperplastic Fibroid Degeneration."

Naked eye appearances.—The organ is, as a rule, increased in size, the surface is finely granular, feeling like a piece of morocco leather, and the substance of the liver is hard or even brittle. On section the liver tissue may be bile-stained in patches, of different hues (yellow to dark green), or may be pigmented or blood stained, the fibrous tissue remaining grey or greyish red. It is often extremely difficult to make out where the fibrous tissue ends and the liver substance begins, as the young fibrous tissue in this form passes round and encloses individual lobules. The portal veins may in some cases, though not usually, appear to be distended. Harden (§§ 58 and 59), stain (§§ 98 and 103).

(× 50).—The capsule is not necessarily thickened; but in the small portal or interlobular spaces and in the interlobular fissures there is marked increase in the amount of new cellular or fibro-cellular tissue. There is in fact an interlobular or monolobular cirrhosis.

In the newly formed tissue are a number of double rows of nuclei, which evidently belong to the epithelial cells of the small bile ducts. These bile ducts are apparently much increased in number, and where the disease is advanced they are seen running along with fibrous tissue into the substance of the lobule. This increase is not so great as at first sight appears, as even in the normal condition bile ducts run for some distance into the lobule, where, however, they are not readily distinguished. The fibrous bands, running at right angles to the periphery of the lobule, may encroach from all sides, and split up the lobule into small masses of cells, which gradually become atrophied, and finally, may disappear.

(× 300).—The connective tissue resembles that found in common cirrhosis, but appears to be formed in connection with the walls of the smaller bile ducts rather than around the branches of the portal vein. The larger branches of the bile ducts are also constricted by the growing and contracting tissue, in consequence of which there is increased pressure in, and slight distention of, the smaller branches. These small bile ducts are also apparently much more numerous at those points where the connective tissue is invading the lobule from its margin. Near the advancing portion of the newly formed bile ducts the liver cells appear to undergo atrophic changes, the nuclei divide, and the liver cells split and become flattened.

It may be well here to describe more minutely the structure of the bile ducts, commencing at the larger branches and passing backwards.

The largest bile ducts are lined by a layer of well formed columnar cells, external to which is a limiting membrane, or *membrana propria*, probably composed of endothelial cells; surrounding this again is a coat of non-striped muscular fibre. (See Figs. 20 and 39.) The lumen of one of these tubes is large, and after death its walls are thrown into folds by the contracting muscular fibre. The smaller bile duct has a comparatively thick wall and a small lumen; the epithelial cells are not so distinctly columnar, and there is now no muscular coat. At or in the margin of a lobule the small ducts are much branched; the epithelial cells form a single flattened layer, but there is still a distinct *membrana propria*. This, the intermediary portion of the duct, opens directly

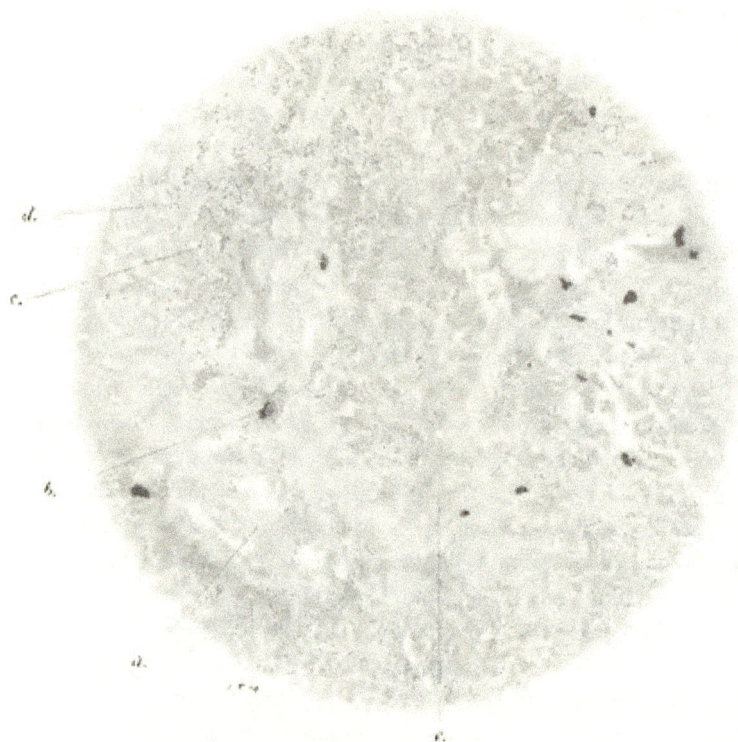

Fig. 40.—Section of Liver in which biliary cirrhosis had been developed. Stained with logwood. (× 50.)
  a. Mass of new fibrous tissue in which
  b. may be seen a bile duct filled with dark bile pigment.
  c. Smaller bile duct at the margin of a lobule, where there is a kind of transition stage between the liver cells and the epithelium of the bile ducts.
  d. Normal liver cells.
  e. Young cellular tissue where there is an increase of interstitial tissue.

and suddenly into the bile capillaries, which appear to consist simply of channels formed by the apposition of the grooved surfaces of several liver cells. Thus, a bile capillary is generally placed at the

angle between three or four liver cells, a groove or depression in
each cell forming its share of the capillary channel; still more
minute channels run in the substance of the liver cell. It is

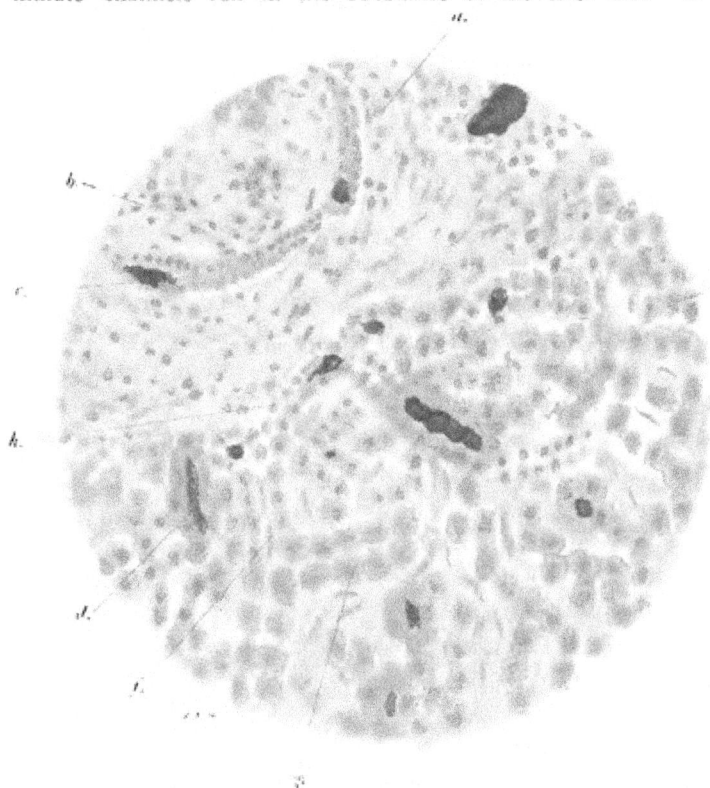

FIG. 41.—Section of Liver, in which biliary cirrhosis has been
developed. Stained with logwood. (× 300.)
  a. New fibrous tissue.
  b. Imperfectly developed new bile duct in new tissue.
  c. Well formed bile duct, previously existing, containing pigment
     or inspissated bile.
  d. Column of liver cells, now converted into a channel containing
     altered bile.
  e. Normal or slightly cloudy liver cells.
  f. Modified liver cells, intermediary portion of bile duct between
     ordinary liver cells (g.) and bile duct proper (h.).

much easier to understand the mode of formation of the new bile
ducts if the structure of these normal bile ducts is thoroughly
grasped, and if we assume that they are in the centre of the lobule,

and not at its periphery as usually described. In the coarse new connective tissue, as it penetrates the periphery of the lobule, the liver cells are divided and flattened, and, quite close to, and continuous with, the columns are the small bile ducts running for some distance into the lobule, so that it may be safely concluded that the new bile ducts are formed from the splitting up of these liver cells—a process of division of the nucleus and then of the cell,—followed by further subdivisions,—until in place of the three or four cells surrounding the bile capillary, there are numerous small flattened cells resembling those around the smaller bile ducts ; the process consists, in fact, of a reversion of the liver cell to its embryonic or epithelial type.

The condition is due in all probability to an inflammatory change set up around the branches of the bile duct, either by some chemical irritation, or by irritation caused by obstruction to the outflow of the bile from the ducts.

In certain cases monolobular cirrhosis may be set up by a periphlebitis; but this form is much less common, and appears to be unaccompanied by any new formation of bile ducts.

From the above short descriptions of some of the forms of interstitial hepatitis it will be evident that they are due to the action of some irritant matter conveyed by the blood vessels or contained in the bile ducts. In the common alcoholic form it would appear that the irritant is carried along the portal vein, the characteristic changes taking place along the course of the medium-sized branches ; in other cases, however, the irritant may be conveyed, not through the portal system specially, but from the systemic arterial circulation, in which case the new tissue is developed around the finer branches of the hepatic artery; we then have a much finer cirrhosis than in the previous case. Lastly, the new growth may be due to irritation of the tissue along the course of the bile ducts—obstruction, catarrhal inflammation, and perverted excretion by these channels apparently preceding this form. It is found that between these three forms there may be various intermediate stages or combinations. It has also been observed that the parenchymatous tissue is affected both primarily and secondarily, so that during the earlier stages we may have all the characteristic signs of an acute inflammatory process in the liver cells before the interstitial changes become well marked; whilst in the later stages, owing to the interference of the connective tissue with the vascular supply, or with bile excretion, further degenerative or atrophic processes may supervene.

It is usually assumed that it is possible to draw a sharp line of demarcation between these various forms, and that definite atrophic or hypertrophic conditions of the liver are invariably met with. It must be borne in mind, however, that the hypertrophic form is simply the result of a widely diffused increase of connective tissue, where the amount formed is more than sufficient to make up for the atrophic and degenerative changes that take place in the liver cells, *i.e.*, although there is a large increase of connective tissue, this does not affect the nutrition of the liver cells so profoundly as to induce their degeneration, death, and removal more rapidly than the connective tissue is formed. In the atrophic forms which are usually more chronic, the connective tissue is usually not so widely diffused, but it interferes so seriously with the nutrition of the glandular cells of the liver, that they atrophy more rapidly and in greater proportion than the new connective tissue is formed; of course the more acute and the more widely diffused the interstitial process the greater apparent hypertrophy there will be, whilst the more chronic and the greater the interference with the nutrition of the liver cells the more marked will the atrophy appear.

It will thus be seen that, although it is not possible to distinguish sharply or to give any clinical signs and symptoms by which it is possible to differentiate absolutely between the above forms of cirrhosis, it is nevertheless true, generally, that where the branches of the portal veins are specially involved, we shall probably find dropsy and the associated conditions, and that where the bile ducts are affected, jaundice may be looked for. The following list of comparative differences, then, must be accepted as having only a general application. It may, however, prove useful in drawing attention to the different forms, it being distinctly borne in mind that there are hypertrophic forms of cirrhosis in which the branches of the hepatic artery, rather than the bile ducts, appear to be the structures around which the interstitial changes are specially localised.

In Common Cirrhosis.

1. The bile ducts appear to be but little involved in the growth of connective tissue, there is little or no jaundice or bile-staining of the liver tissues, and few new bile ducts are found on microscopic examination.

2. In consequence of the new growth of tissue taking place along the course of the portal veins, especially the medium sized branches, ascites is a very common complication, as are also hæmorrhoids, varicose conditions of the veins of the œsophagus, congestion, or even hæmorrhage in the gastro-intestinal tract.

3. In the early stages, in consequence of the increased amount of young connective tissue in the portal spaces, there may be considerable enlargement of the organ ; but in the later stages, where this tissue is becoming fibrous but cicatricial and contracting, there is, as a rule, a considerable diminution in the size of the liver.

4. The liver is rough, with projections about the size of a hobnail on its surface. The capsule is thickened and opaque, especially at the bottom of the fossæ which surround these projections.

5. The masses of liver cells vary very much in size, some consisting of several lobules, whilst others are smaller than a single lobule. Each of these masses forms a distinct area with a rounded outline and surrounded by a fibrous zone.

6. On microscopic examination, it is seen that the process is going on chiefly at the periphery of groups of lobules, masses of liver cells being " shaved " off by the invading fibrous tissue.

In Biliary Cirrhosis.

1. The structures round the bile ducts are those first involved, the jaundice and bile-staining of the liver substance are, as a rule, well marked, and there is a new formation of bile ducts.

2. The portal veins are not so frequently involved, and ascites, hæmorrhoids, etc., are rare.

3. In consequence of the large amount of new tissue diffused throughout the organ, it is considerably increased in size, the increase of new tissue being greater than the atrophy of the parenchyma of the liver.

4. The surface of the organ is smooth (morocco leather feeling), and the capsule is not so markedly thickened.

5. The masses of liver cells consist of single lobules, which are, however, considerably diminished in size, and the cut surface has a more or less uniform or finely granulated appearance.

6. The single lobules above mentioned are surrounded by bands of fibrous tissue, which bands, however, are not confined to the periphery, but "invade the substance of the lobules."

SYPHILITIC CIRRHOSIS (CONGENITAL) OF THE LIVER.

185. This condition is met with in children who come into the world still-born, or who die shortly after birth, with all the marks of syphilis upon them, but also in children in whom the symptoms of syphilis may be almost absent. In well marked cases the liver, *on naked eye examination,* is found to be enlarged; on its surface there are frequently purplish nodular projections; the tissue is firm, tough, and pale, the pallor being more marked at certain points which

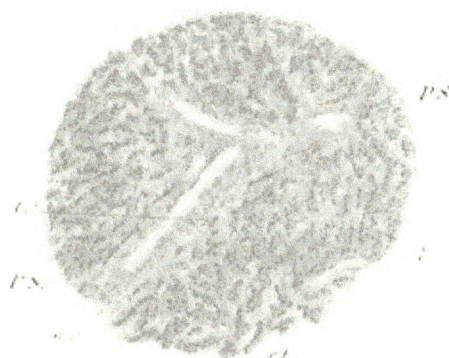

FIG. 42.—Drawing from a section of syphilitic cirrhotic liver, stained with carmine and methylaniline violet. (× 50.)

 P.S. Increase of fibrous tissue in portal spaces. This increase of fibrous tissue is seen to extend from the space for some considerable distance into the lobules, the columns of liver cells (*l.c.*) are more atrophied at the margin than at the centre of the lobule (*l.c¹*).

 c.t. Nucleated fibrillated tissue between the atrophied liver cells.

are pearly white, surrounded by a yellow and then by a more vascular zone. These pale areas are about half an inch in diameter, and in them the largest amount of new connective tissue is found. If the disease be very far advanced, the lobules are almost entirely obliterated, and no definite structure remains, the parenchyma appears yellow, mottled with reddish or greyish brown, and delicate looking striæ run irregularly through it. It is to be remembered, however, that to the naked eye the structure of the liver may appear to be little altered, even when grave microscopic changes are present; then the only gross evidences of a diseased condition are the increased weight and firmness of the organ. Harden (§§ **57** and **58**). To stain sections satisfactorily, add one part ammoniacal carmine solution, and a similar quantity of methylaniline violet, to 24 parts of water. Allow the sections to stand in this solution for several hours, wash thoroughly in water, and mount (§ **152**).

(× 50).—Near the portal spaces, in which is an increase in the amount of fibrous tissue, there may be seen, apparently continuous with the perilobular tissue, a quantity of clear looking material with numerous rounded nuclei. Between the clear bands are small linear or Y-shaped masses stained deep purple; these are separated from

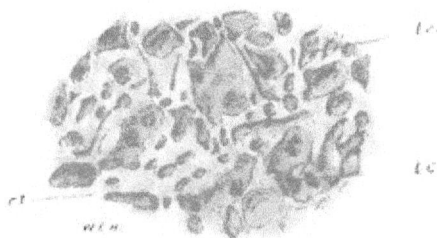

FIG. 43.—Drawing from a section of syphilitic cirrhotic liver. Stained with carmine and methylaniline violet. (× 440.)
l.c. Small masses of granular and somewhat atrophied liver cells, between which is the increased amount of nucleated and fibrillated connective tissue (*c.t.*).

one another by spaces, two or three, or even more, times the diameter of the deeply stained masses, which are always smaller where the clear spaces are wider. Further away from the portal spaces the tissue becomes more and more like that seen in a normal liver, until at certain points the structure is almost normal.

(× 300).—The deeply stained masses are now seen to be rows of liver cells undergoing more or less marked changes. Where the rows of liver cells are comparatively broad, the structure of the cell is as yet little altered; there is simply a slight compression of the cell. Where the rows are narrow, there are more extensive changes in the cells; they are angular, shrunken, and granular looking, and are evidently undergoing atrophic degeneration; the nuclei are obscured, or in certain cases are altogether lost. The substance between these bands of atrophied liver cells consists of a nucleated connective tissue. Around the connective tissue cells, and apparently formed by them, is a delicate fibrillated periplast, of which the transparent tissue seen under the low power is composed. The enlargement of the organ is due to the great increase in the amount of intralobular connective tissue. In order to understand the nature of this change, it must be remembered that, communicating with the interlobular lymphatics at the margins of the lobules are "minute spaces extending between the liver cells and the capillary blood-vessels, and containing numerous branched connective tissue corpuscles." The capillary vessels are lined by a layer of endothelial cells, which, like the connective tissue corpuscles, are of mesoblastic origin. This form of cirrhosis consists essentially in a proliferation (*a*) of the endothelial lining of the capillary vessel (endarteritis obliterans), and (*b*) of the connective tissue corpuscles or endothelial cells, which may be said to line the lymph spaces between the capillaries and the liver cells. Around these proliferated cells a fibrillated periplast is formed; then follow the gradual compression and atrophy of the proper parenchyma of the organ, giving rise to a continually increasing interval between the columns of liver cells, which are thus cut up into short, detached, granular, angular, or linear masses; the vascular supply is greatly altered.

Syphilitic Gumma of the Liver.

186. The syphilitic gumma, closely related to the above form of cirrhosis, is usually seen in the caseous stage; but it is to be remembered that here caseation is merely a degenerative process taking place in the gumma. In the livers of adults this syphilitic lesion is usually met with in the caseous form only. To find a gumma in process of growth it is necessary to examine the liver of a syphilitic child, in which they are frequently found in connection with the syphilitic form of cirrhosis. Such a growing gumma is a tumour, varying in size (from the size of a pea to that of a marble, or even larger), of a rosy-grey colour when seen on section, and *containing vessels*: it gradually merges into the surrounding tissues with which it is intimately connected. This surrounding tissue is made up of very vascular fibro-cellular bands.   On the surface of the liver are irregular patches, deep red in colour (redder than the rest of the liver substance).

The caseous gumma is usually met with in the adult, situated near the surface of the liver, enveloped in a fibrous capsule, which sends out long radiating processes into the surrounding liver substance.   It occurs on the upper surface of the organ, and is most frequently found near the suspensory ligament.   In consequence of the contraction of the fibrous capsule surrounding the mass, there is a distinct depression at the periphery; and the caseous nodules appear to be contained within fibrous cicatrices situated near the surface of the liver.   The liver tissue is usually brown or bile stained, and is evidently undergoing atrophic changes.   Harden (§§ 57 and 58); stain (§§ 77, 98, 103, and 185).

(× 50).—On examining a section of a nodule taken from the liver of a syphilitic child, it is seen that the growth is situated in newly formed intralobular fibrous tissue; in other words that the formation of a gumma is preceded by a syphilitic cirrhosis identical with that already described; at certain points the development of fibrous tissue has taken place to such an extent that there are numbers of strongly marked fibrous bands intersecting the lobules and cutting up the liver tissue.   These fibrous bands are highly vascular, vessels in all stages of development being seen in their substance.   In the fibrous band and around the vessels the first trace of the developing gumma appears in the form of a number of deeply stained embryonic cells, forming a ring which gradually increases in diameter; as this extends peripherally, the cells near the centre become angular, granular, atrophied, and (stained with picro-carmine) yellow.

In this stage the gumma is an actively growing mass of connective tissue, for it may be observed that around the embryonic cells at the periphery is a delicate fibrillated stroma.   Whilst the growth is going on in the gumma, certain changes are also to be observed in the vessels in the immediate neighbourhood.   If one can be examined in transverse section, it will at once be seen that its walls are thickened, and that the increase in thickness takes place principally in the "intima," or within the internal elastic lamina (which in the picro-carmine stained specimen is bright yellow). In some cases this thickening of the "intima" is so great that the lumen of the vessel is almost obliterated ; and it is to be noted that even where the obliteration is not complete there is frequently a coagulum fixed in the lumen, which might prevent the passage of blood through the vessel.

(× 300).—(1.) The granular shrivelled cells in the centre of the mass are readily made out ; they are small in size, are closely packed together, and are frequently stained yellow, even before caseation has actually set in. (2.) Surrounding these central atrophied cells is a zone of larger embryonic cells, or of endothelioid cells very similar to those met with in tubercle ; they are of various shapes and sizes, and many of them contain several nuclei. (3.) Between these endothelioid cells, or surrounding them, is a fibrillar periplast. (4.) External to this zone are numerous small round cells (leucocytes) or nuclei, which, as in the case of the nuclei of the endothelioid cells, take on the carmine or logwood stain very readily. In the vessel, with the outer wall of which the gummatous growth is practically continuous, the endothelial cells of the "intima" have undergone enormous proliferation, and the flattened cells are so arranged layer upon layer, that they may almost block the lumen of the vessel. Within the narrowed tube a coagulum of fibrin is frequently found, with a few white blood corpuscles at the periphery of the clot, adhering to the wall. It is highly probable that the caseation which almost invariably ensues in gummata is brought about (1.) by the specific action of the syphilitic poison on the tissue elements ; (2.) by the contraction of the tissue at the periphery of the gumma itself and of the fibrous tissue surrounding it ; (3.) by the *endarteritis obliterans* (*see* § 214) causing the stoppage of the vessel either alone or (4.) in conjunction with a coagulum which forms on its roughened and inflamed walls. The change in the artery may take place at some point outside the gumma, but so long as the blood supply to the gumma is cut off the effect is the same—fatty degeneration of the tissues, followed, first, by caseation, and later, by absorption and cicatrisation. The section of the gumma is then hard and firm, and cuts almost like gritty india-rubber.

Where caseation has taken place, as in the gummata found in the adult, harden (§ 57 or 59) and stain (§§ 98, 106, and 110).

o

(× 50).—The centre of the mass is seen to be stained yellow, the caseous material taking on the picric acid stain, but not any carmine. Around the caseous portion is a distinctly fibrous zone, by

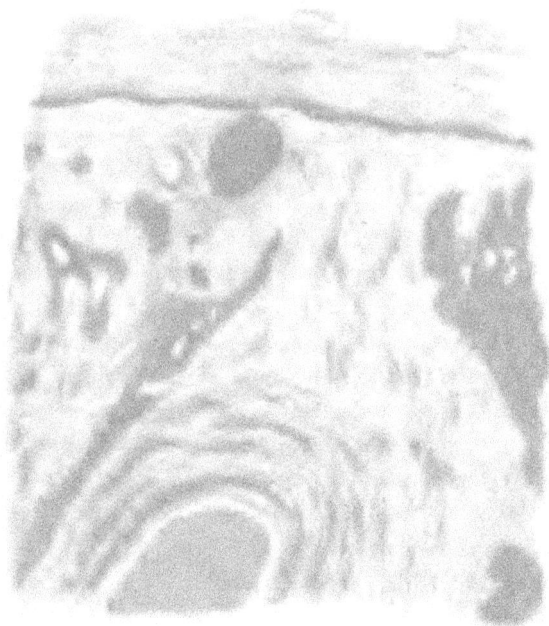

FIG. 44.—Drawing from a section of liver with hepatitis gummosa. Stained with picro-carmine. (× 20.)

C. V. Thickened capsule, pink and fibrous in appearance.
a.a. Arteries becoming obliterated by thickening of both internal and external coats.
f.t. Continuation of the fibrous tissue from the capsule into the substance of the liver, in which are numerous sections of embryonic vessels (v.e.).
l.c. Small patches of liver tissue left between the bands of fibrous tissue.
C.G. Fibrous external zone ; and Cas. g., caseating central zone of softening gumma just below the capsule.

the contraction of which the indentation of the capsule of the liver at the outer margin of the growth is brought about. The fibrous capsule gradually shades off and sends out long radiating processes into the surrounding cirrhotic tissue, between the bands of which may be seen the Y-shaped trabeculæ of atrophied liver cells. The "adventitia" of the vessels in the neighbourhood is considerably thickened, whilst the proliferation of the endothelium lining the vessel is also well marked.

(× 300).—The caseous yellow mass is made up of shrivelled granular *débris*, into which run bands of fibrous tissue, apparently continued from the capsule of the gumma. Crystals of cholesterine and of stearic acid are met with, as well as fat granules, or even globules—readily recognised with the aid of osmic acid staining. In the fibrous capsule are a number of lymph spaces which contain blackened globules, these being, in all probability, carried from the caseous mass. In this way the gumma may be gradually absorbed, the surrounding fibrous tissue being exceedingly vascular. Under this power the changes already described as seen in the neighbouring vessels may be again noted, as may also those described as being identical with the changes in syphilitic cirrhosis.

The middle coat may undergo the lardaceous or waxy degenerative change, so common a result of syphilis in its various forms.

It is difficult to look upon the whole process as anything more than a caseation of parts or areas of newly formed fibrous tissue, brought about by the action of the specific poison, and by the cutting off of the blood supply as a result of *endarteritis obliterans*, as pointed out by Friedländer, Heubner, and Greenfield.

SYPHILITIC CICATRICES.

187. Syphilitic cicatrices appear to be the result of the two previous lesions. The liver may be cut up into a series of small masses by bands of fibrous tissue. These bands run in from the thickened Glisson's capsule, the thickening being due to perihepatitis, or inflammation of the capsule, as a result of which the liver is often found to be firmly adherent to the diaphragm. If a section be made through one of these fibrous bands, numbers of small gummata may be found scattered through it. Harden (§ 58 or 57) and stain (§ 98).

(× 20).—The cirrhosis is seen to begin at the surface—in the capsule—from which bands of pink fibrous tissue run irregularly through the organ. Between these fibrous bands, especially near the margins of the mass of fibrous tissue, are the thin rows of atrophied liver cells similar to those seen around gummata, and in the syphilitic cirrhotic liver. All this should be verified (× 300).

ACUTE YELLOW ATROPHY.

188. In the stage at which, in acute yellow atrophy, the organ comes under examination, the liver is usually considerably atrophied; the capsule is markedly wrinkled, and may be caught up between the fingers. The organ is soft and flabby, in some cases almost of fluid consistence; the surface is mottled, yellow ochre with dark red patches. On section the colour and appearances are much the same, and as a rule, all traces of the individual lobules are lost, though there may be some in which the centre is red, the outer zones being yellow or greyish yellow. Under the capsule, in addition to the larger red or brownish-red patches, irregular in outline, varying in size, often appearing almost like infarcts or blood clots, are small punctiform hæmorrhages similar to those found on other serous surfaces in this condition.

On examining scrapings from the cut section (× 300) a number of liver cells in various stages of degeneration and atrophy are observed. They are almost invariably bile-stained and extremely granular; the nucleus is obscured, and in the protoplasmic substance are found numerous small granules of pigment. Along with these cells are a number of red and white blood corpuscles, and often crystals of leucin, tyrosin, and xanthin. (These may be seen in the blood and urine of the patient during life, where their presence appears to be due to the fact that the perfect oxidation of the proteid substances does not take place, these substances being formed as incomplete oxidation products.)

Harden (§ 56), stain (§ 100), and mount (§ 152).

(× 80).—In the portal spaces, especially around the vein, a number of round cells can be seen as pink nuclei. This is evidence of an interstitial inflammation taking the form of an interlobular exudation. From the interlobular spaces and fissures, however, the process extends into the lobule between the columns of liver cells.

The liver cells are shrunken and angular, are stained bright yellow, and appear to be very irregularly arranged ; very frequently they have

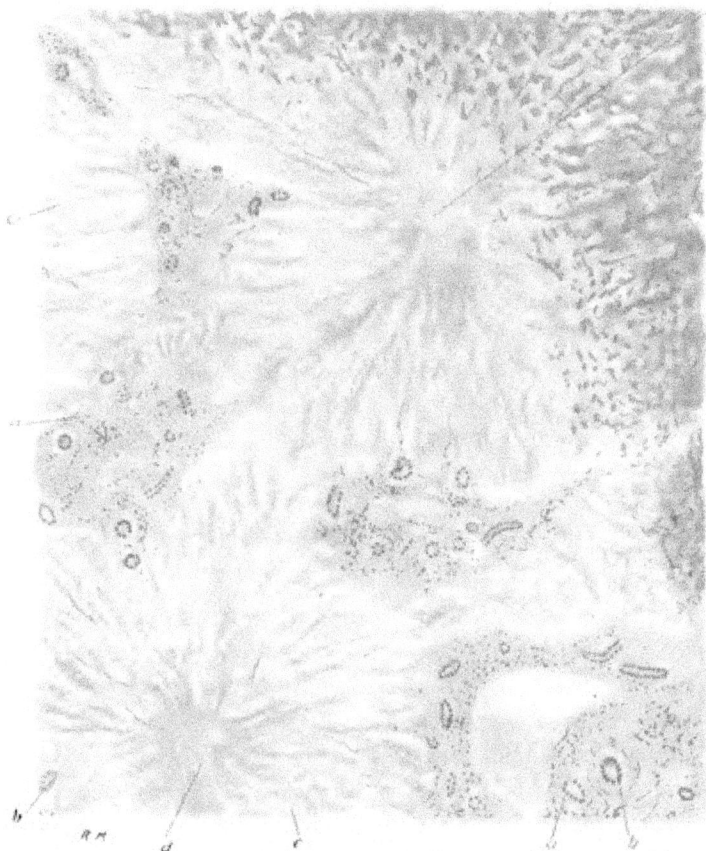

FIG. 45.—Acute yellow atrophy of the liver, section stained with picro-carmine. (× 80.)

    a.a. Interlobular spaces in which is a considerable amount of small-celled infiltration and some œdematous swelling of the connective tissue fibrils. In this the bile ducts (*b.*) appear to be increased in number.

    c. Portal capillaries containing much blood, a few round cells between, but the liver cells have almost disappeared.

    d. Hepatic venule surrounded by swollen fibrillar tissue. A few nuclei of small round cells should also be seen (not brought out in drawing).

    l.c. Liver cells, many of them atrophied and shrivelled, especially at the margin of the mass, between the red and the yellow areas.

disappeared from the centre of a lobule or from several lobules. In the hæmorrhagic patches the tissue may be quite disorganised.

(× 300).—In the newly formed tissue, made up of leucocytes and young connective tissue cells, a number of small bile ducts may be recognised as elongated double rows of nuclei ; some of these are pre-existing bile ducts, enlarged, whilst others appear to be of entirely new formation. The liver cells are shrunken and the protoplasm is atrophied, so that the outlines are irregular ; they are of a yellow colour, even when they contain no brown pigment. Many of these, however, contain much granular pigment, as noted in the examination of the scrapings. In a fresh section, in addition to the above appearances, the crystals of leucin and tyrosin are readily distinguishable. In the early stages of the disease micrococci of considerable size have been demonstrated[1] lying "in the portal canals, filling the arteries, and in the peripheric part of the lobule between the liver cells, filling up apparently the capillaries between them."—(Dreschfeld.)

TUBERCLE OF THE LIVER.

189. The liver is one of the best organs in the body in which to study the structure and development of tubercle ; the growth being uncomplicated by catarrhal changes, such as occur in the lung, the formation of any fibrous tissue can be more easily followed.

Tubercular nodules in the liver are first seen as small grey or caseous granulations, either in the capsule itself, or near the surface of the organ. It is only in the very earliest stages that these tubercle masses are grey ; when the growth has become fully developed, it is no longer vascular, and rapidly becomes caseous, and bile-stained. Harden a section of the liver with one of these small grey granulations (§ 56), stain (§ 98), and mount (§ 152).

(× 50).—In an interlobular space, or just at the margin of a lobule, may be seen a granular looking mass pushing aside the liver cells, and apparently gradually infiltrating the surrounding tissues. This mass, the tubercle follicle, is usually pink in colour, but towards

---

[1] A case of Acute Atrophy of Liver.—*Lancet*, April 5, 1884.

the centre is a bright orange ring, about the size of a small pin's head, which surrounds a light canary yellow centre—a giant cell.

(× 300).—The elements of which the tubercle follicle is composed

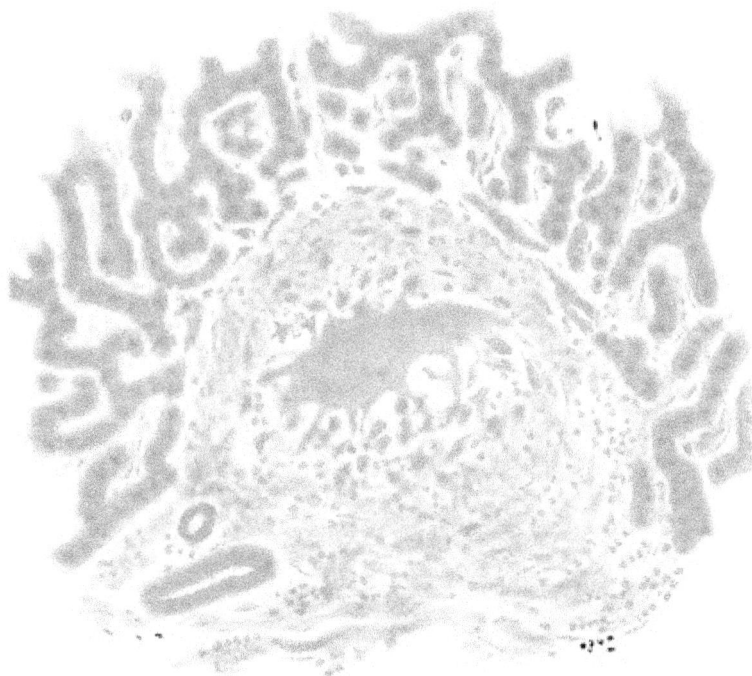

FIG. 46.—Drawing from section of tubercle of the liver. Stained with picro-carmine. (× 300.)

g. Giant cell, with nuclei at the periphery, and sending off branching processes.

e.c. Endothelioid cells, lying on fibrillæ of the network of connective tissue, with which the branching processes of the giant cell appear to anastomose.

r.c. Round cells, young connective tissue corpuscles, and leucocytes appearing towards the periphery of the mass.

f.t. Fibrous tissue, forming a kind of capsule to the tubercle. In this capsule are a number of rounded nuclei.

l.c. Columns of liver cells, those near the tubercle somewhat flattened and atrophied ; between them are rounded nuclei, &c., extending from the growing tubercle mass.

b.d. Small bile duct. *a.* Branch of hepatic artery.

are now well seen. (1.) At the periphery of the growth, and spreading in between the liver cells, which are pushed aside and gradually atrophy, are numerous small round cells ; these take on the pink staining, and appear to be little more than young connective tissue nuclei with some leucocytes. (2.) Nearer the centre, or rather running amongst the inner layers of these small cells, is a felted mass of fibrous tissue, stained pink ; in some cases, especially where the nodule is still young, there is very little of this fibrous tissue. (3.) As the centre is neared, the tissue opens out into a kind of network, in the meshes of which are found a number of larger cells of various shapes. Many of them contain two, three, or even more nuclei. (4.) These appear to be endothelioid cells, such as are found lying on all bundles of connective tissue, especially where growth is rapid. (5.) The centre of the tubercle is occupied by the giant cell which is seen as a large branching cell, from the periphery of which processes run to join the fibrous reticulum ; in the liver these processes can often be very distinctly seen. (6.) At the periphery of the giant cell are numerous rounded, deeply-stained nuclei, each about the size of one of the small cells found at the periphery of the tubercle, but they appear to be somewhat more deeply stained. They form a distinct belt or zone around the cell, as a single or double row, and they bound the bright canary yellow area already spoken of, which occupies the body of the cell, and is, as a rule, perfectly homogeneous and translucent. In this there may be one or more clear spaces or vacuoles.

The tubercle follicles (giant cell systems, as they are called), are developed in the interlobular or portal spaces. Around the primary follicle numerous other follicles may be formed ; these being non-vascular cut off the supply of nutriment from the central part, which rapidly undergoes death and caseation. The small bile ducts are involved in the caseous mass, into which bile is poured, and it is found that tubercle in the liver, except in the very earliest stages, is invariably of a greenish yellow colour (all dead matter in the liver becoming bile-stained).

These tuberculous areas may gradually enlarge until they form yellowish green masses of considerable size, the centre of which caseates and softens, forming large cysts with fibrous or gelatinous-looking walls. In the gelatinous-looking wall are found numerous tubercle follicles. Contained within the fibrous capsule is a green, soft putty-like mass, composed of granular *débris*, fatty globules, and angular shrivelled and atrophied cells. Sometimes the caseous material is replaced by a clear watery fluid—bile from which the bile acids, pigments, and salts have been absorbed. The dense lymphatic system around the bile ducts may account for the special affection of these ducts by tubercle.

In one form of tubercle the larger bile ducts are specially affected. If the wall of the bile duct be examined in such a case, tubercle follicles are found in the submucous layer; these rapidly caseate and ulceration ensues as the blood supply to the epithelium is cut off by the non-vascular tubercular growth beneath. The process extends along the lymphatics, but it also spreads by direct infection, by application of the specific material to the opposite wall of the duct or to the surface at some distance. This form of tubercle should be studied along with tubercular ulcer of the intestine and tubercular pyelonephritis, both of which, in many respects, it closely resembles. Very frequently other conditions are found associated with tubercle of the liver, such as cirrhosis—which is especially met with in the livers of tuberculous children—waxy changes in the vessels, fatty infiltration or degeneration with atrophy and shrivelling of the liver cells; in examining a tubercular liver these complications should be borne in mind, and such changes carefully searched for and noted.

A peculiar lymphoid growth similar to the above, differing, apparently, only in the fact that it contains no giant cells, is also sometimes met with in the liver. Harden (§ 56), stain (§ 98).

(× 50).—The granular pink-stained mass is seen lying in the interlobular spaces, but no orange ring can be made out in the centre. The liver capillaries appear to be relatively much enlarged, whilst the rows of liver cells are thinned and appear irregular. In an unstained specimen, small, bright, strongly refractile bodies (globules of fat) are observed in the liver cells; these in a specimen stained with osmic acid (§ 110) are blackened.

(× 300).—The granular pink mass is seen to be composed of rounded cells which, at the periphery are small, but nearer the centre are larger, multinucleated, and often irregular in shape. Running through the mass are strands of delicate pink-stained fibrous or reticular tissue, on which larger cells appear to be lying. The liver cells are distinctly atrophied and angular, their nuclei are obscured, and the protoplasm of the cell appears to be converted into fatty globules, which are seen as highly refractile or blackened bodies, according as they are examined unstained or stained with picro-carmine or osmic acid. In some of the cells there is an appearance of vacuolation, which is probably due to the presence of these fat globules. This condition is met with where there are similar changes in the lymphatic glands, changes in which the naked eye appearances are like those presented in tubercle.

Lymphadenoma of the Liver.

(*Hodgkin's Disease.*)

190. In Hodgkin's disease the organ is enlarged, smooth, and pale (Goodhart, in "New Sydenham Society Atlas"); in it growths usually occur as small, pale pink or grey nodules, which are seen specially affecting the portal canal, spreading thence into the lobules. They may be numerous or few in number. Sometimes the masses are larger, when they assume a "greyish yellow colour," and are tough, but in some cases they are undergoing caseation and softening. Each of these masses, varying in size from a pin's head to a sixpence, is surrounded by a zone of reddened tissue, which appears to be made up of dilated venous capillaries. There is a different form, or a more advanced stage, where grey streaks appear not only on the surface under the capsule but also on the surface of a section. This condition of the liver is almost invariably associated with a similar condition of other organs—spleen, kidney, &c. &c., with induration and enlargement of the lymphatic glands, first those of the neck, then those of the axilla, and so on throughout the body. Harden (§ 59), cut (§ 82 *et seq.*), stain (§ 98). The appearances presented are very similar to those described under the heading of lymphoid growth. The growth begins in the portal spaces, and gradually extends into the substance of the lobule running from the periphery towards the centre, apparently along the walls of the capillaries, the endothelial cells of which become increased in size, and are often multinucleated; it consists of a network of fibrous tissue packed with leucocytes, small connective tissue, or lymphoid cells and endothelial plates; at the margin of the growth the liver cells are atrophied.

LEUCOCYTHEMIA OF THE LIVER.

191. The liver is usually enlarged, in some cases markedly so, and is firm and fleshy to the touch; the surface is smooth and pale. Small subserous hæmorrhages are often seen, but these are lighter red than usual. On section, we have the same pale smooth surface; between the lobules, in the interlobular fissures and spaces, the pallor is more distinctly marked, and we have a network or "irregular

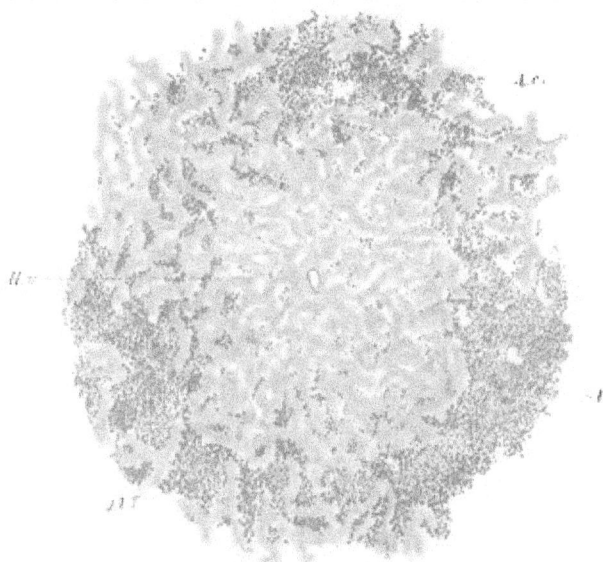

FIG. 47.—Section of leucocythemic liver stained with logwood. (× 70.)
H.v. Central or Hepatic vein.
l.   Leucocytes, especially numerous at the periphery of the lobule.
l.c.   Rows of liver cells between the capillary vessels.

veining of pearly white colour," the tissue enclosed in the meshes of which is more or less fatty or anæmic looking; the margin of the lobule appears to project beyond the general surface of the section.

Harden (§ 57 or 59), and stain (§ 103).

(× 50).—In the interlobular spaces and fissures there are enormous collections of deeply stained nuclei (leucocytes), by which the lobules are very distinctly outlined. Masses of these leucocytes are also seen between the liver cells in the peripheral zone of the lobule, in the spaces and tissues surrounding the vessels, and the intercolumnar capillaries themselves are crowded with them. In advanced cases the whole lobule may be infiltrated, and small hæmorrhagic masses, in which are large numbers of leucocytes, are scattered at irregular intervals throughout the liver substance, but especially under the capsule.

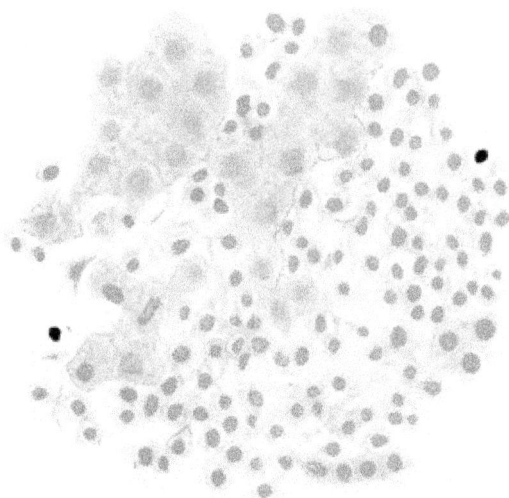

FIG. 48.—Section of leucocythemic liver, taken from the periphery of a lobule. Stained with logwood. (× 600.)
l.c. Liver cells, with intranuclear and intracellular plexus.
f. Strands of fibrin or displaced connective tissue fibrils between (*l.*) leucocytes and (*c.t.*) connective tissue corpuscles.
e.c. Large round cells with two nuclei.

(× 450).—The infiltration around the vessels is readily observed; the capillaries are crowded, both inside and out, with the deeply stained cells, so that in many places the liver cells appear to be atrophied, and even destroyed, by the pressure of the leucocytes, though otherwise they may remain unchanged.

These small cells, when carefully examined, are in all respects like the so-called wandering cells or leucocytes, and are surrounded by no stroma of any kind, though a few delicate threads of *coagulated fibrin* may sometimes be seen lying in the normal connective tissue spaces of the part; in this respect leucocythemia differs very markedly from lymphadenoma, in which condition a distinct stroma or network of *fibrous tissue*, containing small round, and larger endothelioid, cells is seen.

In many cases of leucocythemia, pigmentation of the liver cells in the peripheral half of the lobule is a characteristic feature. A similar condition has been observed in the liver in pernicious anæmia.

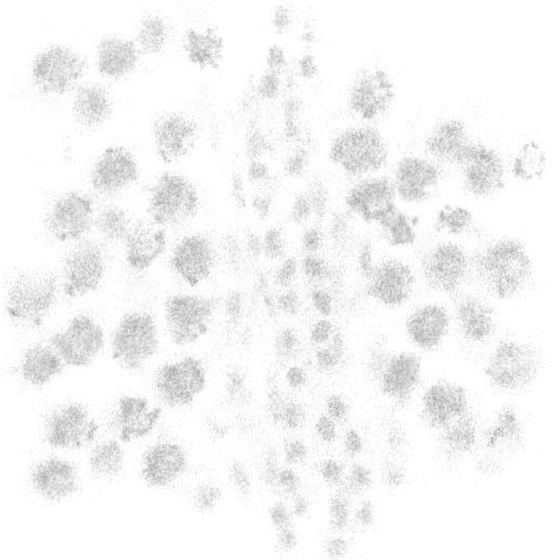

FIG. 49.—Section of liver from a case of leucocythemia. Stained with alum carmine. (× 350.)

　　a. Nucleus of liver cell, deeply stained, and standing out prominently.
　　b. Golden brown pigment accumulated round the active nucleus. There is no marked degenerative change in the cell.
　　c. Nuclei of cells of bile duct. This marks the position of the portal canal, so that the liver cells seen are in the portal or peripheral zone.
　　d. Connective tissue of portal space.

The pigment differs somewhat from that met with in chronic venous congestion. It is essentially an iron pigment, for when a section is soaked in a weak solution of ferrocyanide of iron for a few minutes, and then washed in water, to which a few drops of hydrochloric acid has been added, the yellow or golden brown colour is replaced by a beautiful transparent blue.

Typhoid Lesion.

192. There is a condition of the liver induced in typhoid fever of long-continued standing and of severe type, which is, however, probably common to this and other diseases. It appears to be a peculiar inflammatory change due to the impaction of some bacterial thrombus in the capillaries of the intermediate zone of a lobule. In addition to the general cloudy swelling of the liver cells, common in febrile conditions, we find scattered throughout the substance of the liver a number of small yellow or grey specks, each about the size of a pin's head, situated in the above-mentioned position, or in some cases involving the whole of the lobule. Harden (§ 56), stain (§ 98), and mount (§ 152).

(× 50).—Note that parts of some of the lobules are more deeply stained than the surrounding liver tissue. These deeply stained patches are not met with in every lobule, but only here and there, one or two comparatively normal lobules intervening between the affected areas.

(× 300).—One of two conditions will be observed in the deeply stained portions. In the early stage there is extreme cloudy swelling of the liver cells, which are so swollen and pressed against one another that their outlines cannot be distinctly discerned. The protoplasm of the cells is extremely granular and somewhat opaque, so that the nucleus is frequently partially obscured, or even lost sight of. The cloudy swelling is more or less marked in the cells of the whole of the lobule, but is most characteristic in the situations mentioned. In the later stages both protoplasm and nuclei of the liver cells appear to undergo complete disorganisation, until in the intermediate zone of each lobule only a mass of granular *débris* may be seen. This mass takes on the pink staining somewhat distinctly, unless it has undergone marked degeneration before the death of the patient, in which case it takes on a more yellow stain (with picro-carmine), as do all necrosed tissues (it is bile-stained when seen *en masse* with the naked eye). This condition appears to be similar to that met with in some cases of dysentery, where the formation of abscesses in the liver is commencing.

Abscesses of the Liver.

193. (1.) *Tropical Abscess.*—This is a form of suppuration of the liver met with in hot climates, sometimes associated with antecedent dysenteric disease of the bowel, but frequently occurring without any assignable cause. It may occur as a single abscess (or at most two or three), deeply situated in the right lobe of the liver. The walls are ragged, and shreds of liver tissue are found hanging into the cavity. There is no trace of a membrane, or even of a condensation of the surrounding tissues. On examination of the contents they are found to consist of a creamy, pus-like material, tinged pink by the presence of a small quantity of blood: this material has a peculiar characteristic sickly odour, but is not putrid.

(× 300).—On examination of the fluid in a neutral solution (¾ per cent. salt, § 34, 5) numerous pus corpuscles are found, which are cleared up by the addition of a drop of acetic acid, and several nuclei are made evident; mixed with the corpuscles is a quantity of *débris*, consisting of liver cells in various stages of disintegration, delicate shreds of connective tissue, and very frequently numerous red blood corpuscles. Around the abscess there is no sign of inflammation. It appears as though the liver tissue is simply completely broken down around one focus, with little or no hyperæmic or surrounding inflammatory changes.

(2.) *Pyæmic Abscess.*—This form of abscess is comparatively rare in the liver, unless there is some source of putrefactive infection in the tract from which the portal blood comes—such as a putrid ulcer of the mucous surface of the stomach or intestinal canal, or septic disease of the pelvic organs, uterus, rectum, &c.; it may be caused by phlebitis, due to the presence of a calculus in the portal vein. In all these conditions there is absorption of some septic material from the primary infecting source by the portal vein. It is said that in injuries to the cranial bones, where there is suppuration extending to the open veins of the diplöe, there is a tendency to the formation of pyæmic abscess, but this has been denied by several authors, who have examined numerous cases of this form of disease and of injury of the cranial bones.

Such abscesses are usually small and multiple, and are more or less wedge-shaped. They appear to be limited to certain branches of the portal vein, and are found especially near the surface of the organ. On opening into one a quantity of very foul smelling, ashengrey or greenish pus is evacuated ; this is found to be made up of ordinary pus corpuscles and shreds of tissue in the last stages of disintegration. The walls of the abscesses are sloughy and ragged looking, and are sodden and infiltrated with serum and pus; surrounding this sloughy and sodden zone is an area or zone which appears to be highly injected and vascular.

These abscesses are probably the result of septic inflammatory changes in the corresponding branches of the portal vein, in which septic thrombi are frequently found. Harden a piece of the liver near the abscess with a part of the wall (§ 56), and stain and mount (§§ 98, 106, and 155 a).

(× 50).—Around the vessels in this position there are numerous leucocytes stained pink with picro-carmine.

(× 450).—In the section stained in methylaniline violet look for micrococci, which, when present, are seen as violet stained granular masses, in some cases forming a considerable part of the "clot" in the vessel. In the neighbourhood of these septic thrombi the liver cells are usually granular, or it may be completely broken down ; the nuclei are also lost, as they now take on the stain very feebly. In the portal spaces the appearances are similar to those already described as occurring in acute fevers (§ 183, p. 195, and § 192), in fact, the whole condition resembles very closely those described under the heading of typhoid lesion. In both of the above abscesses, whether in the single or in the multiple form, it is to be noted that the walls are sloughy and that there are ragged shreds of tissue projecting into the abscess cavity. This is an important diagnostic feature, for in the next form of abscess it will be found that the walls are usually smooth and well defined.

(3.) *Suppuration in Hydatid Cyst of the Liver.*—Where suppuration takes place in a hydatid cyst as a result of direct violence, or from any other cause, the hydatid membrane becomes swollen, and may be entirely broken down and evacuated, but even then the false fibrous capsule formed by the condensed tissue of the organ remains for a considerable time, and bounds the cavity as a smooth, well-marked wall; hooklets are usually to be found in the discharge by which this condition may be distinguished from either of the above forms of abscess.

Cysts of the Liver.

194. (1.) Hydatid cyst, usually found as a single cyst, though there may be several, in the right lobe of the liver.—(See Hydatid Cysts under "Parasites.")

(2.) Simple serous cysts. As a rule, single; probably due to the distension of a bile duct, often brought about by obstruction from pressure of a cancer or some similar growth; as from all collections of bile in the liver, the bile salts, acids, and colouring matter are gradually absorbed, and a clear fluid is left.

(3.) Similar cysts formed by the distension of bile ducts resulting from tubercular growths, softening and ulceration in their walls. These have a caseous and somewhat ragged lining, and contain a clear watery fluid.

(4.) True cystic disease of the liver, associated with a similar condition of the kidney. The cysts vary in size from microscopic spaces to cavities the size of a walnut. The walls are thin, smooth, and fibrous, and within the cavity a clear watery or serous fluid is collected. The mode of origin of these cysts is somewhat doubtful; some hold that they are formed by vacuolation of the liver cells, whilst others maintain that they are dilated bile ducts, the dilatation being caused by constriction of the ducts at certain points by a growth of fibrous and non-striped muscular tissues.

(5.) A form of cyst said to be due to *post mortem* decomposition, occurs especially in hot weather (putrefactive emphysema). The liver tissue is converted into a kind of cavernous tissue by the rapid formation, in its substance, of putrefactive gases.—(Moxon, Goodhart).

Tumours of the Liver—Angioma.

195. Angioma is not very frequently met with in the human subject, but in the liver of the cat it is of common occurrence.

P

When present it is usually found near the surface, and may be seen shining through the capsule as a purple or dark claret coloured patch. The patch may be single, and about a third of an inch in diameter ; or the growth may be multiple. At the site of the tumour there is a slight depression, in which there is a mass which has the appearance of an extravasation of blood sharply defined from the surrounding tissues, though it can be partially injected from any of the vessels of the liver. On making a section, after hardening a

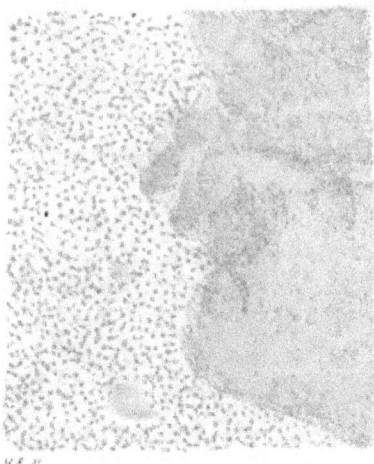

FIG. 50.—Drawing from a section of a cavernous angioma of the liver. Stained with picro-carmine. (× 50.)
    c.a. Fibrous capsule marking off the angioma pretty sharply from the normal liver substance, *l.*
    f.t. Fibrous trabeculæ running from the capsule into the substance of the tumour, forming spaces (*c.s.*) lined with flattened nucleated cells, and containing, apparently, nothing but blood—coloured and colourless—corpuscles.

piece of the liver (§ 59) in which there is an angioma, the tumour is seen to be round or wedge-shaped ; it is sharply marked off from the liver tissue, at first sight appearing little more than a mass of coagulated blood.   Stain (§ 98.)

(× 50).—Around the tumour, and circumscribing it sharply, as already seen, is a fibrous capsule, in which are numerous nuclei. Running in from this are bands or trabeculæ of similar fibrous tissue stained pink, in which are deeply stained nuclei. The bands form a network, the spaces or meshes of which communicate with one another. In these spaces, under this power, a granular greenish mass (red blood capsules) is seen, with here and there a small pink dot (a leucocyte). This blood fills the cavernous structure.

(× 300).—The delicate pink fibrous capsule and trabeculæ are seen ; a large number of more deeply stained nuclei—of young connective

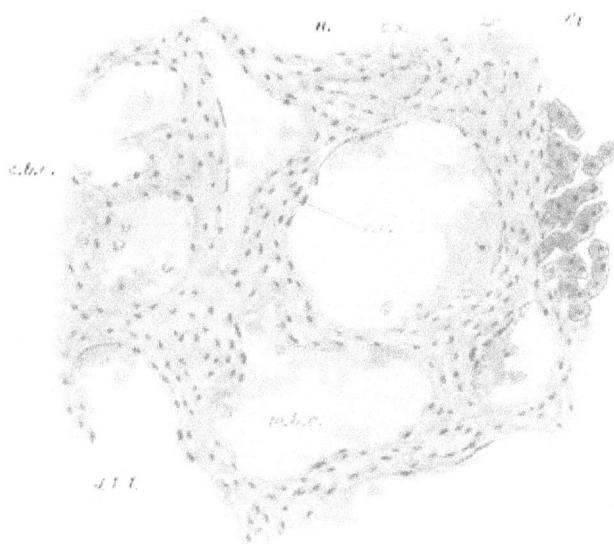

FIG. 51.—Drawing from a section of cavernous angioma of the liver. Stained with picro-carmine. (× 300.)

f.t. Fibrous trabeculæ surrounding (c.s.) cavernous sinuses.
l.c. Nuclei of liver cells between sinuses (n.) connective tissue nuclei.
e.c. Endothelial cells lining the sinuses, and in contact with
c.b.c. The coloured and (w.b.c.), the colourless blood corpuscles.
lc². Liver cells at margin of the tumour.

tissue cells—lie amongst or on the fibres. In some of the trabeculæ a few atrophied liver cells may be seen apparently enclosed and compressed between the bands of fibroid tissue ; but in most of the bands there are no such cells. Lying on the bands of fibrous tissue, and evidently lining the cavernous spaces, are flattened endothelial cells, which, seen in section, are spindle-shaped ; each cell contains one or more rounded nuclei. These cells have very much the appearance of the endothelial cells which form the smooth lining surface of blood-vessels. Lying in the cavities are the coloured blood corpuscles stained sage green, whilst here and there may be seen a pink-stained cell, which will at once be recognised as a colourless blood corpuscle. These tumours appear to be formed by the dilatation of capillary vessels and atrophy of the intervening liver cells. The walls of the vessels become thickened, but in some places they give way, and additional intercommunications are formed. It appears, in fact, to be a similar (but very advanced) condition to that described in "nutmeg liver" (§ 182).

OTHER TUMOURS OF THE LIVER.

196. Tumours of the liver are similar in their structure to those found in other parts or organs of the body; here it will be necessary only to state what tumours may occur in this organ, and to give a few of their naked eye characteristics.

Of the primary forms, malignant adenoma was first described by Greenfield, and it is probable that most of the primary cancers of the liver have their origin in this form, which appears to be developed primarily in connection with the bile ducts.

Malignant pigmented tumours of the liver are invariably sarcomatous.

Cancers, secondary to primary tumours of the breast, uterus, or of the alimentary canal, are of frequent occurrence; they may be either diffused or nodular. In the diffused form the liver is usually much enlarged, and markedly bile stained. Throughout the organ there is a peculiar veining or mottling, caused by the presence of bands of glue-like material, very like the bands of young fibrous tissue seen in certain forms of cirrhosis, more especially to the naked eye, and in some cases even under the microscope. On more careful examination, however, these bands are found to have a more or less characteristic carcinomatous structure. Of the nodular forms, the harder masses, sharply defined from the surrounding tissues, rounded but *umbilicated* in the centre, pink at the periphery, and yellower and fatty looking towards the centre, with, in some cases, fatty looking patches, and but few hæmorrhagic points, are generally cancerous. In some cases firm nodular sarcomatous masses are met with. These, however, are rare, and may usually be recognised by the presence of a larger number of minute hæmorrhages.

The softer nodules occurring in the liver may be either cancerous or sarcomatous, the latter comparatively rarely in adults. The liver is enlarged in both cases. They are both of rapid growth, and are sharply circumscribed; they project from the free or from a cut surface, are pink in colour, and frequently are somewhat translucent. The points of difference are, that in the sarcoma, hæmorrhages into the tissues of the tumour occur more frequently, in consequence of which red, brown, or yellow patches, according to the date of the hæmorrhage, are scattered throughout the substance of the tumour, and that there is no umbilication, while in the cancer this is almost invariably present.

Beyond the evidence to be derived from these general characters, it is, as a rule, impossible to collect with the naked eye any information which will enable one to state with certainty what is the nature of the tumour, and a careful histological examination (for the method of conducting which, see section on Tumours) should always be made.

CHAPTER V.

THE HEART.

Microscopic Structure of the Wall of the Normal Heart.

197. If a section be made through the wall of the left ventricle, and a thin layer of the tissue, embracing both the outer and inner surfaces, be prepared for microscopic examination, the following appearances may be made out with the low power (× 50). The epicardium, or visceral layer of the pericardium, is seen as a mass of pink tissue (if the section has been treated with carmine or picro-carmine), much more dense at its outer surface than near the muscular tissue, where we see an open connective tissue network, with small pink nuclei scattered throughout its substance. Bounding the muscular tissue is a layer of connective tissue, the cells of which are usually infiltrated with fat. This layer of adipose tissue, almost invariably present, varies considerably in thickness, sometimes being exceedingly thin. In the more open parts of the pericardium, the open mouths of vessels are readily seen, and, by special prepara-tion, the presence of numerous nerves and lymphatics may be demonstrated. Beneath the pericardium are numerous bundles of yellowish-brown muscular tissue; in these bundles pink-stained nuclei are seen between the muscular fibres. Bands of pink connective tissue run between the larger bundles of muscular fibre, and form a kind of supporting framework for the muscular tissue. The muscular bundles are seen in both longitudinal and transverse section. When the former, they appear as a reticu-lated mass of fibres, in some cases with meshes of considerab size.

On the endocardial surface are small elevations or irregularities—sections of the musculi papillares. The endocardium itself, under this power, appears to consist of a very thin layer of connective tissue, with here and there throughout its substance a few *small* bundles of muscular tissue.

(× 400).—The epicardium consists of ordinary connective tissue, with bands of yellow elastic tissue in the condensed part near the surface. Covering this is a single layer of flattened nucleated endothelial cells, which, seen in section, appear to be spindle-shaped; and beneath, as already seen under the low power, is a quantity of looser and more vascular connective tissue, beneath which again are the "signet ring"-like fat cells, the nucleus in the angle of the cell being supposed to represent the seal.

The muscle elements of the heart resemble those of ordinary striped or voluntary muscle, in that they are striated both longitudinally and transversely. Each fibre is composed of a series of muscle elements, each of which, in turn, is made up of the following :—(1.) a nucleus containing an intranuclear plexus ; (2.) a thin film of what usually appears to be more or less granular protoplasm, the two together forming the muscle corpuscle of Max Schultze, which is placed in the centre of (3.) a mass of striated, contractile, formed material, or the functionally active part of the substance of the heart. This formed material (on treating as in § **41**, 4, or 5) is broken up into a series of fragments or muscle elements, more or less cylindrical in form, each having for its central point a muscle corpuscle. The extremities of the muscle element are serrated, and in many cases at least one of its ends is bifurcated, each branch joining the serrated end of another, or part of another, element. When a number of these branching cylindrical muscle elements are examined *in situ*, it is seen that they make up the peculiar reticulated mass of fibres above referred to, and on examining transverse sections the different fibres are seen to be of different diameters. In one case the section of a whole fibre is seen, in another the section of one of the branches only. Nuclei occupying the centres of the fibres are seen in transverse as well as in longitudinal sections, but only when the plane of section happens to pass through the muscle corpuscle. If it passes through one of the branches only, or through the end of the element, the nucleus cannot be seen through the mass of formed material. At the poles of these nuclei (especially when the heart is from a subject somewhat advanced in years) are small accumulations of golden yellow or brown pigment.

Around the muscle fibres of the heart there is no sarcolemma, and the highly vascular connective tissue which lies in the interstices of the muscular network is in direct contact with the muscle elements.

The connective tissue has a rich vascular supply, and is completely honeycombed by lymph spaces and lymphatic vessels. The nuclei of these various tissues are readily seen in stained sections. (§§ **100** or **103.**)

On the inner surface of the endocardium is a single layer of flattened nucleated or endothelial cells. In the human heart this layer is seldom seen, as the organ is usually not removed within twenty-four hours after death, by which time the endothelial cells have disappeared. Beneath this layer is a network of flattened branched cells lying on a stratum of elastic tissue, and from it trabeculæ run to join the connective tissue between the muscular fibres, whilst in its substance are to be found muscular bands which, though small, are in all other respects similar to those found in the myocardium.

Cloudy Swelling.

198. Cloudy swelling of the muscle fibres of the heart appears to be the result of an inflammatory condition of the myocardium maintained for a short time, or, in some cases, it may be looked upon as the precursor of fatty metamorphosis of the muscular tissue. It frequently occurs during the course of certain specific or organic fevers, where the temperature is very high, as in typhoid fever, scarlatina, septicæmia, and similar conditions. In one case a severe burn, causing death in six hours, is recorded by Weber as having induced this condition in the muscle fibres of the heart and in the epithelium of the tubules of the kidney. It is in such cases that this condition must be looked for.

Naked eye appearances.—A heart so affected loses much of its firmness and toughness. Its muscular wall is softened, and in some cases even friable, and may be broken down by squeezing between the tips of the fingers and thumb. The tissue is of a dirty grey colour, in place of the usual purple red, and appears as though it had been slightly boiled.—(Perls.) A fresh section of the muscle presents the same grey colour, and has a peculiar translucent appearance. Harden a piece of the muscular tissue, about three-quarters of an inch square, from the wall of the left ventricle (§ 59), examine one section unstained (§ 34), and stain others (§§ 98, 103, and 110).

(× 50).—In longitudinal section the spaces between the individual fibres of the network are somewhat smaller than in the normal heart. This is especially the case near the endocardial surface. Even under this power the fibres look slightly opaque. Find a thin part of the section and centre it.

FIG. 52.—Muscle fibres of the heart in a state of cloudy swelling. Stained with picro-carmine, and mounted in Farrant's solution. (× 300.)

c.s. Part of fibre in a condition of advanced cloudy swelling; transverse striation lost.
t.s. Indistinctly marked transverse striation.
f.c. Commencing formation of small fat globules.

(× 400).—In the unstained specimen the fibres are somewhat opaque. The transverse striation, which in the normal fibre is so distinctly marked, is lost, or obscured, and in place of it there is a granularity of the whole of the formed or striated material of the muscle element. The granules are exceedingly minute, and the appearance of the striated muscle is described as seen through a thin layer of dust or a sheet of ground glass. In such cases the nucleus is obscured and sometimes cannot be distinguished at all.

If instead of the neutral solution a drop of water be added to a few of the fibres spread out on a slide, the granular cells break down, and the nucleus becomes distinctly visible. Again, if a drop of acetic acid is run under the cover glass from the edge, the granular appearance fades away, and an almost normal looking fibre remains.[1]

Ether, chloroform, or strong alkalies run under the cover glass in the same manner leave the cloudiness unaffected.

Examining the osmic acid stained specimen, nothing is found which cannot be observed by the above methods, as with this reagent there is no blackening of the fine granules ; from this fact it is to be inferred that they are not yet of a fatty nature.

Picro-carmine and logwood do not stain the muscle elements deeply ; but they are useful for bringing into prominence the nuclei of the interstitial tissue and of the muscle corpuscles. The nuclei of the connective tissue are frequently more numerous and more deeply stained than in the normal heart, especially where the condition arises during the course of an early inflammatory process. These nuclei are then seen as deeply stained bodies lying between the bands of muscular fibres, arranged most frequently along each side of the small blood-vessels.

This cloudiness of the fibre is not equally distributed throughout the wall of the heart, but is much more advanced in some places (usually near the endocardial surface) than in others. This is specially the case where the cloudy swelling is to be looked upon as the precursor of fatty degeneration.

FATTY INFILTRATION OF THE HEART.

199. Fatty infiltration of the heart, or Adipose Heart, must be carefully distinguished from fatty degeneration of the muscular walls of the heart. In fatty infiltration there is at first simply an increase in the amount of the epicardial fat to which reference has already been made (§ **197**). Subsequently, the fat extends from the epicardial surface into the muscular wall of the organ between the various bands of fibres. Although the two processes of fatty infiltration and fatty degeneration are frequently associated (as in cases where the

---

[1] If a heart in which there is cloudy swelling (especially in the early stages) be kept in alcohol for some time, the cloudiness may disappear, or nearly so. The alcohol appears to abstract water from the tissues, or otherwise so to change the protoplasm as to restore the refractive indices of the various elements to the normal.

pressure of the invading adipose tissue on the muscular fibres causes their degeneration), it will be well to describe the two conditions separately.

The adipose heart, as seen with the naked eye, appears to be larger than normal, the increase in size being due mainly to an increase in the amount of subpericardial fat: there is usually some flabbiness of the muscular tissue, more especially near the outer surface. Small yellow streaks run down in the somewhat pale muscular tissue, evidently merely continuations of the adipose tissue from the subpericardial layer. Unless there is also advanced fatty degeneration, the flabbiness does not extend beyond the gross lines of fatty tissue.

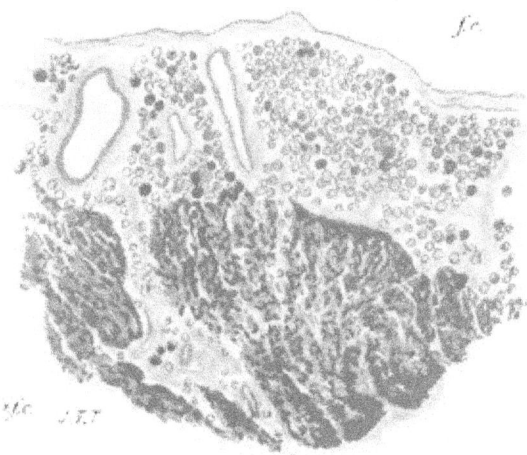

FIG. 53.—Section of adipose epicardium. Stained with osmic acid and carmine. (× 40.)

    e.c. Superficial epicardium.   *f.c.* Deeper layer, enormously thickened, connective tissue cells distended with fat.
    v. Vessels. *m.* Muscular tissue.
    i.f.c. Fatty infiltration of connective tissue between muscular tissue near the surface of the heart.

Harden (§ 59), cut (§ 82 *et seq.*), and stain (§§ 98 and 110).

(× 50).—The epicardial tissue is completely infiltrated with fat globules, which are of considerable size. The connective tissue cells have become filled and distended with fat, and present the appearance of fat cells in ordinary adipose tissue; the highly refractile globules have a double outline, and are stained black with osmic acid. The nucleus is situated at one angle of the cell, and is stained pink or olive green, as the case may be. These large cells extend in rows for some distance between the muscular fibres, but are entirely outside them; the condition is in fact one of fatty infiltration of the connective tissue framework of the heart, and not of the muscle substance proper. In very marked cases this fatty infiltration of the connective tissue cells may extend as far as the endocardial surface, when, however, it is invariably associated with true fatty degeneration of the muscle fibres.

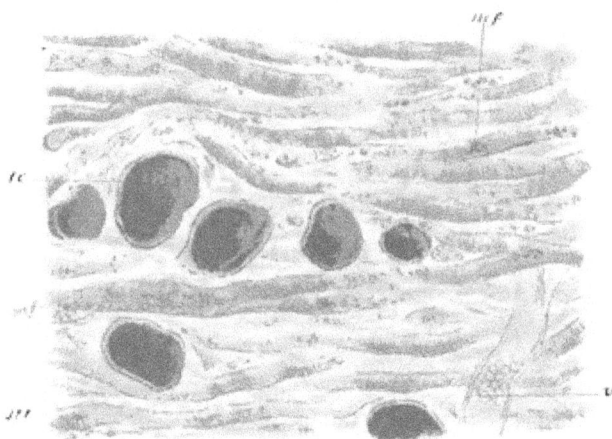

FIG. 54.—Fatty infiltration of the connective tissue between the muscular fibres of the wall of the heart, stained with osmic acid. (× 300.)

f.c. Large fat cells between the muscle fibres.
m.f., m.f. Muscle fibres—slight fatty degeneration.
v. Small vessel filled with blood.

(× 400).—The cells of the adipose tissue are closely packed together, and the following parts may be observed in each. The protoplasm of the cell forms a mere film, except at one point or angle, where there is usually a triangular mass of protoplasm containing a nucleus, which, when stained, stands out very distinctly. Surrounded by the thin wall of protoplasm is a large, strongly refractile globule with a double outline, clear in the centre, but with a dark ring at the margin, or the reverse, according to the part that is focussed. With picro-carmine the globule remains unstained, but with osmic acid it is stained black. Between the muscle fibres they have exactly the same appearance; in no way do they affect the fibre itself, except by actual mechanical pressure. As before stated, this condition must be carefully distinguished from fatty degeneration, which is an affection of the muscle substance proper.

Fatty Degeneration of the Muscle Wall of the Heart.

200. Fatty degeneration occurs in patients who have succumbed to various exhausting diseases, such as phthisis, anæmia, leucocythemia, Addison's disease, and disease generally in which there is a deteriorated condition of the blood. It occurs also as a sequel to scarlatina and diseases of that type, and to various septic conditions. Lastly, it is met with in patients who have died from phosphorus or arsenic poisoning, or in a minor degree from alcohol, antimony, and sulphuric ether poisoning (§ **177**). In some few cases, fatty degeneration appears to be due to the partial occlusion of the coronary arteries, affected with endarteritis deformans, which has extended from the aorta, or to some other obstructive lesion. It also occurs as a sequel to endocarditis and pericarditis.

To the naked eye the heart has a characteristic appearance. It is somewhat dilated; on section it is pale and smooth, especially near the endocardial surface, which is considerably paler than normal. As a rule, this pallor is not equally diffused over the whole surface, but appears in patches, especially in the musculi papillares and the columnæ carnæ.

On examining one of the musculi papillares, taking it as a typical specimen of an affected part, it is found that there are numerous small cream-coloured areas, which stand out distinctly from the reddish brown background. This has been very aptly compared to a "thrush's breast," and also to "faded leaves." In very advanced cases the cream-coloured patches have spread so far as to meet one another, in which case the "thrush's breast" simile does not hold good. Where this form of degeneration is due to phosphorus or arsenic poisoning, or to scarlet fever, or leucocythemia, small hæmorrhages are frequently seen immediately beneath the epicardium. The muscular tissue is flabby, and slightly, or in some cases very, friable, so much so, that the thumb and fingers may be easily pushed through the muscular wall.

Harden (§ 59), stain, and mount (§§ 34, 98, 103, 104, and 110).

(× 50).—Very little is to be discerned beyond the fact that the muscle fibres appear in some cases to have become slightly enlarged. This is especially the case where the fatty degeneration follows upon an inflammatory condition ; but in the pure degeneration, such as that brought about by metallic poisoning, the fibres are seldom increased in size. The enlargement of the fibres cannot be

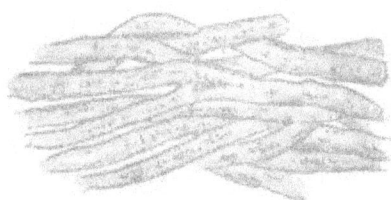

FIG. 55.—Muscle fibres of the heart. Fatty degeneration Mounted unstained in Farrant's solution. (× 300.)

f.   Muscle fibre in which there is slight dimming of the transverse striation.

f.c. Small fatty granules and globules along the lines of longitudinal striation, especially around the nuclei and near the centres of the cells.

definitely determined, but it should be remembered that as the fibres increase in size the spaces between them become somewhat narrower, and the contained tissue elements more crowded together.

(× 300 or 400).—The nuclei between the muscle fibres are usually increased in number and distinctness. The transverse striation of the fibres has, to a great extent, disappeared ; in some not a trace of it is left, whilst in those in which the change is not so far advanced the striation is seen only at the margins. In such cases where the centre of the muscle element of the fibre is most affected, the transverse striation is replaced by a number of small round granules, or in some cases small globules, which never, however, reach even a medium size. These granules and minute globules first make their appearance at the poles of the muscle corpuscles (the oval mass of protoplasm with its nucleus in the centre). From these points the process gradually extends through the length of the fibre, until, eventually, the whole of it is involved. The fibre then appears to consist of a series of rows of small round granules and globules, each row corresponding more or less to one of the fibrillæ of which the fibre is made up, so that at this stage the fibre, though perfectly well defined, has lost its transverse striation, and appears to be built up of rows of small, highly refractile bodies (like so many strings of beads). This condition resembles cloudy swelling in many respects, but may be distinguished from it by the following features : the granules and globules are larger, and, in the section stained with osmic acid, are black or brownish black, which is not the case with the

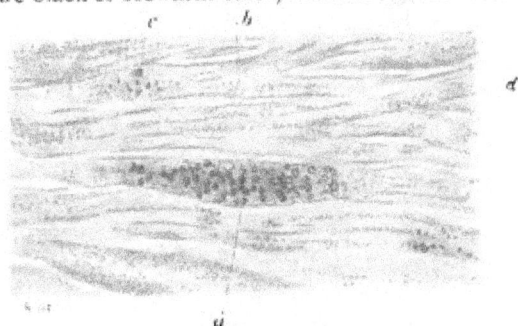

FIG. 56.—Muscle fibres of a heart taken from a case of advanced pernicious anæmia. Well marked fatty degeneration. Section stained with osmic acid. Mounted in Farrants' solution. (× 300.)
a. Fibre in which there is advanced fatty degeneration. Oil globules much larger than usual.
b. Healthy part (nucleus well seen).
c. Fatty part of same fibre.
d. Nucleus of muscle corpuscle in a comparatively healthy fibre.

granules in cloudy swelling. On the other hand, the fattily degenerated muscle is unaffected by a drop of acetic acid run under the cover glass from its margin. Treated with chloroform, ether, &c., the fatty material is dissolved, whilst the granules of cloudy swelling are unaffected. The transverse striation in this condition may be almost lost. As already noticed, the fatty degeneration occurs in localised patches, and as the section is examined under the high power, the same fibres may be fatty in parts, whilst in other parts they are to all intents and purposes healthy. With the microscope these areas can be localised much more accurately than with the naked eye.

240THE HEART.

Fatty infiltration is frequently associated with fatty degeneration. In fact, as already pointed out, the infiltration when extensive may so compress the muscular fibres that their nutrition and function are very seriously interfered with, and a degenerative change in their substance is brought about.

PIGMENTARY DEGENERATION, OR BROWN ATROPHY OF THE HEART.

201. This condition is also met with most frequently in cases of general wasting disease, where the process of exhaustion has been long continued. Consequently it is often found associated with fatty degeneration of the muscle in such conditions as phthisis, or more markedly still in Addison's disease. The pure brown atrophy is more frequently met with in the hearts of old people; but marked pigmentation is often present in hypertrophied hearts.

The naked eye appearances vary somewhat in different cases. When it is found in connection with atrophic conditions, the heart is dark brown in colour and considerably smaller, the walls are thinner, the cavities are contracted, the coronary arteries are tortuous, and are more prominent than normal, and the epicardium is frequently thrown into folds. If the condition is unaccompanied by fatty degeneration, the muscle may be firm or even tough, or it may be "brittle;" but when associated with that condition, it is friable and soft, in which case, too, there are paler patches scattered in the dark brown background. Where it occurs along with hypertrophy, the colour is not so dark, the tissue is firmer, and it may be that few of the characteristic features of the atrophic form are present.

Harden (§ 59), mount a section unstained (§ 152), and another stained (§ 98). A section taken from a heart removed from a patient affected with Addison's disease is described below.

(× 50).—The fibres are thinner than normal, and are not so closely packed as in the healthy heart. They are considerably broken up, the constituent muscle elements or muscle cells, with their serrated ends, being separated by intervals more or less marked in different places. Near the centre of each muscle element is a dark brown spot; if a bundle of fibres is examined in transverse section, a similar dark spot can be distinguished in most of the fibres, occupying the centre of the section of the fibre.

(× 400).—Where the pigmentary degeneration is unaccompanied by fatty degeneration, the transverse striation of the fibres is extremely well marked. The end of the segments, into which the fibres are divided, are distinctly serrated. In the centre of the segment the largest mass of pigment is observed occupying the position of the muscle corpuscle around which it is collected, especially towards the poles. In relation to this it will be remembered that even in the

FIG. 57.—Brown atrophy of the heart. Muscle fibres broken up into short segments. Mounted unstained in Farrant's solution. (× 400.)

    a. Fibres splitting up into short detached fragments.
    b. Pigment collected around the nucleus.
    c.c. Pigment scattered along lines of longitudinal striation.
    It will be noted that the transverse striation is very distinctly marked in this condition.

normal heart there is a small quantity of golden brown pigment collected at each pole of the muscle corpuscle. So far, then, there is simply an exaggeration of a normal process. Where the condition is advanced, as in the section now under observation, the pigment appears in elongated patches, following more or less regularly the lines of longitudinal striation. These patches are not confined to any part of the muscle element, but are more frequently seen at some distance from the periphery than near the margins. The granules of which the patches are composed vary, slightly, in size,

Q

but all, alike, are of a beautiful golden yellow colour, when seen under a high power and by a strong light. In a transverse section of one of the muscular fibres the pigment is seen as a golden yellow mass, occupying the centre of the section of the fibre, whilst the smaller masses appear as minute points scattered throughout the substance of the fibre. In the picro-carmine stained specimen the nuclei may, in some few instances, be seen as pink bodies; but in most of the fibres the accumulation of pigment is so great that the nucleus is completely obscured.

The pigment is some altered form of hæmoglobin; but whether

Fig. 58.—Muscle fibres from a heart in which there was acute myocarditis. Stained with picro-carmine, and mounted in Farrant's solution. (× 300.)

    a. Fibres, comparatively healthy, in a condition of cloudy swelling.
    b. Fibres broken down into an almost granular mass. These fibres are slightly but irregularly swollen.
    c. Parts of the fibres as yet only in the condition of cloudy swelling. These are placed between parts which are in the more advanced stage of disintegration.

there is any accession from the blood, or whether there is simply a concentration of that which already existed in the muscle, is as yet merely a matter for conjecture.

ACUTE MYOCARDITIS.

202. Acute myocarditis may occur either as a primary or secondary condition, but it occurs much more frequently as the latter, extend-

ing from the epicardial or endocardial surface into the substance of the muscle proper, or along the course of the connective tissue framework which supports the muscular structure. The presence of acute myocarditis is suggested by the symptoms during life, and after death by the racemose reddening of the endocardium, the friability, the deepened colour, and the yellow patches on, or mottling of, the muscular wall. Harden (§ 59), and stain (§§ 98, 102, and 110). In very acute cases (septic) abscesses similar to those already described are found in the ventricular wall (§ 165).

(× 50).—The fibres are swollen and closely packed together. If the disease has been very acute, small areas of extremely opaque bluish-grey (or pink) material are scattered throughout the yellow muscular tissue; between the individual fibres, or around the smaller vessels, are numerous very small pink points (nuclei). (In the logwood-stained section these come out even more distinctly as blue points.)

(× 400).—The bluish-grey areas are composed of swollen and bulging fibres which have lost all trace of striation; they present the appearance of broken down, glassy-looking protoplasm (the result of the so-called vitreous degeneration), having in some parts almost angular depressions and bulgings; or the muscle fibres have become broken down, and there is simply a mass of more or less granular *débris*. These are the fibres in which the degenerative process is taking place most rapidly; some of the yellower-looking fibres appear quite normal, whilst others are in an advanced state of cloudy swelling (§ 198). The nuclei in the connective tissue spaces are considerably increased in number, most of them (leucocytes) lying around the vessels from which they have probably emigrated. Some of the nuclei, however, are those of the connective tissue cells, which in this condition are more highly stimulated, and are undergoing rapid proliferation. The vessels are usually somewhat dilated. In the section stained with osmic acid not a single black granule can be distinguished, showing that, as yet, fatty degeneration has not set in. If the condition is not so acute, and the patient has survived rather longer, the black reaction with the osmic acid is given at some points in the mass of extremely granular *débris*.

CHRONIC MYOCARDITIS.

203. The more chronic form of myocarditis, which is rather an interstitial inflammation than a true inflammation of the muscle, like

FIG. 59.—Section of fibroid degeneration of the heart. Stained with eosin and logwood. (× 50.)

    a.a. Mass of fibrous or cicatricial tissue which may be looked upon as thickened perimysium, embedded in, or rather surrounding, the muscular fibres. Few nuclei in this new tissue.
    b. Small new blood vessel in this tissue.
    c.c¹. Atrophied muscle fibres, in this case somewhat pigmented.
    d. Blood vessel with thickened adventitia in which are numerous deeply stained nuclei.

most of these diseases, is found only on the left side of the heart, and especially in the wall of the left ventricle. The muscular wall is firm and hard, and can not be broken down with the fingers as can the muscle of a normal heart. Running through, or sometimes almost replacing the muscle fibre, especially near the apex, are grey semi-translucent or opaque fibrous bands, to which the muscular structure owes its firmness. Under the microscope the principal change observed in the first instance is probably a more acute process, in which there is proliferation of the intermuscular connective tissue cells, this being followed by the development from the new tissue of fibrous bands, often of considerable thickness, which intersect and compress the muscle tissue proper, in which case we have what is known as fibroid degeneration of the heart. The connection between the acute and chronic forms is very similar to that described as existing between acute interstitial hepatitis and common chronic cirrhosis.

(× 50).—In the early stages, lines or accumulations of deeply stained bodies, following pretty closely the lines of the vessels, are seen. In some cases these nuclei form bands almost as broad as the bands of muscular tissue. The smaller vessels are often increased in size, and their walls, especially the adventitia, undergo consider-able thickening. In the later stages this cellular tissue has, except immediately around the blood vessels, given place to well developed dense fibrous tissue, with only a few deeply stained nuclei scattered here and there. These fibrous masses are often of considerable size, and in them atrophied patches of muscular tissue, sometimes fatty, but more frequently pigmented, may be seen. Usually the fibrous tissue has running through it a few small blood vessels, the walls of which are somewhat imperfectly developed.

(× 400).—The muscle fibres may be perfectly normal in appearance, but between them the deeply stained nuclei are very numerous, and the dilated blood-vessels, with their thickened walls, are also well seen, the thickening being due, chiefly, to an increase in the number of cells in the adventitia. Where the condition is more chronic, or where the patient (say in acute rheumatism) pulls through the first stages of the disease, the young cells become organised into fibrous tissue, which stains pink with picro-carmine, and in which are seen a number of spindle-shaped connective tissue cells. Where this stage is reached, the muscle fibres are usually undergoing atrophy and sometimes fatty degeneration, though neither of them is by any means invariably met with. These conditions appear to be due to malnutrition of the fibres, brought about, first, by the altered condition of the blood which has induced the cell proliferation, and, second, by the mechanical pressure of the newly formed fibrous tissue on the muscular fibres. The fatty fibres are similar in appearance to those previously described (§ 200). A condition spoken of as cardiac sclerosis is described by Cornil and Ranvier, in which the essential details are similar to those above described. It occurs very frequently during the course of interstitial nephritis, more especially in patients who are at the same time suffering from maniacal symptoms.

In a heart in which there is aneurism at the apex of the left ventricle (by far the commonest position), the muscle fibre usually undergoes some local softening, such as fatty degeneration, myocarditis or endocarditis; it may be the result of acute (rarely of chronic) myocarditis, or of stoppage or obstruction of the blood supply through diseased coronary arteries. Even in the aneurisms near the base of the heart, in the interventricular septum, which are often continuations of valvular aneurisms, the muscle fibres in the immediate neighbourhood usually undergo fatty degeneration.

ENDOCARDITIS.

204. The structure of the endocardium has already been briefly described (§ 197). The results of endocarditis are most evident in connection with the valves of the various orifices, and it will be well to see what parts of (and in what proportions) the endocardium enter into the structure of the valves. The layer of flattened connective tissue cells, with the fibrillated tissue and yellow elastic fibres, which has already been described as lying immediately under the layer of endothelium, is continuous from both the auricles and the ventricles on to their respective valves. The endothelial covering is also continuous, and is further prolonged over the chordæ tendineæ, which are composed of yellow elastic and white fibrous tissues, so that any process affecting the surfaces of the valves is most frequently continued along the chordæ tendineæ. The aortic and pulmonary valves are, in the same manner, covered with a layer of endothelium, that of the heart becoming continuous with that of the vessel, and the subjacent condensed layer of fibro-elastic tissue of the one becoming continuous at the margin of the valve with that of the other.

ACUTE ENDOCARDITIS.

205. Acute endocarditis is seen in patients who have succumbed during the early stages of an attack of acute rheumatism. The most marked evidences of the disease are in the form of verrucous growths, which are found along the lines of contact of the valves, chiefly in the left side of the heart, on the mitral and aortic valves —the former on the auricular aspect near the margins, the latter on the ventricular aspect, and at some little distance from the margins of the cusps. These warty growths are much more rarely met with on the tricuspid and pulmonary valves, but when they do occur the same rules as regards their position hold good. The growth or vegetation is "soft, friable, and semi-transparent." In the more acute form it never reaches any very great size, but smaller growths occur all along the points of contact of the valves. If separated from the valve, a small portion of the subjacent tissue is brought away, leaving an ulcer the size of the base of the vegetation. If the patient has survived the early stages of the disease, the growths may increase considerably in size, but they have much the same structure as the smaller forms. Along with these vegetations, at the points of contact of the valves, others may occur on the whole of the auricular surfaces of the valves, the process radiating from the primary focus. The chordæ tendineæ, which, as already observed, are simply continuations of the endocardial covering of the valves, are very much swollen, and are extremely brittle.

Harden a piece of a valve, on which is a good vegetation (§§ 56 and 59). Cut sections (§ 93) through the vegetation and the valve at right angles to the plane of the valve. Stain (§§ 98, 103, and 106).

For full description of these vegetations, see § 170, but here note that (× 300) the cells of the endocardial tissue appear to have proliferated very rapidly, and that from them most of the tissue composing the growth arises; the proliferation is so rapid and so great that, just as in the case of a granulating wound, the mass of cells passes beyond the level of the endocardium, and a small projection is the result. The yellowish mass on the surface is made up of two factors, degenerating cells and coagulated fibrin, both of which may be readily distinguished with the aid of picro-carmine and other stains.

In the section stained with methylaniline violet, a number of micrococci may sometimes be seen, forming a deeply stained granular layer on the surface of the disintegrating cells and fibrin. In ordinary acute endocarditis these micrococci do not appear to give rise to any serious changes, even when they are carried off, along with parts of the degenerating mass near the surface, to form minute embolic infarcts in other organs.

Chronic Endocarditis.

206. As in the case of all other inflammatory processes, acute endocarditis tends to become chronic—especially if not extremely acute at the commencement. The vegetations occurring in the positions already mentioned then become firm, hard, fibroid masses, having a broad base ; they are not so prominent as in the acute form. The edges of the valve are thickened, especially along the lines of contact. At certain points the thickened valves have become adherent at their extremities by the organisation of the inflammatory products, and are usually puckered and retracted. As in the case of acute endocarditis, the valves of the left side of the heart—the auricular surface of the mitral valve, and the ventricular surface of the aortic valve—are the parts specially affected. The right side is only affected where the disease commences *in utero*. In some few cases the thickening extends so that the walls of the cavities as well as the valves are affected. The chordæ tendineæ are shortened, thickened, and opaque, and look almost like pieces of firm cartilage. In place of being brittle, as in the acute form, they are extremely tough. In the mass of thickened fibroid tissue, calcareous plates may frequently be observed immediately under the endothelial covering, or pultaceous or fatty granular material may occupy the same position.

Harden (*a*) one of the valves, on which is one of the flattened vegetations, and (*b*) one with some of the fatty and calcareous patches (§ 59), and stain (§§ 98 and 103).

(× 50).—In place of the round cells which, in the acute form, were observed in the vegetation, and in the endocardium beneath it, there are now a number of spindle-shaped (as seen in section) cells, the nuclei of which are stained with carmine. Between these flattened cells (for flattened branched cells they will be found to be if examined from the surface) are layers of fibrillar substance arranged in regular lamellæ, giving rise to the appearance of a very much thickened endocardium. This lamellated tissue is stained pink with picro-carmine, and gives all the reactions of fibrous tissue. On the surface of the vegetation there is frequently a deposition of fibrin, but it is usually freshly deposited, and does not stain, although the few cells entangled in the fibrinous meshes are usually deeply stained. This fibrin has therefore been deposited whilst the blood current was slowing, and as the patient was dying. In fact, in almost all sections of vegetations examined, any deposit of fibrin on the surface appears to have been deposited in great part during the last few days of the patient's life.

Examine the section in which are the fatty and calcareous plates (× 300). In the spaces originally occupied by the flattened cells, there is now more frequently a mass of yellow stained granular material. In the deeper endocardial layer this granular material is replaced by a number of highly refractile granules, which, on the addition of a drop of hydrochloric acid, evolve bubbles of gas (carbon dioxide) and then disappear. These highly refractile granules are small calcareous particles deposited in the fatty material. In some few places the fibrous tissue is also undergoing fatty degeneration and calcareous infiltration, as a result of which large calcareous patches have been formed. In the very early stages, however, the change is confined to the spaces in which the flattened cells lie, the intercellular fibrous tissue being stained a beautiful pink. This condition should be studied along with endarteritis deformans, to which it bears a very close resemblance (§§ 212, 213) especially in the more chronic forms in old people, when it occurs on the aortic surface of the semilunar valve. We might compare the vegetation in

the early stages with a mass of granulation tissue growing on a free
surface, that of an ulcer, for example. In the later stages the
vegetation may be likened to the fibrous cicatrix which is left when
the ulcer has healed. If such tissues are examined together, it
will at once be seen how closely the two stages of the one
correspond to the two stages of the other.

ACUTE ULCERATIVE ENDOCARDITIS.

207. This condition, which in many respects resembles the acute
form of endocarditis already examined, and is by many writers
considered to be the same disease, differs from it, apparently, in the
two following points :—1*st*, That it is more destructive in its local
action ; and 2*nd*, That the fragments detached and carried into the
circulation give rise to a much more rapid and widespread mischief
than do emboli from the simple acute form (§ 165). To the naked
eye the vegetations appear to be very similar to those described in
the simple form, but they tend to occur more indiscriminately over
the endocardial surface of the valves or of the heart wall. They also
appear to be much more liable to break down and to leave ulcerated
patches. The vegetation itself, taken, for example, from a case of
ulcerative endocarditis occurring during the course of a case of
pyæmia), if stained and examined as in the acute form, will be found
to present exactly the same character under both low and high
powers, as already described (§ 169), the micrococci in the superficial layer being especially well seen. Harden (§ 56), stain (§§ 98,
103, and 110).

(× 50).—The floor and margins of the ulcer are infiltrated with a
great number of small round cells, which take on the carmine stain,
except at the surface, where there is a distinct yellowish tinge, which
points to the fact that the tissues are here undergoing degenerative
changes. In the section stained with osmic acid this same area
appears to be much darker than the deeper tissue.

(× 300).— The pink-stained cells are closely packed together,
forming the floor and margins of the slight depressions or even
roughened elevation. Directly in contact with the blood is a layer of
extremely granular looking cells, the granules in some cases appear-

ing almost like small globules. This layer is stained more or less yellow with the picro-carmine, and the small globules (which are often free) and granules are stained black with osmic acid. Here, too, small quantities of free blood pigment may be observed. Mixed with this layer of degenerated tissue is, frequently, a quantity of granular looking fibrin, in which, in a section stained with methyl-aniline violet (§ 106), may be seen colonies of micrococci, some of them, colonies of considerable size. It has recently been maintained that all these forms of endocarditis are the result of the action of micro-organisms, but this is not yet proved.

SIMPLE PERICARDITIS (see § 166).

PURULENT AND TUBERCULAR PERICARDITIS

Are also sometimes met with. In the latter form, the covering of lymph is usually of great thickness, is yellow, and has pus on the surface. On microscopic examination tubercle follicles with large well marked giant cells are seen throughout the new fibrinous layer, but they are specially numerous near the surface.

NEW GROWTHS MET WITH IN THE HEART.

Tubercle in the pericardium (rarely in other tissues), syphilitic gummata, secondary cancers and sarcomas (rarely primary), fibroma, myoma (congenital), and lipoma.

CYSTIC PARASITES.

Hydatids of *Tænia echinococcus*, and *Cysticercus cellulosæ* of *Tænia solium.*

CHAPTER VI.

BLOOD-VESSELS.

NORMAL HISTOLOGY.

208. Capillary vessels consist simply of a single layer of more or less flattened endothelial cells. Each cell contains a nucleus, by the double rows of which the capillary vessel is most easily recognised. Between the cells is a cement substance, which is stained brown with nitrate of silver. The cement substance is

FIG. 60.—Drawing of capillary vessel, with surrounding adenoid tissue. (× 300, after Klein and Noble Smith.)
    a. Nucleus of flattened endothelial cell, forming the inner layer of the vessel.
    b. Flattened cells (really connective tissue cells) surrounding a capillary vessel (perithelium).
    c. Lymphoid cells in meshes of the network.

supposed to have considerable pathological importance, for as we have already seen, in the process of inflammation where the vessels are distended, the cement substance gives way, and openings are said to occur in it, through which the coloured and colourless blood corpuscles escape from the vessel.

Around some of the capillaries there is a second sheath, sometimes spoken of as the perithelium, which is composed of "a network of branched connective tissue cells" (Klein). Between these two layers is a reticular or fibrillated layer, which is of great pathological importance, as it is in the fibrils (forming a kind of basement membrane) on which the epithelial or perithelial cells rest that the process of waxy degeneration is supposed to occur.

209. A medium sized artery is made up of three layers or coats— the "intima," the "media," and the "adventitia."

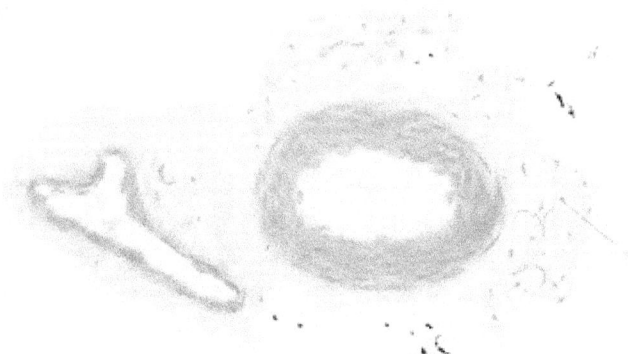

FIG. 61.—Transverse section of normal artery and vein from the finger of a child. Stained with picro-carmine. (× 150.)

A. Artery, with (*a.*) lining nucleated endothelium resting on a delicate laminated connective tissue.
b. Internal elastic lamina thrown into folds by the contraction of
d. The thick muscular coat, composed of non-striped muscular fibres, the nuclei of which are seen as deeply stained rod-shaped nuclei.
e. Fibro-cellular adventitia.
V. Vein, with (*a.*) flattened endothelial cells.
b. Thin intima.
d. Thin muscular coat.
e. Fibro-cellular adventitia.
f. Fatty tissue.

The tunica intima is composed (1.) of a layer of endothelial cells, very similar in appearance to those already described in the capillaries; (2.) subendothelial connective tissue or intima proper, which consists of longitudinal and transverse laminated tissue with branching connective tissue cells lying between its layers; (3.) the so-called internal elastic lamina, an elastic homogeneous layer, which is usually wavy owing to the contraction of the muscular tunica media of the wall, which takes place during the hardening of the vessel. It is composed of interlacing bands of elastic tissue, between which are openings or fenestræ; through these the vessels of the media may make their way into the lumen of the vessel during the process of organisation in a thrombus.

The middle or muscular coat is composed of non-striped muscular fibres, arranged, principally, transversely to the axis of the vessels. Where more than one layer is present, they are arranged regularly, rod-shaped nuclei being seen in the fibres. Between the individual layers of non-striped muscular tissue are laminæ and networks of elastic tissue; in the larger branches these elastic laminæ are especially prominent. Vasa vasorum are found passing from the adventitia for some distance into the substance of the media, the capillaries of these vessels stopping short at the part of the coat next the endothelial lining of the intima, which rarely receives capillaries from this source. In the smaller vessels the adventitia is in direct contact with the media, but in the larger arteries there is an elastic network, spoken of as the external elastic lamina, separating the two coats.

The tunica adventitia is composed of connective tissue, with numerous cells, between which are bundles of pink-stained (with picro-carmine) fibrous tissue, with here and there, especially near the media, longitudinal bundles of yellow elastic fibres; the elastic laminæ are stained yellow. Small vessels invariably run into the adventitia of the larger vessels to supply the walls with nutriment.

210. The structure of the aorta differs somewhat from that above described. The adventitia is comparatively thin; the media contains relatively little muscular tissue; the internal elastic lamina of the smaller vessels is apparently represented by a number of thin layers of elastic tissue interspersed through the muscular tissue, networks of elastic and connective tissue running along with the vasa vasorum. Here, too, the intima is thicker than in any other vessel; it is composed of an endothelial layer and a thickened subendothelial layer, in which are numerous flattened nucleated connective tissue cells, with reticulated elastic tissue beneath.

The coats of the veins correspond to those of the arteries, but here the adventitia is the most important coat; the media is composed of irregular bundles of non-striped muscular fibre, with little or no elastic tissue, simply a basis of connective tissue; the various parts of the intima are very delicate. The valves are formed of folds of the intima, in which a portion of the muscular coat is invaginated.

In all vessels numerous lymphatic spaces lined with endothelium are found in the adventitia, and in the larger vessels, tubular lymphatics in the same position. Lymph spaces between the bundles of muscular tissue are also met with; these communicate with the lymph spaces of the adventitia.

ACUTE ARTERITIS.

211. This form of inflammation is met with principally in the aorta, but it may also occur in the smaller vessels, especially in those near wounds. *The naked eye appearances* are very characteristic. On the inner surface of the first part of the aorta, say, especially near the coronary arteries, are one or more patches of soft elastic or gelatinous looking material of a yellowish, or, it may be, of a pearly pink colour. The patches vary in size, but are usually from a quarter of an inch to half an inch in diameter, and are sharply defined from the surrounding intima, which is almost normal, or only slightly swollen and thrown into small folds in the immediate neighbourhood of the swelling. The outer surface of the vessel is inflamed; a mass of semi-gelatinous or œdematous-looking tissue, having a pink tinge, is seen, from which it is evident that the acute endarteritis is accompanied by periarteritis. In some cases the tunica media is also swollen and infiltrated.

Harden (§ 59), cut sections transversely to the long axis of the aorta (§ 82 *et seq.*), and stain (§ 98).

(× 50).—Where the thickening is marked, the cells of the deep layer of the intima, undergoing rapid proliferation, are extremely numerous, and are separated only by thin layers of the laminated tissue. Even where the thickening is as yet not well marked, flattened cells, with somewhat elongated nuclei, may be seen in the deeper layers. All these cells take on stains readily.

Where the condition is advanced, there is also an increase in the number of cells in the adventitia; the increase in some cases becomes so marked that the adventitia looks more like a mass of granulation tissue than anything else. In some few cases small, round, deeply stained cells are scattered through the muscular tissue, but usually the middle coat is comparatively unaffected.

(× 300).—The cells in the intima, immediately under the endothelial lining, composed of nuclei, surrounded by thin films of protoplasm, all give evidence of great vegetative activity. Their growth is maintained at the expense of the fibrous laminæ. In the deeper layers, or where the process is not so far advanced, the flattened nucleated cells may still be seen, but they are cloudy and granular. In the adventitia the capillary vessels are more prominent and are distended, and new loops are frequently sent through the media into the thickened intima. Along the course of these vessels, which may be seen as double rows of flattened cells, are numerous small round cells, some composed of little but a nucleus, others having around the nucleus a quantity of protoplasm. As these cells are developed, and the connected tissue fibrils and yellow elastic fibres are swollen, softened, and absorbed, the wall of the vessel may become considerably weakened; where these patches occur in the very acute form in minute vessels, aneurisms may result from the wall of the vessel giving way at the weakened point. (*Acute Multiple Aneurisms.*)

As in all cases where there is a formation of granulation tissue, the process may become more chronic, in which event there is a formation of fibrous tissue. This occurs especially around the mouths of the branches of the aorta,—*e.g.*, in the coronary arteries, which are frequently surrounded by constricting bands of fibrous tissue formed by the organisation of the round-celled tissue.

Chronic Endarteritis—"Endarteritis Deformans"—"Atheroma."

212. This may be described first as it occurs in one of the smaller vessels, and then as it occurs in the aorta. It is found especially in the vessels of aged people, and is to be looked upon as a degenerative process, following a low form of inflammation. In the vessel (one of the larger vessels at the base of the brain) from which the section described is taken, are patches of opaque, pale, firm tissue, in some cases quite hard and gritty when cut, scattered at irregular intervals along the course of the vessels.

These patches vary from one-sixth to one-third of an inch in

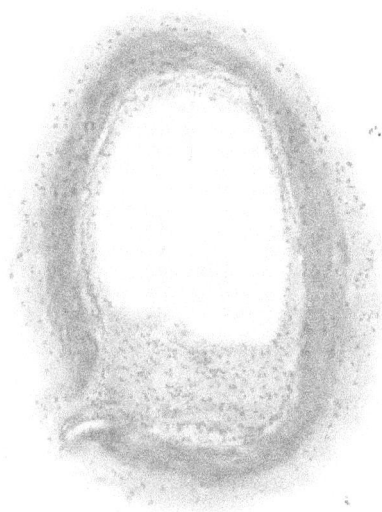

FIG. 62.—Section of one of the medium-sized cerebral vessels affected with chronic endarteritis deformans (atheroma). Stained with logwood and eosin. (× 40.)

    a. Thickened tunica intima.
    b. Internal elastic lamina.
    c. Muscular tunica media.
    d. Tunica adventitia.
    e. Endothelial lining covering
    f. Localised thickening of the tunica intima.
    g. Two small points at which calcification has occurred. Immediately around the calcareous patches the nuclei are present in considerable numbers.

length, and are usually confined to one side of the vessel, so that on section one side of the vessel wall is seen to be much thicker than the other, and the lumen is eccentric. On cutting into these masses, they are firm, hard, and in many cases calcareous and gritty feeling, some of them "cutting" almost like cartilage or fibrous tissue ;

frequently they are softened and yellow in the centre. The lumen is very much narrowed in places, whilst at one part the vessel is completely blocked by a clot of blood which has become adherent to the thickened and roughened wall.

Harden (§ 59 or 57), and stain (§§ 98 and 103).

(× 50).—The wall of the vessel is very unequally affected. The change takes place almost entirely within the internal elastic lamina which may be recognised as a wavy yellow line (with picro-carmine) situated immediately within the muscular layer, this latter being known by its regular lamination and the rod-shaped nuclei. The patches are very unequally distributed on the wall of the vessel, so that in transverse section the vessel has somewhat the appearance of a signet ring.

At the point where there is least change we have simply a thickening of the laminated part of the intima, in which there is proliferation of the flattened cells which lie between the fibrous laminæ. There appears to have been no proliferation of the endothelium ; from this point the thickening gradually increases until it is very marked, involving about half the circumference of the vessel. Where it is most marked, the intima may split into two layers, each of which is composed of laminated, fibrous looking tissue ; between the two laminæ is an open space. It will perhaps be advisable to examine the different layers, from the lumen to the intima, in order.

Near the lumen the fibrous tissue, as in the thinner part, is stained pink, showing, occasionally, the nucleus of a flattened cell. The cells in this position are increased in size and take on stains very readily.

Beneath this layer comes a mass of similar flattened laminated tissue, but the spaces in which the cells lie are much larger ; the cells are very granular and do not completely fill the spaces. In the deeper part of this layer, these spaces usually run into one another, and are filled with a bluish grey, highly refractile material, which disappears on the addition of hydrochloric acid, with the evolution of bubbles of carbon dioxide. Then comes a mass of homogeneous looking material, stained—but very unequally—a dirty pink, in which are numerous irregular slits or openings running in all directions, which contain granular or semi-crystalline bodies identical in appearance with those in the more regular spaces. Some of the irregular openings are of considerable size, and contain granular *débris* in addition to the bluish grey material. In most cases the line of demarcation, formed by the internal elastic lamina (between the diseased and the healthy tissues) is very distinct; but in the more advanced condition this bounding lamina has given way, and a process similar to that described in the deeper layers may be observed in the tunica media, the muscular layer becoming broken down and atrophied.

In a logwood stained specimen very similar details come out, but the nuclei near the lumen appear much more prominent than those in the deeper layers.

(× 300).—The earliest indications of the advancing change can be best made out immediately under the endothelium. The laminæ seen so distinctly under the low power are separated from one another, the intervals being occupied by cells, which, near the surface, are numerous, rounded, and deeply stained, lying in rows between the separated laminæ. Some of these are merely resting nuclei, others are undergoing swelling and proliferation, whilst others again are surrounded by a thin film of protoplasm. The laminæ in this position are also swollen. As the distance from the surface increases, the proportion of cells to fibres diminishes, the cells become flattened, they are not so deeply stained, and in many cases

FIG. 63.—Section of medium sized vessel (cerebral artery), endarteritis deformans. Stained with picro-carmine. (× 250.)

a. Placed in the lumen of the vessel.
b. Small round cells immediately under the lining endothelium.
c. Thickened intima, with flattened laminæ, and flat cells (corneal structure), cells and laminæ both swollen.
d. Region in which cells and intercellular laminæ are both becoming granular and swollen (fatty and calcareous deposit).
e. Broken down tissue, in which are large cracks and fissures, calcareous salts, crystals, &c.
f. Layer next to internal elastic lamina, similar in appearance and structure to *d*.
g. Yellow internal elastic lamina.
h. Muscular tunica media, perfectly healthy.

they are granular, the granular material becoming more abundant as the surface is left. In the deeper parts these granules stain black with osmic acid. Later, a number of similar granules make their appearance in the swollen fibrous tissue. The spaces around the granular areas are much enlarged, as though they had at some time been distended ; but now they contain only the *débris* of such tissue as originally caused the distension. When cells and matrix have both become granular, the whole mass may break down, and large spaces containing the calcareous looking material (some parts of it granular, others crystalline) are seen. In some of the spaces or cavities a few crystals of cholesterin may be found ; these are recognised by the fact that when a section is stained with iodine and then transferred to a weak solution of sulphuric acid (§ 91), they are stained blue, especially at their edges.

Where the calcification has passed into the middle coat, the appearance presented is exactly that seen in the deeper layer of the intima—a homogeneous or granular matrix, in which are numerous large spaces containing the granular *débris* and highly refractile crystals. This is usually accompanied by an increase in the number of cells in the adventitia, an indication that there is an accompanying condition of periarteritis.

The principal points to be noticed are, that part only of the circumference of the wall of the vessel is affected, and that the change takes place in the subendothelial tissue, commencing as a swelling and proliferation of the cells, followed immediately by a swelling of the fibrous matrix. These in turn, and in the same order, undergo fatty degeneration and calcareous infiltration, the most marked changes taking place in the deepest layers of the swollen and proliferating tissue, and the most recent changes always near the lumen of the vessel. The process commences near the internal elastic lamina, and extends through the intima towards the lumen of the vessel. Usually the internal elastic lamina defines, sharply, the diseased area, but this is not always the case ; when the media is invaded, the adventitia may also become secondarily affected.

ATHEROMA OF THE AORTA (ENDARTERITIS DEFORMANS).

213. *Naked eye appearances.*—Endarteritis deformans is most frequently met with in the first part of the aorta, where also it is seen
in the most advanced stage, but it may occur in any part of the
vessel, often around the openings of its branches, especially about
the orifices of those branches springing from the arch, and then
around the other vessels, in pretty regular order from above
downwards. It appears to affect those parts of the aorta at which
the strain is greatest, and the movement most continuous. For the
sake of convenience it may be divided into four stages, but all the
four stages may be observed in the same vessel. In the earliest stage

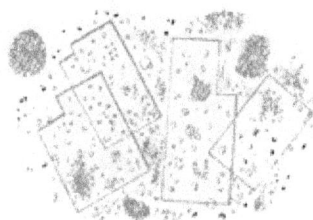

FIG. 64.—Cholesterin crystals, compound granular corpuscles, oil
droplets, and granular *débris.* (After Cornil and Ranvier.)

it takes the form of a pale pinkish opaque, translucent or opalescent,
somewhat gelatinous-looking, swelling of the intima. Though these
swellings vary considerably in size they are seldom more than half an
inch in diameter; they are rounded or oval, and have a perfectly smooth
surface, so that they evidently lie beneath the endothelium which
lines the vessel. In some cases these rounded patches are so near
together, that as they spread they meet one another, and form
irregularly shaped pearly masses, each of which very early acquires a
yellow centre. On cutting into one of the swollen patches, at this
stage, the pearly tissue is found to be firm and fibrous, whilst the

yellow centre is softer and more readily broken down. The mass may remain firm and tough, but as a rule the softened yellow patch becomes larger until it comes almost to the surface ; in this calcareous salts are deposited, and eventually a calcareous patch is formed which is covered by a single layer of endothelial cells resting on a

FIG. 65.—Atheroma of the aorta. Stained with picro-carmine. (× 50.)

    a. Position of lumen of vessel..
    b. Layer in which there is proliferation of cells and swelling of fibres.
    c. Commencement of fatty degeneration.
    d. Fatty degeneration and calcification in both cells and fibres.
    e. Muscular and elastic coat.
    f.   Do.   do.   teased out a little, to demonstrate the muscular and elastic layers.
       (Note that here there is no internal elastic lamina.)

thin membrane of laminated tissue, these separating the calcareous patch from the blood stream. The swollen or calcareous patches may be separated from the tunica media with the finger nail at almost any stage, leaving the media intact.

(× 300).—Examine the contents of one of these small softened centres. Spread out the fatty or cheesy looking material on a slide in a drop of Farrant's solution (§ **152**), and press a cover slip firmly down on it, with the handle of a needle. Note (1.) fatty granules and shrivelled fatty-looking and granular cells and fibres ; (2.) highly refractile granules, which disappear on the addition of hydrochloric acid (calcareous granules) ; (3.) fatty acid crystals ; and (4.) crystals of cholesterin, which may be recognised as rhomboidal plates, from one corner of which a small rhomboidal chip is wanting.

In more advanced cases the middle coat may be invaded, just as in the case of the cerebral artery already described. Where this occurs aneurism very frequently results, owing to the weakening of the vessel, the media being the true resistant coat.

Harden (§§ **59** or **57**), and stain (§ **98**).

(× 50).—The intima is now on the convex surface of the wall of the vessel ; the elastic tissue in the media and adventitia causes them to contract, and the outer surface of the vessel becomes the concave surface. The next point to be noted is that there is no distinct internal elastic lamina, and consequently no distinct line of demarcation between the intima and the media. In the media, as already stated, fenestrated elastic membranes separate the bundles of muscular fibre one from another.

Immediately under the endothelium, the appearances are very similar to those described in the smaller vessels, except that the cell proliferation is not nearly so well marked. Some of the spaces are undoubtedly enlarged, and the once flattened cells have now become swollen and are proliferating. The fibres are also swollen. Passing down further, the changes are still very similar, except that the granular and shrivelled looking cells are arranged in more regular layers with the pink fibrous laminæ between,—first a layer of cells, then a layer of fibres, and so on. Deeper still, the fibrous tissue also becomes granular looking ; and lastly, just before the muscular tissue is reached, is seen a homogeneous yellow-stained layer, with calcareous material (black or bluish-grey) deposited in the cracks and spaces. These spaces vary very much in size ; some are about two or three times the size of an ordinary cell space only, whilst others are so large that they occupy a considerable part of the thickening of the intima.

(× 300).—The flattened cells close to the surface are so granular that they appear to form long, flattened, regular rows of granules. Between these the fibrous tissue is swollen, but it is not markedly granular until some little distance from the surface. After this the changes are almost identical with those examined in the smaller vessel, and the appearances may be interpreted in the same manner. It will be noticed that in the earlier stages of the disease there is a layer of homogeneous pink tissue intervening between the media and the lower and more advanced portions of disintegrating tissue. The changes take place in the following order, the most recent being again near the surface, the more advanced deeper. Near the lumen, we see swelling and proliferation of the deeply-stained cells; then come swelling of the fibrous laminæ, fatty degeneration of the swollen cells, and similar changes in the fibres. This tissue either breaks down at this stage, or there is a deposit of calcareous material, first in the cells, and then in the fibrous tissue. As these parts become fatty, they no longer take on the pink stain, but are stained yellow by picric acid. The calcareous particles are more highly refractile, and have a bluish-grey colour when examined under the high power. The pink tissue intervening between the broken down calcareous material and the intima is very frequently found to be undergoing fatty degeneration, and small oil droplets are seen throughout its substance, which, although not sufficiently numerous to affect the pink colour appreciably, may be very readily seen scattered at intervals, either in or between the bundles of fibrous tissue. Further evidences of slight fatty degeneration may be seen in the interstitial tissue of the media, in some few cases affecting the internal muscular fibres of that coat.

ENDARTERITIS OBLITERANS.

214. There is a more or less acute inflammatory process, which not only affects the intima, but also involves the endothelial lining of the arteries. This condition occurs most frequently as (1) a syphilitic endarteritis; (2) the form which is found in healing wounds and in interstitial inflammations, very frequently, for example, in stone-mason's phthisis; and (3) a similar form, which is found in the vessels of the kidney during the course of Bright's disease (really a form of No. 2).

In syphilitic disease this endarteritis is of extremely common occurrence, and is, according to several authors—Heubner, Friedländer, Greenfield, and others—the determining cause of the caseation of gummata in syphilitic interstitial growths. It occurs especially in the cerebral arteries—medium sized vessels—but it may occur in smaller vessels in almost any organ of the body. In the basilar artery, for instance, so affected, small nodular thickenings are seen,

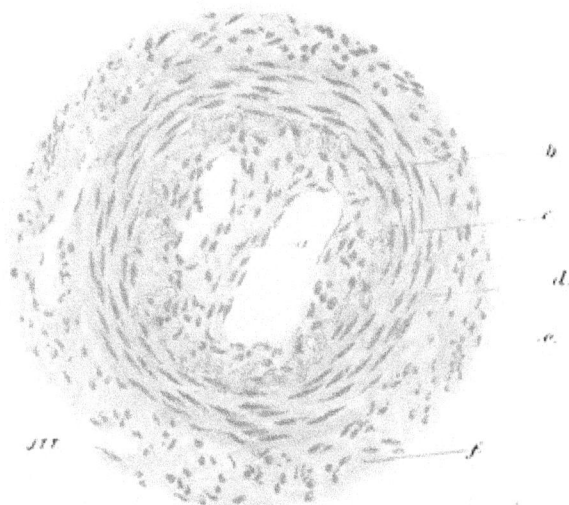

Fig. 66.—Section of small artery from the boundary area of the kidney from a case of subacute interstitial nephritis. Well-marked endarteritis obliterans. Stained with picro-carmine. (× 200.)

    a. Enormous thickening of subendothelial and endothelial tissues, the letter pointing to a process passing from wall to wall, and dividing the lumen into two channels.
    b. Yellow internal elastic lamina.
    c. Well-marked muscular coat.
    d. Delicate external elastic lamina.
    e. Fibro-cellular adventitia increased in thickness.
    f. Epithelium of one of the straight tubules.

the lumen of the tube affected becoming very irregular in shape and very much contracted. In some cases clots are found in the lumen, but these are frequently *post mortem.* Harden (§ 57), and stain (§ 98).

(× 50).—The thickening is mostly in the intima, internal to the internal elastic lamina. At the same time there appears to be some slight infiltration of the adventitia with cellular elements. The middle coat is usually irregularly thinned.

The thickened intima is made up of numerous cells, which appear to be formed by proliferation of the endothelial cells, and of the flattened cells of the intima. As already stated, this proliferation may become so great that the lumen of the vessel may be almost obliterated.

(× 300).—Lining the vessel is a layer of more or less flattened cells, which are spindle shaped or rounded when seen in section. Beneath this is a layer of irregular cells, some with rounded, others with elongated nuclei, whilst deeper still, and next to the

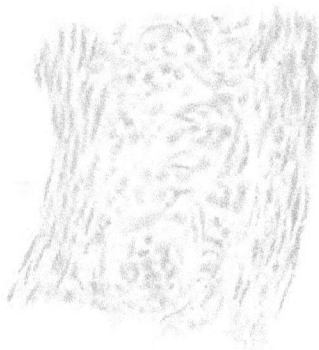

FIG. 67.—Section of the inner coat of a small syphilitic artery. (× 170, after Greenfield.)

   a. Lumen of the vessel.
   b. Internal elastic lamina.
   c. Thickened and cellular inner coat.
   d. Situation of muscular coat.
   e. Layers of cells representing endothelium.
   f. Transverse section of a small vessel in the deeper part of the inner coat.

internal elastic lamina, is a layer of flattened cells, with here and there a group of rounded cells. Pushing their way into this mass of cells are numerous capillary blood-vessels, which pass through the internal elastic lamina, from the capillaries of the inner layers of the media. It will be at once noticed that this is a process of organisation of a granulation tissue; and, as a matter of fact, we find that where the process has lasted for any considerable length of time, imperfectly developed fibrous tissue is formed (*see* Fig. 68 near *a*, where there are fibrous laminæ, between which are spaces, some

containing cells, others empty).   There is no fatty degeneration.
Organisation in a clot in a vessel differs in no essential detail from

FIG. 68.—Drawing of small segment of section of a syphilitic
artery. (× 170, after Greenfield.)
  a. Lumen of the vessel.
  b. Internal elastic lamina.
        Between *a.* and *b.* the enormously thickened intima, *c.*, is
        divided into two areas by a secondary elastic lamina, *g.*
  d. Muscular coat thinned near *b.*, considerably encroached upon
        by the small round-celled growth in the intima.
  e. Adventitia, cellular and thickened, in which are numerous
        blood-vessels, *h.*, prolonged through the media, and into the
        deeper layer of the intima, *i.*

that described in the chapter on Inflammation, Organisation, and
Repair (§§ 166-170).

In almost all cases of *endarteritis obliterans syphilitica*, as in the similar condition in interstitial nephritis, there is also marked thickening of the adventitia and even of the surrounding connective tissue. This thickening consists either of a small round-celled growth, or of such a mass which has become organised into fibro-connective tissue, more or less fully developed, which may be readily recognised under the microscope.

CHANGES WHICH TAKE PLACE IN THE MIDDLE COAT OF ARTERIES.

215. Of these several have been already mentioned as occurring in connection with disease of the intima, and the only one to be mentioned here is calcification of the middle coat, which occurs especially in the medium sized vessels of elderly people suffering from endarteritis deformans in the aorta. First there is fatty degeneration of the muscular wall of the artery; this makes its appearance in yellow patches or circles in the deeper part of the wall, and gradually spreads, but before the patches run together a deposit of calcareous material usually takes place in the yellow fatty rings. Later, the whole muscular wall becomes first fatty and then calcareous, when it is represented by nothing but a brittle tube. If this be macerated a perfect cast of the muscular coat remains.

Harden (§ 59), stain (§§ 98 and 110).

(× 50).—The muscular coat is seen to be undergoing fatty degeneration, the tissue appearing yellower (with picro-carmine), or blackened (with osmic acid). The intima and adventitia are almost normal in appearance.

(× 300).—The tunica media is undergoing fatty degeneration at certain points, the muscular fibres and connective tissue are granular and much yellower than normal, whilst with osmic acid a number of the granules are stained black.

At other parts highly refractile calcareous granules are seen. These, when treated with hydrochloric acid, disappear, and carbon dioxide bubbles are evolved. The intima and adventitia are comparatively healthy, though the adventitia in some cases appears to become infiltrated with cells and considerably weakened; this latter condition usually follows rupture of the brittle tube.

A similar calcification often occurs in the smaller arteries, such as those at the base of the brain, where, however, the patches have a peculiar annular arrangement. The microscopic appearances of a transverse section are exactly the same as above. Fatty degeneration of the vessels is met with in phosphorus poisoning (§ 180). It occurs especially in the capillary vessels, where first the protoplasm around the nucleus becomes granular; then droplets of fat are formed in the cells of which the wall of the vessel is built up. These droplets are stained black with osmic acid, and may come to occupy the whole of the cell. Punctiform hæmorrhages are found where the vessels have given way under increased pressure. The fatty degeneration may extend to the smaller arterioles, and, like the condition next to be described, greatly predispose to the formation of aneurisms or even ruptures of vessels. Waxy degeneration in the middle coat, the parts specially affected being the delicate connective tissue fibrils between the muscle tissue proper, is met with, especially in the small arterioles. (See descriptions of waxy organs.)

Chronic Periarteritis, or Inflammation of the Adventitia.

216. Chronic periarteritis is usually associated with endarteritis, especially in interstitial inflammations of the Kidney, Lung, &c., in the description of which conditions it will be mentioned. It is met with in syphilitic interstitial inflammations, forming a marked feature in such cases; but the most important form of the disease is that which occurs in the small arteries of the brain, where we have a chronic inflammation of the adventitia, usually associated with endarteritis, and a gradual atrophy and degeneration of the middle coat, evidences of which may be readily seen under the microscope. The outer coat is formed of laminæ of fibrous tissue, between which the connective tissue cells may be seen as flattened corpuscles; the middle coat becomes granular, and very much compressed and condensed. With this condition multiple aneurisms and hæmorrhages are frequently associated.

217. Whilst the subject of vessels is under consideration, it may

be well to give very briefly the various forms of aneurisms which
are met with as a result of injury to, or disease of, the walls of
the vessels.

True Aneurisms.

A true aneurism is a dilatation of a vessel so arranged as to form a
kind of sac, the walls of which are formed by some or all of the coats
of the vessel, but generally by parts of the intima and the adventitia
.only. The blood is thus confined within its proper walls, but not
within its proper bounds. Anything which weakens the wall of the
vessel, such as endarteritis, slight injury, overstrain, &c., predisposes
to this condition.

The wall of an aneurism is composed almost entirely of laminated
fibrous tissue. Between the laminæ are flattened cells. Some of
this tissue is the persisting intima, another part, the more important,
the altered adventitia. Patches of granular and fatty tunica media
may be seen near the undilated vessel, or where the dilatation is but
slight, but in most parts it has almost entirely disappeared. In some
cases the wall of the aneurism is calcified.

Cylindrical and fusiform aneurisms are rounded or elongated symmetrical dilatations of the vessel. They occur in atheroma and
arteritis, affecting the whole wall of the vessel for a shorter or longer
distance. This condition is accompanied by (1.) flattening of the
intima, (2.) thinning of the media, and (3.) distension of the adventitia, the last-named coat forming the chief part of the wall of the
aneurismal sac.

Sacculated aneurism is a unilateral dilatation of the wall of the
vessel, the opening being usually smaller than the cavity into which
it opens. The muscular coat disappears from the wall, the intima
appears as a modified flattened coat, and the adventitia, which is
composed of thickened fibrous laminæ, between which are flattened
connective tissue cells, forms the principal part of the wall of the
aneurism, which in turn is usually lined by or filled with a laminated
clot. This frequently occurs as a result of localised endarteritis in
the second part of the arch of the aorta, at points where the large
branches are given off from it or along their course, especially at the

point where the cœliac axis or other large branches are given off from the abdominal aorta, in the popliteal vessels, &c.

A *dissecting aneurism* is the aneurism formed when blood, escaping through a weakened and ruptured intima, makes its way between the layers of the tunica media. The escaped blood may pass for some distance down the vessel, and then again make its way into the lumen. Such an aneurism may be developed as one of the results of the fusiform dilatation, or it may be found where there has been chronic inflammation of the wall of the vessel, especially of the intima; it comes on very suddenly, and is due in most cases to the rupture of the brittle intima.

A *saddle clot aneurism* is a sacculated aneurism, developed at the bifurcation of a vessel. It is usually due to the endarteritis, and consequent weakening of the wall, set up by an embolus arrested at the point of bifurcation of the vessel.

Miliary aneurisms are multiple sacculated aneurisms, occurring in the brain as a result either of fatty degeneration or of periarteritis, in which conditions the coats of the vessels are weakened at many points.

False Aneurisms.

A false aneurism is a cavity formed in connection with the lumen of a vessel. This cavity, however, is not bounded entirely by the coats of the vessel; it may communicate with some other cavity, or its walls may be formed by the surrounding extra vascular tissues.

A *traumatic aneurism* is formed where a vessel is wounded and the blood escaping into the tissues around the vessel, gradually displaces them until they form a limiting wall. If the wound in the vessel wall be large, there may even be pulsation in a cavity so formed. A true aneurism may, by rupturing, form a false aneurism, the blood then escaping into and distending the surrounding tissues until a false aneurismal cavity is formed outside the true aneurism.

Varicose aneurism results from the opening of a true aneurism into a vein, or from a false aneurism communicating with a vein. When venesection was more frequently practised varicose aneurism was especially common at the bend of the elbow.

Aneurismal varix is the condition in which a false aneurism is formed in a vein. There is a direct communication between the vein and the artery, and whilst the latter remains comparatively undilated, the vein becomes enormously distended, in consequence of the direct throwing in of the arterial blood and the resulting increase in the intravenous pressure ; in time its walls become thickened.

Other conditions which simulate aneurism, but which do not come under either of the above headings, are—

(1.) The *cirsoid aneurism*, which consists of a number of small arteries, capillaries, and even veins, which are elongated, dilated, and frequently varicose. The whole mass of vessels forms a pulsating tumour, usually on the face or head.

(2.) *Aneurism by anastomosis*, where, along with enlargement of existing arteries, new arteries are formed, and a pulsating tumour is the result, also most frequently met with on the head.

Diseases of Veins—Phlebitis.

218. The commonest diseases of the veins are those met with as the result of inflammation. In acute phlebitis we may have the walls infiltrated with cellular tissue, with small granulations in the intima, and eventually thrombosis ; in the whole of this new tissue organisation takes place ; or, in consequence of the nature of the irritant which sets up these changes (micro-organisms), the tissues may suppurate and we have what is known as suppurative phlebitis. (*See* Formation of Abscess, § **165.**)

Varix.

219. In varix the superficial veins, especially those of the lower extremities and of the mucous membranes, become distended and tortuous. Irregular dilatations, or ampullæ, occur along their course, whilst here and there calcification of the wall takes place. On slitting open such a vein, the valves are found to be obliterated by the stretching of the intima, the valvular folds being drawn out. Surrounding the tortuous and dilated veins is usually a dense mass of connective tissue, which mats the vessels together. Harden (§ **59**), and stain (§ **98**).

(× 50).—The inner coat is composed of laminated tissue, almost identical in structure with that described in endarteritis deformans. The longitudinal and transverse bands of muscle fibre, stained yellow, are surrounded by pink connective tissue, often containing golden-brown altered blood pigment. The adventitia is also somewhat thickened. Where the dilatation is very great and irregular, the muscular bands may have entirely disappeared at the points of dilatation, or they can be seen as granular or fatty masses scattered throughout the laminated connective tissue.

(× 300).—The above appearances must be verified.

Organisation in clot in veins takes place in the same manner as in arteries and in healing wounds or on serous surfaces (§§ 165-170).

CHAPTER VII.

THE KIDNEY.

220. The normal kidney is "smooth, and of a deep red colour." It weighs about four and a quarter to four and a half oz. (§ **18**); is about four inches long, two and a half inches broad, and one and a quarter inches thick, though the left kidney is somewhat longer and narrower than the right, and is also rather heavier. On close examination of the surface of the organ, small injected stellate veins are seen beneath the capsule. Make a longitudinal incision from the convex border to the hilus, then lay hold of the capsule with the forefinger and thumb and detach it. In a normal kidney this is readily done; the smooth surface is then seen to have a homogeneous or *slightly* mottled appearance, from which the stellate veins stand out prominently. On examination of the section, the kidney is seen to consist of (1) the cortex, forming the outer layer of tissue; (2) the medulla, or the part between the cortex and the pelvis; and (3) the pelvis, or funnel shaped collecting basin into which, drained by the ureter, the papillæ converge (for relative thickness of cortex and medulla, see § **18**). Radiating from the medulla to the cortical surface are numerous sets of parallel straight lines. These, on close examination, are found to be small arterial trunks, on each side of which are arranged, very regularly, a number of small round shining, almost translucent, points—the Malpighian bodies. Between them are opaque conical bundles of straight tubules. The straight tubules are longest midway between the rows of Malpighian bodies, and reach nearly to the surface, but nearer the Malpighian bodies they are considerably shorter. This structure will be examined more in detail under the microscope. On each side of the bundle of straight tubules is a somewhat irregular tissue, composed of sections of convoluted tubules. At the line where the cortical substance joins the medulla are numerous sections of vessels of considerable size, from which branches pass both upwards and downwards.

The medullary portion of the kidney is, for the sake of convenience, divided into two layers, the boundary layer, or that nearer the cortex, and the papillary portion, or that near the apices of the

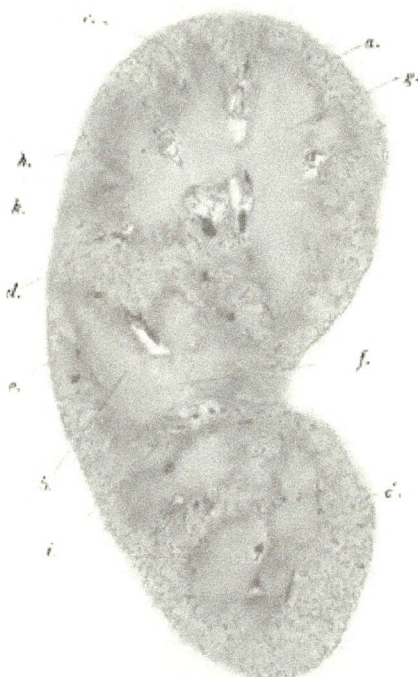

FIG. 69.—Section of a small normal kidney injected with carmine gelatine.

a. Cortex ; *h.* "superficial" cortex ; *i.* interpyramidal cortex.
b. Medulla ; *e.* boundary layer ; *f.* papillary portion, with a chink where it opens in a calyx of the pelvis of the kidney—the only part of the calyx seen in the section.
c. and *c'.* Lines of interlobular arteries, with rows of Malpighian bodies—red dots—on each side.
d. Arteries of supply in boundary area.
g. Comparatively non-vascular part of the medulla.
k. Straight vessels. The relative vascularity of the cortex and medulla is well seen.

pyramids, dipping down into the pelvis. The pyramids of Malpighi, of which about eight are usually seen in the section, extend as inverted cones from the papillary portion, dipping into the pelvis, up to the superficial cortex (or that which does not dip down between the pyramids), and, between the bases of these pyramids, the cortex

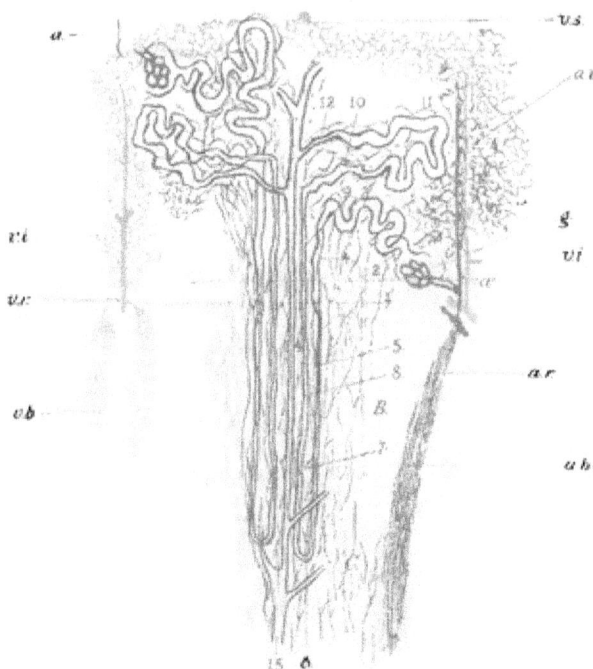

FIG. 70.—Diagram showing the course of the renal tubules, the arrangement of the vessels, and the Malpighian bodies. (Modified from Klein and Noble Smith.)

v.s. Stellate vein.
v.i. Interlobular vein.
a.i. Interlobulary artery.
g. Glomerulus of Malpighian corpuscle.
a.r. Arteria recta.
v.r. Vena recta.
a.b. Bundle of arteriolæ rectæ.
v.b. Bundle of venæ rectæ.
A. Cortex.
a. Subcapsular layer, not containing Malpighian corpuscles.
a¹. Inner layer of cortex, not containing Malpighian corpuscles.
B. Boundary layer.
C. Papillary part.

1. Bowman's capsule.
2. Neck.
3. Proximal convoluted tubule.
4. Spiral tubule.
5. Descending limb of looped tubule of Henle.
6. The loop.
7. Ascending limb.
8. Spiral part of ascending limb.
9. Narrow part in medullary ray.
10. The irregular tubule.
11. Distal convoluted tubule.
12. Curved collecting tubule.
13, 14, 15. Straight collecting tubule.

dips down for some distance, forming the so-called interpyramidal cortex. The pyramids are made up of a series of alternating light and dark lines, the light lines being the urinary tubes which are continuous with the conical bundles of tubules which have been described in the cortex, and the dark lines the straight vessels, proceeding from the boundary area to the apices of the papillæ.

The papillary portion of the pyramid is considerably lighter in colour than the cortex, which is described as being "light crimson brown;" it consists of striated tissue, the striæ being regular, and at right angles to the orifices of the papillæ as they open into the calyces or subdivisions of the pelvis. Much is to be learned from a naked eye examination of the kidney, which should always be most systematically carried out.

For the purposes of the pathologist, the kidney may be described as consisting of a series of lobules, and any change which is found in one of these lobules may confidently be looked for in any other. But before describing the lobule, it will be necessary to have some idea of the various structures of which it is composed. These are—(1) The blood-vessels; (2) the secreting urinary tubules; (3) the collecting urinary tubules; and (4) the connective tissue framework (§ 223).

221. *Blood-vessels.*—The renal artery breaks up into a number of branches which, running from the pelvis along the sides of the Malpighian pyramids in the submucous tissue, enter the substance of the kidney at the boundary layer, at once breaking up into a number of arches, the convex surfaces of which are towards the cortex; from these arches in the boundary layer two sets of vessels pass, one upwards, the interlobular arteries, and one downwards, the straight branches which subdivide to form the arteriolæ rectæ. The interlobular arteries give off a series of lateral branches (afferent arterioles) almost at right angles, each of which passes to a Malpighian body where it breaks up into a tuft of small capillary vessels — the glomerular tuft. These are again collected into a single vessel, the efferent arteriole, which carries the blood from the Malpighian body and then breaks up to form a network of capillaries; these capillaries surround the various tubules, and afterwards open into veins, which gradually unite to form the interlobular vein. In addition to the above branches of the artery and vein there are interstitial and capsular branches to

the connective tissue and capsule of the organ, and the interlobular vein commencing as the stellate vein already mentioned. It is necessary to remember this arrangement of the veins in connection with chronic venous congestion of the kidney.

Passing downwards into the medulla from the arches in the boundary layer are numerous short vessels, which speedily break up, each one into a tuft or pencil of small straight vessels, the arteriolæ rectæ ; these form a network with elongated meshes around the bundles of urinary tubules ; they pass down as far as the papillæ. Beginning at the apices of the papillæ are small veins which return to the boundary layer, and take a similar course to the arteriolæ rectæ, around the bundles of straight tubules ; in the boundary layer the blood from these meets the blood from the interlobular veins, and is conveyed away from the kidney by large venous trunks running in the submucous tissue to the hilus, and thence by the renal vein.

222. *Urinary tubules.*—These form the parenchyma, or substance proper of the kidney. Klein describes them as commencing " with a cœcal extremity in the Malpighian corpuscles," and terminating "with an opening on the free surface of the papilla." He then describes the tubules as composed of sixteen different segments, the first of which—(1) the Malpighian corpuscle, is in reality the invaginated and distended end of the blind tube (like the finger tip of a glove turned inwards, *see* Fig. 76). Pushed into the invagination is a tuft of capillary vessels communicating on the one hand with the afferent arteriole, and on the other with the efferent arteriole, both of which pass into the involuted "tip." The outer coat of the double covering of the capillary tuft is known as Bowman's capsule. It is composed of a basement membrane, bounded on its external surface by a connective tissue (which plays a most important part in certain pathological processes), whilst internally it has a layer of flattened endothelioid cells. Continuous with this layer of Bowman's capsule is a similar layer of flattened cells covering the tuft of capillaries, forming what is in fact a reflection of the capsule. Supporting the capillary vessels is a delicate connective tissue framework (also very important), the nuclei of the cells of which are easily distinguished in stained specimens. Between the tuft of capillaries and Bowman's capsule is a space which communicates by (2) a narrow opening, or neck, with the tubule proper. The tubule throughout its whole length is composed of a basement membrane, resting on which is a layer of epithelial cells. These epithelial cells vary considerably in both form and structure in the different sections of the tubule. In the neck of the tubule they are slightly cubical in form, but those nearest the glomerulus are flattened. Immediately following the neck, and therefore still near the Malpighian body, comes (3) the first

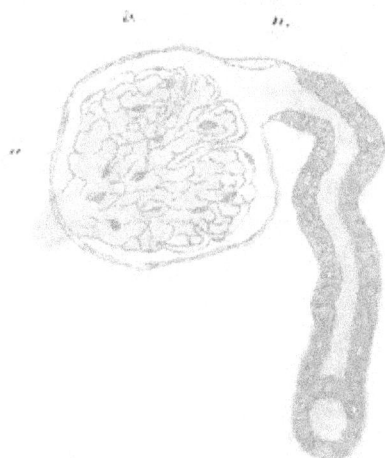

FIG. 71.—Malpighian body, and part of convoluted tubule of kidney of dog. (× 350.) (After Klein and Noble Smith.)

a. Capillaries of the glomerular tuft arranged in lobules.
b. "Bowman's capsule, with its lining of flat epithelial cells, and the flat epithelial cells covering the glomerulus."
s. Stalk of the glomerulus, composed of afferent and efferent arterioles.
n. "Neck of the Malpighian corpuscle."
c. Longitudinal section of the first part of the convoluted tubule.

part of the convoluted tubule, which, with the following part, (4) the spiral tubule, runs entirely in the cortex. In these the epithelium is columnar but somewhat irregular, especially in the spiral tubule, and each cell has a rounded nucleus situated in its centre. The upper part of the cell, that near the lumen, is finely granular, but the part between the nucleus and the basement membrane is distinctly striated, the striæ running longitudinally from the base of the cell to the nucleus. The next part of the tubule (the looped tubule of Henle) is principally within the medulla. The descending limb and the loop itself, (5) and (6), are lined by a layer of flattened epithelial cells. After the loop the ascending limb of the tubule (7) is lined with a layer of columnar cells, each of which has its nucleus placed near the lumen. Passing further upwards (8) the lumen becomes narrowed, but the epithelium

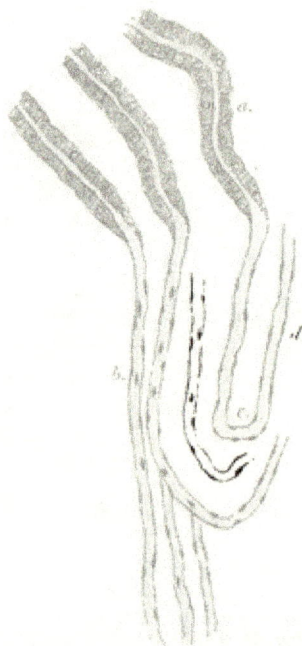

FIG. 72.—Looped tubules of Henle cut longitudinally in both the boundary layer and the papillary portion of the pyramid. (× 300.) (After Klein and Noble Smith.)

  a. First part of the ascending limb of the looped tubule of Henle, in which the epithelium is columnar.
  b. Part of the ascending limb.
  c. The bend.
  d. The descending limb and loop of the looped tubule of Henle, in all of which the epithelium is flattened and squamous. The tubules at these points are very like young blood-vessels in appearance.

remains columnar. In the cortex (9) the ascending tube is narrower, and its epithelium more cubical or flattened. Still in the cortex is (10) the irregular tubule, lined by columnar cells, which vary very much in height, always, however, leaving the lumen of this part of the tubule very narrow. Then follows (11) the second or distal convoluted tubule, which is "identical" in position and structure with the first part of the convoluted tubule. After this, still in the cortex, are (12) the curved parts of the collecting tubule, and (13) part of the straight tubule, the lining of which is an irregular epithelium, with some of the cells cubical, others spindle-shaped, but all having well-marked nuclei. Lower down in the medulla (14) the lumen of the tube is larger and the cells are cubical or slightly columnar, and each contains a spherical nucleus. (15) The lower parts of the collecting tubule, and (16) the large papillary duct are lined by epithelium of a cubical type, leaving a lumen of considerable size.

From the accompanying diagram and description it will be seen that, the straight collecting tube being taken as a central point, the looped tubules of Henle are arranged on each side, whilst further out come the sections of the two convoluted tubules, and lastly the Malpighian bodies as they spring from the interlobular arteries. A lobule of the kidney is composed of the tissues between two interlobular arteries and the prolongations of these down into the medulla.

In the cortex the lobule of the kidney may, like the lobule of the liver, be divided into three zones—peripheral, intermediate, and central. In the peripheral zone are the Malpighian bodies, with regular sections of the convoluted tubules. The intermediate zone, much narrower, is made up of the irregular and spiral portions of the convoluted tubules, the central zone containing the straight tubules and the larger collecting tubules.

The central zone only is continued into the medulla, where it is composed, as in the cortex, of the straight tubules of the descending limbs of the looped tubule, and of the straight collecting tubules. In the greater part of the papillary portion of the medulla the lobule is represented by the collecting tubes alone.

223. Examine a section of the cortex of an injected kidney (§ 47) made in the plane of the convex outer surface.

(× 50).—A number of polygonal areas may be observed, bounded by vessels, with here and there Malpighian bodies, in which the capillaries are injected. Within this vascular ring are numerous sections of tubules, some of them cut obliquely, others more transversely. Note that the lumen of each tubule is small and irregular; the epithelium is columnar, and each cell has a rounded nucleus near the lumen; the vascular meshes around these tubules are of considerable size. Nearer the centre are the tubules described as making up the intermediate zone, and here the loops of vessels are smaller, as the tubules are not only smaller, but are more regularly cut transversely, the cells are more cubical, and the lumen is still narrow. In the central zone the meshes of the network of vessels are again somewhat larger: the openings in the tubules are larger, the epithelium being cubical and occupying less of the tubule.

(× 50).—Examine a section cut at right angles to the above (this is the direction in which sections of the kidney are usually made). The zones of the lobules, as above described, can be made out in both the cortex and the medulla. Notice especially the large vascular meshes around the convoluted tubules in the peripheral and intermediate zones, the more elongated meshes around the straight tubules (seen now in longitudinal section) of the central zone; in the medulla, the long vascular bundles and meshes running down, between, and around the bundles of straight tubules.

(× 300).—Examine the arrangement of the tubules with their contained epithelium, the structure of the Malpighian bodies, the amount of connective tissue around the capillary loops of the glomerulus, around the glomerulus itself, around the tubules, and around the vessels.

Tube Casts.

224. In our examination of the kidneys, various forms of casts and cysts will be met with, and in order that the student may understand something of them, it may be well to consider these intratubular formations somewhat systematically before we take up the principle diseases in which they occur.

Casts may be divided into four groups—(1.) those derived from hæmorrhages into the glomeruli or tubules; (2.) those composed of altered epithelium; (3.) those formed of urinary secretions; (4.) those made up of other materials not normally found in the tubules.

(1.) *Casts derived from Blood.*—Under the first form come the various *blood casts* which are met with in acute nephritis—especially the scarlatinal form—in chronic venous congestion, or in acute congestion of the kidney. In the acute diseases they are most frequently composed of but slightly altered red blood corpuscles, and are commonly met with in the first part of the convoluted tubule. In the more chronic forms of disease they may be met with in the same position, but they are also seen as pigment casts in the lower parts of the tubules, where they may be golden-brown in colour, in which case they are composed of hæmatoidin crystals or granules ; in the straight tubules they usually occur in the form of extremely black material, or melanin. In either case they are derived from blood which has escaped from ruptured glomerular, or less frequently, intertubular capillaries.

Hyaline fibrinous casts occur especially in acute inflammatory conditions, but they may be met with in health. They are usually seen in the looped and collecting tubules as delicate homogeneous casts filling a considerable length of the tube. They are extremely difficult to recognise in an unstained specimen, but may be seen as very delicately stained homogeneous masses in carmine (§ 100), or logwood (§ 103), stained sections. They form the basis of a great number of other casts. In very acute cases we may actually find fibrinous lymph, and even leucocytes, in these casts ; but more commonly the casts are quite homogeneous, and appear to consist of coagulated serum albumen, which has made its way from the glomerular capillaries into the tubules.

(2.) *Casts derived from Epithelium.*—The most common cast of this form is the *colloid* (or glue-like) *cast*, a homogeneous, yellowish, translucent mass, found especially in the lower parts of the convoluted tubules in almost all cases of kidney disease where there are marked epithelial changes, as in waxy kidney, and in subacute and chronic interstitial nephritis. In some cases the casts present the dim outlines of the cells of which they are composed, but most frequently they appear to be composed simply of a glue-like material, which gives a yellow reaction with picro-carmine (§ 98), a brown reaction with iodine (§ 107), but a bluer purple with methylaniline violet (§ 106) than is given with "waxy" material. They stain deeply with other reagents. They are usually surrounded by a layer of flattened epithelial cells, which appear to proliferate and add layer after layer of degenerated cells to the surface; consequently, the cast may in some cases present faint traces of lamination.

Granular casts are met with in the convoluted tubules in inflammatory conditions, or where marked atrophic changes are taking place in the epithelium. They are composed of a hyaline centre, with granular protoplasmic material, which appears to be derived from degenerating epithelial cells around; these casts are larger than the ordinary hyaline cast. Some authors term only those casts granular that are derived from degenerated blood or dissolved blood pigment which is deposited in the epithelium, and forms the basis of the brown granular tube casts.

Fatty or oily casts are hyaline casts around which are fatty or albuminoid globules. (Not always fatty.)

Epithelial casts are usually found in the looped and straight tubules when these are in a condition of acute catarrh. Each has a hyaline basis, and is covered with a number of cells, derived either from the epithelium of the straight tubules or from exuded leucocytes. Only those casts which are formed in the looped or straight collecting or excretory tubules come unchanged to the urine, but similar casts may be found in the upper parts of the tubules in sections of the kidney.

(3.) *Casts formed from Urinary Salts, &c.*—As seen in the case of the granular contracted kidney, crystals of acid urate of soda accumulate in the tubules of all the regions of the kidney, giving rise to the yellow patches mentioned under that disease.

Similar deposits of uric acid, or urate of ammonia or soda, are frequently met with in the excretory tubes near the apices of the papillæ in children who die within from two to fourteen days after birth, as "yellowish or brick-red lines," running from the apices for some distance towards the bases of the pyramids. Ziegler says that apparently the rapid metabolic changes which take place after birth are accompanied by the production of so much uric acid, that the urine is incapable of holding it all in solution, and it is deposited as casts.

(4.) *Casts of foreign material.*—*Bilirubin casts* are dark granular casts, occurring chiefly in the straight tubules during the course of long-continued jaundice. They are probably closely allied to blood casts

Calcareous casts are met with in the straight tubules in aged people, and in cases of osteomalacia, where there is a rapid absorption of the calcareous salts from bone. These salts are deposited as white masses in the looped tubules or in the excretory tubules near the apices of the papillæ. "They consist of dark, strongly-refractile globules or nodular masses, which join together to form nodular rods." In a second form there is "an albuminoid basis, infiltrated with carbonate of lime." These stain deeply, but irregularly. On the addition of a weak acid they disappear, and carbon dioxide is given off. They are composed principally of carbonate of lime.

Cysts in the Kidney.

225. *True secondary cysts* may be formed in one of three ways.

(1.) By distension of Bowman's capsule of the Malpighian body, owing to the obstruction of the narrow outlet or neck, frequently by a plug of colloid material, or, more rarely, by constricting fibrous bands. These cysts are seldom of large size, as the outflow of the watery part of the secretion from the capillary tuft ceases as soon as the pressure in the cyst equals that in the blood-vessels. The capillaries atrophy when their function is lost, and a cyst is left. These may be filled with watery material, or with colloid material derived from the degenerating epithelial cells.

(2.) Simple cysts in the tubules are formed in the same manner.

(3.) Rows of cysts are formed where the convoluted or straight tubules become irregular, varicose, and tortuous, forming a chain of small cysts. They occur especially in the granular contracted kidney, and in the tubules which are situated near the margin of the wedge-shaped mass, where the convoluted tubule is alternately outside and within the granular patch. Colloid plugs are formed at certain points, usually where there is already slight constriction from the pressure of fibrous bands; above this point there are other slight constrictions, and as the tube becomes distended it becomes so unequally—especially where it lies outside the solid area— and a row of cysts is formed, the dilatations and constrictions alternating.

For cysts to increase in size there must be two factors at work :—

(1.) the watery secretion must be going on above the constricted point ; and (2.) epithelium must be growing, must be shed, and then, undergoing degeneration, must be washed by the urine until it eventually forms colloid material.

The contents of these cysts may be—

    (1.) Serum, or the watery part of the blood along with its salts. This occurs most commonly.

    (2.) Colloid ; a gelatinous, homogeneous material, derived from degenerated epithelium.

    (3.) Urinous salts or urates, which are by no means uncommonly met with.

Cysts are most frequently found in the granular contracted kidney, and in the various forms of interstitial nephritis.

Primary Cysts.—These are found in the so-called cystic degeneration. There are two forms—the congenital, and that which occurs during adult life.

In the first form, which occurs during fœtal life, the kidney may be enormously increased in size, or it may be smaller than normal. Both organs are affected. The cysts, which form the greater part of the organ, are probably distended tubules and glomeruli, the secretions of which cannot escape, owing to constriction of the efferent tubes in the atrophied papillæ. These cysts, unlike the following form, contain urinary fluid and salts.

The second form is very frequently unsuspected during life, and usually gives rise to no symptoms until late in life. Both kidneys are enlarged, and are converted into numerous cysts, which vary very much in size, from that of a millet seed up to two-thirds of an inch, or even more, in diameter. They are filled with a fluid containing albumen and blood-pigment in various stages of alteration, so that they present all shades of colour, from yellow, through green and blue, up to purple. Cholesterin crystals are also met with, and in rare cases, oxalate of lime and leucin—rarely any urinary salts. The fibrous cyst walls " are partially lined with flattened polygonal cells." It is quite possible that this may be the slowly growing or fully developed congenital form, but as yet little is known of the mode of development of either of the forms of cystic degeneration.

CHRONIC VENOUS CONGESTION OF THE KIDNEY.

226. *Synonyms.*—" Cyanotic " Kidney (not a good term), "Congestive Induration," " Passive Hyperæmia " of the Kidney.

In chronic venous congestion of the kidney, we have distension and thickening of the veins and venous capillaries with wasting of the parenchyma, brought about by pressure and malnutrition.

This condition is met with in conjunction with valvular disease of the heart, more especially with mitral disease, in chronic fibroid phthisis, chronic bronchitis, emphysema ; in fact, it occurs under just the same conditions as does chronic venous congestion of the liver (§ **182**), to which it is analogous, and with which it is frequently associated.

In cases of heart disease, during the course of which albumen in the urine or slight hæmaturia has been present, this condition may very frequently be found after death.

Naked eye appearances.—In the earlier stages of the congestion the kidney is enlarged ; it may be as much as seven or eight ounces in weight, and is firm and elastic. Under the capsule, the venæ stellatæ are considerably distended and are very prominent. On section the capsule is readily removed ; the cortex is smooth, markedly congested, and has at first a deep purple colour, which rapidly turns to crimson.

On examining the section of the cortex more carefully, its thickness is seen to be slightly increased, the Malpighian bodies stand out as red spots, arranged regularly in parallel rows on each side of the prominent interlobular vessels (distended interlobular veins). The most marked changes, however, are in the medulla, where the venulæ rectæ stand out prominently, especially near the bases of the pyramids, which are deeply congested ; the tissue has a distinctly striated appearance, the congested vessels shining out very prominently between the bundles of uriniferous tubules. In old-standing congestion, irregular pale patches (due to fatty degeneration of the epithelium in the tubules), may make their appearance, and the organ may feel almost fibroid.

Harden (§ **59**), cut (§ **82** *et seq.*), and stain (§ **98**). The following description applies to the later stages of the disease (in the earlier stages we see simply the distension of the vessels without any of the structural changes).

(× 50).—The interlobular veins in the cortex are filled with a greenish material,—coloured blood corpuscles. Following the course of these veins, it is seen that the capillary plexus between the convoluted and straight tubules, the afferent arterioles and the glomerular

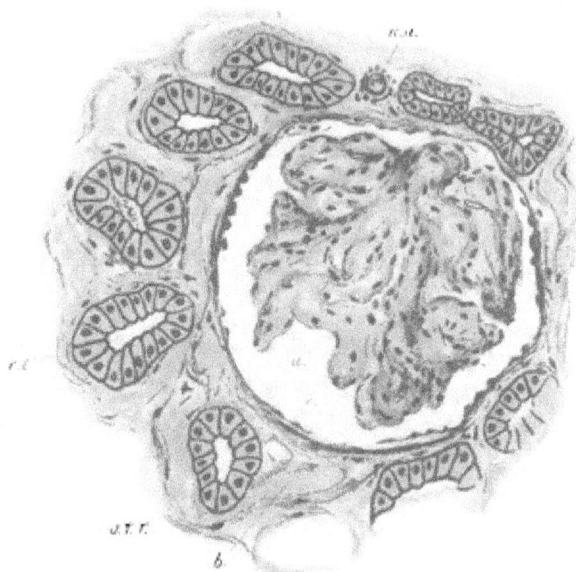

FIG. 73.—Drawing of a section of cortex of kidney in a state of chronic venous congestion. Stained with logwood. (× 300.)

  a. Capillaries of glomerular tuft distended with blood.
  b. Intertubular capillaries in a similar condition.
  a.a. Afferent arteriole seen in transverse section.
  c.t. Convoluted tubules.
  c. Flattened cells lining Bowman's capsule.
  It will be noticed that there appears to be a considerable thickening of the walls of the vessels between the sections of the convoluted tubules.

capillaries are all distended with this same greenish material. The glomeruli are, in some cases, very much increased in size, and the connective tissue nuclei are increased in number. In the medulla the straight vessels are extremely prominent, being all distended with coloured blood corpuscles.

Next examine the tubules. Very frequently the capillaries in the

Malpighian bodies show signs of rupture, small extravasations of blood are found within the glomerular capsule, and large masses of altered blood may be seen in the convoluted tubules. In the straight tubules in the medulla small masses of golden brown pigment (derived from the blood) are met with, and here and there almost inky black "melanin" casts occupy a few of the tubules in the papillary portion of the medulla. The epithelium may be

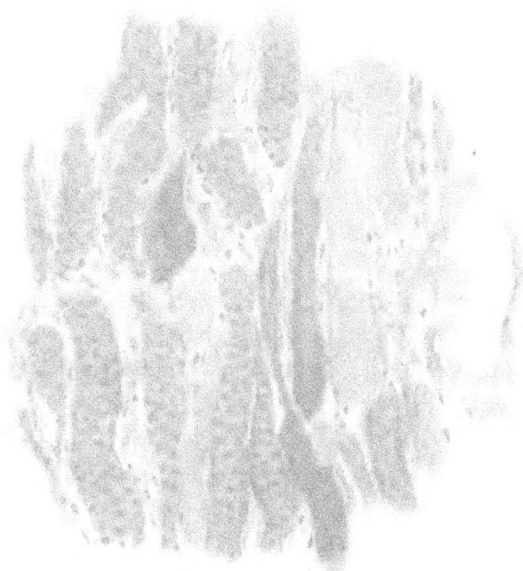

FIG. 74.—Drawing of section of kidney (boundary layer) in a state of chronic venous congestion. Stained with picro-carmine. (× 300.)
v.c. Vessels distended with coloured blood corpuscles.
a.l.H. Ascending limb of looped tubule of Henle. Spiral portion and collecting tubule.
d.l.H. Descending limb.

granular, with small globules of fat in the protoplasm of the cells, which in some cases nearly fill the tubules. Very frequently there are wedge-shaped pink patches of fibro-cellular tissue under the capsule, the base of the wedge being near the surface, the apex extending for some little distance into the cortex ; they extend along the lines of the interlobular vessels, and enclose some of the Malpighian bodies, which then become atrophied and fibroid. The tubules involved in these masses are atrophied and small, and their epithelium

T

is flattened. This is said to be an intercurrent inflammatory condition, but it is one which frequently occurs in this disease.

(× 300).—The capillary tufts in the Malpighian bodies are greatly enlarged, the vessels being distended with red blood corpuscles ; between the tuft and Bowman's capsule, blood corpuscles in various stages of disintegration are seen. Frequently there appears to be a slight increase, not only in the number of connective tissue nuclei, but also of the pink fibrillated tissue around the walls of the capillaries. In the convoluted tubules the epithelium is comparatively healthy, though in some cases it is in a condition of cloudy swelling, or even fatty degeneration. In the lumen small collections of broken-down blood corpuscles, or of golden brown pigment derived from the small hæmorrhages within Bowman's capsule, are frequently seen. The vessels between the tubules are greatly distended ; their walls are thickened, and take on a pink reaction with carmine, just as in the case of the thickened vessels in "Nutmeg Liver" (§ 182). In the medulla the longitudinal and transverse sections of the straight vessels are filled with blood, the walls are thickened, and are stained pink. In the tubules the epithelial cells may be undergoing degenerative or proliferative changes. There may be fatty globules in the cells. Here, too, are found the "melanin" casts already referred to as composed of the altered blood pigment.

The wedge-shaped patches in the cortex consist of pink fibrous tissue, with a few round cells at the margin. The Malpighian bodies in them are atrophied and fibrous looking (*see* Interstitial Nephritis, § 238), whilst the enclosed tubules are small, and the epithelial cells lining them are flattened, extremely granular, and atrophied, and some contain small globules of fat, which stain black with osmic acid. The study of these sections will give an exceedingly good idea of the vascular supply of the kidney.

The above, mostly mechanical, changes are first seen in the veins —the interlobular and the straight veins being first affected—then in the capillaries, and lastly in the arteries. Distension and thickening of these take place as in "Nutmeg" liver. The changes in the epithelium are seen only in the later stages, and are due, in great measure, to pressure and malnutrition.

FAT EMBOLISM OF THE KIDNEY.

227. Fat embolism is met with in certain cases of diabetic coma, or in the similar coma following fracture of bones, especially of the bones of the head and of cancellated bones. In both these conditions fat is set free to circulate in the blood, and is eventually arrested in some of the smaller vessels.

The naked eye appearances vary considerably, but the points to be specially looked for are pallor, increased size, and flabbiness of the organ, and minute hæmorrhages under the capsule or on the surface of the sections.

Where fat embolism is suspected, make a microscopic examination in the fresh condition. To make a more exhaustive examination harden (§ 59), and stain a section with osmic acid (§ 110) and then with picro-carmine (§ 98).

(× 50).—There is evidently some congestion, especially at certain points near the surface of the cortex. Near the congested areas, filling some of the vessels between the tubules, are black masses, evidently fat stained with osmic acid. Similar black masses are also seen in some of the capillaries in the glomerular tuft, and in the straight vessels. Near these congested areas are small hæmorrhages along with which some of the fatty material may have escaped into the surrounding tissues, or even into the tubules, especially where rupture of the capillaries in the Malpighian tuft has occurred.

(× 300).—The above appearances are to be verified, special care being taken to localise the fat in the positions above mentioned.

WAXY OR LARDACEOUS DISEASE OF THE KIDNEY.

228. This disease is frequently associated with other marked changes of the tubules and of the interstitial tissue, but as these are rather superadded conditions, it will be well to confine the description to the waxy change, and take up the other conditions separately. For example, waxy disease is frequently associated with interstitial nephritis, in which case the changes due to the waxy condition are to a certain extent masked by those due to the interstitial

processes.   For conditions under which this disease occurs (*see*
§ 181).

FIG. 75. — Drawing
of section of waxy
kidney, injected with
soluble Prussian blue.
Stained with methyl-
aniline violet, and
treated with oxalic
acid. (× 50.)

   t.c. Thickened cap-
        sule, underneath
        which new inter-
        stitial tissue may
        be seen.

   w.g. Malpighian tuft,
        completely
        waxy, through
        which the injec-
        tion has not
        passed.

   i.g. Tuft, in which
        capillaries are
        not so much
        affected, the in-
        jection passing
        into most of
        them.

   a.a. Afferent vessels,
        waxy.

   w.a. Larger artery in
        boundary area,
        and, *a.r.*, *a.r.*,
        arteriolæ rectæ
        seen in both
        longitudinal and
        transverse sec-
        tion, all waxy.

   The small inter-
tubular waxy capil-
laries seen as delicate
red violet streaks
throughout the section.

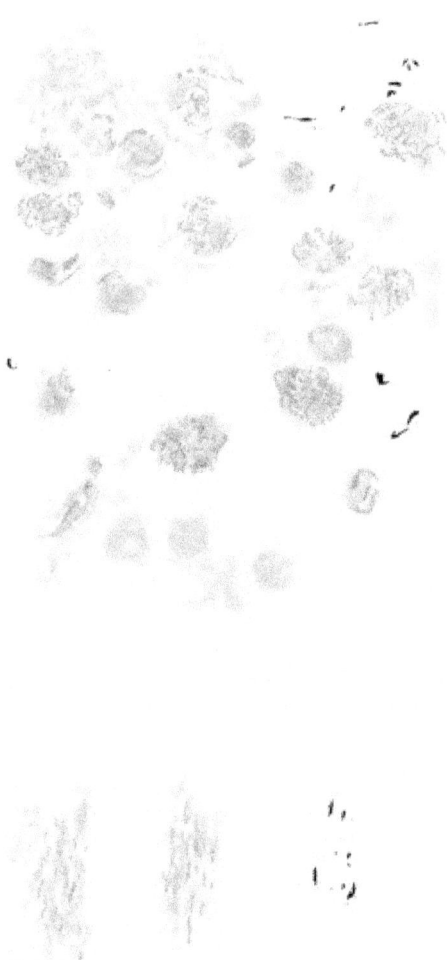

Naked eye appearances in the early stage. — The kidney is

usually slightly enlarged, and the capsule strips off very readily; the surface is smooth, glistening, anæmic, and often yellow.

On section the cortex is pale and anæmic, and the Malpighian bodies are seen as glistening rounded masses, arranged regularly in parallel rows; the surrounding tubular tissue has a peculiar mottled look, though there are no very marked evidences of fatty degeneration.

In the medulla the appearances are also very characteristic. The striation at the base of the pyramid is slightly exaggerated, the congested straight vessels standing out prominently from the pale tubules, and there is usually, even in this early stage, a comparatively deep colour, due to congestion ; the apices of the papillæ remain pale.

Pour iodine (§ 107) over the fresh surface of the section, and note that dark mahogany lines make their appearance in the position of the straight vessels, and that the glassy looking Malpighian bodies also take on a brown stain. In an earlier stage, where otherwise no naked eye changes are distinguishable, the iodine staining frequently brings out the fact that there is slight waxy degeneration in the Malpighian bodies and in the walls of the straight vessels.

Harden (§ 57) and mount one section unstained (§ 152). Stain others (§§ 106 and 107).

(× 50).—In the unstained specimen the Malpighian bodies are enlarged, and have a translucent appearance. This translucence does not extend throughout the whole of the capillary tuft, but certain of the capillary vessels only are affected. Their walls are thickened, homogeneous, and glassy, and have a yellow tinge ; the transverse diameter of the vessel as a whole becomes increased. Parts of the tuft remain perfectly healthy, so that there is a kind of picking out of the tuft with the waxy material. The afferent arteriole is also affected, small areas of the middle coat being quite glassy looking ; in the medulla the arteriolæ rectæ are undergoing similar changes.

In the iodine stained section the waxy parts are seen as mahogany brown patches when examined by reflected light, whilst the normal tissues appear yellow ; with methylaniline violet the waxy parts stain *red* violet, whilst the normal tissues and fattily degenerated cells take on a *blue* violet or slaty blue colour. In this stage the changes in the epithelium lining the tubule are comparatively slight, but in the advanced stage they are far more marked. As a result of these changes, colloid casts may be found even in this early stage. They are perfectly homogeneous, and fill up the lumen of the tubule, whilst the epithelium around them is usually considerably flattened. Such a cast, unstained or stained with iodine, appears to be very like waxy material, but, stained with methylaniline

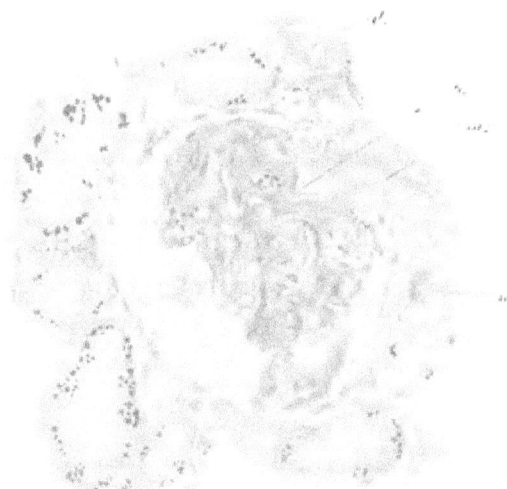

FIG. 76.—Section of waxy and fatty kidney. Stained with methyl-aniline violet and osmic acid. (× 350.)

a. Afferent arteriole, waxy. Stained red violet.
b. Capillaries of Malpighian tuft, waxy in patches.
c. Waxy intertubular capillaries.
d. Colloid casts, stained intermediately between waxy and healthy tissues.
e. Fat granules and globules in epithelium, stained black with osmic acid ; healthy tissues stained blue ; red blood corpuscles unstained, seen as yellowish green corpuscles in the capillaries.

violet, it gives an intermediate colour between the *blue* violet of normal tissues and the *red* violet waxy reaction.

(× 300).—Note the patches of waxy material in the walls of the capillaries in the glomeruli, and that the flattened cells and the basement membrane of Bowman's capsule are unaffected. In the muscular coat of the afferent arteriole observe the swollen and translucent (or red violet) patches; and that the diameter of the whole vessel is increased, although the lumen is greatly diminished in size. Note, too, the marked changes in the arteriolæ rectæ, and that the vessels near the papillæ are more affected than those near the base of the pyramid. If this be remembered when the naked eye examination is made, it will be readily understood why the base of the pyramid is almost invariably relatively deep in colour. The consequent diminution in the diameter of the vessels also suggests the cause of the pallor of the organ, even in the early stage. Further, not only is the quantity of blood passing through the organ lessened, but, from the nature of the causes of the disease, its quality is very much deteriorated. To these two conditions the fatty changes which occur during the later stages of the disease are also to be referred. The appearances of the colloid casts, as above described, must be verified under the high power, and the chemical and colour reactions again observed. The epithelium is usually comparatively healthy throughout, though slight fatty degeneration may be met with.

Waxy Kidney—More advanced Stage.

229. In the later stages the kidney is very soft and flabby; it may be enormously enlarged, even to twice its usual size. The capsule strips off readily, the surface is smooth and pale, having a dull brown or brownish-yellow colour as a groundwork, mottled with numerous paler patches. On section, the great increase in size is seen to be due, in great measure, to the increase in the thickness of the cortex. The Malpighian bodies are enormously swollen, and stand out prominently as large glistening masses. With a hand-lens the vessels between the tubules are also seen to be glistening and swollen, whilst the tubules themselves are pale and fatty looking. The striation of the medullary rays is distinctly marked, and there is marked congestion at the bases of the pyramids, near the boundary layer. The tips of the papillæ are extremely pale. With a watery solution of iodine (§ 107), the mahogany brown staining is very extensive. The Malpighian bodies, the interlobular arteries, the intertubular plexus, and the straight vessels in the medulla are all

affected.   Harden (§ **57**), examine one section unstained, stain others
(§§ **106** and **107**).

(× 50).—The change is wide spread.   In the Malpighian
body the capillary tuft may be very extensively affected, the smaller
waxy patches running together.   In the basement membrane of
Bowman's capsule, and rarely, apparently even in the flattened cells

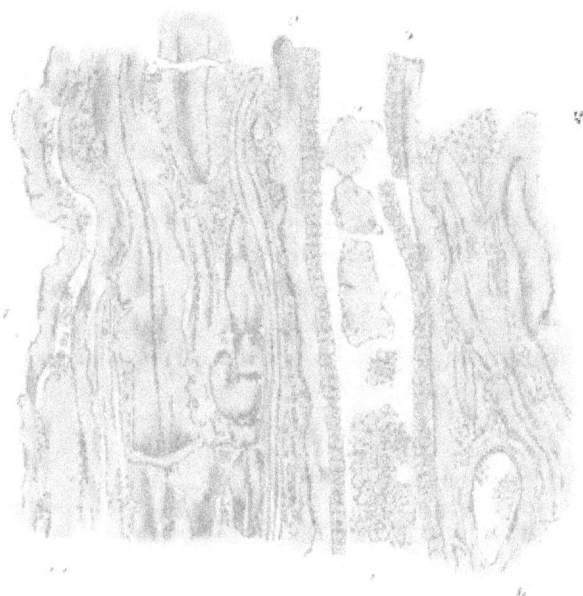

FIG. 77.—Section of medulla of waxy kidney.   Stained with iodine
and sulphuric acid.   (× 310.   After Kyber.)
 a.   Straight tubule with colloid cast
 c.c.   in lumen.
 b.   Epithelium.
 d.   Shed epithelium, fatty and colloid.
 e.   Basement membrane ; waxy (blue).
 f.   Descending limb of looped tubule of Henle.   Waxy basement
          membrane.   Cells fatty.
 g.   Vessel, the walls of which are in an advanced stage of waxy
          degeneration.

which line the capsule there may be a similar waxy material.   The
interlobular and afferent arterioles are markedly affected, as are
also the efferent arterioles, and, in a less degree, the intertubular
capillary vessels.   A similar change may be noted in the basement
membrane of the convoluted tubules ; waxy change in the epithelial

cells is very rare indeed. In these cells, however, owing to mal-nutrition, fatty degeneration is of frequent occurrence, the cells becoming angular and shrivelled, and when treated with osmic acid (§ 110) numerous black globules and granules of fat are seen in them.

In the medulla, from the boundary layer to the apices of the papillæ, the waxy change is in the walls of the vessels and the basement membrane of the straight tubules. It is always most marked in the muscular coat of the vessels; but in the later stages the intima may be involved, the endothelial lining in such cases undergoing fatty degeneration. Nearer the tips of the papillæ the connective tissue fibrils between the bundles of muscular fibres, which, in the normal kidney, run from the tips of the papillæ for some distance towards the boundary layer, are affected, apparently quite apart from the vessels; this change may occur where the other tissue elements of the kidney are comparatively unaffected. The colloid casts are somewhat numerous throughout the whole section; they have been already described in the earlier stage. True waxy casts are described as occurring in extremely advanced cases, but this must be a very rare condition.

Greenfield gives the order of affection of the various parts by the waxy change as follows:—(1.) Afferent arterioles; (2.) Groups of glomerular capillaries, especially those of the superficial cortex; (3.) Arteriolæ rectæ; (4.) Efferent arterioles, and the capillaries into which they break up; (5.) Capsule of Malpighian body; (6.) The capillaries which run between the bundles of straight tubules; (7.) The basement membrane of the convoluted tubules; (8.) Large interlobular arteries; (9.) Walls of the straight tubules, especially near the papillæ; (10.) Large branches of arteries and veins in the boundary area; (11.) The connective tissue around the collecting tubules at the tips of the papillæ; and (12.) The epithelial cells, rarely.

GENERAL TISSUE CHANGES IN BRIGHT'S DISEASE.

230. In considering the following forms of kidney disease, it is essential that the changes which take place in the various tissues under different conditions, and that the interdependence of certain of the acute forms of Bright's disease, and corresponding chronic forms, should be understood. Inflammation of the kidney differs in no respect from inflammation of any other organ, except in so far as the different arrangement of the tissues and the distinct function of the organ may lead to such differences. Here changes are met with in the vessels, in the connective tissue, and in the epithelial lining of different tubes and cavities. The vascular and connective tissue changes present special features and induce distinct phenomena, because these tissues are arranged around the tubules, and in and around the Malpighian bodies. In the same way, the various epithelial changes have different characteristics, simply because the epithelium is divided into three groups, viz. :—(1.) that covering the capillaries of the Malpighian tuft and lining Bowman's capsule of the glomerular body ; (2.) the secreting epithelium of the upper part of the urinary tract ; and (3.) the epithelium lining the excretory ducts.

Here, as in inflammatory diseases of the liver, although the nutrition of *all* the tissues is affected, the degree in which the different tissues suffer varies materially. It may be found, for example, that in one form the changes in the connective tissue predominate, and that only very slight alterations are met with in the secreting epithelium, though these always tend to become more marked as the disease advances. On the other hand, the epithelium may undergo grave changes in cases in which it is difficult to make out any vascular or connective tissue lesions. Again, there may be marked affection of the tubular portion of the kidneys, whilst the Malpighian bodies manifest little evidence of inflammatory reaction. Note, however, that the Malpighian bodies may be the seat of considerable alteration before the tubules beyond them give any very definite evidence of inflammatory disease, though such evidence invariably follows at a later stage.

With all this, it may be that the epithelium of the excretory tubules may remain entirely unaffected ; in fact, evidence of disease in the excretory tubules is of comparatively rare occurrence. It will be evident, then, that in making any examination of the kidney for inflammatory lesions, our attention should invariably be first directed to the secretory portion of the kidney, the cortex, as only in very rare cases is it found that the tissues in the bundles of straight tubules participate in the inflammatory changes; it must be borne in mind that the secretory portion of the kidney extends into what is spoken of as the interpyramidal cortex.

In consequence of the peculiar relation of the Malpighian body to the remainder of the tubule, we may have marked inflammatory changes in the tissues in and around the glomerulus, which lead to interference with the proper discharge of its functions; the tubules below are no longer called upon to perform their special functions, and they undergo atrophic changes. These atrophic changes may or may not be associated with inflammatory changes in and around the tubules; and, according as the inflammation is present or absent, very marked differences, to which reference will be made in the description of inflammatory forms of kidney disease, are found.

Briefly, the special conditions met with in inflammation are the following: first, those which occur around the vessels and in the connective tissue; secondly, those met with in the Malpighian body; and, thirdly, those that are found in the tubules.

In the interlobular arteries and in the afferent arterioles in acute septic conditions, bacteria may be found in small embolic masses; these may make their way into the surrounding connective tissue, and will be more fully described later. In certain forms of interstitial nephritis, thickening of the intima leading to endarteritis obliterans (§ 214) may occur. Far more important, however, than these conditions is the hyaline swelling of the middle coat of the vessel, and also, in certain cases, of the intima and even of the adventitia, which is probably due to an increased absorption of fluid by the elements of which the various coats of the vessel are composed. It occurs especially in the early stage of acute inflammatory disease, and may lead to considerable diminution in the size of the lumen of the vessel in which it takes place. It is almost invariably associated with the escape of leucocytes from the small vessels immediately behind it, and also with the proliferation of the fixed connective tissue cells in its neighbourhood.

In the complicated glomeruli there are, as one would expect, several sets of changes, two or three of which, however, are usually associated. In certain cases, owing to slight hyaline thickening at the point of entrance of the afferent arteriole, there is slight constriction, followed by exudation of leucocytes; then, too, the connective tissue which surrounds or forms the outer part of the capsule may participate in the general connective tissue changes, as a result of which the glomerular capsule—Bowman's capsule—is distinctly thickened. In other cases the basement membrane may become swollen or thickened, or, as we have already seen (§ **229**), it may undergo waxy degenerative change. The layer of epithelium lining the capsule may proliferate, and layer upon layer of cells being formed, they may ultimately assume an almost fibrous appearance, or they may become hyaline. Thickening of the capsule may from these several causes be so marked that the capsule and the vascular tuft are almost obliterated. Within the capsule albuminoid casts may be met with, or extravasations of blood (the result of hæmorrhage), or, in leucocythemia, large numbers of leucocytes have escaped from the glomerular tufts, the blood in some cases becoming degenerated *in situ*, or, far more frequently, finding its way into the convoluted tubules, where it undergoes degenerative changes; the pigment is set free and taken up into the epithelial cells. The cells investing the capillary tuft may also undergo proliferation, fatty or more acute degenerative changes, or may even be detached bodily. The connective tissue cells supporting the capillary network are sometimes seen to proliferate. Coming now to the capillaries themselves, we find that the endothelium may undergo fatty degeneration, the basement membrane may become swollen, or it may undergo waxy degeneration, whilst, actually within the vessels, thrombi or emboli—simple, or containing micro-organisms —may sometimes be found.

The connective tissue must be looked upon as a kind of lymphatic sponge formed of a net-work of fibrils covered with flattened endothelial cells; through the lymph spaces so formed is a free circulation of fluid, in which float numerous lymph cells. In inflammation two sets of changes are set up in this connective tissue:—
(1.) There is an escape of fluid lymph and white corpuscles from the blood-stream into the lymph spaces; when this becomes greatly exaggerated, a few red blood corpuscles may also escape, and in very acute cases the spaces may become distended with fibrinous

lymph, which clots in them, and gives rise to a very characteristic appearance. In most cases, however, the only evidence of inflammatory exudation is an increase in the number of round cells in the lymph spaces, and a swelling of the fibrils of which the connective tissue network is composed. (2.) In more chronic cases there may be a proliferation of the endothelial cells covering the fibrils, as a result of which there is an increase in the amount of connective tissue between the tubules, just as in the healing of wounds or in common cirrhosis of the liver. Wherever this takes place we may expect to find cicatrisation, contraction of the fibrous tissue, and compression of the tubules leading to atrophy or to irregular dilatation.

In the tubules, as in other positions, the basement membrane may undergo hyaline or waxy change, and the epithelium may be affected by all kinds of degenerative changes. In the very early stages of inflammatory processes the cells become swollen, they lose their normal shape, the striation at the base of the cell is lost (*see* Fig. 79), the protoplasm becomes more coarsely granular, and the nucleus is less distinctly stained ; this may become so marked that ultimately a great part of the cell is broken down, and the nuclei remain entirely unstained, clear spaces making their appearance in the degenerated protoplasm.

231. In certain acute forms of kidney disease, and even in subacute and chronic nephritis, there frequently occurs what is known as " catarrh ;" this consists really of active proliferation of the epithelial cells lining the tubules; and as those cells near the lumen are formed, they are cast off and are washed away by the urine. It will be noticed in such cases that not only the cast off cells, but also those that remain attached to the basement membrane, assume very irregular shapes,—some are pear-shaped, others globose, others flattened and spindle-shaped, and more like endothelial cells. This process of catarrh should be very carefully studied. Wherever there is catarrh there is also usually fatty degeneration, though this may occur where there is no marked evidence of catarrhal change. In a section stained with osmic acid, small black globules and granules may be seen distributed throughout the protoplasm of the epithelial cells,

but in all cases it will be observed, especially in the convoluted

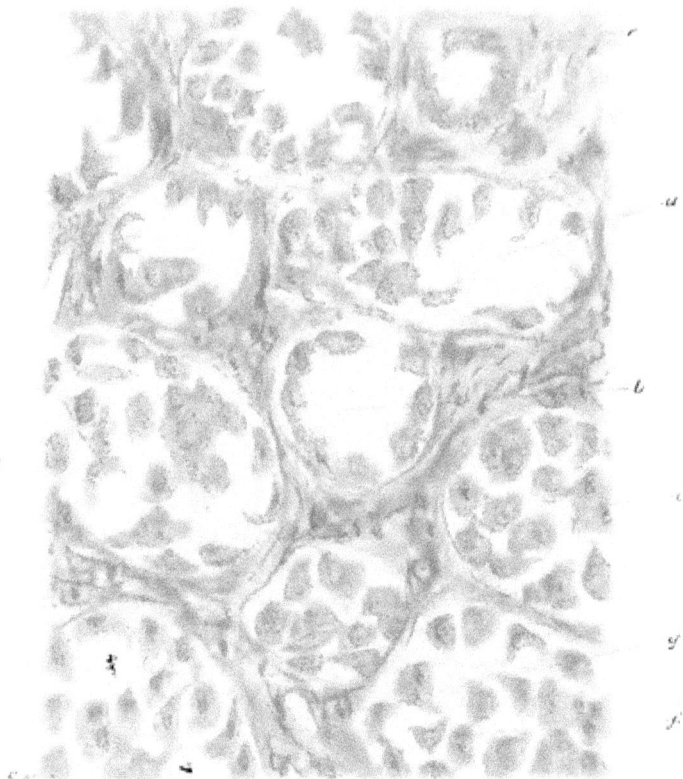

FIG. 78.—" Catarrhal " nephritis in which interstitial changes may also be observed, stained with picro-carmine. (× 300.)

 a. Oblique (b) transverse section of a convoluted tubule in which there is well marked catarrh.
 c. The proliferating cells have assumed a cubical character, the layer which remains attached to the basement membrane being that from which new cells are developed.
 d. The cells are more irregular in shape, but even here is a flattened or spindle-shaped layer from which, under certain conditions, new secreting cubical or columnar cells might be developed. Even in the most advanced stages we find some trace, however imperfect, of an epithelial lining left.
 e. Section of straight tubule, in which there is little catarrh.
 f. Swollen fibrous tissue ; in addition to swelling, however, there is an actual increase of fibres formed by proliferating connective tissue cells (g).
 g. Leucocytes and connective tissue nuclei.

tubules, that the larger globules are usually situated near the base of the cell (*see* Fig. 80). Fatty degeneration, like catarrh, is usually met with in the upper part of the secreting tubules, the straight and excretory tubules being much more rarely affected; the same applies to the presence of glycogen, which is sometimes seen in diabetic kidneys in which a number of clear globules, which give no reaction with osmic acid, but which give a distinct reaction with iodine, may be demonstrated in the epithelial cells. In the tubules, casts having a hyaline basis (probably serum albumen), around which are epithelial cells in various stages of degeneration, sometimes containing granules of blood or bile pigment, may be seen. Blood casts in various stages of degeneration, or masses of leucocytes, the result of acute inflammation or of leucocythemia, may take the place of epithelial cells in these casts. The tubules may become distinctly atrophied, such atrophy being invariably associated with impairment or loss of function; this may be due to an altered blood supply and an increase of connective tissue around the tubule, in which case it may be spoken of as *primary* atrophy. When the loss of function is due to the fact that the Malpighian body is no longer in a normal condition, and does not separate the fluid elements of the blood, and the tubule below has comparatively little work to do, there ensues that series of atrophic changes in which the tubules become small and the epithelial lining shrivelled and atrophied. This may be looked upon as *secondary* atrophy, and is certainly quite distinct, both in course and causation, from the primary atrophy above mentioned.

When it is remembered what part the kidneys play in the separation and excretion of effete and poisonous matter from the blood, it can be readily understood how different parts of the organ may become affected. If a poisonous substance is rapidly secreted by the epithelium, it may, in its passage through the secreting cell, so modify the structure, or so over-stimulate the protoplasm of the cell, that cloudy swelling or catarrh is rapidly and certainly developed, whilst the nutrition of the cell may be so interfered with that ultimately it undergoes fatty or other degenerative changes. If, on the other hand, any poisonous or irritant substance is poured out with the fluid elements of the blood from the capillaries of the glomerular tuft into Bowman's capsule, it may easily be understood how fibrin may make its way into that space, or there may be proliferation of the cells around the vessels and lining the capsule. Returning to the vessels, constriction of the afferent vessel may lead to diminution in the size of the tuft, followed by a kind of compensatory thickening of the capsule—all this leading to the secondary atrophy of the convoluted tubule connected with that Malpighian body.

Lastly, should the connective tissue be specially affected, *i.e.*, should the poisonous material circulate freely in the lymphatic system, and not pass at once into the secreting cells, a series of connective tissue changes, such as those met with in the various forms of interstitial nephritis, may be the result. As already stated, these forms merge one into another; in some cases the connective tissue changes predominate, although epithelial changes are always present; whilst in others the epithelial or glomerular changes are most marked; the interstitial changes, however, though attracting comparatively little attention, always accompanying them.

Cloudy Swelling of the Parenchyma of the Kidney.

232. Cloudy swelling or "Molecular," or "Parenchymatous," degeneration of the kidney is one of the first results of altered nutrition and function of the renal epithelial cells, especially those lining the convoluted tubules. It may occur as an early stage of an inflammatory lesion, or it may simply be the precursor of fatty degeneration of the cells. The causes are much the same as in cloudy swelling of the liver (§ 177) and heart (§ 198).

Naked eye appearances.—The kidney is enlarged and rounded, the capsule strips off readily, leaving the surface with a peculiar shining opalescent appearance and pink colour. On section the cortex is seen to be enlarged and pale, though there is usually considerable hyperæmia, and the Malpighian bodies stand out prominently. The medullary rays are distinctly seen, and the pyramids are deep in colour. The vessels in the boundary area appear to be filled with blood; otherwise the boundary and papillary layers are normal in appearance.

Harden (§ 63 or 59), (spirit alters the appearances of the cells, and should not be used as a hardening fluid for this tissue), and stain (§ **98**).

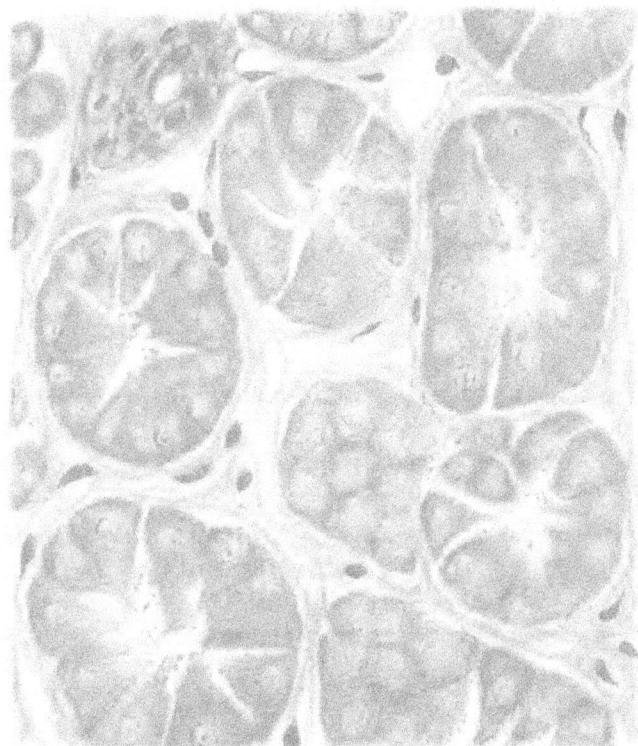

FIG. 79.—Cloudy swelling of the kidney, where death has taken place at a very early stage of the process. Stained with picro-carmine. (× 500.)

a. Swollen columnar epithelial cells of a convoluted tubule. Outlines somewhat obscured; nuclei not very distinct; protoplasm coarsely granular.

b. Swollen epithelial cells, with apices projecting into the lumen of the tubule, giving rise to the radiate or stellate fissures very characteristic of this condition.

c. Coarsely granular protoplasm breaking down.

d. Lumen of intertubular capillary blood vessel.

e. Basement membrane of capillary vessel and delicate connective tissue fibrils, hyaline, and much swollen.

(× 50).—The principal changes are found in the cortex, where the sections of the convoluted tubules present a greater surface than in the normal condition. The lumen is very irregular, and often appears to be little more than a stellate fissure. The epithelial cells are swollen, so that the diameter of each cell is increased; its outline is irregular but very well defined.

(× 300).—The epithelial cells are greatly enlarged. They are angular, and so project into the tubule that sometimes the lumen is almost obliterated. The outlining of the cells is distinct, the protoplasm is extremely granular, much more so than in the normal condition, and the nucleus is obscured, though in a few cases it takes on the carmine stain very deeply, and may thus become more prominent. Treat a section with acetic acid (§ **146**) or caustic potash (§ **147**); the cloudiness disappears, and, with the exception of the change in size and shape, the epithelium regains its normal appearance.

If the change has been going on for several days, a few clear highly refractile fatty globules stained black with osmic acid (§ **110**), by which the nucleus is almost obscured, may be seen in the swollen cell. From this it is evident that the cloudy swelling is being superseded by fatty degeneration, a condition met with in all cases of acute Bright's disease. The intertubular capillaries appear to be compressed, and around them a few leucocytes, which take on the carmine stain very deeply, may have escaped. In the medulla the vessels are more distended, and there is frequently slight catarrh, swelling, proliferation and budding off of young cells, but no other changes in the epithelium of the straight tubules.

FATTY DEGENERATION OF THE KIDNEY.

233. Fatty degeneration of the epithelium of the kidney is usually associated with imperfect nutrition, due to defective blood supply, or to the action of certain materials circulating in the blood; it very frequently appears to follow cloudy swelling, and, although it is sometimes said to be a simple condition, we must, from the nature of the change, and from the conditions with which it is associated, look upon it as being closely related to, if not identical with, the inflammatory processes. It is met with especially in patients who have succumbed to wasting diseases, such as cancer, phthisis, pernicious anæmia, Addison's disease, and diabetes; to certain fevers, such as scarlatina, typhoid or yellow fevers, and small pox; or to poisons, such as alcohol, sulphuric ether, phosphorus, arsenic, or antimony.

Naked eye appearances.—These differ according to the stage of the degeneration. The kidney in the later stages is usually slightly smaller and paler than normal, and is extremely flabby. The capsule strips off readily. On section, the cortex may be normal in thickness, or slightly wasted, mottled, and somewhat yellow, and the surface is flabby and greasy. On the yellow background the interlobular arteries with their double rows of Malpighian bodies stand out prominently, giving a distinctly striated appearance, especially when the organ contains much blood (in phosphorus poisoning there may be small punctiform hæmorrhages in this position); in the medulla the striation is also well marked. Where this condition is associated with anæmia and wasting diseases, the pallor is more uniform than in those cases where inflammatory processes play a more prominent part.

Stain a section with osmic acid (§ 110), and then with carmine (§ 100).

(× 50).—In the convoluted tubules the epithelial cells are swollen, and contain droplets of fat (stained black with osmic acid) of various sizes, principally at the bases of the cells, or near the basement membrane and blood-vessels. Similar black dots are seen in the Malpighian bodies, and in the epithelium lining Bowman's capsule. In the straight tubules the fatty change is not so well marked, and the globules are scattered throughout the substance of the cell; the collecting tubules are usually unaffected.

(× 300).—The ring of dark globules at the periphery of the tubule is seen more distinctly. It is composed of fat droplets of various sizes, some occupying a considerable portion of the cell, others being simply embedded in the surrounding protoplasm; the nuclei in such cells are frequently obscured. The cells are very unequally affected, and a few are comparatively healthy. Observe the granules in the epithelium lining Bowman's capsule, and in the walls of the capillaries. In the straight tubules the fat droplets are distributed irregularly throughout the protoplasm of the cell.

In metallic poisoning the fatty degeneration is much more marked,
the whole of the protoplasm of the various cells may become fatty,

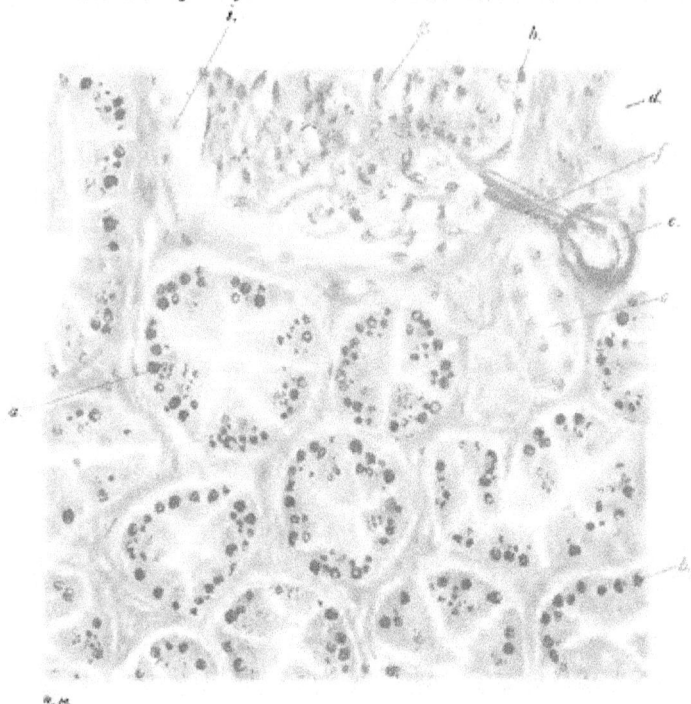

FIG. 80.—Fatty degeneration of the kidney, from a case of diabetes.
Stained with osmic acid and picro-carmine. (× 300.)

    a. Epithelial cells in the first part of a convoluted tubule, in
        which is well marked fatty degeneration ; smaller globules
        near the middle of the cell, larger globules near the base-
        ment membrane.
    b. Cells in which there is infiltration, with large globules only, near
        the base of the cells.
    c. Irregular, and *d* straight tubules, in the cells of which there is
        no fatty degeneration.
    e. Interlobular vessels, from which the afferent arteriole *f* runs to
        supply the glomerular tuft *g*, supported by a delicate con-
        nective tissue framework, and surrounded by an investing
        layer of epithelium *h.*
    i. Layer of flattened epithelial cells lining Bowman's capsule.
    k. Thickened connective tissue and basement membrane of
        Bowman's capsule.
    l. Slight increase of connective tissue at the point of entrance of
        the afferent arteriole.

not only in the tubule, but also in the capillaries and connective tissue ; in such cases, small patches of blood corpuscles are met with as interstitial hæmorrhages, or as hæmorrhages into Bowman's capsule, or into the tubules. In many varieties of this disease the degeneration is accompanied by fatty infiltration of the cells. As evidence of this, note the position of the fat globules, especially at the bases of the epithelial cells in the secreting or convoluted tubules. Treat sections with caustic potash (§ 147), and with acetic acid (§ 146). The fat is entirely unaffected.

Fatty degeneration, with atrophy of the epithelial structures of the kidney, is an extremely common condition ; it has already been seen in waxy degeneration of the kidney ; and it plays a very prominent part, not only in all those inflammatory lesions which come under the heading of nephritis, but also in the numerous atrophic changes which are so commonly met with in this organ.

KIDNEY OF "ACUTE" OR "ACUTE PARENCHYMATOUS" NEPHRITIS, "ACUTE BRIGHT'S DISEASE." — ACUTE "DESQUAMATIVE," "TUBULAR," OR "CATARRHAL" NEPHRITIS.

234. Of these names acute parenchymatous nephritis is undoubtedly the best, as it refers rather to the physical conditions met with in the diseased organ than to any theory as to the processes which go on during the course of the disease.

It is found in patients who, during life, have high arterial tension, and pass albuminous and smoky urine, containing hyaline and blood or other casts. Causes,—sudden congestion, and overwork of the kidneys, irritant poisons, febrile conditions, pneumonia, and similar diseases. The earliest condition has already been described as cloudy swelling of the epithelium or "parenchyma" of the kidney (§ 232).

Naked eye appearances in early but well pronounced acute Bright's disease are — the kidney is flabby and considerably increased in size, especially in thickness, so that it is more rounded ; the capsule is tense, but strips off, even more readily than usual ; the surface is pale and œdematous, and has a peculiar mottled appearance, and on this pale background the venæ stellatæ stand out prominently ; there are usually no cysts present. On section the cortex presents a peculiar granular mottling; it is both relatively and absolutely much increased in thickness, and, although large quantities of blood escape from the cut vessels, it is pale when the blood is washed away; on the pale pink background, are "opaque pinkish points" and "markedly injected dots, due to the swollen vessels and glomeruli." If the process is very acute, small hæmorrhages are found in the cortex, the whole of which may be intensely injected and red. The medullary portion of the kidney is simply congested, and is rarely affected by the graver changes at this stage. The mucous membrane of the pelvis of the kidney, however, is much injected.

Harden (§ 59), and stain (§§ 98 and 110).

(× 50).—In the cortex, and that part of the boundary layer in which the epithelium of the (convoluted) tubules is columnar, the following changes may be noted. There is cloudy swelling (§ 231) to be seen in some of the cells; other cells are undergoing rapid proliferation, and the large swollen cells are dividing (the early stage of catarrh) (Fig. 78). In these dividing cells there is evidence of degenerative change—the swollen protoplasm is granular; in many cases this is so marked that the epithelium is opaque and the nuclei are obscured. In the opaque masses of protoplasm small oil droplets are frequently seen, especially if stained with osmic acid. Blocking up some of the tubules are masses of broken-down fatty cells, which accumulate to form a kind of plug. The interlobular vessels and afferent arterioles are distended; the Malpighian bodies also appear to be considerably larger from the increased quantity of blood which is contained in their capillaries. Around the glomerular capsules, and between the convoluted tubules, especially near the surface of the cortex, small pink dots (leucocytes, and nuclei of young connective tissue cells) are more numerous than usual, pointing to the fact that along with the parenchymatous inflammation there is, even at this early stage, some interstitial change. In some of the Malpighian bodies, and in or around some of the convoluted tubules, are masses of blood corpuscles, which have passed out from the vessels ruptured by the high blood pressure. In some cases a mass of brown pigment is all that is left to represent this blood, especially in the straight tubules. Tube casts (hyaline fibrinous, blood, and a few fatty casts (§ 224)) are met with in the convoluted tubules, and also in smaller numbers in the straight tubules, whither they have been washed down. The vessels in the medulla are filled with blood.

(× 300).—All the above conditions are more readily recognised. The congestion of the vessels in both cortex and medulla, the crimson nuclei around the Malpighian bodies, the slight separation of the convoluted tubules, the swollen, extremely granular or proliferating and slightly fatty cells in the convoluted tubules and ascending tubule of Henle, the casts of various forms—hyaline, seen as very transparent material, fatty, in which the outlines of the cells may still be made out—and the blood casts or masses of altered blood, in the convoluted and straight tubules (§ 224 (1.)).

ACUTE SCARLATINAL NEPHRITIS.

235. The description of scarlatinal nephritis here given is based on the appearances presented in a kidney taken from a case fatal at the end of the first week after the onset of the fever, convulsions and death following suppression of urine.

Naked eye appearances.—In some cases, except for a little hyper-æmia, the kidney is perfectly normal in appearance. It has the same appearance as in cloudy swelling, but it is more congested ; whilst on section, at the bases of the pyramids, and scattered through the cortex, are small hæmorrhagic patches. The Malpighian bodies are readily distinguished.

Harden (§§ 58 and 59) and stain two sections (§ 100), mount one (§ 152), and a second (§ 155 *a*).

(× 50). —The most marked changes are seen around the interlobular arteries. Examine these at their origin in the boundary layer and as they pass towards the cortical surface ; around each are deeply-stained granular looking areas, especially along the lines of the afferent arterioles. They also occur around the Malpighian bodies, and extend from them for some distance between the sur-rounding convoluted tubules. Beneath the capsule and around the terminal branches of the interlobular arteries the granular areas are wedge-shaped, the base of the wedge being towards the cortical sur-face ; whilst in the boundary area are wedge-shaped granular patches, each with its base resting on the medulla, and its apex running upwards to meet the apex of the corresponding patch at the surface. The vessels in these patches are very prominent. Around the glomerular tuft, forming a kind of bounding line between the tuft and the enormous mass of granular material, Bowman's capsule is seen as a distinct, hyaline, translucent lamina, within which

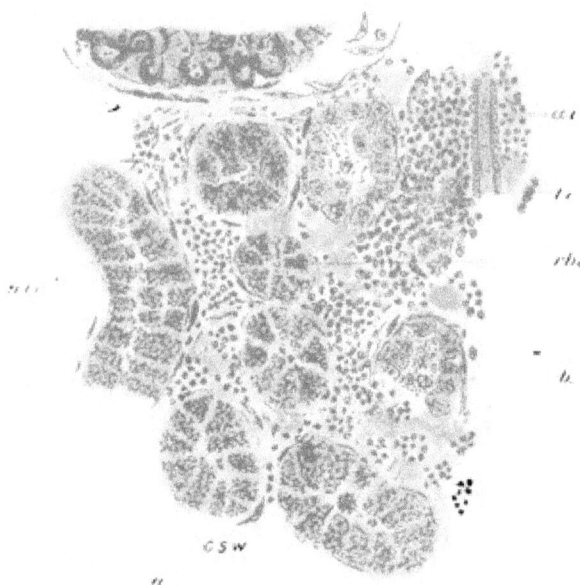

FIG. 81.—Acute scarlatinal nephritis; death on eighth day. Section stained with carmine, and mounted in Farrant's solution. (× 300.)

    a. Epithelium in an advanced state of cloudy swelling.
    b. Commencing catarrh in the tubule, cells proliferating, some detached from the deeper cells which are more or less flattened.
    a.i. Interlobular artery, around which is a great amount of round cell infiltration.
    r.b.c. Coloured blood corpuscles.
    t.c. Section of atrophied tubule, compressed by the round celled exudation.
    n.i.c. Nuclei of intertubular capillaries, near which the round cell infiltration is also well marked.

are numerous small pink dots. At the point where the afferent arteriole enters the thickened Bowman's capsule there is frequently some thickening of the walls of the vessel. The tubules are filled with epithelium in a most typical condition of cloudy swelling (§ 231).

(× 400).—*Changes in the walls of the vessels.*—The interlobular arteries and the afferent arterioles stand out more prominently than in a normal kidney. Their transverse diameter is increased. This is especially well marked at the points where branches are given off, and near Bowman's capsule, and is said to be due to—(1) hyaline swelling of the intima, which takes place irregularly along the course of the vessel ; (2) infiltration of the muscular coat with leucocytes and connective tissue nuclei, and consequent thickening : this takes place especially near the entrance of the arteriole to the Malpighian body. Klein describes emboli in these narrowed vessels.

Changes around, and in connection with, the vessels.—The distribution of certain pink granular material was followed out under the low power. It will now be seen to be composed of small round cells which have all the appearances of leucocytes. Many of these cells have undoubtedly escaped from the blood-vessels, for alongside them are found numerous coloured blood corpuscles ; it is probable, however, that some of them are young connective tissue cells, derived by proliferation from pre-existing cells. This exudation should be observed around the glomeruli, and also running in between the neighbouring tubules.

Changes in the Malpighian bodies or glomeruli.—The glomeruli are usually enlarged, and deeply stained. The capillaries forming the tufts are swollen, whilst the intercapillary nuclei are increased in number. These are similar in all respects to those seen outside the glomeruli, and are probably exuded leucocytes resulting from the acute inflammatory process.

The basement membrane, or Bowman's capsule proper, is considerably thickened, and is homogeneous. At this stage cloudy swelling, and even proliferation of the flattened cells lining Bowman's capsule, is frequently seen.

The changes in the tubules are exactly those of cloudy swelling (§ 232) and slight catarrh (§ 231). In some of the tubules hyaline and blood casts are met with.

If the above conditions be looked upon as occurring in a less acute, and as gradually merging into a more chronic, form, the other conditions met with in scarlatinal kidney will be much more readily understood. The changes which appear to be of the greatest importance are those which take place in and around the vessels and glomeruli, but they are always accompanied or followed by secondary changes in the epithelium.

SCARLET FEVER KIDNEY (NO. 2).

236. Found in cases where death has taken place at from the seventh to the fourteenth week of the disease.

Naked eye appearances.—The organ may be even smaller than normal, or only slightly enlarged. It is tough and dense, the capsule is readily removed, leaving the surface of the cortex pale or of a "pinkish colour, and more translucent than natural, on which the angular glomeruli may frequently be seen as brownish-red dots." (It will be remembered that in the normal kidney the glomeruli are never seen on the surface.)

On section the superficial cortex may be normal in thickness, or it may be considerably narrowed, and is of much the same colour as the surface. The interpyramidal cortex, on the other hand, is usually swollen, in some cases markedly so, this often leading to compression of the bases of the medullary pyramids, which do not stand out so prominently as usual; it is of "opaque yellowish or pinkish-white colour, mottled with opaque yellowish-white points."

The enlarged glomeruli are usually distinctly seen in double rows on each side of the prominent interlobular artery. Some of them are translucent greyish, others brownish-red, angular dots. Where the brownish-red dots are seen, patches of inflammatory exudation will be found surrounding the glomeruli. There are also angular yellowish patches, which represent to the naked eye the fatty and degenerative changes taking place in the epithelium of the convoluted tubules. The medulla presents a comparatively normal appearance, with the exception of the bases of the pyramids, where there is some compression and irregularity.

Harden (§§ 57 and 59), cut (§§ 55 *a*, 82, *et seq.*), and stain (§§ 98 and 103 *d.*).

(× 50).—The principal changes take place in and around the Malpighian bodies, and along the course of the afferent arterioles and interlobular arteries, around which, and extending for some distance between the neighbouring tubules as in the acute form, are pink-stained nuclei (leucocytes and connective tissue nuclei), especially at the point of exit of the afferent arteriole. This increase of connective tissue nuclei and leucocytes may be enormous. Within the capsule they may also be increased in number, when, by pressure, they cause diminution in size of the vascular tuft. Some only of the Malpighian bodies are affected, and these very irregularly, according to the severity of the inflammation. The convoluted tubules immediately around the Malpighian bodies appear to be compressed by the inflammatory growth around them, and exhibit marked catarrhal changes (§ 231).

Many of the convoluted tubules, and some of the straight tubules, are choked with broken-down or fatty catarrhal cells.

(× 300).—The swelling of the intima of the interlobular and afferent arterioles, described as occurring in the acute stage, may also be distinguished in this form. The nuclei of the inflammatory cells surrounding the vessels are, in many cases, in process of organisation into more or less highly developed connective tissue. Similar cells are present in great numbers around the Malpighian bodies, radiating from them between the interlobular vessels, or along the lines of the capillaries between the tubules. Bowman's capsule is swollen, hyaline, and homogeneous looking, though in the later stages it may become distinctly laminated. Within the capsule there seems to be an increase first in size, and then in number, of the flattened cells lining it, and within this again there is proliferation and partial organisation of the connective tissue cells supporting the capillaries, which become compressed and atrophied. The tubules near the Malpighian bodies are also atrophied or compressed, and the epithelium is flattened; whilst, as seen under the low power, there is, both in the straight and in some of the convoluted tubules, an accumulation of catarrhal cells, forming the so-called fatty and granular casts (§ 224 (2.)). Along with the above conditions there is frequently simple catarrh in the straight collecting tubules. In this form the atrophy of the superficial cortex is said to be due to the obstruction in the arterial system (§ 231).

There is a form of acute interstitial nephritis met with at about

the sixth week of an attack of scarlatina, in which the naked eye
appearances are very similar to those seen above. The microscope
reveals an extremely diffused form of acute interstitial and glomerular
nephritis. The whole of the Malpighian bodies are affected, and
between the convoluted tubules there is an extraordinary increase
in the amount of young cellular connective tissue. In consequence of this the tubules are atrophied and widely separated,

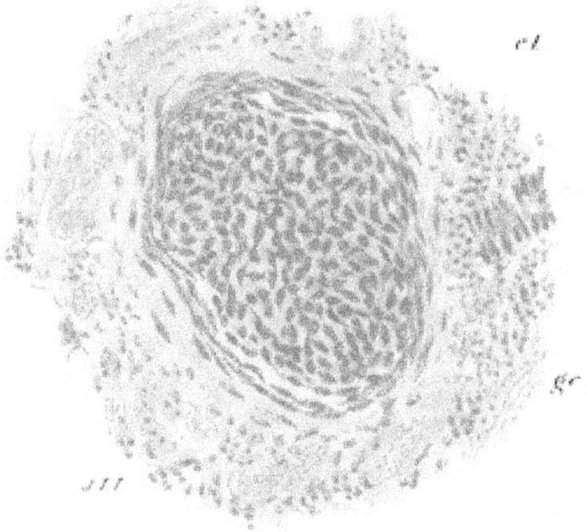

FIG. 82.—Post-scarlatinal nephritis; death at about the sixth week.
Stained with picro-carmine. (× 260.)
  a.a. Afferent arteriole, surrounded at its point of entrance to the
      glomerulus by a large number of leucocytes.
  g.c. Thickened Bowman's capsule, the endothelioid cells proliferating
      rapidly, and forming a distinct lining to the thickened and
      laminated capsule.
  c.t. Nuclei of connective tissue, supporting glomerular capillaries,
      greatly increased in number.
      Around the glomerulus are sections of tubules, surrounded by
      leucocytes, &c.

and the epithelium lining them is in a state of active proliferation.
Fatty casts may be seen in both the convoluted and straight tubules.

The more chronic forms of scarlatinal nephritis, occurring from six
months to a year after the fever, are so like those met with in subacute interstitial nephritis, that it is unnecessary to give a separate
description of them. The observer, however, should bear in mind
that in the scarlatinal forms the glomerular changes, and the changes

along the line of the interlobular vessels predominate, whilst in the other forms the interstitial changes are usually more "diffuse."

"LARGE PALE" (?) KIDNEY OR "FATTY" KIDNEY, SUBACUTE OR CHRONIC PARENCHYMATOUS NEPHRITIS.

237. The acute form of Bright's disease may be cured ; sometimes it is followed by a series of more chronic changes, when we have what is spoken of as the "Large Pale" or "Fatty" Kidney. These are both faulty names, as the waxy kidney, and the kidney of subacute interstitial nephritis, which is even paler than that of chronic parenchymatous nephritis, are both spoken of as large pale kidneys, whilst the fatty change in the epithelium is common to this and to many other forms of disease. Of the two names, however, the latter is preferable. Although this form of Bright's disease may follow the acute form, it is far more frequently met with as a subacute condition from the beginning, when it runs a very definite and usually fatal course.

Naked eye appearances.—The kidney is considerably enlarged. The capsule is still readily separable. The surface is pale, mottled, and somewhat anæmic. On section, the cortex is swollen, and is mottled pink and yellow. The Malpighian bodies are not more prominent than usual. On taking scrapings from the cut surface and floating them in water, greasy streaks are seen. There is now no congestion of the pelvis of the kidney.

Harden (§ 59), cut (§§ 55 *a*, 82 *et seq.*), and stain (§§ 98 and 110).

(× 50).—In the section stained with osmic acid, fatty globules may be seen in the degenerated epithelium of the convoluted tubules of the cortex. The vascularity between the tubules is not great, but the nuclei around the Malpighian bodies, and around the tubules, are increased in number, and have given rise to an increase in the amount of connective tissue. Some of the tubules are comparatively open, and are lined by a layer of flattened cells which take on the carmine stain very readily (*see* Fig. 78 *d*), even those which are choked with the blackened epithelium are seen to have this layer of flattened cells lining the tubule. The casts in the tubules are more colloid and fatty than in the earlier stages of the disease. They are especially numerous in the lower part of the convoluted tubules, and in the first part of the straight tubules.

(× 300).—The epithelium lining the convoluted tubules is flattened, and forms a thin cellular layer around the lumen, or around the mass of fatty material occupying it. These flattened cells are young epithelial cells, and, as a rule, are not granular or fatty. This layer is seldom or never thrown off, *i.e.*, complete degeneration does not take place, the cells remain, and from them any new epithelium that is formed is reproduced. The colloid and other casts (§ 224 (2.)) are stained yellow. Verify the other conditions seen under the low power, more especially the cellular increase around the Malpighian bodies and around the tubules. Look for dilated tubules blocked up at points by the tube casts.

In the straight tubules the cells may also present this flattened appearance, and casts of small cells are frequently met with.

SUBACUTE INTERSTITIAL NEPHRITIS,

Or the Large, Pale, Smooth Kidney following Acute Bright's Disease.

238. From the description given of the second stage of paren-chymatous nephritis, the student will be quite prepared to meet, at a still later period of the disease, with considerable increase in the amount of connective tissue (formed from the prolifer-ating cells around the vessels), especially between the convoluted tubules.

Naked eye appearances.—The organ is usually slightly enlarged, and is firmer than normal. The capsule may be somewhat thickened and adherent; the surface is pale with yellow mottlings, but the venæ stellatæ are congested. On section the cortex is seldom thickened, and is usually atrophied, the Malpighian bodies are not prominent, and the tissue of the cortex is firm, dense, and translucent. Small cortical cysts are sometimes met with, but not nearly so frequently as in the granular contracted kidney.

The arteries of the boundary layer have rigid and thickened walls, and always remain patent and prominent, and there is some con-gestion at the bases of the pyramids.

Harden (§ 59) and stain (§§ 98 and 103).

(× 50).—The Malpighian bodies have the normal arrangement, but they are undergoing very important changes. These changes will be more readily understood if a general description of the appearances of the cortex is first given.

In the deeper part of the cortex, along the lines of the interlobular arteries, are wedge-shaped masses of solid looking tissue, with the base directed towards the medulla. Dipping down from the surface is a similar wedge, the base of which is at the cortical surface, the apex running down to meet the apex of the other pyramidal mass. Between these more solid looking areas are oval patches of comparatively normal and open tissue which are situated midway between the interlobular arteries, and consequently are composed of sections of straight tubules in the centre, and of convoluted tubules at the margin. The convoluted tubules, especially those near the margin of the denser tissues are considerably dilated. In the denser areas the small openings are lined with flattened fatty and atrophied cells ; these are sections of compressed and atrophied convoluted tubules. Arranged fairly regularly along each side of the interlobular arteries are the Malpighian bodies, in some of which very marked changes have taken place, whilst others are apparently healthy. The healthy ones are almost invariably situated in the open, more normal, tissue. Those which are situated between the open and denser tissue, or just within the margin of a denser area, are often somewhat increased in size, owing to an increase in the connective tissue of the glomerular tuft, and to distension of the capsule by an accumulation of colloid matter or fluid. In the middle of the denser wedge-shaped area the Malpighian bodies are usually much diminished in size, and are closer together than usual. Bowman's capsule is seen to be very much thickened and fibroid, and the glomerular tuft in many cases cannot be discerned at all, or only as a small knot of fibrous tissue. Between the atrophied tubules and the altered Malpighian bodies there is an enormous amount of small round-celled or young connective tissue which tends to become organised ; this does not seem to affect the Malpighian bodies specially, but is distributed along the lines of the interlobular and intertubular vessels. It is this tissue which gives the solidity to the wedge-shaped masses. In the boundary layer the larger branches of vessels have thickened walls; there appears to be thickening in all three, in consequence of which the lumen is somewhat narrowed.

(× 300).—Within Bowman's capsule note the layers of new fibrous or hyaline tissue, and within these again numerous cells. At

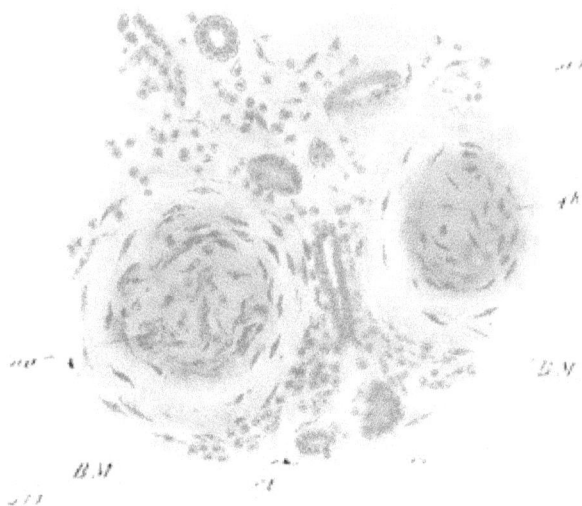

FIG. 83.—Section of a couple of fibroid Malpighian bodies from a case of subacute interstitial nephritis. Section stained with picro-carmine and mounted in Farrant's solution. (× 300.)

B.M. Thickened Bowman's capsule, laminated and fibrous.
c.k. Central fibrous knot, which is all that is left to represent the capillary tuft.
a.a. Point of entrance of afferent arteriole.
a.t. Atrophied tubule, one of which at *c.c.* contains a cast rapidly becoming colloid.
c.t. Periglomerular new formation, tissue becoming fibrous. At certain points the tubules are not so much atrophied, and the epithelium is more natural in appearance.

some points the fibrous tissue may be absent, and there is simply a thicker, often irregular, layer of cells lining the capsule. The thickening may be due—(1.) To a growth by multiplication of the layers of flattened cells within the capsule; (2.) to proliferation of the connective tissue cells around Bowman's capsule, which thus brings about a thickening of the "adventitia" of the Malpighian body; (3.) to a deposition of inflammatory coagulable lymph in layers between the glomerular tuft and Bowman's capsule; the leucocytes or detached epithelial cells standing out distinctly from the granular or hyaline fibrin in all stained specimens; this is not very frequently met with, but it undoubtedly occurs in certain cases; or (4.) to the thickening of the basement membrane of the capsule. The periglomerular infiltration is well marked, as is also the rapid proliferation of the connective tissue cells, which support and invest the glomerular capillaries. This latter may be so marked, indeed, and its organisation so far advanced, that the capillaries are atrophied by pressure, and nothing but a firm fibrous knot remains, around which the capsule may be firmly contracted; this knot may be situated at one side of the capsule, which is then distended to form a small cyst filled with colloid or watery material.

Changes in and around the Tubules.—The basement membrane may be swollen and hyaline-looking; the epithelium, though proliferating rapidly in the earlier stages, and forming irregular cells, does not desquamate, for in carefully hardened sections a distinct epithelial layer is always seen, the cells of which may be somewhat irregular in shape and size, but which, in the later stages, become extremely flattened. Numerous fatty and colloid casts are found in the various parts of the convoluted and straight tubules.

Changes in the Connective Tissue.—Along the lines of the capillaries, and between them and the basement membrane of the tubules, embedded in the small round cell tissue, are numerous branching cells or more fully developed connective tissue cells, of which there are so many in an undeveloped condition around the Malpighian bodies and the atrophied tubules; they may form a firm fibrillated connective tissue. Secondary to this fibrous tissue formation, the capillaries become atrophied, though some of the intertubular vessels still remain patent. It must be remembered, however, that these connective tissue changes are often secondary to changes in the vessels.

Changes in the Arteries and Arterioles.—The inner coat within the internal elastic lamina is frequently thickened. (*See* " Endarteritis Obliterans," § 214.)

w

Frequently there is pseudo-hypertrophy of the muscular coat, due to an increase in the number of connective tissue cells between the muscle fibres, which may be much atrophied.

As already noticed, there is a general increase in the interstitial connective tissue; and the tunica adventitia of the arteries, which is really a part of, or is directly continuous with it, takes part in the general thickening.

It is held by some authorities, with a considerable show of reason, that this form of interstitial nephritis is but an early stage of the granular contracted kidney. As this seems to be especially the case as regards the large granular kidney, it will not be necessary to say anything of that form beyond referring to the diminution in size of the organ, especially of the superficial cortex, the granular surface, the thickening, lamination, and adhesion of the capsule, the more advanced glomerular, vascular, and interstitial changes, and the more numerous casts.

GRANULAR CONTRACTED KIDNEY.

239. Chronic Interstitial Nephritis? "Cirrhosis" of the Kidney? "Small Red" Kidney, or "Gouty" Kidney is found especially in alcoholics, in gouty patients, and in cases of chronic lead poisoning.

Naked eye appearances of the small or typical form.—The kidney is very much diminished in size and its substance is extremely tough. The capsule is thickened, opaque, and laminated, and is firmly adherent to the subjacent tissue, so that it comes away in layers, shreds remaining adherent to the cortex, or else bringing away with it fragments of the parenchyma, leaving a very granular surface which feels like a piece of moist morocco or shagreen. The granules are pale, small, and fairly regular in size, each corresponding to a lobule; the fossæ around them are usually injected, and much redder in colour than the elevated patches or granules. It is to these red patches that the capsule is most firmly adherent, as at these points small vessels appear to run from the capsule into the tissue beneath. Over the surface of the kidney there may be deeper and more irregular sulci, which divide it into areas, these usually corresponding accurately to the outlines of the lobes of which it is made up. On the surface numerous cysts are seen; the sizes of which vary from a pin point to a walnut, or even larger; small brick red or yellow points (uratic deposits) are also seen scattered over the surface.

On section, the cortex, which is tough and leathery, is found to be much contracted, and may be only a sixth of the normal thickness; the thinning of the cortex is most marked at the bases of the pyramids. The edge of the cut surface is sharply marked, but uneven, the elevations corresponding to the granules already

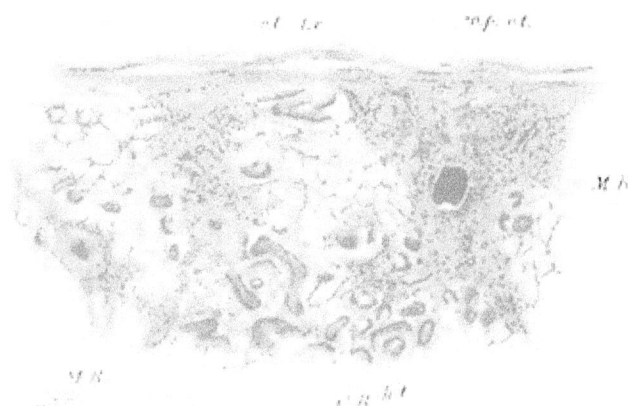

FIG. 84.—Part of cortex of granular contracted kidney. Stained with picro-carmine. (× 40.)

    t.c. Thickened capsule, laminated and adherent, especially over the dense wedge-shaped areas.

    w.p. Wedge-shaped patch, composed of atrophied tubules (*a.b.*) and fibroid Malpighian bodies (*M.B.*)

    o.t. Ovoid patch of open tissue composed of dilated convoluted tubules, from which most of the epithelium has fallen out.

    C.B. Enlarged Malpighian body, forming early stage of cyst, situated at the margin of the more solid patch.

    h.t. Comparatively healthy tubules.

described. The section varies very greatly in colour, but in a very large proportion of cases it is brick red, and is not specially anæmic. Small cysts, most of them filled with a yellow gelatinous material, and brick red or yellow lines (deposits of urates in the tubules), are scattered at irregular intervals over the cortical surface; similar yellow lines, but straight, are also seen in the medulla. Notice further that the parallel radiating lines, composed of the straight tubules and double rows of Malpighian bodies, are either altogether obliterated, or are tortuous and irregular, and that the interlobular arteries are thickened and much distorted. This irregularity is characteristic of this disease, and even in the early stages, when no other naked eye evidence can be made out, it is quite sufficient to indicate the presence of atrophy. The large branches of the renal artery are rigid and atheromatous, those in the boundary layer have their walls thickened, and the lumen patent, so that they stand out much more prominently than in the normal kidney. The interpyramidal cortex is pale, often swollen, and atrophied only in the very late stages of the disease. The medullary pyramids are usually somewhat atrophied, especially near their bases, but present no marked naked-eye changes. In the pelvis there is frequently more fat than usual around the calyces.

Harden (§ 59), and stain (§§ 98 and 103 *d*).

(× 20).—The free cortical surface is very irregular, with elevations and depressions corresponding to the granules already mentioned ; the capsule is thickened, firmly adherent to wedge-shaped patches beneath, laminated and stained pink with picro-carmine. Running from the depressions down along the lines of the interlobular arteries are wedged-shaped patches of dense granular looking tissue, the base of the wedge being situated towards the cortical surface. Between these dense areas are patches more or less oval, which are evidently composed, as in the case of subacute interstitial nephritis, of sections of the straight and some of the convoluted tubules, either normal in size or greatly distended. It will be sufficient for our purposes to describe one of these dense patches and one of the open networks along with the vessels in the boundary layer. Begin at the centre of the patch, and work outwards ; it will be noted that the centre is occupied by the interlobular artery, which is somewhat thickened and tortuous. Around this the Malpighian bodies appear to be massed closely and much more irregularly than normal. The Malpighian bodies nearer the surface of the kidney and nearer the interlobular vessel are represented by a yellowish dot only, whilst those situated nearer the margin of the dense mass are surrounded by thickened capsules, and may be smaller than normal, or their atrophied tufts of vessels may be contained each within a large cyst, formed of the distended and thickened Bowman's capsule. In the centre of small rounded areas of granular material, which are not so opaque as the surrounding tissue, are some very minute openings. These are the atrophied convoluted tubules, which are lined with flattened epithelial cells. The tubules in the open network between the denser patches are in some instances enormously distended, and are also lined with flattened epithelial cells. The irregularity and tortuosity of the medullary rays as they pass to the surface are in great measure due to the unequal dilatation of some of these tubules, combined with the contractions which take place in the fibroid or denser patch.

(× 300).—The thickened capsule has a peculiar hyaline appearance. The dense patch is composed principally of atrophied tubules and Malpighian bodies. Between these, however, there is a slight increase of small round cells which, in certain forms, appears to follow the atrophy of the tubules ; but in others the process is similar to the subacute interstitial change, though of a more chronic nature. It is frequently exceedingly cellular or almost granular in appearance, even under the high power, and very little fully-formed fibrous tissue is observable. In this denser patch the intertubular capillaries may be obliterated at points, but, to make up for this, there is an accession of small branches from the capsule ; these run into the patch at the most retracted parts, and appear to communicate with the terminal branches of the interlobular arteries. The Malpighian bodies, as already seen, present three distinct forms :—(1.) the pink ring composed of fibrous concentric laminæ, in the centre of which is the yellow atrophied knot of capillaries; (2.) the enormously thickened and fibrous capsule, with the capillary vessels of the tuft still patent ; and (3.) the thickened and distended capsule, with the capillary tuft lying within, but only partly filling it. The method of formation of the thickened capsule has already been referred to.— (*See* Subacute Interstitial Nephritis, § 238.) The tubules found in the dense mass are in various stages of atrophy. The lumen is small, the epithelium is flattened or irregular, and is undergoing fatty degeneration, whilst numerous colloid casts (stained yellow with picro-carmine) are seen in the tubules. The basement membrane is swollen and hyaline. Casts of a similar nature are found in some of the dilated tubules which form the open network, and which are lined by flattened, often fatty, epithelium. On careful examination, the larger arteries will be found in a condition similar to that met with in subacute interstitial nephritis (§ 238). The intima is thickened—endarteritis obliterans (§ 214); there is an apparent hypertrophy of the middle coat, consisting in an increase of the connective tissue cells and a hyaline swelling of the connective tissue fibrils between the muscular fibres, which are often somewhat atrophied; the adventitia, which is continuous with the surrounding connective tissue and Bowman's capsule, is also hyaline and increased in thickness.

Notice that here we have an exceedingly chronic process, which appears to consist primarily of an atrophy, first of the Malpighian bodies and then of the tubules, followed very gradually by a slight increase in the amount of connective tissue. The changes in the Malpighian bodies are, in turn, due to the changes in the terminal branches of the interlobular arteries, around which, near the surface, the first indications of the disease are seen; the process gradually spreads down to the medulla, which thus, at a later stage, may become involved. This atrophic form of granular contracted kidney appears to be quite distinct from the so-called large granular kidney, in which the process is preceded or accompanied by a considerable increase in the amount of connective tissue, and which is more like the subacute interstitial nephritis, of which it is more than possible that it is the chronic continuation, more or less acute exacerbations occurring at intervals. In such a case, the interstitial changes are more diffuse than in the true granular or atrophic form; there is not the same tendency to contraction, though the newly-formed connective tissue undoubtedly does contract, and so may give rise to secondary atrophic changes. It is, in fact, essentially a chronic interstitial nephritis.

TUBERCLE OF THE KIDNEY.

240. Tubercle occurs in the kidney as one of two forms:—(1.) Disseminated or acute miliary tuberculosis; or (2.) Tubercular pyelo-nephritis.

(1.) The disseminated form occurs most frequently as part of a general tuberculosis; in which case the affection of the kidney is, as a rule, late, and of comparatively little importance.

Naked eye appearances.—The organ is not enlarged or markedly altered in any way. On stripping off the capsule, small grey granulations, about the size of a millet seed, are seen projecting, very slightly, above the surface. On section these grey granulations are wedge-shaped, and extend down into the cortex for some distance along the lines of the interlobular arteries. Similar masses may be more deeply situated in the cortex, where they assume an elongated or oval form; deeper still in the boundary layer they are rounded; they are seldom found in the medulla. In some cases they are surrounded by a distinct hæmorrhagic zone, especially in the later stages, when they become opaque, and white or yellow in the centre. Nodules (fibromas) similar in appearance, but more translucent, are frequently found in the centre of the pyramids; but these are much firmer, and, on microscopic examination, are found to be composed of fibrous tissue.

Harden (§ **56** or **59**), and stain (§ **98**).

(× 50).—It is at once seen that the tubercular process is going on around, and in connection with the distribution of the interlobular arteries. Each of the small opaque looking nodules, around which are evidences of interstitial inflammation, is made up of several tubercle follicles. The tubercular giant cell structure can rarely be made out, as in this organ caseation takes place at a very early stage of the process. The cells—of which the young non-caseated tubercle follicles (when present) are composed—may be seen to differ very considerably in both size and structure. In the centre are numerous so-called endothelioid cells of irregular shape, each containing several nuclei, and frequently lying on delicate filaments of pink tissue. Around are numerous smaller cells, between which the pink fibrillated tissue is distinctly marked, especially at the outer part of the follicle, where it forms a kind of capsule. Small homogeneous or granular yellow caseous patches may usually be seen in the centre of the follicle, even in the very early stage of the growth, when nothing can be made out but a mass of small rounded cells, with here and there a few of the larger endothelioid cells near the centre. In some few cases the typical giant cell formation (*See* Liver, § **189**) may be developed before caseation sets in; but in the kidney this is comparatively rarely met with. The softened points gradually increase in size, until several of them run together, and small cavities are formed; this is not of very frequent occurrence. Notice especially the arrangement of the tubercular nodules along the lines of, and in the perivascular sheaths of, the interlobular arteries.

(× 300).—Examine the constituent elements of the tubercle follicle more carefully, the endothelioid cells of various shapes and sizes with several nuclei, between and supporting which is delicate fibrillar tissue; at the periphery of the mass the small round cells with denser pink fibrous tissue between them are well seen. If there is a true giant cell system, the structure is similar to that met with in the liver (§ **189**). Note carefully that these tubercle masses have no vascular supply, the arteries having become obstructed, and that the caseation takes place in the centre of the nodule, or in those follicles which are furthest removed from the blood-vessels at the periphery of the nodule.

(2.) Tubercular Pyelo-Nephritis—[synonyms, "Genito-Urinary Phthisis," "Genito-Urinary Tuberculosis," "Scrofulous" or "Strumous Pyelitis," "Renal Phthisis" (not a good term), "Chronic Localised Tuberculosis," &c.]—is usually associated with tuberculosis of the ureter, of the trigone of the bladder, and of the vasa deferentia and vesiculæ seminales (scrofulous testicle). Both kidneys may be affected, usually, however, unequally.

In the earlier stages of the disease small yellow caseous nodules, with small cavities in the centre, are situated towards the bases of the pyramids; these extend upwards and downwards in the calyces and in the pelvis along the lines of the lymphatics in the submucous tissue. Ulceration soon follows this caseation; similar grey nodules, which rapidly caseate, are also found in the pelvis of the kidney, the surrounding injection of the mucous membrane often being a very marked feature.

Harden a piece of the wall of a cavity (§ **56** or **59**), and stain (§ **98**).

(× 50).—The caseous material is stained yellow, and is composed of a mass of granular *débris*. Beneath this are seen tubercle follicles which appear to undergo caseation at a very early period of development. Giant cells are rarely met with in the kidney, but if a piece of a tubercular testicle from the same case be examined, giant cell systems are exceedingly numerous. The origin of the disease is as yet imperfectly understood; but it appears that there is a local tubercular process beginning in the mucous membrane (the result of impaction of tubercle bacilli in one of the small blood-vessels), followed by early caseation and rapid ulceration; after which the process may spread by the blood-vessels, the lymphatics, or by direct infection. It is possible, however, that catarrh may be the starting-point of the disease, this being followed by a tubercular infection.

In the fully developed disease the kidney is very much enlarged and lobed, a marked depression existing between the projections, which vary in diameter from three-quarters of an inch to one and a quarter inches. The capsule may strip off readily, leaving a pale smooth surface from which the venæ stellatæ stand out prominently, or it may be slightly adherent. On section each nodule is found to correspond to a caseous mass or to a rounded or irregular cavity, and each depression to a kind of septum, which corresponds in position to the interpyramidal cortex, the cavities occupying the position of the Malpighian pyramids. Each cavity contains a yellowish or purulent-looking fluid, in which float caseous fragments; its walls are rough and finely nodulated or papillated, or are ragged looking; they are lined by a soft, dirty yellow or caseous material, which may be readily removed with the finger-nail, as a soft putty-like mass. The pelvis of the kidney is lined by a similar material, and is usually considerably distended. The ureter, too, has its walls thickened, is blocked with the same caseous material, and feels like a hard firm cord.

SUPPURATIVE NEPHRITIS.

241. Surgical kidney, a condition of suppurative nephritis, occurs very frequently in connection with stricture of the urethra, or renal or vesicular calculus, causing pyelitis (inflammation of the pelvis of the kidney), or cystitis (inflammation of the bladder), in which the contents of the bladder undergo putrefactive changes, as the result of the entrance of bacteria from without. The septic inflammatory process is supposed to pass back along the ureter to the pelvis of the kidney, and thence by the collecting tubules to the secreting tubules. It is probable, however, that the lymphatics and blood-vessels are really the channels by which the bacteria are carried to the kidney parenchyma from the mucous membrane of the pelvis. It is also known by the following names:—"Disseminated Suppuration" of the Kidney, "Multiple Abscesses" of the Kidney, "Suppurative Pyelo-Nephritis."

The kidney is usually, though not always, irregularly swollen, it is soft, sodden, and friable, and the capsule strips off readily. The vascularity varies very considerably at different parts. On the surface small projecting yellow points may be seen surrounded by deeply injected or hyperæmic zones. On pricking one of them a small drop of pus escapes.

On section most of the yellow points are found in the cortex, where they assume a wedge shape, but a few elongated abscesses are also seen in the pyramids. Around each abscess the hyperæmic zone is well marked; where the condition is more advanced, the kidney may have the above characteristics exaggerated, whilst the small cavities have run together, and may replace a considerable part of it. Where the abscesses are of considerable size they usually communicate with the pelvis of the organ, and contain ammoniacal phosphates mixed with the pus (pyo-nephrosis), or they may extend into the surrounding tissue, giving rise to the so-called peri-nephritic abscesses, which, however, most frequently occur quite independently of this condition. The mucous membrane of the pelvis is usually extremely infected, even before the abscesses are well formed in the kidney itself, and there may be seen small grey swollen points or yellow specks of pus in the submucous connective tissue.

Harden (§ 56), and stain (§§ 98 and 132, or 106).

(× 50).—In the cortex a large quantity of granular material (deeply stained with carmine) may be seen running along each side of the interlobular arteries surrounding the Malpighian bodies, and also in between the convoluted tubules, which thus become widely separated from one another. This is most marked at the bases of the pyramids. Within the tubules the epithelium is granular, and appears to be undergoing a process of disintegration. Similar changes are taking place in the medullary portion of the kidney along the lines of the vasa recta, thence extending between the straight tubules. In some cases the changes are so grave that

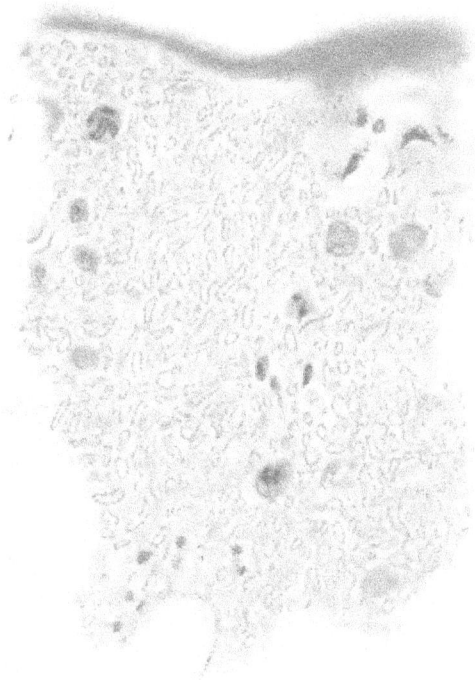

FIG. 85.—Section of the cortex of a kidney from a case of suppurative nephritis, the result of ulcerative endocarditis. Stained by Gram's method—gentian violet and eosin. (× 40.)

a. Swollen and hyaline capsule.
b. Distended capillaries of glomerular tuft crammed with micrococci ; *b'*, do. do. with swollen capsule.
c. Intertubular capillaries ; and *c'*, interlobular artery plugged with micrococci.
d. Masses of micrococci making their way from the vessels into the surrounding tissue, in which are numerous leucocytes surrounding the partially peptonised and rapidly breaking down kidney tissue.
e. Masses of micrococci in the straight vessels in the boundary layer. The epithelial lining of the tubules, except in the immediate neighbourhood of the commencing abscesses, is comparatively healthy, or is simply undergoing cloudy swelling.

a mass of deeply stained granular material is all that can be made out in these positions.

(× 300).—The granular material along the course of the vessels and around the Malpighian bodies is seen to be composed of small round cells; they cannot be distinguished from leucocytes or from pus corpuscles, and appear to be the result partly of inflammatory exudation, and partly of active proliferation of the connective tissue corpuscles. In many cases the cellular mass has fallen away from its position, leaving a small cavity, whilst in the more acute forms these cavities communicate with one another. In a section of the true surgical kidney, stained with methylaniline violet, the small rod-shaped bacteria, which are very similar to those met with in decomposition products, may be distinctly seen. Note too that these are frequently in the tubules, the epithelium of which is undergoing marked fatty degenerative changes; there may be no regular catarrh in these tubules, although in the early stages cloudy swelling of the epithelium is invariably present.

242. In a second form of suppurative nephritis, frequently associated with ulcerative endocarditis, there can be no doubt that the multiple abscesses result from the impaction of septic emboli in the interlobular vessels, and in the intertubular and intra-glomerular capillaries. These emboli consist of scraps of fibrinous lymph in which are embedded micrococci, which latter multiply rapidly and set up abscess formation as already described (§ 165), as, in addition to the condition above described, masses of deeply stained micrococci may be found in all these positions (in a section stained with methylaniline violet).

Under certain conditions nephritic abscesses become more chronic, in which case large caseous masses, encapsuled by firm fibrous tissue, may be met with. On microscopic examination, the tissue around is found to be atrophied, whilst chronic interstitial inflammatory changes are also met with. — (*See* Interstitial Nephritis, § 238 *et seq.*)

DILATATION OF THE PELVIS AND CALYCES OF THE KIDNEY.

243. Dilatation of the pelvis and calyces of the kidney may be due (1.) to tubercular thickening of the walls of the ureter; (2.) to obstruction of the ureter during the course of abscess

of the kidney. This may be due (*a.*) to the presence of a calculus in the ureter,[1] or (*b.*) to the existence of some obstruction to the outflow of the urine from the bladder, accompanied by decomposition of the urine (stricture, enlarged prostate, and a dirty catheter). (3.) Simple obstruction of the ureter, or of its orifice, or of the outlet from the bladder, by any of the above agencies, without the decomposition of the urine may give rise to simple hydro-nephrosis, in which there is dilatation of the pelvis of the kidney with gradual

---

[1] Forms of Renal Calculi—

(1.) Reddish or brownish-yellow uric acid calculi, in the form of gravel or rounded smooth masses, the size of a pea, or larger. These occur in great numbers, and are composed of uric acid mixed with urate of sodium or other alkaline urates.

(2.) Calculi filling the pelvis and calyces of the kidney, irregular and branching, with a somewhat rough surface, and composed of phosphates and uric acid or urates.

(3.) Oxalate of lime calculi, small, smooth, or mulberry masses, dark grey or purple in colour, and extremely hard. Soluble in the mineral acids.

(4.) Carbonate of lime calculi are found in the kidneys of old people. When pure they are usually yellow and hard. Carbonate of lime, like the following, enters into the composition of many of the other forms of calculi.

(5.) Phosphate of lime calculi are met with as small, smooth, facetted, nodular masses, usually much whiter, softer, and more friable than the calcium carbonate calculi.

(6.) Triple phosphate of ammonium and magnesium may be found deposited on any of the various other forms of calculi, or on an inflamed surface, especially where there is decomposition of the urine. It forms a soft grey or dirty white layer, and when examined under the microscope is found to be made up, principally, of the characteristic "knife-rest" crystals.

(7.) Cystine calculi are rarely met with. They are light yellow, ovoid, crystalline masses, soluble in ammonia. From the solution so made the crystals may be obtained in the form of hexagonal plates by evaporation.

(8.) Xanthine calculi are also occasionally, but very rarely, met with as white waxy-looking masses. They are soluble in hot nitric acid. When the solution is evaporated, and the residue heated with caustic potash, "a beautiful violet-red colour" is obtained.

(9.) Bile pigment calculi are sometimes met with in people suffering from icterus, especially in the case of new-born children. The bile pigment is deposited in granules in the epithelium of the tubules, or it may form distinct calculi, composed of flakes of bile pigment or of crystals of bilirubin.

atrophy of the papillæ from the pressure of the urine as it accumulates; they gradually disappear, and leave the interpyramidal cortex
projecting to form septa. (*See* also Tubercular Pyelo-Nephritis,
§ **240** (2.)).   Externally, the kidney presents a lobed appearance.
Running down from the depressions are septa, more or less perfect,
composed of membranous-looking fibrous tissue only.   The cortex
may be extremely thin and atrophied, and nothing may remain but
a thin crust enclosing cavities of considerable size, which are
usually filled with water and urinous salts.   If the disease is of long
standing, a mucous fluid only is found in these cavities.

Rarer Diseased Conditions of the Kidney.

244. *Syphilitic gummata* are very rarely met with.   They are
situated near the surface of the cortex, are of small size, and present
all the characters of gummata in other organs.

Leucocythemia.—Changes are sometimes met with in the kidney in
this general condition.   Both kidneys are affected, and are then
considerably enlarged; each may weigh as much as fourteen ounces
or even more.   The capsule strips off easily, leaving a pale grey
smooth flabby surface, mottled with numerous grey or cream-coloured
patches and minute hæmorrhages.   On section, both cortex and
medulla are enlarged; and it is often difficult to make out where
one begins and the other ends.   The cortex is pale, and, in addition
to the smaller hæmorrhages, a few larger ones are occasionally met
with.   There may be a few small cysts present.   The striation of the
pink medullary pyramids is distinctly marked, and grey lines, with
enlargements at intervals, alternate with red or pink streaks.   In the
boundary area the grey predominates, and here the medulla gradually
merges into the cortex, from which in this region it is almost indistinguishable, except by the position of the larger vessels and the
swelling of the medulla.   The minute hæmorrhages are most
numerous in this superficial portion of the medulla, and here, too,
the grey patches stand out most prominently; there are frequently,
however, numerous hæmorrhages at about the level of the looped
tubules of Henle, and also in the mucous membrane of the pelvis.

Harden (§ **59**), and stain (§ **103** *d*).

(× 50).—Along the lines of the intertubular capillaries, and within Bowman's capsule, also in the medulla between the straight tubules, and even in some places in them, there is an enormous

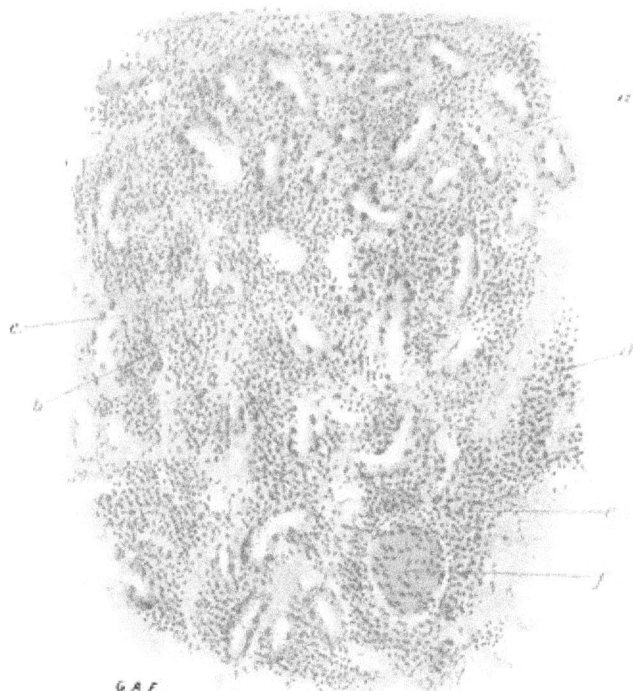

FIG. 86.—Section of kidney from a case of leucocythemia. Stained with picro-carmine. (× 70.)

a. Comparatively normal convoluted tubule.
b. Small vessels filled with leucocyte thrombi, and surrounded by leucocytes.
c. Small vessel surrounded by leucocytes, but with a clear lumen.
d. Hæmorrhagic mass of leucocytes around a tubule.
e. Do. at the point of entrance of an afferent arteriole.
f. Glomerulus in which are a few extra leucocytes.

The whole of the lymphatic spaces of the connective tissue are filled with leucocytes. In this part of the section there are no leucocytes in any of the tubules.

increase of deeply stained nuclei. At intervals, too, they form small plugs in the blood-vessels, and behind these may be seen small hæmorrhages. The connective tissue spaces are simply crammed

with these nuclei. There may be a few fibrils of coagulated fibrin
between them, but there is never any proper reticulum formed.

(× 300).—The nuclei are leucocytes which have escaped
along numerous red corpuscles from the ruptured vessels. The
so-called hæmorrhages, however, are composed very largely of
leucocytes. The epithelium in the tubules may be comparatively
healthy.

TUMOURS OF THE KIDNEY.

245. Of primary tumours the following forms may be met with in
the kidney :—

(1.) *Lymphadenoma.*—(*See* " Lymphadenoma " under Tumours.)

(2.) *Lympho-sarcoma* and small round-celled sarcoma are usually
congenital. They both lead to enormous enlargement of the organ ;
they are pale, and filled with numerous hæmorrhages scattered
throughout spindle-celled sarcomas, in which, frequently, a few
fragments of striped muscle fibre may also be found. They are very
similar in appearance to other forms of sarcoma.

(3.) *Fibroma* occurs as a firm hard nodule about the size of a
millet seed, somewhat rounded or elongated in form, situated
usually about the centre of the pyramids, but it may occur in almost
any part of the kidney, its pelvis, or its capsule. Under the microscope
it appears to be more cellular than most fibromas ; otherwise it
corresponds to the description of a soft fibroma given in the section
on Tumours.

(4.) *Non-striped muscular tumours—myomata*—are also found,
usually near the apices of the papillæ.

(5.) Simple *adenoma* has been described, but the malignant form
is much more frequently met with. The former is said to begin
in the collecting tubules. It appears as a small pale pink or grey
mass about the size of a filbert. The epithelium lining the spaces is
columnar and well formed, almost like renal epithelium.

(6.) The malignant form, which is really a cancer, usually begins
in the cortex, where the growths are at first not very large ; ultimately the whole organ appears to become infiltrated, when it may
attain an enormous size. The typical structure of the kidney is lost,
and we have in its place a large encephaloid pinkish mass, with

yellowish and grey patches, and numerous softened hæmorrhagic patches, from which blood and cancer tissue may make their way to the urine. The tissue, examined microscopically, resembles, very closely, the malignant adenoma already mentioned. (*See* section on Tumours.) It is probable, however, that cancer of the kidney is by no means so common a condition as was formerly supposed, and that many so-called cancers are, in fact, sarcomatous growths.

Secondary Tumours.

246. The most common of these are the various forms of *cancer* and *sarcoma*, which may or may not attain considerable size. They are usually multiple.

Parasites.

247. (1.) Hydatid cysts of all sizes and in various stages of degeneration are met with, though comparatively rarely.

(2.) In the mucous membrane of the pelvis of the kidney, the matured *Bilharzia hæmatobium* is sometimes met with, in which case the ova may always be discovered in the urine.

(3.) The *Filaria sanguinis hominis* occurs in the kidney, and has been found in the urine during life in cases of chyluria.

(4.) A few instances of the presence of other parasites in the kidney, such as *Cysticercus cellulosæ, Eustrongylus gigas,* and *Pentastoma denticulatum,* have been recorded, but such cases are of extremely rare occurrence.

Infarction.

248. Embolic infarcts, the result of the impaction of emboli,—detached fragments of fibrin, or young granulations, usually from the left side of the heart,—may be met with in all stages of development, from the swollen, red, conical, or wedge-shaped patch in the cortex, or the dense, pale-veined area, surrounded by a hyperæmic zone, to the caseous mass or cyst surrounded by a fibrous capsule, or the simple, puckered, and retracted scar which marks the position of the old infarction. The description of an embolic infarct will be given in the section on Diseases of the Spleen, to which the reader is referred, as here the process is essentially the same as in that organ.

CHAPTER VIII.

THE LUNG.

249. In order thoroughly to understand the various morbid processes in the lung, and to interpret aright the appearances presented by the tissues of the lung in disease, it will be necessary first to examine the healthy organ, and to describe, briefly, its structure.

Naked eye appearances.—The lung, when taken from the body in the normal condition, should weigh about one-and-a-half pounds in the male, and one pound in the female. It is enclosed within a fibrous sac or capsule, the outer surface of which is smooth, glistening, and serous. In people who live in the country, the lung has a pink colour (Shetlander's lung); but in the lungs taken from the inhabitants of towns the pink colour is lost, and is replaced by a dull bluish or pinkish grey, with a series of darker streaks (carbon pigment) outlining the lobules. A healthy lung crepitates under the finger. On section a quantity of blood, mixed with air, may be squeezed out; when the section is first made, it presents a bluish purple, and not a bright arterial red colour (though this makes its appearance when the cut surface is exposed to the air for a short time). The open bronchi contain only a small quantity of frothy mucus, covering a mucous surface somewhat wrinkled longitudinally.

The lung may be compared to a bunch of grapes, the stalks being the bronchi and the grapes the air vesicles. These bronchi divide regularly and dichotomously, but the division of the two largest bronchi takes place in a different manner in the two lungs. The left bronchus runs for some distance before dividing, and then one branch goes to the upper, and the other to the lower lobe. The right bronchus divides almost immediately into two branches, the lower of which goes to the lower lobe of the lung, whilst the upper one is subdivided, the lower branch going to the middle lobe and the upper one to the upper lobe. These bronchi divide and sub-divide until they come down to the smallest or terminal bronchi, each of which has around it a system of bronchioles and air vesicles, all communicating with it, and together forming what is known as a lobule. Accompanying the bronchi, at the root of the lung, and passing into the organ along with them, is a mass of connective tissue, which supports a series of structures, to which reference will afterwards be made. On examining the pleural surface of the lung, it is found that this division into lobes and lobules is not at all an artificial one, the lobules being readily enough discerned as a series of polygonal areas, each of which is bounded by a series of black lines. The air vesicles which form this lobule all communicate with a terminal bronchus. On section these black lines will be found to represent bands of connective tissue (interlobular septa), from which finer septa run between the smaller groups of air vesicles. These form a strong supporting network of connective tissue, the large bands of which are situated at the root of the lung running along the bronchi on the one hand, and on the other forming a strong covering to the lung, from which bands of considerable size run into the substance of the organ, to meet the bands of connective tissue prolonged along the bronchi from the root of the lung. (See Fig. 88.)

This connective tissue framework, as in other organs, not only supports the characteristic epithelial structure of the lung, but serves also as a medium in which the blood-vessels, nerves, and lymphatic vessels and spaces may ramify before they come into direct relation to the alveoli or air vesicles.

In order to understand the openings in the tissue which may be seen in any specimen of normal lung under a low power, it will be well to describe the structure of one of these lobules, as the structure has a very important bearing on the formation of cavities in certain diseases, such as emphysema and phthisis. When the terminal bronchi, or the last branches resulting from the dichotomous division of the bronchi, are reached, it is to be noted that numerous small branches, more or less at right angles to the terminal bronchus, or continuous with it at its termination, are given off (Fig. 88). These vary in number somewhat, but there appear to be at least six of them. Each of these divides into two branches, the terminal bronchioles. At the end of the terminal bronchiole is a tuft of two or three small tubes, each of which continues as such for a short distance, and then suddenly opens out into what is known as an alveolar passage. The walls of this alveolar passage are delicate, and are really made up of a series of air vesicles, which have

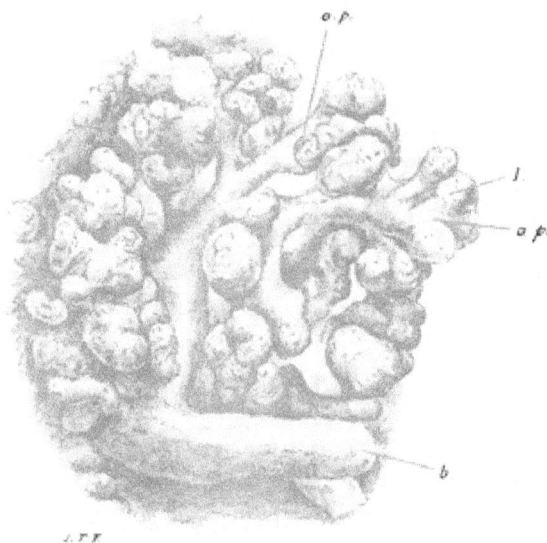

Fig. 87.—Drawing from fusible metal cast of the air cavities of a fœtal lung, made and kindly lent by C. W. Cathcart. (× 30.)

b. Terminal bronchus, from which lateral branches are given off at right angles.

$\left.\begin{array}{c}a.p.\\a.p.\end{array}\right\}$ Alveolar passages, opening into which are the infundibula (*I*).

On the surface of some of the casts of the infundibula the markings corresponding to the septa of the air vesicles may be seen.

a somewhat different arrangement at different points. Along each side of the passage are larger pouches, which in turn consist of a series of air vesicles; between the openings of the pouches the air vesicles surround the alveolar passage, from which point they are continued as the walls of the larger pouches. At the end of the alveolar passage, similar large pouches, also composed of a series of air vesicles, are met with. The pouches at the sides are spoken of as the lateral infundibula, those at the end as the terminal infundibula. The *alveolar passages* in connection with a *terminal bronchiole*, with their *infundibula* and *air vesicles*, make up a *lobulet* or *acinus*, whilst the whole of the acini in connection with a *terminal bronchus* make up a single *lobule*, the base of which is seen on the surface of the lung, as the polygonal area surrounded by the dark pigmented connective tissue. Supporting the walls of these various cavities is the *connective tissue*, first of all between the various lobules, as the interlobular septa; also as prolongations from the peribronchial connective tissue, running towards the centre of the lobule, and from the centre to meet that from the periphery derived from the pleural sac and the interlobular septa. There is thus formed a network of connective tissue which supports the blood-vessels and nerves of the lung, and in which are the lymphatics and lymph spaces.

Alongside the larger bronchi, embedded in the peribronchial tissue, run not only the large pulmonary artery and vein, but also the smaller bronchial vessels (*See* Fig. 88); with the smaller bronchi, however, only the pulmonary artery runs, the pulmonary vein being situated at the periphery of the lobule, so that, on making a section through a larger bronchus and its accompanying vessels, three openings of considerable size are seen; whilst on making a section through one of the terminal bronchi, only two openings are seen together — the bronchus and the pulmonary artery, the third opening—the pulmonary vein—being situated some little distance away.

Harden a section of healthy lung (§ 59 or 64) and stain (§ **98**).

(× 50).—Note (1.) the pleura at one margin of the section—the smooth surface; (2.) the interlobular septa; (3.) the bronchi with their accompanying vessels; and (4.) the air-chambers, into which these bronchi open.

(× 300).—(*a.*) The *pleura* is seen to be divided into two distinct layers—(1.) the superficial, seldom pigmented, and (2.) the deep layer. Covering the superficial layer, in very carefully made preparations, may be seen a layer of endothelial cells—large flattened nucleated cells—which, seen in a section taken from a fully expanded lung, are spindle-shaped. Both layers of the pleura

are made up of fibrous (pink) and elastic (yellow) tissue arranged in
bundles. The superficial layer contains a number of blood-vessels,

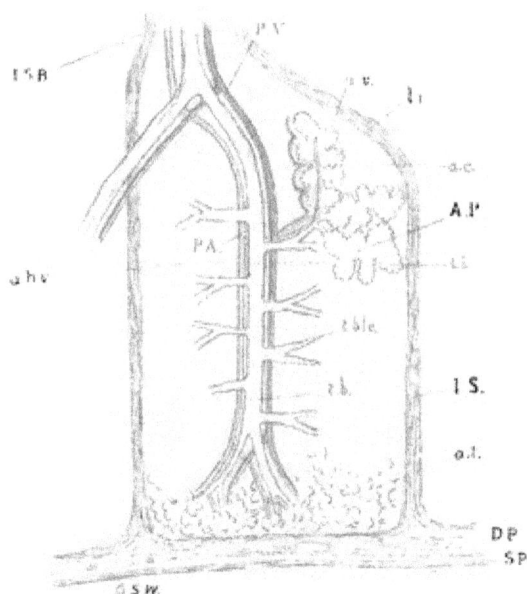

FIG. 88.—Diagram of a lobule of the lung.

a.b.v.	Line of section where artery bronchus and vein are cut across.
a.c.	Line of section where the artery is placed at some little distance from the vein.
t.b.	Terminal bronchus.
t.ble.	Terminal bronchiole, from which open the small alveolar ducts.
A.P.	Alveolar passage.
l.i.	Lateral infundibulum.
t.i.	Terminal infundibulum.
a.v.	Air vesicles.
a.t.	Alveolar tissue near surface.
P.A.	Branch of pulmonary artery.
P.V.	Branch of pulmonary vein.
I.S.	Interlobular septum.
I.S.B.	Do. prolonged from peribronchial connective tissue.
D.P.	Deep layer of the pleura.
S.P.	Superficial layer of the pleura.

The three alveolar passages constitute an acinus; the parts between
the interlobular septa, a lobule.

whilst between the bundles are numerous small plasma spaces or
lymphatics. Between the lymphatics of the superficial and deep

layers there is not a free communication, but those of the superficial layer communicate freely with the pleural cavity.

Beneath the superficial layer of the pleura is a delicate elastic layer which, in pleurisy, becomes swollen and very distinct; then comes the deeper or subpleural layer, which is considerably thicker than the superficial layer, but which is made up of more areolar-looking fibro-connective tissue. It is freely supplied with blood-vessels, some of them of considerable size (filled with greenish corpuscles). The lymphatics in this layer can be readily distinguished, as they contain small quantities of carbon pigment, even in the healthy lung.

Continuous with this more open subpleural layer, and of similar structure, are the interlobular septa, which send off small branches, to support the parenchyma of the lung, and are prolonged to meet the connective tissue surrounding the bronchi, so that several bands of connective tissue are seen in direct continuity between the subpleural layer and the walls of one of the bronchi. In all these bands the lymphatic vessels and spaces are numerous.

(*b.*) *The structure of the bronchi.*—(× 300).—(1.) Lining the tube is a layer of *ciliated* epithelium, the cells of which are distinctly columnar in the larger bronchi, but are shorter, though still ciliated, in the smaller bronchi. A few of these are seen as goblet cells lying between the ciliated cells. (2.) Between these, and at a lower level, are a number of ovoid cells, which appear to be imperfectly developed ciliated cells. (3.) Whilst still deeper is a layer of flattened cells, of which Debove's membrane is composed. (4.) These cells rest on a delicate homogeneous layer or basement membrane (which stains pink (§ 98)), found only in the bronchus of man (Hamilton). This appears to play a very important part in bronchitis and bronchiectasis. It is very elastic, may be stretched to an enormous extent, and is not easily affected by reagents. (5.) Beneath is a fibrous coat, in which are nuclei of connective tissue cells and a number of white blood corpuscles, whilst running through the tissue are some yellow elastic fibres. (6.) Then comes the muscular coat, made up of circular bands of non-striped muscular fibres, in which the rod-shaped nuclei may be readily distinguished. It is to the contraction of these fibres that the longitudinal folds

described under the heading of *naked eye appearances* are due.
(7.) External to this, again, comes the outer fibrous or connective
tissue coat, in which are the bronchial cartilages (between which
are the mucous glands, extending inwards), and the bronchial
artery and vein, sections of which are seen.   (8.) Continuous
with this outer fibrous coat are the interlobular septa. Around
the smaller bronchi the quantity of yellow elastic tissue in the
outer fibrous coat is considerable, but the glands and cartilages
are fewer in number, becoming less numerous as the branches
become smaller.

(*c.*) The terminal *air cavities* can be best seen in a silvered preparation (§ 118), say of the lung of a cat, but they can be made out in all
healthy lungs.

(× 50).—Note the air cavities. Some of them are seen as
small polygonal openings, bounded by a slightly tortuous line, on
each side of which is a network of tortuous lines ; resting on these
lines are a few small round nuclei (of epithelial cells) ; other cavities
with similar boundaries are considerably larger, and instead of being
polygonal in shape, appear almost like the section of part of a racemose gland ; others, again, are more or less rounded or oval, with a
series of indentations along their walls.   These correspond to
sections through alveolar systems, infundibula, and air vesicles, and
the student should make a careful study of these various openings, in
order to be able to recognise the parts of which they are sections.

(× 300).—The irregular lines running at the margins of the
air vesicles, or in the angles between the septa, are blood-vessels.
The network of capillaries forms the floor of the air vesicle,
and between its meshes are seen delicate bands of elastic fibre.
Separating the blood-vessels from the air are epithelial cells, of
which there are two kinds :—(1.) More or less cubical cells, which
are situated chiefly in the alveolar duct, or at the entrance to the
alveolar passage, at the angles between adjacent infundibula and
adjacent air vesicles, and a few, in groups, at intervals on the floor of
the air vesicle ; and (2.) between these groups of small cells, large
flattened cells, each of which has a rounded nucleus ; the outline of
each cell is marked out distinctly by the cement substance which
is stained brown by the nitrate of silver.   At intervals along the

lines of cement are clear areas—the so-called stomata—which are apparently due to the heaping-up of cement substance at these points.

A complete air vesicle, then, is a cup-shaped cavity lined with epithelium, either flattened or cubical, which rests on a fine network of capillary vessels. Supporting the capillaries is a delicate connective tissue. These cups placed side by side form the walls of the pouches or infundibula, which are given off from the alveolar passages ; they also make up the walls of the alveolar passages in the intervals between the infundibula. In the angles between these cups are larger vessels ; the walls of the cups cut transversely appear as the outlines of the air vesicles. (*See* Fig. 88).

ACUTE PNEUMONIA.

250. *Synonyms*—"Common," "Lobar" (from the fact that, as a rule, the whole of one or more lobes becomes affected), "Sthenic" (from the type of the symptoms), "Fibrinous," "Exudative," or "Croupous" (because the exudation appears to be similar to that which forms the false membrane in croup—"Croupous" is not an appropriate name) ; and lastly, "Pleuro-Pneumonia" (as this form of pneumonia is almost invariably accompanied by pleurisy, with an exudation of fibrinous lymph on the pleural surface).

The process may be divided into four stages :—

    1st. Stage of congestion or engorgement, during which there
        are (*a.*) hyperæmia ; (*b.*) effusion.
    2nd. Stage of red hepatization.
    3rd. Stage of grey hepatization.
    4th. Stage of resolution.

Only very rarely can the lung be examined in the early stages. The changes which occur in the first stage are characterised by the following appearances :—

STAGE OF CONGESTION.

251. *Naked eye appearances.*—In this stage, there is marked congest on of the vessels in the pleura at the base and posterior margins of the lung. Under the pleura small hæmorrhages are seen, and the substance of the lung is here somewhat firmer than it is towards the apices, but it is not solidified, and does not sink in water. It is rather more friable than the normal lung tissue. On section, the surface is of a bright arterial red colour, owing to a retardation of the blood flow, in consequence of which the blood is longer in contact with the air, which still freely enters the lungs before death ; it is owing to this retardation of the blood flow also that the tissue is somewhat œdematous. On pressure, a bright red or watery fluid mixed with air is forced out ; this fluid, examined under the micro-

Fig. 89.—Drawing of section of congested lung. Stained with picro-carmine. (× 300.)
    c.v. Distended capillary vessels of vascular network in the wall of the air vesicle.
    e.c. Detached epithelial cells.
    e.m. Elastic membrane.

scope, is found to contain a considerable number of red blood corpuscles, but these appear to come directly from the blood-vessels.

Harden (§ 59 or 64) and stain (§ 98).

(× 50).—A peculiar beaded appearance of the vessels bounding the air vesicles is observed. The capillary network is distinctly marked out, whilst, in the space bounded by these vessels, a number of small pink nuclei (of the epithelial cells) may be discerned ; similar nuclei are seen studding the beaded vessels.

(× 300).—The capillary vessels are distended with closely-packed greenish cells—red blood corpuscles—a few of which may have escaped into the air vesicles, where they may be recognised by their double outline and pale green colour. The epithelial cells are swollen at some points, and at others are undergoing proliferation, or some of the large flattened cells are simply separated from the capillaries, and are lying free in the air space. Only here and there throughout the whole section is there any further effusion into the air spaces, but when this does occur, its characters are similar to those presented during the next stage ; it may be in the form of slight hæmorrhages from ruptured capillaries. There comes a point, however, at which this effusion into the air vesicles becomes a very marked feature ; and as soon as this is reached, and the material has coagulated, the stage of true red hepatization is reached.

Stage of Red Hepatization.

252. *Naked eye appearances.*—The lung, or a lobe of the lung, has become solid, and now sinks in water ; all the air vesicles are filled with a coagulated fibrinous effusion. As a rule, it is found that this solidification is confined to one of the lobes—the lower one—especially at the posterior portion. This arises from the fact that, as at first the effusion is fluid, it gravitates to the most dependent parts, where it consolidates. The affected portion is sharply marked off from the rest of the lung tissue, in which, however, there is, as a rule, marked congestion and œdema. Sometimes the whole of the organ may be hepatized, in which case the lung, instead of weighing about a pound and a half, may weigh two or three pounds, or even more, in consequence of the large amount of exudation that has accumulated in the air cavities. There is frequently considerable injection of the superficial vessels of the pleura, or there may be a layer of fibrinous lymph thrown out on its serous surface ; in the later stages of the disease this evidence of pleurisy may invariably be met with. When handled, the lung feels somewhat firm, almost like a piece of leather, but it is so friable that the fingers may be made to meet in its substance much more readily than in a normal lung. On section, the tissue feels tough and elastic ; but, as it is quite solid, it "cuts" readily, and does not give way before the knife. The cut surface is often compared to red granite, as it has a dull, or, after a time, a bright red, smooth, glistening appearance, mottled with paler and grey spots—older coagula ; in some cases, this glistening gives way to a somewhat granular appearance, especially in the later stages, as the exudation contracts slightly. On pressure, only a very small quan-

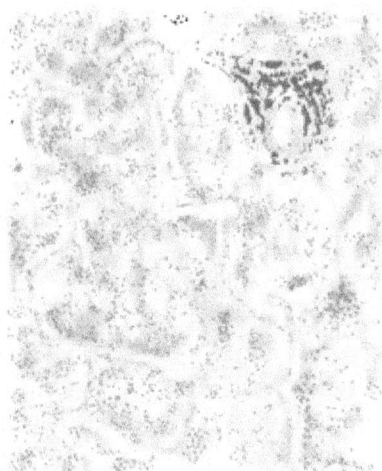

FIG. 90.—Drawing of section of lung in a condition of acute pneumonia, stage of red hepatization. Stained with picro-carmine. (× 70.)

In the air cavities the delicate strands of fibrinous lymph and the cellular elements of which the coagula are composed are seen. The capillary blood-vessels are readily distinguished. Note the transparency of the clot, and that it does not take on the staining material at all readily. Observe also that the clot completely fills the air vesicle. The tunica adventitia of the small vessel seen in section is infiltrated with carbon pigment.

tity of bloody serum exudes. The mucous membrane of the bronchi is injected, and is covered with a layer of bloody, frothy, or viscid fluid. In the smaller bronchi small firm casts may be found, similar to those met with in the air vesicles.

Harden (§ 59) and stain (§ 98).

(× 50).—The air cavities, in place of being empty, are completely *filled* with a delicate looking film, through which *light is readily transmitted.* In this film are seen numerous nuclei. The blood-vessels forming the outlines of the air vesicles are less distinctly seen than in the normal lung, and sometimes contain a comparatively small amount of blood. ′

The vessels in the deep layer of the pleura and in the interlobular septa are engorged with blood, and there is thickening of the fibrous tissue (due to œdema); on the surface, often above the flat cell layer,

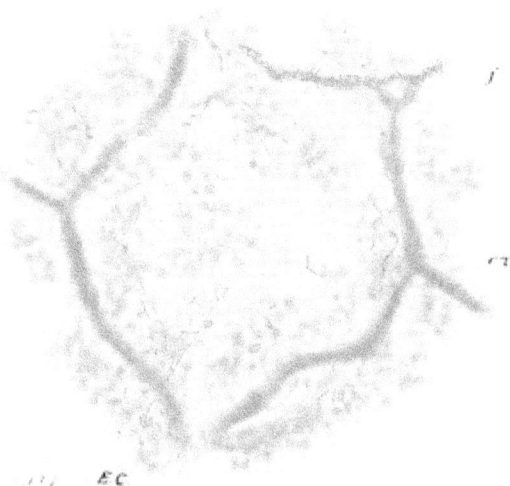

Fig. 92.—Drawing of air vesicle with contained fibrinous exuda-tion. Red hepatization. Stained with picro-carmine. (× 300).

    c.v.   Blood-vessels in interalveolar septa, in this case somewhat distended with blood.

    f.   Filaments of fibrinous lymph attached to the wall of the air vesicle, and not deeply-stained.

    E.C. Large nucleated epithelial cell.

    The white and red blood corpuscles may also be seen entangled in the meshes of the fibrinous network, the white, stained pink, and the red, with a double outline, green.

is a quantity of coagulated fibrinous lymph, which has all the charac-teristics of that seen filling the air cavities and the smaller bronchi, except that it is stained somewhat more brown, is more granular, and is not quite so transparent.

(× 300).—The exudation completely fills, and even distends, the air vesicles; it is composed of a delicate meshwork of coagulated fibrin (exuded from the capillary vessels), the fibrils of which are attached to the walls of the air vesicle.   Entangled in this meshwork are—(1.) numerous coloured blood corpuscles, again recognisable by their double outline and greenish colour; (2.) numerous colourless blood corpuscles, stained pink; and (3.) some larger nucleated (detached epithelial) cells.   At certain points there are larger groups of blood corpuscles, which have been poured out through ruptures in the walls of the vessels.   The more scattered corpuscles, as they have come through the walls of the vessels by diapedesis, have become entangled in the coagulum formed from the exuded blood elements.

The other cells met with are the large nucleated cells, similar to those lining the air vesicles.   They are derived from the swollen and proliferating epithelial cells, or are simply flattened cells separated during the first stage of the process and entangled in the fibrinous network; the majority of these cells are near the wall of the air vesicle, though a solitary one may be met with here and there throughout the network.   Around the blood-vessel is an exudation of leucocytes into the delicate connective tissue in the wall of the air vesicle, and there is probably, at the same time, a proliferation of the connective tissue cells; here, then, the first indication of an interstitial process, which in some pneumonias may become a very prominent feature, is met with.   There is no difference in appearance between the leucocytes and the connective tissue cells, both of which are seen in the early stage as small rounded carmine-stained bodies.   The exudation on the pleural surface is made up of similar elements—coagulated fibrin, red and white blood corpuscles, with, in some cases, a few flattened cells derived from the endothelial layer which covers the pleura.   In a section stained by Gram's method (§ 132), pneumococci or diplococci of pneumonia may be brought out.   They are seen not only in the cells filling the alveoli and embedded in the mucin in that position, and in the lymphatics in the walls of the air vesicles, but also in the expectoration, especially during the early stages of the disease, where they are very numerous.

STAGE OF GREY HEPATIZATION.

253. *Naked eye appearances.*—The lung is considerably heavier than normal.   The exudation is found in the same positions as in red hepatization. The affected part of the lung is solid, but does not appear engorged ; frequently the lobe above that in which there is grey hepatization is in the red stage, or is deeply congested. On the surface of the pleura a layer of coagulated lymph is invariably present. The tissue is heavy, firm, solid, sinks in water, "cuts" readily, and is extremely friable, breaking down very easily under pressure between the finger and thumb. The red colour has given place to a yellow or reddish grey or grey granite mottling. The cut surface is finely granular, an appearance very characteristic of this condition. The bronchi in this stage of the disease, if not in the red stage, are usually somewhat congested. Examine a scraping from the surface of the section (× 300), and note that the yellowish particles which come away with the muco-purulent material consist of small casts of the air vesicles, alveolar passages, infundibula, or even of the small terminal bronchioles. On adding acetic acid to the masses mixed with water, there is a precipitation of mucin ; and if some of the casts be treated with osmic acid (one-sixth per cent. solution) for a few hours, teased out and exposed to the light, and mounted in Farrant's solution, they are stained black (fat) ; with picro-carmine or logwood they are also stained deeply. Harden (§ 59 or 64), and stain (§ 98).

(× 50).—The exudation in the air vesicles does not now completely fill them ; it has shrunk, leaving a distinct interval between it and the wall ; it is stained brick-red, and is granular and opaque, not allowing the transmission of light to the eye, as in the red stage. The vessels apparently contain little blood, but are, nevertheless, distinctly seen. The pleura is thickened as in the stage of red hepatization, and around the engorged blood-vessels of the interlobular septa and the pleura a considerable number of deeply-stained small round cells (leucocytes and young proliferated epithelial cells) are seen. On the pleural surface is a layer of coagulated fibrin, which is opaque, granular, and stained brick-red.

(× 300).—A mass of brownish pink cells (degenerated leucocytes) may be observed in each air vesicle. The fibrin filaments are broken down and have become granular, and the red blood corpuscles have disappeared. The white blood corpuscles, or leucocytes, have become much more abundant, and are evidently undergoing de-

generative changes, for they now appear to contain three or four
nuclei, thus resembling pus corpuscles.   The whole mass is separated
from the wall of the air vesicle by a distinct interval, as seen above,
and is brick-red, more or less granular, and obstructs the passage
of light.   Examine the wall, in which the vessel is somewhat

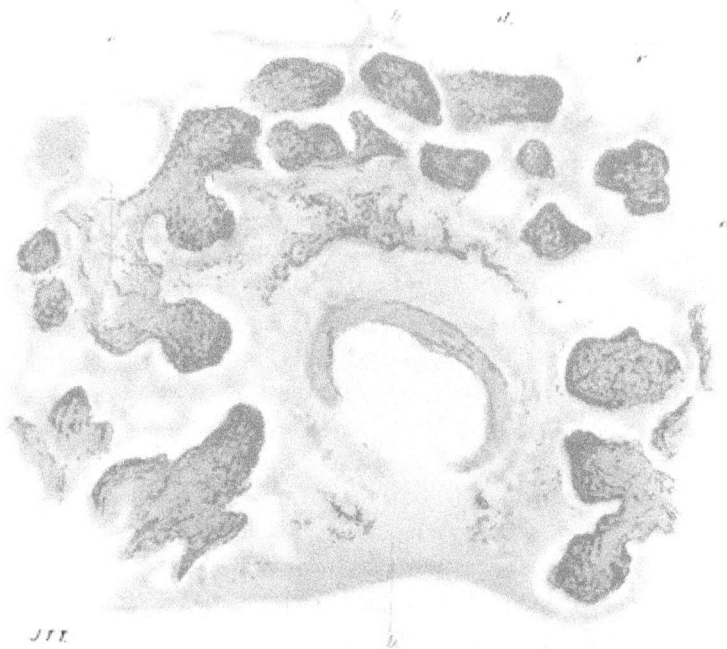

Fig. 92.—Section of lung ; acute pneumonia ; grey hepatization.
Stained with picro-carmine.   (× 50.)
a.   Small artery cut transversely.
b.b.   Interlobular septum, in which small cell infiltration is well
        marked.   (Early interstitial pneumonia.)
c.   Thickened interalveolar septa.
d.   Opaque, deeply-stained, retracted clot in air vesicle.   (Grey
        stage.)
e.   Coagulum passing from red to grey stage, more translucent,
        and not so deeply stained.   This occupies one of the larger
        terminal air cavities.

compressed, and contains but little blood.   Here are seen more
of the rounded cells (leucocytes) stained pink, lying around the
vessel, with a few young connective tissue cells becoming slightly
elongated or spindle-shaped.   Young epithelial cells may also be seen

on the wall of the cavity. Around the vessels in the interlobular septa, and in the pleura, are similar small round cells; whilst on the surface, in the deeply-stained, opaque, granular looking lymph, loops of blood-vessels are frequently to be distinguished passing from the vessels of the pleura. The vessels in the peribronchial tissue are engorged, and surrounded by a number of leucocytes and young connective tissue cells.

In a section stained in osmic acid (§ 110) it may be seen that all the leucocytes are more or less fatty, and that between them are fatty granules and globules all stained black; in certain cases, the lymphatics around the air vesicles are marked out by the black-stained fatty particles lying within them.

STAGE OF RESOLUTION.

254. *Naked eye appearances.*—In this stage the tissues are still pale, but they are softer and more flabby to the touch; a considerable quantity of a soft muco-purulent material may be squeezed out, and along with this small fatty casts of the air vesicles. Harden (§ 59 or 64), and stain (§ 110).

(× 50).—The granular mass in the air vesicle is much further removed from the walls than in grey hepatization, is deeply stained, and the black particles and globules are especially numerous. The whole section is granular, and the blood-vessels are more prominent.

(× 300).—The material in the air vesicles consists of fatty granules and globules, some of which have evidently been taken into the lymphatics around the air vesicles. The blood-vessels contain numerous red blood corpuscles as they are again opening up. New epithelial cells cover the capillary network, taking the place of those which were shed; they appear to be derived from the small cubical cells which have already been described (§ 249 c.). The walls of the air vesicles are much more prominent during this stage, owing to the distension of the lymphatics, the return of the blood to the capillary vessels, and the new formation of epithelium.

Other terminations of pneumonia may be — (*a*) death during one of the earlier stages; (*b*) abscess formation where the inflammatory condition is very acute; or (*c*) gangrene, where the blood supply is rapidly and completely cut off by the great amount of effusion into the air cavities, and where the irritant action of the micro-organisms (in septic conditions) is allowed full play.   In this condition there is a characteristic sloughy appearance, and an intensely fœtid odour.

BRONCHIAL CATARRH OR ACUTE BRONCHITIS.

255. Bronchitis in adults is essentially a catarrhal inflammation of the larger and medium-sized bronchi, and is usually associated with a similar condition in the larynx.   In children the capillary bronchi are specially affected, the disease then often spreading to the air vesicles, and giving rise to catarrhal or lobular pneumonia.

As an uncomplicated disease, acute bronchitis is seldom met with on the *post-mortem* table ; it is usually associated with chronic bronchitis, with heart disease, with some of the various dust diseases of the lung, or with one of the acute specific fevers.   In children it is most frequently met with as an accompaniment of or sequel to measles, whooping-cough, scarlatina, and similar conditions.

Naked eye appearances. — The lung is congested, and on exposure of a section to the air for a few minutes assumes a bright-red colour.   In the bronchi there is redness and swelling of the mucous membrane, with evidence of increased secretion and exudation ; at first the mucous surface is covered with a glairy, transparent, tough, mucous fluid, which later becomes a " yellow muco-purulent fluid which covers the surface of the mucous membrane, and can be pressed out in the form of a tough tenacious pellet." [1]   The adventitia of the bronchus is greyish-white ; the intense injection of the mucous membrane is readily seen when the tenacious mucus is removed, there is also some swelling and œdema of the injected membrane.   The smaller bronchi are apparently in a similar condition, and may be filled with the muco-purulent secretion.

Harden a piece of lung with several of the larger bronchi in it (§§ 59 and 64), and a thin section (§ 65) ; and stain (§§ 98 and 103 *d*).

(× 50). — Next the lumen is a layer of small round cells, with here

---

[1] " The Pathology of Bronchitis," p. 26, D. J. Hamilton, 1883.

and there one rather more elongated, generally placed at right angles

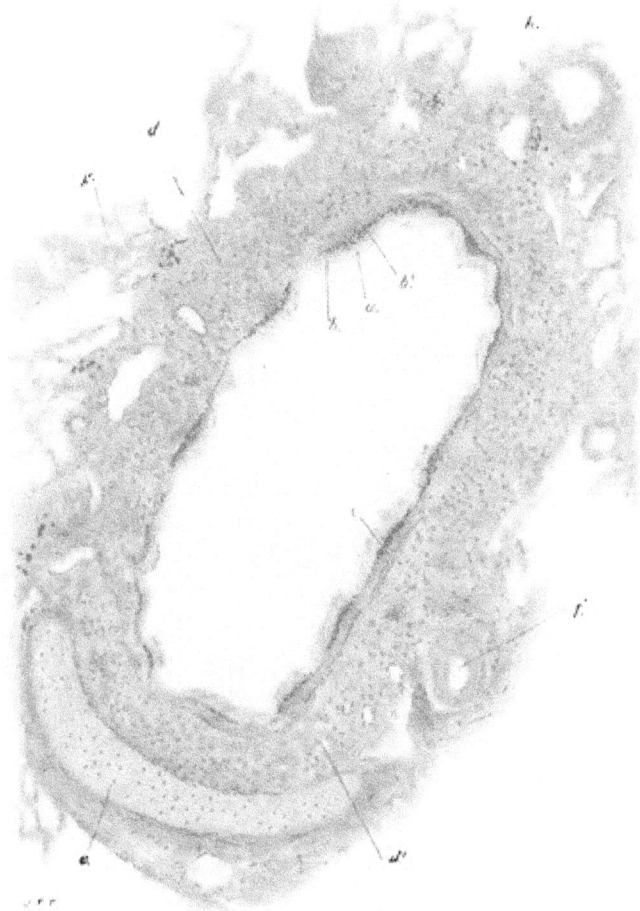

Fig. 93.—Section of a bronchus in which there is acute bronchitis. Stained with picro-carmine. (× 50.)

a. Single elongated cell resting on
b. The swollen and hyaline basement membrane. At other points the cells are more numerous, and are more rounded. b'. Submucosa thickened and pigmented.
c. Muscular coat of bronchial wall.
d. Adventitia of bronchus infiltrated with small round cells. In this may be seen the dilated vessels, d'.
e. Peribronchial cartilage.
f. Artery with thickened walls.
g. Lung tissue.
h. Carbon pigment in peribronchial lymphatics.

to the surface of the mucous membrane. Beneath this is the basement membrane, which is enormously swollen, hyaline, and œdematous looking. Pushing their way for some distance into the basement membrane are numerous distended blood-vessels, which lie principally in the inner fibrous coat of the bronchus. Around the vessels, and separating the fibrous laminæ, are numerous cells, seen as deeply-stained (pink) granules. These are especially numerous around the vessels, but are to be met with throughout the greater part of this inner fibrous layer. The muscular coat may also contain a few of these cells, and the outer fibrous coat is often infiltrated with similar cells. This, which is evidence of peribronchitis, is usually not a very marked feature in acute bronchitis.

(× 300).—In a section taken from a case in which death has occurred within a few hours of the first attack, the blood-vessels in the inner fibrous coat are distended, pushing their way into the basement membrane towards the lumen of the tubule. Later, in from sixteen to twenty-four hours, the basement membrane becomes swollen and œdematous, this change being followed almost immediately by a separation of the ciliated and columnar epithelium, which, on microscopic examination, may be found in the frothy expectoration. After this no columnar cells can be seen until the mucous membrane returns to the healthy condition. There are now also marked changes in the mucous glands, the cells of which undergo cloudy swelling, and secrete mucus more actively, the clear goblet-like cells being very numerous, and in the centre of the gland there is a considerable amount of granular material. After a few days the typical catarrhal condition is reached. Lying on the swollen basement membrane, are seen the flattened cells of Debove's layer, whilst above these are numerous rounded or peg-top shaped cells, which are evidently derived by proliferation from them. As these cells become detached, they, along with the mucus from the active glands, go to make up the muco-purulent discharge, the greyish parts being composed of mucus, the yellow or purulent material of the separated round cells. The changes in the inner fibrous coat are chiefly around the blood-vessels, which are distended with blood, and surrounded by a number of leucocytes and young connective tissue cells, which stain very readily with carmine and logwood.

Extending into the muscular coat are similar round deeply-stained cells, and it is to the presence of these cells, as a result of inflammation, that the weakening of the muscular coat, especially in the later stages, is due; for, as in the case of blood-vessels, as soon

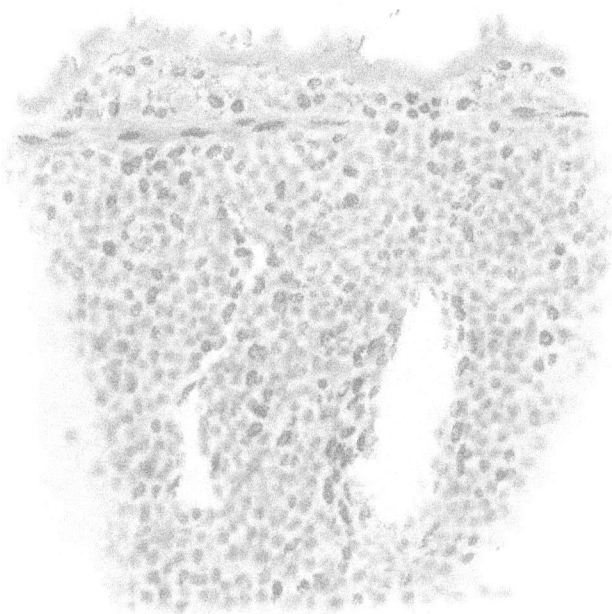

FIG. 94.—Portion of a section of the wall of a bronchus in a case of acute bronchitis. Stained with picro-carmine. (× 300.)

   a. Irregular columnar and rounded cells resting on
   b. The swollen and hyaline basement membrane.
   c. Submucosa infiltrated, and with small hæmorrhages in it.
   d. Muscular layer of the wall of the bronchus, through which the cells of the adventitia have made their way at one point.
   e. Peribronchial tissue (adventitia) in which are very numerous inflammatory cells (leucocytes and connective tissue). Here and there are small hæmorrhages (masses of cells stained green).
   f. Dilated capillary.
   g. Larger vessel, much distended.
   h. Lung tissue.

as the muscular coat is involved, it gives way; there is dilatation of the bronchus, and we have bronchiectasis. The outer fibrous coat is usually involved only as the disease becomes more chronic and there is extreme cellular infiltration. In the medium-sized bronchi the changes are much the same, except that there are no mucous glands present, and consequently no mucus.

CHRONIC BRONCHITIS.

256. This usually occurs in old people who have been subject to acute bronchitis during earlier life. It is often associated with emphysema, with valvular disease of the heart, in which there is venous engorgement and œdema, and with interstitial pneumonias of various kinds.

Naked eye appearances.—The most marked feature is emphysema, the air cavities of the free margins of the lungs are very much distended, and the other characters of this condition are readily recognised.—(*See* Emphysema, § **259.**) On squeezing the cut surface, a quantity of muco-purulent discharge is expelled from the bronchi, which, on examination under the microscope, is found to be composed principally of small round cells. Slit open a bronchus, and note that the mucous membrane is deeply congested, is usually of a dark-red colour, and except that it is thrown into longitudinal folds, is smooth and glistening in appearance; the mucous glands are often greatly enlarged, and may be seen as small glistening grey points, studding an injected or patchy surface. The smaller bronchi are usually dilated, and stand out more prominently than normal.

(× 50).—Note that the bronchial wall is greatly thickened and extremely granular, especially around the distended blood-vessels, the cartilages are not so prominent as in the normal bronchus, and the muscular coat is almost obscured. Lining the bronchus is a layer of rounded or peg-top shaped cells, similar to those described in § **255.** Columnar cells are seldom seen.

(× 300).—Examine first the epithelial cells lining the walls of the bronchus. They consist simply of rounded or incompletely developed columnar cells, and are very similar to those met with in the later stages of the acute form. The basement membrane is swollen, œdematous-looking, homogeneous, and hyaline, whilst its under surface is recessed at points by the pushing in of the vessels of the inner fibrous coat. These vessels never come to the surface of the basement membrane. The small round cells in the inner fibrous coat vary slightly in size; the smaller ones are simply exuded leucocytes, but the larger ones are derived from the connective tissue cells by proliferation. These do not pass to the surface of the basement membrane, though a few may be found around the vessels in its deeper part. The cartilages and muscular fibres are shrivelled and atrophied as a result of the great increase in the number of the round, deeply-stained, inflammatory cells.

In the outer fibrous coat, and extending along the lines of the interalveolar, and even of the interlobular septa, there is a similar new cell formation extending around the bronchi for some distance, which may thus give rise to a kind of interstitial pneumonia. These changes are most marked along the lines of the bronchial vessels and lymphatics, extending from them to the lymphatics of the surrounding tissues.

CAPILLARY BRONCHITIS.

257. Capillary bronchitis, or inflammation of the smaller, terminal or capillary bronchioles, is usually met with in broncho-pneumonia, and is frequently a result of the more acute form of bronchitis, not, probably, as the result of an extension of the inflammatory process, but rather of the application of the catarrhal products directly to the mucous membrane, or by the formation of a small plug of secretion in the bronchus. The changes are really those of bronchitis, peribronchitis, and catarrhal pneumonia combined:— accumulation of catarrhal cells in the bronchi, proliferation of the epithelium, swelling of the basement membrane, dilatation of the bronchus; small cell infiltration of the peribronchial tissue extends to the interalveolar septa. Capillary bronchitis is so closely related to catarrhal pneumonia, that the other changes may be best studied under that head (§ 261).

EMPHYSEMA OF THE LUNG.

258. As seen in chronic bronchitis and in old persons, emphysema is said to be atrophous, from the fact that there is frequently in such cases considerable wasting of the tissues of which the walls of the air cavities are composed; the emphysema met with in broncho-pneumonia along with collapse of patches of lung tissue is spoken of as compensatory, as some of the air cavities appear to be expanded to make up for the filling up of others. Emphysema may also be classified as follows:—(1.) vesicular emphysema, in which there is simply dilatation of the larger air cavities, some of which appear to be expanded to compensate for the filling up of others; and (2.) interstitial emphysema, in which the air has passed from the cavities in which it is normally contained into the surrounding or interstitial tissue. Of the latter form it is necessary to say little, except that to the naked eye the change is observed along the lines of the interlobular septa, in which a number of small clear air-filled spaces make their appearance. These spaces are never of any great size, but groups of them form beaded lines at the free margins of the lung under the pleura, or even between individual lobules. This form appears to be an extension of the vesicular process, and may be due (1.) to rupture of air vesicles, or (2.) to a wound in the larger air passages or in the pleura.

VESICULAR EMPHYSEMA.

259. *Vesicular emphysema* is usually met with where there is impaired nutrition of the lung tissue, which, when weakened, allows of the air cavities being more easily dilated. It is therefore specially common in chronic wasting diseases, in chronic lead poisoning, and in old people. In addition to these predisposing causes, however, there must be a direct or exciting cause, such as coughing in the case of old people who suffer from chronic bronchitis. In the case of children the predisposing causes seldom play a very important part. Here coughing in whooping-cough often leads to it; there is forced expiration, with closure of the glottis during the act of coughing, which, when repeated and continued for some time, gives rise to well marked emphysema. The causes then, are long continued and often repeated high pressure in the air cavities, especially when accompanied by weakening of their walls by impaired nutrition.

Naked eye appearances.—On opening the chest cavity the lungs are found to be considerably more voluminous than normal, the anterior margins of the lung extending much further than they usually do—in some cases overlapping—when the sternum is removed. The lung may weigh several ounces less than in health. The whole of the outer surface has a deep red colour, except near the apex, down the anterior margins, and around the margin at the base, where it is greyish pink. In these areas the outlines of the lobules are not so distinctly visible, but when made out it is seen that the lobules are considerably increased in size. There is great distension of the lung tissue, and what are called emphysematous bullæ, in which the tissue appears to be light and spongy, and feels almost like a mass of feathers in a silk bag, are formed. Squeeze the dilated portion, and observe that the air can be driven from one point to another along the margin of the lung; if a single incision is made, the air in the whole of the emphysematous portion may be driven out at the one opening.

On section, the tissue "cuts" with a peculiar gritty or harsh feeling, and to the touch the cut surface is harsh and dry. The bullæ consist of large cavities, across which run thin non-vascular trabeculæ, evidently the remains of interalveolar septa. No blood oozes from the section where the bullæ are well marked. Throughout the whole of the non-emphysematous part of the section there is more blood than one meets with in the healthy lung; on pressure a yellow catarrhal fluid exudes from the bronchi, as in this condition there is usually bronchitis, often of old standing.

With a piece of string tie firmly one of the emphysematous bullæ, so as to keep in the air, and remove it. To the string attach a weight sufficient to sink the mass. Harden (§ 59 or 64) and stain (§ 98).

(× 50).—All the changes are most marked immediately under the pleura. Instead of the angular and polygonal openings of air cells, the openings are round, and are somewhat increased in transverse diameter. These rounded openings, however, are much fewer in number than are the polygonal openings in the healthy lung, in place of a number of which, there are large irregular openings, usually surrounded by cup-shaped depressions. In a favourable section the capillary blood-vessels are

seen to form a network, with wider meshes than in the normal
lung, and the transverse diameter of the vessel is not so great,

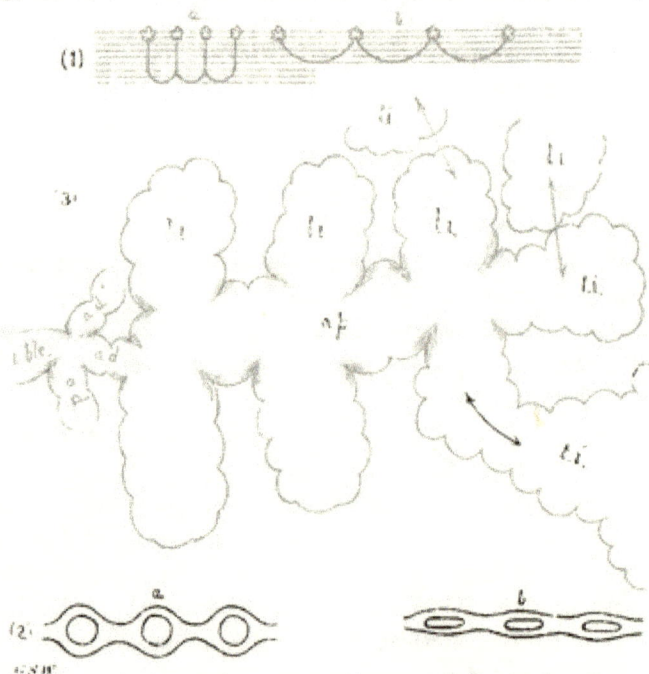

FIG. 95.—Series of diagrams illustrating the changes which take
place in emphysema.

(1.) *a.*   Normal air vesicles through which a series of imaginary
            sections are made at right angles to the wall.
b.   Air vesicles flattened out. Sections pass obliquely
            through their walls, which therefore *appear* to be
            thicker.
(2.) *a.*   Sections of capillaries in normal lung.
b.   Sections of compressed capillaries in emphysematous
            lung. The pressure is due to the flattening out of
            the air vesicles.
(3.) *a.p.* Dilated alveolar passage.
            Infundibula, terminal, *t.i.*, and lateral *Li.*, dilated; air
            vesicles flattened.
t.i^1. Terminal, and *Li^1.* lateral infundibula of other alveolar
            passages into which ruptures, indicated by double
            arrows, take place; between *l.i.* and *l.i.* infundibula
            of the same alveolar passage, rupture may also occur.
t.ble. Terminal bronchiole.
a.d., a.d., a.d. Alveolar ducts.
            Hypertrophied muscular tissue at the mouths of infundi-
            bula, &c., is indicated by shading.

the vessels apparently being stretched over an expanded surface.

Although there is evident dilatation, and probably thinning of the walls, the thinning is not at first sight apparent, for the sections of the walls between the individual cavities are sometimes even broader than in the normal lung. This may be accounted for as follows :— In emphysema the individual air cells are not distended; there is rather a distension of the infundibula and the alveolar passages, and, as a result of this distension, a flattening out of the air cells which form their walls; the greater the distension of the larger cavities the more marked becomes the flattening of the air cells, the walls of which also become considerably stretched. Consequently, if the normal air vesicle be imagined as represented by a cup with a thickened rim, the embryonic epithelial cells at the edge of the cup, forming this rim, the flattened out emphysematous air vesicle may be compared to a saucer, also with a thickened rim. If the cup be cut down in transverse sections, a considerable number—say eight or ten—are cut almost at right angles to the septa, and therefore in a direction showing least thickness of the wall. In cutting down the saucer, on the other hand, the number of sections must be fewer—only two or three—and each section passing obliquely through the wall appears thicker (though the wall may be actually thinned), and the relative, but not the absolute, number of sections through the bottoms of the concavities appears to be increased. Hence the apparent thickening of the walls of the spaces, and the numbers of membranous patches over which the capillary vessels are stretched. It will be remembered that when the section was made into the lung, there was in the emphysematous portion no exudation of blood, even on pressure; this was due to the fact that the pressure on the vessels, and the stretching of them over an increased area, frequently bring about their occlusion. By this fact, too, is the absence of hæmorrhage after rupture of the septa during life accounted for. The breaking down of the septa follows a regular plan. The septa between individual air cells never give way, they are simply stretched out; but the septa between adjacent infundibula of the same alveolar system, or between infundibula of adjacent alveolar systems, are often broken down.

(× 300).—Verify all the above appearances, and note in addition a few fibres of muscular tissue around the openings of the infundibula.　In emphysema, these fibres are more distinctly seen than in the normal lung, as they are somewhat hypertrophied.　Besides the changes in the walls already noted, there are marked changes in the epithelium lining the air vesicles.　It is granular and atrophied, and is evidently undergoing fatty degeneration.　The atrophic changes are brought about by the cutting off of the blood supply through the constriction of the capillary blood-vessels—the greater the constriction, the greater the amount of fatty degeneration and atrophy of the epithelial cells.　Another change, due to the same cause, is thickening of the walls, and even atheroma of the larger branches of the pulmonary artery.　(*See* § 212).

In this condition, owing to the obstruction to the passage of blood through the lungs, the right side of the heart has more work to do, is usually dilated, and somewhat hypertrophied.

COLLAPSE OF THE LUNG.

260. Collapse is met with under three or four different conditions.

(1.) In patients who, before death, have been extremely exhausted, and have not had sufficient strength left to take a full inspiration. In such cases the collapse is in the lower and posterior, or least moveable, portions of the lung.　The tissue has a firm and fleshy feeling, is non-vesicular, and sinks in water.　There is usually congestion of the collapsed and surrounding parts, and eventually the alveolar walls, at first merely in apposition, become adherent.

(1.) In weakly new-born children it occurs in conoidal patches of one or more lobules at the periphery, especially near the root and at the base of the lung, and is known as *atelectasis* or *apneumatosis.*　The collapsed patches are of a bluish or slate colour, and the tissue is so solid that it sinks in water.　This is *imperfect expansion,* due to pressure on, or to blocking of the bronchus leading to a lobule or group of lobules.

(3.) Where there is an effusion of fluid into the pleural cavity, as in pleurisy, leading to collapse of the whole lung.　This may disappear if the fluid is absorbed ; but where at the same time there is a thickening of the pleura, and organisation is taking place in the lymph, the lung may be bound down to the postero-internal wall of the pleural cavity, and the collapse remains. The lung is anæmic, though it may be somewhat œdematous. Spinal curvature, aortic aneurism, or distension of the pericardium, may bring about similar results.

(4.) It may also be due to a wound in the chest wall, when the visceral pleura is also involved. Here the lung is first congested and solid, but after a time it may become more anæmic than the other lung; which, however, in such circumstances, has a tendency to become congested and even emphysematous.

In all the above forms the tissue feels firm and fleshy, there is no crepitation, and no air can be squeezed out on pressure; a part of the solid lung will sink in water, and, though in the earlier stages of collapse the lung is congested, in the later stages it becomes anæmic, as its function is left more and more in abeyance.

(5.) *Lobular* collapse takes place in broncho-pneumonia (§ 261) as leaden-looking patches, each consisting of a lobule, or of a group of lobules, frequently depressed below the surface of the surrounding lung. This form of collapse is said to be determined by a plug of mucus which acts as a ball valve, allowing air to pass out, but falling back to the mouth of one of the smaller openings at the bifurcation of a bronchus at every inspiration. It is accompanied by congestion of the capillary vessels of the collapsed parts, and by emphysema of the lobule supplied by the corresponding smaller branch of the bronchus, which is not plugged, and of the air vesicles immediately around it; in such cases there is often a distinct ring of distended air cavities around the collapsed area. This is usually situated at the base and posterior border of the lung, or along the free margins, but the depressed patches may be present at almost any part of the surface.

CATARRHAL PNEUMONIA.

261. Synonyms—"Broncho" Pneumonia, "Lobular" Pneumonia.

This condition, in its simplest and most typical forms, is met with in children who have suffered from capillary bronchitis (§ 255), during the course of some of the exanthematous fevers, or whooping-cough. It is also met with in hypostatic pneumonias, where the contents of the alveoli are to a great extent catarrhal, though the distribution of the process is then not necessarily lobular.   During the earliest stage of catarrhal pneumonia, there is seldom any extensive pleurisy; in this respect it differs from the lobar form, in which pleurisy is a well-marked feature.   On the surface of the lung, which usually appears somewhat congested, are seen a number of firm, solid, purple patches, varying in diameter from one-tenth to one-fifth of an inch.   These are angular, and are frequently retracted slightly below the surrounding surface (collapsed lobules, § 260 (5.)).   In addition to these, there are a number of patches of similar appearance and consistence, which usually project beyond the surrounding surface (pneumonic patches).   Around each of these the interlobular septa may be readily distinguished; the lobules in the immediate neighbourhood appear to be distended with air, and in some instances there is marked emphysema.

On section, the lung is found to be congested throughout; the small angular patches coincide in extent with the lobules, and near the surface they are of a pyramidal shape; the solid patches are not very sharply defined from the surrounding tissue, are smooth and non-vesicular, and very little fluid can be squeezed from them; the walls of the surrounding dilated air vesicles evidently contain a considerable amount of blood, as the tissue appears very congested, and both blood and air may be squeezed out from these vesicles in considerable quantities.

Either during this stage, or more frequently during the next, the solidified and purple pneumonic patches may run together, and so form a solid mass with irregular outline, involving a considerable part of a lobe of the lung.   A careful examination in such a case, however, enables one to say at once that this is a condition of acute or lobar pneumonia.   In addition to this irregularity of the outline, there are usually a number of lobules and smaller patches which have as yet not become fused to the main mass.   Between the solid-looking patches, which are not granular, the lung tissue, though deeply congested, is otherwise normal.

The larger bronchi are deeply congested, whilst in the smaller ones there is acute catarrh, and on squeezing (§ 255) a quantity of muco-purulent material is pressed out from them.

Harden (§ 59 or 64), and stain (§ 98).

(× 50).—Examine a single lobule in which the catarrhal pneumonic process has been detected with the naked eye. It may be divided into three zones. In the centre is the small bronchus, recognised as a large rounded tube, with thickened granular-looking walls. In it there are usually a number of small cells, seen as small granules. Near the bronchus runs the branch of the pulmonary artery, known by the thickness of the adventitia and the quantity of pigment deposited in its lymph spaces.

In the narrow area immediately around the bronchus, the air vesicles are filled with a semi-transparent mass of delicate fibrils and cells, which differs from the exudation in the red hepatisation stage of acute lobar pneumonia only in the fact that it contains a greater number of cells. Where this process is not of long standing, the walls of the alveoli are thickened owing to the distension of the capillaries; near which a number of larger cells are usually found situated within the air vesicle. Outside this narrow zone the air vesicles are filled with catarrhal cells, with little or no fibrin between them. These, or their nuclei, are deeply stained, and are not nearly so transparent as the exudation in the central zone. Here, too, the capillaries in the walls of the air vesicles are distended. The catarrhal change may extend to the periphery of the lobule, but in many cases there is an outer zone in which there is merely congestion of the capillary vessels, accompanied by slight proliferation or detachment of some of the alveolar epithelial cells.

Examine the interlobular septa, and observe that they are more prominent than normal, are swollen, and that their vessels are considerably distended; around the vessels small inflammatory cells are frequently seen. The deep layer of the pleura is in a similar condition and in it small greenish patches (small hæmorrhages composed of red blood corpuscles) are seen. There is some bronchitis (*see* § 255).

(× 300).—The plug of muco-purulent material in the lumen of the bronchus is composed principally of small purulent-looking cells; in which, on the addition of acetic acid to a fresh section, several small nuclei appear. The epithelium of the bronchus is proliferating, and is usually seen only as a layer of irregular or flattened cells lying on the basement membrane ; beneath this the vessels of the bronchial mucous membrane are distended ; and around them, and in the peribronchial tissue, there is a great increase in the number of small round pink-stained cells (*see* Fig. 94). This condition of infiltration with small round cells and thickening of the walls extends down to the minute bronchioles.

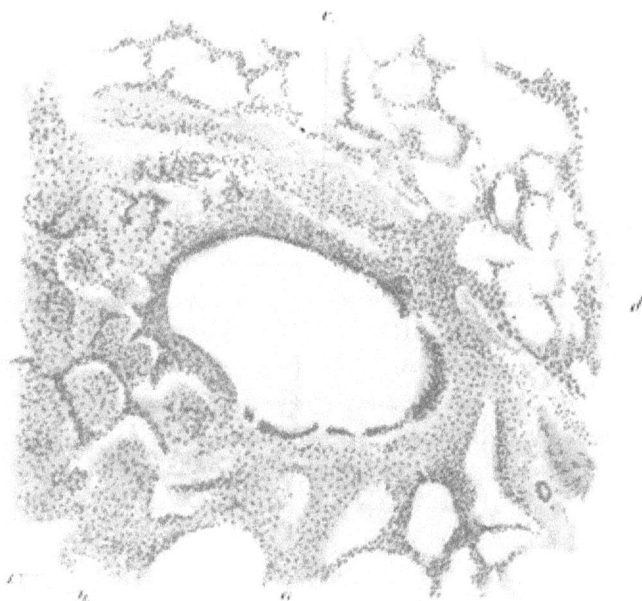

FIG. 96.—Section of lung ; catarrhal pneumonia.   Stained with logwood.   (× 50.)
> *a.* Section of small bronchus with infiltrated walls, proliferating epithelium well seen.
> *b.* Air vesicle filled with catarrhal cells, wall of vesicle thickened, and epithelium very prominent.
> *c.* Infiltrated interlobular septum, in which are distended blood-vessels, *d.*
> The catarrhal proliferation is well-marked in the whole of the air vesicles.

The air vesicles in the central zone are filled with fibrinous exudation, along with the clear unstained strands of which numerous corpuscles, which differ considerably in size, are seen.—(1.) Small round corpuscles with a double outline, and stained green with picro-carmine—red blood corpuscles ; (2.) Granular corpuscles a little larger than the above, stained pink—colourless blood corpuscles; and (3.) Rounded or oval cells, found in greatest numbers towards the periphery of the exudation. These are usually much larger (two to six times) than either of the preceding, and are made up of delicately-stained granular protoplasm, in which one or more nuclei stand out as deeply-stained bodies. The nuclei vary considerably in size, even in the same cell. Such cells are all derived from the epithelium lining the air vesicles by a process of catarrhal prolifera-

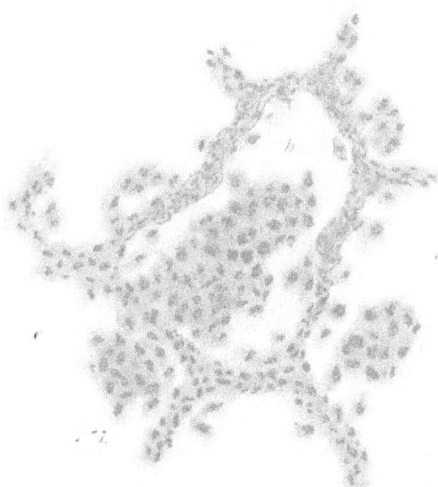

FIG. 97.— Catarrhal pneumonia; drawing of air vesicle. Stained with picro-carmine. (× 300.)

  a. Proliferating epithelial cells still attached to the interalveolar septa.
  b. Pear-shaped cell held in position by a peduncle.
  c. Mass of catarrhal cells, lying free in the alveolus. Smaller groups in the adjacent alveoli. These large epithelial cells are quite distinct from the small cells seen in the exudation in acute pneumonia.

tion. Though most of them are lying free near the edge of the alveolus, some are still adherent to the wall, and seem to be in a state of active proliferation; many of them are still attached to the parent cells by thin bands of protoplasm, which act as peduncles until they are set free.

In the next zone the air vesicles contain only catarrhal cells with a small quantity of granular matrix (mucin, fat granules, and granular protoplasm); the coloured blood corpuscles and the fibrin appear to be absent. On the addition of acetic acid the mucin between the cells may be brought out more prominently, but it is always a difficult matter to differentiate this intercellular material. In the very early stage of the catarrh, the proliferating process may be well seen in this intermediate zone; the cells lining the air vesicle are swollen, multinucleated, and in many cases dividing; and are seen in all stages of detachment from the alveolar wall. Where this is taking place the blood-vessels are distended, and there is slight thickening of the alveolar wall, quite apart from the increased thickness of the epithelial layer. In what has been described as the outer zone, this proliferative layer of epithelium and the distention of the blood-vessels may be all that is present, though in other cases the catarrhal products fill the cells at the margin of the lobule. It will be noted, even where the catarrhal process has been going on for a few days only, that the large detached epithelial cells are becoming more granular, less deeply stained, and are studded with small highly-refractile bodies, which stain black with osmic acid (§ 110), showing that the cells are undergoing fatty degeneration. The interlobular septa, as already seen, are considerably thickened; the vessels running in them are distended with coloured corpuscles (stained green with picro-carmine); there may be small extravasations around the vessels, and in addition there appears to be proliferation of the connective tissue cells, and an exudation of leucocytes. The strands of fibrous tissue of which a septum is composed are somewhat separated from one another; and in the lymphatics, granular-looking masses of fibrin and cellular *débris* may frequently be observed. The deeper layer of the pleura is usually in a similar condition.

The condition above described is the first stage of acute *lobular* pneumonia; but just as in the case of acute *lobar* pneumonia, the exuded and proliferated products may pass through a series of changes, as a result of which both the naked eye and microscopic appearances are somewhat altered. In this form the various stages are described under the terms of red and grey splenization and resolution, corresponding to the stages of red and grey hepatization and resolution of the acute lobar form.

GREY SPLENIZATION.

262. Grey splenization corresponds very closely to the grey hepatization of acute pneumonia.

Naked eye appearances.—The lung is not nearly so deeply congested as in the earlier stages, and in some cases it may appear, as a whole, even paler than normal, this being due to the pallor of the more solid patches. In the centre of each of the solid patches there is frequently a greyish point, or the grey colour may extend throughout the whole lobule. On palpation, the patches are not always firm and solid.

On section, note the slight congestion around the greyish-yellow lobules. On pressure, a quantity of muco-purulent material which, on microscopic examination, is found to consist of pus corpuscles or of fat globules of various sizes, which are blackened by osmic acid, exudes from even the very small bronchi. On the addition of acetic acid, this material becomes stringy, owing to the mucin it contains. The mucous membrane of the bronchi is deeply congested.

Harden (§ 59 or 64), and stain (§§ 98 and 110).

(× 50).—The exudation in all the zones of the lobule is broken down, and in place of the catarrhal cells, smaller pus cells and large compound granular cells are seen in considerable numbers; these, when stained, are dirty brown and opaque, or stained with osmic acid are almost black—due to fatty degeneration.

(× 300).—The pus cells and compound granular cells are very distinctly seen at the centre of the air vesicle; whilst at the margin there are usually a few small flattened epithelial cells growing, and forming a covering for the interalveolar septa. The other appearances are much the same as in grey hepatization of lobar pneumonia (§ 253).

Later, the microscopic appearances are much the same as in the stage of resolution in acute pneumonia; the whole of the catarrhal products are broken down and softened; they form a fatty pultaceous mass, part of which is expectorated, and part absorbed by the lymphatics. In a section stained with osmic acid, the fatty material may be traced in the lymph spaces in the interalveolar and interlobular septa. The epithelium is regenerated during this stage, and is seen first as a layer of cubical cells lining the air vesicle; in the interalveolar septa there is some increase in the number of connective tissue cells.

As in the case of lobar or acute pneumonia, it is impossible to go into all the forms of disease which may follow acute catarrhal pneumonia, but the following more common sequelæ may be mentioned as referred to by several writers.

SEQUELÆ OF ACUTE CATARRHAL OR LOBULAR PNEUMONIA.

263. (1.) Acute suppurative broncho-pneumonia, in which the pneumonia is set up by retained bronchial secretion. This condition is so acute, and the infiltration with leucocytes of the tissues around the bronchus is so great, that an abscess is formed, which may involve the whole of the tissue in the immediate neighbourhood of the bronchus. To the naked eye, the lung presents the characteristic features of ordinary lobular pneumonia, with here and there points of suppuration.

(2.) Chronic broncho-pneumonia appears to be little more than an interstitial pneumonia, set up by the irritation of the absorbed broncho-pneumonic products. It occurs as a diffuse form especially in children, and as a nodular form in old people. The appearances, both naked eye and microscopic, are very similar to those of interstitial pneumonia (§ 267).

(3.) Caseous broncho-pneumonia, of either the nodular or the diffuse form, is as yet not exactly localised; it was formerly classified as a true catarrhal pneumonia; but it is now referred to the tubercular diseases, and will be more conveniently described along with phthisis (§ 272).

(4.) Owing to the changes in the walls of the bronchi in bronchopneumonia, a form of ulcerative bronchiectasis (of the small lobular bronchi) is sometimes met with, in which irregular cavities containing softened or purulent material are seen. This form is apt to be mistaken for caseous tubercle (Greenfield).

THE PNEUMONO-KONIOSES, OR THE DUST DISEASES OF THE LUNG.

264. The most important of these are—

1. Anthracosis—Coal-miners' phthisis.
2. Siderosis—Needle-grinders' phthisis.
3. Silicosis—Stone-masons' phthisis.

But there are numerous other forms, such as those due to inhalation of vermilion, particles of wool, cotton, clay, or similar finely divided irritant dust particles.

Of these it will be necessary to examine specimens of the first and third only ; in both of which, however, may be found characters distinctive of the special disease or of the whole group.

"ANTHRACOSIS," OR COAL-MINERS' PHTHISIS.

265. This disease is the result of the inhalation of coal or carbon particles, which find their way into the air passages, air vesicles, and hence into the surrounding connective tissue, in all of which they set up irritative changes, catarrhal or interstitial, as the case may be.

Naked eye appearances.—The lungs of a coal-miner are invariably deeply pigmented ; they are increased in size, fill the *opened* pleural cavity more completely, and are heavier, much firmer, and more solid than normal. The pleural surface at first sight appears to be uniformly black, but on closer examination small dark spots, or accumulations of pigment, from which lines radiate in various directions may be seen, these lines corresponding to the lymphatics of the interlobular septa. Very frequently in the centre of these spots there is a lighter coloured point. Such a spot, with its light centre and dark periphery is firm, hard, and fibroid, and is about the size of a mustard seed, or a little larger.

On section, the lung is firm and tough ; it has a peculiar harsh emphysematous feeling, whilst small nodules, similar to those seen on the pleural surface, are scattered throughout its substance, but in smaller numbers. Between the nodules the pigmentation is not nearly so well marked, though there is a considerable deepening of the colour of the tissue, especially along the course of the lymphatics of the interlobular septa. From the cut surface a large quantity of inky black fluid exudes, which in the fresh condition stains the hands. The bronchial glands when incised are firm, hard, and deeply pigmented. The mucous membrane of the bronchi is pink and not black; the particles of carbon can gain no foothold—either in consequence of the currents set up by the active cilia of the cells of the healthy epithelium, or of the active proliferation and secretion of mucus which occurs on a catarrhal surface, the secretion washing away all foreign particles as they are deposited—it is often

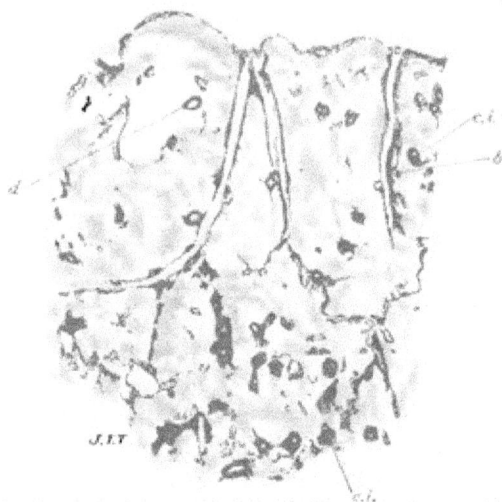

FIG. 98.—Section of coal-miners' lung, to show position of carbon pigment. Unstained. (× 6).

    a. Deep layer of pleura, in lymphatics of which a large quantity of pigment has accumulated. The magnification is not sufficient to bring out the superficial non-pigmented layer.
    b. Interlobular septum, pigmented at margins. (In lymphatics of connective tissue.)
    c.i. Small bronchi with thickened and pigmented walls.
    d. Vessel with pigmented adventitia.
    In all these pigmented areas there is great increase in the amount of connective tissue, so that they are hard and firm, and, from the amount of pigment that has accumulated in the lymph spaces, gritty.

pink or red, as it is considerably injected. At one or two points, if the disease be far advanced, the tissue presents the appearance of a solid black mass, or in the blackest part of this there may be a ragged cavity bounded by sloughy looking walls.

Harden (§ **59** or **64**) stain (§ **98**), and mount a section,—on which should be a piece of the pleura, and which should pass through several lobules,—unstained (§ 152).

(× 50).—The pleura is divided into two distinct layers, the more superficial of which is but slightly pigmented at any point, and is apparently little changed. Between it and the deep layer, which is sometimes three or four times the normal thickness, is a sharp line of demarcation. Throughout this thickened layer are black patches, which evidently follow the lines of the lymphatics, especially around the blood-vessels ; these patches are sharply bounded by the walls of the lymph spaces or sinuses.

The interlobular septa continuous with the deep layer of the pleura are also considerably thickened, and their lymphatics are similarly injected with black pigment. From them the black lines and patches may be traced into the perivascular and peribronchial tissue, as the peribronchial lymphatics are in direct communication with those in the septa, and so with those in the deep layer of the pleura. The mucous membrane of the bronchus is entirely free from pigment of any kind, though it is frequently swollen and in a condition of catarrh (see § 255).

The interalveolar septa are considerably thickened and pigmented, and the walls of the air vesicles are thickened and contain numerous dark-coloured patches. In the air vesicles coal particles are found in considerable numbers, some of them lying free on the surface of the epithelium, others contained within detached epithelial cells, whilst others again are found within swollen epithelial cells, still attached to the wall. In addition to these are numerous nucleated cells lying free in the cavity. In the lymphatics around the small branch of the pulmonary artery, the masses of carbon pigment are specially numerous. Here they act as irritant bodies and set up proliferation of the connective tissue cells, and so thickening of the adventitia or outer coat, fibrous nodules being formed around the vessel. Then endarteritis (§ 214) setting in, layer upon layer of proliferated cells (derived from the flattened cells of the intima lying directly in contact with the blood current) is developed until the lumen is narrowed, or in some cases obliterated, and only a solid fibrous nodule remains. This eventually may undergo degenerative changes, soften and break down in the centre, leaving a small cavity bounded by ragged fibrous deeply-pigmented walls. From the fact that the above changes are most marked where the nodules are most numerous, it appears probable that most of them have an obliterated vessel in their centre, the process of degeneration being due to the obstruction to the lymph and blood flow.

(× 300).—Follow the course of the pigment in the lung. It is not found in the mucous membrane of the bronchi, which frequently, however, shows well marked evidences of acute bronchitis (§ 255). In the air vesicles it is found in the different positions mentioned above; the lymph spaces in the walls of the air vesicles are in many cases packed with it; the connective tissue cells in the walls of these spaces, and some cells lying free in the lymph channels, are also pigmented. The cells in the air vesicles, as seen above, vary from the size of a colourless blood corpuscle to three or four times that size, and some of them may have several nuclei. Occasionally, too, a few coloured blood corpuscles may be recognised.

There is evidently considerable proliferation of the connective tissue cells, for nuclei are much more numerous than usual, and there is a great increase in the amount of fibrillated tissue around the capillary vessels, which are usually considerably dilated and are distended with blood corpuscles. Small fibrous nodules are sometimes seen in the interalveolar septa. Similar changes, but on a larger scale, are met with in the interlobular septa. The lymphatics contain pigment; there is marked increase in the amount of interstitial connective tissue, many of the cells containing granules of carbon. The blood-vessels may be distended, or, in some cases, the lumina, though filled with blood, are considerably contracted, owing to thickening of both the intima and the adventitia. In this position the fibrous nodules are pale and firm in the centre, but towards the periphery they contain, in the spaces between the bundles of fibrous tissue, a considerable quantity of pigment. From the alveoli near the surface the pigment is carried by the more superficial lymphatics of the interalveolar and interlobular septa to the deep layer of the pleura, and as seen above the thickening and pigmentation are both extremely well marked; all the changes observed in the interlobular septa are here repeated. The superficial layer of the pleura is usually unaffected; there is no marked pigmentation, and but little increase in thickness. The lymphatics of this layer do not appear to communicate with those of the subpleural layer.

From the lymphatics surrounding the alveoli nearer the root of the lung the pigment is carried to the perivascular and peribronchial lymphatics, giving rise to changes similar to those described in the above positions. Around the bronchi the changes are not so marked, but even here the fibrous tissue may be invaded, but never the mucous membrane proper.

To sum up: the small black nodules may be found in the interalveolar and interlobular septa, in the deep layer of the pleura, and in the perivascular and peribronchial tissue. Pigment is found in all these positions, and also in the air vesicles, either lying free or contained within the proliferating epithelial cells.

"SILICOSIS," OR STONE-MASONS' PHTHISIS.

266. *"Lithicosis,"* or *"Chalicosis."*—In essential details this process is similar to anthracosis; but all the changes are more marked and more rapid, the particles of stone being much more irritating, give rise to greater proliferation of both epithelial and connective tissue cells, the catarrhal and fibroid changes go on more rapidly, and the changes in the vessels are more prominent, and lead to greater destructive processes. In consequence of the fibroid changes, bronchiectatic cavities are also met with here, though not in coalminers' lung. The clinical history is that of ordinary phthisis, but the pathological process is quite distinctive. It is met with especially amongst stone-masons and quarrymen who work in dry silicious stone, from which the dust particles are very fine and are therefore readily inhaled.

Naked eye appearances.—As soon as the hand is introduced into the pleural cavity, evidences of the disease present themselves. Over the surface are patches of adhesion in different stages of organisation, but most of them are exceedingly tough and fibroid, and it is often necessary to strip away the costal pleura in order to remove the lung. The pleura is much thickened.

The organ feels firm throughout, and the surface is studded with small, hard, fibrous nodules, about the size of a split pea (larger than those seen in anthracosis), which have a very characteristic appearance.

The centre of the nodule is frequently yellowish in colour, and is surrounded by a grey, or bluish or pinkish grey, fibroid ring; outside this again is a pigmented zone, in some cases very distinctly marked.

On section, numbers of these nodules are seen scattered regularly throughout the tissue. Between them there is great increase of interstitial tissue, which becomes so marked in certain cases that the lung feels almost like a cirrhosed liver. On cutting into one of the nodules, which to the touch feel like small beads, it is found to consist of hard fibrous tissue at the periphery, with a gritty centre, the pigmented zone around this varying in size and colour with the age and work of the patient.

Bounded by fibrous bands are numerous large cavities (bronchiectatic cavities); these are pyriform in shape; the apex usually communicates with a bronchus (of which it appears to be a dilatation), and the base is towards the pleural surface; the walls are hard and thickened, and are lined by a pink, glistening, or translucent membrane, which is continued from the bronchial wall. Radiating from the thickened wall are numerous fibrous bands, some continuous with the deep layer of the pleura, others with the peribronchial and perivascular tissue more deeply situated. These fibrous bands are the thickened and fibrous interlobular septa. In them the fibrous nodules, although met with around the bronchi and vessels, are much more numerous and are more prominent. The septa, then, in this case, may be looked upon as the true position of the various changes. (For the nature and mode of formation of bronchiectatic cavities, see § 268.)

Harden a piece of the lung with pleura and a cavity (§ 59), a second (§ 57 or 64), stain (§§ 98 and 103 *d*), and mount one section unstained (§ 151).

(× 50).—It will be at once observed that there is an enormous increase in the amount of fibrous tissue, more especially along the lines of the interlobular septa, in which also the rounded nodular masses are seen. These latter consist usually of a number of fibrous layers concentrically arranged, the nuclei of which take on the picro-

carmine stain very deeply. In the centre of the mass there is
frequently a "core" of yellow, somewhat homogeneous, or granular
material; the result of degeneration and breaking down of the cells,
which at this point derive little nutriment from the surrounding
tissue. Around the yellow centre is a zone of imperfectly

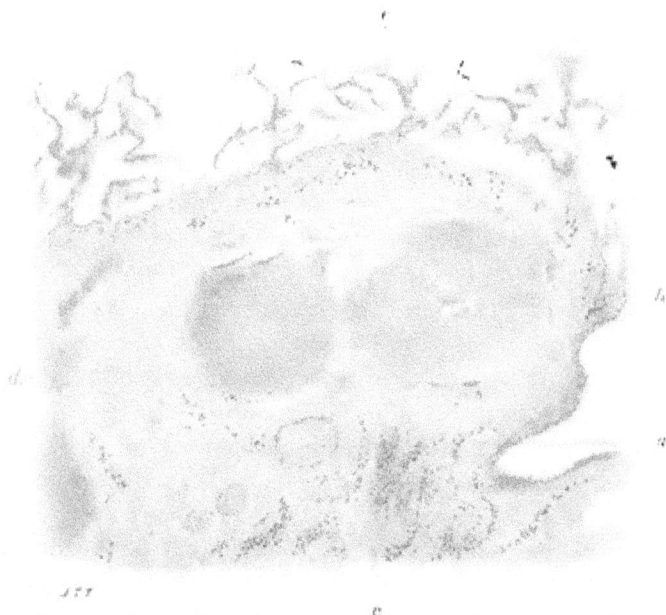

FIG. 99.—Section through small fibrous nodule in stone-masons'
lung. Stained with picro-carmine. (× 50.)
  a. Small artery completely occluded. Endarteritis obliterans.
  b. Caseous centre.
  c. Pigment deposited in lymphatics, &c., of young fibrous tissue,
      marking out position of stone particles.
  d. Young fibro-cellular tissue, near the margin of the nodule.
  e. Comparatively healthy lung tissue.

vascularised fibrous tissue, whilst still further out is a zone of
exceedingly vascular and cellular connective tissue. At some points
this appears to be little more than a mass of young rounded deeply-
stained connective tissue cells, in which the greatly distended larger
vessels and capillaries stand out very prominently. The adventitia
of the walls of the larger vessels is thickened and cellular,
whilst in the intima there is great proliferation of the cells,

some of them of considerable size, and many containing granules of carbon pigment. In the walls of the alveoli, the vessels are engorged, and there is some interstitial new formation along the lines of the capillaries. In the air vesicles there is marked evidence of catarrh, and the large epithelial cells contain small granules of black pigment. The air vesicles appear to be smaller, and the epithelium in them in some cases is becoming more or less cubical (Fig. 99)—*i.e.*, it is reverting to the embryonic type. In the peribronchial and perivascular tissue there are similar but less marked changes, pigmentation usually being the most prominent feature. The changes in the bronchi themselves are very similar to those found in coal-miners' lung, but are frequently more acute. (§ 255).

(× 300).—The fibrous tissue in the septa is almost fully developed, though at certain points, especially near the nodular masses, there appears to be very rapid proliferation of the connective tissue cells. The pink fibrous bands, with the elongated nuclei deeply stained, are readily distinguished in the carmine-stained specimen.

In the larger vessels the adventitia, in common with the surrounding connective tissue, is undergoing active proliferative changes. The cells are more numerous, and this part of the coat is thickened. In some of the elongated spaces in the thickened adventitia small granules of black pigment and particles of stone may be observed; these silicious particles are usually grey in colour, especially at the margin, but the centre appears to be clear and highly refractile. Pigment is found both in the spaces and in large cells. In the intima we have the processes seen in connection with obliterative endarteritis (§ 214). In such vessels as have not yet become obliterated the lumen is filled with blood corpuscles. In the rounded fibroid nodules the centre is usually yellow and extremely granular, and is undergoing degenerative changes, as it no longer receives a supply of blood from the obliterated vessels, and there is a condition almost identical with that of the caseating gumma (§ 126). Around the yellow mass is well-formed fibrous or cicatricial tissue, to the contraction of which the puckering around the centre of the nodule is due. In the cicatricial tissue few, if any, vessels are visible. In some of the elongated ovoid spaces in the fibrous tissue the black pigment granules and refractile stony particles are seen. These particles are usually unaffected by hydrochloric acid.

In the zone outside the cicatricial tissue, there is nothing but a mass of connective tissue cells in all stages of development. Some of them are merely rounded nuclei with scarcely a trace of surrounding protoplasm. Others are elongated, and have a delicate periplast, whilst others again are fully formed connective tissue cells, with a distinct, often fibrillated, periplast. In some of the cells pigment granules and silicious particles may be distinguished. Here the vessels are extremely numerous, and are very similar in appearance to those already described in the septa. It is by this zone that the tissue of the nodule is continuous with the tissue of the interlobular and interalveolar septa. The interalveolar septa are somewhat thickened (1.) by the distended vessels; (2.) by the increase of the interstitial tissue, in the form of small round cells (proliferated connective tissue cells); and (3.) by the distended lymph spaces, in which may be found cells containing pigment and stone particles. The epithelium in the air vesicles is undergoing rapid proliferation. Some of the detached cells contain the foreign particles, as do also some of those still *in situ ;* others again are undoubtedly free from any of these particles. Some of the epithelial cells are more cubical than in the normal condition, and the air vesicle thus appears to lose part of its lumen. The changes in the interlobular septa are continued on to the peribronchial and perivascular tissue. Bronchitic changes similar to those met with in coal-miners' lung, but usually more acute, are present (§ **255**).

The pigment granules are simply those which are met with in every lung, but by their presence they aid us very greatly in localising the silicious particles.

In *siderosis,* or needle-grinders' lung, changes very similar to those above-mentioned, but of a still graver type, are induced.

Chronic Interstitial Pneumonia.

267. The forms of disease above described are all forms of interstitial pneumonia, but, as already noticed, interstitial inflammation is very frequently a result of acute or lobar, and of catarrhal or lobular pneumonia. It may also occur in the lungs of children affected with congenital syphilis, whilst the most common form, which is probably also due to syphilis, or to tubercle, is met with in persons in more advanced life.

In the more common form, cirrhosis of the lung (synonyms, "Fibroid" phthisis or Corrigan's lung), one lung only may be affected, or the disease may be more advanced in one lung than in the other.

Naked eye appearances.—On opening the thoracic cavity the affected lung is found to be considerably smaller than the healthy one. It feels firm and fibrous; the visceral pleura is enormously thickened and firmly adherent to the costal layer, though here and there between the two are soft fibrinous masses. On removal it feels almost like a piece of indiarubber, but at some parts, especially towards the base, there may be patches of compensatory emphysema (§ 258). On section, it "cuts" with a firm fibrous feel, the pleura is found to be enormously thickened, especially in the deeper layer, which is pigmented, and in which may usually be seen small tubercular nodules. In some cases, however, these nodules are absent, especially where the condition is supposed to be of syphilitic origin. Similar nodules may also be found along the lines of the septa and around the bronchi. From the deep layer of the pleura firm fibrous bands pass into the substance of the lung, and run to join the thickened walls of the bronchi and blood-vessels. There is often considerable pigmentation of these bands, and also of the peribronchial and perivascular tissue. The vessels and bronchi appear to be crowded together and are dilated. The lining membrane of the dilated bronchus is smooth, pink, and translucent, and is continuous with the mucous membrane of the healthy bronchus.

These dilated bronchi or bronchiectatic cavities are even more common here than in silicosis. They are usually irregular in shape or somewhat oval, and around the large central cavity we have usually a number of smaller sacs, all communicating with it; these sacs, as a rule, contain a "quantity of pultaceous material, consisting of inspissated catarrhal secretion" (Hamilton).

The bronchial glands are enlarged and often caseated; other caseous or gummatous looking masses, about the size of a marble, are often found in the fibrous bands. These are especially common in the syphilitic form, but they may also occur in the tubercular condition.

In some cases the interstitial changes appear to be superseded by an acute pneumonic process, which, to a certain extent, masks to the naked eye the fibroid change, but in which the interstitial changes are very evident. Prepare as above (§ 263).

To avoid useless repetition, it may be stated at once that here the microscopic changes are very similar to those met with in silicosis. The thickening of the pleura, the changes in the interlobular septa, and in the peribronchial and perivascular connective tissue; the proliferation of connective tissue along the lines of the lymphatics, along which the irritant material—whether it be stone particles or specific virus—travels; the changes in the vessels—endarteritis obliterans giving rise to the gummatous-like masses in the fibrous tissue, just as in syphilitic disease of the liver (§§ 185 and 186)—and proliferation of the adventitia, are all very similar. The air vesicles are considerably diminished in size, their walls are thickened, and the epithelium is markedly cubical, more so here indeed than in silicosis. The fibrous tissue is extremely vascular towards the margins of the septa, and at the periphery of the peribronchial and perivascular tissue, where also it is extremely cellular.

(× 50).—The superficial layer of the pleura is little affected, but the deeper layer is thickened and pigmented. The vessels in it are numerous, are distended with blood, and are surrounded by a number of small pink granules (nuclei of young connective tissue cells and leucocytes). The interlobular septa are very vascular, and contain a large number of cells and much fibrous (pink) connective tissue. At the margins of the septa the capillary vessels are numerous, and appear to be those of the thickened interalveolar septa, which are becoming gradually involved in the advancing fibrous mass (§ 266); in this region, too, are evidences both of acute and of catarrhal pneumonic processes. In the wall of a bronchiectatic cavity, there may be recognised some of the elements of the bronchial wall, which have, however, undergone considerable change. There is a formation of new cell elements, by which the proper connective tissue may be gradually displaced, with the result that there is weakening of the wall.   The cartilage cells are undergoing either fatty or proliferative changes, the matrix gradually disappears, and there is left simply a mass of small round cells.   This is a process similar to that which goes on in the absorption of the connective tissue matrix.   These cartilage cells appear to be granular under the low power, but under the high power their true fatty nature may be

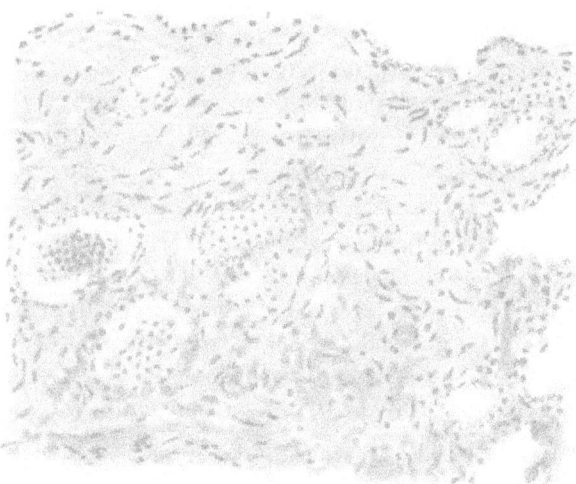

Fig. 100.—Drawing of section of lung; interstitial pneumonia. Stained with logwood. (× 200).
  a. Mass of dense fibro-cellular tissue formed in the position of the interalveolar septa.
  b. In this fibrous tissue are small air vesicles, lined with cubical epithelial cells, and containing numerous catarrhal cells.
  c. Similar cubical epithelium, near the margin of the mass, where too, the air vesicles are larger.
  d. Well-formed blood-vessels, near the margin of the mass.
  e. Nearer the centre the vessels are not well defined.

distinguished, especially when the section is stained with osmic acid (§ 110).   On the lining membrane of the cavity a few columnar cells, with their deeply-stained nuclei, can still be distinguished.   Running into the weakened cellular wall of the bronchus are the interlobular septa, several of which converge around each bronchial tube.

(× 300).—Note the contracted air vesicles, with their thickened and fibrous looking walls, and their lining of cubical epithelium (the air vesicles outside the fibrous mass are frequently somewhat dilated), the surrounding blood-vessels, the changes in the septa and pleura,

and lastly, the changes in the wall of the bronchus.   Any ordinary
case of cirrhotic lung, from syphilis, or any other cause, presents
most of these features in such a marked degree that there can be
very little doubt as to the nature of the disease, if the examination
be carefully made.

BRONCHIECTATIC CAVITIES.

268. Bronchiectatic cavities have already been mentioned as
occurring in silicosis, and in the various forms of chronic interstitial
pneumonia.   They are also found in almost all forms of chronic
phthisis, where interstitial inflammatory changes are set up.

Naked eye appearances.—These cavities are usually of moderate
size, and are frequently sacculated or globular in form, especially
when they are due to the weakening of the bronchial wall by inflam-

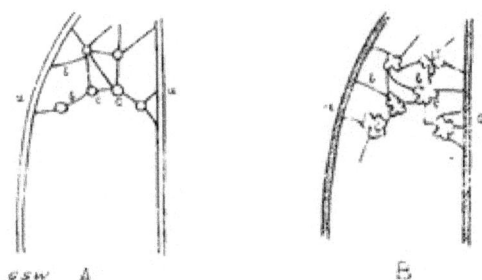

FIG. 101.—Diagram to represent the method of formation of
bronchiectatic cavities by the traction of the cicatricial tissue in
the interlobular septa on the weakened bronchial walls.

matory changes, such as have been described in the two previous
sections.

Angular cavities are caused by traction exerted on the walls of the
bronchi by the contracting fibrous bands—the cirrhotic interlobular
septa—a process which may be best explained by means of a
diagram.

The lines *a.a.* represent the walls of the chest to which the pleura
is adherent, naturally because the cavities are air-tight, but also
through inflammatory thickenings and adhesions.   The lines *b.b.*
are supposed to represent the interlobular septa, running first from

2 A

the one wall of the chest to the wall of a bronchus, *c.*; then on to another bronchus, and lastly, to the opposite chest wall. As these fibrous bands contract, there is traction on the walls of the bronchi, and also on the walls of the chest; and as the latter are much more rigid than the former, the former have to give way at a point where the septa run into their walls. At the same time the chest wall becomes slightly flattened, especially at the upper part, but this is not nearly so noticeable as is the change in shape, and increase in size, of the bronchial tube. In the cavity the lining membrane is smooth, glistening, and translucent, and has a pink tinge, owing to its extreme vascularity.

There is another form of bronchiectatic cavity, caused by the accumulation of catarrhal products in the bronchus. This leads first to distension, and then to the formation of a cavity of moderate size, as inflammatory processes are set up in the walls by the irritant accumulated material. Such cavities are usually met with in considerable numbers; they are more or less fusiform, or spindle-shaped, and may have the same pink, glistening, lining membrane as the above form, or they may be lined by a soft caseous material, especially in cases of tuberculosis.

Still another form is that met with in ulcerative bronchiectasis following catarrhal pneumonia. In this there is ulceration of the bronchus and a giving way and distension at the weakened point.

Whilst on the subject of cavities, or vomicae, the form in which there is extensive softening of the lung tissue, as a result of various inflammatory and caseous processes, may be mentioned. A large cavity is formed, and into this one or several bronchi open, by which are carried away from the cavity the softened contents. Such a cavity may usually be recognised by its greater size, the more or less irregular outline, the "several openings of the bronchi into it, and by the bands of more resistent fibrous tissue which run from side to side of the cavity" (Hamilton). These are not blood-vessels, as generally supposed, but are bands of fibrous tissue or thickened interlobular septa,—very frequently, however, containing branches of blood-vessels embedded in their substance. Small aneurisms have been described as occurring in connection with some of these vessels. It is now held by most authorities that these large irregular cavities are the result of the running together of several smaller cavities, many of which are formed during the course of rapid phthisis. When a cavity is once formed it rapidly dilates, as the surrounding fibrous tissue is comparatively non-resistent, so that even repeated coughing brings about a rapid distension. The pleura over a cavity is almost invariably much thickened.

BROWN INDURATION OF THE LUNG.

269. Synonyms, "Brown Œdema," "Chronic Venous Congestion" of the lung. This condition is most frequently associated with disease of the valves of the heart, especially of the mitral valve, though it often occurs in connection with aortic disease.

Naked eye appearances.—The lung is generally somewhat more voluminous than usual. The pleura has a peculiar reddish-purple colour, through which the deeply pigmented interlobular septa stand out very prominently. At the free borders of the lung there is frequently some emphysema; here also are hard, firm, deeper coloured, wedge-shaped patches of a deep plum colour, sometimes with a tinge of brown, which project above, and are sharply defined from the surrounding tissue. They are solid and sink in water, and constitute the so-called pulmonary apoplexies. On section, in place of the bright arterial red colour of acute congestion, there is a peculiar brownish or brick-red colour, and, on pressure, there exudes brownish-red serum, mixed with air; there is œdema, and at certain points, marked emphysema. Scattered over the section, especially at the posterior and lower part of the lung, and not sharply marked off from the surrounding tissue, are firm patches, varying in diameter from half-an-inch to an inch. They are not solid, but are much firmer, harsher, and drier feeling than the surrounding tissue; when cut into they have a peculiar gritty feel, and from them also reddish-brown serum, mixed with air, may be squeezed.

Examine this exudation (× 300).—It consists (1.) of granules of golden-brown pigment; (2.) of large flattened cells, in which are numerous similar granules; and (3.) of coloured blood corpuscles in various stages of disintegration. The interlobular septa, the deep layer of the pleura, and the bronchial glands, are deeply pigmented, and stand out very prominently, and the latter are also often enlarged and indurated. On the surface the dilated branches of the pulmonary vessels stand out more prominently, and therefore appear to be more numerous than in the normal condition. (*See* Nutmeg Liver, § 182.)

The mucous membrane of a bronchus is usually deeply congested, folded, and corrugated, and has a characteristic watery or œdematous appearance.

Harden two pieces, one of a brown patch, a second with a wedge-shaped pulmonary apoplexy or hæmorrhage, some of the pleura, and a small bronchus (§ 59), and mount unstained (§ 152).

(× 50).—The pleura is greatly thickened, especially the deeper layer, which is also deeply pigmented. The pigment is black and golden-brown. The interlobular septa, the perivascular and peribronchial tissues, are also thickened and pigmented. In the solid wedge-shaped mass the air vesicles also have their walls thickened and pigmented, but this is partially masked by the enormous number of red blood corpuscles which have escaped. On the pleural surface there may be slight inflammatory changes, but these are by no means constant.

In the portions in which brown induration is well marked, the changes are very characteristic. The walls of the air vesicles are thickened and pigmented, and have a peculiar beaded or varicose appearance; in the beads (or loops) there is a greenish granular material—coloured blood corpuscles. Within the air vesicles similar small green granules may be observed, and also a number of large flattened cells, many of which contain pigment. Most of these cells are lying free in the alveolar cavity, but others are attached to the beaded-looking wall; the interlobular septa are thickened.

In the walls of the bronchus the small blood-vessels are enormously distended. There is, throughout, an increase of fibrous tissue, which in a picro-carmine stained specimen is very prominent. The mucous membrane is thrown into folds, and the tortuous blood-vessels, which come very near the surface, may even, in a small bronchus, rupture into the lumen. As a rule, there is but little of the bronchial epithelium left, as it is detached by the serum exuded from the distended blood-vessels almost as rapidly as it is formed.

(× 300).—First examine the air vesicles, in which are numerous flattened cells lying free, or closely applied to the wall; the former, comparatively few in number, may be seen in section as nucleated spindle-shaped cells. Most of them contain granules of beautiful golden-brown pigment, which stand out very prominently. Along

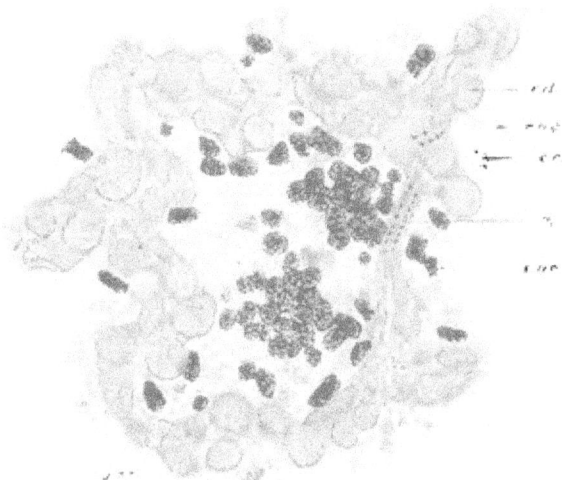

FIG. 102.—Drawing from section of brown induration of the lung. Unstained. (× 300.)

c.d.   Distended capillaries of interalveolar septa.
c.b.c. Coloured blood corpuscles lying free in the air vesicle.
e.c.   Epithelial cell, detached.
e.p.c. Epithelial or catarrhal cell, containing large quantity of altered blood pigment.
p.   Pigment in lymphatics of interalveolar septum.

At the point from which this was taken the pigmentation was very well marked; the varicosity of the vessels is here well seen.

with the large detached cells are a few coloured blood corpuscles. Lying beneath the attached epithelial cells are the capillary vessels of the wall; they are much distended and varicose, and appear as loops or sections of vessels projecting into the air cavity. They were long mistaken for epithelial cells, but by the aid of picro-carmine staining, the coloured blood corpuscles may be demonstrated lying in the lumen of the pink-walled vessel. These vessels have a double outline, and in some cases there appears to be enormous thickening of their walls, as described in Nutmeg Liver (§ 182). In the wall of the vesicle—that is, along the course of the lymphatics—pigment, much deeper in colour than that in the cells, but still golden-brown, is deposited. A small proportion of it is black, and is simply carbon pigment derived from without, but most of it is pigment derived from altered red blood corpuscles; it is seen to be lying in the lymph spaces, free or enclosed, either in epithelial cells from the air vesicles, or in endothelial or connective tissue cells.

Similar pigments are met with in the interlobular septa and in the deep layer of the pleura, to both of which they have been carried from the air vesicles by the lymphatics. The peribronchial and perivascular lymphatics are also filled with pigment. In all these situations there is, as seen above, an increase of fibro-cellular tissue, an increase which is brought out very decidedly in the picro-carmine stained specimen; after the pigmentation, the enormous distension of the vessels is the most marked change, and it is to this dilatation especially that the thickening of the pleura and the increase in volume of the lung are due.

In the walls of the smaller bronchi note the great congestion of the mucous membrane. The vessels here, as in the walls of the alveoli, are distended, lengthened, and varicose, and their walls are thickened. At certain points they are so much dilated that they form a cavernous structure, almost like that seen in the centre of a lobule in advanced nutmeg liver. The muscular coat is usually somewhat atrophied, owing, apparently, to distension and consequent pressure. The basement membrane is swollen and œdematous, and the few cells covering it are flattened or cubical, or irregularly columnar. The most marked vascular changes take place around the bronchi and beneath the pleura, towards the base of the lung, but that they are by no means confined to these situations. In the naked eye examination it was observed that there was dilatation and prominence of the vessels of the lung. This is evidently due partly to distension, but also partly to the same cause as in the granular contracted kidney, *i.e.*, hyaline or fibroid thickening of the tunica intima, which in this condition is tolerably well marked.

The solid wedge-shaped plum-coloured or brick-red patches—pulmonary apoplexies, as they are called,—frequently coincide with the distribution of the bronchus; the bronchus, as well as the terminal air cavities, in such cases being filled with blood. Otherwise they have all the appearances presented in the remainder of the lung. It must be remembered that hæmorrhages are usually met with only where the brown induration is due to valvular disease of the heart, especially of the mitral valve. Brown induration of the lung is simply a secondary condition induced by a primary disease of the heart. It first appears as a chronic venous congestion, in which there is an exudation of serum from the capillaries; this causes separation of a considerable part of the epithelium in both air vesicles and bronchi. At the same time blood corpuscles escape into the alveoli, and are taken up by the altered epithelium; these are taken into the lymphatic system of the interalveolar septa, from which the pigment is distributed to all the positions above mentioned, including the bronchial glands. The vessels become more distended, more tortuous and thickened, and so the condition of brown induration is gradually developed. A small portion of the pigment is carbon pigment; but by treating a section with a solution of ferrocyanide of potassium, and then with a dilute solution of hydrochloric acid, a blue reaction is obtained, even with some of the perfectly black pigment, which indicates that it contains iron and is probably derived from the blood.

Between this brown induration and rapid venous congestion are many intermediate stages. The rapid venous congestion is characterised by the water-logged condition of the lung, the lymphatics being unable to carry off the fluid as it is exuded. On section there is usually marked congestion, whilst from the cut surface there exudes an enormous quantity of frothy, watery fluid. The air vesicles are filled with fluid very rapidly. On examination under the microscope the epithelium is found to be detached, and usually lying free in the alveolar cavity, the vessels being distended with blood.

Fat Embolism of the Lung.

270. There are few naked eye changes in the lung in this condition beyond some œdema and congestion, which are specially marked

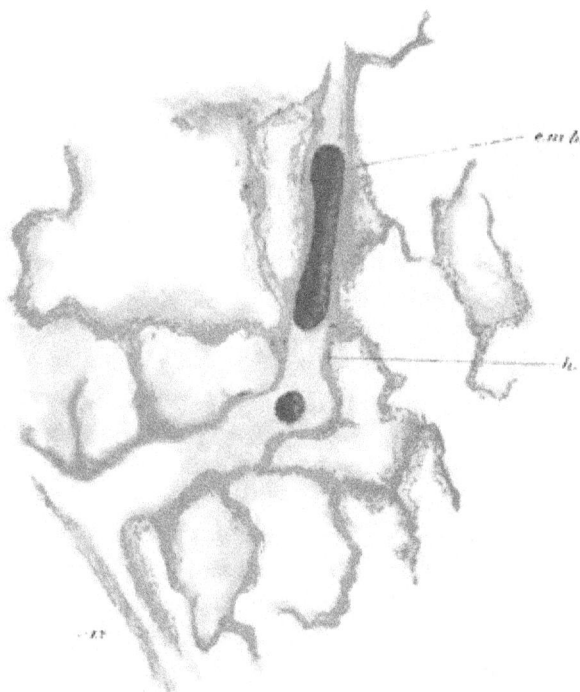

FIG. 103—Fat embolism of the lung. Stained with osmic acid. (× 100.)

emb. Fat embolus stained black, filling one of the larger vessels.
h. Mass of coloured blood corpuscles in an air vesicle, the result of rupture of some of the smaller blood-vessels behind the embolus.

where the embolism follows diabetic coma or fracture of a bone, especially of one of the cranial bones.

Naked eye appearances.—The following case was diagnosed during life as a case of fat embolism, due to fracture of one of the cranial bones. There was deep congestion of both lungs, accompanied by a number of bright subpleural hæmorrhages which, though small, were very distinctly seen. On examination of a fresh section (§ 34, × 50) bright refractile globules were observed in a number of the capillary vessels, and also in some of the larger branches of the pulmonary artery. These were stained black with osmic acid. In the stained specimen some of the emboli in the larger vessels were distinctly seen as elongated masses, completely filling the vessel, and ending at its point of bifurcation. Sometimes, at the proximal end of the fat embolus, the vessel had ruptured, and there was an extravasation of blood into the surrounding air vesicles; most of the emboli and hæmorrhages were situated near the surface, as the terminal branches of the blood-vessels are usually distributed there.

Harden (§ 57) and stain (§ 110).

(× 50 and × 300).—Confirm the above points, and observe the different sizes and positions of the fatty globules stained black by osmic acid. Some are extremely small, and are in the centre of the blood mass. Others, larger and crescentic, are adherent to the wall of the vessel ; whilst others again completely fill the lumina of vessels of very various diameters.

Similar small hæmorrhages are met with in cases of phosphorus poisoning, in septic fevers, anthrax, &c., and frequently even in cases of active hyperæmia.

TUBERCULOSIS.

271. Within recent years there has been a complete change of opinion as to the meaning that is to be attached to the terms tuberculosis and phthisis. These conditions are now known to be intimately connected with one another, and the differences in the course and appearance of the different forms of these diseases have been more or less completely reconciled. Tuberculosis may be defined as an infective disease brought about by the activity of a specific bacillus, which is enabled to live within the body, where, by its presence, it sets up irritative and proliferative changes in either epithelial or endothelial cellular tissues, such changes being followed by fibroid or caseous changes, according (*a*) to the number and activity of the bacilli ; and (*b*) to the state of nutrition and powers of resistance of the tissues attacked.

Phthisis.

272. In consequence of these irritative inflammatory and degenerative changes there are set up the conditions of pulmonary phthisis. Phthisis may be defined as a disease of the lung, characterised first by consolidation, the result of the formation of tubercle of different kinds, accompanied by the various forms of pneumonia—interstitial, croupous and catarrhal—with obliteration of the blood-vessels and disturbance of the lymphatic circulation, leading to fibrous tissue formation, or to caseation and ulceration, as the case may be. Changes in the walls of the bronchi lead to weakening, or even to ulceration; those in the septa may lead to fibrous tissue formation, whilst similar changes or caseation may result throughout the whole of the lung substance. Caseation and cavity formation are most frequent in the upper part of the lung, where, too, the process is, as a rule, more chronic, but more advanced.

Tubercle Bacilli.

273. The association of the tubercle bacillus with tubercular disease cannot now be doubted; it is found in the lungs and sputum in various forms of tuberculosis and phthisis; it has also been demonstrated in tuberculosis of the intestine; around the vessels in tubercular inflammation of the membranes of the brain; in tubercle of the liver, and of other organs of the body; and in tubercular eruptions of the skin. It may be well at this point to examine the tubercle bacillus, in order that it may be recognised in the various specimens of tuberculosis and phthisis that have to be examined.

Prepare a specimen of sputum (§§ 128 and **130**) and stain (§ **140**). When thus prepared tubercle bacilli may be seen (× 450) as delicate rods or threads, 1.3 to 3.5 μ in length, and about 2 μ in thickness, though they may appear to be somewhat thicker. Speaking roughly, the length is equal to from one quarter to one half the diameter of a red blood corpuscle. The bacilli are usually slightly curved, or two are arranged end to end, so as to contain an angle. At first sight they do not appear to contain any spores; but, on more careful examination, and with specially high powers, from two to six pseudo-spores or small ovoid or rounded clear spaces may be seen at intervals in the stained thread; and in some cases these are so prominent that they appear to project beyond the straight outline of the bacillus, an appearance that has led to the thread being sometimes described as a chain of cocci or coccothrix. The bacilli are quite motionless. Sometimes they may be imperfectly stained or the protoplasm may appear granular, and almost as a little rod of *débris;* usually they are lying free near the epithelial and pus cells, but in some cases they are actually embedded in the protoplasmic substance of these cells. They appear to exert an influence on the tissues even

FIG. 104.—Tubercle bacilli in sputa. Stained with gentian violet. Contrast stain Bismarck brown, Weigert's method. (× 450.)

at a distance, and where they are present in considerable numbers there will usually be found in the immediate neighbourhood a small portion of tissue that has undergone marked degenerative changes, evidenced by the fact that the cells are now imperfectly stained with carmine or the aniline dyes. After a time they lose their outlines; they become more and more indistinct, and eventually nothing but a shadow of the cell is left, this occurring where the caseous degeneration is advanced. Even outside the zone in which the bacilli are numerous the cells become hyaline and take on stains imperfectly, although the bacilli have not yet advanced into this area; on the other hand, in the zone in which they are found, some semblance of form is still seen in the

tissue cells, and many are comparatively normal ; whilst, in the zone
that they have left, caseation is now well marked, and there is little
evidence of the nature of the tissue from which the caseous material
is derived. These facts should be borne in mind in making any
examination of tuberculous tissue.

DISSEMINATED MILIARY TUBERCULOSIS.

274. *Disseminated Miliary Tuberculosis* is met with in acute general
tuberculosis, especially in children and in young adults.

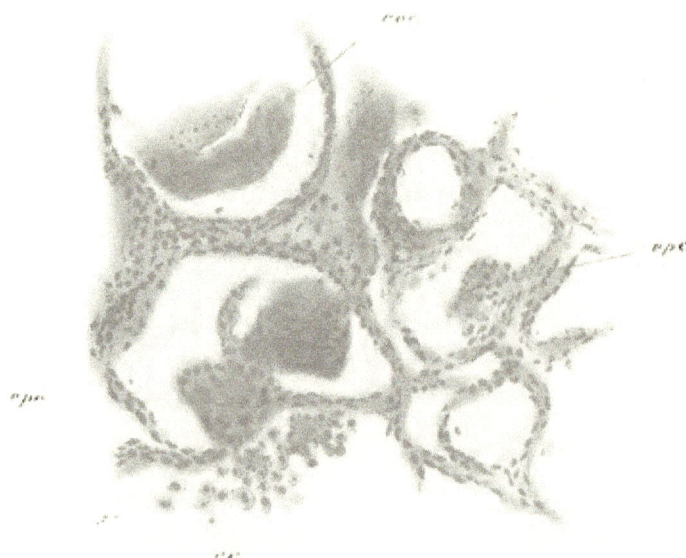

FIG. 105.—Section of lung. Acute miliary tuberculosis. Stained
with picro-carmine. (× 300).
    e.c. Growth of large endothelioid cells.
    ep.c. Growth of epithelial cells into alveolus. These cells are
        arranged somewhat in columns, and are undergoing rapid
        caseation. Mass is yellow and homogeneous at surface.
Between the air vesicles the septa are somewhat thickened, and
some of the air vesicles are apparently diminished in size by the
encroaching epithelium.

Naked eye appearances.—The lung is usually deeply congested ;
scattered over the congested surface are numerous pale, pearly,

translucent or gelatinous-looking nodules about the size of small shot, which stand out very distinctly from the surrounding tissue; there is usually little or no pleurisy. At first sight the nodules appear to be scattered indiscriminately over the surface of the lung; but on more careful examination, it will be found that they are situated in the lines of the interlobular septa, especially at their points of junction. A fresh section, like the surface, is deeply congested and of a bright scarlet colour; the nodules are usually more numerous in one lung than in the other, and affect one lobe more than the other. They are found in the deeper layer of the pleura at the points where the septa run into it, and also along the lines of the larger septa, though some are in the lobule itself. A few of these may be grouped together, but this is comparatively rare. Harden (§ **56** or **59**), and stain (§§ **98** and **137** *et seq.*).

(× 50).—Note that the tubercle masses are growing in the interlobular septa, or in some cases from an interalveolar septum, and that each is composed of one or more follicles. In all essential points they resemble the tubercular masses in the liver (§ **189**); but giant cells, containing a large number of nuclei, are comparatively rarely seen, and usually in place of them there is a granular yellow caseous mass. Around it is an open reticular tissue, the meshes of which are somewhat elongated, and are concentrically arranged. In the elongated spaces there are but few small round cells, but there are numerous endothelioid cells, somewhat irregular in shape, many of them containing two or more nuclei. At the periphery of the tubercle nodule, numerous small round cells are found, which appear to be arranged in rows, these rows enclosing spaces. The spaces appear to be contracted alveoli, of which the rows of round cells form the thickened walls. Projecting into the air vesicle from the thickened wall are similar masses of endothelioid cells, pushing before them the epithelial layer. In the immediate neighbourhood of the solid area the thickening of the alveolar walls is proceeding, the cavities are smaller and appear collapsed.

Examine an artery and a bronchus, and notice that in some cases slight round cell infiltration is the only evidence of tubercular affection.

(× 300).—The caseous centre is easily made out. Around it are numerous endothelioid cells; these are very irregular in shape and size, some containing but one nucleus, whilst others have as many as four. The reticulum is not very readily distinguished under this power, but the round cells, along with the larger cells, are well seen. Towards the periphery of the mass the appearances are very distinctive. Collapsed air vesicles are bounded by the greatly thickened alveolar walls, in which there is evidently active proliferation of the connective tissue cells. The masses of large endothelioid cells are, however, distinctly pushing their way into the cavity, forcing before them the epithelial lining. The cells of which this lining is composed are in a condition very similar to that met with in interstitial pneumonia, but they are hyaline or granular and swollen. They are cubical, and in some cases are of very great size (§ 267). In the immediate neighbourhood of the tubercle nodule the interalveolar septa are considerably thickened, and epithelial changes are beginning; the air vesicles appear to be collapsed, but there is no marked catarrhal or croupous inflammatory exudation. The caseation in the centre of the tubercle mass is similar to that met with in caseation of gummata. The tubercular masses are purely extravascular, as may be proved by injecting such a lung; and as fresh tubercle follicles are formed around the primary one, that in the centre is cut off from its nutritive supply, and undergoes caseous degeneration. In most cases this caseation comes on before the formation of a giant cell has taken place, or immediately after the abnormal growth of the large endothelioid cells; this is especially the case where the disease is very acute, when there may be a condition almost like that to be described as broncho-pneumonic phthisis. In the specially stained specimen now look for the tubercle bacilli, which may be seen as violet-stained rods lying in the lymph spaces. Some of them may be in the giant cell, but they are best seen as they lie in the meshes of the network surrounding the giant cell. (For appearance of these bacilli, see Figs. 104 and 106.)

The larger masses of tubercle will be best described under chronic phthisis (§ 277), in the production of which they play a very prominent part.

Caseous Broncho-Pneumonic Tubercle.

275. Up to the present, discussion has waged fast and furious in regard to this condition, and even now there are various opinions as to the nature of the process. It will be difficult to omit from the description all theoretical or controversial statements, and to confine what is said to a simple description of the appearances which may be met with; but as far as possible this will be done.

Caseous broncho-pneumonic tubercle is met with in children as what appears to be a form of acute tuberculosis, specially confined to the lung, or, at any rate, more advanced in this position than in any other organ in the body.

Naked eye appearances.—The lung is congested and sometimes slightly œdematous, with here and there patches of collapse; whilst standing out prominently from the congested surface, either through the pleura or from the cut section, are a number of small nodules, one-twelfth to one-sixth of an inch in diameter. They are most numerous at the apices and towards the roots of the lung, and may be rounded or irregular in outline, some of them appearing to be branched and elongated. Each has a typical appearance; at the periphery the tissue is firm, greyish, and gelatinous, whilst the centre is softer, pale yellow, and granular.

On squeezing the section a quantity of tenacious, muco-purulent material is pressed from the various sized bronchi, especially from the smaller ones (§ 255 and 256).

Harden (§§ 56 and 59), and stain (§ 137 *et seq.*).

(× 50 or × 20).—All the patches of the solidified tissue have a similar arrangement, the details differing only according to the direction in which the section is made through a bronchus, with its dependent air vesicles. In a transverse section of a terminal bronchiole, the following features may be observed:—Towards the centre, or a little to one side of the solid area, is a rounded opening, or what was an opening, containing a plug of small rounded catarrhal or purulent-looking cells, which look like granules. In the centre is a quantity of more or less homogeneous material, which stains yellow with picro-carmine; in this yellow material the outlines of the individual air vesicles can only in a few cases be discerned.

Around the caseous centre there is a zone of air vesicles in which there is no caseation, but in which there are evidences of catarrhal (§ 261) or acute (§ 251 and 252) pneumonic deposits; the interalveolar septa are thickened, and stand out somewhat prominently. Around the bronchi there is also an amount of thickening of the adventitia, due apparently to peribronchitis, similar to that met with in catarrhal pneumonia (§ 261). Fully developed giant cell tubercle is comparatively rare, caseation taking place before the organisation of the follicle has reached that stage. The changes can best be observed where the process is beginning, or just at the margins of the caseating area.

(× 300).—Examine a small bronchus or an alveolar passage, and note that it is filled with cells which very closely resemble the catarrhal cells—seen under the low power as granules. Amongst these in the specimen stained with gentian violet and Bismarck brown are numerous rod-shaped tubercle bacilli. In the centre of the acinus, where the caseation is most advanced, a mass of granular *débris*, stained yellow, may be observed. Near the margin, tubercle bacilli are found in the interalveolar septa, and in some cases are exceedingly numerous. At the margin of the caseating mass the epithelial cells are undergoing other changes than simple catarrh; they appear to be arranged in columnar processes—(this is especially well seen in a fresh section stained in picro-carmine)—extending into the alveolus for some little distance. The cells of which these columns are composed have a peculiar hyaline appearance; they are stained yellow with the picric acid of picro-carmine, and they very rapidly become caseous. In those cells which are the result of a true catarrhal process, there is frequently an œdematous condition or a simple fatty degeneration—changes quite distinct from the caseous condition.

Examine the fibrous septa near the caseous centre, and note that in them and in the interalveolar septa there is a great amount of small cell infiltration; nutrition is cut off by the occlusion of the vessels, and this assists the caseous metamorphosis. In very thin sections tubercle bacilli may be distinguished, not only in the lymph spaces in the thickened interalveolar septa, but also in the epithelial cells which line the air vesicles at the point where the proliferation is taking place.

It should be noted that the air cavities in connection with the terminal bronchioles are the areas in which these changes are observed ; and if a vertical section be made through the bronchiole with its terminal cavities, the caseous mass is always situated near the bronchiole, and the pneumonic zone nearer the periphery.

ACUTE PHTHISIS.

276. Acute, rapid phthisis is a condition in which there appears to be a process almost like broncho-pneumonic tubercle, but associated with more extensive changes.

Naked eye appearances.—The pleura is, as a rule, somewhat thickened, especially over the apex. The whole of the lung is solid,

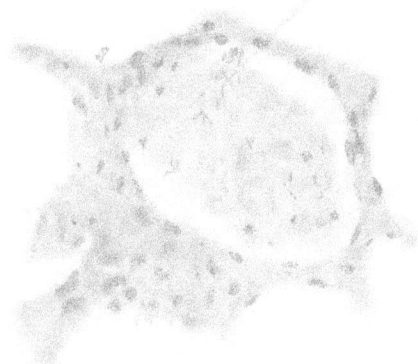

FIG. 106.—Section of acute miliary tuberculosis of the lung, stained by Gram's method with gentian violet and Bismarck brown to bring out the tubercle bacilli.

   a. Epithelial cell lying on the section of the wall of an air vesicle.
   b. Similar cells forming a membrane seen from above.
   c.   Do.   cells becoming degenerated, not deeply stained.
   d.   Do.   degeneration not far advanced.
   e.   Do.   nuclei and cells imperfectly stained.
   f. Tubercle bacilli.

and beneath the pleura large pale yellow patches are seen, radiating from which are numerous similar solid bands. On section, there is usually evidence of a more chronic process at the apex. There may be a cavity of considerable size, the walls of which are firm, indurated, and pigmented; over it the pleura is thickened. Around the cavity the changes are more acute, but the appearances are evidently considerably modified by the presence of the more chronic changes. In the lower part of the lung, however, the acute changes are more prominent and characteristic.

Scattered over its surface are large, rounded, pale yellow patches, from which processes run out in the same manner as under the pleura. Between the yellow patches, which in shape may be compared to bunches of grapes, of which the bronchioles form the "stalks"—are bright red lines, in which the caseous process has not as yet become marked. Towards the base the yellow patches are so large and so numerous that they run together, and obscure every other change.

On pressure there exudes a thick, tenacious, muco-purulent material from the bronchi, the walls of which are thickened and somewhat gelatinous looking; the bronchial glands may be swollen and œdematous, or softened and caseous.

The yellow patches, and even the appearances of a great part of the lung, may be similar to those met with in broncho-pneumonic tuberculosis, except that the destructive processes are more pronounced; or there may be patches of grey granulations, wedge-shaped near the surface, racemose, or in clumps in the substance of the lung, all of which are surrounded by pneumonic patches, are in various stages of caseation, and are more chronic than the form first described; the microscopic changes vary considerably, but will be readily traced out.

Harden pieces of the different parts of the lung (§§ 56 and 59), and stain (§§ 98 and 137 *et seq.*)

(× 50).—Examine one of the pale yellow patches, and note that it is made up of a series of areas, each of which has a caseous centre, in which are involved the walls of the alveoli as well as their contents. At this point there are no vessels. Further from the centre is a zone, in which the alveolar walls are somewhat thickened, and where the blood-vessels are not very readily seen. There is considerable catarrh in this position; parts of the products being stained black

if a section be treated with osmic acid. Still further from the centre
are early catarrhal or acute croupous pneumonic patches—readily
recognised—and in this region the capillary vessels are usually
considerably distended. These areas have frequently become fused
by the extension of the pneumonic process; in such cases great
destruction of tissue occurs. The pleura is thickened and extremely
vascular, with a considerable number of granulation loops passing
to the surface, and at points the two pleural surfaces have become
adherent. In tissue taken from near the apex there are usually
evidences of the presence of a chronic interstitial pneumonia, with
chronic tubercle, to be afterwards described; whilst around the parts
thus affected the tissues may be in an advanced state of caseation,
and smaller cavities are formed by the breaking down and evacuation of the caseous material. The vessels around these patches,
as in interstitial pneumonia (§ 267), are in an advanced stage of
endarteritis obliterans.

Around the bronchi are changes similar to those met with in
broncho-pneumonia; tubercle nodules in an early stage of development may sometimes be met with in this position.

(× 300).—Confirm the above appearances. The course of the
disease is apparently very rapid, but the rapidity varies in different
cases. If the patches are more or less separated, and the caseous
changes are taking place only at intervals, the course of the disease
is comparatively slow, and the appearances, both naked eye and
microscopic, closely resemble those found in broncho-pneumonic
tubercle; but when the masses run together rapidly, owing to the
rapidity of the catarrhal and croupous pneumonic changes, and there
is formation of cavities of considerable size, the course of the disease
is usually extremely acute. In whichever form the disease is met
with, tubercle bacilli are found in large numbers, especially at the
points where the proliferation of epithelial cells is greatest, and
also where the connective tissue cells are undergoing rapid proliferation. Where the caseation is advanced the bacilli are not so
readily distinguished. To find them, it is necessary to use a somewhat higher power (× 600) than that used in the examination of
sputum.

COMMON CHRONIC PHTHISIS.

277. This form of lung disease may run a very slow course, the symptoms during life being very well marked, and the pathological changes extremely characteristic.

Naked eye appearances.—On opening the chest it will be noted that the lungs are firmly adherent to the surrounding tissues, especially at their apices (if the disease occurs on both sides); frequently one lung only is affected. The adhesions may be so extensive that the pleural cavity is almost obliterated, or this may occur especially at its upper part. The pleuræ are much thickened, and are fibrous looking, and on the surface of the visceral layer, bluish-grey gelatinous nodules may be observed. On palpation the surface of the lung near the apex feels hard, firm, and fibrous, but somewhat irregular, whilst lower down are a number of hard wedge-shaped or nodular masses near the pleura or in the substance of the lungs.

On section, the thickening of the pleura near the apex is found to be very great, reaching as much as a quarter of an inch, or even more in some cases. Under the thickened pleura, and usually very near the apex, are cavities, one or more in number, each of which is bounded by firm fibrous walls, with a glistening lining, and usually containing a soft caseous-looking mass, which partially fills the cavity. These cavities vary greatly in size, "from that of a hazel nut up to that of a small orange." The fibrous wall of the cavity is deeply pigmented, and appears to be continuous with the thickened pleura. Throughout the whole lobe are bands of fibrous tissue, most numerous around the above-mentioned cavities, but also following the lines of the interlobular septa, the deep layer of the pleura, and the peribronchial and perivascular tissues. In the fibrous tissue are small yellow caseous-looking masses, similar to, and formed in the same manner as, those seen in silicosis, (§ 266). Now examine the wedge-shaped masses under the pleura. They are in the form of bunches of grapes, the base of the pyramidal mass being situated towards the pleura. From the apex of the mass, the stalk consisting of a line of small round nodules is seen to extend. In the substance of the lung, irregularly rounded masses of similar appearance are met with, packed closely together in the upper part of the lung, but with large highly vascular areas of lung tissue between them towards the base. These larger masses are composed of small rounded or ovoid shot-like bodies, hard and firm to the touch, and of a bluish-grey colour ; the centre usually being very fibrous and deeply pigmented, and the peripheral zone gelatinous and even pink. In some cases the centre, in place of being hard and fibroid, is somewhat softened, and may be yellow, but where this is the case the growth appears to have been somewhat more rapid than in the above typical form. Around the bronchi similar masses are seen. These are the so-called tubercle masses, but it must be borne in mind that each of these is not a simple body, but is made up of several tubercle follicles. Around the larger masses are a number of smaller points which are usually surrounded by a pneumonic zone. These changes are always most marked in the upper lobe of the lung, where the solidified areas may have become so fused that they present a solid area, in which, however, are caseous or calcareous nodules the result of degenerative changes ; the tissues, of which the solidified parts are composed, are very fibrous and deeply pigmented. In the lower lobe the several tubercle masses are more distinct, have not undergone fibroid or caseous changes, and have between them more or - less congested lung tissue.

In some few cases the lower lobe or base of the lung is solidified, yellow, and caseous, and exactly in the condition described as advanced acute phthisis (§ **276**). This appears to be quite a secondary condition, and usually occurs in one lung only.

Harden pieces of the lung from various positions (§§ **56** and **59**), and stain (§§ 98 and **137** *et seq.*).

(× 20 or × 50).—Each nodule contained in one of the grape-like masses is composed of a number of giant cell systems or tubercle follicles, each of which has the structure previously described (§ **189**), the oldest follicles being near the centre, the youngest at the periphery.

In the extremely chronic condition the giant cell systems are most perfectly developed at the periphery of the nodule, the central part being caseous ; more frequently, the centre has become quite fibroid, whilst the peripheral fibrous network has become compressed, then forming a mass of dense fibrous tissue. The younger tubercle

follicles around the primary degenerating follicle are readily distinguished by their more typical structure. Under this power observe
the positions in which the nodules occur in the deep layer of
the pleura, in the interlobular and interalveolar septa, and the
caseous and stained yellow; passing further outwards there may be
peribronchial and perivascular tissues, all of which are greatly
thickened. It is a significant fact, as often pointed out, that
the tubercle nodules follow very much the same course as the pigmented nodules and pigment injection in the dust diseases, *i.e.*, the

FIG. 107.—Section of chronic tubercle of the lung. Stained with
picro-carmine. (× 50.)
g.c. Giant cells in centre of tubercle follicles, yellow homogeneous
centre of cell, with deep crimson ring of nuclei.
The whole group of follicles forms a tubercle nodule, surrounded by comparatively healthy lung tissue.

course of the lymphatics. Note, too, that the tubercle follicles are
growing into the air vesicles from the interalveolar septa. These
tubercle follicles may be seen in various stages of development. One
may be represented by thickening of the septum only, in which a
number of small round cells and some large endothelioid plates are
seen occupying the space around the capillary vessel. At other
points the cellular mass appears to be projecting into the air vesicle,
pushing the epithelial lining of the wall before it. Usually a giant cell

is to be observed in the centre of such a follicle, the centre stained bright yellow, the nuclei at the periphery, crimson. Around the tubercular nodules are numerous patches in which are catarrhal or fibrinous exudation. There may be an actual tubercular growth in the walls of the bronchus, extending into its lumen and diminishing its size, and even causing ulceration of the mucous surface ; a similar condition on the walls of the vessel may lead to partial obstruction of its lumen. In addition to these changes in the wall of the vessel, there is frequently endarteritis obliterans. The acute or croupous form of pneumonia is in these cases more commonly met with than the catarrhal.

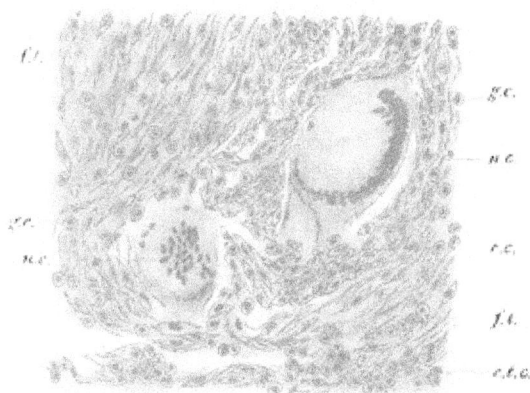

FIG. 108. Giant cells from a case of chronic tuberculosis of the lung. Stained with picro-carmine. (× 300).
    g.c. Branching giant cells with yellow homogeneous basis.
    n.c. Nuclei of giant cell.
    e.c. Endothelioid cells lying on the delicate network around a giant cell.
    f.t. Fibrous stroma, here more fully formed, comparatively few endothelioid cells near the periphery, but a considerable number of smaller and rounded (*c.t.c.*) cells are seen. These are simply such cells as are seen in rapidly proliferating connective tissue.

(× 300).—Observe the tubercular and fibroid masses in the deep layer of the pleura, in the interlobular and interalveolar septa, and in the peribronchial and perivascular tissue. In the wedge-shaped patches of tubercle near the surface, the individual nodules, each surrounded by pneumonic zones, should be further examined ;

these patches may be taken as typical of the patches in the whole
of the lung, with the exception of those at the apex, where fibroid
changes are more marked.

Each patch is made up of tubercle nodules, which again are composed of tubercle follicles.   In the centre of the nodule the tissue is
seen masses of granular *débris*, in which are a few angular and
shrivelled cells, with here and there fatty globules or granules, which
are stained black by osmic acid (§ 110).   Around the central caseous
mass, which is simply caseous tubercle, is a zone of tubercle follicles,
each of which has the regular giant cell structure.   Further out again
is a zone in which are tubercle follicles, growing principally into the
air vesicles, and usually accompanied by pneumonic exudation.
Examine one or two of the tubercle follicles in the interalveolar
septa, the endothelioid cells of various forms and sizes, and the small
round cells, all formed by proliferation of the endothelium of the
lymphatics and of the connective tissue cells.   As this mass grows
it is seen to make its way into the air vesicle, pushing before
it a regular layer of epithelium, which afterwards desquamates as the
connective tissue grows further into the vesicle ; the giant cell makes
its appearance and the full tubercle follicle is developed.   Around
the tubercle nodules there is, as seen above, an inflammatory exudation—croupous or catarrhal, especially in the more acute forms.

Tubercle bacilli are much more rare in chronic phthisis than in the
more acute process, but they may be found in the specially stained
specimens, particularly during the earlier stages of the disease.   They
must be looked for with a high power (× 600) in the lymph spaces,
where the proliferation is taking place most rapidly.

In exceedingly chronic tubercle (fibroid) there may be only slight
surrounding inflammatory changes, the giant cell becoming fibroid,
and the process remaining quiescent.

The bronchial glands, on microscopic examination, are found to
be tuberculous, pigmented, fibroid, or, frequently, caseated.

ELASTIC TISSUE IN SPUTUM.

278. Before concluding this short description of the pathological
conditions of the lung, it will not be out of place to say a few words

as to the treatment of sputum (the contents of phthisical cavities, &c.), in order to demonstrate the presence of the elastic membrane of the alveolar walls, which resists pathological disintegration far longer than most of the tissues.

To separate the elastic tissues Fenwick's method is undoubtedly the best. He boils the sputa in a beaker with an equal quantity of a strong solution (at least 20 grains to the ounce) of caustic soda or potash, until all the mucin and cement substance is dissolved. A quantity of water is then added to the fluid, and the whole is put aside in a conical glass. All other tissues are dissolved or separated, but the elastic fibres remain unaffected; they sink to the bottom of the glass, whence they may be removed by means of a pipette, transferred to a slide, and examined. The elastic fibres are seen as translucent, curled yellow fibres, sometimes in regular bundles, at others in short fragments. Their peculiar curliness is their chief characteristic.

In certain cases crystals are met with in sputa, especially long, delicate, colourless, acicular, fatty acid crystals, which are sometimes mistaken for elastic fibres; they may, however, be easily differentiated by adding ether, which dissolves fatty acid crystals, but does not affect elastic fibres. Charcot's crystals, which are met with in cases of asthma and chronic bronchitis, are delicate, colourless, long and spindle-shaped. They are soluble in dilute acids or alkalies, but are unaffected by alcohol. Various other disintegration crystals, such as cholesterin, leucin, tyrosin, and hæmatoidin, may also occur in the sputum.

OTHER PATHOLOGICAL CONDITIONS MET WITH IN THE LUNG.

279. Pyæmic abscess is sometimes met with in connection with a general condition of pyæmia. In such a case the abscesses are near the surface, and over the inflamed and degenerating tissue there is usually acute pleurisy. Similar small abscesses are sometimes met with where there has been pressure on a bronchus, by an aneurism for instance, leading first to pneumonia, pleurisy, and, ultimately, to small abscess formation. Examine the vessels in the deep layer of the pleura and near the abscess. They and the lymph spaces in the

neighbourhood are distended, and in many cases masses of micrococci are found in them.

In farcy, there are frequently evidences of catarrhal pneumonia, fat embolism of the lung, &c., and small bacilli are also described both around air vesicles and bronchi. Small abscesses are met with in actinomycosis; in or near which the characteristic mycelial fungus is usually found. (*See* section on Parasites).

OTHER PARASITES MET WITH IN THE LUNG.

Hydatids, Filaria bronchialis (especially in sheep), and sometimes, but rarely, the *Cysticercus cellulosæ.*

PRIMARY TUMOURS OF THE LUNG.

280. *Lipoma, osteoma,* and *fibroma,* the latter especially near the bronchi, are sometimes met with.

Chondroma or *enchondroma* occurs in connection with the bronchial cartilages.

Cylindrical or *columnar-celled epithelioma* grows as a primary tumour in connection with the bronchial glands and ducts.

Squamous epitheliomas are also described, but are very rare.

SECONDARY TUMOURS OF MALIGNANT TYPES.

281. Ziegler says of secondary tumours in this position, that "examples of every tumour that gives rise to metastases at all, have been found in the lungs." Of these, from the extreme vascularity of the organ, the most common are the *sarcomas,* especially the more malignant forms. (*See* section on Sarcoma).

The *melanotic sarcoma,* which appears as a somewhat flattened or rounded mass, immediately below the pleura, is deeply pigmented, and the structure is the same as when it occurs in other positions.

The same may be said of the other forms of sarcoma as regards structure, but these occur much more frequently in the substance than near the surface of the lung.

Lymphosarcoma, lymphadenoma, which usually spread from the mediastinum.

Small round-celled sarcoma, and *small spindle-celled sarcoma, osteo-osteoid,* and *myeloid sarcomas.*

Malignant enchondroma, secondary to the same condition in the testicle.

Myxochondroma, secondary in one case to myxochondroma of the periosteum of the scapula (Greenfield). This is met with as semi-gelatinous bluish cartilaginous masses in the branches of the pulmonary artery, the branchings of which they closely follow.

Cancers—scirrhous, encephaloid, colloid, and *adenoid* (or the columnar-celled epithelioma), and *squamous epithelioma* (which is usually secondary to that of the tongue when it spreads through the mediastinal glands).

These forms of cancer may all occur in the lung, as there is a very free distribution of lymphatics and lymphatic glands in this organ and in its pleural covering. They are almost invariably multiple.

In this position it is somewhat difficult to distinguish them from the sarcomas, especially in the earlier or softer forms ; but later, and in the harder forms, puckering of the pleura and umbilication frequently occur, just as in scirrhous cancer of the breast. Microscopically they resemble the same tumours in other organs. (*See* section on Tumours).

CHAPTER IX.

THE SPLEEN.

NORMAL HISTOLOGY.

282. The spleen is a flattened, somewhat crescent-shaped organ, from five to five and a half inches in length, three to four inches across, and one to one and a half inch in thickness; these measurements vary considerably in different cases. The weight is usually from five to seven ounces, though this also may vary considerably, as, "even when perfectly free from disease, it may fluctuate between four and ten ounces" (Quain's Anatomy). The anterior margin is notched; these notches persist, however large the organ may become. On the concave surface of the spleen is a vertical fissure, termed the hilum, at the bottom of which are numerous openings, where the blood-vessels enter and emerge.

Investing the organ is (1) a serous coat, which is simply a reflection of the peritoneum. This forms a capsule, and is covered with a layer of flattened endothelial cells which, seen in section, are spindle-shaped. Beneath this is (2) a layer of connective tissue, in which are elastic fibrils. Beneath this again is (3) a denser mass of connective tissue, in which are blood-vessels, nerves, and a few non-striped muscle fibres. Running in from the hilum on the one hand, and from the deeper layer of the capsule on the other, are numerous septa or trabeculæ, composed of connective tissue and of bands of non-striped muscular fibre, evidently continuous with those of the capsule. These trabeculæ divide and subdivide until the ramifications become very small, and the terminal filaments of the trabeculæ from the capsule meeting those from the hilum form a supporting framework of connective tissue.

The arteries of the spleen enter at the hilum, and together with the veins run along the fibrous trabeculæ, in which position there

are numerous perivascular lymphatics. The artery soon leaves the
vein, and at once breaks up into a tuft or pencil of small arterioles.
These leave the trabeculæ, and are continued into the splenic substance proper. After leaving the fibrous trabeculæ, each arteriole
is invested with a mass of tissue known as an adenoid sheath, a
beaded-looking column with irregular enlargements, bulgings, and
constrictions, in which the artery is usually placed somewhat
eccentrically. This column with the artery in the centre, seen in
transverse section, is the so-called Malpighian corpuscle. It is com-

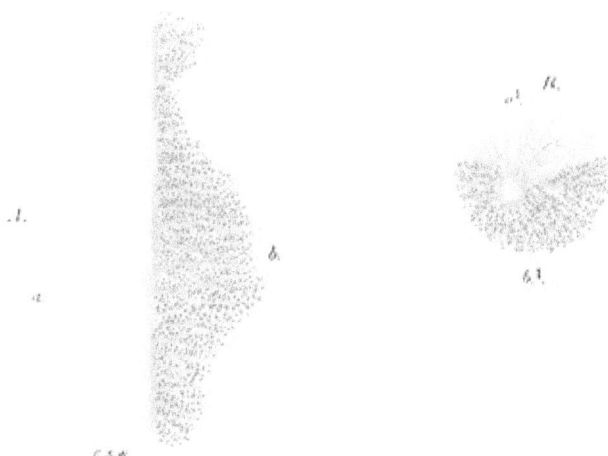

FIG. 109.—Diagram representing the arrangement of the capillary
vessels in the adenoid sheath (Malpighian corpuscle).
 A. Longitudinal section of the arteriole, with its sheath.
 B. Transverse section.
 a.a¹. The capillary vessels which convey the blood from the small
    arterioles to the splenic sinuses.
 b.b¹. Adenoid tissue between these capillary vessels.

posed of a reticular stroma, lying on the bands of which are endothelioid cells, whilst lying in the spaces are numerous small round
corpuscles or lymph cells. This tissue is very dense, and even under
the naked eye is usually readily seen, as are also the fibrous trabeculæ.
Proceeding from the central artery are "elongated meshes of capillary
blood-vessels," which run nearly at right angles to the long axis of
the sheath, until they come to its margin, when they open out into
the pulp tissue, first into a series of small sinuses, and then into

larger venous sinuses, after which the blood is collected into the venous trunks, and carried from the organ along the trabeculæ to the hilum, and thence to the portal vein.

The splenic pulp—the tissue between the adenoid sheaths or Malpighian corpuscles,—is composed of a mass of sponge-like structure, in which are small open spaces communicating with the capillary vessels as they emerge from the adenoid sheath; they are bounded by large transparent endothelial cells or plates, containing one or more

FIG. 110.—Part of a Malpighian corpuscle of the spleen of man. (× 350.) (After Klein and Noble Smith.)

a. Arterial branch seen in longitudinal section.
b. Adenoid tissue, consisting of adenoid reticulum, in which the nuclei of the lymph corpuscles may still be seen.
c. Reticular structure, from which the lymph cells have been removed accidentally.
d. Muscular fibres of the middle coat of the vessel seen in transverse action.
e. One of the endothelial cells lining the vessel.

large nuclei, and lying on a trabecular tissue. In the sinuses themselves are numerous lymphoid cells, in which, as well as in the endothelial cells, blood corpuscles, or pigment derived from them, are frequently found imbedded. There may be a few large cells partially attached to the epithelial cells by stalks or pedicles (the cells proliferating by budding). Opening out from these smaller sinuses of the pulp are larger tubular sinuses, lined with similar endothelial cells, and containing large and small nucleated cells, and usually some coloured blood corpuscles. Supporting the walls of the larger sinuses are bands or fibrils of yellow elastic tissue, which are arranged almost like barrel hoops. From these larger or venous sinuses the blood is poured into the venous trunks.

Harden a section of a healthy spleen (§ 59), and stain (§ 98).

(× 50).—Note the capsule with the trabeculæ running at right angles to it. Between the trabeculæ the rounded masses of denser looking tissue appear to be made up of small cells (lymphoid tissue). These denser masses are Malpighian corpuscles; they vary considerably in size and shape, according to the direction in which the section through the adenoid sheath is made,—rounded if cut transversely, oval if cut obliquely, and elongated, or even bifurcated (at the point of bifurcation of a vessel) if cut vertically; the size varying according as the section passes through an enlarged or a constricted part of the sheath. The vessel is usually situated at some distance from the centre, and may even be near the margin of the sheath. Surrounding the Malpighian corpuscles (sections of the adenoid sheaths) the splenic pulp is recognised as a spongy open network, containing sinuses of various sizes, those nearest the Malpighian corpuscles being considerably smaller than those further away. Running through the splenic pulp, as will afterwards be better observed in the waxy spleen, are numerous small arterioles, which are apparently not in direct communication with the arterioles of the Malpighian corpuscles.

(× 300).—The various features above described must be observed, and special attention paid to the capillaries in the Malpighian corpuscles, the lymphoid tissue of which these corpuscles are composed, the arterial sinuses, with their endothelial lining, the large round and nucleated cells, the smaller lymphoid cells, and the coloured blood corpuscles. Note the similar structures in the large venous sinuses, and the encircling elastic bands in their walls. Examine also the connective tissue and non-striped muscular fibre in the trabeculæ.

ACTIVE HYPERÆMIA OF THE SPLEEN.

283. In this condition the spleen undergoes changes which are very evident to the naked eye, but which, under the microscope, are less characteristic.

Hyperæmia is met with as a result of continued high temperature, but the most acute form is met with in septic, specific, and malarial fevers, and in syphilis. The organ is enlarged, in some cases to two or three times the normal size, and the capsule is stretched. On section the substance is soft, diffluent, contains much blood, and is of a dark red colour, which rapidly turns to a bright arterial red when the cut surface is exposed to the air for a few minutes. In the more acute septic conditions, such as typhus or acute septicæmia, the hyperæmia is more acute, and the tissue, especially in the early stages of the disease, is bright red or even pink, when the organ is first cut into ; if the patient lives for a time, the tissue still remains soft, but it becomes paler and almost creamy, and the trabeculæ and Malpighian corpuscles cannot be easily distinguished in the mass of soft creamy-looking pulp.

In the most acute form, *i.e.*, that met with in malarial fevers, the enlargement of the spleen may be so great and so rapid that the organ may actually rupture.

In smallpox, scarlet fever, and typhoid fever, especially in the later stages, the spleen may, instead of being diffluent, be comparatively firm. In such cases it may be enlarged even to as much as four times its normal size. The Malpighian corpuscles are considerably increased in size, owing to swelling of the adenoid tissue. The whole surface has a peculiar greyish, or sometimes yellowish tinge mixed with the red.

This active hyperæmic stage may be followed by a stage of resolution, as seen in a spleen taken from a case of acute pneumonia, in which death supervened during the stage of grey hepatization or early resolution. The organ is considerably smaller than normal, the pulp appears to be greatly diminished in quantity, and the trabeculæ stand out very prominently as white fibrous bands passing in from a somewhat thickened and greatly wrinkled capsule.

Harden (§ **56, 59,** or **66**) and stain (§ **98** or **103** *d*).

(× 50).—The most prominent feature is the increased quantity of blood, seen as green masses in the pulp sinuses ; scattered throughout these are numerous leucocytes which appear as small pink points. The Malpighian corpuscles are enlarged, though this enlargement cannot always be recognised, as relatively to the increased pulp the corpuscle may be smaller. The small round lymphoid cells are numerous, and take on nuclear stains very readily. Where the Malpighian corpuscles stand out prominently, as in diphtheria,

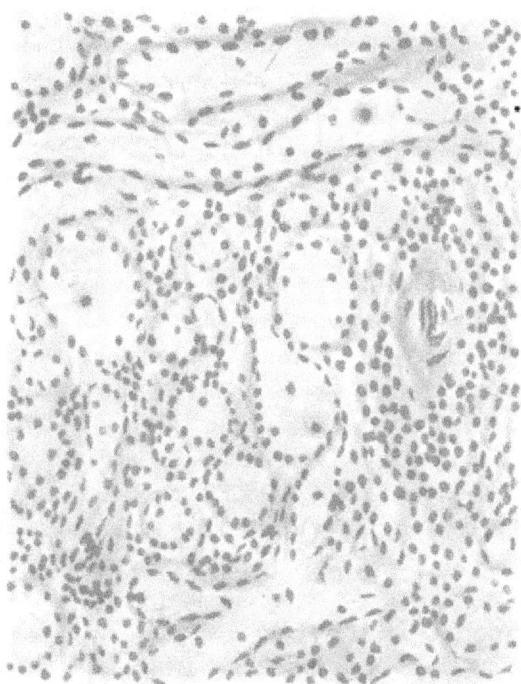

FIG. 111.—Acute congestion of the spleen, stained with logwood. (× 300.)

   a. Large pulp sinus cut longitudinally, lined with flattened nucleated endothelium, and filled with red blood corpuscles, with here and there a deeply stained leucocyte.

   b. Do., seen in transverse section. Large uninucleated corpuscle seen lying in centre.

   c. Smaller sinuses.

   d. Vessel in centre of (*e.*) Malpighian corpuscle. Walls of vessel somewhat swollen, adventitia hyaline. The lymphoid and other cells of adenoid sheath (Malpighian corpuscle) are well seen.

   f. Around the sinuses in this position there are regular accumulations of small round cells in the walls.

typhoid, and scarlet fevers, this increase in the amount of adenoid tissue becomes a very marked feature in the field of the microscope.

Along the lines of the smaller trabeculæ there is frequently proliferation or exudation of leucocytes (deeply stained), which arises from the increased blood pressure and from the other inflammatory processes.

(× 300).—When the congestion is comparatively simple, little more can be made out than distension of the sinuses with red blood corpuscles, with here and there a few colourless blood corpuscles and a number of larger nucleated cells, which appear to be derived from the proliferating endothelial cells which line the pulp sinus. These endothelial cells are all swollen, and appear cloudy; some contain several nuclei, and others contain a number of red blood corpuscles, or a quantity of golden brown pigment, which is evidently derived from the blood. In the adenoid sheath of the vessel the lymphoid corpuscles are numerous, and, in addition, the endothelioid plates, lying on the trabeculæ of the adenoid network, are increased in number; this is not nearly so marked as in those cases in which there is inflammation in addition to the congestion, where, also, the changes in the trabeculæ and sinuses are more distinct. Rapid proliferation of the endothelial cells takes place, and consequent accumulation of leucocytes in the sinuses, exudation of leucocytes along the lines of the trabeculæ, in which the vessels run, and other evidences of an inflammatory condition ensue. As a result of this, abscesses may form, especially in or near the Malpighian corpuscles when we have rapid accumulation of leucocytes, pus formation, and general breaking down of the tissue elements. The abscesses sometimes appear as small yellow points on the surface of a section, but more frequently they are single and are of larger size. In many cases they are of septic embolic origin, as in acute ulcerative endocarditis, pyæmia arising from whatever cause, and typhoid fever. Such abscesses run an acute course, beginning as dark red hæmorrhagic looking patches which rapidly suppurate.

CHRONIC CHANGES.

284. In those cases in which the febrile condition is prolonged, or where there are repeated attacks, as in malarial fevers, the spleen may become permanently enlarged. It is then firm, and of a dirty

greyish red, with pigmented patches seen through the capsule. On section the capsule is thickened, and running from its deeper layer are numerous thickened trabeculæ. The Malpighian corpuscles may also be enlarged, though it is often very difficult to distinguish them from the surrounding firm pulp tissue, which is very brittle,

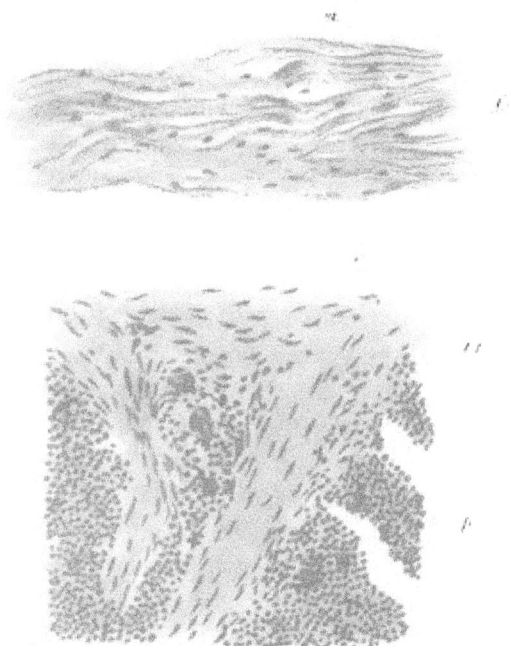

FIG. 112.—Drawing of spleen and capsule in which there was chronic fibroid thickening of the capsule and trabeculæ. Stained with magenta. (× 200.)

f.c. Fibroid thickening of the capsule (flat fibroma).
n. Connective tissue nuclei.
c. Deep layer of the capsule in which are elongated nuclei, some of which are nuclei of non-striped muscular fibres.
t.t. Thickened trabeculæ prolonged downwards·from the deep layer of the capsule to which they are similar in structure.
p. Splenic pulp.

and not nearly so full of blood as in the normal condition; whilst scattered over the whole of the surface, evidently the result of pigmentation, are grey, or even black patches. In malarial diseases the pigmentation is more marked than in any other chronic form of enlarged spleen; but enlargement and fibroid change may be noted in a variety of conditions, not only in those mentioned above, but in rickets, congenital syphilis, or, more rarely, in the later stages of acquired syphilis.

Harden (§ 57 or 59), and stain (§ 98 or 103 *d*).

(× 50).—Note the thickening of the capsule and of the fibrous trabeculæ, and the increased size of the adventitia of the vessels. The pulp tissue is altered, the spaces are not necessarily larger —frequently they are even smaller than normal—but their walls are thickened. The adenoid sheaths of the arteries—the Malpighian corpuscles—are pinker and more fibrous in appearance, and the number of small round lymphoid cells is in many cases considerably diminished. At the margins of the adenoid sheaths and in the pulp proper are numerous accumulations of golden brown pigment imbedded in the fibrous tissue or in the cells.

(× 300).—Observe the thickening of the fibrous capsule and of the trabeculæ, and the elongated or rod-shaped nuclei of the hyper-trophied bands of muscular fibre. The Malpighian corpuscles are more fibroid, and large quantities of dark altered blood pigment may be seen at their margins. Note the thickened walls of the pulp sinuses, in which the endothelial cells often contain large quantities of blood pigment, as do also the rounded cells lying free in the cavity. There may also be considerable pigmentation of the tissue, of which the walls of the sinuses are composed.

CHRONIC VENOUS CONGESTION OF THE SPLEEN.

285. There is another form of chronic interstitial thickening, which is due more directly to mechanical causes. This is met with wherever there is any obstruction to the outflow of venous blood from the spleen. It is consequently found in cases of long-standing heart disease, especially of the mitral valve; in common cirrhosis of the liver, where there is obstruction to the portal circulation; in fibroid phthisis and emphysema, where there is impeded flow of blood through the lungs, and consequently impaired systemic venous circulation; or where there is direct pressure upon the splenic vein.

The chronic venous congested spleen is usually slightly enlarged.

It is also heavier, firmer, and more fleshy than normal. The capsule is thickened, and, like that of the liver in the corresponding condition, may have villous projections or hard cartilaginoid patches on its surface. The cut surface presents a peculiar fleshy appearance, and a bluish-red or purple colour; and although there may be thickening of the trabeculæ, there is no evidence of it to the naked eye. The edge of the cut section is quite sharp and well defined.

Harden (§ 59), and stain (§ 98).

(× 50).—The changes are essentially the same as those met with in similar conditions in other organs—nutmeg liver (§ 182), chronic venous congestion of the kidneys (§ 227), or lungs (§ 269).

The venous sinuses are distended with blood, which is seen as greenish granular material occupying a considerable part of the section. From the splenic pulp the pink fibrous trabeculæ stand out very prominently, but the adenoid sheaths are not so readily distinguished as in the normal condition. They are more fibroid, and the lymphoid cells are not so numerous. The walls of the vessels are usually somewhat thickened. The cellular elements of the pulp are obscured, but delicate strands of fibrillated tissue in the walls of the enlarged venous sinuses may be seen running through the section.

(× 300).—The venous sinuses are greatly distended. In them lie numerous coloured, with here and there colourless, corpuscles in which may be seen granules of altered blood pigment. The cells lining the venous sinuses are often flattened, and contain altered blood pigment. Between the sinuses there frequently appears to be very little tissue, but careful examination reveals the existence of pink fibrous strands, on which rest the lining endothelial cells. The Malpighian corpuscles contain more fibrous tissue than usual, and fewer lymphoid cells are seen. Perhaps the most marked changes are in the fibrous trabeculæ, which appear to be considerably thickened, and around the vessels running in them are usually a number of small round pink cells or leucocytes. There is also fibroid or cartilaginoid thickening of the capsule (Fig. 112). These latter are merely masses of fibrous tissue (the flat fibroma described in the section on Tumours). The villous projections are young masses of connective tissue or granulation tissue, with a quantity of lymph on the surface.   In the trabeculæ and in the capsule there is also marked hypertrophy of the muscular tissue, the elongated nuclei of which can be easily distinguished.

EMBOLIC INFARCTION OF THE SPLEEN.

286. An infarct is the area of tissue supplied by a terminal artery the small vessels of which are filled with stagnant blood ; this unchanged is unable to supply nutriment to the tissues, which rapidly undergo degenerative changes.   In the spleen, infarction occurs in its most typical form.   It will therefore be well to take the description of this condition from the appearances here presented.

In its earlier stages the infarction appears as a slight projection running transversely across the convex surface of the enlarged spleen ; it is deep purple or brick red, according to the stage which it has reached ; it is firm, and, on palpation, is readily defined from the surrounding softer splenic tissue ; it may pass for a considerable distance into the organ, or it may be situated close to the surface.   On section it is found to be wedge-shaped, with a rounded base at the capsule, the apex pointing towards the hilum.   The surrounding pulp is highly congested.   Of these wedge-shaped masses there are usually three, four, or more, but there may be only a single large one involving a considerable part of the organ.   Examined at various later stages, the centre is paler ; then a yellowish pallor spreads towards the periphery, until the whole mass, with the exception of a zone at the outer margin, is completely involved.   An outer congested zone persists for a considerable time, and eventually there is formed in this position a capsule of fibrous tissue, which, as it becomes more and more cicatricial, slowly retracts, and draws on the capsule at the margins of the infarct, so that a kind of fossa or depression is formed around the yellow fatty mass. Following fatty degeneration, absorption and caseation set in.   If the process of absorption continues, the whole of the necrosed tissue may be removed, when there is left to mark the position of the infarct merely a fibrous cicatrix.   In many cases, however, all that remains is a cyst, or a cheesy or calcareous mass, surrounded by the retracting fibrous capsule.

Harden (§§ 56, 57 or 59), and stain (§ 103 *d*).

(× 20).—In a section taken from a very early infarct there is little to be seen beyond an enormous distension of the various vascular

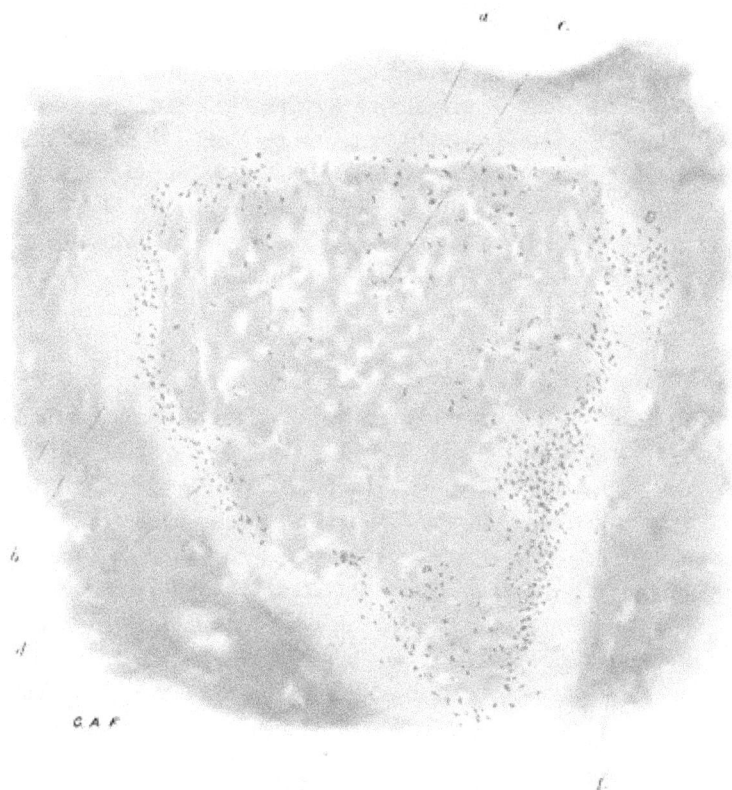

Fig. 113.—Section of small infarct of the spleen. Stained with eosin and logwood. (× 20.)

a. Surface of spleen.
b. Fibrous capsule formed in or within
c. Congested zone.
d. Pigmented cells, &c., most numerous in the inner layers of the fibrous capsule.
e. Pulp sinus with swollen and degenerating walls. The dead splenic tissue in which the infarction has taken place.

channels and sinuses. At a later stage fatty degeneration of the various tissues supervenes, especially towards the centre of the infarct; this is readily observed in a section stained with osmic acid

(§ **110**). At the periphery of the swollen mass there is an enormous accumulation of leucocytes or young connective tissue cells in the position of the hyperæmic zone. Later these cells are organised into connective tissue, which, becoming more and more fibrous, forms bands of pink stained tissue ; these run up to a puckering in the capsule, around the caseous mass, in which, at this stage, pigment granules, and fatty granules and globules, are the principal constituents; but crystals of cholesterin, hæmatoidin crystals, some fat crystals, or even calcareous salts, may also be found. The salts disappear on the addition of hydrochloric acid. Pigment granules are also to be seen in the fibrous capsule, especially near its inner surface. The capsule of the spleen frequently presents evidences of localised inflammatory thickening over the infarct.

WAXY SAGO SPLEEN.

287. Waxy degeneration occurs more frequently in the spleen than in any other organ in the body, with the sole exception of the kidney. It takes one of two forms—(1.) the sago waxy spleen, and (2.) the diffuse waxy spleen. In the first the process is confined to the adenoid sheaths of the vessels—the Malpighian corpuscles ; in the second the pulp is the part specially affected. A careful examination of these two forms of waxy spleen will enable the student to understand the structure of the spleen, and to note the part which the various elements play not only in this, but in other pathological processes. For this reason a somewhat detailed account of waxy disease is here given.

In the sago form, the spleen is usually, though not invariably, somewhat enlarged ; it is hard, firm, and elastic, and in this respect resembles the liver and differs from the kidney in the waxy condition. On section, the general appearance varies in different cases. Sometimes, where there is a large quantity of blood in the organ, it is red, and the Malpighian corpuscles appear as dark shining masses studding the surface. In other cases the pulp is paler, and then the Malpighian corpuscles appear lighter in colour. They are transparent and gelatinous in appearance, and have been aptly compared to grains of boiled sago, which, on the addition of iodine (§ **107**) give a mahogany brown reaction; the surrounding healthy tissue giving a yellow colour. (For other reactions, see §§ 108 and 109.)

Harden (§ 57), mount one section unstained (§ 152), stain others (§§ 106, 107, and 108).

(× 50).—Each Malpighian corpuscle is stained red violet, with the exception of a small blue ring in the centre, surrounded by a thin zone of blue tissue. Where the condition is advanced, the red

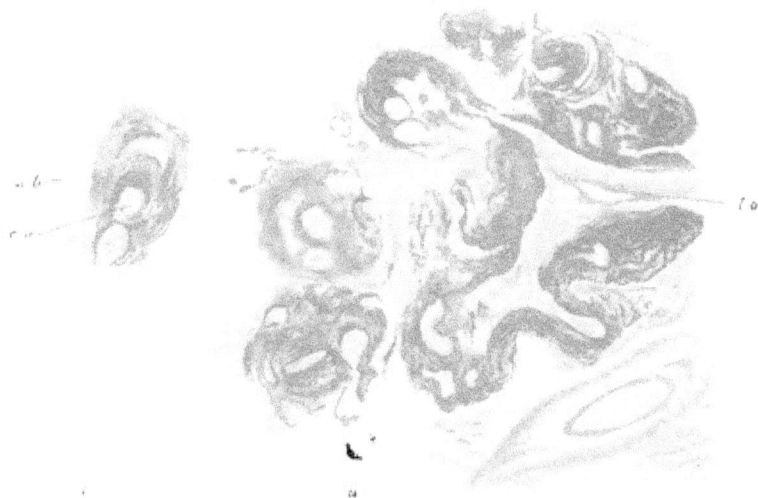

FIG. 114.—Waxy sago spleen. Stained with methylaniline violet. (× 30.)

   l.a. Large arteriole, giving off branches around which the waxy adenoid sheath is readily seen.

   m.b. Malpighian body or adenoid sheath with (*c.a.*) its healthy arteriole in the centre; the two seen here are evidently near the point of bifurcation of the arteriole.

   a. Small waxy vessel in the splenic pulp.

   p. Splenic pulp.

violet mass appears to be almost homogeneous; but near the central blue patch, the unaffected larger central artery of the adenoid sheath, or at the periphery of the sheath at its junction with the splenic pulp, delicate red lines may be seen running from the solid violet mass into the surrounding blue tissue. The central blue ring is surrounded by a thin zone of comparatively healthy adenoid tissue. Around the waxy Malpighian corpuscle the splenic pulp (sinuses, cells, and vessels) is at first sight apparently unaffected, and is stained blue,

although running from the margins of the waxy mass are small
capillary vessels, the walls of which are undergoing the waxy change
—the thin red violet lines already mentioned. A more careful
examination of the splenic pulp reveals, however, a few small red
violet lines, rings, and dots running through it. These are evidently
sections of waxy blood-vessels—small arterioles. In an iodine
stained section, examined by reflected light, the parts seen above as
red violet now appear brown, whilst the blue parts are canary yellow

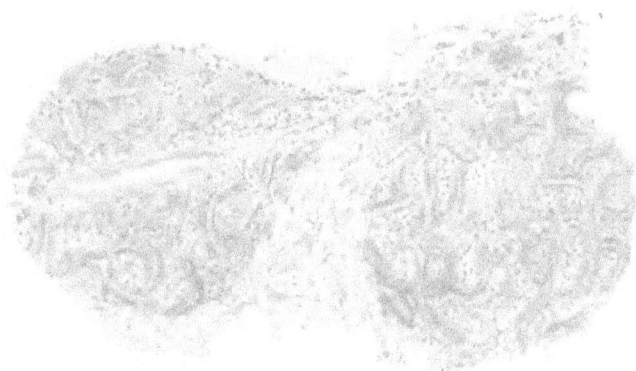

FIG. 115.—Waxy sago spleen, early stage. Stained with iodine
and sulphuric acid. (× 70, after Kyber.)
x. and *y.*　Enlarged Malpighian corpuscles, in which the thickened
　　　　　　waxy vessels may be seen stained blue.
a.　　　　Smaller part of a Malpighian corpuscle, in which the
　　　　　　central artery is not seen.
b.　　　　Splenic pulp unaffected by the waxy disease.

in hue. In an unstained section the waxy portions are glistening,
translucent, and hyaline, and have a faint yellow tinge.

(× 300).—Unless the waxy condition be very far advanced, the
walls of the central artery of the Malpighian corpuscle are quite
healthy and are stained blue ; the intima is thrown into folds by the
contracting muscular coat, from which it may be inferred that the
muscle is functionally as well as optically healthy. As yet, too,
there is no change in the adventitia, and it is only at some little distance from the vessel that any is noticeable. The " degeneration "
begins in the walls of the capillary vessels, which run through the

Malpighian corpuscle. These vessel walls are seen as thin, homogeneous, red violet lines, between which the lymphoid cells, stained blue, stand out prominently. Further away from the centre, the vessels are more affected, and not the vessels only, but the delicate strands of fibrillated tissue which compose the network of the adenoid sheath. The strands are swollen, homogeneous, and are stained red violet. Most of the lymphoid cells between them are comparatively healthy, and are stained blue ; but where the condition is very far advanced some of these cells appear to be waxy, though it may be that the swollen vessels and fibres have, by pressure, caused them

FIG. 116.—Drawing of small capillary vessels and connective tissue fibrils undergoing waxy degeneration. Stained with iodine and sulphuric acid. (× 600, after Kyber.)
These vessels were isolated by pencilling from one of the Malpighian corpuscles of the spleen from which Fig. 115, was drawn.
The degenerated parts are stained blue ; the unaffected connective tissue fibrils and capillary walls are stained yellow.

to become atrophied. Certain it is that the cells are not at all readily discerned. At the periphery of the Malpighian corpuscle, the delicate waxy bands are more readily distinguished, and the process may be seen to extend for a short distance in the walls of the vascular sinuses beyond it, where there is a condition very similar to that met with in diffuse waxy spleen.

Running through the blue splenic pulp are numerous small arterioles, the walls of which are in an advanced stage of waxy degeneration, and the walls of some of the sinuses may be slightly affected. Where this waxy change in the wall of the sinus has once set in, there is usually fatty degeneration of the endothelial cells lining the wall of the sinus.

In this position, perhaps, better than in any other, may the waxy change in the vessel be seen.

(× 300).—Note (*a*) that the waxy change is confined to the middle coat, especially during the early stage of the disease ; (*b*) that the middle coat is picked out in patches by the disease :

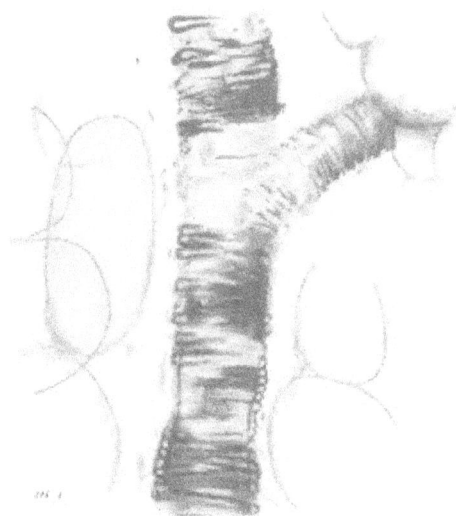

FIG. 117.—Drawing of a vessel in which the middle coat is slightly affected. Stained with methylaniline violet. (× 600.)

   m.f.   Circular muscular fibres of the middle coat cut transversely.
   w.c.f. Between the muscular fibres the connective tissue fibrils are swollen and waxy ; stained red violet. Within the vessel the nuclei of the endothelial cells are readily recognised.
   c.t.   Connective tissue cells.
   c.f.   Fat cells.

(*c*) in these patches the tissues are not affected throughout, for on careful examination it will be seen that only between the muscular fibres is there the waxy change, the longitudinal or transverse sections of the muscular fibres being stained blue, whilst between them are red violet streaks,—the swollen connective tissue fibrils. At the margin of the Malpighian corpuscle the walls of the sinuses are affected, but not extensively. In the pulp the small arterioles and the walls of a few of the sinuses are waxy. As these become more and more swollen, the muscular fibres are atrophied by pressure, and ultimately they may be obliterated. Later, the intima is involved, but the endothelial lining of the vessels then becomes granular and fatty, never waxy. Here, then, is a condition in which the waxy disease affects specially the walls of the small arterioles soon after they are given off from the large central arteriole, then the connective tissue fibrils around them, and it is possible that the lymphoid cells may ultimately be involved.

Diffuse Waxy Spleen.

288. This is often stated to be an advanced form of the foregoing, but such is not even usually the case. Where it is simply an advanced sago spleen, the Malpighian bodies are most markedly affected, and the walls of the sinuses of the greater part of the pulp tissue are involved. In the true diffuse waxy spleen the change is confined almost entirely to the pulp tissue, and the Malpighian corpuscles are unaltered or are apparently only somewhat atrophied.

Naked eye appearances.—The spleen is very greatly enlarged, much more so than in the sago form. Its substance is firm and elastic, and the margins, as in those of a waxy liver, are somewhat rounded. On section, the surface has the peculiar glistening appearance so characteristic of waxy disease in most organs. The edges of the sections are sharp and well defined ; the colour is usually a deep red. The trabeculæ and Malpighian corpuscles are very indistinctly seen, except in an iodine stained specimen, where they may frequently be distinguished as yellow points, each of which has a mahogany-brown centre. The yellow points are on all sides surrounded by a mahogany-brown glistening material. It will be noted that the central mahogany brown point corresponds to the arteriole, the yellow area round it to the adenoid sheath (Malpighian corpuscle), and the mahogany-brown glistening material around this again to the waxy splenic pulp.

Harden (§ 57), and stain (as in § 286).

(× 50).—Examine the methylaniline violet stained specimen, and note that in many parts of it the Malpighian corpuscles are quite unaffected, and are stained blue, though some of them appear to be somewhat fibroid, the number of cells being then greatly diminished. At some points, however, there is a thin ring of red violet material near the central arteriole, in which position the adenoid tissue is most fully developed. The pulp tissue is markedly affected. The walls of the sinuses are in an advanced stage of waxy degeneration, are stained red violet, and are homogeneous and glistening. Within the sinuses the endothelial cells may be seen as small blue granules

FIG. 118.—Drawing of diffuse waxy spleen. Stained with iodine and sulphuric acid. (× 400, after Kyber.)
a. Waxy splenic pulp (between the Malpighian corpuscles).
b. Venous sinuses lined with unaltered endothelial cells.
c. Small arteriole, unaffected.
d. Capillary, opening into the venous sinus.

near the walls, the coloured and colourless blood corpuscles lying free in the spaces.

(× 300).—The central artery of the adenoid sheath is frequently, though not invariably, found to be undergoing waxy degeneration. Around the affected arteriole the capillaries in the sheath may be undergoing the waxy change, but the process seldom extends beyond the immediate neighbourhood of the central vessel. The remainder of the Malpighian corpuscle is fibroid, and may be considerably atrophied, in which case the lymphoid cells are particularly scanty. At the margins of these Malpighian corpuscles the waxy change begins at once. It appears to take the form of swelling of the fibres of those trabeculæ which are in immediate contact with the endothelial cells lining the pulp sinuses. Around the venous sinuses the bands of yellow elastic fibre (the fibres resembling barrel hoops) are seen on section to be considerably swollen and undergoing the waxy change. The rounded cells situated between the sinuses are atrophied, or fatty and granular, though some appear to be swollen and waxy. It is extremely difficult to give an explanation of this latter appearance, and it is just possible that the waxy, cell-like masses may be sections of some of the swollen fibrous bands. Examine the endothelial cells, many of which are in immediate contact with the swollen sinus walls. These cells do not take on the waxy reaction with methylaniline violet, but give a blue colour. Nevertheless, they are sometimes extremely granular and fatty; this is more readily brought out on the addition of osmic acid (§ 110). In other cases the cells are greatly atrophied, and are detached from the walls of the sinuses, most of which are distended with blood corpuscles, both coloured and colourless.

LEUCOCYTHEMIA OF THE SPLEEN.

289. In the spleen in leucocythemia we have an enormous accumulation of leucocytes in and sometimes around the pulp sinuses; the spleen is usually enormously enlarged, and may weigh as many pounds as normally it weighs ounces. The enlargement takes place in all directions, so that the organ retains its relative proportions, and the notches on the anterior border remain strongly marked. The organ is firm, pale, and tough, but not leathery. Under the capsule, which is often irregularly thickened, there are sometimes purple patches, the result of hæmorrhages. These stand out very prominently from the surrounding tissue.

On section the tissue presents a firm homogeneous appearance. The pulp is solid, firm, and of a peculiar grey colour, with small hæmorrhages scattered irregularly through it, but especially near the capsule. Scattered over the surface are cream grey nodules and lines, which represent the Malpighian corpuscles. Embolic infarcts, of very various sizes and in different stages of degeneration (§ 285), may also be observed as yellow wedge-shaped masses situated near the surface.

Examine a scraping from the cut surface (× 300), and note that it contains numerous leucocytes, a number of coloured blood corpuscles, and some larger cells, composed of a mass of protoplasm, in which are imbedded nuclei, sometimes a single one, sometimes several.

Harden (§ 57 or 59), and stain (§§ 98 and 103 *d*).

(× 50).—Note, first, that although the trabeculæ are considerably thickened and the Malpighian corpuscles may be slightly enlarged, they do not form very prominent features in the section. The splenic pulp in the logwood stained section appears to consist of one mass of deeply stained cells, some of which are much larger than the ordinary leucocytes, or even than the normal endothelial cells. The Malpighian corpuscles may contain more lymphoid cells, but in certain cases they are more fibroid. In some cases the lymphoid cells of the pulp proper are very few in number.

(× 300).—Note the above changes in the Malpighian body and in the trabeculæ, both of which may be somewhat hypertrophied. In the former the condition varies slightly in different cases. There is frequently an increase in the number of small round lymphoid cells, together with an increase in the number of endothelioid cells, in which case there is, in this position, a marked increase in the amount of fibrous tissue. These changes are never so well marked as in lymphadenoma, the condition which will be next considered.

In the pulp tissue the most striking feature is the enormous distension of the sinuses. The endothelial cells lining them are swollen and multinucleated, and project somewhat from the walls. To them a number of large cells are attached by a pedicle ; these, like those lying free in the sinus, being probably derived by proliferation from the attached endothelial cells. In these cells there may be only a single nucleus, but very frequently there are several. They usually contain a quantity of altered blood pigment, which is confined principally to those positions, though in some few cases the golden brown pigment granules may be seen lying in the trabeculæ. In addition to these large cells the sinuses usually contain a number of ordinary leucocytes. In the lungs, in the intestine, and on serous surfaces embolic hæmorrhages are usually very numerous in this disease, as are also fatty degenerative changes in the various organs. For long lymphadenoma, or Hodgkin's disease, was classed as a form of leucocythemia, and even now the pathological changes are in many text-books stated to be the same. This is an error which

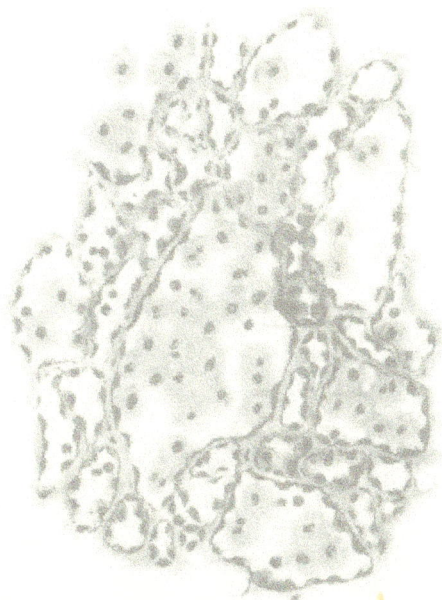

Fig. 119.—Drawing of leucocythemic spleen. Stained with log-wood. (× 300.)

v.s. Large venous sinus lined with a regular layer of endothelial cells, and containing leucocytes (*l.*) and large cells with one or two nuclei each (*c.*).

e.e. Endothelial plates lining the walls of one of the smaller or arterial sinuses.

must be carefully avoided, as the changes are essentially different in the two conditions. In leucocythemia the splenic pulp is the part affected; whilst in lymphadenoma it is, primarily, the adenoid sheath of the vessels, whence the affection spreads into the surrounding tissue until a considerable part of ·the pulp may be involved.

LYMPHADENOMA OF THE SPLEEN.

(*Hodgkin's Disease.*)

290. In Lymphadenoma there is great enlargement and induration of the lymphatic glands, but there is no great increase in the number of white corpuscles found in the blood.

Naked eye appearances.—The spleen is usually enlarged, seldom to the same extent as in leucocythemia, though in some cases

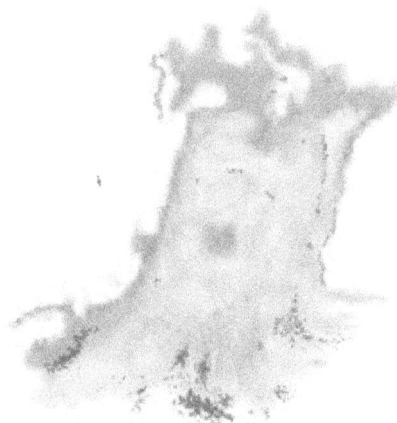

FIG. 120.—Drawing of thickened adenoid sheath in lymphadenoma of spleen. Section stained with picro-carmine. (× 60.)
f.t. Fibrous Malpighian corpuscle.
p. Pigment near the margin of a Malpighian corpuscle.
s.p. Pulp tissue of spleen as yet unencroached upon.
s.p.[1] Mass of pulp involved by growth of fibrous tissue.

it is stated to have weighed from fifty to eighty ounces, or even more.

As in leucocythemia, the increase in size takes place symmetrically; the notches on the anterior border remain well marked; the outer surface is dark in colour, and over the dark surface there are frequently numerous darker purple spots; the tissue is firm and tough, and in many cases feels quite fleshy, or even fibrous.

On section, the appearance is very characteristic. The general surface has a deep red colour, but scattered over it are numerous small, angular, translucent, yellow masses, almost like small masses of suet. Some of these are rounded, but others are elongated and branching. There may also be large tumour-like masses of adenoid tissue. These, like the first-mentioned, are simply altered adenoid sheaths or Malpighian corpuscles.

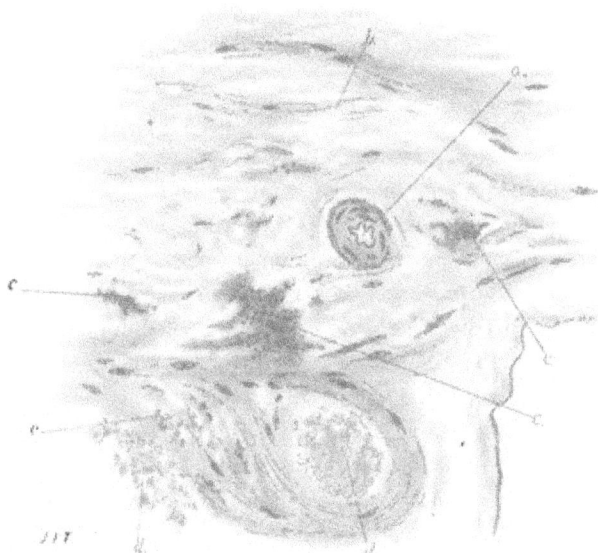

FIG. 121.—Drawing of section of lymphadenomatous spleen. Stained with picro-carmine. (× 250.)

The drawing is taken from the margin of one of the fibroid Malpighian corpuscles.

   a. Small arteriole with walls considerably thickened.
   b. Well-formed fibrous tissue.
   c. Pigmented masses—derived from endothelial and other cells containing coloured blood corpuscles in various stages of alteration.
   d. Cells contained within sinuses in process of being cut off by the encroaching fibrous growth.

Harden (§ 57), mount a section unstained (§ 152), and stain one (§ 98).

(× 50).—All the fibrous trabeculæ are increased in size and thickness. They take on the pink stain very readily, and evidently contain more fibrous tissue than normal.

The Malpighian corpuscles appear to participate in this fibrous change. They are much enlarged, are firm, solid, and fibrous, and the lymphoid cells are comparatively few in number. A few larger cells, some containing several nuclei, may be seen arranged in rows between the bundles of fibrous tissue. These (better seen × 300) are not the lymphoid cells, but are endothelioid plates, or growing connective tissue cells. At the margin of the fibroid Malpighian corpuscle there is usually a large deposit of golden-brown pigment, very characteristic of this disease. The pulp tissue is considerably altered, and looks much more solid, especially near the fibroid masses. Away from these the trabeculæ of the pulp are thicker, the endothelial cells are larger, and frequently contain granules of altered blood pigment.

(× 300).—Observe carefully the fibroid Malpighian corpuscles. The lymphoid cells are few in number, and appear atrophied and angular. The spaces between the bands of fibrous tissue are very small indeed, but in them are multinucleated endothelioid cells, which are evidently the cells by which the large mass of fibrillated periplast is formed. The pigment is usually contained in well-defined spaces (pulp sinuses), and is derived from altered blood corpuscles. Fig. 121 illustrates the process by which it comes to be situated in the fibrous mass. The fibrous tissue grows in all directions around the adenoid sheath, and processes are sent out between the sinuses, which, with their contained blood corpuscles and endothelial cells, are gradually surrounded. The contained blood corpuscles are disintegrated, probably by the endothelial cells, and the blood pigment is set free. The various transition stages are not well represented in the drawing. In the pulp the thickening of the trabeculæ and the proliferation of the large endothelioid cells are easily distinguished ; but there is no cramming of the pulp sinuses with leucocytes, as there is in leucocythemia.

TUBERCLE OF THE SPLEEN.

291. Tubercle is seldom or never found in the spleen as a primary growth. It occurs in two forms, either (1) miliary tubercle, or (2) larger caseous masses.

(1) The first form is met with in acute general tuberculosis as minute grey, gelatinous, prominent, shot-like bodies in the capsule of

the spleen, or near the surface of the organ ; a minute yellowish point in the centre of this small mass usually indicates the commencement of caseation. It is a local manifestation of a general disease, and hence is of comparatively little importance.

Harden (§ **57** or **59**) and stain (§ **98** or **103** *d*).

The microscopic appearances are much the same as in miliary tuberculosis of the liver, but it should be noted that here there is frequently well-marked congestion.

(2) The second and more chronic form is the more typical, especially in children. The spleen may be either enlarged or diminished in size. On section, the pulp is usually red and congested, whilst scattered over the surface are bodies which can scarcely be distinguished from the suet-like masses seen in lymphadenoma ; as a rule, however, they are yellower and more caseous looking, and are about the size of a small pea. The organ in this condition is, like the lymphadenomatous spleen, frequently spoken of as a " hardbake " spleen.

Prepare as above, and note that the appearances are simply those of caseous, or, in rare cases, fibroid tubercle (§ **277**).

Other growths mentioned as occurring in this organ are *secondary cancers* and *sarcomas, syphilitic gummata, hydatid cysts, dermoid cysts* (very rarely), *simple serous* or *mucous cysts*, and one case of *Pentastoma denticulatum* within a calcified cyst.

CHAPTER X.

THE ALIMENTARY CANAL.

292. In the examination of the first part of the alimentary tract for pathological changes, it should be remembered that the epithelium in the oral cavity, in the lower part of the pharynx, and in the œsophagus, is of the pavement, stratified type, which differs only from that on the cutaneous surface in the fact that it is more delicate and has little or no horny layer. In the upper part of the pharynx, however, the epithelium is columnar and ciliated, and extends down into the folds or depressions in the mucosa. The mucosa differs somewhat in thickness in different parts of the tract, but throughout it has the same structure. It consists of dense connective tissue, from which are upward prolongations, forming papillæ, on which the deeper cells of the epithelial layer rest. It is intersected or channelled by a dense network of lymphatics and lymph spaces. The mucosa is continued into the submucosa (except in the œsophagus, where it is separated by a few delicate bundles of non-striped muscle cells), which is composed of a looser and more lamellar connective tissue, and "contains masses of fat cells, the large branches of vessels and nerves, the glands, and striped muscle, and, extending outwards, forms a continuity with the connective tissue of the surrounding organs as muscle, periosteum, skin, &c." (Klein and Noble Smith). The large mucous glands, imbedded in this submucosa, are identical in structure (compound tubular glands) throughout, varying only in number and size in the different regions of the first part of the tract ; they are largest and most numerous in the mouth, and least numerous in the œsophagus.

As on the cutaneous surface, these structures are affected, in inflammation, according to the intensity of the process; there may be simply a transient redness, or there may be such marked vascular and interstitial changes that removal of epithelium or sloughing of the deeper tissues may ensue.

THE APHTHOUS PATCHES WHICH OCCUR DURING THE COURSE OF TEETHING AND A VARIETY OF INFLAMMATORY DISEASES.

293. These are most frequently met with on the inner surface of the lips, on the gums, tongue, and soft palate in children.

Naked eye appearances.—They vary in size from a pin-head to a small wafer, and are white or yellowish-grey, dull and opaque; the mucous membrane around them is injected, red, or sometimes purple, and has a peculiar glistening, semi-transparent appearance. Several of the smaller patches may coalesce to form larger ones.

The peculiarity in this condition is, that although the white patches may be separated from the subjacent tissues, there is seldom any well-marked ulceration. The reason of this will be apparent when the microscopic examination is made.

Harden (§ 57 or 64), cut sections at right angles to the surface, and stain (§§ 98 and 103 *d* or 105).

(× 50). — The changes are almost entirely confined to the epithelial layer. There is undoubtedly congestion of the small vessels of the mucosa, accompanied by an exudation of leucocytes, some swelling of the connective tissue, and even infiltration of the superficial layers of connective tissue fibrils with fibrin; but the most prominent changes are swelling of the epithelial cells, and exudation of fibrinous lymph and leucocytes, first between the epithelial layer and the mucosa, and then between the individual epithelial cells. The swollen epithelial cells, with the fibrinous exudation beneath and around them, form the opaque aphthous patch; the epithelium is regenerated very rapidly.

(× 300).—Note the slight swelling of the connective tissue of the mucosa and the increased number of leucocytes around the distended vessels. In the patch the fibrinous lymph, in which are frequently numerous leucocytes beneath and between the swollen epithelial cells, is considerably increased in amount.

There are changes in the epithelial cells, in addition to the mere increase in size; some of them are vacuolated, the nucleus then being placed at one side of the vacuole, whilst others, especially those in the immediate neighbourhood of the patch, are undergoing rapid proliferation, as is evidenced by the large number of cells in which two nuclei are seen, or in which division of the nucleus has begun.

Mucous Patches.

. **294.** Mucous patches, due to infiltration and proliferation of the epidermis and true skin beneath, are met with in cases of syphilis, and may be taken as fairly representative of a more extensive inflammatory process. They are usually found at the angles of the mouth, on the tips and side of the tongue, and frequently on the tonsils; but they may be seen on almost any part of the mouth, or near any of the orifices of the body where the skin is kept moist and in folds.

Naked eye appearances.—They are small, flattened, opaque, white patches, with a peculiar, moist, silvery grey or glistening surface. On passing the finger over one, it is found to be slightly indurated, or, if of long standing, the induration is well marked, and the thickening very distinct. The formation of the patch may be followed by ulceration, beginning at the centre (in the tonsil this, according to Cornil and Ranvier, is comparatively rare).

Harden and stain as for the aphthous patch (§ 293).

(× 50).—The appearances presented are somewhat similar to those seen in the aphthous patch, but the changes are more extensive. Near the margin, the horny epithelial layer extends for some distance only over the patch, and even where it is present the squames are swollen and are separated by leucocytes and small masses of fibrin. Nearer the centre there is enormous swelling of the polygonal cells of the rete Malpighii, some of which are rapidly breaking down; whilst around these cells, or infiltrating the spaces between them, is an exudation of fibrin, stained red with eosin, and leucocytes, stained violet with logwood. Near the surface the fibrin appears to predominate, whilst in the deeper layers the leucocytes are in excess. At the margins of the patch, and near the mucosa, the epithelium is in a state of rapid proliferation, giving rise to part of the thickening seen with the naked eye. In the mucosa, and in some cases even in the submucosa, the distention of the vessels is well marked. Around the vessels the accumulation of small round cells may be very great; there is also considerable swelling of the connective tissue, and at the same time an accumulation of fibrinous lymph between the swollen fibres, in the lymphatic vessels and lymph spaces. This affection of the deeper tissues is here extremely well marked, and in this respect the microscopic appearances differ from those presented in the aphthous patch.

(× 300).—Confirm the above appearances.

DIPHTHERIA OF THE PHARYNX.

295. In diphtheria there is exudation of a false membrane on to the mucous membrane of the upper part of the pharynx, palatal arches, tonsils, and especially on the posterior surface of the soft palate or uvula. The last-named is one of the best positions in which to examine it. The appearances vary according to the date of the disease at which the patient succumbs. If there are simply swollen greyish patches scattered over a dull red background, the epithelium is usually still present, though very much altered.

Harden a piece of the uvula with the membrane on its posterior surface (§ 56), and stain (§ 106).

(× 300).—On the surface of a section, and extending for some distance into the tissues, are masses of micrococci, which take on the methylaniline staining very deeply. The epithelium forms merely a heavy network, of which the margins of the cells apparently form the meshes. Beneath this altered epithelial layer the connective tissue is infiltrated with fibrin and leucocytes, most of which are accumulated around the distended blood-vessels. Around these distended vessels hæmorrhages are frequently seen, but there are as yet few masses of micrococci in the lymphatics and in the deeper tissues generally, and the cell infiltration is confined to the tissues immediately beneath the epithelium at the point of infection.

At a later stage, when the false membrane has formed, and perhaps has sloughed, leaving a grey, sodden, sloughy, and infiltrated looking surface, examine a piece of the tissue prepared as above.

(× 450).—The connective tissue of the mucosa is transformed into a mass of fattily degenerated or homogeneous material, which is very characteristic of the diphtheritic condition. A fibrinous exudation, in which the masses of micrococci and bacilli are situated, make up the false membrane on the surface. The blood-vessels are distended, and are surrounded by a number of round cells or leucocytes. This accumulation of cells takes place especially at the point of junction between the mucosa and the deeper tissues. The lymphatics for some distance round are choked with fibrin in which are imbedded a few leucocytes, or more frequently they are filled with masses of bacilli and micrococci, which also may be found in any part of the slough.

The grey sloughy part is usually teeming with masses of deeply stained micrococci, but there is now no trace of epithelial structure left. In addition to micrococci, in fact occurring almost invariably in the early stages in cases of true diphtheria, are groups of short, straight, or curved rods 3 to 6 μ in length, with ends sometimes pointed, sometimes rounded and thickened. They often contain small glistening points in their substance. These have been described as spores, but they consist merely of altered protoplasm. Where the disease is more advanced, the rods do not stain so equally, many pear-shaped and club-shaped bacilli are present, and in some very old membranes it is difficult or impossible to distinguish any characteristic rod-shaped bacilli, the micrococci and other micro-organisms becoming more numerous, especially as the surface becomes fœtid and softened. In such cases the rod-shaped bacilli can only be found entangled in the deeper network.

The distinctive characteristics between this condition and the so-called croup are :—that in diphtheria the specific micro-organisms and the slough are almost invariably present, but the marked fibrinous exudation, though usually present, is not essential ; whilst in croup the exudation is essential, and any micro-organisms that may be present are found only on the surface, do not invade the membrane or the surrounding lymphatics, and so do not get into the system to give rise to constitutional symptoms ; of these micro-organisms the "specific" Klebs Loeffler bacillus is said never to be one.

Diagnosis of Diphtheria during Life.

296. In the diagnosis of diphtheria during life, the following methods of staining and cultivation are employed. Remove a portion of the membrane from the patient; to do this tie a piece of cotton wool firmly to a pair of forceps or to a penholder, and with this scrape off a small fragment from one of the grey patches. Remove this with a bit of blotting paper and place it between two cover glasses, where it is broken down as finely as possible; the cover glasses are then separated and heated over a flame in the ordinary fashion (§ 128), and stained with Kühne's or Loeffler's methyl blue (§§ 131 and 133), or with Roux and Yersin's stain, composed of equal parts of aqueous solutions of violet dahlia and methyl green with water added until a clear but not too deep blue is obtained. A drop of the staining fluid is placed on the slide, the cover glass on which the fragments are dried is inverted and lowered on to it, the superfluous fluid is then removed with a piece of blotting paper.

Stain another fragment of the membrane, freshly teased out, with picro-carmine (§ 98).

Roux and Yersin make diagnostic cultures as follows:—with a platinum needle beaten out at the end to form a kind of spatula, they detach a particle of the false membrane, and then make stroke cultures on the surface of tubes of prepared blood serum made according to the following formula:—

Blood serum,	3 parts.
Neutralised broth,	1 part.
Peptone,	1 per cent.
Common salt,	5 per cent.

The same needle is used without being recharged to inoculate some half-dozen tubes. When these are incubated at from 33° to 35° C., colonies of bacilli are visible at the end of twenty hours, and within forty-eight hours they appear as small rounded greyish-white points, the centre of each of which is more opaque than the periphery, they spread rapidly, form greyish rounded discs, and continue to develop so quickly that they are usually well formed before the other organisms have begun to form a colony at all visible to the naked eye.

THE STOMACH.

297. *Normal Histology.*—The wall of the stomach, like that of the œsophagus, is composed of mucous, submucous, muscular, and peritoneal coats. Here, as in the small and large intestine, the secreting glands are confined to the mucosa, the epithelium covering this layer and lining the various gland ducts of the stomach is distinctly columnar; it rests upon a basement membrane composed of flattened endothelioid cells. At the cardiac end the simple peptic glands are straight or slightly curved tubular glands lined with columnar cells, with here and there at the outer margin large spherical or angular cells. At the pyloric end the glands are larger and more complicated, each dividing into several wavy and convoluted tubes; they are lined with the regular columnar epithelial cells, and have none of the large spherical or angular cells near the basement membrane. Supporting the gland tubes is a delicate mucosa similar to that described in the œsophagus, and beneath or in this is a *muscularis mucosæ* separating it from the submucosa. The submucous tissue consists of a delicate supporting connective tissue which rests upon the non-striped muscular wall of the stomach, which has both inner, circular, and outer longitudinal layers. Covering the stomach is a fold of peritoneum, which is similar in structure to that covering the organs already described,—the liver for example. A most interesting fact in connection with the vascular supply of the walls of the stomach is put prominently forward by Cornil and Ranvier,[1] who state that the arteries which supply the mucous membrane "all enter by the peritoneal surface, and ramify in the successive layers of the stomach, so that the zone of distribution of each arteriole in the mucous layer forms a cone, the apex of which reaches the submucous tissue, and the base the surface of the mucous membrane of the stomach."

---

[1] "Manual of Pathological Histology," by Cornil and Ranvier. English translation by A. M. Hart, vol. ii. pt. i.

Inflammation of the Mucous Membrane.

298. The stomach is one of the least satisfactory organs with which the pathologist has to deal. *Post-mortem* changes take place in it so rapidly that any pathological processes of recent date are at once masked, and even those of longer standing are considerably altered. It is, therefore, impossible to give an exact and non-arbitrary account of either the naked eye or microscopic appearances in many diseased conditions.

In acute inflammations of the stomach—in acute catarrhal gastritis, for instance—it is an extremely difficult matter to determine how far the appearances presented are induced by the inflammatory condition, and how far they are due to *post-mortem* changes. Even in a healthy stomach, the epithelium has almost entirely disappeared, being digested by the gastric juice, by the time a *post-mortem* examination can be made, so that in acute gastritis, beyond the changes usually taking place in acute inflammations, little is to be observed. As one would expect, however, the secretion of mucus is greatly increased, and the swollen and dark-red mucous membrane is covered with a layer of mucus, with, here and there, small extravasations of blood.

(× 300).—Distention of the blood-vessels, often accompanied by small hæmorrhages, extravasation of leucocytes, and swelling and proliferation of the endothelial cells of the lymphatics, are the most noticeable points, epithelial changes as a rule being indistinguishable for the reason above given ; but, where they can be made out, the epithelial cells contain large globules of mucin, are desquamating or undergoing disintegrative changes, whilst the epithelial cells of the peptic glands are usually granular and often detached.

Chronic changes, where there is an atrophied condition of some structures, or where there is a new formation of fibro-cellular tissue, are more readily identified.

'Common," "Chronic," "Circular," "Perforating," or "Simple" Ulcer of the Stomach.

299. This ulcer is usually single, though from two to four sometimes occur. It is situated in most cases on the posterior wall,

or on the lesser curvature near the pyloric end, and sometimes in the
duodenum, and measures from one-half to two-thirds of an inch in
diameter.

The *naked eye appearances* are very characteristic. The edges are
seldom much injected or raised from the surrounding tissue, the
margins are quite vertical, and the floor is smooth, pale, dry, and
fibrous. It is rounded or oval in shape, and the formation gives one
the idea that it might have been punched out with a wad-punch.
The depth varies greatly in different cases. In some instances the
mucous membrane only is involved. The punched-out appearance
is in such cases very well marked. If the ulcer extends deeper, so
as to eat through the muscular coat, there is a peculiar terraced
appearance, as though a smaller punch had been used for the deeper
layer, and a somewhat funnel-shaped opening, corresponding in
shape to the conical distribution of the artery already mentioned, is
the result. In some cases the acute ulcerative process has ceased, but
the ulcer has not healed, and slight thickening of the surrounding
tissues has resulted. When these ulcers perforate, it may be only
by an exceedingly small hole, they may open into the pancreas,
liver, or spleen; or into the peritoneal cavity,—when abscesses or
peritonitis usually result,—or into some of the surrounding blood-
vessels, such as the coronary arteries or the large splenic vessels.
Adhesions and fistulous openings may also occur into the duodenum,
transverse colon, or the pleural or pericardial sacs. Even after
perforation the ulcers may heal, and healing may take place so
perfectly that, except on very careful examination, no scar can be
distinguished. This is especially the case where, though the ulceration has been acute, the destructive process has not been extensive.
Where the loss of tissue has been great, the contraction of the new
cicatricial tissue formed during the process of healing gives rise to a
puckered or radiate scar. It is generally agreed that the cause of the
solution of continuity is the cutting off of the blood supply from a
certain area, which, deprived of its nutrition, is acted upon by
the gastric fluids and softened. That the process is acute is also
agreed, but there is some difference of opinion as to the cause of
obstruction to the flow of blood. Spasm of the vessels, atheroma
and thrombosis and embolism—each has its advocates; but it

appears probable that any of these may be the cause of the cutting off of the blood supply, and that the digestive action is then allowed to go on in the patch of tissue originally supplied by the obstructed vessel.

Several cicatrices may occur together, especially in the middle of the stomach, when by their contraction they give rise to what is known as the hour-glass stomach.

Harden such a thickened ulcer (§§ **53** *a* and **57**), and stain (§ **98** or **103**).

(× 50 and × 300).—Around the ulcer, in its immediate neighbourhood, there is little increase in the number of small deeply-stained cells, either in the mucosa or submucosa, and the glands are little altered, except that they stand out more prominently than in the normal condition. Further changes, such as thickening of the walls of the vessels near the ulcer and diminution of their calibre ; and where the muscular coat is invaded, fatty degeneration and fraying out of the muscular fibres are described (Cornil and Ranvier).

Post-mortem Digestion of the Wall of the Stomach.

300. We have already seen that in gastric ulcer, when the blood supply is cut off from any part, such part is rapidly digested. It has also been observed that in certain diseases, especially in inflammatory diseases of the brain, and where the process of digestion is going on vigorously from the large quantity of acid gastric juice present, the whole mucous wall may be partially digested. Far more commonly we find, however, that digestion is continued after death, especially when the stomach " contains an excess of gastric juice, or of acid products of decomposition "—(Ziegler). In such cases the colouring matter is dissolved out from the red blood corpuscles, the various coats become softened, and are readily broken down. There is never any thickening or redness of the parts where the softening is taking place, in fact there are no signs of inflammation of any kind. Where perforation has taken place the margins of the opening are ragged, friable, and pale or dark grey according to the amount of blood that has been in the parts before death. This condition is perhaps best seen in children in whose stomachs much undigested food is left. I have seen it well marked in two cases examined on one day, and in warm weather as many as four out of five cases have given some evidence of this condition.

THE SMALL AND LARGE INTESTINE.

301. *Normal Histology.*—In the wall of the small intestine the coats are the same as those of the stomach, but there are one or two differences which must be noted. The mucosa is thrown into a series of crescentic folds, which form valve-like projections along the course of the tube. These, the *valvulæ conniventes*, have essentially the same structure as the rest of the mucosa. Over the whole surface are small rounded finger-like projections or villi, in the centre of each of which are large lymphatic spaces or chyle vessels, surrounded by longitudinal muscular fibres and a loop of capillary blood-vessels. Between and at the bases of the villi are simple gland tubes, known as the crypts of Lieberkühn. Extending over the whole mucous surface, covering the villi and lining the crypts, is a layer of columnar epithelium, with here and there a few goblet or mucous secreting cells. The base ment membrane, composed of endothelioid cells, separates the epithelial cells from the connective tissue of the mucosa. The *muscularis mucosæ* is here an important structure, but is similar to that of the stomach, and the submucosa, the internal circular muscular fibres, the external longitudinal fibres, and the peritoneal covering have all their homologues in the stomach. The Bruner's glands (compound racemose glands) are imbedded in the submucous tissue of the duodenum, whilst the lymph follicles, in the form of solitary glands and Peyer's patches, are contained partly in the submucous coat and partly in the mucosa. These glandular masses are simply single masses of adenoid tissue, or collections of the single glands. The solitary glands have the structure of ordinary lymphatic glands, having a trabecular framework and the adenoid tissue proper; these are composed of a delicate fibrillar and membranous reticulum, on the strands of which rest flattened endothelioid cells, and between which are the lymph corpuscles. Covering these masses of adenoid tissue is a layer of cubical epithelial cells.

The Peyer's patches are elliptical, run in the longitudinal axis of the intestine, project slightly above the general surface, and are composed of numerous solitary glands. They are found on the side of the intestine away from the mesenteric attachment, and are most numerous at the lower part of the ileum.

In the large intestine there are no villi and no Peyer's patches, but the solitary glands are larger than in the small intestine.

TYPHOID LESION OF THE INTESTINE, LEADING TO THE FORMATION OF THE TYPHOID ULCER.

302. In this condition there is first marked swelling of the elements of the adenoid tissue of the intestine—the solitary glands, and the Peyer's patches. The disease is therefore most marked in those positions where the glands are most numerous—at the lower end of the ileum. It may spread upwards and, though rarely, downwards; in the earlier stages—during the first week—there is a progressive swelling of the solitary glands, which at first are pink and semi-transparent, soft and pulpy in appearance and to the touch; later they become paler and firmer. All the Peyer's patches at the lower part of the intestine become involved throughout their whole extent, as do also the solitary glands. These patches are sharply raised, "and winding ridges not unlike the cerebral convolutions in miniature" (Ziegler), appear on their surface, especially where the mucous membrane is swollen and somewhat paler than the surrounding tissue. In the earlier stages the patches are very vascular, and small hæmorrhages may appear on the deeply congested surface. The mucous membrane near the swollen patch, owing to infiltration of the mucosa, distension of Lieberkühn's follicles, and obliteration of the villi, is smooth. The gland is swollen, and projects into the lumen of the intestine, pushing before it the epithelial layer of the mucous membrane. The swelling is composed of round or lymph cells, which also, to some extent, infiltrate the surrounding mucous and muscular tissue.

If a small portion of the swollen gland be teased out, a number of much larger multinucleated cells, derived from the endothelioid cells lying on the retiform tissue of the gland tissue, are brought into

2 E

view. Rod-shaped bacilli are present during this stage of the process, both in the adenoid tissue of the mucous membrane and in the mesenteric glands. To see these, take fresh scrapings or sections, rinse in a one per cent. solution of corrosive sublimate, stain with gentian violet (§§ 131, 132, 133, or 134), and mount (§ 152 or 155).

When the swollen patches have become very tense and pale, the stage of sloughing sets in. The slough involves the mucous, and usually also the submucous tissue. It is invariably bile-stained, and very frequently blood-stained, from rupture of some of the small blood-vessels in the muscular coat. It comes away in fragments;

Fig. 122.—Diagram to represent the various stages of the typhoid lesion in Peyer's patches. (After Thierfelder.)
 a. Section through the patch in the early or swollen stage.
 b. Stage at which a line of demarcation is forming between the slough and the subjacent tissue.
 c. Ulcer from which the slough has separated. The walls of the ulcer are vascular and infiltrated.

but if violence of any kind is used, the slough dragged away from the softened tissues beneath may cause their laceration, and so bring about perforation of the intestine. Notice that, although all the glands and patches are swollen, comparatively few are ulcerated; and even these latter may not slough throughout their whole extent. In the Peyer's patch, for instance, the ulcer may involve the central width of the patch, but may extend for some distance on each side, as one would be led to expect from the infiltration of the neighbouring tissues. On the other hand, the ulcer very frequently has the shape of the Peyer's patch, or of the solitary gland, as the case may be. Where the whole of the patch is involved, the ulcer is oval, and its long axis corresponds to that

FIG. 123.—Section of typhoid ulcer of intestine—ileum, specially stained with gentian violet (§ 302). (× 450.)

a. Gland tubules.
b. Groups of typhoid bacilli.
c. Single bacilli. (These are represented rather longer and not quite so rounded at the ends as they appeared in the specimen.)
d. Small lymphoid cells in reticulum.
e. Large endothelioid cells.

of the bowel. The floor, which is usually composed of the circular muscular coat of the intestine and of granulation tissue, is smooth, injected, and glossy, but there is comparatively little thickening. The margins are ragged, much undermined, and can be readily floated out in water. They are made up of the mucous membrane and submucous tissue, though where the ulceration has extended through the circular muscular coat, the longitudinal fibres may form the floor of the ulcer, and the free ends of the circular fibres may then form part of the overhanging margins. The peritoneum is seldom much thickened.

The ulcer may heal without leaving a marked cicatrix, the edges simply falling down and uniting with the floor; there is no new formation of glandular tissue, the epithelium grows over from the margins, and a smooth, greyish, very characteristic patch is left. On the other hand, perforation may result from extension of the ulcerative process, and is usually accompanied by hæmorrhage.

Harden (§§ 55 *a* and 56), stain (§ 98, or as above).

(× 50).—Note the shape of the ulcer, the overhanging margins, with the follicles and papillæ of the mucosa on the upper surface. In all the tissues bounding this ulcer—the overhanging walls, and the smooth muscular floor—there is evidently a considerable amount of small cell infiltration extending throughout the mucosa, and giving rise to the swelling between the villi, which are partially obliterated.

(× 450).—Confirm the above. Note also that in the swollen adenoid tissue, solitary or small groups of bacilli may be seen lying in the lymph spaces, and sometimes, though rarely, in the substance of the large endothelioid cells.

The mesenteric glands and the adenoid or Malpighian corpuscles of the spleen must also be examined for similar congestion, for infiltration with round cells and multinucleated endothelioid cells, and, in specially stained sections, for the specific bacilli.

TUBERCULAR ULCER OF THE INTESTINE.

303. Tubercular ulcers are found especially in connection with the solitary glands and Peyer's patches, but they are not confined to these positions. They occur most frequently at the lower end of the ileum, but may extend above this point, and down below the ileo-cœcal valve, sometimes as far as the rectum. In its most common form the tubercular ulcer is met with in very nearly half the cases that succumb to chronic phthisis.

Naked eye appearances.—The first evidence of the process is the appearance of small greyish or yellowish points in the substance of the glands, or in the submucous tissue. These rapidly undergo softening, the mucous membrane covering them sloughs away, the caseous material is evacuated, and a small deep ulcer, with thickened and overhanging edges, remains. In the infiltrated area are numerous caseous tubercular nodules, which give the thickened edge a nodulated appearance. There is usually no great undermining of the edges, as in typhoid ulcer, and in the smaller ulcers they may even be terraced. The floor and edges are pale in the majority of cases, but there may be slight injection extending from the floor, which is then somewhat vascular. The floor is roughened and nodulated, the nodules being most frequently tinged with yellow, from caseation or bile staining, or both. Several ulcers may be found situated close together, separated only by strips of thickened mucous membrane. They extend laterally until they merge into one another, and a large ulcer is formed, which again spreads in a similar way. In consequence of this method of formation, the large ulcer "presents a sinuous or scalloped outline."—(Bristowe.) Though the ulcer usually runs transversely, and may spread so as to encircle the intestine, it may run in the direction of the long axis of the bowel.

On the serous surface note the following appearances. Immediately under the ulcer, or in its floor, are numerous firm grey or yellowish rounded bodies, which are evidently situated in the subserous lymphatics. Radiating from this point—the floor of the ulcer—are similar lines of tubercle nodules, forming a many-rayed star. There is considerable thickening of the floor of the ulcer beneath the serous surface, and in this the nodules may be felt as hard shot-like bodies. The ulceration usually extends through the mucosa and submucosa, the muscular tissue then forming the floor. Eventually the muscular tissue may also be involved.

In consequence of this progressive thickening, perforation very seldom occurs ; in some cases there may even be cicatrisation of the ulcer. Where there is great loss of substance the contraction is very great, and a stellate puckered scar results, the puckering being especially well seen on the serous surface. Where the loss of substance has been very extensive, the cicatrisation may cause considerable narrowing of the bowel.

Harden (§§ 55 *a* and 56), and stain (§ 98 or 140).

(× 50).—At the point where the ulcer is situated there is a particularly noticeable increase in the thickness of the submucosa. The edges of the ulcer are covered with mucous membrane up to their margin, but this mucous membrane is markedly infiltrated, so that the villi, which are packed with small round cells, stand out

Fig. 124.—Section of tubercular ulcer of the intestine—ileum, stained with picro-carmine. (× 30.)

m.c. Mucosa, which at points *u.u.* has given way.
v. Villi, infiltrated and enlarged.
m.m.c. Slightly altered muscularis mucosæ.
s.m.c. Submucosa, in which (*t*) the tubercle follicles are present. In this layer too (*g*) the blood-vessels are considerably dilated.
r.m. Circular muscular fibre at *r.m*[1] swollen and enlarged, and degenerating.
u[1]. Tubercle follicles situated in this layer.
l.m. Longitudinal muscular fibres.
s. Thickened and vascular serous coat.

very prominently ; beneath the layer in which the crypts are found there is a very great amount of round-celled infiltration, scattered through which are tubercle nodules composed of one or more tubercle follicles. Some of these tubercle follicles are beginning to caseate in the centre ; others are well formed, and show the regular giant cell system, with its reticular framework and endothelioid and small cells. The floor of the ulcer is rough and nodular, owing to the presence of similar nodules, which in some cases extend into the muscular coat, and also for some distance laterally.

(× 450).—Confirm the above appearances; also try' to find tubercle bacilli in the giant cells and near the caseating areas.

The mesenteric glands are also usually affected, the tubercle follicles growing in the cortex. They become enlarged and then caseate.

Typhoid Ulcer.	Tubercular Ulcer.
1. Direction often longitudinal.	1. Direction transverse (frequently). This distinction is not so characteristic as is sometimes held.
2. Edges undermined, ragged, and can be floated out on water; thin, vascular, and composed of mucosa and submucosa—red.	2. Edges not undermined; thick, prominent, nodulated, terraced, or sloping — pale or red, composed of tissue infiltrated with tubercular nodules.
3. Floor smooth and vascular.	3. Floor nodular, thickened, irregular, vascular, with pale or yellow points or areas.
4. Peritoneal surface unaltered, except that it may be inflamed. No thickening and no grey or yellow patches.	4. Peritoneum thickened — small yellow or grey points in the floor of the ulcer running along the lines of the lymphatics.
5. Mesentery unaltered; glands enlarged, vascular, pink, and softened.	5. Mesentery thickened at its attachment to the bowel; glands enlarged, firm and gelatinous · on section, or caseous.
6. Perforation more common, both by separation of slough and by direct extension of the ulcerative process. Small opening by which fæces may escape. Peritonitis. Hæmorrhage may occur during either of these processes.	6. Perforation, peritonitis, and hæmorrhage, all rare.
7. Microscopically: A specific inflammation affecting the adenoid tissue; blood-vessels distended, and increased vascularity of the mucosa and submucosa. Dense masses of small round cells—lymphoid cells and leucocytes—with some large multinucleated cells, the latter of which are derived directly from endothelioid cells. A line of demarcation is formed, and abscess results, beginning in the solitary glands and other lymphoid tissue of the mucosa and submucosa.	7. Microscopically: A specific inflammatory affection also of the adenoid tissue and the mucous membrane, ending in caseation and connective tissue formation; vascularity of mucosa and submucosa; increase of connective tissue cells and lymphoid cells; tubercle nodules typical or caseating. It begins in the mucous membrane, and, like the typhoid lesion, is due to direct contagion or infection.

8. Extension takes place laterally, or in depth.

8. Extension usually takes place laterally.

9. Heals by granulation, the thin edges falling on to and uniting with the granulating floor of the ulcer.

9. Very rarely heals.

10. Leaves a smooth, often depressed, pale, anæmic or pigmented cicatrix, covered by a layer of epithelium, but no gland tissue. Seldom breaks out afresh, relapse being due to the affection of adenoid patches previously little damaged.

10. Leaves a puckered cicatrix in which are grey or white nodules. Often breaks out afresh.

WAXY INTESTINE.

304. Waxy degeneration of the intestine very frequently occurs in general waxy disease. It gives rise to watery diarrhœa and exhaustion, to which the patient succumbs. The change is most frequently and first seen at the upper part of the ileum and the lower part of the jejunum, though the mucous membrane of the whole alimentary tract may be more or less affected.

Naked eye appearances.—The mucous membrane is pale, and has a peculiar smooth and glossy look, and a fine velvety feel. On pouring a watery solution of iodine (§ 107) over the surface, a number of dark mahogany brown points, corresponding to the vascular loops of the villi, make their appearance. Between these points the normal tissues are stained yellow by the iodine. In the large intestine the dark staining is more diffuse, owing to the absence of villi and the presence of a dense vascular plexus in the mucous membrane.

Harden (§§ 55 and 57); mount one section unstained (§ 152), and stain one (§ 106).

(× 50).—The waxy change is most marked in the capillary plexuses of the villi, the vessels of which have their walls swollen, hyaline, and stained red-violet by methylaniline violet. In consequence of this swelling of the wall, the lumen is considerably narrowed. Some of the larger and deeper vessels are also affected, especially in their middle coat. There are still a few blood corpuscles to be seen within them. The epithelium on the surface of the villi is often detached and granular, but seldom waxy. In some cases there is waxy degeneration of the delicate connective tissue fibrils between the bands of non-striped muscular fibre, leading in advanced cases to their atrophy; this may be readily recognised.

(× 300).—The evidences of waxy degeneration of the loops of vessels in the villi may be readily made out. The middle coats of both larger and smaller vessels are similarly affected. The waxy material may be observed between the bands of atrophied non-striped muscular fibre, which latter, however, are seldom or never waxy; the endothelium may be fatty, but never waxy. The epithelium on the surface of the villi, as already seen, is fatty, granular, and detached, but rarely waxy.

Dysentery (Tropical Form).

305. This disease affects primarily the large intestine, especially its lower part; but in some cases it occurs higher up, in the lower part of the ileum.

The first indication of the process is swelling, accompanied by redness, of the mucous membrane, on which accumulates a viscid or tenacious mucus, streaked with blood. The swollen mucous membrane is thrown into folds, along the ridges of which there is well marked vascularity. At this stage the solitary glands are firm and swollen, and here and there are small hæmorrhages. After a few days sloughs, which again occupy the ridges of the mucous membrane, are formed. These are blood-stained, bile-stained, or ashen grey and, on separating, they leave the submucosa bare, and very intractable ulcers result, which, if the patient lives, are evidence of the chronic form of the disease. Small ulcers are also found in the position of the solitary glands. These ulcers in the acute condition are deep, from the thickening of the surrounding mucous membrane, and around each is a zone of active congestion, and frequently, also, a number of small hæmorrhages. The contents of the intestine in this condition, consisting of mucus, altered blood, and shreds of sloughy tissue, emit a very foul odour. These shreds of sloughy tissue are found to be teeming with micrococci.

In still more acute forms the mucous membrane is deep red or livid, and may come away in the form of an almost complete cast of the bowel, usually accompanied by profuse hæmorrhage.

Harden (§ 56), and stain (§§ 98 and 106).

(× 50 and × 300).—There is first a very great amount of small round cell infiltration in the tissue around the Lieberkühn's follicles. There is similar infiltration of the solitary glands. Near the margins of the ulcers the infiltration is well marked, especially around the distended blood-vessels. Some of the solitary glands are breaking down, and in this way smaller ulcers are formed. The glands of Lieberkühn are elongated, and are alternately constricted and bulging, and the epithelium is frequently in process of being shed. Among the cells around the vessels are the elements of a coagulum —coagulated fibrin, and red and white blood corpuscles. Around an ulcer, both in its floor and at its margins, are numerous round cells, infiltrating the whole of the tissues, whilst large swollen endothelial cells are sometimes described as being present in the lymph vessels in the neighbourhood of the ulcer. In the methyl-aniline violet stained specimen, masses of micrococci are met with, still attached to the surface of the mucous membrane, especially where sloughing is beginning.

TUMOURS OF THE ALIMENTARY TRACT.

306. *Lipoma* is met with in the mucous membrane of the cheek and lips, in the œsophagus and stomach, and in the intestine.

Fibroma, in the tonsils and salivary glands, and in the other parts of the alimentary canal, affected by lipoma.

Myoma, in the œsophagus, stomach, and intestine.

None of the above three forms are common in the œsophagus ; they are more frequently seen in the stomach, but are comparatively rare in the mucous membrane of the intestine, where, however, they may form polypoid tumours.

Myxoma, in the form of mucous polypus, in the uvula and soft palate, in the nares and in the œsophagus. Myxomatous tumours also grow in the salivary glands, in which also *chondroma* frequently makes its appearance.

Lymphangioma is found in the tongue, and *Angioma* in the lips, tongue, and intestine.

Papilloma is rarely seen in the œsophagus, but is comparatively common in the stomach.

Simple adenoma usually occurs in such structures as the mucous glands, but it is also found in the intestine, especially in the rectum.

Ranula and other *cysts*, the result of distension of ducts or glands, —as, for example, of small mucous glands—occur in the mouth.

Of the malignant growths, various forms of *Sarcoma* grow from the jaws, in connection with either the periosteum or bone marrow ; in the salivary glands, and very rarely in the œsophagus, stomach, and intestine. *Lympho-sarcoma* is also found in the wall of the stomach.

Squamous epithelioma (primary) develops in the lips, tongue, and gums, very frequently in the œsophagus, especially in its lower two-thirds, and in the rectum near the anus.

Malignant adenoma or *adenoid cancer*, like the other cancers, is usually found at the pyloric end of the stomach. In the colon, where it frequently occurs, it specially affects the flexures.

Carcinoma may occur in the salivary glands and tonsils, but its most frequent positions are the stomach—the pyloric end—and the rectum. In both positions it is usually primary, and may be scirrhous, encephaloid, or colloid. It will be described in the section on "Tumours." In carcinoma of the stomach the tendency to softening and hæmorrhage must be specially borne in mind. Cancerous infiltration of the submucous tissue is frequently very clearly marked. In most cases of cancer of the pyloric orifice there is, naturally, as the result of irritation, catarrh of the stomach, with dilatation and hypertrophy of the muscular walls, owing to the obstruction of the pyloric orifice.

Mixed tumours specially affect the jaws and the salivary glands. The occurrence of *gummata* in the tongue and pharynx, and of *tubercle* in the tongue and tonsils, should be borne in mind.

For *parasites* of the alimentary canal, *see* section on Parasites.

PERITONEUM.

307. For structure and inflammation of the peritoneum, *see* § **163**.

TUBERCULOSIS OF THE PERITONEUM.

308. A non-caseating tubercular process is very frequently met with in the peritoneum in general tuberculosis of children. This is perhaps one of the best possible positions in which to examine young tubercle.

Hold a piece of the peritoneum up to the light, or lay it out on a dark background, and in it will be seen a number of minute white or cream-coloured points, very like those met with in tubercle of the pia mater. Spread out on cork, harden in Müller's fluid, diluted with water to one half the ordinary strength, and stain (§ 98).

(× 50).—Along the course of the small blood-vessels, at irregular

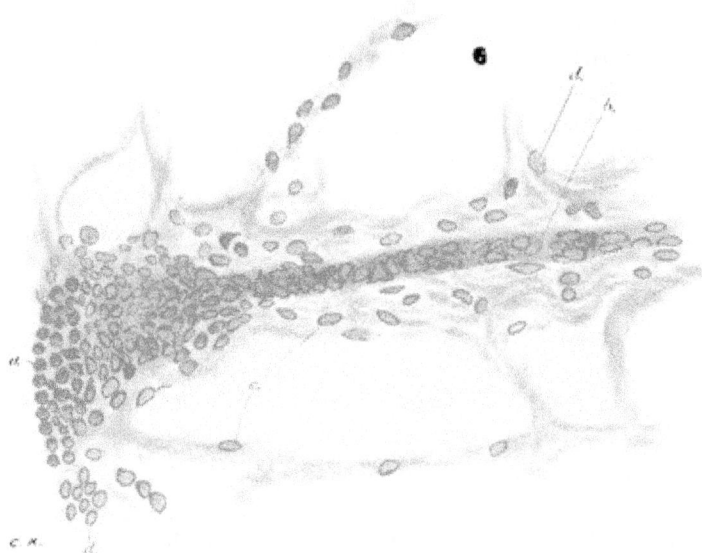

FIG. 125.—Early acute tubercle of the peritoneum, from a child. Stained with picro-carmine. (× 300.)

    a. Young tubercle growth. Endothelial cells growing within the peri-arterial sheath, and also on the peritoneal surface.
    b. Artery, along the course of which the proliferating endothelial cells may be seen.
    c. Fibrous trabeculæ.
    d. Proliferating endothelial cells lying on these trabeculæ.

intervals, are masses of cells which appear to be enclosed by a boundary line. The cells vary in size; some are small round cells, whilst others are endothelioid, and contain several nuclei. Along with these masses there are lines of cells which apparently still follow the course of the vessel, whilst at other points there appears to be proliferation of the endothelial cells on the trabeculæ.

(× 300).—It appears that the endothelioid cells in the perivascular lymphatic spaces are at certain points undergoing proliferation, and that this cell growth is really the early stage of tubercle formation, already described (§ **189**). There are no giant cells, properly so called, and the greater number of the changes take place at intervals along the line of the artery, but not of the vein.

309. Chronic tuberculosis of the peritoneum, characterised by matting together of the intestines, and puckering and thickening of the omentum, occurs very frequently in connection with tubercle of the intestine. The principal features of this condition are extremely slow growth, perfectly formed giant cell systems, and chronic peritonitis.

310. Waxy change in vessels may be readily studied in the peritoneum, as may also the vascular changes in septicæmia, anthrax, and similar conditions.

311. *Cancer*, especially the colloid form, and *sarcoma* both occur as secondary growths in the peritoneum.

CHAPTER XI.

BONE AND JOINTS.

STRUCTURE OF NORMAL BONE.

312. In order that the pathological changes in bone may be understood, it may be well to give a brief *resumé* of the appearances present in normal bone (*a*) in a cartilaginous basis, and (*b*) in connection with periosteum.

Naked eye appearances.—On vertical section through a normal developing bone, the radius, say, in which the epiphysis has not yet become continuous with the shaft, the end and the peripheral part are seen to consist of cancellated or spongy bone ; the former is invested on one side by articular cartilage, on the other by a narrow blue line of what is known as the intermediary cartilage. In very early or fœtal life this latter is much thickened, and is made up of two kinds of cartilage, hyaline—the remains of the fœtal epiphysis—and the intermediary cartilage proper, in which calcification is sometimes taking place. Beneath this comes the bone of the shaft.

Soften the bone (§ **75** or **76**) and stain (§ **98** or **107**).

The epiphysis is made up of spongy bone in which, on the homogeneous looking trabeculæ, lie numerous small nucleated cells—known as osteoblasts. Running through spaces left between the trabeculæ are blood-vessels, all of which are surrounded by small nucleated cells,—connective tissue cells, and leucocytes. When development has not gone far, these trabeculæ, in place of being homogeneous, are evidently bars of cartilage in which calcification is beginning ; as development becomes more complete, the bony matrix is gradually laid down on these trabeculæ and the cartilage disappears (by absorption). Beneath the bony trabeculæ of the epiphysis is (in the fœtus) a layer of hyaline cartilage, composed of a homogeneous matrix, in which the dividing cartilage cells, with their distinct capsules, may be readily seen. Then comes the intermediary cartilage, in which the matrix is distinctly calcified at its lower part, and the flattened cells have a very characteristic arrangement in longitudinal

FIG. 126.—Section of end of long bone taken from a three months' old fœtus, showing development of bone from cartilage. Stained with eosin and logwood. (× 50.) (H. A. Thomson.)

  a. Columns of cartilage cells at the end of the bone.
  b. Periosteum with its fibrous and cellular layers.
  c. Transition of cartilaginous into bony matrix. In this the cartilage cells are small and atrophied. Immediately above this the cartilage spaces open into spaces containing bloodvessels and osteoblasts.
  d. Bony trabeculæ.
  e. Vessels in spaces.
  f. Osteoblasts or bone forming corpuscles lining these spaces.
  g. Muscular tissue.

rows or columns. Near the surface these cells are comparatively small, but as we approach the developing bone of the shaft, they are much larger and usually cubical in shape. They are contained in spaces of considerable size, the lowest of which open into long marrow cavities, as the spaces between the bony trabeculæ are called.

In the bones of very young children the trabeculæ are composed of calcified cartilage; they are covered with osteoblasts, whilst here and there are large multinucleated cells—chondroclasts—similar in all respects to the absorbing giant cells or osteoclasts (to be

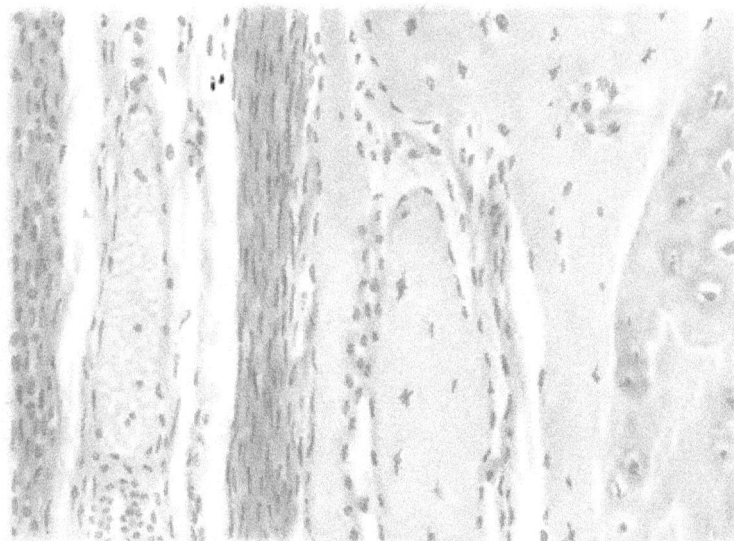

FIG. 127.—Section of periphery of long bone taken from a three months' old fœtus, showing development of bone from periosteum. Stained with eosin and logwood. (× 300.) (H. A. Thomson.)

a. Fibrous layer of periosteum.
b. Osteogenic layer of cells by which bone matrix is formed.
c. Blood-vessel in periosteum surrounded by leucocytes.
d. Outer fibrous (or muscular) layer.
e. Cells lining one of the marrow cavities in which a vessel runs.
f. Do. seen in transverse section.
g. Bone corpuscle not branched.
h. Branched bone corpuscle.

described immediately), and to the giant cells met with in myeloid sarcoma.

In the older bone, or further away from the cartilaginous surface, are regular osseous trabeculæ on which are arranged the small nucleated bone-forming osteoblasts, and the large multinucleated bone-absorbing osteoclasts. In the longitudinal marrow spaces are well-formed blood-vessels. Wherever there is a *cartilaginous* matrix, we have the same conversion of the cartilaginous trabeculæ; first they become calcified through a deposition of lime salts in the matrix and in the capsules of the cells, and then, laid down on these cartilaginous trabeculæ, and gradually taking their place, are regular bony layers covered with osteoblasts, which play an important part in the formation of the bone proper. Osteoclasts or giant cells, rest in the pits or lacunæ described by Howship, each of which appears to have been hollowed out by its own cell.

Around the bone is the periosteum which forms a vascular fibro-cellular sheath, a most important factor in the nutrition of the bone. Its outer layer is dense and fibrous, and contains but few cells, but within this is a bone-forming or osteogenetic layer which is composed of nucleated cells arranged in a *fibrous* matrix. The cells near the surface are rounded and comparatively small; near the centre they become much larger and often more or less spindle-shaped. In this region the fibrillated matrix becomes distinctly osseous, and there are marrow or Haversian spaces lined with osteoblasts; surrounding each Haversian space is a somewhat laminated bony tissue, with lacunæ containing branched bone corpuscles or modified osteoblasts.

The different modes of bone formation (in cartilage and periosteal) must be carefully borne in mind in the study of bone repair and of rickets. In both modes, whether in the periosteum or in the Haversian canals, the osteoblasts are associated with growth, they form a matrix which is ultimately converted into bone; the osteoclasts, on the other hand, play an important part in the removal of bone already formed. There is a continual bone formation, always accompanied by bone absorption.

REPAIR OF BONE.—CALLUS.

313. Callus is the new or cicatricial tissue that is formed to make good a fracture in a bone. Although met with every day by the surgeon in cases of simple fracture, it very rarely comes under the observation of the pathologist, unless produced experimentally upon the lower animals. The conditions under which experimentally

produced callus occurs differ very materially from those under which
it is formed in the human subject. Of these conditions the most
important is the impossibility of maintaining the fractured limb of an
a nimal in one position for any length of time. In consequence of
this, it is almost impossible to obtain accurate and permanent
apposition of the fractured ends of the bone ; the external, provisional, or supporting callus, *i.e.*, that produced around the bone,
forming a kind of natural splint, is formed in excess (owing to excessive irritation of the surrounding tissues), and it and the tissue
between the ends of the bone become cartilaginous. The part
between the ends of the bones is spoken of as the intermediate
or permanent callus ; that in the hollow of the shaft—the internal
callus—is also provisional in character, and is ultimately absorbed.

Naked eye appearances.—Examine the callus from the tibia of
some small animal—a rabbit, for instance—ten or twelve days
after fracture. Make a longitudinal section through the centre
of the bone. The extravasated blood, which was thrown out at
the time the bone was broken, and which, as in a healing wound
of the soft tissues, is such an important feature during the first
six or eight days, has now to a great extent disappeared ; it
has been absorbed, having played its part as a scaffolding. Around
the fractured ends of the bone, and merging into the periosteum,
is a pale, spindle-shaped mass which extends for some distance
above and below the fracture, and apparently involves the surrounding tissues to a considerable extent. At first this mass
consists almost entirely of cartilage, developed from the granulation tissue which is formed around the broken ends of the
bone, just as in any other healing wound (§ **166**). Between the
cartilaginous mass and the bone itself the soft vascular subperiosteal
tissue may still be made out as a pink line or zone, though very
frequently this is somewhat obscured, blending, as it does, with the
remainder of the callus. The outer surface of the provisional callus
is usually much pinker, as it is more vascular, than any other part ;
it thus early appears to form a provisional periosteum.

Passing for some distance into the medullary cavity is a mass
of granulation tissue, in which may be found traces of cartilage.
The only evidence of ossification as yet met with is in the position

in which one would expect it, *i.e.*, near the sound bone where the periosteum is least altered, and near the vascular surface, at the extremities of the spindle-shaped callus ; and here delicate trabeculæ of bone may be distinguished, with the aid of a magnifying glass, running apparently from the sound bone, at right angles to the surface, in the line of the new blood-vessels.

Prepare (§ 75 or 76), and stain (§ 98 or 107).

(× 20 and × 50).—Notice that at the fractured ends the bone has become decidedly more porous, and there is a condition practically of rarefying ostitis (§ 316). The trabeculæ are thinned, the canals are wider, and are filled with a mass of granulation tissue which passes also for some distance into the central medullary cavity, and, unlike the provisional callus, remains non-cartilaginous. It is made up of a mass of young cells, which can scarcely be distinguished from the ordinary subperiosteal and medullary cells ; in this tissue ossification goes on, just as in the growth of a normal bone. Between the ends of, and around the bone, the callus is composed principally of a mass of young cartilage cells embedded in a distinct matrix, the cells undergoing proliferation and the matrix becoming darkened and granular as calcareous salts are deposited. This cartilaginous mass is for the most part well supplied with blood-vessels. It is extremely vascular near the surface of the bone, and still more so on the free surface, where there is a species of new periosteal tissue developed in the form of a layer of dense pink fibrous tissue. Beneath this is the subperiosteal tissue, a layer of small round cells, unlike the cartilage cells in that they are not surrounded by a regular homogeneous matrix. In these two vascular areas of the new cartilage the process of ossification begins, then bony trabeculæ may be seen (in a picro-carmine stained specimen) as green lines running parallel with the vessels. In this section nothing further can be seen ; but if the process be followed out in other preparations, made where the union is more advanced, it will be found that the provisional callus eventually becomes bony throughout, the process of ossification extending from its two extremities, along the inner and outer surfaces, forming two layers, which at first (until they meet in the centre) enclose a mass of cartilage.

(× 300).—In the medullary canal, near the fracture, the amount of
fatty medulla is usually somewhat diminished ; the internal callus is
composed of embryonic connective tissue, made up of cells with
large nuclei, and only a small quantity of periplast. These cells are
very similar to the cells met with in the subperiosteal layer. This is
the only position in which the tissues are perfectly at rest, and
therefore is the only position in which, as a rule, ossification goes
on directly in fibrous tissue without the intervention of cartilage.

Next examine the intermediate callus, or that between the ends of
the bone. It is composed, at this stage, principally of cartilage, the
cells of which are undergoing a process of division, whilst the matrix
is usually calcified, and therefore extremely granular. In some cases,
however, the amount of cartilage is comparatively small, and its place
is taken by a fibro-cellular structure, almost like that found in a
young cicatrix.

The external provisional callus, or that outside the bone, like
the intermediate callus described above, is almost entirely cartilaginous. In this observe the gradual transformation of the proliferated
cartilage cells into bone corpuscles ; the granular appearance first of
the cartilage capsule, and then of the matrix, is due to the deposition of calcareous material. Near the bone the embryonic blood-
vessels, composed of double rows of cells, as in ordinary granulation
tissue, run at right angles from the Haversian canals of the bone into
the callus. Similar vessels run from the surrounding tissue on the free
surface. Note the appearance of the green spicules of bone along
the course of these vessels. The further ossification goes on regularly, and may be studied along with that of normal bone.

If the bone can be kept perfectly at rest, the amount of irritation,
and consequently the amount of callus is small, and the process of
repair takes place without the intervention of a cartilaginous splint.

In a compound fracture, on the other hand, there is the formation
of an excess of medullary and subperiosteal (granulation) tissue as the
result of greater irritation, and thus ossification goes on just as in the
the growth of the normal bone, rapidly and simply, without the formation of any cartilage. Absorption of excess of bone ensues, and
the outlines of the medullary cavity and of the bone may be
restored.

Rickets.

314. Rickets must be looked upon as a disease of an essentially constitutional character, the result of malnutrition. It is most frequently observed in badly nourished children, from one year old and upwards, the period during which the bones in which the changes associated with rickets are most marked, are being most rapidly developed. These changes are best seen in the long bones, especially at their points of junction with the various cartilages, but the flat bones of the head, and even the spongy bones of the spinal column may undergo considerable alteration.

The ends of a rickety bone are enlarged and clubbed, and the shaft is often thickened, especially in the concavity of its curve, which is usually greatly exaggerated, and there is thus formed a buttress of new bone. In the chest of a rickety child it may be observed that at the junction of the ribs with the cartilages on both sides of the sternum there is a series of enlargements or knobs, giving rise to the well-known "rosary" or beaded appearance. External to the "rosary" is a groove, which is due to the retraction of the softened and less resistant ribs during the inspiratory effort. As the softened ribs are flattened or drawn in, the sternum is rendered more prominent. In a typical rickety bone, such as the radius, the enlargement extends above the thickened and irregular epiphyseal cartilage. If the muscles be stripped from the shaft of the bone, the periosteal layer will be found thickened and very vascular; and the shaft in place of being dense is almost like the spongy tissue of the extremity. In consequence of these changes the bones are very soft and friable, are readily bent, and may be easily cut with a knife; they are usually much shortened. Infractions, or greenstick fractures, frequently take place, especially in the upper limbs, and the epiphyses are often displaced.

Make a vertical section through the shaft with its epiphyses, and notice the great increase of translucent or bluish cartilage, which, in place of forming thin regular layers on the articular surface and between the epiphyses and the shaft, forms broad, irregular, somewhat porous belts (in which small islets of calcifying tissue are scattered) dipping into the main mass of calcifying tissue. In these

islets of calcifying tissue pink and yellow points are seen; these
are the calcifying centres, the pinker ones containing numerous
blood-vessels. The cut surface of the shaft is exceedingly red and
vascular, the bony lamellæ are thin and friable, and it is evident
that rapid absorption is going on; the marrow is relatively large
in amount, and is red and gelatinous instead of being yellow and
fatty.

Treat pieces of the cartilage and bone from near an articulation
(§ 65), and a small piece of the shaft, with the periosteum attached
(§ 66), stain (§ 98 or 107).

(× 50).—In the thickened belt of cartilage with the irregular calcareous and bony layer beneath, there is enormous proliferation of
the cartilage cells, some of which have a regular arrangement, but by
far the greater number are grouped without any attempt at arrange⸱
ment, either as regards columns or size, and in many cases there is
comparatively little matrix. In the small yellow opaque points calcification is going on both in the matrix and in the capsules of the
cells. The patches of calcified cartilage are not arranged regularly, but
crop up indiscriminately. Blood-vessels also make their appearance
at irregular intervals in the cartilage, and, closely following them,
appear spaces similar to those met with in ordinary bone, many of
which are lined with a regular layer of pink cells or osteoblasts, and
thus true bone, or a structure which very closely resembles it, is
formed. Even in the midst of the bone formed in this position,
masses of irregular cartilage cells may still be seen.

(× 300).—The above appearances must be observed more closely,
the great irregularity in the size of the cells, in the matrix, and in the
calcification of the matrix; the calcification of the cartilage cells at
certain points, their proliferation and apparent transformation into
osteoblasts. Even where true bone is formed, it appears to be laid
down without any attempt at order or regularity, and bone, calcified
cartilage, and true cartilage are mixed up, apparently indiscriminately.
Here we see, then, that the chief points to be noted are the enormous
and irregular increase of cartilage, with irregular and deficient bone
formation.

(× 50).—Now examine the piece of the shaft. Under the fibrous
layer of the periosteum there is a great increase in the number of

small round cells or osteoblasts, which form a thick deeply stained layer. In the deeper part of this cellular mass a few trabeculæ, partly fibrous (stained pink) and partly calcified (stained green), may be seen. These trabeculæ form an open network, and are seldom or never perfectly ossified; they consist rather of a calcified fibrous matrix. Beneath this *osteoid* tissue (very like that seen in an osteoid sarcoma) comes the true bone, somewhat loose in texture and irregular in structure, in some cases almost like spongy bone. In this tissue the number of vessels and osteoblasts is always very great, but the osteoclasts are not markedly increased in number.

(× 300).—The pink round cells, or osteoblasts, along with the numerous blood-vessels, are readily seen, not only beneath the fibrous layer, but between the granular looking trabeculæ, and in the spaces between the osseous trabeculæ. In normal bone these osteoblasts grow slowly, and form around them periplasts, which gradually become calcified. In the case of rickets, however, these osteoblasts are formed in very large numbers, but any periplast which they may form is always small in quantity and only imperfectly calcified; there is also fine fibrillation of the intercellular substance, parts of which remain fibrous in place of being converted into bone.

In the flattened bones, such as those of the skull, a process similar to that which goes on under the periosteum of a long bone is met with; but where the weight of the brain presses upon the soft tissue, the bone does not develop, and the skull at that point (occipital or parietal bone) remains very thin. The pelvis may also be deformed in this condition, and curvature of the spine is often met with as a result of the softening and mal-development of the vertebræ.

It is evident from the above description that, although there is great proliferative activity in the cells, both of the cartilage and of the periosteum, calcification and ossification go on slowly and incompletely. Although little new bone is formed, the process of absorption goes on as usual (sometimes even more rapidly than normal, as the increased quantity of granulation tissue, or red cellular marrow, aids in this process); but as the old trabeculæ are absorbed new ones are formed to take their place. At the end of the developmental period, however, or where the disease gives way to treatment, the bones, when ossification does set in, may become very thick and strong from the fact that the osteoplastic tissue is present in such large quantities. The bones may be stunted and deformed; this is owing to the fact that ossification sets in so rapidly that the epiphyses unite at an earlier date than usual, and the child remains stunted and dwarfed. The muscular attachments are very well marked, being drawn out during the *soft* stage.

Dr. Barlow has described an exceedingly acute form of rickets, known as scurvy rickets, which is supposed to be due to constitutional disturbance, associated more or less directly with the administration of unsuitable food. It is characterised by sudden swelling of the bones, especially of the femur (over which there is tenderness or even great pain), œdema, a spongy condition of the gums and petechial hæmorrhages in the skin. After death similar hæmorrhages may be found in most of the soft tissues and under the periosteum, especially at the junctions of the epiphyseal cartilages with the long bones. These hæmorrhages are sometimes very extensive, though it is somewhat remarkable that necrosis seldom or never seems to follow this condition. We have the same cellular proliferation both in cartilage and in the bone, rapid absorption, and irregular and imperfect calcification.

OSTITIS.

315. In bone, as in all other tissue, the manifestations of inflammation are very various, and because of the rigidity of its structure the results are very different, according as the process is acute or chronic, occurs in the periosteum or in the bone itself, or is simple or specific.

From the fact that the shaft of the bone, especially its surface, is to a great extent nourished by vessels that run into it from the periosteum, whenever the periosteum is separated from the bone by accumulations of pus, the nutritive supply being cut off from the shaft, the bone dies, leaving a sequestrum or dead mass. The periosteum, still carrying on its bone-forming functions, often somewhat irregularly, forms a case around the sequestrum, which, acting as a foreign body, keeps up a certain amount of irritation; and suppuration

FIG. 128.—Section of bone taken from the lower end of the tibia of a patient suffering from septic osteomyelitis. Stained with eosin and logwood. (× 20.) (H. A. Thomson.)

 a. Cartilage cells and matrix.
 b. Bone trabeculæ surrounded by osteoblasts.
 c. Small abscess (embolic) near the end of the bone.
 d. Compressed and fibrous tissue around the abscess.
 e. Marrow spaces filled with leucocytes along the line of the vessels.
 f. Transverse section of one of the trabeculæ with leucocytes and proliferating osteoblasts around it.

—the result of the admission of micro-organisms to the area of dead tissue—is again set up, or, it may be, is kept up from the first. The pus makes its way to the surface by the shortest available route, an opening or sinus is formed, and the constant discharge keeps this open. Abscess may also form in bones, especially in the spongy tissue at the ends. Such abscesses, occurring in septic osteomyelitis or inflammation of the bone marrow, are usually embolic, the result of the impaction of septic emboli in the vessels which run in the marrow spaces of the open cancellous tissue.

In certain chronic inflammations where the process of bone formation goes on more rapidly than the process of absorption, the trabeculæ may become enormously thickened, and sclerosis of bone may result. In other cases the process of absorption predominates, resulting in a rarefying ostitis; whilst in other cases again—as in tuberculosis or caries—there is, as the result of the formation of tubercular nodules, a gradual absorption of bony trabeculæ (see § 317), cutting off of the blood supply from other portions of the bone, caseation, and formation of a cold abscess.

Rarefying Ostitis.

316. Rarefying ostitis must be looked upon as a process rather than as a distinct disease, since it occurs in a great variety of inflammatory conditions. It is almost invariably met with at the end of a bone after amputation, in absorption of the vertebræ by pressure of aneurisms or tumours, or as a general condition sometimes known as osteoporosis—a term which refers simply to the naked eye appearances.

Whether the rarefaction be due to general or local inflammation, the results are much the same.

Naked eye appearances. — The periosteum is usually thickened and fleshy, and may be highly vascular. On longitudinal section the bone is found to be extremely vascular, the dense layer near the surface may be very thin, the marrow spaces are large, and the trabeculæ are not only diminished in thickness, but are exceedingly rough and irregular, and the spongy tissue is open and friable. Within the spaces the medulla is red and gelatinous.

Prepare a piece of the porous bone taken from the end of a stump (§ **65** or **66**), and stain (§ **98** or **107**).

(× 50).—Near the free extremity of the bone the Haversian canals are usually undergoing great enlargement, and their walls are ragged and irregular. This is most marked at the very extremity, at which point the trabeculæ project as fine spicules, and the spaces open into one another. The vessels are dilated, and are

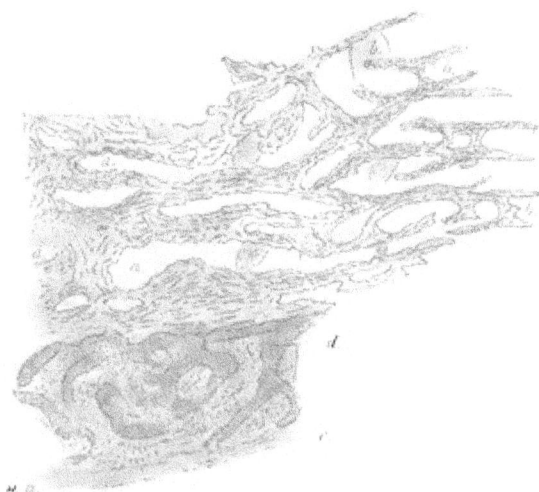

FIG. 129.—Rarefying ostitis. Portion of a vertical section of the first phalanx of the middle finger after amputation. Stained with picro-carmine. (× 30.)

    a. Haversian canals undergoing enlargement.
    b. Free distal extremity of bone, with irregular surface and fine
        projecting spicules.
    c. Periosteum.
    d. Newly formed periosteal bone.

surrounded by a large number of leucocytes, seen as small pink points. These leucocytes appear to be playing the part of osteoclasts. The whole structure of enlarged vessels and leucocytes gives one the idea of a granulation tissue. In addition to the leucocytes, the true osteoclasts (or multinucleated giant cells) are very numerous. In the periosteum the vessels are dilated, there is great extravasation of leucocytes and proliferation of the osteoblasts. Very frequently there appears to be a superficial formation of bone going on in connection with the deep layer of the periosteum, and blood-vessels may be seen dipping down into the newly-formed bone, and running in between the trabeculæ, which are being eroded by the large multinucleated osteoclasts.

The absorption of bone is going on more rapidly than its formation, so that the trabeculæ are thin, or in some cases broken down, several canals opening up into one. This absorption appears to be due to the phagocytic or scavenging action of leucocytes that have escaped from the vessels under stimulation during the process of inflammation, and it has even been suggested that many of the giant

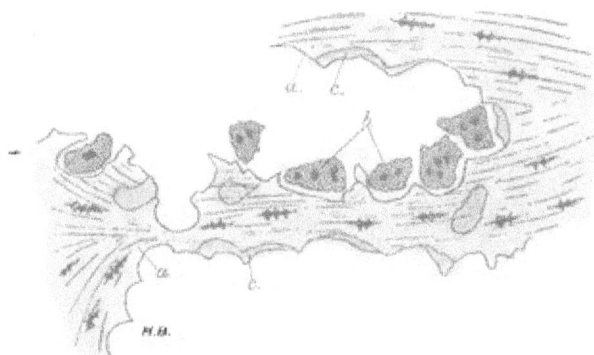

FIG. 130.—Rarefying ostitis. Section of bone stained with picro-carmine. (× 250.)
  a. Howship's foveolæ,
  b. in which are lying giant cells or osteoclasts.
  c. Hyaline border, due to oblique direction in which the section is made.

cells may be nothing more than leucocytes that have combined to form a plasmodium or multinucleated mass of protoplasm, by which the bone is attacked more readily. Under excessive stimulation the osteoblasts are said to act in the same manner.

(× 300).—Note the fibrous layer of the periosteum stained pink with picro-carmine ; beneath this the osteogenetic layer is extremely vascular, and from it small vessels, accompanied by a number of small round cells, may be seen passing in between the bony trabeculæ. Lying on the trabeculæ are numerous deeply-stained round cells, which appear to be partially embedded in a layer of pink tissue : these are the osteoblasts, which eventually become transformed into the branching bone corpuscles. In this region the giant cells or osteoclasts are rare.

Nearer the rarefied bone the Haversian canals are much enlarged and very irregular; this irregularity is due to the excavation which extends from the main cavity outwards into the bone of the surrounding Haversian system. These cavities, whether shallow or of considerable depth, usually contain an excessive number of leucocytes, especially in the immediate neighbourhood of the distended vessels. Where the excavation is going on very rapidly, or where it is far

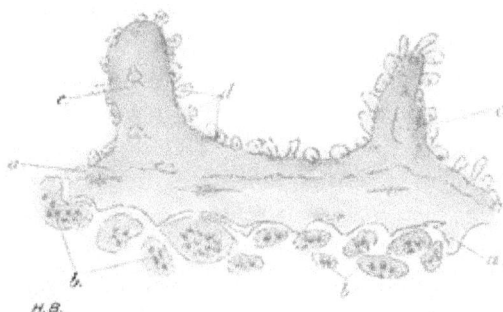

FIG. 131.- Simultaneous destruction and new formation of bone in a piece of bone found in a malignant epulis. Stained with picrocarmine. (× 250.)

   a. Older bone, with
   b. Osteoclasts in Howship's foveolæ.
   c. Newer bone, with
   d. Osteoblasts.

advanced, numerous osteoclasts may also be seen lying in large cup-shaped depressions (Howship's foveolæ) all along the line of erosion. These numerous foveolæ, with their contained giant cells, are simply an exaggerated phase of what is met with in normal bone, which is always undergoing a certain amount of absorption. In the pathological condition, however, the striped margin which is seen in the giant cell of the normal bone is very frequently absent. In the immediate neighbourhood of the giant cell the lime salts are apparently removed before any other elements of the bony tissue.

In rarefying ostitis there is increased absorption of bone, unaccompanied by a corresponding new formation; but it must be remembered that new formation of bone invariably goes on to a certain extent in the deep or vascular layer of the periosteum, and that after the rarefying process has continued for some time the formative process may again predominate, an osteo-sclerosis resulting. This occurs especially in ostitis deformans. In a section of malignant epulis, prepared as above, and examined (× 300), the two processes of bone formation and rapid absorption may be seen going on simultaneously (*see* Fig. 131).

Tubercular Caries of Bone.

317. Tubercular caries may be looked upon as a rarefying ostitis, accompanied by, or rather the result of, the formation of rapidly caseating tubercle. It is found most frequently in the spongy bones, especially in the vertebræ, in the bones of the tarsus, in the phalanges of the fingers and toes, in the acetabulum, and in the os calcis ; more rarely at the ends of long bones. With this condition is frequently associated suppuration, resulting in what is known as cold abscess of bone.

Naked eye appearances.—There is usually a diffuse yellow infiltration, especially of the spongy tissue ; this appears to invade the bone, causing absorption or destruction of the bony trabeculæ.

In a vertebra the whole of the body may be carious, the disease passing entirely through the invertebral discs into the vertebræ above and below. In advanced cases there is nothing left but a mass of soft caseous or putty-like material, which may be scooped away with the handle of a knife. This is surrounded by a quantity of grey or pink gelatinous granulation tissue, which gradually extends into the bony tissue, filling up the spaces as the trabeculæ are absorbed. In consequence of the softening and absorption the bones may be very much deformed ; they give way to external pressure, and in the spinal column, where the weight of the upper part rests on the softened vertebral bodies, they are crushed, and spinal curvature is the result.

Harden (§ 56), or if it is not desired to search for tubercle bacilli (§ 76), and stain (§§ 98 and 140 or 142).

(× 50).—At some distance from the healthy bone the medullary

spaces become larger and more vascular, and the giant cells along
the margins of the trabeculæ are more numerous.   In place of the
fat cells of the medulla, a mass of granulation tissue is seen, gradually
filling the somewhat enlarged Haversian spaces.   It is composed
principally of small round cells, and is traversed by a number of
vessels.   In the mass of granulation tissue are small tubercle follicles,

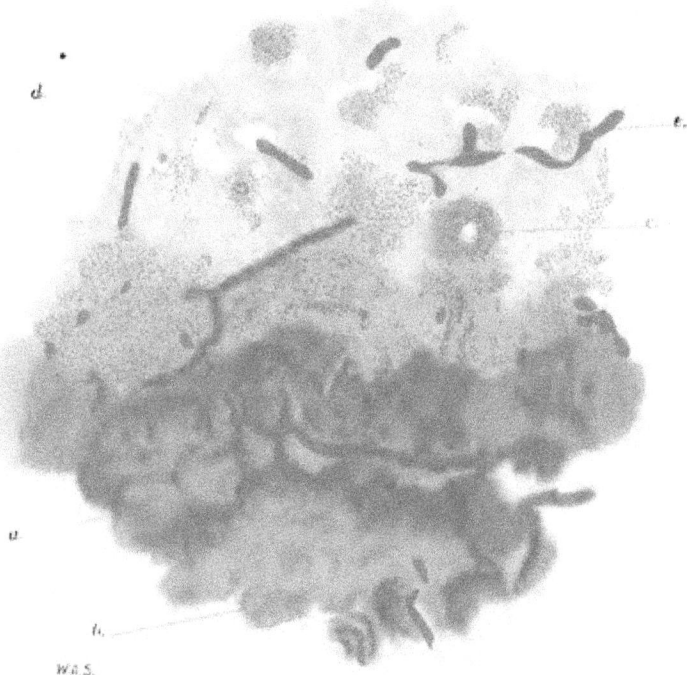

FIG. 132.—Caseating tubercular infiltration of the spongy bone in
the lower end of the tibia.   Stained with picro-carmine.   (× 14.)
(H. A. Thomson.)
  a. Caseous infiltration enclosing trabeculæ of dead bone.
  b. Tubercular granulation tissue with giant cells.
  c. Miliary granulation around medullary blood vessel.
  d. Normal marrow.
  e. Trabeculæ of spongiosa, stained with carmine.

either single or in groups, with their giant cells and typical structure.
(*See* § **189.**)   This tissue corresponds to the area of gelatinous tissue
seen with the naked eye.   Where caseation is complete, the bone
has entirely disappeared, or is represented by small detached fragments or spicules, between which are granular shrivelled cells, drop-

lets of fat (stained black with osmic acid, § 110), in fact, simply a mass of caseous *débris*.

(× 300).—Confirm the above appearances. In the granulation tissue tubercle follicles are developed, after which the whole undergoes caseation, as is the tendency in all tubercle formations. Near the centre of the caseous mass the absorption of the trabeculæ is complete.

There are also described in connection with bone three other forms of tubercular lesion :—(1) Miliary granulations found in

Fig. 133.—Tubercular necrosis of bone. A vertical transverse section of the upper end of the femur from a case of tubercular arthritis of the hip, showing a wedge-sequestrum in the cervix, abutting by its base on the epiphyseal cartilage. (H. A. Thomson.)

    a. Position of epiphyseal plate.
    b. Articular surface of head.
    c. Trochanter major.
    d. Sawn section.

general tuberculosis. (2) The chronic circumscribed tubercular focus of König which "varies in size from that of a pin head to that of a cherry, has a translucent periphery of a reddish-grey colour, and appears well defined to the naked eye" (H. A. Thomson). These nodules have all the characteristic appearances of tubercle. They appear to be formed by a fusion of several smaller nodules, which bring about erosion of the bone, caseation takes place in them, and they break down in the centre, just as do all other caseous tubercle nodules; extension takes place at the periphery. (3) A third form is that in which a sequestrum, often of considerable size, is formed; this, in place of being detached, remains continuous with the living bone. These sequestra are wedge-shaped, with the base turned towards the articular surface (they are generally near the ends of the bones); they can usually be seen only on section, and then must be carefully sought; they are yellow, very dense in structure, and in the spaces tubercular structure may be made out under the microscope; they are separated from the healthy bone by a zone of granulation tissue, which may, however, in chronic cases be replaced by fibrous tissue.

Before the question of caries is dismissed, it must be mentioned that somewhat similar conditions are met with in syphilis. Here gummata and gummatous granulation tissue may be read instead of tubercle nodules and tubercular granulation tissue. We have the same processes of bone absorption, ulceration, and sclerosis, and, so far as can be seen, the processes by which these are determined are almost identical.

"Tumour Albus," or Tubercular Arthritis.

318. Synonyms: Tubercular Inflammation of the Synovial Membrane; White Swelling; Gelatinous or Pulpy Degeneration of Joints.

Tubercular arthritis may be compared with the tubercular inflammation of other serous membranes, just as tubercular disease of the bone may be compared with tuberculosis of the lung; it is most frequently met with in delicate children above three years of age, and occurs in the following joints; most frequently in the knee, then in the hip, elbow, ankle, wrist, and least frequently in the shoulder.

Naked eye appearances.—There is usually no fluid in the joint; where the disease is somewhat advanced the synovial membrane is invariably thickened; it is soft, œdematous, and gelatinous, and is usually grey or greyish white in colour. In some cases exuberant red granulations may be seen projecting from the general swollen mass; the surface may be rough and shreddy, or it may be smooth, in which case small tubercules may be seen standing out prominently from the gelatinous mass.

2 G

The other structures in and near the joint become soft and gelatinous, and frequently appear as a mass of pinkish gelatinous material held in position only by the skin. The gelatinous material may fill up the whole of the joint cavity and gradually cause distension; in such cases the bone is also attacked, the articular cartilages being gradually eroded, and as this takes place the tubercular tissue gradually makes its way between the bone and the cartilages, slowly detaching the latter from their bony beds. In the knee the semilunar discs may become so infiltrated that they cannot be distinguished from the general mass of tubercular tissue. This is always best seen at the periphery of the articular surfaces. On section small yellow tubercular points embedded in the gelatinous mass, may be readily distinguished; these seldom open into the joints unless suppuration has occurred.

The granulations pass into the cartilage, pitting, and in the long run absorbing it. They also pass into the articular end of the bone, giving rise to a condition exactly like that already described as rarefying ostitis with tubercle (§ 317). The change then begins in the synovial membrane as a formation of vascular granulation tissue, which gradually invades the surrounding structures. In the granulations are tubercle follicles, which caseate and suppurate.

Harden one piece of the joint, comprising synovial membrane in its fungating condition, a piece of the cartilage, and a thin layer of bone from beneath the cartilage (§ 56 or 76), and a piece of the granulation tissue (§ 56), and stain (§§ 98 and 107), or for tubercle bacilli (§ 140 or 142).

(× 50).—The granulation tissue consists of a mass of small round cells, through which a number of blood-vessels are ramifying; embedded in it are numerous specially well-developed tubercle follicles. Passing from the under surface of the granulation tissue in the synovial membrane are small processes, which may be seen to run into the substance of the cartilage, gradually absorbing it. In the cartilage itself the matrix appears to be diminished in quantity, whilst there is proliferation of the cells within their capsules, which gradually disappear, so that the cells are no longer encapsuled. The central part of the cartilage is least affected, but as the bone is again approached the process is repeated, until between bone and cartilage there appears another mass of granulation tissue, which extends not only into the cartilage, but also into the bone. In the bone all the appearances are the same as those described in § 317. It must be remembered, too, that tubercle beginning in bone may give rise to tubercular granulations under the cartilage, absorption of the cartilage, and ulceration into the joint, in which case there is also a form of white swelling. In both cases tubercular granulations are found in the tissues around the joint. Endarteritis obliterans is always a well-marked feature in these cases of synovial tuberculosis.

(× 300).—All the above appearances should be confirmed—the tubercle nodules in the swollen synovial membrane, the encroaching of the granulation tissue on the cartilage, the proliferation of the cartilage cells, and the gradual disappearance of the capsules and the matrix. The tubercle follicles are very well formed, the appearance of typical giant cells being very characteristic of this condition ; the granulations in the rarefying bone, the points of commencing caseation and the proliferative changes in the cells of the intima of the vessels are also well seen. In these tubercular masses tubercle bacilli may be found under a higher power. Examine a few of the muscular fibres from near the affected joint, and note that they are undergoing fatty degeneration, and that in some cases this is succeeded by great atrophy of the muscle.

In some forms of this disease it will be found that the cartilage cells, after proliferation, undergo rapid fatty degeneration, and are then, along with the softened matrix, absorbed.—(Billroth.)

Chronic Articular Rheumatism, or "Arthritis Deformans."

319. This condition, known also as rheumatic gout, is really a chronic inflammatory process. It is characterised by proliferation and destruction of the articular cartilages, thickening of the synovial membrane, sclerosis, eburnation of the bony articular surfaces, and formation of granulations which become cartilaginous, calcified, or even ossified.

Naked eye appearances.—At the point where there is greatest friction the cartilage may have disappeared, and there remains simply an area of dense polished bone ; around this a ring of cartilage is often present, the articular surface of which is peculiarly soft and velvety to the touch and in appearance; on examination with a magnifying glass this velvety appearance is seen to be due to the presence of a number of villous processes. In or under the synovial membrane, which is found only near the margins of the articular surface, small nodules, evidently the result of proliferation of the cartilage cells, are seen. These nodules in some cases are of considerable size, but later they disappear, and an ulcer is formed which gradually spreads. Around the joint itself, in the periosteum and tendons and in the synovial fringes, which are increased both in size and number, a process of ossification is going on. In the later stages of the disease, the muscles, at first fatty, may become calcified; eventually the joint is surrounded by a number of characteristic smooth dense bony masses, partly formed as above, but partly the result of a pressing out of the soft granulation tissue from between the two articular surfaces, this soft tissue afterwards becoming first cartilaginous, and then ossified.

Prepare a piece of the cartilage from such a specimen (early stage) (§ 57 or 65), and stain (§ 98).

(× 50).—At some parts there has been proliferation of the cartilage cells; those within an enlarged capsule are well formed and of considerable size, but those near the margin of the ulcer are extremely granular. Notice, too, that there is an entire absence in the floor of the ulcer of the horizontal layers of cartilage cells, which have apparently been removed by the rubbing together of the two rough surfaces, the swollen cartilages in this process playing merely a passive part. Between the vertical rows of proliferating cells near the surface of the bone, the matrix is softened, and some of it has disappeared, and the villous processes already seen with the hand-glass, can now be further examined. Near the margin of the ulcer the process of cell proliferation is more marked, but the horizontal rows are still seen. Observe the thickening of the synovial membrane and the formation of the small mass of vascular granulation tissue.

(× 300).—Granular cells, which are evidently fattily degenerated cartilage cells are well seen; note the well formed proliferated cells, and the splitting up of the cartilage into villous processes. The matrix between the rows of cells is seen to be finely fibrillated, the axis of fibrillation running down towards the bone. The villous layer consists simply of the deeper or vertical rows of cartilage cells, with a fibrillated matrix between. The bone beneath the cartilage, as well as that formed around the joint, is very dense and smooth; this is the result of a chronic ostitis.

FIG. 134.—Section of ulcer of cartilage from a case of arthritis deformans. Stained with picro-carmine. (× 80.)

   a. Columns of cartilage cells, with accompanying matrix from between which some of the fibrillated matrix has been removed, after undergoing softening. (The velvet pile.)
   b. Cartilage cells near the surface, fatty and granular.
   c. Proliferating cartilage cells.
   d. The deeper and more normal layer of cartilage.

In more *acute inflammation of cartilage*, the cells formed in the capsules are much more numerous, but are not nearly so large, whilst the matrix, after softening, may gradually disappear as the disease advances, and a mass of granulation tissue is left; suppuration may also occur.

GOUTY INFILTRATION OF JOINTS.

320. This is an infiltration of the articular cartilages with urate of sodium chiefly, mixed with other urates, carbonates, and phosphates.

These, when the infiltration is complete, form a chalk-like covering
to the joint, or where the deposit takes place in the surrounding
ligamentous and soft tissues, they form chalk-like masses, which may
project through the skin. These latter, the so-called chalk-stones,
by their presence may give rise to considerable inflammation, either
of acute or of chronic form. On cutting into a gouty joint, soft chalky
masses are first exposed, and the surfaces of the joint itself are found
to be white, smooth or grooved and chalky, from the rubbing together of the two infiltrated surfaces.

(× 300).—In the fresh condition (§ 37), in a piece of the cartilage
where the change is not far advanced, a number of acicular crystals
may be seen arranged in stellate groups, the centre of each group
being a cartilage capsule. The crystals are so arranged around this
that the whole mass presents the appearance of a thorn apple.—
(Cornil and Ranvier.) The distribution of the urates differs considerably in different cases, and it is held by some that the chalky
deposits begin in the centre of the cartilage and then pass outwards, whilst others hold that they are most numerous near the
surface, and that they gradually spread downwards to the bone.

Here, as in most of the diseased conditions of cartilage already
examined, the altered cartilage plays a comparatively passive part.
As the infiltration which follows inflammation or depression of
the cartilaginous tissues takes place, the mass is rubbed down by
simple friction, as in fatty degeneration of the cartilage cells, where
the cartilage matrix is softened or becomes fibrillated, and is
worn away ; or in acute inflammation of cartilage, where the cells
proliferate, the matrix softens and is removed, and the cartilage disappears. The more active the proliferation of the cells, the greater
is the divergence from the appearances presented by the ordinary
type of cartilage.

Tumours of Bone and Joints.

321. The principal tumours of bone are *exostoses, osteoid chondroma,
fibroma, myxoma, cystic tumours,* especially in the jaws ; *sarcomas* of
various forms, more especially the myeloid or giant celled sarcoma
and the mixed sarcoma found in the lower jaw, as one of the most

frequent forms of malignant epulis; osteoid and osteo sarcoma. *Primary cancer* is comparatively rare, but *secondary cancer* and *secondary epithelioma* are frequently met with, when they grow at the expense of the bone substance proper; the bone eventually becoming very brittle or fragile.

Primary malignant tumours growing in connection with joints are very few in number, though secondary tumours, extending from bone or from the surrounding soft tissues, are by no means uncommon.

Of the primary simple tumours the most common are *ecchondroses*, which are found growing principally in the intervertebral discs; *fibromas* forming the so-called loose cartilages of joints (especially in the knee); and *lipomas*, rarely met with as arborescent growths from the fatty synovial fringes.

CHAPTER XII.

NERVOUS SYSTEM.

TUBERCULAR MENINGITIS—ACUTE HYDROCEPHALUS.

322. Tubercular meningitis, or inflammation of the pia mater, due to tubercular deposit in the sheaths of the small vessels which ramify in it, is very frequently the cause of death in children in whom there is general tuberculosis.

Naked eye appearances.—The surface of the membrane is congested; beneath it there is considerable flattening of the convolutions, owing to the distension of the ventricles, in consequence of which, too, the whole upper surface of the brain has a peculiar dry appearance, the fluid having been squeezed from the subarachnoid space. At the base of the brain, and extending along the fissures of Sylvius and Rolando, along the superior crura cerebelli, and between the occipital lobes, the inflammatory process with its accompaniment of tubercle can be well made out. In these positions the various soft structures are matted together by a slightly opaque yellowish lymph; when this is torn away, a quantity of turbid fluid, in which flakes of lymph are floating, exudes from the subarachnoid space. A similar fluid may also be found distending the ventricular cavities, the distension being especially well seen in the lateral ventricles. This is due to the interference with the flow of lymph; there is often also an enormous accumulation of fluid at the base of the brain. This leads to flattening of the convolutions and compression of the brain substance. The accumulation takes place so rapidly that the pressure can exert little influence on the bones of the cranium. In consequence of this accumulation of fluid the condition is known as acute hydrocephalus. In most cases, on separating the parts at the base of the brain, the small grey or white tubercle nodules may be seen to stand out prominently from the injected pia mater. The pia mater is seen to be thickened between the tubercular points; it is somewhat cloudy, and is covered by a thin yellowish, almost purulent, layer. Around the blood-vessels there is the same peculiar opacity, which, as will afterwards be found, is due to a small cell infiltration into the sheath of the vessel.

"To find tubercle, the pia mater should be removed from those regions where it is most frequently found, such as the fissure of Sylvius and the superior crura cerebelli. The piece of the membrane should then be agitated in water till the adhering fragments of cerebral tissue are separated, and, on holding it up to the light, small whitish spots will be seen in the membrane. This examination must not, however, be considered sufficient. The pia mater should be carefully spread upon a glass slide, when, with a low power, granulations will be perceived which were not before recognisable with the naked eye" (Cornil and Ranvier).

Harden a piece of the pia mater, with a piece of the brain tissue attached (§§ 55 *a* and **59**), and stain (§ **98**).

(× 50).—Note first the general proliferation of cells, especially around the blood-vessels, and then the tubercular granulations which are situated most frequently near the points of bifurcation of the vessels, or at irregular intervals along the course of the smaller vessels. Each of these tubercular masses consists of cells, varying very greatly in size and shape. They accumulate around the vessel and distend the perivascular sheath. The vessel itself is frequently blocked by a coagulum at the point of swelling, and a peculiar process of endarteritis with a form of giant cell formation may often be seen.

(× 300).—The large endothelioid cells in the perivascular sheath vary in shape, and contain from one to four or more nuclei. Along with them are numerous small round cells, each containing a single nucleus. There is little or no reticular formation, and giant cells are entirely wanting. This structure, therefore, presents a very good example of rapidly growing tubercle.

A chronic form of tubercle, which does not usually give rise to acute hydrocephalus, is sometimes found in the substance of the brain, but much more frequently in the cerebellum. It appears to begin in connection with the pia mater, from which it extends rapidly into the substance of the brain. A typical mass in the cerebellum may be an inch or more in diameter; it projects from the surface, and also passes for a considerable distance into the grey matter; it is firm to the touch, and is somewhat tough. On section the outlines are seen to be irregular and sinuous or lobulated, as though several tubercular masses had become fused; the centre of the mass is cheesy, and may be readily broken down with the fingers, but around the centre is a grey gelatinous zone, which gradually merges into the surrounding nerve tissue.

Harden (§ 59), and stain (§ 98).

(× 50).—Observe the typical caseous material in the centre of a well-formed tubercular growth extending outwards in all directions. The tissue surrounding the tubercular masses is pink and fibrous, and there is a marked increase of the neuroglia cells. In the sheaths of the blood-vessels there is a process similar to that already described as occurring in acute tuberculosis, infiltration of the perivascular sheath with small cells, and obliteration of the lumen of the vessel.

(× 300).—Verify these appearances.

GUMMATA OF THE BRAIN AND ITS MEMBRANES.

323. In tertiary syphilis, inflammatory gummatous patches involving the membranes and the cerebral cortex, especially near the base of the brain in the interpeduncular space, are frequently met with.

Naked eye appearances.—Where the process is well advanced, there may be single or multiple growths appearing first in the membranes, in the larger sulci or spaces, or gradually invading the subjacent cortex. These growths are surrounded by a firm fibrous capsule, bands from which run for short distances into the surrounding brain substance, which is usually somewhat firmer than normal. Within this fibrous capsule is a zone of pinkish gelatinous-looking tissue, pinker at the margin, but grey or yellowish-grey nearer the centre, where it gradually merges into yellow caseous points or patches. In all cases the pia mater is bound down to the cortex.

Harden (§ 56), and stain (§ 98 or 103 *d*).

(× 25).—It is at once seen that the process extends along the course of the vessels that, after ramifying in the pia mater, run into the cortex. The pia mater is greatly thickened, and around each artery and vein accumulations of small round cells may be seen. The intima of the larger arteries is usually thickened by proliferation of its cells. Similar changes may be seen around the vessels in the cortex. The gelatinous zone is now seen to be made up of small masses of granulation tissue composed of nucleated cells. Where these masses of cells are undergoing degeneration they become first hyaline, then granular, and ultimately leave nothing but a mass of granular *débris* corresponding to the yellow caseous points and masses. The fibrous-looking capsule still contains numerous cells, except in very old gummata, where it consists simply of well-formed fibrous tissue. Shooting out from the gumma are numerous small vessels, each surrounded by numbers of small cells similar to those above described.

(× 300).—Confirm the above appearances. Note that the cells around the vessels are usually in the perivascular spaces, that although many of them are small cells each with a single nucleus, there are also large endothelioid cells, often containing several nuclei. The changes in the vessels are specially well marked in the brain. The proliferation of the intimal cells, atrophy of the muscle fibre of the middle coat, with increase of the cellular elements and proliferation of the cells in the adventitia, are all well-marked features. The gradual cutting off of the blood supply, the hyaline and then fatty and granular degeneration of the new masses of cellular tissue, or their conversion into fibrous tissue, are well seen. Around the gumma, especially near the vessels with their infiltrated walls, the brain substance is undergoing degenerative and atrophic changes.

CEREBRAL HÆMORRHAGES.

324. Fresh hæmorrhages are the result of increased pressure within arteries the walls of which have undergone fatty degeneration, or fibroid thickening, especially of the muscular coat (if present) and of the adventitia ; such hæmorrhages may also result from the rupture of a single aneurism of a larger vessel, or of a group of miliary dilatations, which may be readily recognised by the ragged walls, and the dilatations on the vessels in the immediate neighbourhood of the clot. Hæmorrhages occur most frequently in the corpus striatum, optic thalamus, and internal capsule; more rarely in the white substance of the convolutions; and least frequently in the pia mater, cerebellum, pons varolii, and medulla oblongata.

To examine the vessels around a hæmorrhagic focus, the result of rupture of miliary aneurisms, open into it and cut it away with the surrounding brain tissue. Carefully macerate the whole in water, changing every three or four days, until the brain substance is soft enough to be easily removed by small jets of water. When the vessels are thoroughly cleansed they may be spread out on a glass slide and examined.

Harden a small piece of the brain tissue, taken from near the hæmorrhage, with its altered vessels (§ 59), and then (§ 57), and stain (§ 98 or 103 *d*). Another piece should be hardened entirely in methylated spirit, to do away with any chance of the chrome colouring matter from the Müller's fluid being mistaken for altered blood pigment.

When a large amount of blood has been effused, it is first broken down and absorbed, as is a clot in any other part of the body; but changes are also set up in the surrounding tissue which result in the formation of either a cyst or a cicatrix. When a cyst is formed the walls are tough and fibrous, owing to chronic inflammatory or irritative changes being set up, the solid constituents of the clot have all been removed, and there remains a more or less clear fluid with a yellowish tinge. In the immediate neighbourhood of the fibrous wall there is a peculiar yellow opaque tissue, the result of the deposition of altered blood pigment in the lymphatics and cells of the altered brain tissue.

Examine small scrapings from the inner wall (× 600), and observe that there are numerous small round cells which contain crystals in the form of rhombic plates or needles, evidently hæmatoidin crystals derived from altered blood pigment. Similar larger free crystals may be seen, and also a number of granular cells (compound granular corpuscles), which stain black with osmic acid (§ 110). A number of fat globules are also usually met with in this position.

If a thin section of the wall be examined unstained, it will be found to consist in great part of neuroglia cells, the processes of which are closely matted together, with here and there a few altered nerve fibres, many of which are varicose and fatty. Between these are crystals or granules of altered blood pigment. The crystals are especially numerous in the opaque yellow zone surrounding the capsule, where also the fatty granules are more numerous. In the sheaths of the vessels fatty granules and altered coloured and colourless blood corpuscles are found, whilst in the larger cells lining the lymph spaces, or more frequently lying free in them, blood crystals may be seen. In a cyst formed as the result of an embolic softening no blood crystals are found in the walls of the sac, as there has been *no great*

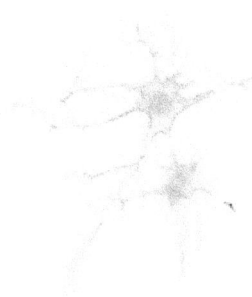

FIG. 135.—Drawing of connective tissue or Deiters' cells, from dense connective tissue of the wall of a cyst. Stained in carmine and half cleared up. (× 600.)
 a. Single or double nuclei.
 b. Delicate branching processes.

escape of blood from the vessels. In embolic softening there is simply fatty degeneration of the tissues ; and a mass of granular *débris* and fat crystals is all that is found under the microscope, save that there may be an increase in the number of leucocytes, along with other evidences of slight inflammatory changes around the vessel. Where the softened area is due to thrombosis, in which the cutting off of the blood supply is gradual, there is true fatty degeneration or yellow softening. The so-called red softening of the brain appears to be an inflammatory process leading to fatty degeneration, in which there is very marked congestion of the vessels. In such a condition

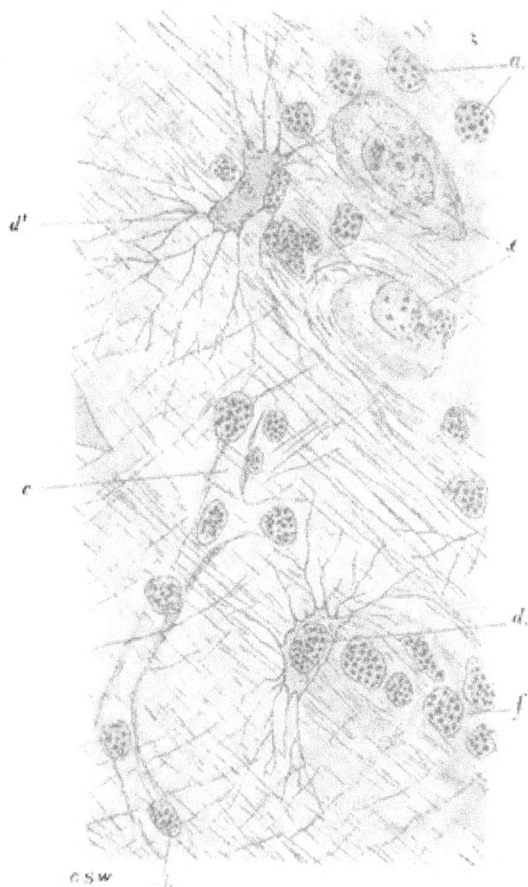

FIG. 136.—Drawing of connective tissue, &c. of medulla oblongata in case of chronic inflammation. Stained with carmine and half cleared up. (× 800.)

a. Connective tissue nuclei, around which there is as yet no formed material. Contractile nucleus well marked.

b. Nucleus of wall of (c) capillary vessel.

d.d¹. Connective tissue corpuscles in different stages of development. (Deiters' cells.) Note the branching processes.

e. Nerve cells, with pigmented nuclei. Each contains a nucleolus.

f. Young connective tissue nuclei or leucocytes lying in lymph space.

note the proliferation of the neuroglia cells, the exudation of leucocytes, and the hæmorrhages into the perivascular sheath. In connection with the various degenerative changes which occur, the amount of blood in the part, the amount of infiltration with leucocytes, and the extent and rapidity of the fatty change in the nerve fibres and connective tissue cells, must all be remembered when an attempt is made to explain the causes of the yellow or the red forms of cerebral softening. The cicatrix left is made up of fibrous tissue or condensed neuroglia. Its structure is very readily made out.

Another section of the wall of the cyst may be stained in carmine (§ 100), but, instead of being completely cleared up, it should be treated with methylated spirit (instead of absolute alcohol), and left in this long enough for part only of the water to be driven out ; clear up partly in clove oil, mount in dammar mounting fluid, and examine at once, as preparations made in this way do not for long retain their characteristic appearances. Such a method is especially useful for demonstrating neuroglia cells with their delicate branching processes.

OTHER PATHOLOGICAL APPEARANCES.

325. Of the other pathological conditions met with in the brain, may be mentioned the various inflammatory changes in the membranes; these, making allowances for the different structures affected, correspond with those set up by inflammation in other positions. There is distension of the vessels, exudation of leucocytes and fluid into the perivascular lymph spaces, proliferation of connective tissue cells, and a gradual formation of fibrous tissue. We find also pigmentation and small hæmorrhages. In the brain substance beneath, either in the cortex or in the ventricles, there is also evidence of inflammation ; one of the most marked of these, whether the inflammation be due to injury or to disease, is the presence of what are known as colloid bodies ; these are apparently droplets of myelin set free from the inflamed or degenerating white substance of Schwann, or, in some cases, it may be even from the degenerating axis cylinders; they stain deeply with picro-carmine, and may be readily distinguished in many pathological conditions.

The amyloid bodies which, in appearance and reactions differ somewhat from these colloid bodies, derive their name from the fact that they take on a deep brown stain when treated with iodine, and a bluish violet with iodine and sulphuric acid; they are also deeply stained by logwood. They are somewhat like starch granules also, in that concentric circles are seen in them where the staining is not too deep, the centre always being much darker than the periphery. These amyloid bodies are of different sizes; they appear to be formed from red and white blood corpuscles, or even from connective tissue corpuscles which first become swollen and granular or homogeneous.

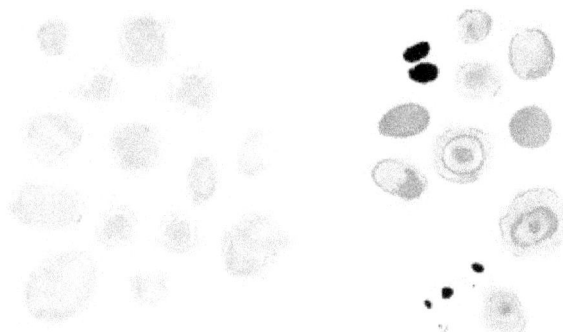

FIG. 137.—Amyloid bodies from epileptic medulla. (× 700.)
   1. Unstained.
      a. Normal blood corpuscles.
      b. Swollen blood corpuscles.
      c. Granular blood corpuscles.
      d. Enlarged granular blood corpuscles.
      e. Enlarged homogeneous corpuscle.
      f,g. Amyloid bodies.
   2. Stained with iodine and sulphuric acid.
   Here the stages of development from the blood corpuscle to the amyloid body may be seen.

In the walls of the ventricles there are formed in the connective tissue of the lining membrane of the ependyma, small granulations or masses of round cells, which grow up beneath the epithelium of the ependyma, and project or break through the epithelial layer, until they form papilliform masses in which may be seen spindle-shaped cells, fibrillæ, and small vessels similar to those in the floor of a granulating wound. Pigmentation of the nerve cells is of frequent occurrence, not only in the ganglion cells at the base, but also in

those of the cortical layers. The pigment is usually collected round
the contractile nuclei ; these cells may be undergoing fatty degeneration and even calcification, they may be vacuolated, or their processes
may be much shorter than usual, and their protoplasm atrophied
and granular, and these may all be the signs of atrophic change
resulting from overwork, from prolonged stimulation and impaired
nutrition. Earlier changes in the cells, such as cloudy swelling,
have been observed, but these are seldom met with in specimens
brought under the notice of the general pathologist. Wherever
inflammatory changes are present in the brain, the Deiters' cells or
neuroglia cells are always more abundant than usual. Between the
connective tissue cell, consisting of a nucleus with little protoplasmic
substance around it, which must be looked upon as a scavenging cell,
and that with a large number of finely-branched processes, may be
seen cells in all the various stages of development.

ANATOMY OF THE SPINAL CORD.

326. In order to render more intelligible the descriptions given of the
pathological conditions found in the spinal cord, it may be well to
describe very briefly the primary tracts of the cord, as the arrangement of these has to be constantly referred to in our study of the diseases of such a complicated structure. As many of the physiological
data now at our command have been obtained by a study of
pathological conditions met with in secondary degenerations (§§ 333
and 334), it may be stated generally that such secondary degeneration of the white matter of the cord runs in the same direction as the
impulse which travels along the special tract in the normal cord ;
from this it may be deduced that the trophic centres are usually
near the point at which the stimulating impressions are received or
reflected. This may be best explained with the aid of a diagramatic
section of the cord (Fig. 138).

In certain spreading lesions or secondary degenerations—locomotor
ataxia, for instance—in which the primary lesion appears to be connected with the sensory nerves or the posterior nerve roots, there is
an ascending degeneration along those definite tracts, marked in the
diagram with an arrow pointing upwards. In lesions of the motor

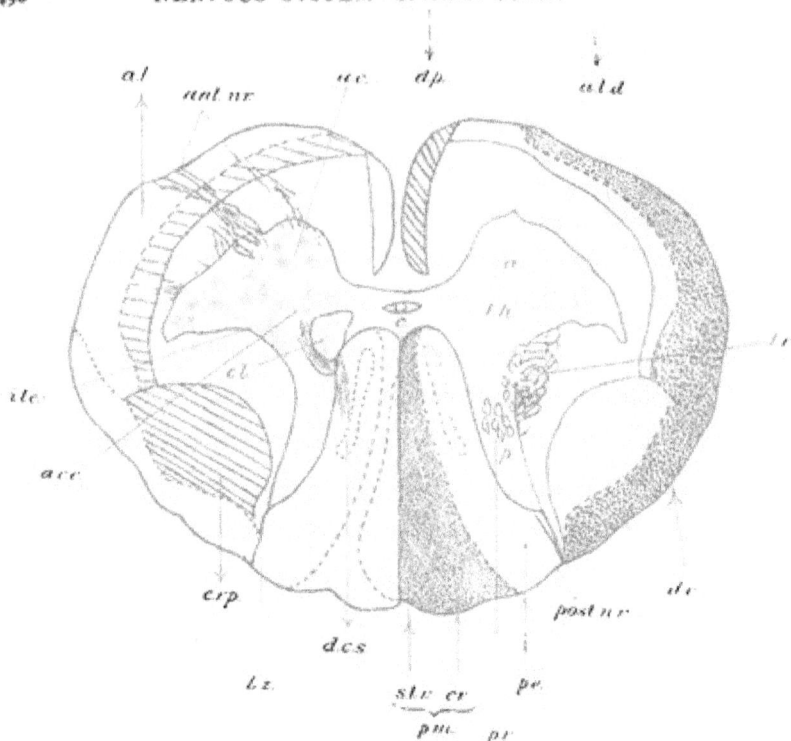

FIG. 138.—Diagram to illustrate the general arrangement of the several tracts of white matter, and of the multipolar cells in the grey matter in the spinal cord. Made up from a series of diagrams prepared by Dr. Sherrington, and given in Foster's *Physiology*.

c.r.p.	Crossed pyramidal tract.
d.p.	Direct pyramidal tract.
a.l.d.	Antero-lateral descending tract.
d.c.s.	Descending "comma"-shaped tract.
d.c.	Direct cerebellar tract.
p.m.	Postero-median column, made up of sacral, lumbar, and dorsal root fibres, *s.l.r.;* and cervical root fibres, *c.r.*
a.l.	Ascending lateral, or Gowers' tract.
p.e.	Postero-external column.
L.z.	Lissauer's zone.
a.	Anterior horn of grey matter.
a.c.	Multipolar ganglion cells of anterior horn.
ant. n.r.	Anterior nerve root.
p.	Posterior horn of grey matter, in which are a few nerve cells.
post. n.r.	Posterior nerve root.
l.h.	Lateral horn of grey matter.
a.c.c.	Cells of the anterior cervix.
c.l.	Clarke's column (or vesicular column).
i.l.c.	Cells of the intermedio-lateral tract, or lateral horn.
c.	Commissure or isthmus, in which is seen the central canal.
l.r.	Lateral reticular formation.
p.r.	Posterior reticular formation.

area of the brain, such as laceration produced by hæmorrhage, softening, or tumours, all of which are invariably followed by descending
degeneration, we have the changes travelling along the tracts of white
matter in the direction of the motor impulse—those tracts marked
with an arrow pointing downwards. If there be injury to the cord at
any definite level, an injury which may be traumatic or due to
hæmorrhage or the growth of a tumour, a secondary degeneration
may be found passing from it upwards in the columns marked
with an ascending arrow, and downwards in those marked with the
descending arrow.

Descending Tracts.—The most important of these is the *crossed
pyramidal tract*, which, coming from the brain, crosses in the medulla
oblongata at the decussation of the pyramids, and runs along the whole
length of the cord in the position marked *c.r.p.* The *direct pyramidal
tract (d.p.)* comes down from the brain through the medulla, but
does not cross over to the opposite side ; it forms a small strip which
bounds the anterior median fissure and is found in the upper half of
the cord only. Between these two pyramidal tracts, forming a kind
of connecting link, is a crescentic strip midway between the surface
and the anterior horn of grey matter. This is not a well-marked
band, but it is spoken of as the *antero-lateral descending tract (a.l.d.)*,
as in it a number of altered fibres may be found in cords in which
there is descending degeneration.

The only other area in which descending degeneration may be
traced is the *descending "comma"-shaped tract (d.c.s.)*, which is
situated in the middle of the postero-external column. It probably
represents part of the posterior root which first of all descends
in the cord ; degenerations in this area are, as a rule, extremely
localised, running down only as far as the root fibres descend in
each series of segments.

Ascending Tracts.—The *direct cerebellar tract (d.c.)* is a mass of
coarse white fibres, lying outside the lateral or crossed pyramidal
tract immediately under the pia mater ; it begins in the upper
lumbar region, gradually increases in size as it passes upwards to
the medulla, and ends in the restiform body or in the fibres that
pass from that body to the cerebellum. Running along the whole
length of the cord is a tract of very fine fibres arranged along each

side of the posterior median fissure ; it is spoken of as the *postero-median tract* (*p.m.*), the *postero-internal column* or column of Goll ; it also ends in the medulla.

The *ascending antero-lateral tract*, or Gowers' tract (*a.l.*), is a comma-shaped area, the head of which lies between the direct cerebellar tract and the crossed pyramidal tract ; this extends to the surface, and as far forward as the antero-lateral descending tract, outside of which it lies. It is made up of fibres of very different sizes. Outside the postero-internal column is the *postero-external tract* (*p.e.*), or Burdach's column.

The *posterior zone* (*L.z.*) or Lissauer's zone is a small tract just outside and behind the posterior horn of grey matter ; it really belongs to the posterior root.

The parts of white matter immediately bounding the grey matter are not yet fully understood. The fibres do not degenerate either upwards or downwards, and, as suggested by Foster, they may be connecting fibres, each of which may be in communication with two trophic centres.

Speaking roughly, the *grey matter* of the cord is divided into anterior (*a.*) and posterior (*p.*) horns and a commissural part (*c.*). It is made up of delicate nucleated neuroglia, in which bundles of medullated nerve fibres run in various directions, all apparently passing from large multipolar nerve cells either across the commissural part or out into the nerve roots. There are also single nerve fibres, varying very much in size.

In the *anterior horn* (*a.h.*) embedded in the reticulum are cells of very considerable size (*a.c.*), which send out numerous processes into the surrounding grey matter ; these cells are divided into smaller groups, named according to their position in the horn.

Clarke's column, or the vesicular column (*c.*), made up of cells, not quite so large as the above, embedded in a mass of fine fibrils, is situated outside the postero-external column, near the end of the commissural part of the grey matter. In it the fibres of the direct cerebellar tract are supposed to take their origin.

On the outer side of the grey matter, about the level of the commissural part, is the *lateral horn* (*l.h.*), the cells of which are somewhat spindle-shaped, " with their long axis placed transversely "

(Foster). It is found as a special group only in the thoracic and lumbar regions.

Behind Clarke's column the cells of the *posterior horn* are few in number and comparatively small ; they are branched and are found in all parts of the cord.

FIG. 139.—Section of cord to show the structure of the anterior horn of grey matter, stained by Weigert's method. (× 300.)
a. Large multipolar nerve cell with branching processes.
b. Nerve fibres of white matter with myelin sheath stained.
c. Fibres running through the neuroglia in which the multipolar cells are embedded.
d. Process in which fibres of the anterior nerve roots run.

The cells of the *anterior cervix* (*a.c.*) are found, in the thoracic region only, as a group of small cells at the base of the anterior horn, just where it runs into the *commissure* or *isthmus* (*c*).

PATHOLOGICAL CHANGES IN THE SPINAL CORD.

327. The pathological changes in the spinal cord may, for our purposes, be divided into five groups:—1st. Inflammation of the meninges; 2nd. Inflammations of the grey matter or poliomyelitis (in which changes are set up in the ganglion cells, especially in those of the anterior horn); 3rd. Atrophy, primary or secondary, of the tissues in the grey matter; 4th. Primary inflammation of the white matter of the cord; and 5th. Secondary degeneration of the white matter.

1. INFLAMMATION OF THE MENINGES.

328. Here the processes correspond very closely to those met with in inflammation of the cerebral membranes; they may be confined to the membranes themselves; this is rarely the case, owing to the intimate connection of these membranes with the surface of the cord; secondary inflammation in the periphery of the white matter of the cord, and also of the connective tissue of the nerve roots, usually supervenes, and these, in turn, may set up secondary degeneration.

2. INFLAMMATION OF THE GREY MATTER.

329. The only cases of this condition that I have seen have occurred in children; it is certainly a disease of early life, though cases are recorded in which it has occurred in the young adult. It appears to be due either to actual hæmorrhage, or to a suddenly increased blood pressure in a localised area, accompanied by great œdema of the surrounding tissues.

The permanent symptoms are the result of destruction followed by absorption of a localised patch of grey matter; the fugitive symptoms are due, apparently, to pressure in the area around that in which the tissues are actually destroyed. On examining a cord in which there is inflammation of one or both of the anterior horns of grey matter, especially as is often the case where the patient has survived the onset of the disease for some time, there is usually a marked atrophy in some segment of the cord corresponding to the area and side of the muscles affected clinically; the affected side of the cord is considerably smaller, a diminution in size which appears to be due entirely to the atrophy of the anterior horn. This small horn is pinkish grey and more gelatinous looking than usual; it may be slightly pigmented.

Harden (§ 59 or 62) and stain (§ 123 or 124 or [1]).

(× 20).—The horn on the affected side is atrophied and shrunken; the large ganglion cells can scarcely be made out; the network of the

---

[1] A method devised by Marchi for the differentiation of degenerated nerve fibres in the cord and brain removed *at once* from experimental cases is the following :—

Harden for one week in Müller's fluid; or, better still, plunge into hot Müller's fluid (Mott); in the case of the brain use Hamilton's injection method (§ 10*b*). Then cut into thin slices 3-4 mm. each, and harden for another week or more in a fluid made up of 2 parts Müller's fluid, and 1 part of 1 per cent. osmic acid. Wash thoroughly in water. Then embed in collodion in the ordinary fashion, after passing through alcohol and ether. Mount the sections without further stain in Canada Balsam. For the description of this method I am indebted to Professor Schäfer. It certainly gives admirable results. Schäfer has devised a capital modification of Pals' method of staining the myelin sheath. Harden for a month in Müller's fluid, cut sections, and then put into Marchi's Müller and osmic acid fluid for twenty-four hours. He stains in the following for a few hours. (Leave overnight.)

Hæmatoxylin, . . . 1 grain (dissolved in a small quantity of absolute alcohol).
Acetic acid, . . . 2 cc.
Distilled water, . . 100 cc.

The sections become black. Bleach by Pals' method (§ 124), allowing the sections to remain for as much as ten minutes in the permanganate solution, and then continue the bleaching in oxalic acid.

Golgi's method is used when the naked axis cylinders and nerve-cell processes before they are covered with myelin are to be stained.

He hardens the nerve centres (cut into thin slices) for 20-30 days in 2 per cent. solution of bichromate of potassium, and then in ·75 per cent. solution of nitrate of silver for 30-40 hours. Another method—Harden for 4-5 days in the bichromate solution, then for 24-30 hours in a mixture of 1 per cent. osmic acid 1 part, and 2 per cent. bichromate solution 4 parts, and then in ·75 per cent. solution of nitrate of silver as above.*

Kölliker uses the following modification of Golgi's method. He hardens for one and a-half days in large quantities of 3 per cent. solution of bichromate of potassium 4 parts, and 1 per cent. perosmic acid solution 1 part. The fluid is changed at the end of four or five hours. He then washes for 30 minutes in ·25 per cent. solution of nitrate of silver, and transfers the specimens to ·75 per cent. silver solution, where they are left for 30-40 hours; and then to 40 per cent. spirit (for not longer than 3-6 weeks). Place in absolute alcohol for one hour, and then in thin celloidin syrup for an hour, and cut *at once*. Clarify in creosote for 15 minutes, transfer to turpentine, and mount in xylol balsam.†

---

* *Fortschritte der Medicin*, Bd. V., p. 545. 1887.
† *See* W. A. Turner in *Journ. of Anat. and Phys.*, vol. xxv., p. 443.

nerve fibres has almost disappeared, and its place has been taken by
a connective tissue made up of proliferating neuroglia cells which
take on the picro-carmine stain very readily. The anterior roots are
somewhat smaller than normal, and there is usually evidence of
great congestion, the vessels being patent and filled with blood.
In some cases small spaces filled with serous fluid may be seen.

(× 300).—Confirm the above appearances. The atrophy of the
cells is well seen ; these cells are irregular in shape, their processes
are far less distinct than usual, there is an accumulation of pigment around the nuclei, and the spaces in which they lie may be
considerably enlarged. Around the vessels there is an accumulation
of young cells, though in some cases masses of small granules may
be seen. In the later stages where atrophy is very far advanced, the
whole of the nerve tissues, both cells and fibres, may be broken
down, when, as in the brain, one of two things, or both, may happen,
viz.:—the cyst (or series of minute cysts) containing serous fluid
remains, or there is an enormous increase of the neuroglia which,
becoming fibrillated and dense, and followed by contraction, is much
more like ordinary cicatricial tissue than neuroglia usually is.

3. Simple Atrophy of the Grey Matter.

330. This is usually well marked in the anterior horns. Little can
be made out on naked eye examination beyond the fact that the two
sides of the cord are unequal, and that this inequality appears to
be due to a diminution in the size of the anterior horn. This atrophy
of the grey matter is found both in the cord and in the medulla
oblongata, giving rise to various well-known forms of motor paralysis.

Harden (§ 59 or 62) and stain (§§ 98 and 123 or 124).

(× 50).—The anterior horn is atrophied, the ganglion cells are
small, and have lost their plump outlines and processes. The nerve
fibres are diminished in number, and many of those that remain
take on stains very imperfectly. The anterior roots of the spinal
nerves are smaller than usual, and in some cases nothing may be
seen but a mass of pinkish (when stained with picro-carmine)
neuroglia.

(× 300).—Confirm the above appearances. The imperfectly stained cells, with their atrophied protoplasm and short blunted processes, are well seen; the nuclei, however, stain badly, and around each there is often deep pigmentation of the protoplasm; sometimes these large ganglion cells are represented merely by small granular masses of pigment. There is also a considerable quantity of pigment around the perivascular spaces, from which it may be gathered that at some earlier period inflammation or congestion must have played a prominent part in the process. There is also an increase of connective tissue around the nerves of the anterior spinal root, and in some cases we have a secondary degeneration of the descending or ascending columns of white matter, according to the position of the primary atrophy. When this atrophic process occurs in the medulla, descending degeneration of the pyramidal tracts is almost invariably met with.

4. INFLAMMATIONS OF THE WHITE MATTER.

331. It is a somewhat difficult matter to determine how far inflammatory processes play any special part in the degenerations that take place in the nerves and in the columns of white matter in the cord. It has been found that in acute inflammation produced experimentally, there are changes both in the axis cylinder and in the myelin sheath which are said to be characteristic, but owing to the progressive nature of most of these inflammatory diseases, it is extremely difficult to follow the course of events. It may be taken for granted, however, that in inflammation of the white matter there is distension of the vessels, exudation of leucocytes, impaired nutrition, degeneration of the myelin sheath, which may be gradually broken down, and irregular swelling and nodosity of the axis cylinder, followed by interruption at some point of its course, and ultimately by its disappearance, all this being accompanied or followed by a great increase of the neuroglia. Although some of these conditions are said to be primary, they may be best examined in secondary degeneration, such as is found in locomotor ataxia, the only difference being that in primary sclerosis the degeneration of the nerves and the increase of neuroglia go on simultaneously, whilst in secondary degeneration the increase of neuroglia appears to follow the changes in the nerve fibres.

MULTIPLE SCLEROSIS.

332. This may be looked upon as one of the forms of primary degeneration of the cord; it may also occur in the brain.

Naked eye appearances.—On examining a cord in which there is multiple sclerosis, we find small grey gelatinous or opaque yellowish

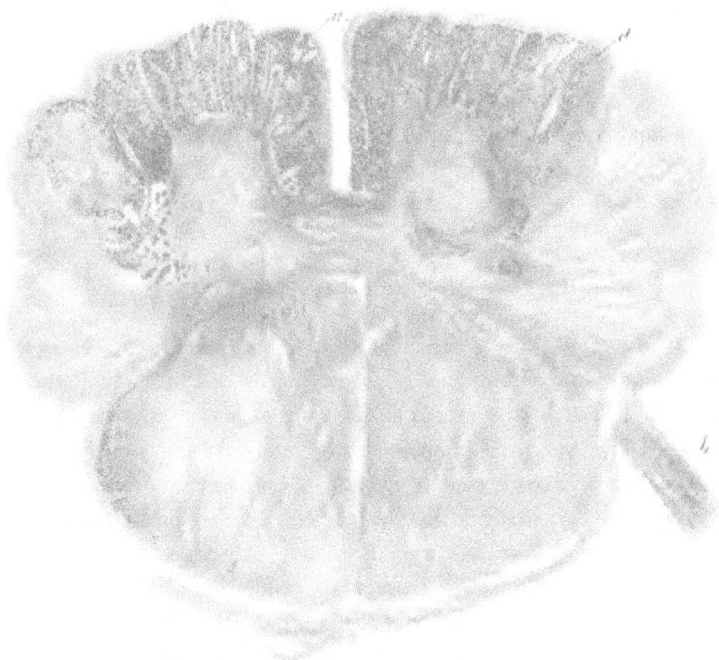

FIG. 140.—Section in the cervical region of the spinal cord from a case of multiple sclerosis. Stained by Weigert's method. (× 15.)
    In this section there is sclerosis more or less marked in every part of the cord, except in the direct pyramidal tracts (*a*) on each side of the anterior median fissure.
    b. Posterior nerve root.
    c. Posterior median fissure.
    d. Anterior horn of grey matter.

white patches, which stand out very prominently from the white matter of the columns.

On making sections at different levels, it will be found that these patches do not correspond in their localisation in the different parts of the cord; at one point they may be in the pyramidal tracts near the surface, at another, deep down, affecting one side or the other, whilst at a third level, some little distance away, the columns at the opposite side, or the posterior columns, may be affected. The grey matter may also be attacked, but this is somewhat more difficult to make out with the naked eye. The patches are usually rounded, though they may be somewhat irregular; they are gelatinous and marked with opaque areas, or they may be firm, sometimes almost like cicatricial tissue.

FIG. 141.—Portion of the postero-internal column of a sclerosed cord from a case of locomotor ataxia. Stained by Weigert's method. (× 300.)
    a. Comparatively healthy fibres, of which the myelin sheaths are stained.
    b. Reticulum of neuroglia unstained by the hæmatoxylin.

Harden (§ 59 or 62) sections from different levels, and stain (§ 123 or 124).

(× 15).—Note the irregular distribution of the patches in the different specimens. It is evident that the disease is not confined to any special tract or series of tracts, either descending or ascending. In carmine-stained specimens the degenerated areas stand out very prominently, the new connective tissue being deeply stained.

(× 50).—In the centre of one of these patches it is impossible to distinguish any nerve fibres lying in the dense felt-work of new connective tissue. Near the margin of the patch, however, a few comparatively normal nerve fibres, or fibres in which the myelin is undergoing granular degeneration, may be seen. The lumen of the vessel is somewhat more patent than usual, and there may be hyaline thickening of the inner coat, or thickening of the adventitia.

(× 300).—Confirm the above appearances. Note first the dense felted network of neuroglia in which the nuclei of the cells may be distinguished surrounded by a small quantity of protoplasm from which run out numerous branching processes (see Figs. 135 and 136). Embedded in this network are a number of compound granular corpuscles which give a black reaction with osmic acid. The axis cylinders of the nerve fibres may be seen in the margin of the patch, and between them the increased amount of neuroglia can be readily made out. Note the hyaline thickening of the intima with a similar change in the connective tissue of the muscular coat ; there is also an increased quantity of connective tissue in the adventitia. The perivascular lymph spaces may be considerably enlarged and filled with small round cells, or with cells containing fatty particles which are well brought out by osmic acid. Corpora amylacea (Fig. 137) may also be made out, whilst where the process is not far advanced, and where the remains of degenerating nerve fibres can still be seen, the compound granular corpuscles and fatty granulations are present in very considerable numbers, not only in the spaces between the neuroglia, but also in the perivascular lymphatics.

5. Descending Degeneration.

333. Descending degeneration follows destruction or injury of the hemispherical ganglia in the region of the fissure of Rolando (the motor area) ; or of the fibres that run from these ganglia as they pass through the corona radiata ; of the internal capsule ; or of the motor tract below this point. If such injury be on the left side, say, the degeneration is found first in the motor area (pyramid) of the same side, in the medulla oblongata. Below the point of decussation of the pyramids the lesion is seen in the following positions—1st, in the direct pyramidal tract on the same (left) side ; 2nd, in the crossed pyramidal tract on the opposite (right) side, situated in the postero-lateral part of the

antero-lateral column, where it does not come quite to the surface, but is bounded externally by the direct cerebellar tract; and 3rd, in the antero-lateral descending tract. When this degeneration depends upon injury of the cord, the direct pyramidal tracts are affected for a short distance only, whilst the comma-shaped tract in the posterior column—the posterior root fibres, which, as already seen, run down the cord for some distance —is also involved.

Naked eye appearances.—The principal change is a peculiar firmness to the touch of the areas mentioned, which assume a much greyer and more gelatinous appearance than the corresponding areas on the opposite side.

Harden (§§ 11, 59-63), mount one section unstained, and stain others (§§ 100, 123, 124, and 324).

Hold the unstained section up to the light, and note that in the crossed pyramidal tract the tissue is much more transparent than the other white matter;—it looks almost like the grey matter. This change is not so readily recognised in the direct pyramidal tract, which is very small;—in some cases it is represented by a few fibres only.

(× 50).—In the carmine-stained specimen note that in the affected areas (the left direct and right crossed pyramidal tracts) the tissue is much pinker than normal white nerve tissue. There appears to be a marked increase in the amount of neuroglia, with a corresponding diminution in the number and size of the nerve fibres.

(× 300).—The increase in the amount of neuroglia can be very readily made out, especially in the carmine and osmic acid stained specimen. The myelin sheath of the nerve is breaking down or has disappeared, but the axis cylinder, deeply stained, can often be easily distinguished. In this section it will be noticed that the affected area is not nearly so deeply stained by osmic acid as is the part where the fatty myelin sheath is still present.

Examine a fresh section of a similar cord—or one in which the degeneration is not so far advanced, which is softer, and not so transparent—(× 300), and notice that in the affected area are numerous bodies about three times the size of a red blood corpuscle. Each of these contains two or three nuclei. Also observe the compound granular corpuscles; myelin drops, rounded or tadpole shaped; colloid masses, few in number—probably derived from the axis cylinder or myelin sheath, and unstained by iodine—and a few small beaded fibres. In the perivascular sheaths fatty globules and granules can frequently be seen, especially in the specimens stained with carmine and osmic acid; but few of the above bodies can be made out in a hardened specimen of the cord.

This descending degeneration, then, is simply a secondary degenerative process of the nerve fibres, accompanied by a formation of neuroglia, which appears as a "substitution" product.

Locomotor Ataxia and Ascending Degeneration.

334. In disease of the peripheral sensory nerves or of the posterior root fibres of the spinal nerves, from which these are given off, or when there is injury of the posterior columns of the cord, secondary degeneration appears in certain areas above the seat of lesion. In locomotor ataxia the process is essentially a progressive one; but in secondary degeneration, due to injury of the cord, the degeneration is very rapidly developed in all the parts that are ultimately affected.

In this latter case both the postero-internal and postero-external tracts degenerate for some distance, but higher up the postero-internal tract, which appears to be the main path of upward conduction, alone is affected, as far up, however, as the funiculus gracilis.

Naked eye appearances.—In a section of an ataxic cord, made at about the level of the last cervical or first dorsal nerve, it will be seen that the dura mater and pia mater are thickened—the posterior nerve roots are small and transparent, and the posterior columns are grey and gelatinous in appearance, but firm in texture. The thickened pia mater is firmly adherent to the posterior columns.

Prepare as above (§ 333).

(× 15).—In the postero-external columns, immediately internal to the posterior roots, there is an increase of fibrous tissue or neuroglia, which takes on the carmine stain deeply; stained by Weigert's method the tissue appears much yellower than normal, and with osmic acid the blackening is not nearly so marked as in the normal white tracts. When the change is confined to this region the disease may be spoken of as locomotor ataxia pure and simple. It will be found, however, that in most cases there is a secondary degenerative process which extends along the sensory tracts, and therefore passes upwards. This gives rise to an increased connective tissue formation, with corresponding changes in the nerve fibres. These changes must be looked for

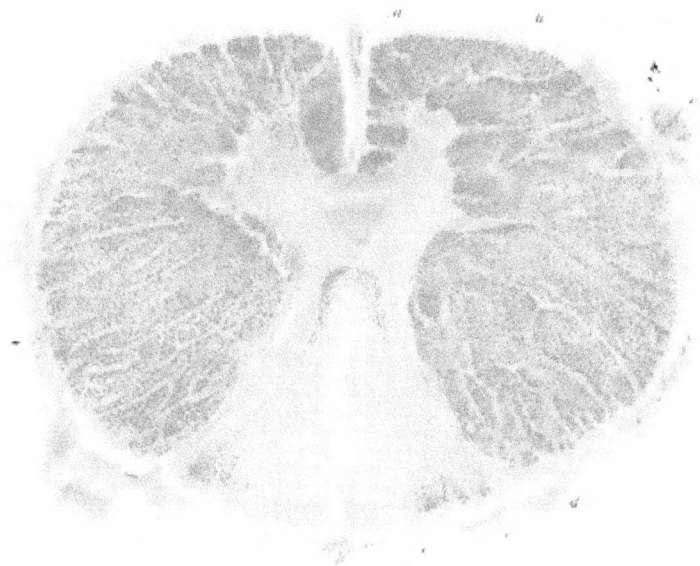

Fig. 142.—Section taken from the dorsal region of an ataxic cord. Stained by Weigert's method. (× 15.)
- a. Anterior median fissure.
- b. Anterior horn of grey matter.
- c. Anterior nerve root.
- d. Posterior nerve root, running from the posterior horn of grey matter.
- e. Column of Burdach, or postero-external tract undergoing secondary degeneration.
- f. Column of Goll, or postero-internal tract in a still more advanced stage of degeneration.
- g. Posterior median fissure.

The direct cerebellar and Gowers' tracts are unaffected.

in the inner parts of the postero-external columns, in the postero-internal columns, and in the upper part of the cord in the direct cerebellar tracts; whilst Gowers and Haddon describe also an affected comma-shaped area opposite the outer angle of the anterior horn of grey matter, either at the surface in the dorsal region, or close to the

surface at the level of the cervical enlargement.   In all these areas
there is a new formation of fibrous tissue which takes on a deep pink
when stained with picro-carmine.

(× 50).—Scattered at irregular intervals through this pink tissue
are more opaque patches — collections of breaking down axis
cylinders or colloid bodies derived from altered nerve fibres.   Near
the surface the vessels are considerably congested, their walls
are thickened, and the perivascular spaces are filled with granular
masses.   Where the disease is furthest advanced, *i.e.,* in some parts

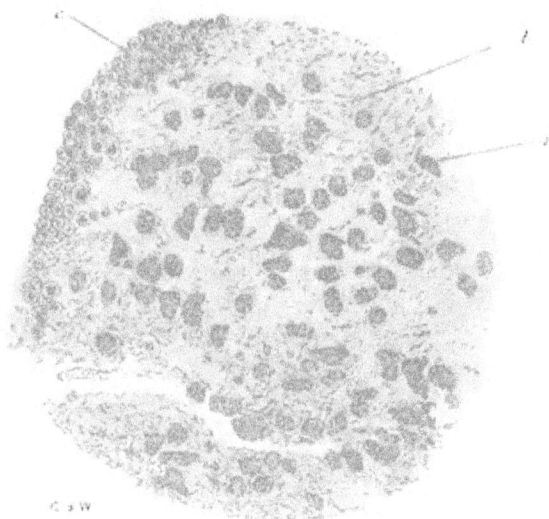

Fig. 143.—Locomotor ataxia.   Small portion of nerve tissue from
the direct cerebellar tract.   Stained with carmine.   (× 120.)
  a. Compound granular corpuscles and colloid bodies.
  b. Newly formed fibro-cellular tissue (pink).
  c. Healthy nerve fibres.

of the postero-external columns, the axis cylinders have disappeared
entirely.

(× 300).—Note the distended vessels.   In the perivascular sheath
there is a considerable quantity of fat in the form of granules and
globules, stained black with osmic acid.   Around the distended blood-
vessels, leucocytes may also be seen.   This loading of the connective
tissue with cells is also seen in the pia mater, where the perivascular
spaces are filled with fatty particles, and in some instances there is,

in the vessel itself, a substance giving, with osmic acid, a black reaction.

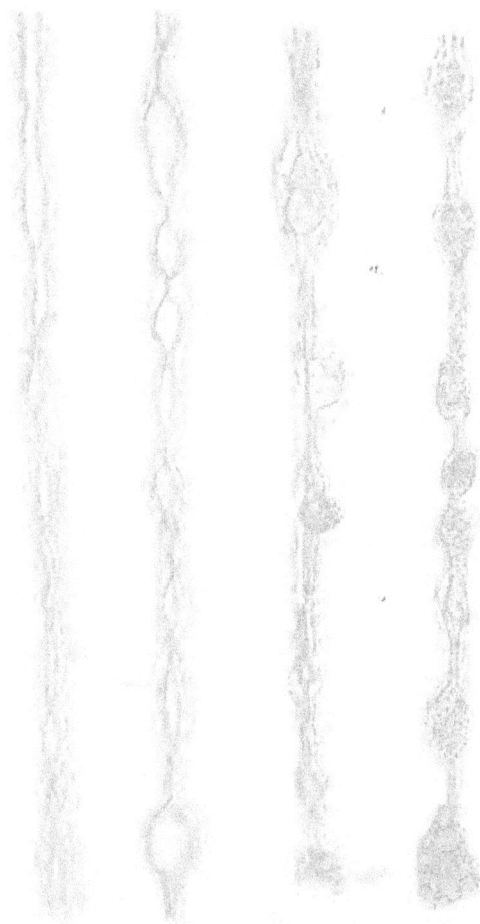

FIG. 144.—Locomotor ataxia. Nerves in various stages of degeneration, from the postero-external columns in the cervical region of the cord. Stained with osmic acid. (× 400.)

    a. The axis cylinders become more and more swollen and constricted, and then undergo fatty degeneration.
    b. Nerve sheath, which gradually loses its distinct outline and becomes fatty and granular.

In longitudinal and transverse sections, examine the nerves of the affected areas. In these there are very marked changes, such as are found in most cases of myelitis or inflammation of the cord. First a number of constrictions may be seen at intervals (in the longitudinal section) along the axis cylinder, the myelin apparently being but slightly affected, in other cases remaining intact. Later, the alternate constriction and swelling are more pronounced, and the varicosity is

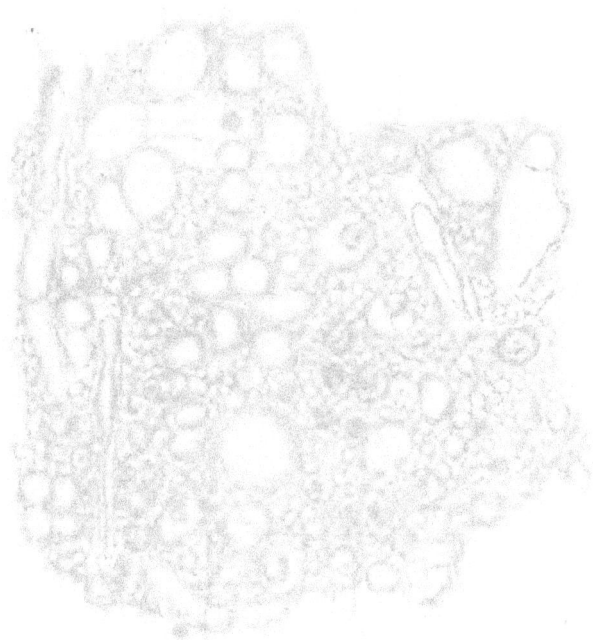

Fig. 145.—Section from valve of Vieussens. Locomotor ataxia. Unstained. (× 700.)
a. Enlarged and colloid axis cylinder.
b. Sheath in process of breaking up.
c. Connective tissue nucleus.
d. Sheath almost disappeared.

very marked. At other points the swollen masses of axis cylinders are seen to be vacuolated, and in other parts they form the granular masses seen scattered throughout the fibrous tissue.—(*See* Fig. 143.) Where these are seen in a transverse section of the cord, or where the disease is not very far advanced, the colloid bodies are very readily recognised from their clear homogeneous appearance, and often from their large size.

In the above condition be careful to distinguish between the area of the primary disease—the outer part of the postero-external columns —and those affected by a secondary ascending degeneration— postero-internal, direct cerebellar, and Gowers' and Haddon's tracts— all of which may be affected *above the point of primary lesion* as the result of any injury to the cord.

In examining this section, a careful search should be made for similar changes in Clarke's column, and for altered conditions in both the posterior and anterior horns of grey matter and for pigmentation, or swelling of the nerve cells.

Varicose swelling of the axis cylinder and hyaline thickening of the sheath, with increase in the amount of neuroglia and colloid bodies, may also be found in the following positions in well-marked cases of locomotor ataxia :—optic tracts and nerves, auditory nerve, and striæ acousticæ, fifth nerve, fourth nerves, at their decussation in the valve of Vieussens, corpora quadrigemina in the roof of the aqueduct of Sylvius, and the roots of the hypoglossal nerves.

WAXY DISEASE OF THE CORD.

335. Waxy degeneration of certain elements of the cord is comparatively rare. Prepare as in (§§ 56-59), stain (§ 106). . Notice first the affection of the middle coat of the vessels, then the degeneration of the connective tissue fibres, of the processes and even of the bodies of the ganglion cells, all of which are swollen and stained red violet.

TUMOURS GROWING IN CONNECTION WITH THE MEMBRANE OF THE BRAIN AND CORD.

336. *Syphilitic gummata* occur in the dura-mater, in the pia mater, and in the cerebral substance, near the base of the brain, especially in the interpeduncular space. *Glioma* and *myxoma* in various forms, *sarcoma*—melanotic, spindle-celled, and small round-celled (the latter usually met with as a primary growth in children), *myxo-sarcoma, angioma, psammoma, fibroma,* and more rarely *osteoma* and *lipoma*—all occur in the central nervous system. *Carcinoma* is almost invariably secondary. In addition to the above—which, with the exception of the glioma, occur in both brain and membranes—*chondroma* is found growing in the meninges. Dermoid cysts are described as occurring in the brain and dura mater. *Parasites—Cysticercus cellulosæ* and hydatid cyst.

Retina.

337. Harden the retina for examination (§ 59). If the whole eye can be obtained, place it intact in the hardening fluid, or make a few minute punctures in front of the attachment of the cornea. Treat as for nerve tissues (§§ **98, 103** *d*, **123** and **124**). If the posterior half of the eye, only, can be obtained, turn the tissues inside out, *i.e.*, have the retina on the convex instead of the concave surface before placing in the hardening fluid. In this way it is kept tense, and much better preparations will be obtained. In place of Müller's fluid, a ten per cent. solution of chloral hydrate may be used in the same way.

The peripheral nerves are to be treated generally in the same way as pieces of spinal cord.

CHAPTER XIII.

THE ORGANS OF GENERATION IN THE FEMALE.[1]

The Pelvic Peritoneum and Connective Tissue.

338. The peritoneum lining the true pelvis is frequently the seat of localised peritonitis. As a result, it is not uncommon to find, on *post mortem* examination, considerable alterations from the normal relationship of the parts, and the presence of bands of adhesion. Such adhesions play an important part in the production of various pathological conditions, notably of the Fallopian tubes. The ovary may become glued to the fimbriated extremity, and, from pressure, obstruction of the tube may be occasioned at some other point in its course. A portion of the tube is thus transformed into a closed sac, in which natural secretions accumulate, and a cystic condition is developed. Adhesions between the uterus and neighbouring parts may lead to displacement and fixation of that organ.

Beneath the peritoneum there is a layer of loose cellular connective tissue. Between the layers of the broad ligaments, especially at their bases and where they are reflected on to the uterus, and around the cervix, especially behind it, the cellular tissue is present in considerable quantity. This tissue is particularly rich in lymphatic vessels and glands, and is frequently the seat of inflammatory action, constituting the condition known as parametritis, or pelvic cellulitis. By direct continuity the process may spread under the peritoneum to the abdominal wall, or up the line of the ureters towards the kidney. Such deposits may suppurate, and occasion pelvic abscesses which may open into the bowel, bladder, or vagina, or through the abdominal wall—rarely into the peritoneal cavity. It should be noted that these conditions of pelvic peritonitis and cellulitis seldom occur entirely

---

[1] Written originally by J. Milne Chapman, M.B., M.R.C.S., for the Second Edition.

independent of one another, and it is sometimes impossible to tell, on *post mortem* examination, which structure was primarily involved.

Pelvic Hæmatocele.

339. This consists in effusion of blood into the pelvis, either beneath the peritoneum or into the peritoneal cavity. The former condition, extra-peritoneal hæmatocele, is usually the result of traumatism during parturition, and the most common situation is beneath the vaginal wall. The causes of intra-peritoneal hæmatocele are more numerous. Again, traumatism may be a cause, as in surgical operations, or blood may regurgitate from the uterus through the Fallopian tubes during menstruation. Probably the most common cause is the early rupture of an extra-uterine pregnancy, especially of one of the tubal variety. Associated with such blood effusions there is always a certain amount of pelvic peritonitis, and the new material thus thrown out, along with the adhesions formed, leads to the shutting off of the effused blood from the general peritoneal cavity. Sometimes such new material and adhesions are in existence previous to the bleeding, which then takes place into a closed-off portion of peritoneum. The blood usually becomes completely absorbed, but sometimes suppuration, followed by sinus formation, takes place.

Microscopic Structure of the Wall of the Normal Uterus.

340. (× 50).—Examine a section made through the whole thickness of the uterine wall (Fig. 146).

The peritoneal lining is seen as a thin layer covering the outer surface. Beneath this is a small quantity of condensed fibrous tissue, but the main bulk of the wall is composed of bundles of non-striped muscle running in various directions, with a supporting framework of connective tissues, partly structureless, partly fibrous. In the wall there are numerous large vessels and lymph spaces. For a depth of 1 to 2 mm. from the internal surface is the "mucous membrane," but no submucous structure is present, nor can the two layers, mucous and muscular, be sharply differentiated. The mucous mem-

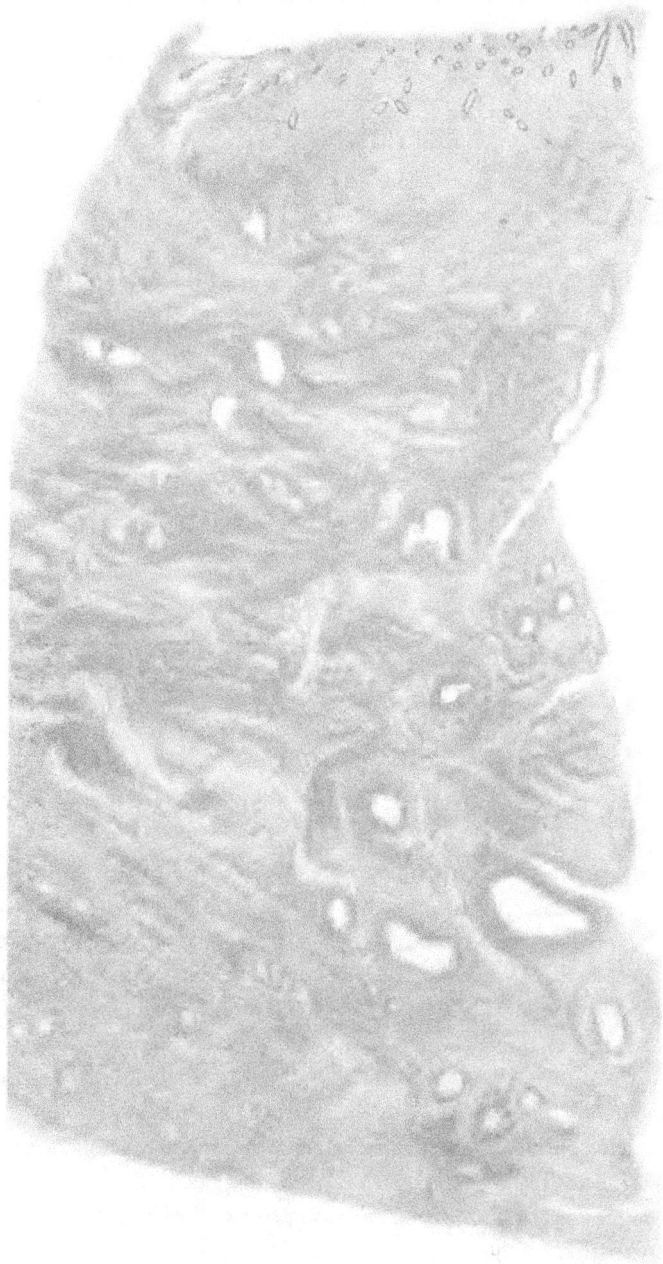

FIG. 146.—Section from surface to surface of the uterine wall of a girl aged sixteen, who had never menstruated. (× 20.) Logwood and eosin.

    a. "The mucous membrane." *b.* Epithelium covering the cavity surface. *c.c.* Uterine glands. *f.* Muscular wall, with muscle bundles cut in various directions. *d.* Vessel. *e.* Lymphatic space. *g.* The peritoneal surface covered with flattened endothelioid cells.

brane consists of connective tissue of the embryonic type, with large nucleated round or slightly spindle-shaped cells. No large vessels are visible, the mucous membrane being supplied entirely by capillaries.

(× 450).—Notice here and there a few ordinary connective tissue fibres and some non-striped muscle cells, especially in the deeper layer. The free surface is covered with a single layer of ciliated columnar epithelium, which is prolonged downwards as the lining of test-tube glands, the deep ends of which are lost sight of among the superficial layers of the muscular tissue. The direction of these glands is very varied, and a complete section of the whole length of one is seldom obtained. They are occasionally somewhat spiral, usually simple, but sometimes slightly branched. The epithelium lining the glands is similar to that covering the free surface, but is devoid of cilia.

NOTE ON THE APPEARANCE OF THE MUCOUS MEMBRANE OF THE UTERUS DURING MENSTRUATION.

341. The lining membrane of the uterus is one of the first structures to undergo *post mortem* decomposition, and it is extremely difficult to know to what extent such decomposition may account for the changes usually found on examination of the uteri of individuals who have died during menstruation.

The greater part of the mucous membrane, including its superficial covering of epithelium, has disappeared. In the remaining portion of the mucous membrane the cells of the matrix and of the glands are swollen and granular, while the superficial layers of the muscular cells are proliferating actively. No trace of fatty degeneration can be made out.

A thickening of the membrane, due to proliferation of all the elements of the matrix, with fatty degeneration (?) of, and hæmorrhage into the most superficial layers, which alone are shed ; and regeneration, occurring from the remaining cells of the stroma and the epithelium of the glands, are all described as occurring during menstruation.

METRITIS.

342. Metritis is an affection of the connective tissue stroma which is present both in the muscular and in the mucous layers of the uterus. When the inflammation is acute, purulent infiltration of the uterine wall may occur. When the affection is chronic, there is first an increase in the quantity of embryonic elements throughout the whole muscular wall, especially in the neighbourhood of the blood-vessels, followed by a development and contraction of connective tissue around the vessels and lymph spaces, leading to dilatation of the latter.

ENDOMETRITIS.

343. Remove with a curette a portion of the endometrium from a case of abortion. Harden (§ 59 or 64) and stain (§ 98 or 107).

(× 50).—If the abortion be recent, the large cells of the decidua, and perhaps also remnants of chorionic villi, may be seen ; but if the abortion has occurred some time previously (Fig. 147), such elements, unless a distinct portion of placental tissue has been retained, are entirely absent. There is usually considerable dilatation of the glands, which, instead of being regularly shaped tubes, with their walls almost in apposition (Fig. 146), appear as convoluted spaces, with the epithelium in a more or less catarrhal condition. The matrix is looser in texture than normal, with here and there spaces and extravasations of blood, the latter sometimes tearing the structures asunder, at other times simply infiltrating them. The individual cells are swollen, granular, and have large and particularly well stained nuclei. Numerous dilated capillaries, some distended with blood, may also be seen.

In more chronic cases of endometritis, the catarrhal condition of the glands often leads to loosening and probably shedding of their epithelium. The cells of the matrix become fibrillated, and new connective tissue develops, apparently at the seat of extravasation, and later the whole matrix becomes fibrous instead of cellular. As this new tissue shrinks, it either, if in large quantity, encroaches on the gland spaces, or, if in small quantity, separates their walls and leads to detachment of the epithelial lining cells.

Polypi of the cervix may be either mucous, fibroid, or channelled. Fibroids are rare; they are similar in structure to fibroids of the body of the uterus. The mucous variety occurs as small papillary outgrowths, with one or more small cysts, resembling the Nabothian

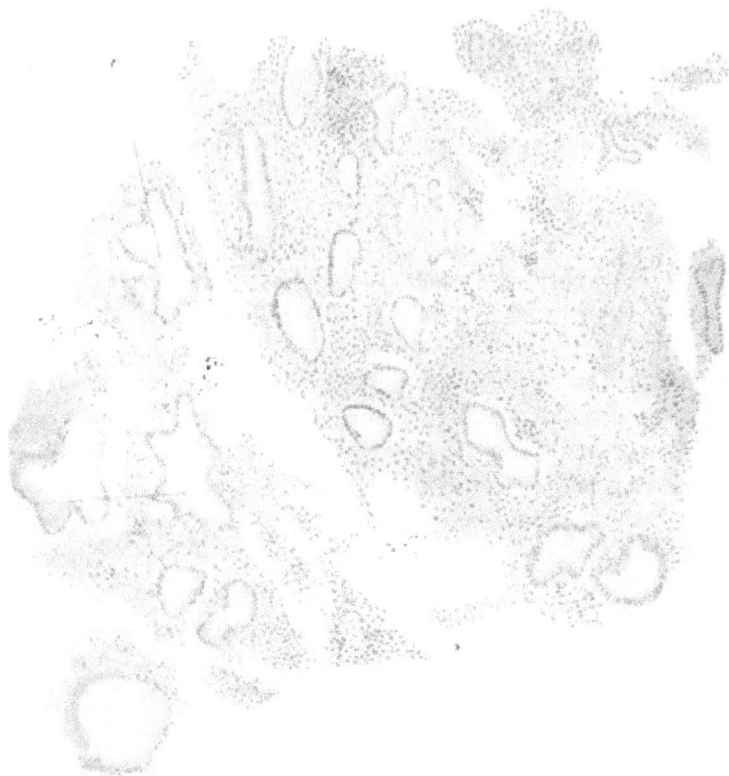

FIG. 147.—Section of curetted fragment from a case of endometritis resulting from abortion, which occurred four months prior to the curetting. Stained with logwood. (× 50.)

    a. Matrix with nuclei deeply stained.
    b. Commencing fibrillation of cells of matrix.
    c. Dilated glands.
    d. Space from which a gland has fallen.

follicles. Channelled polypi are also rare, and consist of hypertrophied mucous membrane, with enormously dilated and branching gland spaces lined with cylindrical epithelium.

Cervical Catarrh; Erosions, Ectropion, and so-called Ulceration.

344. To obtain satisfactory preparations of the above conditions it is absolutely essential that portions of the cervix be removed during life and carefully hardened (§ **58** or **59**), otherwise the epithelial lining of the canal and of the erosions will be lost, and a fallacious appearance produced. On examining sections of a piece of one of these "ulcers" the surface is found to resemble very closely the mucous membrane of the cervix; it is thrown into papillary folds, and is covered by a single layer of cubical epithelium. Deeper down are irregular spaces, lined with similar epithelium, which appear to have been formed from the deep extremities of the foldings between the papillæ. Should the section be made at the point of continuity between the erosion and the healthy vaginal aspect, it will be seen that the change from the one kind of epithelium to the other is very gradual; and, indeed, it is believed that such erosions result from a loss of the superficial squamous layer down to the deepest cells, a single layer only being left. It is more probable that the condition arises from a proliferation outwards of the cervical canal epithelium, which comes to occupy the place of the squamous epithelium on the vaginal aspect. Such erosions are usually associated with catarrh of the cervical cavity. The microscopic appearances of the cervical mucous membrane, under these circumstances, closely resemble those just described as characteristic of erosions. Another way in which cylindrical or cubical epithelium comes to cover the portion of cervix exposed to the vagina is by the healing of lacerations made during delivery. The cubical epithelium proliferates more rapidly than does the squamous. Should the lacerations be extensive and fail to heal by first intention, the lips of the cervix become separated from each other, the lower end of the cervical canal gets everted, and the torn surfaces derive their epithelial covering from that of the latter, and thus become covered with imperfect cylindrical, *i.e.*, cubical cells. In those new glandular structures (erosions) on the vaginal aspect, however originating, there is, in addition to the alteration on the surface, a proliferation of the subjacent connective tissues, and it is to outgrowths of this, rather than to foldings from the surface, that Fischel attributes the papillary formation. When the deep ends of the foldings become shut off, retention cysts are produced, which may

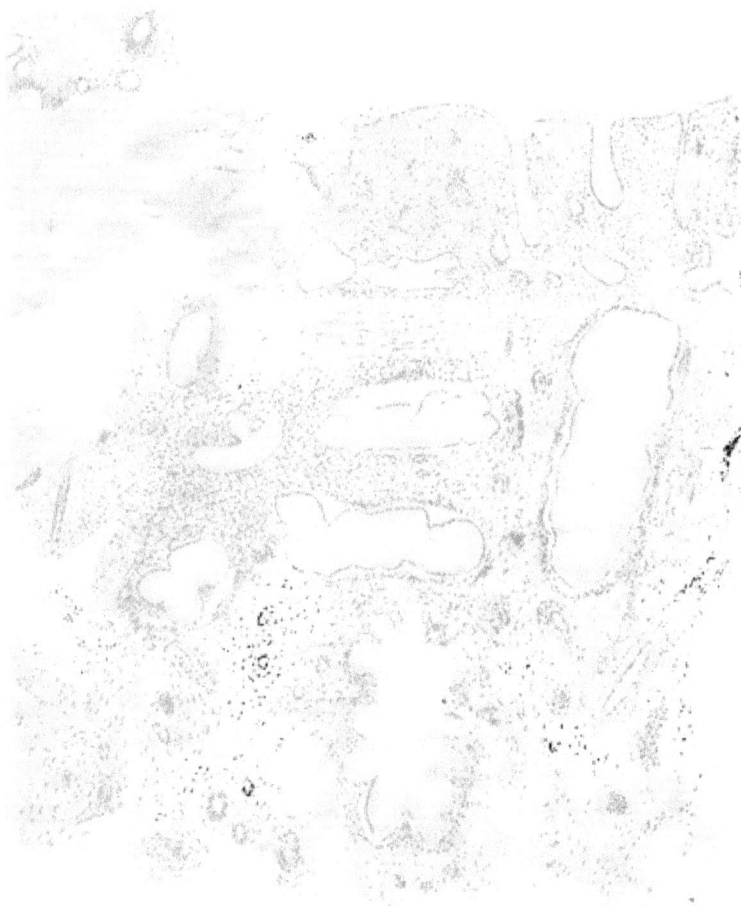

FIG. 148.—Cervical erosion. *a.* Point of junction of healthy cervix with eroded surface ; to the left of *a*, squamous epithelium of the vaginal aspect ; to the right of *a*, eroded surface covered by a single layer of cubical cells (slightly diagrammatic). *b.* Normal tissue of the cervix. *c.* New glandular formation, passing at *d* beneath the healthily covered surface. (× 50.) Stained with logwood.

bulge out the portions still covered by squamous epithelium, reach the surface, rupture, and thus occasion an extension of the altered condition.

Neoplasms—New Growths of the Uterus.

345. Polypi of the cervix uteri have already been referred to. Fibroid tumours—myomas—will be described in the chapter on Tumours. It must here be noted that the myoma is frequently the seat of cystic degeneration ; such a tumour is of rapid, often irregular growth, and it differs from the ordinary fibroid in the fact that its growth frequently progresses after the menopause, and after removal of the ovaries, while the simple myoma almost invariably ceases to grow, and often undergoes retrogressive changes and diminution in bulk under similar circumstances.

Polypi of the uterus may be either simple or malignant. Simple polypi are fibroid tumours which project into the cavity of the uterus, and have either been pedunculated originally, or have become so, as the tumour has increased in size. Malignant polypi are associated with more extensive malignant disease of the uterus, to be presently described.

Cancer of the Cervix Uteri.

346. All varieties of cancer usually described may occur in the cervix, but clinically and pathologically it is only important to differentiate three forms :—*1st*, the diffuse infiltrative, by far the most common ; *2nd*, the sprouting — epitheliomatous — or cauliflower growth ; and *3rd*, that in which the disease is confined chiefly to the mucous membrane of the cavity.

(1.) The diffuse infiltrative form of carcinoma is spoken of as scirrhous or medullary cancer, according to the preponderance of one or other of its constituent elements — fibrous tissue and epithelial cells. The cervix is greatly hypertrophied, and the epithelium on its vaginal aspect, early in the progress of the disease, sends down processes into the subjacent tissues. The pelvic glands soon become affected, and, as the disease progresses, ulceration both of the vaginal aspect and of the cavity occurs, and the vagina and neighbouring organs become implicated. Peritoneal adhesions are produced, which greatly diminish the chance of progress into the abdominal cavity, but the walls of the bladder and rectum are usually invaded.

(2.) The sprouting, epitheliomatous, or cauliflower form occurs as a projecting mass from one or other of the lips of the cervix; it is soft, white, and so broken up on the surface that it presents a peculiar cauliflower appearance. In this form the outward growth is far in excess of that into the substance of the cervix.

(3.) Where the disease is limited chiefly to the cavity of the cervix, the amount of hypertrophy of the cervix is not so great as in the other forms, and the disease spreads upwards through the inner os and into the cavity of the body—which becomes enlarged and elongated—rather than outwards over the vaginal aspect. Here infiltration of the surrounding glands and organs is of later occurrence, but the ultimate history of such cases is the same as that of the other forms.

The microscopic structure of the diseased parts differs in no respect from that of ordinary malignant growths and infiltrations.

CARCINOMA OF THE BODY OF THE UTERUS.

347. This is rarely met with, and is chiefly a disease of advanced life. It occurs either as a nodule formation under the mucous membrane, or as a polypoidal outgrowth, originating probably in the uterine glands, and bulging outwards into the uterine cavity. The progress and ultimate history of these cases is similar to that of the cervical cases already described.

SARCOMA.

348. Tumours of a sarcomatous character in the walls of the uterus often resemble fibroids, except in the fact that they are devoid of any capsule. Portions of a fibroid tumour may undergo sarcomatous degeneration. The sarcomatous spindle cells then differ from the myomatous in their greater size, and in the greater size and more oval shape of their nuclei. Sarcoma also occurs as a primary disease in the mucous membrane, usually in that of the body, rarely in that of the cervix. The mucous membrane is irregularly polypoid, pulpy, and brain-like; the uterus is enlarged, and its cavity elongated. The embryonic connective tissue, forming the stroma of the mucous membrane, is greatly increased in quantity, and is closely packed with round and occasional spindle-shaped, large nucleated cells, while the epithelial surface of the uterine cavity is extensively destroyed, when the diseased structures become exposed or ulcerated.

DISEASES OF THE UTERINE APPENDAGES.

349. Under the term uterine appendages are included the structures contained between the layers of the broad ligaments, along with the ovary which projects through the posterior layer. The Fallopian tube may become blocked and subsequently dilated by inflammation of its lining membrane—Salpingitis. This condition is generally the result of the spreading inwards of gonorrhœal inflammation. The secretion of the tubes becomes increased in quantity, especially during the menstrual periods, and may become altered in character. The fimbriated end often becomes glued to the ovary, and should obstruction of the lumen occur at any other point the secretion accumulates in the intermediate portion, and more or less dilatation results. When this dilatation is extensive the tube bulges downwards and separates the layers of the broad ligament, sometimes altering the relationship of the various parts to such an extent that it is extremely difficult to recognise as tubes the large cysts at the sides of the uterus, especially when, as the result of time and pressure, all trace of ovary and fimbriated end is gone. The fluid contained in such dilatations varies from serum to pus. Sometimes constriction occurs at more than one place, giving rise to two or more cyst cavities.

The tubes are sometimes very much thickened, though not dilated, the thickening being due to inflammatory processes either of their walls or of the peritoneal covering, or of both. Elongation usually occurs along with the growth of ovarian tumours, or of uterine fibroids which have opened out the broad ligaments. Fœtation may take place in a tube, in which case rupture of the sac occurs early in the pregnancy. Should the placenta be attached to the portion of the tube remote from the point of separation of the two layers of the broad ligament, severe and usually fatal hæmorrhage results; but in the event of the placental attachment being over the portion of tube situated between the separating layers, the fœtus, having escaped into the abdominal cavity, may continue to live and grow; and in the event of a *post mortem* examination being made in such a case, most careful dissection will be required to demonstrate the true state of matters.

Other cysts besides those of the tubes develop between the layers of the broad ligament, the Parovarium or organ of Rosenmüller being their usual starting-point. Such cysts are of much more frequent occurrence than the tubular ones, and they frequently attain great size, coming to resemble ovarian tumours. The distinction between them and ovarian tumours may be made out either by the character of their contained fluid; by finding the ovary—probably flattened and atrophied—at some part of the wall; by the fact of their being mono-locular; or by their being covered by peritoneum—derived from the broad ligament;—ovarian cysts, like the ovary itself, being devoid of peritoneal covering.

THE OVARIES.

350. On examining a section of the ovary, there is noticed an outer investing layer, the tunica albuginea, a central vascular and fibrous layer with large vessels entering it from the hilus, and between the two a stroma of fibrous tissue with a few muscle cells; thickly scattered through this are the Graafian follicles in all stages of development and retrogression. Usually a corpus luteum may be found. The Graafian follicles are small cyst-like cavities lined with epithelium, which is heaped up at one part of the circumference around one cell of special size, the ovum. The origin of the Graafian follicles is of sufficient importance, as bearing on the pathological changes of ovarian tumours, to warrant a brief reference to the conflicting theories—those of Waldeyer and of Foulis. Both observers are agreed that the ovum was originally an epithelial cell on the surface of the ovary, which became embedded in the stroma of the organ. Waldeyer holds that the epithelial cells of the Graafian follicle were also at one time cells of the surface, while Foulis regards them as being derived from the connective tissue of the ovary as a result of the irritation set up by the presence of the ovum; as being in fact granulation cells which have become epithelial in character.

351. *Tubercle and cancer* occur in the ovary—usually secondarily, sometimes primarily. Cancer, when secondary, affects both ovaries. When primary, one alone may be affected, but the tumour rarely attains any considerable size. What is spoken of as malignant ovarian tumour is not cancer of the ovary, as will be explained presently. Abscess formation—a rare occurrence—may follow tubercular disease or simple inflammation. In such cases the ovary becomes adherent —in the pelvis or to the abdominal wall—previous to the rupture of the sac, and the relationship of parts becomes greatly altered.

FIG. 149.—Sarcomatous degeneration of ovarian cystic tumour, showing infiltration of the stroma and filling up of small cysts with round cells. (× 50.) Logwood.

352. *Inflammation and cirrhosis of the ovary.*—The ovaries may be found in any stage of inflammation, from the initial congestive stage to that of the formation of new fibrous tissue, which ultimately shrinking gives rise to the condition known as cirrhosis. The size of the organ varies according to the stage of the process, and to the relation of the time of death to the last menstruation. In the later stages the whole ovary may be represented by a mass of dense fibrous tissue in all stages of development, with numerous large vessels, but with only a few small and irregular Graafian follicles, or none at all.

2 K

353. *Cystic degeneration of the ovaries.*—It is quite common to find one or more cysts in the ovaries, especially in those that are partially cirrhosed, but this condition must not be confused with the multiple cystic degeneration which occasions the growth of "ovarian tumours." Such cystic ovaries are almost invariably found where large, rapidly growing, or bleeding uterine fibroids are present.

The multiple ovarian cystic tumour will be described in the chapter on Tumours; here it is only necessary to notice the changes which may occur in it. Sometimes acute inflammation of the interior of one or more of the cysts takes place, and the contents may become purulent, thus occasioning one form of abscess of the ovary. More frequently a degenerative process occurs, and what has been called malignant ovarian tumour, or cancer of the ovary results; but this is better described as a sarcomatous degeneration. This change consists in a new growth, within the tumour, of round cells, scattered throughout the stroma, but more especially in the neighbourhood of the epithelial lining of the cysts. The cysts themselves are closely packed with such cells, and only in a few of them can any trace of the original lining epithelium be seen. From what elements these cells are derived, whether from degeneration and proliferation of the already existing epithelium, or from the connective tissue, is uncertain. Foulis, who holds that the lining cells of the membrana granulosa, and the lining cells of the cysts in cystic degeneration, are derived from connective tissue proliferation, holds the latter view, and hence regards the change as being sarcomatous. The clinical history of these cases is interesting pathologically, and certainly bears out Foulis' views. The new cell growth is at first confined to the tumour mass by the outside limiting membrane. As long as this is so, the tumour may be treated as a simple one, and little fear need be entertained of a return of the affection after the tumour has been removed. The process, however, tends to involve the outer wall of the tumour, and to extend through it, causing rupture, which allows of the escape of some of the cyst contents into the abdominal cavity. When this occurs, portions of the new round cell growth are set free in the peritoneal sac, or attach themselves to the surface of the peritoneum; in either event they continue to grow. On opening the abdomen in such a case new growths will be found studding the peritoneal aspect of the abdominal viscera, and causing adhesions in the abdominal cavity. There is some free ascitic fluid, in which sprouting masses of round cells may be seen. This always recurs after removal.

Dermoid cysts of the ovary are described in the chapter on Tumours.

DISEASES OF THE VAGINA AND VULVA.

354. The mucous membrane of the vagina is frequently the seat of inflammatory affections, and the changes then undergone by it differ in no respect from those occurring in other similar structures. Occasionally small collections of gas are found in the submucous connective tissue meshes, the condition being then called emphysematous vaginitis. In old women a form of vaginitis occurs in which the walls become thinned, dry, and parchment-like. Malignant disease of the cervix frequently spreads to the vagina; occasionally the latter is the seat of primary disease. Cicatricial contractions, especially of the upper part of the canal, are often found as the result of tears, which may have occurred during parturition.

The vulva is the seat of many of the ordinary skin affections, such as eczema, as also of the manifestations of syphilis in its various stages. The natural moist condition of the vulva greatly favours the occurrence of condylomata or warts when syphilis or gonorrhœa are present. In cases of diabetes, where there has been pruritus vulvæ or where that condition has been present from other causes, the external genitals are often found swollen and scratched, and sometimes covered with eczematous eruptions. These changes are purely the result of the scratching, and are not the cause of the pruritus, which affection may be present, even to a most intense degree, without any pathological change being evident. Occasionally there are found studding the neighbourhood of the hymen, the vulva, and adjoining parts, a number of small rounded red spots of apparent ulceration, with numerous cicatrices, the remains of previously affected parts. This condition has been called lupoid disease, but its true pathology is not yet fully understood. Certainly there is not complete loss of epithelium, and, clinically, we know that while in some instances these spots are extremely sensitive, in other, to all appearances undistinguishable cases, no special sensitiveness exists.

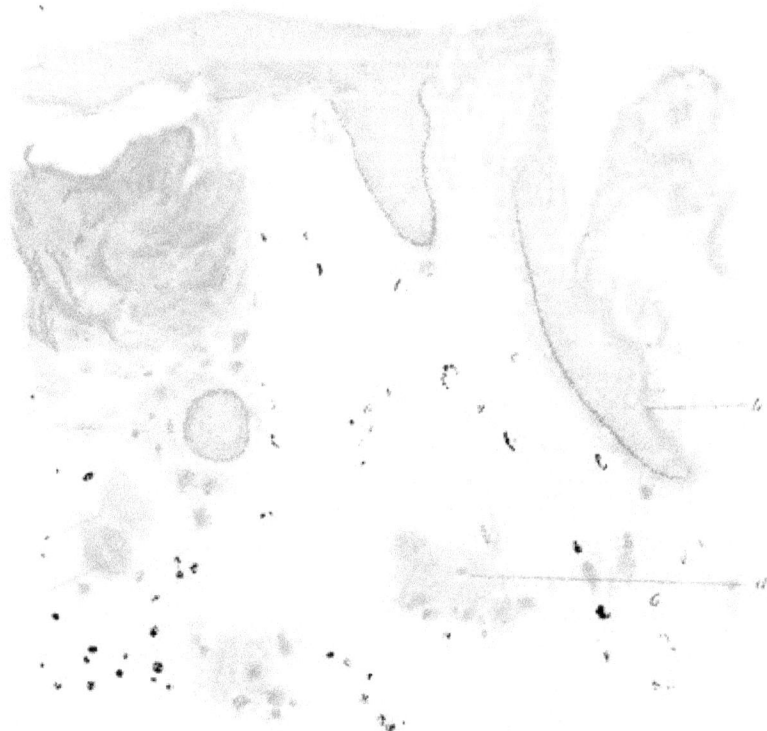

Fig. 150.—Section of a hypertrophic growth from the neighbourhood of the hymen in a case of lupus vulvæ. (× 50.) Logwood.

a. Thickened layer of epithelium.
b. Proliferating mass passing into the corium.
c.   Do.   do. seen in transverse section, both surrounded by proliferating connective tissue cells.
d. Vascular nodule (mass of connective tissue cells around vessels).
e.   Do.   do. without vessels.
f. Mass of disintegrated tissue at the margin of the lupus ulcer.
g.g. Hæmorrhages.
        The blood-vessels, lymphatics, and diffuse infiltration are all well seen.

Clinically, also, we know that it is a most intractable disease to treat, as it constantly recurs even after complete destruction of all existing spots.

355. *True lupus* occurs in the vulvo-anal region, and is extremely

apt to be mistaken for a syphilitic manifestation. It affects both the parts covered by skin and those covered by mucous membrane, and cases have been described in which the process was entirely limited to the vagina. Very probably the so-called "corroding" or "rodent" ulcer of the cervix uteri is of lupoid nature. All the ordinary forms of the disease have been found in this neighbourhood, but the most commonly occurring variety is that which is accompanied by hypertrophies and ulcerations. The hypertrophies are of already existing parts, as of the labia majora or minora, or of the hymen, or they occur as outgrowths, usually finger or club shaped, projecting from the affected surfaces. The disease seems to consist in an infiltration of the connective tissue, with granulation cells, which make a feeble attempt to organise into fibrous tissue, but which usually become so crowded together that they interfere with their own nutrition, and lead to ulceration. Along with this there is proliferation of the epithelial covering.

Fig. 150, in which the changes are very similar to those seen in lupus of the skin, represents a section made across one of the hypertrophic growths taken from such a case. The portion was about the size of the last joint of the little finger, and was completely surrounded by a thick layer of epithelium, presenting a smooth surface externally, but with an irregular deep surface, from which here and there branched prolongations passed into the substance of the mass. The central portion was made up of a meshwork of connective tissue in all stages of development, in which there were numerous spaces, some distended with blood, others containing granular material, probably coagulated lymph, while others, especially those near the surface, resembled gland ducts, and were lined by regular epithelium. Immediately under the epithelial investing layer, notably where the prolongations passed inwards, there were numerous deeply-stained round bodies, which under a high power were seen to be nuclei. These were grouped around the openings above mentioned, and were also sparingly scattered through the connective tissue. The cells, of which these were the nuclei, were very delicately stained, and some of them were of considerable size, and contained more than one nucleus; it was from these cells, apparently, that the connective tissue was developed. They were very similar to those met with as endothelial plates in gummata, tubercle follicles, and similar growths. Sections made from other parts taken from the same case showed a similar condition in evidently a further stage of its history, the cells being present in greater numbers; in one of the specimens they were so crowded together that they appear to have led to breaking down and ulceration. A section made from a hard wart-like structure over the mons veneris had all the characteristics of an ordinary wart or papilloma, with, in addition, a few cells similar to those existing in the other specimens, sparingly scattered through the connective tissue.

356. Malignant growths of an epitheliomatous type may occur in any part of the vulva, but they are especially apt to affect the clitoris. The glands of Duvernay, situated laterally beneath the lower end of the vagina, are frequently the seat of acute inflammation and suppuration, when they bulge into the labia; if they burst, sinuses are left. The canal of Nuck—a developmental prolongation of the peritoneum around the round ligament into the labium majus—may, very rarely, remain as a closed sac, and give rise to a retention cyst in that locality.

CHAPTER XIV.

TUMOURS.

357. In examining tumours, it should always be borne in mind that no new or peculiar structural elements are imported into, or developed in the body, with which to build them up. The tissues of which each tumour is composed have their homologues in some part of the body, at some stage, at least, of the developmental period. Hence it would often be an extremely difficult matter to determine merely by microscopical examination, whether a tissue was taken from a tumour or not. One often hears of "cancer cells." Now it is an absolute impossibility to say with certainty from such examination that the epithelial cells found in "cancer juice" are "cancer cells." The observer is assisted by a microscopic examination, and the evidence so gained, along with that derived from other sources, may enable him to arrive at a definite conclusion; but an examination of so-called cancer cells will enable the observer to say that they merely are epithelial cells.

In the same way it is often impossible to distinguish granulation tissue from round celled or mixed sarcomas; for both are made up of connective tissue cells in an early stage of development, and of embryonic blood-vessels, and so on.

It behoves the observer, therefore, to take great care that he is not led to search for distinctive or characteristic tumour elements. His great aim should be to determine the position, proportion, stage of development, and arrangement of the various tissue elements, which together will give him far more certain indications as to the nature of the growth than he can derive from any amount of study of the mere form of the individual elements.

Definition.—A tumour or neoplasm is an atypical new growth of tissue, which has an existence of its own quite irrespective of the needs of the organ or tissue in which it grows, and which is

independent of all surrounding local conditions. It has an active
vegetative existence and is always growing, but it never takes on any
reparative or functional activity; though it never retrogresses in
type, it never attains any special developmental form, and ultimately
it may undergo fatty or caseous degeneration, calcification, or change
of type of tissue. Such a growth is always composed of tissue
differing in type, sometimes very slightly, from that in which it
grows. Even when the tissue of a new growth is of the same class
of tissue as that in which it springs, it is never precisely the same or
at the same stage of development.

Moreover, the structure is essentially permanent in character,
though seldom perfectly typical. All kinds of tissue may be reproduced in it, and the connective tissue, so characteristic of inflammatory hyperplasia, here, as a rule, acts merely as a framework, and is
not an essential part of the tumour.

It is freely supplied with nerves, lymphatics, and blood-vessels
from the surrounding parts.

In other words, a tumour may be looked upon as a superadded
growth of various tissues, either in the adult or in the young child,
developing abnormally. Its growth is not defined by an obvious
limit, as in the growth of normal tissues. It never reaches a point
at which growth ceases, though portions may suffer involution.

By its presence it may act mechanically by pressure on nerves,
blood-vessels, or vital organs, or it may exert a constitutional influence—cachexia — especially in those cases of malignant tumour,
where there is ulceration or any great discharge.

Tumours may, for the sake of convenience, be considered in three
large groups, which may be taken in the following order :—

I. Simple or histioid tumours are tumours composed of tissues
which deviate but slightly, if at all, from those of which a healthy
body is built up. These tumours are usually mesoblastic in their
origin, and consequently are mainly composed of some form of
connective tissue.

II. Sarcomatous tumours are composed of tissues more or less
embryonic in type, in which there may be some attempt at higher
development—which attempt, however, *is always abortive.* These

are also mesoblastic, and are therefore composed of tissues *imperfectly developed* of the connective type.

III. Cancerous tumours are those in which some or all of the tissue elements may be present in excessive degree or erratic form. There is a loss of balance between the tissues, which are derived from mesoblast and hypoblast or epiblast.

SIMPLE OR HISTIOID TUMOURS.

358. *General characters* of simple tumours.

They all grow comparatively slowly. They are usually single, rounded (rarely flattened), or lobulated, and are surrounded by a fibrous capsule which, like the pseudo-cyst of the hydatid cyst is formed of fibrous tissue, due to proliferation of the connective tissue cells, the result of the chronic local inflammation set up by the presence of the tumour itself. They are non-malignant, and give rise to no inconvenience or injury, except by their weight and mechanical pressure. On section, fibrous bands or trabeculæ can be seen passing in from the capsule, between the individual lobules; along these bands and in the capsule run the blood-vessels.

They are liable to certain degenerative processes, of which fatty degeneration and calcification, ulceration, colloid degeneration of the cells, and mucoid degeneration of the fibrous or connective tissue are the more important. Hæmorrhages also frequently occur in the softer forms, and inflammatory changes may be set up by mechanical injury or by the action of irritant chemical substances or putrefactive products.

MYXOMA.

359. A myxoma is a tumour made up of delicate branching connective tissue cells embedded in a mucoid matrix (myxomatous tissue). Although it is composed of a tissue which is in many respects embryonic, as it is found only in the vitreous humour in the adult, it is non-malignant. This myxomatous tissue is met with in fœtal life as the subcutaneous tissue, from which fatty tissue is later developed. Wharton's jelly of the umbilical cord and young fibrous tissue have a similar structure. Myxomatous degeneration of the

villi of the chorion is spoken of as a form of multiple myxoma. In this case there are rounded or pear-shaped masses of myxomatous tissue, held together by portions of the healthy villi. Myxoma is also found in the submucous tissue as nasal polypi, in the subcutaneous and other connective tissue, in the intermuscular septa, between the bundles of nerves, in periosteum, and in subserous fat. In rare cases it grows on the umbilical cord.

Naked eye appearances.—It grows slowly, and does not often reach any very great size, though occasionally it may do so. It is lobulated, and is surrounded by a delicate capsule, from which trabeculæ run into the tumour mass. On section, the tissue between the trabeculæ, which projects beyond them, is clear and gelatinous, and is often compared to a mass of boiled tapioca. Running along the trabeculæ, and into this gelatinous substance, are small blood-vessels, seen as thin red lines. Usually these have given way, as the mucous tissue does not afford them an efficient support, and small hæmorrhages, red, brown, or yellow, according to their age, may be seen in the clear mass. Examine some of the viscid fluid scraped from the surface (× 300); it contains a number of coloured blood corpuscles, and some nucleated cells, with one or two nuclei and several branching processes. Unless these cells are stained, it is very difficult to distinguish them. Immerse a small piece of the tumour in acetic acid or alcohol, either of which immediately precipitates the mucin between the branching cells, and renders the section opaque.

Harden (§ 60), and stain (§ 98).

(× 50).—Between the trabeculæ, which in most cases are more fibrous, but which may be composed of very cellular material, and in which may be seen running small blood-vessels, is the true myxomatous tissue. This is made up of a number of branching cells, each having one or more deeply stained nuclei, around which is a large quantity of protoplasm; between the individual cells are spaces, in the fresh condition occupied by mucin, with here and there small green masses which will afterwards be recognised as blood corpuscles (small hæmorrhages).

(× 300).—The fibro-cellular trabeculæ are now seen gradually merging into the myxomatous structure. Note the granularity of the

protoplasm of the branching cells, the number and ramifications of
the processes and the intercellular spaces, in which may now be made
out a number of small round cells—leucocytes and young connective
tissue cells. The blood corpuscles which have escaped from the

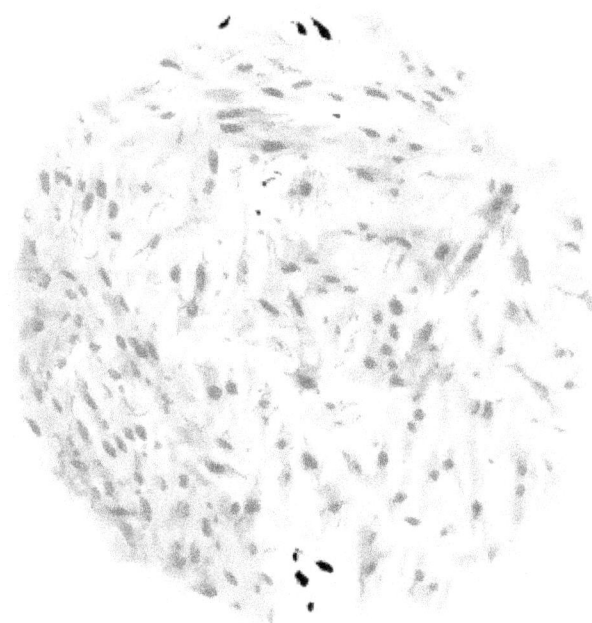

FIG. 151.—Drawing of myxoma. Section stained with picro-
carmine. (× 300.)
a. Branching myxomatous cell with several nuclei.
b. Do. do. with single nucleus.
c. Intercellular spaces containing mucin.
d. Denser portion of the tumour in which the spaces are fewer
    and smaller.

blood-vessels are in various stages of disintegration. In the breast,
the myxomatous tissue may spread between the acini of the gland,
whilst in some specimens it is found to encroach on the acini,
growing into them and distending them, as granulation tissue does
when it forms the so-called cystic sarcoma.

Varieties of myxoma.

(1.) Pure myxoma : (a) Hyaline form, composed of an exceedingly translucent substance, with few round cells between the branching cells; (*b.*) Medullary form, which is more opaque from the presence of a greater number of the small round cells.

(2.) Myxoma containing a quantity of elastic tissue.

(3.) Lipomatous myxoma, in which some of the branching cells are distended with droplets of fat.

(4.) Cystic myxoma, formed by the softening of certain portions of the tumour.

Degenerative changes.

(1.) Hæmorrhagic.

(2.) Mucoid and colloid degeneration of the cells.

(3.) Inflammation which may become gangrenous and ulcerative, especially where the tumour is polypoid, and therefore on a free surface and exposed to mechanical injury.

GLIOMA.

360. Two forms of glioma are usually described, one of which appears to be simply a form of small round-celled sarcoma. The true glioma is a non-malignant tumour composed of connective tissue similar to that found in the nerve centres. It is found in the brain and spinal cord, more frequently in the former than in the latter, and in children than in adults.

Naked eye appearances.—It is a gelatinous looking mass, evidently of slow growth, which gradually replaces the nerve tissue, into which it merges at its margins. On section it has a grey, translucent, or a greyish or dark red colour, according to its vascularity. It may be distinguished from the small round-celled sarcoma, which frequently occurs in the same positions, by the fact that even in the form where hæmorrhages occur (the dark vascular form) the substance is firmer.

Harden (§ 59), and stain (§ 100), half clear up (§ 324), to bring out the processes of the Deiters' or neuroglia cells distinctly, or stain a section (§ 98) and tease out a small fragment of it.

(× 50).—The tumour is composed of neuroglia cells, the nuclei of which are very distinctly seen grouped round the small blood-vessels (of which there may be local or general dilatation, see § **195**) running through the mass. Between them is a tissue, the structure of which cannot be determined under this power.

(× 300).—Examine a few of the cells in the teased out specimen. They are composed of granular looking protoplasm, embedded in

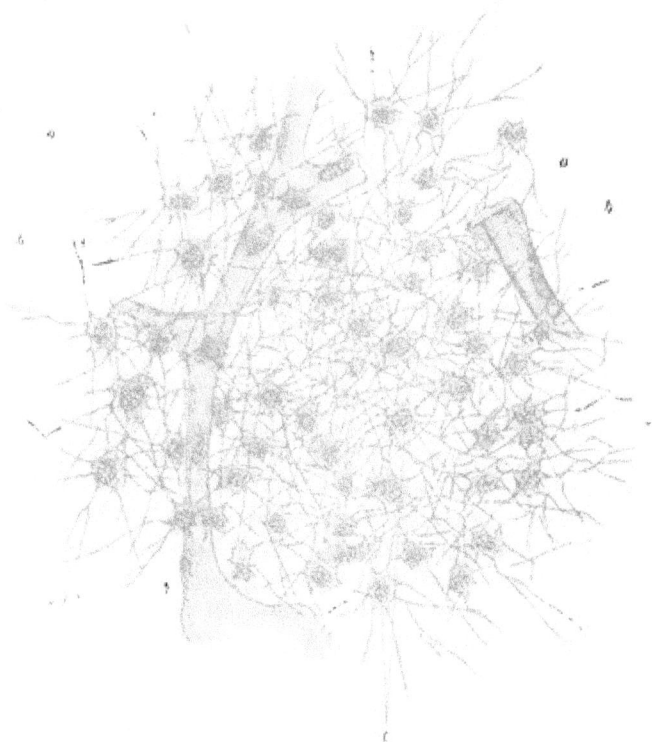

FIG. 152.—Glioma taken from the brain. Section stained with carmine, and half cleared up. (× 600.)

a. Capillary blood-vessels.
b. Nuclei, with intranuclear plexus well seen.
c. Neuroglia cells, or Deiters' cells, with nuclei and long branching processes.

which are one or two rounded or ovoid nuclei. From the main body of the cell run out branching processes, very like those met with in myxoma. In the half cleared up section, observe the capillary blood-vessel with its endothelial plates, and the branching cells with their large nuclei, and their long, delicate, and anastomosing processes. If a section be stained and mounted by any of the ordinary methods, the nuclei can be seen quite readily, but the tissue between appears to be composed simply of a felted mass of fibrils seen in longitudinal section, or as a granular mass, where the transverse sections of the fibrils are numerous. As already seen in various inflammatory conditions in the spinal cord, medulla oblongata, and brain, this gliomatous tissue may be greatly increased, and a similar tissue is found in large quantities in the dense walls of old cysts in the brain.

Degenerative changes.—Hæmorrhagic (as in myxoma), fatty, caseous, or simple softening.

LIPOMA, OR FATTY TUMOUR.

361. This tumour is composed of fatty or adipose tissue, and usually grows in connection with pre-existing fat. It occurs most commonly in the subcutaneous tissue, especially in such parts as are subjected to pressure, as on the shoulders or buttocks, also in the abdominal wall, in the breast, and as the aborescent lipomas of the synovial fringes of joints. It is sometimes found, however, in tissues which do not normally contain fat, as in the dura mater, and in the submucous tissue of the intestine, and rarely in the liver and heart, between muscles and in bone. It is of slow growth, and may be single or multiple.

Naked eye appearances.—It is usually rounded and lobulated, or flattened, or it may be pedunculated when it occurs in the fatty synovial fringes or enlarged appendices epiploicæ. Its size varies from that of a pea up to a growth of many pounds weight. It has a well-formed fibrous capsule, from which septa run in and cut the fatty mass into a series of lobules. On section the surface presents the appearance of a mass of yellow fatty tissue, through which run white and glistening fibrous septa, containing the blood-vessels which supply the tumour tissue, which is much softer and more plastic than ordinary fatty tissue.

Harden (§ **60** or **64**) and stain (§ **98** or **103** *d*).

(× 50).— Note that the tissue resembles ordinary adipose tissue, but that the fat cells are rather larger, that the tissue is

extremely vascular, and that at certain points there are, in addition
to the fully-developed connective tissue cells distended with fat,
numerous embryonic cells, in which the process of fatty infiltration
is as yet incomplete. These latter occur in isolated groups as small,
deeply-stained cells in which there is frequently not a single droplet
of fat.

(× 300).—The swollen connective tissue cell, infiltrated or loaded

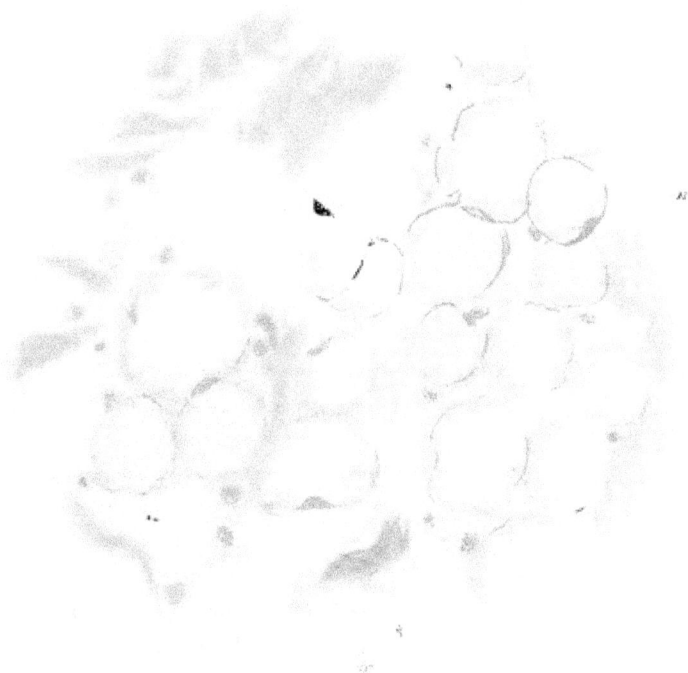

FIG. 153.—Drawing of lipoma. Stained with logwood and mounted
in Canada balsam. (× 250.)
  n.   Nucleus of fat cell.
  n.c.t. Collection of connective tissue nuclei (cells not infiltrated
            with fat).
  p.   Thin film of protoplasm surrounding fat globule.
  m.   Remains of bands of fibrous tissue.

with fat, is seen with its nucleus pushed into an angle, the protoplasm
of the cell forming a thin film or coat around the fatty globule.
Sometimes these cells contain fat crystals, and usually they are so
closely packed together that they assume a polygonal form. Under

this power a number of the uninfiltrated cells are seen to be myxomatous in type (§ 354).

Varieties of lipoma—(1.) Pure lipoma—the form described.

(2.) Myxomatous lipoma, in which the branching myxomatous cells, with intercellular mucoid substance, are very numerous.

(3.) Fibrous lipoma, in which the fibrous trabeculæ are well developed and very numerous.

(4.) Osseous lipoma, described by Cornil and Ranvier, in which the trabeculæ are osseous.

(5.) Erectile lipomas, principally met with as very vascular polypoid growths on serous and mucous surfaces.

Degenerative changes.—The tumour may undergo—(1.) molecular softening, when it becomes opaque and putty-like ; (2.) calcareous degeneration ; (3.) inflammation and ulceration, where young connective tissue cells are formed more rapidly than they are filled with fat.

FIBROMA.

362. The fibroma is a tumour composed of fibrous tissue, and, as a rule, grows where fibrous tissue already exists ; it is of comparatively slow growth, and is non-malignant. It occurs most commonly in the subcutaneous and submucous tissues ; in the upper and posterior part of the pharynx (then probably growing from the periosteum of the basilar process) ; in fasciæ, and in the interfascicular tissue of nerves ; in the ovary ; in the uterus ; as small, firm, rounded masses, about the size of a pin's head, or larger, in the centre of a pyramid of the kidney ; as keloid growths in scars ; and as the so-called loose cartilages of the knee joint.

There are two forms of fibroma, fasciculated and lamellar, of which the fasciculated is perhaps the more characteristic.

Naked eye appearances.—It is usually met with as a firm, dry, glistening, white or brownish, not very vascular tumour. It may be rounded or lobulated, has a capsule, and on section presents a peculiar appearance, often compared to watered silk, or it may be not so firm, when it is somewhat pinker and is more gelatinous looking. Notice the lobular arrangement ; each lobule is composed of a number of concentric layers of fibrous tissue ; they are softer towards their centre, at which point they seem to grow; between them is a quantity of looser connective tissue, in which run numerous blood-vessels. When the cut surface is scraped, small fragments, but very little fluid, are removed. Treat one of these fragments with acetic acid and examine (× 300). It is seen to be composed of small bundles of connective tissue, which swell up, become gelatinous or homogeneous, and enable one to see the connective tissue cells as branching nucleated masses of protoplasm.

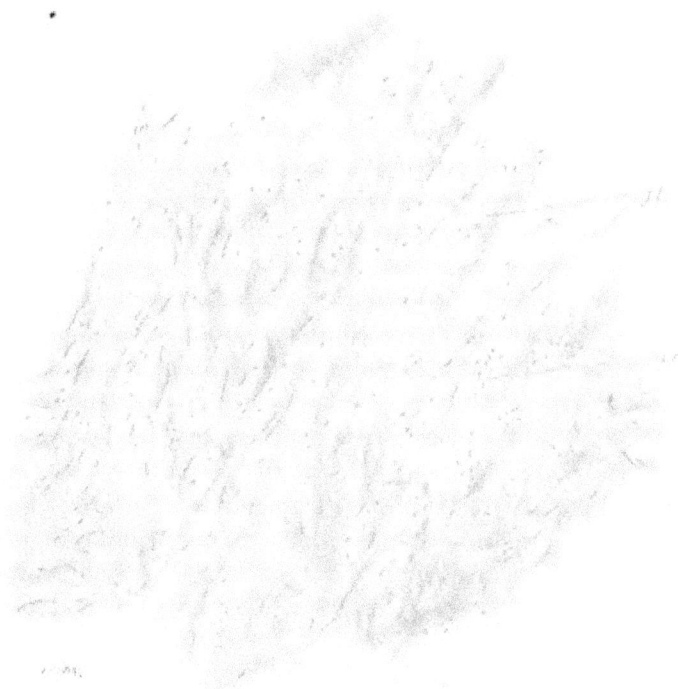

FIG. 154.—Drawing of a hard fibroma. Stained in logwood, and mounted in Canada balsam. (× 50.)
   f.t. Bands of well-developed fibrous tissue, in which are few nuclei.
   n.c. Intervals between the fibrous bands, in which the tissue is more cellular, the strands of formed tissue running obliquely, with well-marked nuclei between them.

Harden (§ 59 or 57) and stain (§ 98 or 103 *d*).

(× 50).—In the picro-carmine stained specimen the tissue is throughout stained a beautiful pink (a reaction very characteristic of fibrous tissue). The fibrous tissue has different arrangements in different parts of the tumour, but it is in great part disposed in bundles, which (1) run in various directions, or (2) are arranged concentrically, or (3) have a peculiar feather-like or ladder-like arrangement. In the last form there are dense pink bundles, which may be said to run longitudinally, whilst running off at various acute angles are more delicate strands. In the dense longitudinal bundles there are few cells; in and between the more delicate transverse strands numerous nuclei of cells are seen. Whatever be the arrangement of the bundles, the cells—small, round, elongated, or branching —are always most numerous in the more open tissue. There are never any yellow elastic fibres present. Observe that the blood-vessels running in the capsule and trabeculæ are all fully developed, but are not very numerous.

In a molluscum fibrosum, where there is a kind of œdema of the fibrous tissue—a distension with fluid of the spaces between the fibres—the arrangement of both fibres and cells is very easily seen.

(× 300).—Look for the pink fibrous bundles, between which are branched cells, the processes of which clasp the bundles. Observe how scanty are the cells in the denser pink fibrous bands, and how numerous they are in the soft open parts of the tumour, especially between the transverse bars of the ladder. Examine the cells carefully; some are embryonic cells, nearly all nucleus; others are surrounded by a quantity of protoplasm; others are elongated, and the formed material around them is becoming fibrillated; others again have several nuclei; and some have well-developed branching processes. In fact, a young or growing fibroma is composed of the purest form of fibrous tissue, and is one of the best structures in which to study its development.

Degenerations.—(1.) Serous infiltration, as in the molluscum fibrosum; (2.) Mucoid degeneration of the fibres; (3.) Fatty degeneration, especially in fibromas of syphilitic origin (Cornil and Ranvier); and (4.) Calcification. The two changes last named occur near the centre of the nodules, or away from the blood-vessels. Inflammatory changes and new cell formation are sometimes set up, especially when the tumour, from its position, is exposed to mechanical injury.

The Lamellar Fibroma or Flat Fibroma.

363. Flat fibromas can scarcely be looked upon as true fibromas. They are rather a thickening of lamellated tissue—the result of a chronic inflammatory process on a serous surface. They are met with as flattened, hard cartilaginoid masses, which vary considerably in size and shape. They occur on the outer surface of the spleen and liver (especially after abdominal dropsy); on the pleura, or in the subpleural tissue in old people; in stone-masons' lung and on the inner surface of blood-vessels in certain conditions. They are usually yellow and translucent, but they may be pigmented; they are cartilaginous in consistence, and are cut with difficulty.

Harden (§ **59**), and stain (§ **98**).

(× 50).—The structure is essentially that of corneal tissue, or of the inner lining of vessels—a series of laminæ of fibrillated tissue, between which are flattened cells.

(× 300).—These flat cells are only flattened, branching connective tissue cells, seen in profile. In order that these cells may be examined fully, a small fragment must be treated with acetic acid, and then stained with carmine (§ **100**), and carefully teased out.

Chondroma.

364. A chondroma is a tumour composed of cartilaginous tissue. It usually grows in the periosteum of bones (especially in the ends of the metacarpal bones and on the phalanges of the fingers and toes); in the bones themselves; in the parotid and other salivary glands; and in the testicle, skin, lung, and mamma.

Naked eye appearances.—Such tumours are usually met with as multiple growths, firm and elastic, though in some cases, owing to mucoid degeneration, they may be soft and even gelatinous; they may be either rounded or lobulated, they are surrounded by a fibrous capsule, with fibrous bands separating the lobules from one another. On section the tumour cuts with the peculiar creak of cartilage, but when calcification is present, there is a also a gritty feeling. Running across the section are white glistening fibrous trabeculæ, between which the cartilage, with its translucent pearly appearance with a bluish or pink tinge, is seen.

Harden (§ 57) and stain (§ 98).

(× 50).—The capsule of the tumour is seen as a pink fibrous band, at one margin of the section. From it a series of fibrous trabeculæ,

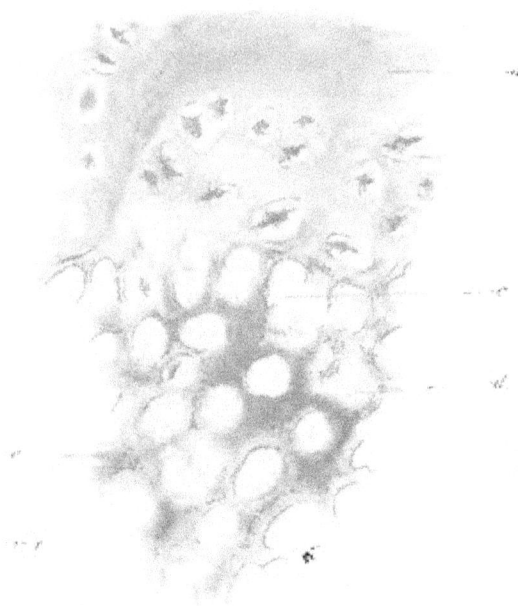

FIG. 155.—Section of a chondroma taken from the parotid gland. Stained with picro-carmine. (× 200.)

    a. Homogeneous cartilaginous matrix, in which are embedded
    b. Branching cartilage cells.
    c. Spaces from which cells have disappeared.
    d. Granular matrix (calcification just beginning).
    e. More advanced calcification.

in which run small vessels, extend between the masses of cartilage. Some of the cells appear to be rapidly developing hyaline cartilage cells, with well-formed cartilage capsules; from others the capsules have disappeared, and they are seen as branching cells sending their processes in all directions into the matrix, which here is soft and mucoid, and takes on a very delicate stain. Near the centre of each lobule where calcification is beginning, the tissue is green, and much less translucent. At the margin of the calcified part granules of calcareous material may be seen embedded in the matrix, whilst in some few cases the calcareous particles appear to have found their way into the cartilage capsules.

(× 300).—The greater part of the tumour is composed of hyaline cartilage, made up of encapsuled and proliferating cells in a matrix, which in this case is not fibrillated. The branching cells in the mucoid matrix, and the fibrous capsule and trabeculæ, with the well developed blood-vessels, and the yellowish green part, with the highly refractile calcareous particles infiltrating the matrix around the distended capsules are all well seen.

In another section of a parotid tumour of softer consistence growing more rapidly and prepared as above, the tissue is composed almost entirely of branching cells embedded in a mucoid matrix, with proliferating gland structure running through it. The epithelium of the gland acini and ducts takes part in the increased activity of the surrounding tissues, and grows so rapidly that it forms solid-looking columns or masses, which intersect the myxochondromatous tissue in all directions. This form of parotid tumour is spoken of as the myxochondro-adenoma.

Myxochondroma.

365. Certain cartilaginous tumours are much softer and more gelatinous than the form last described; they grow with extreme rapidity, and frequently give rise to similar growths in other parts. In the case from which the section described was taken, the tumour grew from the periosteum of the scapula, increased very rapidly in size, and gave rise to secondary growths of a similar nature in the lung, in the branches of the pulmonary artery. It was a soft lobulated tumour, composed of a brown gelatinous material surrounded by a very vascular fibrous capsule.

Prepare as in § 359.

(× 50).—The pink fibrous capsule and trabeculæ are readily seen, and running in them are well-formed blood-vessels. Near the trabeculæ the cells are somewhat flattened, and have a comparatively regular arrangement. Towards the centre of the mass are large cells, very irregular in shape, having long processes, and often two, three, or four nuclei and nucleoli. Between these huge cells, which by Ranvier are compared to the cells of the cartilage found in cephalopods, the matrix is somewhat fibrillated near the periphery, but is

FIG. 156.—Section of myxochondroma. Stained with picrocarmine. (× 200—about.)
　　a. Fibrous capsule from which run in
　　b. Trabeculæ.
　　c. Mucoid matrix, in which are embedded
　　d. Embryonic cartilage cells, proliferating rapidly, and of various
　　　shapes.

mucoid towards the centre. Towards the periphery greenish masses (coloured blood corpuscles) may be seen.

(× 300).—Note the forms of the cells and the structure of the matrix.

All varieties of cartilage between the white fibro- and hyaline forms may be found in these chondromas.

Degenerations.—(1.) Mucoid softening of the matrix; (2.) Calcification of the matrix; (3.) True bone formation.

OSTEOMA.

366. Osteomas, or bony tumours, occur chiefly at the point of junction between a bone and its cartilage. These outgrowths of bone are classified according to their position into *exostoses*, or those growing from the exterior of a bone, and *enostoses*, or those growing in the interior. A more natural classification is that in which they are arranged according to their structure, as (1) eburnated, (2) compact, and (3) spongy osteoma.

(1) The *eburnated osteoma* occurs most frequently as a syphilitic growth from the inner table of the skull. It is extremely hard, and is often multiple and symmetrical.

Prepare (§ **80** or **81**), and stain (§ **98**).

On section notice that the dense bony structure is composed of lamellæ, which are arranged parallel to the surface of the tumour —(Virchow)—*i.e.*, they are arranged in convex layers, which follow more or less closely the free outline of the tumour. In the lamellæ there are no blood-vessels and no Haversian canals; but, according to Cornil and Ranvier, there are canaliculi, similar to those found in the "cement" of a tooth, which run towards the surface.

The *compact osteoma* is composed of ordinary compact bone, similar to that found near the surface of a long bone. It is met with as a nodular growth, usually beneath or in the periosteum, especially of the long bones; but it may be found growing in the substance of a bone, in the meninges of the brain, in the choroid coat of the eye, in the pericardium, in the skin, around glands, in the apices of tuber-culous lungs, even in the nerve centres; also in tendons, in inter-muscular septa, and in other positions where new fibrous tissue formations occur. Make a vertical section through the growth with a saw, and examine with a low power lens, when it will be observed that it differs from the eburnated osteoma in that the vessels and Haversian canals run at right angles to the long axis of the bone.

Prepare (§ **76** or **75**) and stain (§ **98**).

(× 50).—Notice that the structure is essentially that of compact bone, that the vessels run in the Haversian canals at right angles to the long axis of the bone, that there is a periosteal fibrous covering, with a layer of small round cells—osteoblasts—and young bone formation beneath. Around the Haversian canals regular Haversian systems may be readily distinguished.

The *spongy osteoma* differs from the compact form only in the fact

that the trabeculæ are much thinner and not so numerous; that the
medulla is usually more embryonic in character, and appears to the
naked eye as a gelatinous mass; in some cases, however, it is
almost fibroid. The whole tumour is essentially like the spongy
tissue of which the ends of long bones and the bodies of the shorter
ones are composed.

(× 50).—Treat as for compact osteoma. A few fat cells can
usually be observed amongst the small round cells which compose
the embryonic mass.

Myoma.

367. Myoma is a tumour composed of muscular tissue; it is
usually described as occurring in two forms.

(1) That composed of striped muscular fibre, an exceedingly rare
form, probably met with only as a result of the higher development
of sarcomatous tissue, in which case the muscle is imperfectly developed, and never gets beyond an embryonic stage.

(2) The ordinary myoma or leio-myoma, in which there is a formation of well-developed non-striped muscular fibres. This form is
met with so much more frequently in the uterus than in any other
position, that it has been named the uterine fibroid. It may, however, occur in any position in which non-striped muscle is normally
present, as in the gastro-intestinal tract, where it is seen as a polypoid
growth; in the wall of the bladder; in the prostate in old men; in
the skin, especially of the scrotum; and in the kidney, where it is
developed near the apices of the papillæ.

Naked eye appearances.—It may be small and rounded, or it
may grow to an enormous size, when it is usually lobulated.
Like most of the simple and slowly growing tumours, it is enclosed
in a fibrous capsule. It is usually multiple.

The typical uterine fibroid is a firm, fleshy, somewhat elastic mass,
growing in the muscular wall of the organ. On section the tumour
is usually paler, but sometimes brighter in colour than the surrounding muscular tissue. In the smaller rounded tumours the muscular
tissue is arranged in concentric laminæ, an arrangement which can
be easily discerned with the naked eye; but in the larger lobulated
forms each lobule is composed of one of these concentric masses,

and between them, running from the capsule, are bands of fibrous tissue, in which blood-vessels pass to nourish the new growth. In consequence of this laminated arrangement, the appearance of these masses is frequently compared to that of balls of cotton. In the uterine wall the tumours occur in three positions :—(1) Intramural, in the muscular wall itself; (2) Submucous, beneath the mucous membrane; and (3) Subserous, beneath the peritoneum. The two last push the mucous and serous tissues before them as they grow to the surface and eventually become polypoid.

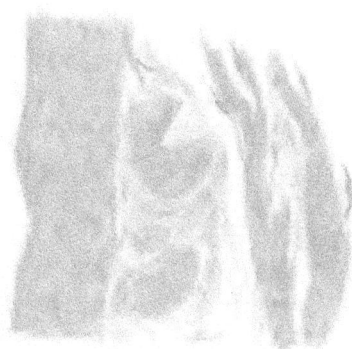

FIG. 157.—Non-striped myoma (uterine fibroid). Stained with picro-carmine. (× 450.)

    a. Mass of non-striped muscular tissue, in which the rod-shaped nuclei and the parallel arrangement of the fibrils are seen.
    b. Similar bundles of fibres cut transversely. The sections of the fibrils have the appearance of rounded cells, the section of the round nucleus is seen as a dot in *some* of the sections.
    c. Spindle-shaped cells, of which the fibrils (*f.*) are composed.
    d. Pink fibrous tissue.
    e. Connective tissue corpuscles.

Harden (§ 59) and stain (§ 98, or 103 *d* and 104).

(× 50).—In the pure myoma the section, instead of presenting a pink appearance, as in the fibroma (stained with picro-carmine), is yellowish-brown with minute crimson points at intervals. In an old myoma, where there is usually a considerable quantity of fibrous tissue, the pink fibrous strands stand out prominently between the yellowish-brown muscular bands. The muscle fibres are so small that it is necessary to use a somewhat higher power than usual to bring out the detail of their structure.

(× 450).—The muscular fibres are identical in appearance with those of ordinary non-striped muscle, but the bundles interlace with one another in every direction. Each bundle is marked by a series of parallel lines; and if the tissue is teased out or if the edge of a section be examined, each fibril marked off by these parallel lines is seen to be composed of spindle-shaped cells, which overlap at their ends to form the fibre. A rod-shaped nucleus may be seen in the centre of each cell. The larger bundles are usually thrown into folds, so that though the lines are parallel, they are somewhat wavy. In certain parts of the section the bundles are cut transversely or obliquely, and in place of parallel lines there are bundles of what appear to be rounded cells, some with, others without, a deeply-stained centre. These are simply the muscle cells cut transversely, the section sometimes passing through the rod-shaped nucleus, and sometimes through the contractile part of the cell.

It is not always an easy matter to distinguish between a true fibroma and a fibro-myoma, and it is therefore well to bear in mind that the fibrous tissue is white, hard, and glistening, whilst the muscular bands may be "pink, reddish-grey, or white," and are not nearly so firm as fibrous tissue. To make the diagnosis certain, a microscopic examination should always be made, for which small fragments of the tissue should be prepared (§ 41, 4 and 5). The fibrous tissue then swells up and disappears, and the muscle fibres may be separated and examined, stained or unstained. The rod-shaped nuclei stand out very prominently in such preparations.

Degenerative changes.—(1.) Fatty change; (2.) mucoid softening; (3.) hæmorrhages frequently follow the above conditions, especially where the vessels are numerous; (4.) calcification, giving rise to the so-called womb-stone; (5.) inflammation in consequence of injury, in which condition the fibres undergo cloudy swelling, and become swollen and granular,—abscess formation frequently following.

NEUROMA.

368. It is necessary to mention this tumour, although it is of comparatively rare occurrence. It may assume one of two forms—

(*a*) composed of nerve fibrils, occurring usually at the cut ends of nerves ; or (*b*) composed of ganglion cells, one case of which is recorded in connection with the supra-renal capsules. Many of the so-called neuromas are in reality fibromas or myxomas on the nerve trunks, or gliomas in the central nervous system.

Prepare as for nerve structures (§ 325).

Angioma.

369. The angioma is a tumour made up of dilated blood-vessels, some of which appear to be of new formation, whilst others are only pre-existing blood-vessels dilated. Along with the dilatation there is frequently an increase in the amount of connective tissue between the vessels.

There are two forms—(1.) Cavernous angioma, and (2.) Simple angioma.

The former has already been described (§ 195), and its structure in the skin is very similar, making allowance for the difference in the structure of the tissue or organ in which it occurs.

Prepare as in § 195.

Simple angioma is distinguished from the cavernous form by the fact that although there are fusiform and sacculated dilatations of the new or pre-existing vessels, the general tubular form of the vessel is still preserved. In the simple angioma of the skin or nævus (mother's mark) the dilatation above described is the principal feature ; there is little thickening of the walls of the vessels.

Naked eye appearances.—Such a tumour appears as a bright red or livid patch surrounded by a number of similar small spots which are not raised from the skin. These tumours are of comparatively common occurrence in glioma, and more rarely they may be met with in the brain, kidney, spleen, uterus, muscles, bones, hollow viscera, and mamma.

In another form of simple angioma the dilatation is not so great, but the increase of tissue around the vessels is more marked, as in hæmorrhoids, which are found in the submucous tissue of the rectum, and consist of masses of small dilated veins with thickened walls, supported by an increased quantity of connective tissue.

Harden (§ 59), cut (§§ 90-93), and stain (§ 98).

On microscopic examination the principal points to note are the dilated saccules, connected by the vascular tubes; the well-marked endothelial lining of the blood-distended cavities; and in some cases the thickening of the vascular walls, chiefly by an increase in the thickness of the adventitia.

A similar condition of the lymphatic vessels is described under the term Lymphatic Angioma, or Lymphangioma.

LYMPHOMA.

370. The true lymphoma is a histioid tumour; along with it must be described two other forms of lymphoid growth, both of which, however, depart somewhat from the true histioid type, and, unlike the true lymphoma, are often very malignant—the lymphadenoma and lympho-sarcoma.

The lymphoma appears, in many cases, to be rather a hyperplasia of lymphoid tissue than a true tumour, and it is always found in positions in which lymphoid tissue is normally present, as in lymphatic glands in the intestine, uterus, kidney, &c.; but occasionally there are true lymphoid tumour growths.

Naked eye appearances.—It occurs as a solitary mass, does not attain any great size, and is usually surrounded by a more or less dense fibrous capsule. On section it is uniformly soft, and white or pale pink in colour. Where small hæmorrhages have occurred, it may have yellow or brownish points (altered blood pigment). From this circumstance, and from the general appearance, it may in some cases be mistaken for a sarcoma, but the history and histological structure will at once set any doubts at rest.

Harden (§ 57 or 59), and stain (§ 98 or 103 *d*).

(× 50).—Note that the tissue is essentially like normal lymphoid tissue. The deeply-stained nuclei of the cells are seen in great numbers; here and there running through the mass are capillary vessels. If one of these vessels near the edge of the section be examined, delicate bands of pink tissue may be seen attached to its walls; and in favourable specimens, where the rounded cells have been displaced, a delicate reticulum may be distinguished. Lying

on the junctions of the strands or fibrillæ of the network, and clasping
them with their processes, are large nucleated branching endothelioid
or connective tissue cells. A number of larger vessels are also
present, with similar fibrils attached to their walls. To distinguish
more clearly the elements of which the tissue is composed, shake a
thin section of the tumour in a test tube containing a small quantity
of three-quarter per cent. salt solution (§ 37); lay out carefully on a
slide and stain (§ 104). The stroma attached to the capillary walls
can then be readily distinguished. It is said that in the lymphoma
the capillaries are distended, but it is extremely difficult to make
this out.

(× 300).—The attachment of the stroma to the capillary walls
is more easily seen. At the junctions of the bands of the stroma
are large branching endothelioid cells with branching processes
which clasp the bands of the stroma and extend along them for some
distance, but are quite distinct from them; each has one or two
nuclei which stain deeply and so stand out prominently. Ranvier
holds that these endothelioid cells are the cells by which the fibrillæ
are secreted or formed. This is a fact to be borne in mind when
considering the other forms of lymphoid tumours. Lying in the
meshes of the network are the small round lymphoid cells, which
are stained almost throughout, showing that they are composed of
a nucleus surrounded by an extremely thin film of protoplasm.
Some of the cells are larger, and may contain a couple of nuclei,
and in a few instances, especially where there have been small
hæmorrhages, they may contain granules of brown pigment. Where
the capillaries have ruptured, the blood may be seen as greenish
corpuscles, lying in the meshes round them.

LYMPHO-SARCOMA.

371. The second form of lymphoma—the lympho-sarcoma—is a
malignant growth, which, from its clinical history and pathological
appearances, is frequently mistaken for sarcoma or encephaloid
cancer. It may grow in any position, but usually begins in the
lymphatic glands or tissue of the viscera, from which it spreads,
especially to the lungs; it may grow to a considerable size and is

often multiple. The so-called primary cancer of the kidney is usually a lympho-sarcoma. The section from which the following description is taken was removed from one of the mesenteric glands.

Naked eye appearances.—The growth resembles an ordinary lymphoma; but is more pink, slightly more vascular, and of a somewhat softer consistence throughout. Around the soft almost diffluent mass is a delicate fibrous capsule. On section are seen numerous yellow or brown spots, due to rupture of the vessels and the presence of extravasations of blood of different ages. On scraping the surface a quantity of creamy fluid is removed. Examine this in a neutral solution (§ 37) × 300, and note that it is composed chiefly of lymphoid cells, similar to those described as occurring in lymphoma.

Prepare as in (§ **370**).

(× 50).—In the hardened section the lymphoid cells predominate to such an extent that no other structures, except a few blood-vessels, and around them at intervals the green hæmorrhagic masses, can be distinguished, either under the low or high power; the tumour resembles very closely the small round-celled sarcoma (§ **380**).

Now examine the pencilled or shaken section. A few of the small blood-vessels may be seen, and at certain points, where the lymphoid cells are washed away, an exceedingly delicate reticulum can be distinguished. This reticulum is similar to that present in lymphoma, but is much more delicate; the meshes are larger, and the endothelioid plates are neither so prominent nor so numerous. In the small round or ovoid cells the nuclei, and therefore the cells, appear to be undergoing more rapid division than in lymphoma.

(× 300).—The increased proportion of small round cells to reticulum, and the relatively small number of endothelioid plates on the network, can now be better appreciated. Note the small masses of coloured blood corpuscles, the result of hæmorrhage from the "embryonic" and badly supported vessels. The delicate stroma at once enables the observer to distinguish this growth from the small round-celled sarcoma, which it otherwise so closely resembles.

LYMPHADENOMA (HODGKIN'S DISEASE).

372. In Hodgkin's disease, as already seen (Liver, § **188**; Spleen,

§ 290), there is an overgrowth of certain elements of the lymphoid tissue. The first manifestation of the disease is a growth in the lymphatic glands, usually of the neck or groin. From the primary centre, the surrounding glands and then the spleen, liver, kidneys, lung, submucous tissue of the intestine, serous membranes, skin, heart, and supra-renal capsules, are all, in turn, involved in a malignant infective process.

Naked eye appearances.—The lymphadenomatous tissue in the lymphatic glands is firmer and not so liable to caseate as that in the viscera, otherwise the growths are identical in both naked eye and microscopic appearances. It occurs either as small firm elastic masses, or as large pinkish-white nodules, though in the liver, spleen, and kidneys, especially where there is a tendency to caseation, there is a yellower tinge from the beginning, and the tumour is doughy and even putty-like. Hæmorrhages, such as those met with in lymphoma and sarcoma, are comparatively rare.

There is here, as described in the Spleen (§ 290), an enormous increase in the number and activity of the endothelioid plates, and a corresponding increase in the amount of fibrous stroma or reticulum, which, however, seems to compress the lymphoid cells out of existence, in consequence of which their number is diminished.

Harden a section of lymphadenoma taken from any of the lymphatic glands (§ 59), and stain (§ 98).

(× 50) and (× 300).—In the growing part of the tumour there is a great increase in the number and activity of the endothelioid cells, followed by an increase of the bands of the reticulum, both in thickness and in number, so that there is a gradual conversion of the reticulum into a mass of fibrous tissue, the lymphoid cells becoming more and more sparse as the fibrous tissue is more fully formed. As in the spleen, the lymphadenomatous tissue gradually invades and destroys the surrounding tissue.

Lymphoma—ordinary lymphoid tissue; both endothelioid plates and reticulum well developed; number of lymphoid cells normal.

Lympho-sarcoma—small number of endothelioid plates; correspondingly scanty reticulum; enormous increase in the number of lymphoid cells.

Lymphadenoma—early increase in the number and activity of the endothelioid plates, accompanied by an increase in the reticular tissue which leads to great diminution of the lymphoid cells.

From the above statement it will be seen that, as in connective tissue, the quantity of the reticulum varies directly as the number of endothelioid plates, but inversely as the number of lymphoid cells.

Simple Histioid Tumours composed of more than one Tissue.

Papilloma.

373. The papilloma—under which heading are classed warts, horns,

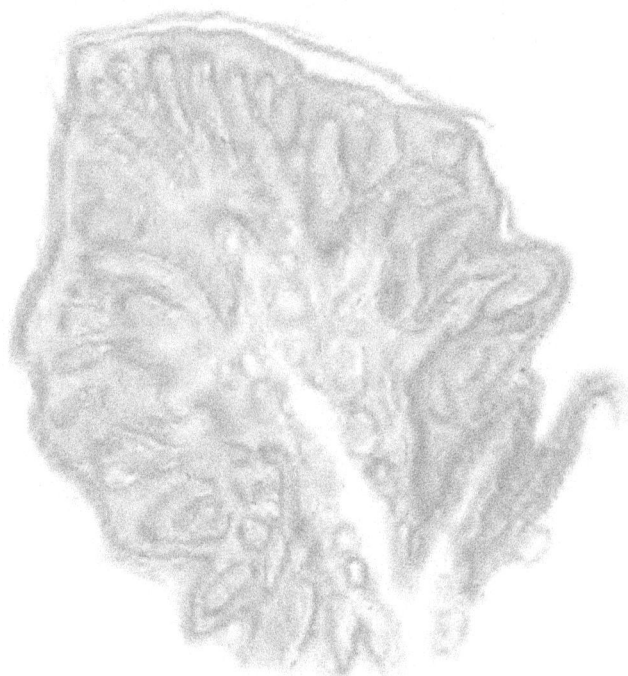

Fig. 158.—Section of papilloma. Stained with picro-carmine.
(× 50.)

c. Horny layer.
R.M. Rete Malpighii.
C.t. Connective tissue basis.
b.v. Blood-vessels of considerable size.

the compound cauliflower excrescences, and such polypoid growths as occur in the bladder and in the larynx—consists essentially of a hypertrophied and often branched connective tissue papilla, covered with a hypertrophied layer of epithelium. As examples may be taken the ordinary wart, the large cauliflower excrescences which are so frequently met with round the anal or genito-urinary orifices in syphilitic and gonorrhœal patients, and the horns seen on the face and neck. Although this tumour may grow rapidly, it is non-malignant, and is of purely local origin.

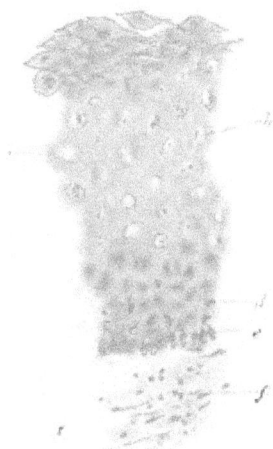

FIG. 159.—Drawing of epithelium from the surface of a papilloma. Stained with picro-carmine. (× 300.)
  a. Layer of flattened cells from near the surface of the rete Malpighii.
  b. Well-formed prickle cells.
  c. Vacuolated prickle cell.
  d. Smaller rounded or polygonal cells, immediately above
  e. The columnar or germinal layer.
  f. Cellular connective tissue of papillary basis.

Harden small pieces of one of the compound cauliflower excrescences (§§ 59, 57, and 71), and stain (§ 98).

(× 50).—The general outline of the growth must first be noticed. In place of the simple papilla there is a branching mass of fibrous or fibro-cellular tissue. This, in the picro-carmine stained specimen, is pink, if fibrous, but more crimson if the cells predominate, as is the case where the tumour is of very rapid growth. Supported in the fibrous basis are numerous blood-vessels, very similar to those in a normal papilla, except that they are usually somewhat larger. At the point of junction with the subjacent tissues these vessels appear to open into large vascular sinuses or dilatations. In consequence of the branching of the connective tissue basis, masses of it may be seen in transverse section, apparently embedded in the epithelium. Lying immediately on the connective tissue is a layer of somewhat columnar epithelial or epidermic cells, which take on the carmine stain very readily; this corresponds to the germinal layer of the rete Malpighii or rete mucosum. Above this is a thicker and yellower layer, in which

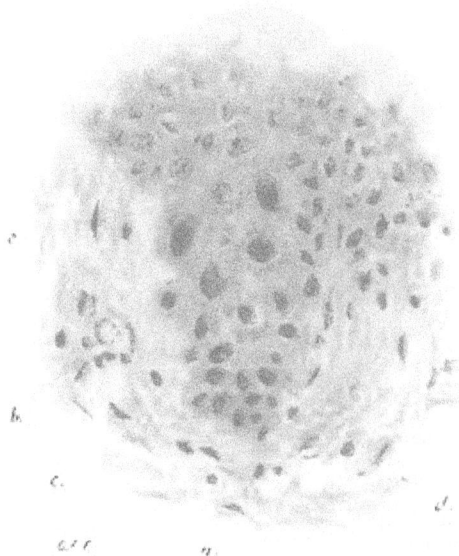

FIG. 160.—Drawing of epithelium from a rapidly growing papilloma. Stained with picro-carmine. (× 450.)

   a. Fibrous tissue of true corium.
   b. Small blood-vessel.
   c. Lymph spaces.
   d. Cells of germinal layer.
   e. Well-formed prickle cells in the rete Malpighii.

the cells are seen to have more formed material, and to be polygonal in shape, corresponding to those in the upper part of the rete Malpighii. Passing further outwards, a second deeply-stained layer is reached—the stratum granulosum of Langerhans. Above this the stratum lucidum is not very distinctly seen under this power, and the stratum corneum is represented only by an exceedingly thin yellow streak.

(× 300).—Examine the blood-vessels distended with blood and the fibro-cellular basis, in the young cells of which the nuclei can frequently be seen undergoing division. Then note the layer of columnar cells, with their deeply-stained nuclei. Above this layer the cells are first irregularly round and then polygonal, and many of them have well-marked " prickles " passing into the body of the cell, these often appearing to be directly continuous with processes from the nucleus, though in some cases the nucleus is surrounded by a distinct vacuole. The processes of adjacent cells are continuous with one another, and may be seen to pass from nucleus to nucleus in all directions. The stratum granulosum is very well developed; its cells are granular and deeply stained at the poles, but in the body of the cell there is a clear bright space. Each cell is more or less spindle-shaped. The stratum lucidum may be distinguished under a high power, but it is never very well developed in the true papilloma, and the stratum corneum, too, is represented merely by a thin bright yellow band of horny squames. Here, then, the distinguishing features are the enlargement and branching of the papillæ, the enormous development of the rete Malpighii and stratum granulosum, and the thinness of the horny layer.

Papillomas of the mucous membrane grow in the same way, but are covered by epithelium, similar to that which is normally present in the position from which they grow. These are the soft velvety growths which are met with in such positions as the bladder and intestine.

Horny Papilloma.

374. If a section be made of a horn taken from the face or the neck, and stained as for papilloma, the stratum corneum is seen as a dense yellow mass, which appears to fill up every crevice on the outer surface of the growth; it forms a layer of very considerable thickness over the stratum granulosum, which therefore does not stand out quite so prominently as in the ordinary papilloma. In order to understand this appearance the situation of these growths must be remembered—face, neck, and those surfaces generally on which there is secretion of a large quantity of sebaceous material. The horny layer, instead of being constantly shed, as from a normal cutaneous surface, or from the surface of an ordinary papilloma, is glued together by the large quantity of sebaceous material, and thus a kind of paste is formed, which, drying and hardening, constitutes the smooth, horny mass. All the other features described as present in the ordinary papilloma are here repeated.

SIMPLE ADENOMA.

375. The simple adenoma of the breast may be taken as the typical form. It is a mass of glandular tissue growing from a separate centre of acini and tubules in no way connected with those of the mammary gland. In the true adenoma there is more than a mere increase in the amount of inter-glandular tissue. There is actual gland formation, accompanied in many cases by a growth of inter-acinous connective tissue, and also by a distension into cysts of the newly-formed acini and tubules. Pathologists differ greatly as to the definition and even as to the nature of adenoma, and cystic sarcomas and primary cancers have been classed under this heading, but it will be well to distinguish the adenoma from the cancer in the same way as the papilloma is distinguished from the epithelioma, though in both cases, under certain conditions, the one may be followed or replaced by the other.

Naked eye appearances.—The adenoma is a rounded or lobulated tumour, varying greatly in size, from a filbert to a child's head, usually surrounded by a fibrous capsule, by which it is sharply defined from the neighbouring tissue. It grows slowly; there is no central umbilication, and no retraction of the nipple, such as is met with in scirrhous cancer, for which only they are liable to be mistaken. There are no secondary growths in the neighbourhood, and there is no implication of the glands.

On section it appears to be composed of a mass of fibrous tissue, over which are scattered small chrome yellow or cream coloured points (the masses of epithelium), and cysts of various shapes and sizes in large numbers, from which a quantity of creamy opaque, serous, gelatinous, or semi-solid material may be expressed. In some cases the adenoma consists of a soft, pinkish mass, through which run vascular bands, surrounded by a fibrous capsule.

Harden (§§ 57 and 59), and stain (§§ 98 and 103 *d*).

(× 50).—A regularly formed fibrous matrix, more or less cellular, according to the rapidity of the growth of the tumour, is seen. Running through this are numerous blood-vessels, and supported by it are tubes or acini in various stages of development, seen as solid columns of cubical epithelial cells, perfectly formed tubes with distinct lumina, or cysts of considerable size; at certain points may be observed the process of the opening out of the lumen from

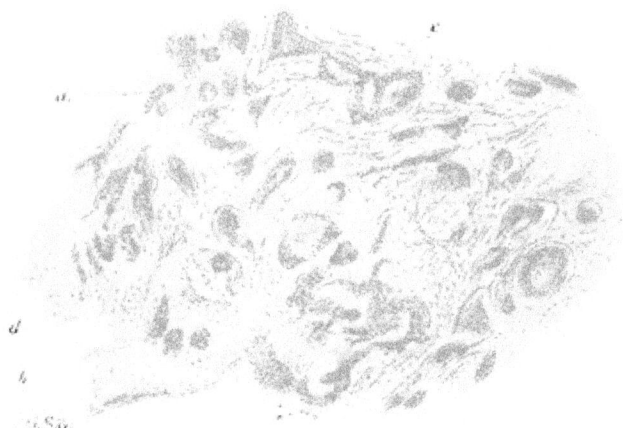

FIG. 161.—Simple adenoma of the breast. Stained with logwood. (× 50.)

    a. Column or double row of cells, of which the nuclei only are seen.
    b. A more irregular mass or cylinder of cells.
    c. Cyst formed by distension of an acinus or tubule.
    d. Connective tissue basis.

the solid mass of cells to the distinct cavity, lined with a layer of regularly arranged cylindrical or cubical cells.

(× 300).—Examine the fibrous stroma in which the blood-vessels are embedded. Lying immediately on it, and apparently taking the place of the basement membrane of the normal gland tissue, is a layer of delicate flattened cells—Debove's layer. Above this layer is usually only a single layer of non-ciliated columnar or cubical cells, each with a distinct and well-formed nucleus. A somewhat deceptive appearance is frequently presented, especially when the sections are not very thin :—in some of the cavities it appears as though there were several rows of cells, because the knife, passing obliquely through the same layer of cells, exposes a somewhat elongated surface view, hence the appearance of several layers. Again, if the section be made through the epithelial lining at the margin of the cyst, an apparently solid mass of epithelium is presented to our view. It is very necessary to remember this fact in making an examination of adenomas.

The adenoma is developed in much the same way as is the mammary gland (probably from a portion cut off from the main mass of this gland), for a description of which the student is referred to works on embryology and histology.

MULTIPLE, COMPOUND, OVARIAN CYSTIC TUMOUR (SYNONYMS— PROLIFEROUS OVARIAN CYSTIC TUMOUR; MULTILOCULAR OVARIAN TUMOUR).

376. The ovarian cystic tumour is a growth which, in its mode of development, simple nature and general structure, may be compared to the adenoma, and may be termed the adenoma of the ovary or of the peritoneum.

It may reach an enormous size, and is composed of a series of cysts, situated in the ovary or in the broad ligament. The tumour is surrounded by a fibrous capsule, and on section the cavities are found to be bounded either by dense fibrous bands or by spongy tissue, which, examined with a magnifying lens, is seen to be made up of a number of small cysts, in which minute glistening or gelatinous specks are to be seen. The larger cysts usually contain a quantity of watery or serous fluid, in some cases almost like the fluid found in hydatid cysts, with chloride of sodium, and but little albumen. This fluid may be variously coloured by altered blood pigment—purple, red, or yellow. The smaller cysts are filled with a gelatinous material, which is rarely blood-stained, but contains more albumen.

Harden a small piece of the spongy part of the tumour, in which minute glistening or gelatinous specks are to be seen (§ 59), and stain (§ **98** or **103** *d*).

(× 50).—Embedded in a somewhat cellular and highly vascular connective tissue stroma are numerous small cysts. The nuclei of the connective tissue cells are deeply stained with the carmine, and stand

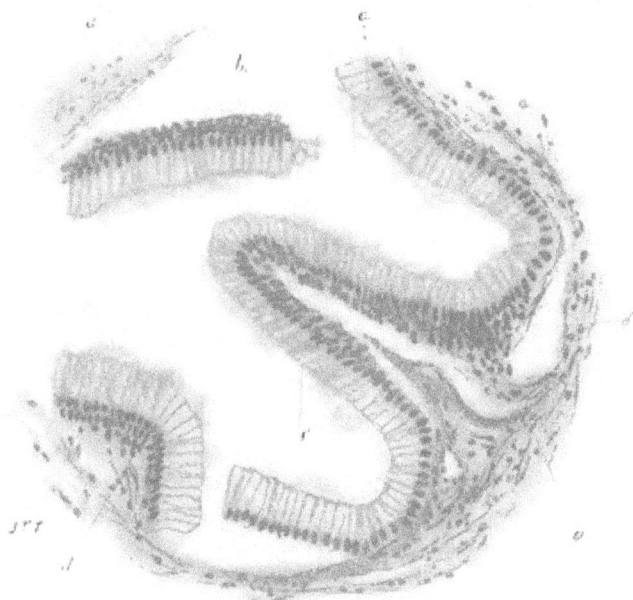

Fig. 162.—Drawing of section of a compound ovarian cystic tumour. Stained with picro-carmine. (× 300.)
  a. Fibro-cellular connective tissue stroma.
  b. Layer of flattened cells, or Debove's layer.
  c. Single layer of chalice cells.
  d. Several rows of cells, of which the nuclei are seen.
  e. Mouths of the chalice cells.
  f. Mucoid material contained within the cyst.

out prominently. The blood-vessels are filled with the greenish blood corpuscles. The cysts are very irregular in outline; some are round or oval and simple; others are subdivided by papilliform processes which run from the connective tissue stroma, and in some cases meet in the centre and divide the primary cysts into smaller compartments.

Lining each cyst is a regular layer of epithelium, columnar and often ciliated, or excavated to form goblet or chalice cells. The nuclei of these cells can be distinctly seen, and are usually situated in the lower third, especially of the chalice cell. Notice that all the papilliform projections are completely invested with this regular layer of epithelium.

(× 300).— Examine the cellular stroma, with its numerous blood-vessels, and then the arrangement and appearance of the epithelial cells. There is no basement membrane ; but, as in the adenoma of the breast, a layer of flattened nucleated cells is found between the columnar cells and the connective tissue—Debove's layer. From these flattened cells spring the larger cells, which are arranged in a single or a double row. The deeper cells are more cubical than columnar, and interlock with those of the more superficial layer. The superficial cells are tall and columnar, a few of them are ciliated, but the greater number are chalice cells, in which the nucleus is placed in the lower third. The nucleus is deeply stained, and stands out very prominently from the more delicately stained cell. In the chalice cell the part above the nucleus bulges out slightly before the mouth of the cell is reached, which may be seen as an ovoid opening. The bulging part is more transparent than the lower third of the cell. Within the cyst a few cells are usually lying free, embedded in a delicately tinted mucoid or colloid material.

Cysts.

377. Cysts have been already described as present in the liver (§ **194**) and kidney (§ **225**), where they are due to the dilatation of obstructed ducts, to the accumulation of various epithelial or fluid materials, and to the distension of pre-existing spaces.

Other cysts have been described in the liver as due to the presence of parasites (hydatid cysts) or foreign bodies.

Others, again, are formed by softening and degeneration in new growths, as in the case of the cystic myxoma (false cysts, or cysts of degeneration).

Cysts of new growth are also met with, as in the adenoma and the compound ovarian cystic tumour.

Peritoneal cysts are found as hydrocele and loculated cysts, in which the peritoneum is prolonged into a small cavity or series of cavities, separated from the main cavity, and then distended to form a cyst or cysts; secondary cysts are budded off, as it were, from the primary sac, and they are in turn distended.

Ranula.—This term is applied to the cysts which are found under the tongue. It includes those large cysts extending forward to the frenum, lined with ciliated epithelium, and filled with thick, somewhat tenacious, fluid containing mucin and sodium albumen, and a few epithelial cells; these are the result of dilatation of the ducts of the sublingual glands, and not of any part of the gland itself, which continues to secrete the material with which the cysts are distended. Other forms of ranula are described, but they are comparatively unimportant.

Endothelial cysts, such as bursæ, occur round tendons, and are caused by distension of their sheaths by exudation.

Distension of a closed cavity may give rise to a cyst formation, as in the case of goître, where large cysts are formed by distension of the normal closed sacs of the thyroid gland, by a proliferation of the epithelium lining the cavity, followed by colloid degeneration of the cells, as in the case of the contents of colloid cysts derived from the renal epithelium (§ 225).

DERMOID CYST.

378. One form of cystic tumour which deserves more than passing mention is the dermoid cyst. It is usually found in or near the ovary in the peritoneum, when it is often large and complicated; smaller and simpler forms are found near the sacrum and at the side of the neck and face.

Naked eye appearances.—The tumour from which the following description is taken was removed from the ovary, and was about the size of a child's head at birth. It was firm at points, but on the surface a number of cysts projected. Some of these contained a quantity of glue-like fluid, others a soft, fatty, or sebaceous looking material, whilst others again were filled with long hairs disposed in coils. When the mass was cut into, the knife "creaked" through nodules of cartilage, and then "grated" through calcareous or calcified patches. In the body of the tumour were larger cysts, though some parts of the growth were simply fleshy. Portions of the mass were hardened (§ 98), and treated as for adenoma (§ 375). On microscopic examination this dermoid cyst appeared to be an attempt at the formation of a fœtus within the ovary itself, as almost every tissue present in the human body could be distinguished—epithelium, squamous, evidently on a cutaneous surface; goblet cells, as from the intestine; ciliated, as from the trachea; hair follicles, with the deeply-stained yellow hair in the centre, in transverse and longitudinal section; cartilage, with well-developed capsules and matrix; muscular fibre, both non-striped and striped; blood-vessels in all stages of development; gland structures similar to those found in the bronchi, in the skin, and in the duodenum; small fragments of bone in process of calcification—in some parts the matrix is pink, in others the peculiar green colour that calcified structures give with picro-carmine; nerve fibres; multipolar nerve cells similar to those met with in the anterior horn of the cord; ganglion cells or large rounded cells with well-marked nuclei and long processes, such as are normally met with in the semilunar ganglia; masses of lymphoid tissue; fat globules; fibrous tissue, and tendon. The large cysts were all lined with ciliated or goblet-celled epithelium, except those into which hairs were growing, where most of the cells were more like ordinary cutaneous epithelium.

Sarcomas.

379. The sarcoma, as already defined, is a tumour composed of mesoblastic tissue in an imperfect state of development; but owing to the fact that there is always an attempt at the formation of some of the higher tissues, there are many varieties of sarcoma. The tumour may be simply a mass of granulation tissue, or there may be in it a partial formation of fibrous tissue, cartilage, bone, striped muscular fibre, &c.; and each of these tissues may modify to a certain extent both the naked eye and the microscopic appearances of the growth.

SMALL ROUND-CELLED SARCOMA.

380. This, the simplest form of sarcoma, is composed of the most elementary type of connective tissue, the typical embryonic or granulation tissue, and is perhaps the most malignant of the group. It grows very rapidly, infiltrates locally, and, spreading by the blood-vessels, gives rise to secondary growths.

It occurs especially in the fasciæ and in the loose areolar and subcutaneous tissues, in the connective tissue of the nerve centres, retina, bones, muscles, testicle, and mamma, as a primary growth; but it does *not* affect the lymphatic structures. As a secondary growth it almost invariably makes its appearance first in the lungs, after which it affects the more vascular organs, especially those in which there is a complex capillary system.

Naked eye appearances.—It is very soft, in some cases almost pulpy, or is like a piece of brain tissue; it is usually rounded, and to the naked eye sharply defined from the surrounding healthy tissue, but has no fibrous capsule. On section it is pale pink, has no glistening white fibrous streaks running through its substance, but yellowish or creamy patches—due to fatty degenerative changes— are frequently observed on the surface. Still more characteristic are the small red, brown, and yellow points—hæmorrhagic patches in various stages of alteration. Hæmorrhages are common in all forms of sarcoma, but especially in this and in the myeloid form (§ **385**).

Harden (§ **59**), and stain (§ **98** or **103** *d*).

(× 50).—Observe the mass of small round cells gradually invading or infiltrating the surrounding tissues; in a sarcoma growing in muscle, the fibres are gradually separated by the infiltrating small round cells. Where the tumour tissue is very distinct, a series of lines of elongated cells may be distinguished, usually arranged in double rows, between which greenish lines may be seen. These double rows of cells are the embryonic blood-vessels, and the green lines lying between them are the strings of coloured blood corpuscles. The great resemblance of this mass to granulation tissue will be at once recognised (§ **166**).

(× 300, or better, × 450).—The elementary cell structure is now easily distinguished. The majority of the cells are from $\frac{1}{3500}$

to $\frac{1}{1000}$ inch in diameter (all larger than a coloured blood corpuscle, which is about $\frac{1}{3200}$ inch). There is no cell wall, but each cell has a distinct deeply-stained nucleus, $\frac{1}{3000}$ to $\frac{1}{2500}$ inch in diameter, within which nucleoli are to be observed as deep crimson dots.

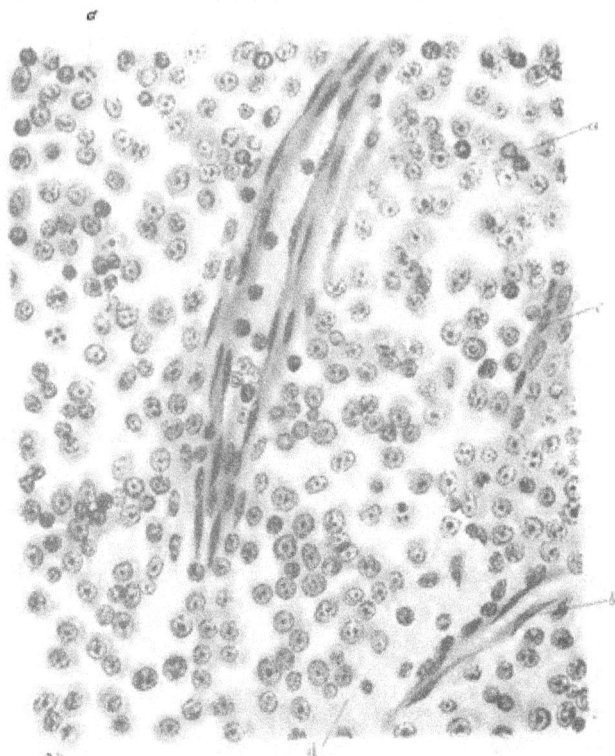

FIG. 163.—Small round-celled sarcoma. Stained with picro-carmine. (× 400.)
  a. Small round cells with large nuclei and distinct nucleoli.
  b. Flattened spindle-shaped cells, forming the walls of embryonic blood-vessels.
  c. Flattened cells between ordinary tumour cells and spindle cells of the vessel wall. Row of red blood corpuscles between.
  d. Hæmorrhage.
  In some of the cells we have distinct evidence of rapid proliferation. Double nucleoli and elongating and constricted nuclei.

Between the cells is a very small quantity of granular homogeneous intercellular substance, which, however, in many cases is almost indistinguishable. The elongated cells seen above are only sarcoma cells, and have taken their present shape because of the pressure to which they have been subjected by the blood corpuscles which appear to have simply been forced in between them. The blood-vessels in this growth are quite embryonic in type; their walls, composed of these modified sarcoma cells, are exceedingly delicate, and the least extra strain causes them to give way, when blood is poured out into the surrounding sarcomatous tissue. Examine a transverse section of a vessel, and note the flattened layer of cells next to the blood current, and the gradual transition in the successive layers from the flattened to the rounded cell, so that the

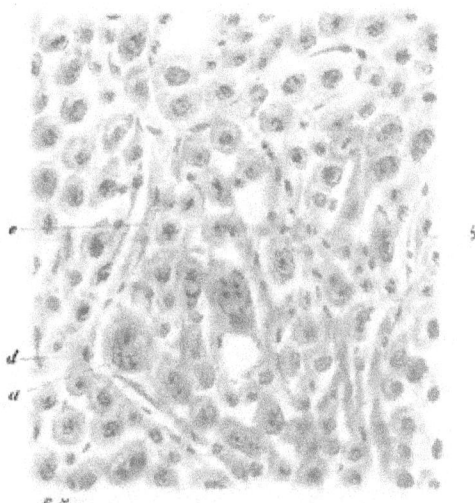

FIG. 164.—Section of mixed large celled sarcoma, stained with picro-carmine. (× 300.)

a. Large irregular cell with three nuclei.
b. Spindle-shaped cell with nucleus dividing
c. Smaller round cell with single nucleus.
d. Delicate intercellular substance.
e. Embryonic blood-vessel, bounded by smaller flattened or spindle cells.

tumour cells are in direct contact with the blood current, by which they are carried to the lungs—where secondary growths first make their appearance—and then to the other vascular organs.

The degenerations to which this variety is liable will be best considered with those of the other sarcomas.

LARGE ROUND-CELLED OR MIXED SARCOMA.

381. The large round-celled sarcoma grows in much the same positions, but affects specially the submucous tissue of the pharynx and posterior nares, where it forms a small, firm, almost fibrous, pale, polypoid mass, sharply defined from the surrounding healthy tissues. It is malignant in a much lower degree than the small round-celled sarcoma, and rarely gives rise to secondary growths.

Harden (§ 59), and stain (§ 98 or 103 *d*).

(× 50) and (× 300).—Note that the rounded cells are about two or three times as large as the cells of the small round-celled form. Each contains from one to four large ovoid nuclei, surrounded by a quantity of protoplasm. Between them is a delicate fibrillated intercellular substance, which at certain points is collected into thicker bands. These, along with thin walled vessels, divide the large cells into groups, which vary considerably in size. At other points, especially where the fibrillar tissue is present in large quantity, elongated or spindle cells may be seen, almost like those in organising granulation tissue. The vessels, as in all sarcomas, are quite embryonic in type, having thin cellular walls.

SPINDLE-CELLED SARCOMA.

382. In the spindle-celled sarcoma there is an attempt at the formation of more highly organised connective tissue than in the small round-celled form. The cells become elongated, in most cases the amount of intercellular substance is increased, and the development of the vessels is carried somewhat further.

Of these tumours the more important are the following.

RECURRENT FIBROID TUMOUR.

383. The recurrent fibroid of Paget, like the other tumours of this group, is found growing from connective tissue in almost any position, but especially in fasciæ, periosteum, the breast, kidney, liver, skin, and dura mater. The cases recorded by Paget appear to grow principally from periosteum and subcutaneous tissue in various parts of the body. They vary in size from half an inch to as much as a foot in one of their dimensions, and are characterised by their tendency to recur locally when imperfectly removed; they have no special tendency to infiltrate.

Naked eye appearances.—In the first instance they do not give rise to secondary growths, but when they have been repeatedly removed, the recurrent mass very frequently comes to resemble the true spindle-celled sarcoma (§ 384). They are rounded or lobulated, and are firmly attached to the tissue from which they grow. On section this

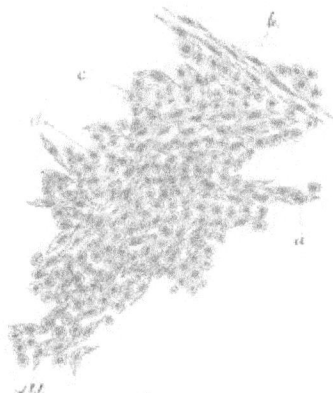

FIG. 165.—Small spindle-celled sarcoma. Stained with picro-carmine. (× 300.)
  a. Well-formed spindle cells.
  b. More elongated spindles bounding one of the vascular channels.
  c. Embryonic blood-vessel cut transversely.
  d. Transverse section of spindle cell. (This transverse section, with the section of the nucleus in its centre, must not be mistaken for a round cell.)

tumour is firm, tough, and irregular, and often has a fleshy look. It may be pale pink or brownish red, almost like a fibroma, and the surface has a streaky look, as if from the presence of bands of fibrous tissue. It is from this appearance that the name "fasciculated sarcoma" is derived.

Harden (§ 59), and stain (§ 98).

(× 50).—Note the fasciculated appearance. A series of bundles of cells may be seen interlacing with one another in all directions; some of these are cut longitudinally, others obliquely, others again transversely. The blood-vessels are fewer but are more highly organised than those in the small round-celled sarcoma.

(× 400).—The bundles are seen to be made up of "narrow, spindle-shaped, elongated, caudate, and oat-shaped nucleated cells." The nucleus is said to distend the body of the cell at the point at which it is present. Some of the cells have bifurcated ends, but the majority of them are oat-shaped, and between them is a small quantity of fibrillated intercellular substance.

TRUE SMALL SPINDLE-CELLED SARCOMA.

384. This tumour grows in much the same positions as the fore-

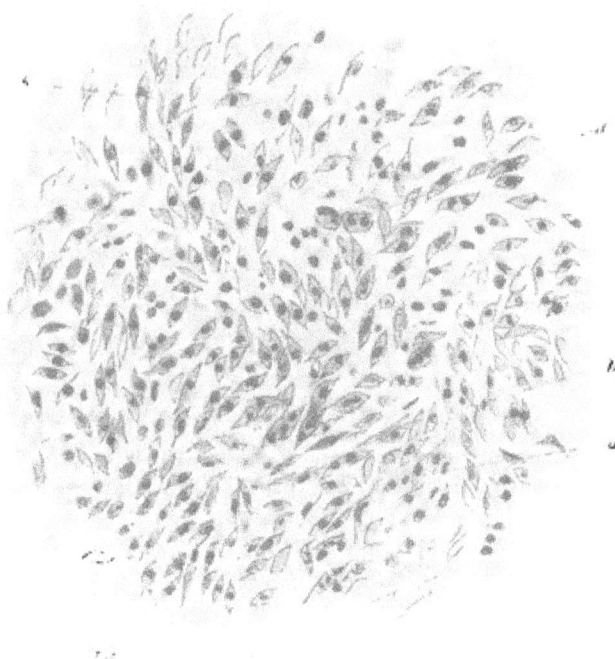

FIG. 166.—Small spindle-celled sarcoma. Stained with alum carmine. (× 350.)
  a. Well-formed spindle cells.
  b.b'. More elongated spindles bounding vascular channels.
  c. Cell cut transversely appears to be a small round cell.
  d. Larger cells in which there is indirect division of the nuclei.

going, and, like it, comparatively rarely gives rise to secondary growths. When these do occur, they are found in the same position (the lung first, and then other vascular organs) as the other secondary sarcomatous growths.

Naked eye appearances.—It may attain a considerable size, is surrounded by a more or less definite capsule, and on section presents a firm, solid, or elastic, pale, fleshy surface ; not so smooth as in the recurrent fibroid form, and with the glistening or fibroid streaks are more pronounced.

Prepare as above, and examine.

(× 50) and (× 400).—The spindle cells are more perfectly formed, and, as a rule, are somewhat larger and more elongated than are those of the recurrent fibroid tumour. They are arranged in bundles, which interlace in all directions, so that they are seen in various sections. Those cut longitudinally are the ordinary spindle cells, with ovoid, or, in some cases, rod-shaped nuclei. Others are cut obliquely, and these appear to be ovoid cells ; whilst others again, cut transversely, appear to be round cells. It must be noticed, however, that these sections are comparatively small, and that some of them have no nucleus, owing to the fact that the sections are made near the end of the cells to which the ovoid nuclei do not extend.

Where the section passes transversely through the centre of a cell the nucleus, of course, is divided, and the rounded section appears to have a nucleus.

Running through the section are embryonic blood-vessels similar in structure to those met with in the small round-celled sarcoma ; but not so numerous.

MYELOID SARCOMA.

385. The myeloid or giant-celled sarcoma, the most common variety of the small spindle-celled sarcoma, is one in which are well-formed giant cells, these being present probably because of the positions in which the tumour occurs, either within the shaft or epiphyses of a bone or under the periosteum, especially in the following positions :—the upper end of the tibia, the lower end of the femur, the upper end of the humerus, on the outer surface, or within the lower jaw—constituting one form of malignant epulis—

or in the antrum. When growing under the periosteum it is surrounded by a fibrous capsule only; but when in the centre of the bone it expands the outer shell, which may become so thin that it crackles under pressure of the finger.

Naked eye appearances. — It grows slowly, and may attain a considerable size, is moderately firm, fleshy, or elastic, pinkish or brownish yellow in colour, and on section has a peculiar "fasciculated" or sometimes a marbled appearance. The peripheral

FIG. 167.—Myeloid or giant-celled sarcoma. Stained with picro-carmine. (× 300.)

   a. Spindle cells, of which the tumour is principally composed.
   b. Cells arranged to form the walls of embryonic blood-vessels.
   c. Giant cell, with large number of nuclei scattered throughout its protoplasm.
   d. Transverse sections of spindle cells.
   e. Extravasated coloured blood corpuscles—escaped from ruptured vessels.

or growing part, in which small fragments of bone may often be found, is usually more pink than the centre, which is pale or brownish yellow, almost fatty looking, and variegated with brown or red patches (hæmorrhages of various ages), whilst at certain points are cysts containing a yellow or brown gelatinous material (derived from softened tumour tissue stained with altered blood pigment). The hæmorrhages and cysts are very common as the vessels are numerous, embryonic in structure, and from the exposed position of the tumour and the unyielding nature of the structure on or in which it grows, are especially liable to injury from external violence.

Harden (§ 59), and stain (§ **98** or **103** *d*).

(× 50.)—The bundles of small spindle cells, well developed, and cut in various directions, are readily observed. Throughout the section are small green granular masses (collections of coloured blood corpuscles). The giant cells, more or less numerous, are seen as areas of protoplasm, about the size of a pin's head, delicately stained, with small crimson specks (nuclei) scattered through them. The delicate green lines indicating the position of the blood-vessels are very numerous.

(× 300).—Examine the spindle cells. The description given of them in the small spindle-celled sarcoma applies in this case also. The blood-vessels are exceedingly numerous, and are composed simply of tumour cells, more or less regularly arranged in rows, between which the coloured blood corpuscles (green) have pushed their way. Around these embryonic blood-vessels green masses of extravasated blood are frequently met with, the red blood corpuscles with their double outlines lying in direct contact with both spindle-shaped and giant cells.

The giant or myeloid cells resemble very closely the osteoclasts of bone. They are large irregular masses of delicately tinted protoplasm, in which are imbedded twelve, twenty, or more, deeply stained nuclei scattered irregularly throughout them. In many cases these cells are vacuolated.

Although this is the typical form of the giant-celled sarcoma, it must be remembered that these giant cells may be met with in any sarcoma which is growing in connection with bone, so that their presence must be looked upon simply as an accident of position of the tumour. Granules of altered blood pigment may usually be seen. In the yellow patches above described many of the spindle cells are becoming granular and fatty, so that the myeloid, like the round-celled, sarcomas frequently undergo fatty degeneration.

The typical form seldom gives rise to secondary growths ; but such secondary tumours as have been examined when found in the position ordinarily affected (the lung), have contained no giant cells, but have been simply small spindle-celled sarcomas.

Large Spindle-Celled Sarcoma.

386. This form, though not absolutely distinct from the small spindle-celled variety, differs from it in many respects, both clinically and pathologically. The primary growth occurs in the same positions, but is found especially in the skin. It seldom reaches a very large size, but its growth may be extremely rapid; it infects locally, and gives rise at a comparatively early stage to secondary growths in the lymphatic glands, followed rapidly by growths in other glands, and in the lungs, liver, intestine, brain, pleura and pericardium.

Naked eye appearances.—The tumour is softer, pinker, and more vascular than even the small spindle-celled form, and hæmorrhagic patches and soft gelatinous cysts similar to those found in the myeloid sarcoma are of frequent occurrence.

Harden (§ 59), and stain (§ 98 or 103 *d*).

(× 50) and (× 300).—The cells are three or four times as large as those of the small spindle-celled sarcoma. They are more like the ordinary fibro-plastic cells (the organising cells in a healing wound), but have between them little or no intercellular substance or formed material. They are very irregular in shape, are frequently bifurcated, and are arranged in bundles, the cells interlocking by their bifurcated ends. The blood channels between these cells are very numerous and of embryonic structure, and green masses of extravasated blood are frequently seen. As some of the bundles are cut transversely, rounded sections, some nucleated, others without nuclei, are scattered over the field.

Melanotic Sarcoma.

387. The most important of the large spindle-celled sarcomas is the melanotic or pigmented sarcoma, which grows especially from the choroid coat of the eye, the skin, and the pia mater.

It is extremely malignant, secondary growths usually making their appearance whenever the primary growth has reached the size of a walnut. These secondary tumours may grow in any of the positions usually affected by sarcomas, especially by the large spindle-celled and mixed forms, and they are frequently deeply pigmented, though in some cases they are entirely devoid of colouring matter.

The special malignancy of this tumour is due to the fact that it extends not only locally and by the blood-vessels, but also by the lymphatics. It appears to be most malignant when growing from the true skin, in which case secondary growths may be looked for in all the positions above mentioned, in the liver, and in the sub-mucous tissue of the intestine, when the primary growth has reached the size of a marble.

Naked eye appearances.—The specimen of which a description is

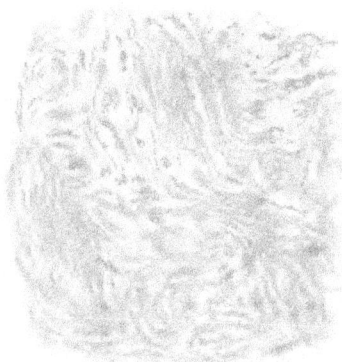

Fig. 168.—Drawing of melanotic sarcoma. Stained with logwood, and mounted in Canada balsam. (× 60.)

a. Small deeply-stained cells.
b. Spindle cells, with protoplasm around the nucleus deeply pig-mented.
c. Large spindle cells, arranged concentrically.
d. Large non-pigmented spindle-shaped or irregular cells.
  Notice the peculiar concentric and reticular arrangement of these cells.

here given was a large fungating blue-black mass, measuring about two-and-a-half inches in diameter, projecting from the orbit, and growing from the choroid coat through the eye-ball at the upper margin of the cornea. It bled on the slightest touch. On section, the mass was deep brownish or blue-black at certain parts; at others it was slaty grey, whilst at others again it was white or pale pink. It was comparatively soft, and extremely vascular.

Harden (§ 59), and stain (§ 98 or 103 *d*).

(× 50).—Note the arrangement of the large spindle cells into an open concentric network, with, in some cases, numerous small round cells lying in the meshes. Remember also that some of the large cells are cut transversely, and that they are frequently arranged in bundles. At certain points pigment may be seen, collected chiefly around the nuclei of the large spindle cells.

(× 300).—Examine the large spindle-shaped or branching cells of which the open network is composed; these may be seen in both

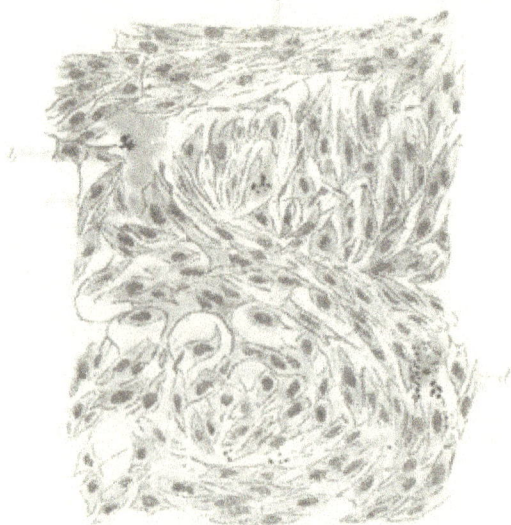

FIG. 169.—Melanotic sarcoma. Stained with logwood. (× 450.)
  a. Large spindle-shaped cell.
  b. Branching cell.
  c. Pigment around nucleus.
  d. Pigment between cells.
    Note the concentric arrangement of the cells which at certain points form a kind of network.

longitudinal and rounded transverse section; note also the great number of small round cells with which, in some cases, the meshes are crammed. The embryonic blood-vessels are surrounded by tissue which presents all the characters of lymphatic tissue. Around some of these vessels are small hæmorrhages, in which there may be altered blood pigment. This altered blood pigment must be carefully distinguished from the melanin proper, which is found as

golden yellow or black granules, situated around the nuclei of the
large spindle cells, more rarely in their protoplasm, and more
rarely still in the spaces between the cells of the tumour. It is
not derived directly from the blood pigment, but appears to be
elaborated by the large cells of which the tumour is composed.
When treated with dilute hydrochloric acid, and then soaked in a
solution of potassium ferrocyanide, this pigment gives no blue reaction ; but if a section be boiled in a solution of caustic potash, the

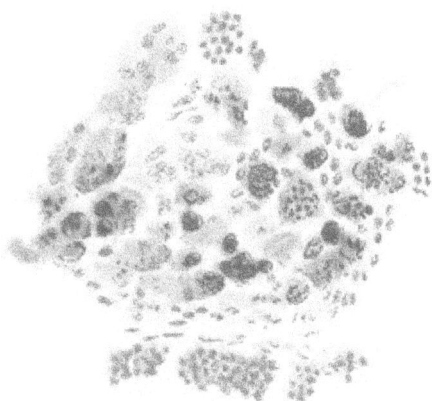

FIG. 170.—Melanotic Sarcoma. Stained with logwood, and
mounted in Canada balsam. (× 300.)

a. Round cell distended with golden brown pigment.
b. Small round cells unpigmented. Some of these may be spindle
cells seen in transverse section.
c. Small spindle cells forming walls of embryonic blood-vessels.
d. Multinucleated giant cells or plasmodia, one containing pigment
the other without.
e. Spindle cell in which the pigment is collected around the nucleus.
f. Similar cell in which the whole protoplasm is crowded with
pigment.

pigment is dissolved, and a brown tinge is given to the solution,
which immediately disappears on the addition of chlorine water.
The pigment seen in old hæmorrhages, in brown induration of the
lung and similar conditions, gives a blue reaction with hydrochloric
acid and potassium ferrocyanide, whilst the coal pigment found in
the lung gives no blue reaction, and is perfectly insoluble in boiling
caustic potash.

In all sarcomas there may be various modifications of structure, and all varieties of combinations of the cells, in form, number, and arrangement, may be met with, and therefore all sarcomas will not present the regular or typical appearances above represented. Where the mixed sarcomas occur, they are both locally and generally malignant, and frequently have a tendency to attempt the formation of some more highly developed tissue.

Alveolar Sarcoma.

388. The alveolar sarcoma, first described by Billroth, is a form of tumour in which groups of sarcoma cells are arranged in alveoli formed by connective tissue, something like the alveoli in carcinoma, the only difference being that in this case we have cells of the connective tissue type instead of epithelial cells. It grows most frequently as a small tumour, which has most of the characteristics of the ordinary sarcoma, in the true skin, and in the pia mater, muscle, and bone.

Harden (§ 59), and stain (§ 98 or 103 d).

(× 50) and (× 300).—This sarcoma at first sight resembles a carcinoma very closely. The cells are of considerable size, and are almost epithelial in character. They are large and rounded, may have a couple of nuclei, each of which has several deeply stained nucleoli. In consequence of the arrangement of pre-existing and newly formed vessels, these cells are divided into groups. Along with the blood-vessels is a quantity of fibrillar tissue, which extends in some cases in delicate strands between individual cells, "but no vessels enter the cell groups."—(Ziegler.) The tumour is formed from lymphomatous tissue, in which the proliferation of the endo-thelial cells takes place rapidly without a corresponding increase in the stroma, the vessels and reticulum forming the thicker bands and more delicate stroma between the groups of cells. The vessels are increased in number as the endothelial cells proliferate. Ziegler describes a similar process in the tissues of the sub-arachnoid space and pia mater, where, he says, the masses of cells are formed from the endothelial covering of the trabeculæ, the cells proliferating and forming thicker and thicker investing layers until the spaces are completely filled. This growth might be described as a lymphadenoma, with but a small formation of fibrillar tissue, in which sense it is an endothelioma (as distinguished from an epithelioma) and a true sarcoma.

389. An *Angio-sarcoma* is a pulsatile tumour, in which the whole mass appears to be converted into embryonic blood-vessels. The process of development of blood-vessels is exactly similar to that already described in other sarcomas, but is carried a step further.

PSAMMOMA OR ANGIOLITHIC SARCOMA.

390. This tumour grows in the fringes of the choroid plexus or in the pineal gland. It consists of a branching mass of spindle cells in which are numerous blood-vessels, at the sides of which are a number of bud-like or club-shaped processes. The vessels themselves, seen in section, are surrounded by layers of spindle cells, or flattened cells, which are prolonged on to the outer surface of the bud. The centre of the bud is occupied by a hard, often cretaceous or colloid mass, either single or composed of several pieces, very like ordinary brain sand. Local infiltration of the surrounding tissues has been described. In some cases similar growths are covered by more fully formed connective tissue; in which case they are undoubtedly non-malignant.

OSTEO-SARCOMA.

391. In the osteo-sarcoma, properly so called, there is an actual formation of true bony spicules, not only in the primary but also in the secondary growths. These tumours vary very much as regards the size and shape of the cells of which they are built up, but in all cases they grow in connection with bone, first as ordinary malignant sarcomas. They spread by the blood-vessels and secondary growths soon make their appearance in other bones, the characters of the primary ones being reproduced.

On section, small hard but delicate spicules, which may be cut through with a knife, are found.

Harden (§ **59**), and stain (§ **98** or **103** *d*).

(× 50).—The softer parts are composed entirely of cells, round or
spindle-shaped, as the case may be. At certain points bands of pink
fibrous-looking tissue may be seen pushing their way between the
masses of cells, showing that the matrix is becoming fibrous. Small
green patches are also seen, in which there is regular bone structure.

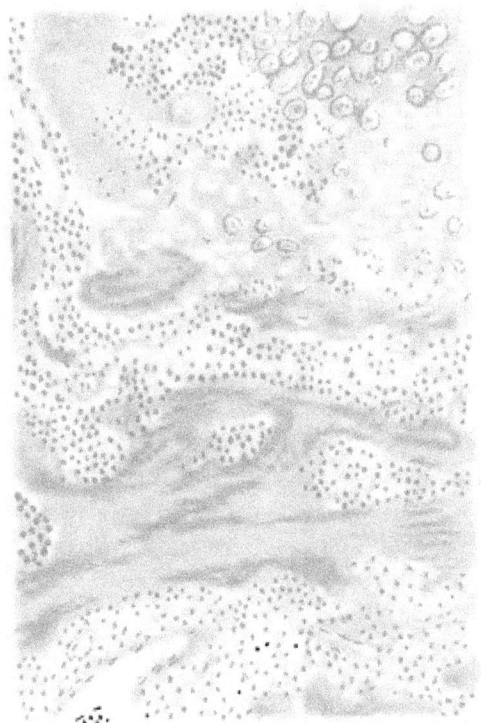

FIG. 171.—Osteo-sarcoma stained with picro-carmine.   (× 80.)
    a. Embryonic blood-vessels.
    b. Sarcoma cells.
    c. Pink bony matrix as yet apparently fibrous.
    d. Cells lying in the fibrous matrix.
    e. Cartilage cells with surrounding matrix. Transformation stages
        very well seen.

In these patches or spicules we have regular lamination, Haversian
canals, and all the essential features of true ossification (§ 312).

(× 300).—The tumour cells take the place of the osteoblasts in
this bone, otherwise the spicules are in all respects like those in true

cancellous bone. In the neighbourhood of these growing centres of ossification the cells are modified, and many have assumed the characters of cartilage cells embedded in spaces bounded by capsules, and surrounded by the pink matrix. Later these tissues seem to become impregnated with lime salts, just as in the growth and development of normal bone.

OSTEOID SARCOMA.

392. This is a very malignant form of sarcoma, in which there is calcification but no true ossification. It grows primarily from the periosteum, and gives rise to secondary growths in serous membranes, the lungs, and other organs.

Harden (§ 59), and stain (§ 98 or 103 *d*).

(× 50).—Note that there is an increase of the intercellular substance, and that the cells are considerably larger than those of a small round-celled sarcoma, and are often multinucleated.

(× 300).—Between the large rounded multinucleated cells is a translucent intercellular substance, delicately stained with the carmine of the picro-carmine; at certain points, especially near the newly-formed blood-vessels, this material is infiltrated with dark or highly refractile calcareous particles. Where the calcification is very marked, the section gives a green reaction with the picric acid. True bone structure is entirely wanting, and the hardness from which the tumour derives its name is due to the calcification of the cartilaginoid matrix.

DEGENERATIONS AND MODIFICATIONS OF STRUCTURE OF SARCOMAS.

393. (1) Fatty degeneration of the cells is due to imperfect nutrition; the cells first become granular, and then may break up altogether. This is readily recognised, even with the naked eye, as the degenerating patches of the tissue become cream coloured or yellow.

(2) Hæmorrhagic degeneration from rupture of the embryonic blood-vessels, often accompanied by the so-called cystic degeneration due to softening and then absorption of the softened and infiltrated tissues described in myeloid sarcoma (§ 385).

(3) Hyaline degeneration, especially of the cells in the immediate neighbourhood of the blood-vessels, gives rise to the formation of a kind of hyaline covering for the vessel.

(4) Myxomatous degeneration of the cells. The tumour becomes mucoid, and, on microscopic examination, clear mucoid globules are seen in the swollen cells. This must be carefully distinguished from mucoid softening of the intercellular substance.

The following are modifications of structure rather than true degenerations :—Fatty infiltration of the cells (lipomatous sarcoma); pigmentation of the cells, as in melanotic sarcoma.

Myxomatous softening, calcification or chondrification of the intercellular substance.

PSOROZOA IN CANCERS.

394. During the last few years many observations have been made on the invasion of epithelial cells by certain forms of parasites. In some of the lower animal forms, viz., certain fish, the snail, the rabbit, etc., zoologists have demonstrated the presence of psorozoa, psorospermæ or coccidia ; and from the nature of the changes set up in these cases, pathologists have been led to examine cancerous tumours for similar organisms.

That such organisms do exist in Paget's disease (demonstrated by Wickham), and even in epithelial tumours of various kinds, is now an undoubted fact ; and in order that those who are engaged in the study of cancer may prepare material in which they can see such parasitic bodies as have been described, it may be well to give a short account of the methods employed by Russell and Soudakewitch in their several researches.

Russell hardens in the ordinary fashion (§§ **57-59**), and gives directions for staining as follows :—Place the section in water, and then stain in a saturated solution, made by dissolving fuchsin in 2 per cent. carbolic acid water, for ten minutes or longer ; wash for a few minutes in water, then for half a minute in absolute alcohol ; from this put the section into a 1 per cent. solution of iodine green (Grüblers) dissolved in 2 per cent. carbolic acid water, and allow it to remain in this, well spread out, for five minutes ;

rapidly dehydrate in absolute alcohol, pass through oil of cloves, and mount in Canada balsam.

(× 50).—In a section stained by this method there may be seen in the epithelial cells, lying in the alveoli, single purple or fuchsin stained bodies, usually rounded and deeply stained, or groups

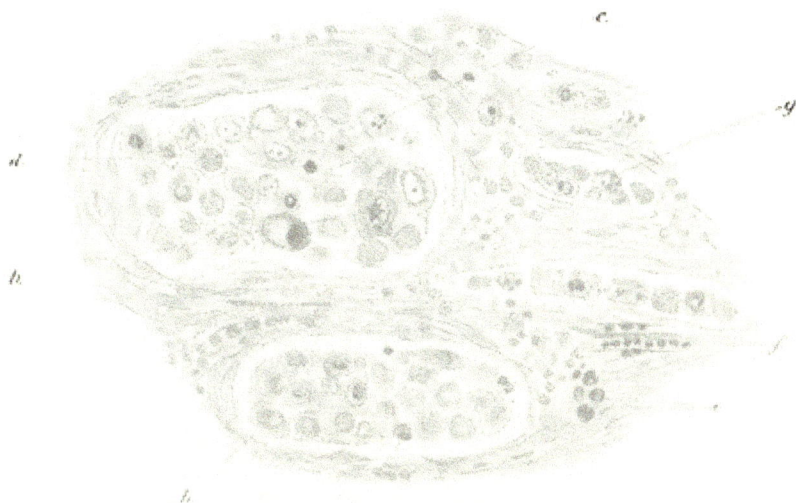

FIG. 172.—Section of cancer of the breast "fixed" with bichloride of mercury, hardened in alcohol, and stained by Russell's method. (× 450.)

a.   Fuchsin stained body pushing nucleus to one side of the cell. It is contained within a capsule.
b.   A somewhat star-shaped organism within a capsule in a large epithelial cell.
c.   Small deeply stained bodies in a homogeneous matrix within a capsule.
d.h.g. Other forms of this organism, probably psorospermæ or coccidia.
e.   "Fuchsin bodies" not contained within epithelial cells. Nature doubtful.
f.   Fuchsin stained red blood corpuscles.

or clusters of similar bodies which stand out very prominently from the greenish-blue epithelial tissue.

(× 300).—These bodies are in the protoplasm of the epithelial cell near the nucleus, and pushing it to one side, or in some cases actually within the nucleus itself. Seen under a very high power they appear to have a somewhat radiate structure, especially at the margin but most of them, where the tissues have been hardened by any of the ordinary methods, are quite homogeneous. The drawback of preparing sections in this manner is that other bodies which take on a similar staining may be observed; these may be merely colloid masses in or near the epithelial cells, though, on the other hand, they may be similar organisms that have undergone change owing to the slowness of the fixing process. A certain number of red blood corpuscles also take on this stain, unless the decolourising method is carefully carried out, so that the organisms described by Russell have often been said to exist in the imagination of the observer only; there can be no doubt, however, that the organisms to which he draws special attention are similar to those described by other observers as psorosperms.

Soudakewitch, working at this subject, has obtained specially good results, and has been able to demonstrate most accurately structures which Metchnikoff declares can be nothing other than psorosperms or coccidia. Taking pieces from rapidly growing cancers in glandular structures Soudakewitch hardens for one or two days in 1 per cent. osmic acid (§ 70), or in Fleming's solution (§ 66), the tissue is then transferred to Muller's fluid, where it is left for five days, after which it is well washed in water for twelve or twenty-four hours, and then passed through spirit of various strengths (§ 58). The sections are stained with hæmatoxylin (§ 103 *d.*).

(× 50).—The organisms may be seen in much the same positions as described by Russell, as small homogeneous or granular stained bodies embedded in the epithelial cells in the alveoli.

(× 450).—It is difficult to distinguish the numerous forms described by Soudakewitch, especially in slowly-growing cancers. At first sight they appear as rounded nuclei, some of them granular, others with a delicate network running through their substance, others again are like nuclei, with well marked nucleoli, which in some cases are stained, in others unstained; but it will be observed that, just as in the fuchsin bodies, these rounded psorosperms are actually within the nucleus of the cell, or have pushed it to one side. Whether these parasites are the causal agents in cancerous infection, or whether they are simply an after effect is difficult to say, but from their invariable occurrence in these epithelial cells, and from the fact that such organisms undoubtedly give rise to proliferative changes in the lower animals above mentioned, we must accept the evidence as, at any rate, indicating the possibility that they may play the *rôle* of one of the causal agents in the production of cancer.

EPITHELIAL TUMOURS.

395. For convenience of description, the epithelial tumours may be grouped together as belonging to a class in which there is " growth

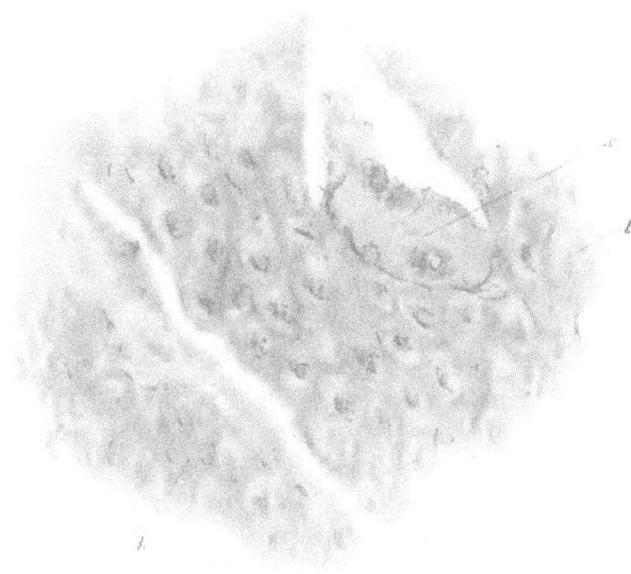

FIG. 173.—Section from near the surface of a papilloma stained with picro-carmine. (× 450.)
a. Delicate connective tissue papilla.
b. Well developed epidermal cells.
c. Mass of colloid substance, derived from degenerated epidermal cells, the remains of which are distinctly seen.

of some or all tissue elements in excessive degree and erratic form, in which there is great vegetative power" (or power of growth as distinguished from functional activity), " the members of which are highly parasitic and malignant, infecting locally by direct transport, and through lymphatics and blood-vessels. Secondary growths may affect any tissue."—(Greenfield).

These tumours grow from the mesoblast, but, unlike the sarcomas, involve at the same time epi- or hypo-blast tissues. The above definition will, to a certain extent, cover the whole group; but there are slight modifications of structures in different species.

EPITHELIOMA.

396. The first of the epithelial tumours to be considered is the epithelioma proper, in which the principal factor is an excessive and irregular growth of epithelium. The epithelial masses invade the subjacent tissues by the lymphatic system, and secondary growths result in the lymphatic glands and other parts.

There are two forms :—(1) Squamous epithelioma ; (2) columnar epithelioma, according as they originate on a surface covered with squamous or with columnar epithelium.

(1.) SQUAMOUS EPITHELIOMA. .

397. This occurs usually at the points of junction of the skin and mucous membrane, or at those parts which, from their movement and position, are exposed to considerable irritation, and where the epithelium is in a state of great proliferative activity—the lips, tongue, mouth, orifice of vagina, rectum, and penis.

Naked eye appearances.—When fully developed an epithelioma is an irregular warty-looking mass, the surface of which is ulcerated, and has an extremely characteristic appearance, generally compared to that of a cauliflower, from the prominence of certain small white points and ridges. From this surface an irritant watery or ichorous fluid exudes. The ulceration takes place only on the more or less rounded main mass of the tumour. At the margin of the central mass there is great induration, whilst surrounding it, but at some little distance, are numerous small firm nodules, each of which is distinctly marked off from the surrounding tissues. On scraping the ulcerated surface with a knife, small white points come away as rounded pellets, leaving behind them distinct pits or depressions. Press one of these pellets between two glass slips, and then examine in neutral solution (§ **34,** 5); it is found to consist principally of large flattened epidermic scales, which stain yellow with picro-carmine.

On section the tumour tissue is firm, and running through the mass, bounding the white or yellowish masses of epithelium, are white glistening fibrous bands ; but, as one would expect from the fact that hæmorrhages are extremely rare, there are very few blood-vessels near the surface.

Harden (§§ 57, 59, or 72), and stain (§§ 98 or 103 *d*).

(× 50).—Examine first the ulcerating surface of the tumour, especially near the margin, where there will be noticed an extra-

FIG. 174.—Epithelioma of the tongue. Stained with logwood.
(× 300.)
    a.   Colloid centre of epithelial globule or " cell nest."
    b.   Larger colloid mass.
    c,c. Flattened layers of cells around these colloid centres, which
          are composed partly of horny squames, such as are met
          with in the stratum corneum of the normal skin.

ordinary development of squamous epithelium, which, instead of merely clothing the papillæ, grows downwards for some distance into the subjacent tissues in finger-like processes, which send out secondary processes in all directions. Around these hypertrophied masses of epithelium there appears to be a considerable increase in the number of small round cells in the connective tissue, and although the vessels do not come near the surface, because of the thick layer of epithelium, in this subjacent tissue they are often of considerable size. In the still deeper tissues the masses of epithelium (stained

2 o

brown) are seen running in all directions, each mass being surrounded by the cellular connective tissue (stained pink). At certain
points in these brown masses of epithelium are yellow areas, evidently
composed of strata or layers of flattened cells, the centre of each mass
being almost homogeneous. These yellow areas are the cell nests
so characteristic of this form of epithelioma.

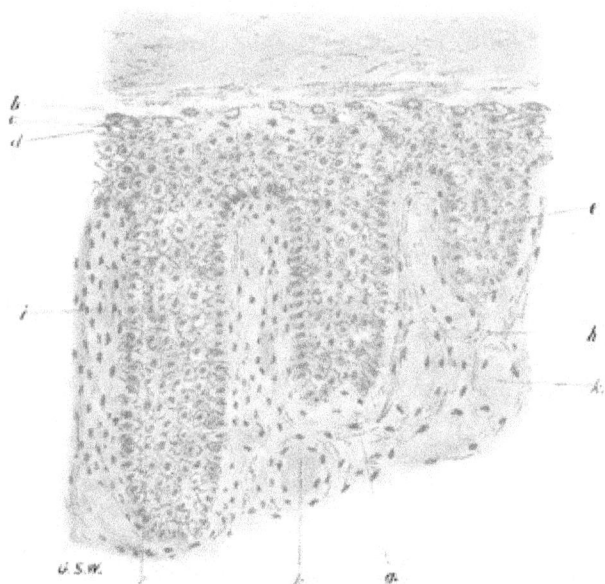

FIG. 175.—Diagrammatic sketch to represent the changes which take
place during the invasion of connective tissue by epithelial columns.

a.	Stratum corneum or horny layer of the cuticle.
b.	Stratum lucidum.
c.	Stratum granulosum.
d.	Rete Malpighii. Superficial, more flattened cells, beneath which are the well-formed prickle cells. Layer of columnar or germinal cells.
e.	Epithelium at normal level.
f. and g.	Epithelial bands passing downwards between the papillæ.
h.	Normal connective tissue papilla.
i.	More cellular and vascular connective tissue.
k.	Blood-vessels.

(× 300).—The epithelial cells of which the penetrating columns
are composed are in all respects like those found on a cutaneous
surface. The rete Malpighii and stratum corneum can be readily
distinguished, and it is to this fact that the tumour owes its charac-

teristic appearance, especially near the surface. The germinal layer and the prickle cells are also easily distinguished, the stratum granulosum and stratum lucidum not so readily. The horny layer is frequently very well developed, especially in the cell nests, which

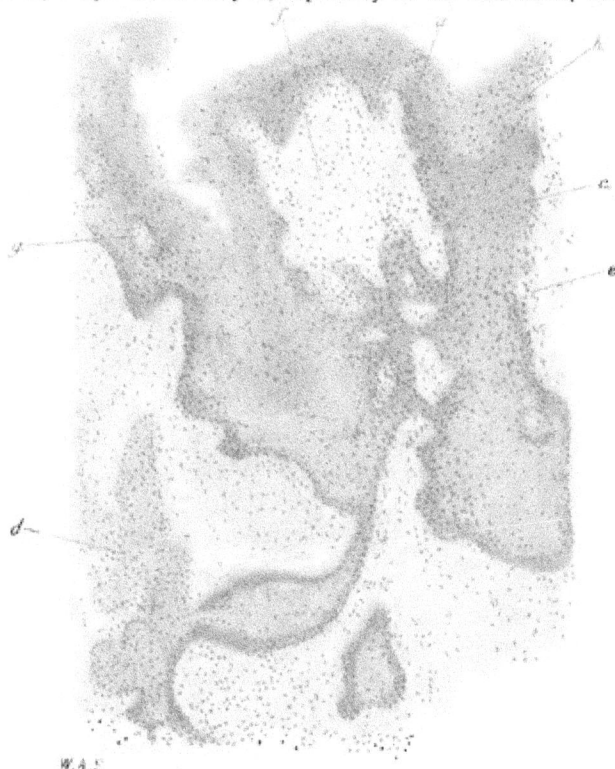

FIG. 176.—Section of the tongue of an old man, in which epithelium is growing down into the deeper tissues as in epithelioma. Stained with picro-carmine. (× 100.)

a. Horny layer of the cuticle.
b. Clear and granular layers of epithelium.
c. Layer of columnar or germinal cells.
d. Mass of epithelium invading the lymph spaces of the deeper connective tissue.
e. Connective tissue basis of true skin ; at *f.* somewhat more cellular.
g. Small vessel in the centre of a papilla of corium.

are seen to be composed of concentric layers of flattened cells arranged around a central colloid mass. In order to understand the method of formation of these cells nests, it must be remembered that, as in the normal skin, the epithelial cells are removed from the germinal layer; they gradually become dry and flattened, and lose their nuclei; these form the horny layer, and are then shed. In the epithelioma, as the cells grow in the pits they are removed from the germinal layer on the walls and are carried to the centre of the "shaft," where, as they cannot be removed as on a free surface, they undergo colloid changes, form a hard centre or core against which succeeding layers of cells are projected and flattened, and the peculiar laminated cell nests are the result.

Notice that near the surface, or where the epithelial projections have not passed for any great distance into the lymphatics of the corium, there are few round cells in the connective tissue, but that where the prolongations have passed further, the round cells become more numerous, the vascularity of the tissue in such cases becoming greatly increased. In the secondary growths the epithelial masses are usually growing more rapidly, have prickle cells well developed, but no horny layer, and are surrounded by more of the new round-celled tissue, though in certain cases there appears to be an entire absence of such tissue.

Squamous epithelioma grows slowly, and, like all cancerous tumours, spreads by the lymphatics, though it is not very malignant. When secondary growths occur, they are found first in the lymphatic glands, where they frequently cause superficial ulceration; after this they may be found in almost any position.

Epithelioma is distinguished from papilloma by the fact that the epithelium, in place of remaining in its normal relation to the subjacent corium and connective tissue, invades these structures by the lymphatic spaces; when this occurs the growth becomes malignant, the vegetative power of the epithelial growth rapidly increasing.

The varieties of epithelioma are due almost entirely to the rate or growth and position of the tumour; it is therefore unnecessary to enter into any detailed account of them, but it must be remembered that where the tumours are of slowest growth, the cell nests are most perfectly formed, and that where the growth of the epithelial columns is very rapid, the cell nests may be absent, especially in the case of secondary growths.

(2.) COLUMNAR-CELLED EPITHELIOMA.

398. The columnar-celled epithelioma, also termed, with almost equal accuracy, malignant adenoma and adenoid cancer, is found, in structure, to occupy an intermediate position between the simple

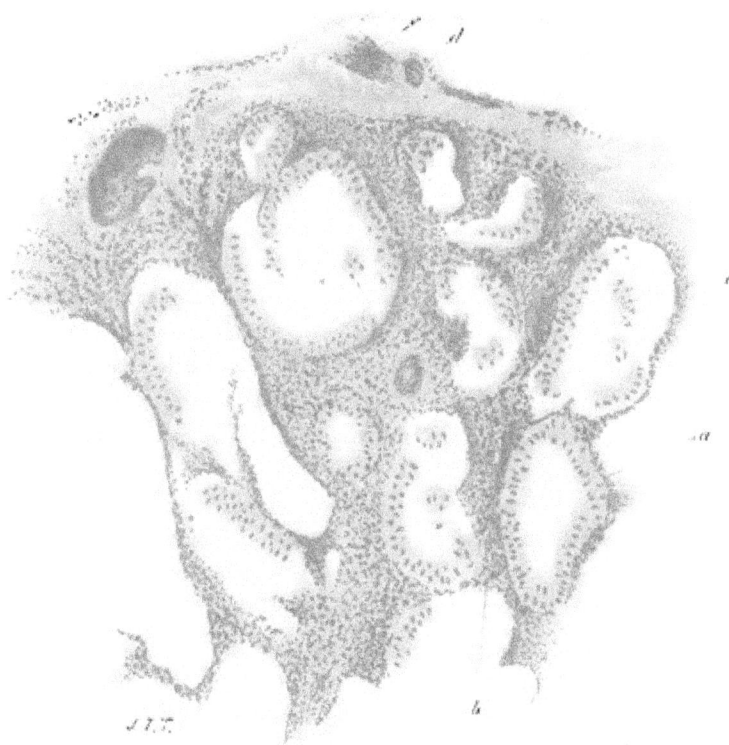

FIG. 177.—Columnar-celled epithelioma (adenoid cancer of the stomach). Stained with picro-carmine. (× 100.)

a. Columnar epithelial cells.
b. Stroma, in which are numerous young connective tissue cells.
c. Alveolus.
d. Blood-vessel in wall of stomach.
e. Muscular fibres from wall of stomach.

adenoma and the true cancer, and also to bear the same relation to a papilloma of the intestine, say, that a squamous epithelioma bears to a cutaneous papilloma.

It may be considered that the invading epithelium, in place of being squamous, is columnar or cubical, that hollow, finger-like processes of epithelium branch or bud, and project into the subjacent tissue, where they are seen lining spaces with a distinct layer of columnar epithelium, which in some cases proliferates, and becomes more or less irregular. Sections of such a tumour have much the appearance of a true cancer of the encephaloid type (§ **401**). Between the hollow epithelial prolongations a variable amount of fibro-cellular connective tissue is formed; this appears to be the result of an irritative overgrowth of the pre-existing connective tissue.

A similar structure is met with as a primary growth in the large intestine—especially at the flexures and in the rectum—as a soft, pale, succulent mass, the surface of which frequently ulcerates, projecting into the intestinal tube. It is so frequently situated at the lower part of the bowel that it is spoken of as the malignant polypus of the rectum. It is also found in the stomach in a more diffuse form, where it is liable to undergo a peculiar softening, almost like that of colloid cancer, for which it may be easily mistaken; in the liver, beginning in the epithelium of the bile ducts; and in the lungs, being there developed, apparently, from the epithelium of the bronchial glands.

In the liver, columnar-celled epithelioma presents to the naked eye very much the appearances of true cancer. Scattered throughout the organ are a number of rounded or irregular masses, each of which has a characteristic appearance, the growing or peripheral part being much more vascular, softer, and more pink than the centre, where the tissue is yellower, and in some cases very fibrous. These masses, therefore, very closely resemble scirrhous cancer in an early stage of development.

Harden (§ **60**) and stain (§ **103** *d* or **98**).

(× 50).—In the purest form, as seen in the rectum, there appears to be first an enormous increase in the size of the gland tubes in the true mucous membrane. From this point there is a gradual invasion of the deeper structures until the whole thickness of the intestinal wall is involved. Between the large gland-like tubes small-celled infiltration may be seen, at certain points only, as in the squamous epithelioma, especially in the deeper parts of the growth. Small outlying nodules of the glandular-looking tissue may also be observed.

(× 300).—Examine the tissue more fully. Each tube is lined by a layer of regular columnar epithelium, the nucleus being usually placed in the lower third of each cell. Beneath the well-formed epithelial cells flattened cells may, in very good preparations, be recognised, but they appear to be very inconstant, even in number. Around some of the tubes, especially those near the surface, the stroma is like normal connective tissue, but in the deeper parts of the tumour, just as in the squamous-celled epithelioma, there is great increase in the number of small round cells.

In the lung the same features may be easily recognised, the tubules invading the lung substance in all directions.

In the liver, in the pink peripheral part of the tumour, the appearances are also very similar to those above described ; but in the

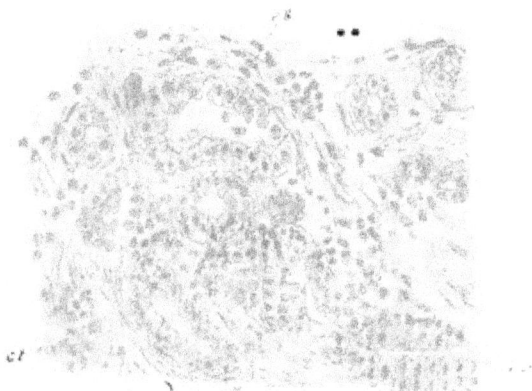

FIG. 178.—Columnar epithelioma. Secondary growth in the mediastinal gland. Stained with logwood. (× 300, after Greenfield.)
e.s. Single layer of epithelium in irregularly shaped space.
e.d. Double row of epithelial cells.
c.t. Young growing connective tissue cells (indifferent tissue).

central harder part there is an enormous increase of the stroma, which is more fibrous and contains comparatively few round cells. In consequence of this increase in the stroma, the gland follicles or tubes are more widely separated, and are much more irregular both in size and shape ; in the tissue in the centre which is still older, the epithelium fills the spaces irregularly, and the lumen of the tubule is entirely obliterated. These points must be carefully kept in view when the growth and development of malignant adenoma and its relation to true carcinoma are under consideration.

CARCINOMA OR CANCER.

399. The true carcinoma consists of a system of connected alveoli or spaces, bounded by fibrous tissue—the stroma—and containing cells of an epithelial type. Imbedded in the fibrous stroma, and quite separated from the epithelial elements, run *well developed* blood-vessels. The alveoli are in direct communication with the lymphatics at the margin of the tumour. Any classification given must depend upon (1) the amount, nature, and arrangement of the stroma, and (2) the number and character of the cellular elements within the alveoli.

SCIRRHOUS CANCER.

400. In the scirrhous or hard cancer the typical carcinomatous structure is well developed. The stroma, with well-formed blood-vessels, is derived from the mesoblast; the epithelial cells are derived most probably either from the epi- or hypo-blast. The alveolar structure is exceedingly well marked; this is due, apparently, to the fact that the growth is slow, and that the fibrous stroma is well developed.

Naked eye appearances.—Scirrhous cancer occurs as a hard, firm tumour, varying somewhat in appearance, according to the position in which it grows—breast, pylorus, œsophagus, rectum, testes, ovary, kidney. In the breast it forms a hard, rounded mass, which is firmly attached to the subcutaneous tissue, very frequently causing retraction of the nipple. The section has a greyish white, glistening, or silvery appearance, with, here and there, yellow patches. This appearance is due to the presence of hard fibrous bands, which run across and between small yellow masses of fatty tissue. In the centre of the section, the retracting fibrous bands cause a depression, whilst the fatty masses project slightly above them. Near this centre are small patches of creamy or doughy tissue, the result of fatty degeneration of the older portions of the tumour. Towards the periphery the tissue is much more vascular, and assumes a pinker

tinge and a softer consistence. Take a scraping from the margin of
the tumour. It consists of a milky fluid, which mixed with water
becomes slightly turbid.

(× 300).—A number of cells, irregular in shape when isolated,
and usually smaller than ordinary epithelial cells, are seen. Each is
surrounded by a cell wall, and has a distinct nucleus in which
nucleoli are easily distinguished. A scraping taken from the fatty
centre is creamy and more opaque, and is found to contain small
shrivelled angular cells filled with small oil globules and granules;

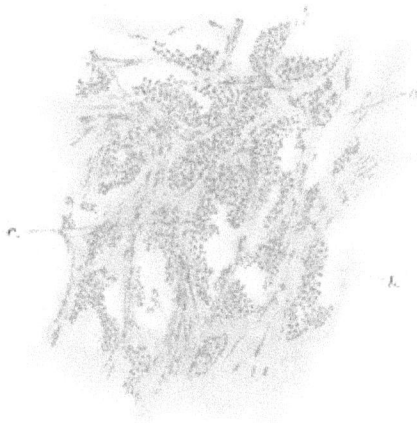

FIG. 179.—Scirrhous cancer of the breast. Stained with picro-
carmine. (× 50.)
  a. Fibrous stroma, in which run well-formed vessels.
  b. Alveolus.
  c. Epithelioid cells.

these cells are epithelial in type, and are undergoing marked fatty
degeneration.

Harden pieces of both the peripheral and central parts of the
tumour (§§ 57 and 59 or 71), and stain (§ 98).

(× 50).—In the section taken from near the periphery, the tissue
is composed of two sets of structures — first, connective tissue,
stained pink or crimson; and second, epithelial elements, which are
stained brown or yellow (the nuclei pink). The connective tissue
is so arranged that it bounds a series of rounded or irregular spaces
or alveoli, in which the epithelial cells are collected. In this section

the stroma is partially fibrous and pink, but at certain points there are great accumulations of deeply stained cells. These occur most frequently near the margin of the tumour, and form the cellular tissue into which the epithelial masses project; wherever the stroma is young and growing, these small cells are present in considerable numbers. They are young connective tissue cells, and of them the outer margin of the tumour is almost entirely composed. In these bands of stroma the well developed blood-vessels, quite separated from the epithelial

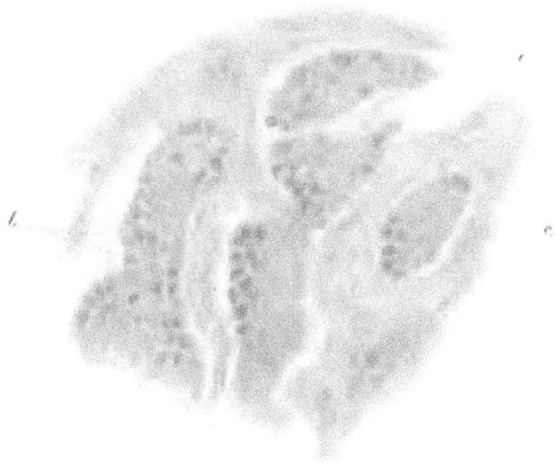

FIG. 180.—Scirrhous cancer of the breast. Stained with picro-carmine. (× 300.)
　　a. Fibrous stroma bounding
　　b. Alveoli.
　　c. Epithelioid cells, some with several nuclei. Note the irregular shape and epithelial character.

masses, are readily distinguished. Although the bands of fibrous stroma are well marked, they are not nearly so thick and dense as are those near the centre of the tumour. The alveolar spaces are filled with angular cells, tolerably regular in shape, and closely packed together.

(× 300).—Note the pink fibrous and crimson cellular elements of the stroma; the position of the blood-vessels, embedded in the fibrous bands; the cellular tissue, in which are no alveoli and no epithelial cells, at the margin of the tumour; and lastly, the angular cells which lie crowded together in the alveoli. The protoplasm is stained brownish yellow, but the nucleus is deep crimson; in this nucleus (or there may be more than one) nucleoli and vacuoles may be seen as deep crimson points and small clear spaces. There is no intercellular substance, or, at most, only a small quantity of fluid material.

To further examine the alveoli, and to determine their communication with the surrounding lymphatics, a thin section of the tumour taken from near the growing margin should be treated at once with nitrate of silver (§ 118), and then mounted in glycerine (§ 151).

In the section from the central part of the tumour (× 50) and (× 300) it may be observed that the fibrous stroma has become exceedingly dense, and in some parts constitutes almost the entire mass of the tumour growth. The alveoli are much smaller than those already examined, and contain only a few shrivelled atrophied and angular cells. These epithelial cells have undergone fatty degeneration, and the greater part of them have evidently been absorbed, as the stroma has become more dense, but less vascular. As the stroma comes to predominate more and more, it becomes more fibrous and cicatricial, and, like all cicatricial tissue, tends to contract. The contracting fibrous tissue drawing upon the nipple, or upon the tissues around the centre of the tumour, gives rise to that retraction of the nipple—umbilication—which is such a characteristic feature of all scirrhous cancers.

ENCEPHALOID CANCER.

401. Under this heading come all those soft, rapidly growing, brain-like or medullary cancers, in which the stroma is very scanty the alveoli large, and the cells numerous.

Naked eye appearances.—The primary encephaloid cancer grows especially from the mucous membranes, testes, and breast; but as a secondary growth, following primary scirrhous cancer, it frequently grows in the more vascular organs. It occurs as soft, pale pink nodules, of various size and shape, which, when scraped, yield a considerable quantity of opaque "cancer juice." Hæmorrhages are frequently met with.

Harden (§ 60) and stain (§ 98).

(× 50).—The pink stroma is exceedingly scanty, and in consequence the vessels, which are relatively numerous, are badly supported though structurally they are usually well developed. The alveoli are very numerous, but vary greatly in size, and with their contained epithelial cells, constitute the greater part of the growth.

(× 300).—The stroma is very delicate, and in many cases exces-

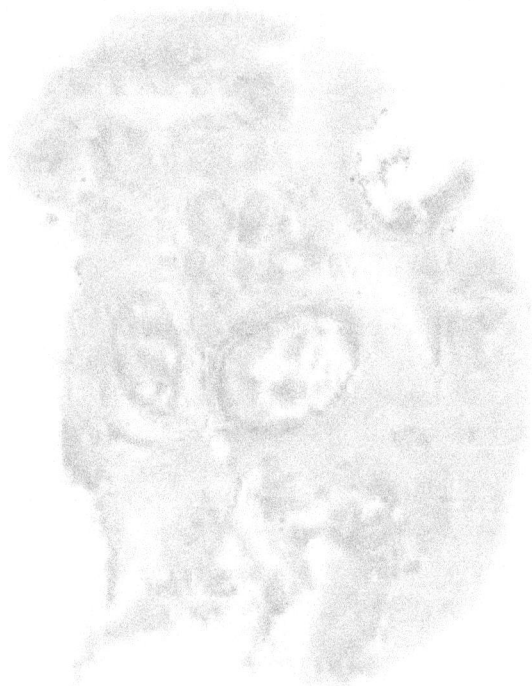

FIG. 181.—Section of encephaloid cancer of the breast.   Stained with picro-carmine. (× 40).
 a. Cellular connective tissue near advancing epithelium.
 b. Well marked alveolus filled with epithelial cells.
 c. Colloid mass derived from cells which usually form milk.
 d. Fatty tissue of breast.
 e. Older fibrinous band of stroma.

sively cellular, so that the blood-vessels are very indifferently supported. At some points there may be extravasations of blood from ruptured vessels, in which case the blood corpuscles find their way into the alveoli.

In the alveoli the cells, stained brown, present great differences both as to size and arrangement, according to the origin of the tumour. In some cases, where the cancer has its origin in a gland duct, the cells are large, almost columnar, arranged regularly near the wall of the alveolus, but grouped indiscriminately near the centre, the arrangement, in this instance, resembling that of the malignant adenoma. In other cases, when the breast is the point of origin, the cells may be large and rounded, having three or four nuclei and nucleoli, or they may be polygonal or irregular in shape, like those found in the developing breast acini.

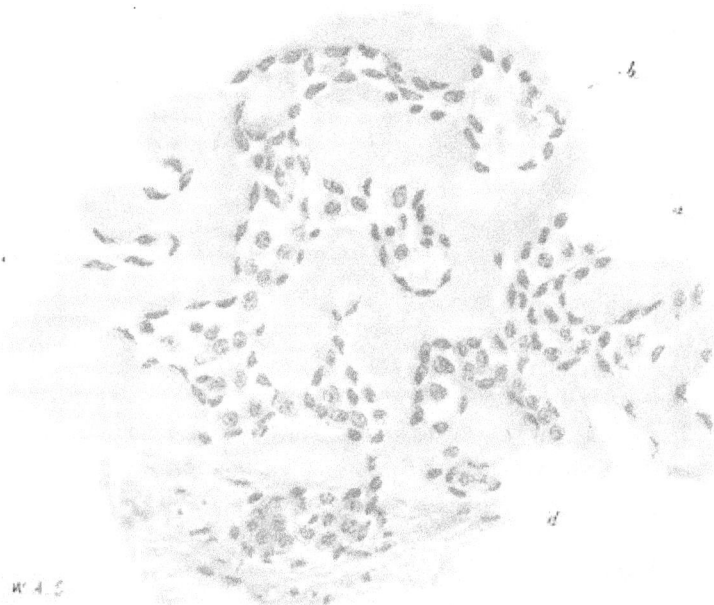

FIG. 182.—Section of colloid cancer of the breast. Stained with picro-carmine. (× 300).

    a. Epithelial cells filling alveolus.
    b.   Do.   undergoing colloid degeneration.
    c. Flattened cells covering fibrous trabeculæ.
    d. Swollen homogeneous mucoid (?) fibrous tissue.
    e. Normal stroma.

The cells of a cancer multiply by indirect division of the nucleus; a process which may be very readily followed out in this tumour.

Colloid Cancer.

402. The colloid cancer may be looked upon as one of the forms of cancer already mentioned, in which the epithelial cells have undergone colloid degeneration. It is especially common in the gastro-intestinal mucous membrane, in the abdominal cavity, in the breast and ovary, and more rarely in other viscera.

Naked eye appearances.—The presence of the colloid change is indicated by a peculiar brownish glue-like or gelatinous appearance. When the growth is diffuse, and occurs on a serous membrane, as in the peritoneal cavity, it may form a gelatinous mass which appears to form a coating over the whole of the abdominal organs, or a gelatine cast of the viscera. In colloid cancer of the breast, the degeneration takes place in portions, only, which have the same peculiar gelatinous consistence.

Harden (§ **60**), and stain (§ **98**).

(× 50).—The pink stroma differs in no respect from one or other of the forms previously described ; but the alveoli are more rounded, and in place of cells there may be simply a yellow colloid mass.

(× 300).—Where the cells are not entirely replaced by colloid material, they are swollen and rounded, and contain yellow drops or globules. In some cells the protoplasm forms a mere film around the colloid globule, and eventually even this may disappear, and the globule joins the main mass. In other cases a few altered and swollen cells may be left in the centre of the colloid material, in addition to which, especially in the breast, this substance may have penetrated between the layers of fibrous tissue forming the wall of the alveolus ; these layers stripped off one after the other by the invading colloid material, give rise to a peculiar laminated appearance. The laminated mass is made up as follows :—In the centre are the altered cells, surrounding them is the colloid material, and around this again are successive alternate layers of pink fibrous tissue and yellow colloid.

From the above description of the various forms of cancer it will be understood that they are all of an exceedingly malignant character. The encephaloid cancer is most malignant, the squamous epithelioma least so. They spread by the lymphatics both locally and to distant parts.

Degenerative Changes in Cancers.

403. These changes modify, in a very marked manner, both the naked eye and microscopic appearances.

(1) Colloid, and (2) fatty degeneration of the cells, and (3) myxomatous or mucoid degeneration of the stroma, have already been mentioned.

(4) A cancer may soften *en masse,* or superficially; this leads to ulceration, by a process of fatty degeneration or necrosis. It occurs especially when the tumour is exposed to the action of irritant or digestive fluids, or to mechanical injury. Such ulceration is usually followed by hæmorrhage.

(5) Hæmorrhage also occurs, as already mentioned, in encephaloid cancers; it is frequently met with in *carcinoma telangiectodes* or erectile carcinoma, where well-developed vessels, on which are small dilatations, project from the stroma into the alveoli, and, being no longer supported, rupture, serious hæmorrhage resulting.

(6) Inflammation of cancerous growths is also very commonly found; the results are very similar to those met with in inflammation of any normal tissue—vascular changes and connective tissue proliferation.

(7) Pigmentation of the stroma of cancerous growths also occurs. Most of the so-called pigmented cancers, however, are nothing but melanotic sarcomas.

Diagnostic Features of Sarcoma and Carcinoma.

404. The following tabular form may prove helpful to the student who has carefully examined both the sarcoma and the carcinoma:—

	SARCOMA.	CARCINOMA.
1. *Origin*	Entirely mesoblastic. (Connective tissue type).	Meso- and epi- or hypoblastic. (Both connective tissue and epithelial types).
2. *Stroma*	Intercellular. Rarely forms alveoli.	Vascular connective tissue, which forms alveoli; these communicate with one another and contain masses of epithelial cells.

	SARCOMA.	CARCINOMA.
3. *Cells* . . .	Granulation tissue or embryonic connective tissue cells, not epithelial (shapes various).	Epithelial cells contained within alveoli, shape and size various. Distinct nuclei and nucleoli.
4. *Intercellular substance*	May be present.	Absent, or merely fluid.
5. *Vessels* . .	Embryonic in character. They are in direct contact with, or rather are composed of, the special cells, slightly modified, of which the tumour is composed.	Well developed, entirely contained within and supported by the walls of the alveoli. Seldom in contact with the cells.
6. *Spreads* . .	By blood-vessels.	By lymphatics, except in the later stages, when they may also spread by blood vessels; they then spread with very great rapidity.
7. *Malignancy* .	Great.	Greater.

CHAPTER XV.

ANIMAL PARASITES.

TREMATODA.

405. *Distoma hepaticum, Fasciola hepatica,* or fluke of liver-rot in sheep, rarely occurs in man. It is found as a flattened leaf like worm, one-half to three-quarters of an inch long, lying curled up in the bile ducts and gall bladder. When flattened out it is broader at the anterior than at the posterior end, and is prolonged into a narrow proboscis in front. It is brownish, with a pink tinge. To inject the worm, kill by plunging it into warm thin gelatine carmine, which is immediately taken into the alimentary canal. To preserve for examination soak thoroughly in glycerine, and mount in a deep cell in the same medium. With a hand-lens examine and note the oral sucker at the anterior extremity of the proboscis; from this runs the injected alimentary canal, which is deeply bifurcated and branched, giving off lateral diverticula, and ending in cœca. Behind the mouth is the genital aperture, and next to this comes the ventral acetabalum or disc; behind this again comes a convoluted tube—the uterus, occupying a considerable proportion of the body cavity. The testes are situated more centrally, and are bifurcated. The body is enclosed in a chitinous cuticle, which is covered with very minute spines. This organism, like many others of the animal parasites, is not developed completely in one host. In one it passes through certain stages of its existence, after which, unless taken up by a second host, it remains quiescent or dies. The first host (in which development is incomplete) is spoken of as the *intermediate* host; the second as the *final* host, and the parasite must inhabit both in order that it may pass through its full cycle of development or generation. The *intermediate host* of the distoma hepaticum is the fresh-water snail;

2 P

the following is its *cycle of generation :* ovum ; ciliated embryo, set free in water by the opening of an operculum ; the embryo then loses its cilia and enters the intermediate host, where it becomes encysted. It then forms a sporocyst or *redia* form, by a process of internal gemmation, by which small-tailed embryos are formed—the cercariæ ; these escape, and after swimming in water by means of the muscular tail, enter the final host, and becoming sexually developed into hermaphrodite forms, lose their tail, and the cycle is repeated.

D. lanceolatum, a longer and narrower form of fluke, also occurs in man.

D. hæmatobium, Bilharzia hæmatobia, or blood-fluke, is an important member of this group, as it is present in the portal and splenic veins, and in the vessels of the mucous membrane of the rectum and bladder ; by its presence in the latter position it gives rise to a condition of hæmaturia. It is met with especially in Egypt, the West Coast of Arabia, Mauritius, and the Cape. Unlike the other trematodes, it is bisexual.

The male is about half an inch long, is somewhat flattened and curved in on its ventral surface, so that a transverse section is crescentic. Both discs, larger in the male than in the female, are placed near the anterior extremity, and the genital orifice lies behind the posterior of these. The female is about one inch in length, is filiform, and is received into the ventral groove and the *canalis gynæcophorus,* formed by a further folding in of the lateral margins at the posterior extremity of the male. In the urine from a case in which this parasite is present, a quantity of blood may usually be found ; although sometimes scarcely a trace can be detected with the naked eye. When some of the sediment is examined under the microscope, large numbers of ova may be distinguished. These ova are about $\frac{1}{120}$ of an inch in length, are oval, and have a spine or beak situated, usually, at the broader end. They are yellow, transparent and smooth, and through the transparent investment the segmented yolk mass may be seen. If to the sediment containing these ova a few drops of water be added, and one of them be watched under a low power for ten or fifteen minutes, a movement of cilia may be observed within the investing membrane. This becoming very active, the membrane ruptures. The released embryo has imperfectly developed organs, but darts about with great rapidity, the cilia working actively.

Stain (§ 98), and mount (§ 151), or better (§ 152).

D. crassum, found in the duodenum ; *D. sinense* and *D. conjunctum,* in the liver ; *D. heterophyes,* in the intestines,—are the other more important members of this group.

CESTODES OR TAPE WORMS.

406. Each so-called tape-worm is really a colony of slightly different individuals, each segment or individual, however, with the exception of those situated at the anterior extremity of the chain, being sexually complete. The whole chain is termed a strobilus, the most anterior modified segment forms the head and neck ; after which come the

FIG. 183.—Head and immature segments of *Tænia mediocanellata* (natural size).
a. Head with four suckers.
b. Neck.
c. Immature segments.

proglottides or segments, first the sexually immature, and then the mature but hermaphrodite segments. In this group alternation of generation is strictly maintained throughout. The fully developed form occurs in the alimentary canal of the final host, and must be looked for in the fæces, which must be carefully broken down with a stream of water, and strained through fine muslin, so as to intercept the various fragments of the strobilus.

TÆNIA MEDIOCANELLATA, T. SAGINATA, OR T. INERMIS.

407. This is probably the commonest form in England and India,

but in Germany it is less frequently met with.   The intermediate
host, in which the cystic form (*Cysticercus bovis*) occurs, is the ox.

Naked eye appearances.—It is found as small yellowish spots in the
muscles, especially in the thin curved muscles of a round of beef, in
the lungs, and in the liver.

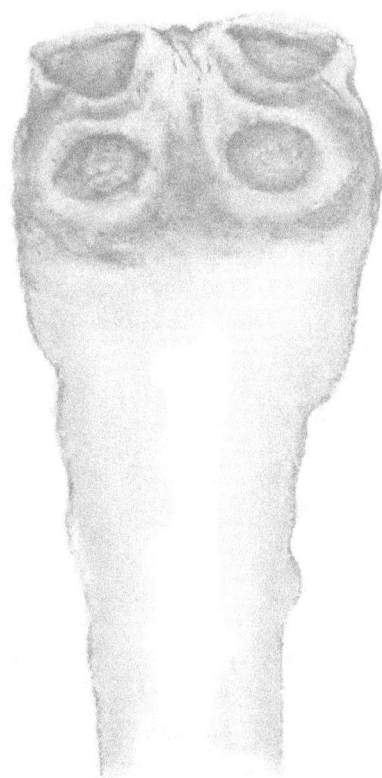

FIG. 184.—Flattened head of *Tænia mediocanellata*, with four
suckers well seen.   Neck becoming constricted.   (× about 30.)

The matured strobilus is a soft, flattened, yellowish white "band"
or ribbon worm, which sometimes attains a length of over twenty
feet.

Examined under a low magnifying power, the head is seen to be
square and somewhat flattened, about one-twelfth of an inch in
diameter, having no beak or rostellum, or only a small proboscis, and

no hooklets. At each corner of the head is a muscular sucker, and from each sucker runs a water vascular canal. In the centre of the head is a rounded opening, surrounded by a circular canal, into which the canals from the suckers open. From the circular canal are two longitudinal branches, running one down each side of the chain of proglottides.

Examine the fully matured proglottides, as they are arranged in a row. Small papillæ with central openings *alternate irregularly* on

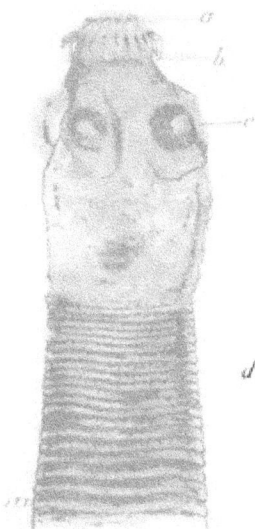

Fig. 185.—Head, neck, and immature segments of *Tænia saginata* (found in the fæces of a dog). Stained with logwood and mounted in Canada balsam. (× about 30.)
  a. Rostellum.
  b. Double row of hooklets; the anterior hooklets appear to be the larger.
  c. Suckers.
  d. Immature segments.

The head of this form resembles that of the *Tænia echinococcus* and that of the *Tænia solium*, which, however, has only a single row of hooklets, and that of the *Tænia acanthotrias*, which has a triple row of hooklets.

each side of the ribbon, a little below the centre of the segment. Running down each side of the flattened segments, which are square, or longer than broad, is the branch of the water vascular canal, whilst at the front part of each segment runs a transverse connecting branch.

By plunging the living worm into a warm solution of carmine, or carmine gelatine, a most beautiful injection of the water vascular system may be obtained. The uterus is very much branched, the diverticula branching dichotomously. The testis consists of a convoluted tube placed in the anterior part of the segment, from which passes a duct ending in a cirrus or penis, which may in some cases be seen protruding through the genital pore; close to this is the opening of the vagina. Near the posterior part of each segment are a couple of small glands—the vitelline glands. Each strobilus consists of three or four thousand segments, the sexually matured proglottides commencing at about the 450th from the head. To preserve these worms for future examination, soak in glycerine and mount in a deep cell (§ 152), or stain (§ 98 or 103 *d*), clear up thoroughly (§ 150), and mount in a cell (§ 155). To mount as a permanent preparation, whilst still moist, arrange it in a series of concentric circles on a piece of clean glass. Begin with the head in the centre and work gradually outwards; allowed to dry *in situ* they adhere firmly to the glass.

Tænia Solium, T. Cucurbitina, or T. Vulgaris.

408. This is the form which occurs most frequently in Germany.

Naked eye appearances.—The cystic form—*Cysticercus cellulosæ*—occurs in pork, where it gives rise to the so-called measly condition. A similar cystic form is met with, more rarely, in man, in the subcutaneous areolar tissue, between muscles, in the eye and in the brain. Like the *T. mediocanellata* the strobilus is composed of head and neck, and proglottides. It is several feet in length, but is shorter than the *T. mediocanellata;* it consists of about 1200 segments.

(× 50).—Around the head are four suckers arranged below a well-marked rostellum; this is armed with a single row of hooklets considerably larger than those of the *T. echinococcus.* The water vascular system near the rostellum is like that met with in *T. mediocanellata*—double, and may be injected in the same manner. The segments are square, or are longer than broad; the uterus—or, more properly speaking, the ovary—has a number of lateral branches (seven to ten), which again subdivide, but not nearly to the same extent as in the *T. mediocanellata.* The cirrus genital pores, which *alternate regularly*, should also be examined. Prepare as for *T. mediocanellata.*

BOTHRIOCEPHALUS LATUS, OR TÆNIA LATA.

409. This form of tapeworm, which is frequently met with in Iceland, Holland, North-east Germany, Geneva, Southern and Eastern Russia, and on the shores of the Caspian Sea, probably has its cystic form in certain species of trout which are especially common in the regions mentioned. The bleak, according to Dr. Fock, quoted by Cobbold, is possibly the intermediate host, when it occurs in the Dutch Jews. The pike, eel, and pout are also mentioned in this connection.

Naked eye appearances.—*B. latus* is the largest of the tapeworms occurring in man; it may be as much as twenty-five feet in length, and from half an inch to one inch in breadth. The head is about $\frac{1}{25}$ of an inch broad, is club-shaped, but slightly flattened; it has no rostellum and no hooklets; and running down each side is a very characteristic groove. Behind the head comes a thin neck, after which come the proglottides, three or four thousand in number. At first these are extremely narrow and short; but as the segments become sexually matured (at about the 600th segment) they are broader and about one-eighth inch in length, whilst at the posterior extremity they again taper off slightly in breadth, but are as much as one quarter of an inch in length. The individual segments are not so much flattened as in the tæniada, but still the worm is flat and ribbon-like. The segments have a brownish tinge, and in the centre of each, or a little nearer the front on the ventral surface, is a distinct, deeply-pigmented elevation or thickening, in the middle of which is placed the genital pore. The pigmentation is due to the presence of numerous dark-coloured ova. The uterus lies in the centre of the segment and is composed of a simple tube which is so coiled that it forms a rosette-shaped mass; on each side of this are small saccules which represent the testes. The water vascular system is similar to that of the other members of the group. For permanent preparations of the head or of the segments, stain and mount as for *T. mediocanellata* (§ 407).

Cycle of development of tape-worms.—Beginning with the sexually matured segments, proglottides are voided from the intestine of the final host; ova are discharged or escape from these as they become disorganised. They are then taken up by the first host, generally from water, into the alimentary canal; here the ovum opens by an operculum, and an embryo, with its three pairs of hooks, emerges, increases in size, becomes vacuolated, the hooklets disappear, a chitinous or horny cuticle is developed, and an imperfect water vascular system makes its appearance. The sac then becomes thickened at one point, and invagination of this goes on until a double-walled sac, open at one end, is formed. At the bottom of the sac, on the inner wall, hooklets are seen (if present in the tape-worm form), then elevations, which eventually form the suckers; this inner part of the floor, looking towards the mouth of the sac, is really therefore the head. All this takes place in the first or intermediate host, while the liberated embryo is passing from the alimentary canal into the intermuscular septa, brain, &c., and during the time that it is becoming encysted in these positions. In some instances, as in the hydatid cysts to be afterwards described, a secondary or even a tertiary internal budding takes place, so that in the primary cysts a large number of scolices, or undeveloped heads, may be formed.

When the muscular or other tissue, with the contained encysted parasites—measly pork, for example—is taken into the alimentary canal of the second or final host, the cyst wall is dissolved by the gastric juice, the head becomes evaginated, attaches itself to the wall of the intestine, proglottides are developed behind it, and the cycle begins again.

When man is the primary host, the "measles" are found in the positions before mentioned. A fibrous pseudo-cyst is formed around the cystic parasite, which may live for a considerable time. On the death of the scolex, however, the cyst becomes calcified, the contents undergo caseation and calcification, and the only evidence of the scolex left are the hooklets, which may almost invariably be found.

Tænia Echinococcus.

410. The *Tænia echinococcus*, or the tape-worm of the dog, is important only in that it gives rise to a cystic form in man, who is the intermediate host. It is a worm measuring about a quarter of an inch in length, one-half of the whole length being taken up by the terminal proglottis, which is the only one that comes to sexual maturity. The head is rather like that of the *T. solium*, but is smaller. It has a distinct rostellum, surrounded by a double row of hooklets, thirty or forty in number, similar in shape to those of the *T. solium* but only about one-third of the size. Here, too, as in the *T. solium*, there are four suckers which may readily be seen. There is a well developed water vascular system; the genital pore is placed a little behind the centre of the matured segment. The uterus occupies the greater part of the segment, and is filled with ova.

Hydatid Cyst.

411. The cystic form of the *T. echinococcus* occurs most frequently in the liver and peritoneum, but also in the lungs, spleen, heart, and pericardium, nerve centres and retina, kidneys, muscles, and subcutaneous tissues. In Iceland, according to Cobbold, "it is the cause of one-sixth of the annual mortality;" and in Switzerland, Southern Germany, and Australia (Victoria) it frequently occurs, but much more rarely in England and Scotland.

Naked eye appearances.—The cysts vary greatly both in size and number, as they may be only the size of a pin's head, or they may grow to several times the normal size of the organs in which they are developed. In some cases they are single, but in others there are several in the same organ, or there may be numerous cysts occurring simultaneously in several organs.

Examine one of the cysts. Before the organ is disturbed there is usually considerable bulging at the point where the cyst is situated (in the liver, most frequently on the upper surface of the right lobe). Make a crucial incision into the bulging part, cutting carefully through a fibrous capsule that is found, and reflect the flaps from the true cyst. This fibrous capsule or pseudo-cyst consists of new or compressed

tissue, the new tissue being the result of pressure irritation of the connective tissue of the organ.   The true capsule now exposed is white
and opaque, almost like boiled white of egg, and from its outer surface, surrounding well lighted objects, such as a window, are reflected.
Open the capsule and remove some of the fluid.   This has a specific
gravity of 1004 to 1013; gives no gelatinous or other precipitate with
heat or nitric acid, and therefore contains no albumen.   With nitrate
of silver a white cloudy precipitate is formed, as the fluid contains
about a half per cent. of sodium chloride (common salt).   When the
fluid escapes the membrane curls inwards in a very characteristic
fashion.   If the fluid be set aside in a conical glass to settle, and
some of the granular looking sediment, mixed with Farrant's solution,

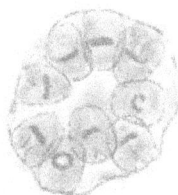

FIG. 186.—A number of scolices contained within a delicate
brood capsule.   Mounted in glycerine.   (× 70.)
     Note the circlet of hooklets retracted within the body of each
scolex.

be mounted in a shallow cell and covered with a cover-glass, the
scolices may be made out under the microscope.
     (× 50).—The scolices appear to be about the size of millet seeds.
Some of them are rounded, others are more elongated, and have at
one end a dark-coloured disc or zone.   The body appears granular,
and small suckers may be observed.   A number of these small bodies
may be grouped together and surrounded by a delicate membrane or
brood capsule, which is attached to the endocyst.
     (× 300).—The structure of the scolices may be further defined:
the circlet of hooks; the suckers placed somewhat laterally; the
body containing the bright-looking globules and particles.   A number of hooklets may usually be seen in any hydatid fluid, and these
should be carefully examined in order that they may be recognised,
even after the other contents of the cyst have undergone suppuration

or other degenerative changes. Examine a scraping of the endocyst removed from the inner surface of the cyst, mixed with Farrant's solution, and pressed between two glass slips. It is found to consist of a granular mass, in which are imbedded the scolices, similar to those above described. From this endocyst or inner layer of the hydatid membrane are developed the scolices, or where the primary cysts are of large size, the secondary cysts. As these secondary cysts grow, tertiary cysts may in turn be developed within them. These of course may be observed during the naked eye examination.

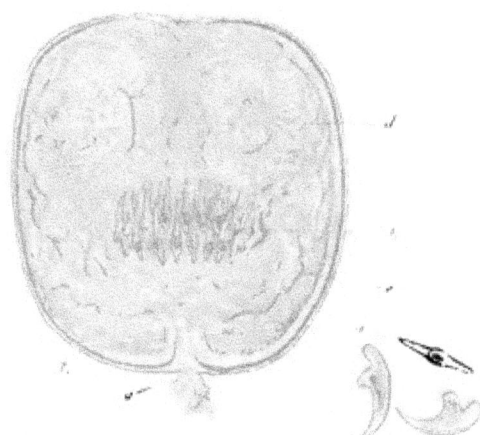

FIG. 187.—*A.* Drawing of *Echinococcus.* Head or scolex. (× 450.)
  a. Pedicle, by which it is attached to the endocyst.
  b. Circlet of hooklets.
  c. Depression at point of invagination of anterior
      segment.
  d. Suckers with radiating fibres.
  e. Vascular canals (?)
B. Detached hooklets. (× 450).

The ectocyst, or thick white of egg-like outer layer, varies in thickness according to the size of the cyst. It is the curling inwards of this layer which causes the incurling of the membrane when the cyst is ruptured. With a couple of pairs of forceps it is possible to strip layer after layer from it, showing that it is composed of a series of laminæ. If a small portion be teased out in glycerine and examined under the microscope, the lamination is easily distinguished ;

and on further examination under a high power each of these laminæ may be seen to be marked by a series of pectinate striæ running at right angles to the plane of the laminæ.

Degenerative changes occur in the hydatid cyst :—

1. Spontaneous cure, due to absorption or evacuation of the fluid. This is followed by death of the scolices, fatty degeneration, caseation, and even calcification.

2. Evacuation after suppuration, or after inflammation of the sur-

FIG. 188.—Laminated ectocyst of the true hydatid cyst. (× 300.) Note the pectinate markings on the laminæ.

rounding tissues, in which there is marked softening of the membrane.

T. tenella (Cobbold)—cystic form, *Cysticercus ovis*, the cause of mutton measles, may be mentioned in this group, but it is unimportant; as is also *T. marginata* of dog—cystic form, *Cysticercus tenuicollis*.

NEMATODES, THREAD-WORMS, OR ROUND-WORMS.

412. These are lumbricoid or filiform parasites, some of which are found affecting man.

Naked eye appearances.—They are covered with a thick elastic cuticle, have a mouth, straight alimentary canal, posterior and ventral anus, and are bisexual. The ovary in the female, and the testis in the male, are seen as more or less convoluted tubes in different species. The genital opening in the female is in the middle, or even a little in front of the middle, of the ventral surface. The male cloaca, with or without a spine, is situated near the posterior extremity of the body.

The most important of this order, perhaps, is the *Trichina spiralis*, which is met with in two positions in man,—one, the mature form, in the intestine ; the second, the sexually immature form, encysted in the inter-muscular connective tissue.

THE ENCYSTED FORM OF TRICHINA SPIRALIS.

413. The immature trichina, either in the pig or in the human subject, is usually found in the thin muscles of the abdomen, thoracic walls, diaphragm, cervical and laryngeal muscles, front of the thigh, and less frequently in the other parts of the muscular system. To the naked eye it appears as small whitish specks, longer than broad, lying in enormous numbers in streaks or lines in the long axis of the muscular fibres.

Examined under a strong magnifying glass, the small specks are seen to be cysts, in which, coiled up, lie the larval trichinæ. Rupture the cyst with a couple of needles, turn out the trichina, and under the microscope examine the specimen, after staining (§ 98) and mounting (§ 152). It is about $\frac{1}{25}$ of an inch long, and is provided with an alimentary canal and imperfectly developed reproductive organs. Some of the white specks are quite hard and calcareous. If these are treated with hot caustic potash or soda, they remain unaffected, but a very weak solution of hydrochloric acid dissolves out the hard material and leaves the capsule soft and pliable.

Harden a piece of the trichinous muscle (§ 58) ; with the aid of a low power of the microscope, find a section in which is at least one cyst, and stain with (§§ 98 or 103 *d*).

(× 50).—The cyst is seen to be placed between the muscular fibres, which in the immediate neighbourhood are somewhat compressed ; it is lemon-shaped, and contains the larval worm rolled up in one, two, or three coils. At each pole, outside the cyst, a few fat globules, with small blood-vessels running amongst them, may be seen. The cyst itself is first fibrous, being derived from proliferated sarcolemma cells. In the specimen from which Fig. 189 was taken, calcification of this fibrous covering was beginning at the poles. Where complete calcification has taken place, a fibrous covering is still present. Within the first cyst is a second membranous or

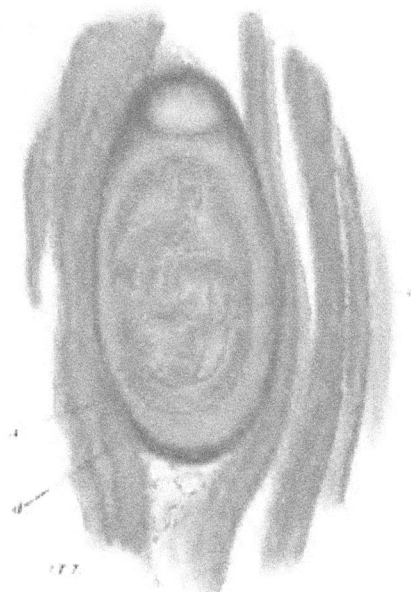

FIG. 189.— *Trichina spiralis* encysted. Stained with picro-carmine. (× 300.)

   a. Atrophied muscle fibres.
   b. Fat cells situated at the end of the cyst.
   c. Capsule becoming calcified.
   d. Protoplasm surrounding the worm.
   e. Trichina coiled up in the cyst.

chitinous covering, which in turn may become calcified, whilst within this again is a quantity of granular protoplasm, in which the worm is imbedded. The complete calcification of the cyst is not completed for about ten months, after which, at an undetermined period, the contained larvæ may undergo fatty degeneration, and even calcification.

   (× 300).—Corroborate the appearances above described.

Cycle of development of Trichina spiralis. — When trichinous pork is taken into the alimentary canal, the encysted larval form is set free by the action of the acid gastric juice. On the second or third day it becomes sexually matured. Both sexes are found. The adult male is about $\frac{1}{18}$ of an inch in length, and may be recognised by the two small processes in which the tail ends. The adult female is considerably longer, sometimes twice the length of the male; its body is also thicker, and the posterior extremity is "broad and bluntly rounded." The cloaca in the male is between the lobes of the tail, whilst in the female the genital orifice is placed at about the anterior third of the body. On the sixth or seventh day the female gives birth to numerous living sexually immature embryos, which make their way into the muscular tissue, cause disorganisation of the muscle fibres, and at the end of fourteen days are completely encysted; calcification ensues, and the cycle is complete.

OTHER ANIMAL PARASITES FOUND IN MAN.

414. The following further list, selected from Cobbold's " Human Parasites," and Leuckart's " Parasites of Man," may prove of use to the student, in so far as it may serve as a guide to him in his search for descriptions of parasites.

NEMATODES.

415. *Tricocephalus dispar,* or whip-worm.—A worm about two inches long, with a narrow head and neck; the posterior two-thirds thick, like a whip-stock, is curled in the male, but straight in the female; the anterior portion is very thin. It is very commonly met with imbedded in the mucous membrane of the cæcum, and is perfectly harmless.

Filaria sanguinis hominis—F. Bancrofti.—The embryo form (*F. sanguinis hominis*) found in the blood is about $\frac{1}{130}$ of an inch in length, pointed at one end, blunt at the other. By its presence in the kidneys it gives rise to chyluria and hæmaturia. In the fully developed form (*F. Bancrofti*) it is a hair-like worm about three or four inches in length, and is met with in the lymphatics, especially those of the scrotum and lower limbs, giving rise to a condition similar to, if not identical, with Elephantiasis. It is found especially in China, Australia, and Brazil.

Dracunculus or *Filaria medinensis—the Guinea worm.*—The female, —from the pathological point of view the more important of the sexes,—cylindrical in shape, measuring from one to six feet in length, and about one-tenth of an inch in diameter, is found in the subcutaneous tissue of the back or legs, giving rise to swelling and subcutaneous abscesses, which burst, allowing the parasite to come to the surface. It is found especially in India, Arabia, Guinea, the West Indies, Egypt, and Brazil.

Eustrongylus or *Strongylus gigas* is found in the pelvis of the kidney of dogs and wolves and other fish-eating carnivora ; only one case is recorded in man. The male is about one foot long, the female twice that length ; the latter is about one-tenth of an inch in thickness ; its body is red.

Strongylus or *Filaria bronchialis*, a small species occurring especially in the lungs of sheep (rare in man). It is about one twenty-fourth the size of the larger form.

Dochmius duodenalis or *Anchylostoma duodenale* is found in the duodenum and upper part of the intestine. The male is about three-eighths of an inch long, the female half an inch. It attaches itself by its ventral mouth, which is situated near the anterior extremity, to the mucous membrane, from which it takes blood. By its presence it thus gives rise to extensive ulceration and hæmorrhage. It is met with in the West Indies, Cayenne, Brazil, Egypt (giving rise to what is known as tropical anæmia, Anæmia Egyptica), and in Northern Italy (St. Gothard Tunnel trichinosis of Perroncito).

Oxyuris or *Ascaris vermicularis* is the small thread worm, found in the cæcum and upper part of the colon, especially of children ; the male is about one-sixth of an inch in length, the female half an inch.

Leptodera or *Anguillula stercoralis.*—A small nematode found in the stools of patients suffering from Cochin-China diarrhœa. It is about $\frac{1}{25}$ of an inch long, and occurs in very great numbers in the whole length of the alimentary canal, along with a much less numerous but larger form, the *L. intestinalis*, which is about one-eighth of an inch in length.

Ascaris lumbricoides or *Lumbricus teres hominis* is a round-worm or maw-worm, found in man, and in the pig, cat, and horse. It has pointed ends, and is light brown in colour. The male is from four to six inches long, and has a curved tail, on which are two sharp spines ; the female measures from ten to fourteen inches in length, and has a straight tail, and no spines. This worm is found in the upper part of the intestine, but may be present in any part of the alimentary canal, in the bile ducts, and in the peritoneal cavity ; it may be ejected with the fæces, more rarely, by the mouth.

Ascaris mystax or *A. alata.*—A small nematode, one-third of an inch in length, found in the alimentary canal of man, and of the cat, dog, and other carnivora.

ARACHNIDA.

416. *Acarus*, or *Sarcoptes scabiei*, or human itch insect, is found in burrows or tunnels in the deeper layers of the skin. The female burrows in the skin, laying her eggs as she goes, and leaving a white track behind her. The irritation so produced sets up ecze-matous or vesicular eruptions. To obtain the acarus for examination the white line should be found, then the point of entrance to the tunnel, which is marked by a black speck ; at the opposite end the female is found. Cut down on this point with a sharp knife, place the parasite on a slide in a drop of Farrants' solution or glycerine, and examine (× 20). It is about "the size of a small pin-head, and somewhat turtle-shaped." On the under surface are four pairs of legs. The two anterior pairs of legs end in stalked discs, but both the hinder pairs of legs end in setæ. The male is about half the size of the female, and the posterior of his two hinder pairs of legs end in stalked discs ; the anterior of the hinder pairs end in long setæ.

Pentastoma tænoides of the nasal fossæ of the dog is the matured form of *P. denticulatum* of the human liver, spleen, and kidney.

P. constrictum.—A larger pentastoma, which infests the liver and lungs of man.

Acarus, or *Demodex folliculorum*, or face mite.—One of the mites met with in the sebaceous follicles of the skin.

Leptus autumnalis, gooseberry bug, or harvest bug.—A small red mite which infests the skin, giving rise to very irritable papules.

INSECTA.

417. *Pediculus capitis,* or head louse.—Found on the scalp.

P. pubis, or crab louse.—Found on all hairy parts of the body, but not on the head.

P. vestimentorum, or body louse, which lays eggs and lives in the clothes.

Culex anxifer, or mosquito.

Glossina morsitans.—Tsetse of Africa, described by Dr. Livingstone.

Hæmatopota pluvialis, "horse fly," or "clegge" of the Western Highlands.

Cimex, or *Acanthia lectularia,* or bed bug.—One of the "free parasites."

Pulex penetrans.—The jigger or chigoe of the West Indies. The female is found in the soles of the feet, beneath the skin.

Pulex irritans.—The common flea. Another of the "free parasites."

CHAPTER XVI.

VEGETABLE PARASITES.

Schizomycetes, Fission Fungi, or Bacteria.

418. In the examination of bacteria it is necessary not only that they should be appropriately stained, but that we should enlist the most accurate microscopic appliances into our service.

These organisms are so minute that it is only by the exercise of the greatest care, and with the aid of the most perfect illuminating apparatus at our command, that a number of them are to be recognised, though masses of them may often be readily enough made out lying in blood-vessels or lymphatics. When once their presence is determined, their position in the tissues has to be further studied, and this can only be done under the most favourable conditions. In all work of this kind, where possible, use an oil immersion lens and an Abbe's illuminator, with which the best optical combination is obtained. This illuminator or condenser has a very short focus, and must therefore be brought up almost to the under surface of the object to be examined. It may also be used as an ordinary condenser, if the lateral or greatly converged rays be cut off by means of a diaphragm with a small aperture, placed below. If a large aperture in the diaphragm be used, the greatly converged rays of light are also allowed to play on the structures, which are lighted from all points, all shadows disappear, and the "structural picture" is lost. As the structural picture is lost, however, the stained elements, such as the micro-organisms, and the nuclei, are brought out prominently, and can be carefully examined. All preparations should be examined with both the small and the large apertures of the diaphragm beneath the condenser. With the smaller aperture the structural elements and the positions of the organisms are observed; as the aperture is increased in size, the organisms become more and more prominent, whilst the structural elements gradually disappear from view.

From a mouse suffering from mouse septicæmia take a specimen of blood, and prepare (§ 106).

Examined under ordinary conditions it appears to contain nothing

FIG. 190.—Blood of a mouse killed by inoculation of the bacillus of mouse septicæmia. A thin layer of the blood has been dried on a cover-glass, carefully heated, stained with a watery solution of methyl blue and mounted in glycerine. (× 700.)

    a. White blood corpuscle with horse shoe-shaped nucleus, and numerous minute bacilli in and around it.
    b. Red blood corpuscles.
    c. Small bacilli between corpuscles.

but white and red blood corpuscles. When, however, it is illuminated by means of an Abbe's condenser, and examined (× 700), a number of exceedingly minute, deeply stained, rod-like bodies may be seen lying between the red blood corpuscles, or embedded in the protoplasm of the colourless corpuscles. These are the smallest bacilli yet described.

A specimen of blood taken from the spleen of a mouse, inoculated with anthrax virus, and examined in the same way, is seen to be charged with much larger, jointed, purple, rod-like bodies, which are recognised as anthrax bacilli. Typhoid bacilli are recognised in the same way in a scraping from one of the enlarged soft mesenteric glands from a case of typhoid fever (§ 302).

A drop of pus from an acute abscess (§§ 164, 173, 205, and 221), similarly treated and examined, presents numerous minute rounded bodies, either in chains or in zoogloea masses, with, here and there, a few elongated or rod-shaped bodies lying free in the fluid, whilst in the pus corpuscles similar organisms are frequently embedded, and can be readily observed.

Examine a section from a case of diphtheria, either of a cervical gland or of the uvula, especially its posterior surface, treated by the caustic potash method (§ 128). Wherever there are micrococci in zoogloea form, they may be seen as small granular strongly refractile layers or masses, arranged on the surface, or contained within the lymphatic spaces, or in the gland follicles near the surface. See also (§§ 295 and 296) for descriptions of the diphtheria bacillus.

Stained with Loeffler's methyl blue (§ 133), they are seen in the same positions, but they then have a blue tinge. Living or well preserved micrococci and bacilli are stained deeply, but when they become disorganised, the granular *débris*, like all dead tissue, is often stained very imperfectly, even though it is composed largely of broken-down micro-organisms. This fact must always be borne in mind, for, although stained organisms may not be present in large numbers in caseous or purulent material, a section taken from the wall of a caseous abscess may be swarming with organisms which readily take on aniline colours, and retain them very tenaciously.

CLASSIFICATION OF THE SCHIZOMYCETES.

Sphærobacteria (rounded bacteria).

(a.) *Micrococcus* and (b.) *Sarcina.*

419. Micrococci are the smallest and most elementary forms of vegetable organisms. They are probably divided into cell membrane and cell contents. They may be isolated, or in fours, as in the

pyæmia of rabbits; in chains, as in the gangrene produced by inoculation of certain soils in the house-mouse or field-mouse; or in
zoöglœa masses, united by a glue-like material, as on the surface of a
diphtheritic membrane; in the lymphatics in acute pneumonia, where
they are surrounded by a kind of capsule (Friedländer); and in the
spreading abscesses of rabbits, as described by Koch.

They may vary considerably in size and shape, the smallest being
rounded and found in the spreading abscess above mentioned,
whilst a larger, more oval form is met with in the septicæmias of
rabbits, fowls, and pigs. They appear to increase in number by a
process of direct division or fission. When in large naked eye
masses, they may be characterised by certain differences of appearance, generally manifested in the colour; for instance, some of them
form brown colouring matter, others white, yellow, pink, red, blue
grey blue or green (as seen in blue pus), and the rest.

FIG. 191.—Vessel from the cortex of the kidney of a pyæmic
rabbit. Stained with methylaniline blue. (× 700, after Koch.)
  a. Nuclei of the vascular wall.
  b. Small group of micrococci between the blood corpuscles.
  c. Dense masses of micrococci adherent to the wall and enclosing
      blood corpuscles.
  d. Pairs of micrococci at the border of the large mass.

Pathogenous micrococci, or those which are supposed to be the
cause of diseased conditions, are met with in many of the specific
infective diseases.

In *septicæmia*, they occur in connective tissue spaces; but also in
capillary vessels at the points of junction between the arterial and
venous capillaries, where the blood is flowing most sluggishly through
the widest area, and where consequently the micrococci are most at
rest, as in the glomeruli of the kidney and in the hepatic capillaries
of the liver.

In certain forms of *pyæmia*, the micrococci are found in similar
masses in the vessels.

In *purulent inflammations*, they are usually found either in the connective tissue or on some one or other of the mucous surfaces.

Erysipelas is caused by an organism which is found in chains or masses in the lymphatics and connective tissue spaces.

Endocarditis (§ **165**), appears to be due to the presence of a streptococcus.

Osteomyelitis (staphylococcus, pyogenes aureus, or micrococcus of osteomyelitis).—(§§ **172, 173**, and **315**.)

Sarcina.

420. The sarcina ventriculi, described by Goodsir, is frequently met with in the acid watery vomited matter from dyspeptic patients. It occurs in the typical wool-sack formation ; the fission taking place so as to form masses of fours of small round micrococcoid organisms. A smaller form, sarcina pulmonum (Virchow), is met with in the lungs, pharynx, and urine. It has a green tinge.

Microbacteria (short bacteria).

421. These are the short rod- or egg-shaped bodies with rounded extremities, which are found in rabbit septicæmia, fowl and hog cholera, and similar diseases. The pneumonia bacillus and the gonococcus, which is made up of two apposed discs, with a clear intermediate band, really belong to this group.

Desmobacteria (ribbon-shaped bacteria).

422. These are ribbon or thread-shaped organisms, which appear at some stage of their existence to be composed of strings of short rods. The strings may be composed of two or three segments only, or there may be a considerable number in each chain, whilst in some cases again, or at certain periods in their life history, the long filament is present, but is quite unsegmented. The most important of these are the following.

Bacillus anthracis—the bacillus associated with splenic fever, malignant pustule, charbon, and intestinal mycosis—is from 4 to 20 micromm. in length, and is about 1·5 micromm. in thickness. In the serous fluid thrown out, in such cases, into the pleura, the rods are as much as 150 micromm. in length (these may have grown after the death of the patient).

This organism is found, especially in the capillary vessels, at the points where the blood flow is most retarded. It may be present in such quantities as to cause plugging, distension, and rupture of the vessels, especially of the abdominal and thoracic viscera. Like the other members of the group it begins as a spore, which goes through certain changes before it assumes the form of a rod-shaped

FIG. 192.—Villus of intestine of a rabbit, stained with methyl-aniline blue, cleared up with carbonate of potassium, and mounted in Canada balsam. (× 250, after Koch.)

The lines of anthrax bacilli corresponding to the course of the capillary blood-vessels are very readily followed in this specimen.

bacillus. Under favourable conditions the threads attain to as much as ten or twenty times the original length of the bacillus; the protoplasm of which it is composed becomes granular; highly refractile spores are formed in this at regular intervals; after which the thread breaks up into lengths, the spores are set free, and the same process again begins. In place of this series of changes the bacilli may undergo simple division, especially in the blood of the

living animal, as in splenic fever and in septicæmia of the mouse.
—(Koch.) The spores are never formed, except in the presence
of free oxygen, in the blood that has escaped from the body, for
example.

Bacillus tuberculosis, already described (§ 273).

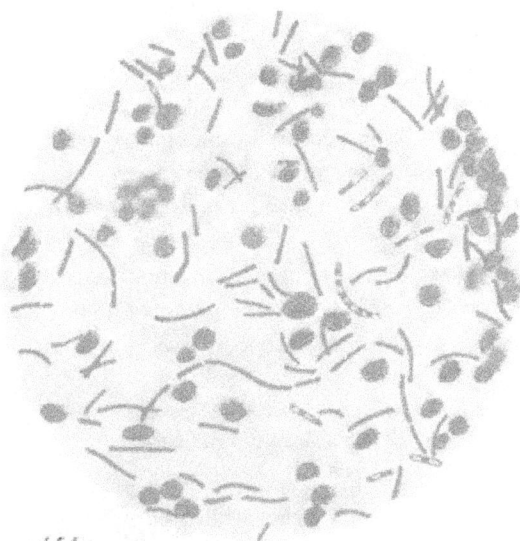

FIG. 193.—Bacillus anthracis from the spleen of a cow that
succumbed to an attack of splenic fever. The specimen was taken
some time after the organ had been removed from the carcase, and
in presence of air spores had begun to form in the bacilli. Specimen was dried, heated, stained by Gram's method, with methyl violet
and vesuvin, and mounted in Canada Balsam. (× 700.)

The anthrax rods and filaments, some of them with bright points
or spores, are stained with methyl violet. The cells of the splenic
pulp are stained brown by the vesuvin.

Bacillus lepræ, which is best stained, as for tubercle bacilli (§ 131),
is 4 to 5 micromm. in length, often contains spores, and is embedded
in the cells of the nodules found in leprosy.

Bacillus of typhoid fever (§ 302), in which, as in the *B. lepræ,* are
small rounded or oval, bright, unstained spots, which may be either
vacuoles or spores. It occurs in two forms; as long and short rods
in the intestinal ulcers, and as short rods in the spleen, kidney, liver,
and blood.—(Koch, Eberth, Gaffky.)

Bacillus of septicæmia (of mice), ·8 to 1· micromm. in length, and about ·1 to ·2 micromm. in diameter (§ **418**).

Bacillus of purpura hæmorrhagica, which may be stained best with methyl blue, was first described as present in certain positions in the small vessels of the pericardium (W. Russell and Watson Cheyne). It is exceedingly small, and appears at first sight to be a micrococcus, but it is a true bacillus. In connection with this organism it must be remembered that micrococci have been already described as present in " Hæmophilia neonatorum," and in one case of acute purpura hæmorrhagica I found enormous numbers of micrococci in different positions, but especially in the blood-vessels.

Bacillus mallei or *glanders bacillus* has been cultivated and inoculated. When inoculated it gives rise to a characteristic attack of glanders.

Bacillus of tetanus.—A minute drum-stick shaped organism, has been described as being the specific organism of tetanus.

Bacillus of syphilis is also described as occurring along with micrococci in hard chancres.

Spirobacteria (spiral bacteria).

423. The *cholera bacillus*, Koch's comma-shaped bacillus, belongs to this group. It is found in the liquid stools during the early stages of the disease. Stain in a watery solution of fuchsin (§ **114**).

To this group also belongs another spiral or screw-shaped organism or spirillum, the *Spirochæta Obermeyeri*, which is found in the blood in cases of relapsing fever. It must be examined in the fresh condition, as it rapidly breaks down, even in such an innocuous fluid as distilled water. Examined in the living blood on a warm stage, it is seen as a very active spiral organism, which is usually two, three, or four times the length of the diameter of a coloured blood corpuscle.

HYPHOMYCETES, OR MOULDS.

424. The most important are—

Achorion schönleinii (favus fungus, forming the yellow cup-shaped masses around hairs), which is found in the root sheath of the hair bulb, in which the jointed hyphæ or rod-shaped filaments, with clear globules within, and rounded spores or groups of spores (conidia) may be found amongst the epithelial cells. It is best prepared by staining in methylaniline violet, washing carefully in distilled water, and mounting in glycerine. It may also be soaked in water, and treated with caustic potash or acetic acid, or it may be treated with a mixture of alcohol two parts, ammonia one part, and mounted in distilled water. Several other fungi have been described as present around the hairs of a favus patch.

Trichophyton tonsurans, Tinea tonsurans, or ringworm fungus, prepared in the same manner, is seen in the form of slender jointed rods and small highly refractile spores ; these rods spread not only into the sheath, but also up the shaft of the hair.

Microsporon furfur, Tinea or *Pityriasis versicolor* occurs as yellowish or brownish red patches, covered with thin scales. Scrape off a few of these scales with a knife, treat as before, and examine under the microscope. The microsporon is seen as thin curved filaments, the conidia are grouped into masses, whilst the short sporebearing filaments form a dense network.

Actinomyces (ray fungus).

425. Actinomycosis is a disease which was long mistaken for tuberculosis, and for other forms of new growth such as osteo-sarcoma.

The fungus itself appears as a rosette-shaped mass, formed of a central body, from which club-shaped masses radiate. As these grow they set up around themselves a proliferative irritation, by which a structure, similar in most respects to that of tubercle, is formed. Some of these masses, especially those of rapid formation, suppurate, giving rise to abscess cavities and fistulæ, from which a pus containing the actinomyces, "small white or yellow (or reddish) greasy looking masses lying among the purulent detritus," is discharged. These may be recognised with the naked eye, but much more readily under the microscope. In cattle the masses do not break down nearly so readily as in man, and sections of the tissues containing the fungus are easily made after hardening in absolute alcohol. Remove all fatty matter with potash or ammonia, and then dissolve out any calcareous particles with weak hydrochloric acid. Then stain (§ **140**) or in Spiller's blue. The nodules are usually of considerable size ; and when this is the case, they are found to be made of several or numerous follicles, as in tubercle.   The tumours may be as large as the fist or even larger.

The granulation tissue, endothelioid cells, fibrous bands, and the rest may all be distinguished (× 50 and × 300) as in tubercle.

Fig. 194.—Fibrous nodule from a case of actinomycosis (from the tongue of a cow).   Stained with Spiller's blue.   (× 50.)
  a. Fungus growing in the centre of a follicle.
  b. Large endothelioid cells near the fungus.
  c. Fibro-cellular tissue away from the centre of the follicle, in which round cells predominate.
  d. More fibrous tissue, still further from the fungus, forming a fibrous capsule.

In cattle the positions in which the disease most frequently occurs are the lower and upper jaws, and first part of the alimentary canal ; in the human subject the soft parts of the neck, the mediastinal tissue, and the lungs are specially affected.

PREPARATION OF FUNGI, ASPERGILLI, &c.

426. For the examination of fungi, aspergilli, mucors, saprolegnia, &c., the following method will be found to be particularly convenient. Place the fungus in a watch-glass containing a mixture of two parts of

FIG. 195.—Actinomycosis. Tongue of cow. Section stained in Spiller's blue. (× 300.)

    a. Centre of mass of conidia (conidiophore).
    b. Pear-shaped conidia.
    c. Endothelioid cells (Compare these with the cells seen near the centre of a tubercle follicle (Fig. 46).)
    d. Fibrillar tissue near the margin of the follicle.
    e. Spindle-shaped cells, seen especially near the margin.

absolute alcohol and one part of liquor ammoniæ. Allow it to remain for two or three minutes, and transfer to a slide on which is a drop of distilled water—or glycerine, if the specimen is to be kept as a permanent preparation—and mount.

ADDENDA.

Ehrlich-Biondi triple staining fluid.

Instead of hæmatoxylin, as in the Ehrlich triple stain (§ 126), methyl green is used as the nuclear stain, along with acid fuchsin (Rubin S.), and orange as ground stains. This combination gives excellent results, and is recommended by Ruffer and J. H. Walker as probably the best for bringing into prominence coccidia and psorospermæ in cancer.   Prepare as follows :—

> Methyl green—saturated watery solution,   5 c.c.
>
> Methyl orange   ,,   ,,   10 c.c.
>
> Rubin S. (acid fuchsin), ...   2 c.c.

On mixing the concentrated fluids a precipitate is thrown down ; it is better, therefore, before mixing, to dilute each solution with about 40 volumes of water.[1]

Stain for from 15 minutes to 12 hours, wash in dilute alcohol, then for one minute in absolute alcohol. Wash thoroughly in xylol and benzol (§ 150), and mount in xylol balsam (§ 155).

Sections, after staining, may be rinsed in a very dilute solution (1-1000) of acetic acid, they must then be very thoroughly washed with the weak spirit.

Stiles' nitric acid method for naked eye examination of cancers (§ 69).

Place thin slices of the fresh cancer (taken from the spreading margins) in a 5 per cent. watery solution of nitric acid for from five minutes to twelve hours. Then wash in water for five minutes or longer, when the connective tissue becomes gelatinous looking ; from this the epithelial columns and masses stand out very prominently as opaque white streaks and points.

In place of a watery solution I have used 5 per cent. nitric acid in methylated spirit with equally good results.

---

[1] See *Methods and Formulæ*, P. W. Squire. 1892.

INDEX.

INDEX.

2 R

2 S

652   INDEX.